New Standard Encyclopedia

S

(S to Slu)

S

New Standard Encyclopedia

VOLUME 15
(S to Slu)

Ferguson Publishing Company

CHICAGO

Pronunciation Guide

Letters with their pronunciation markings are pronounced as follows:

ā as in āte	ă as in ănt	à as in fàst
â as in vâcation	ă̇ as in ă̇bhor	a̍ as in a̍bandon
â as in râre	ä as in färm	

ē as in ēven	ė as in crėation	ĕ as in parĕnt
ę as in fęar	ė̇ as in sė̇lf	ẽ as in farmẽr

ī as in īre	ĭ as in ĭnk	ĭ as in qualĭty

ō as in ōver	ŏ as in pŏcket	o͞o as in po͞ol
ô̇ as in ô̇blige	ǒ as in ǒccur	o͝o as in wo͝ol
ô as in ôrgan	ô̇ as in ôff	

ū as in redūce	û as in occûr	ŭ as in sŭppose
û̇ as in sû̇perior	ŭ as in cŭp	ü as in the French menü

th as in three; t̶h̶ as in these
κ German ch sound as in ach (äκ)
N as in the French bon (bôN); the n is silent and the preceding vowel is nasalized

Syllables are separated by an accent mark (′ or ′) or hyphen (-). The mark ′ is placed after a syllable with primary accent, and the mark ′ after a syllable with lighter, or secondary, accent, Example: prȯ-nŭn′sĭ-ā′shŭn.

A vowel that is not pronounced is replaced by an apostrophe(′), as in fasten (fàs″n).

A consonant that is pronounced very lightly is enclosed by brackets, as in Hampshire (hăm[p]′shĭr).

Library of Congress Cataloging-in-Publication Data

New standard encyclopedia.

    p.   cm.
Includes bibliographical references and index.
ISBN 0-87392-105-4 (set)
1. Encyclopedias and dictionaries. I. Ferguson Publishing Company.
AE5.N64 2001   2001018951
031—dc21

W	𝄢	S
1000 B.C. PHOENICIAN	800 B.C. WESTERN GREEK	50 A.D. LATIN

S s	*S s*
MODERN ROMAN (Bodoni)	MODERN ITALIC (Bodoni)

S, the 19th letter in the English alphabet. It is a *sibilant,* a letter with a hissing sound. Its ancient Semitic name was *shin,* the Hebrew word for "tooth," but which may have meant "mountain ridge" then. In the Phoenician alphabet *shin* had the sound of SH, and its symbol resembled a W. The letter was turned on end and simplified by the Greeks, who called it *sigma* (after a different Phoenician sibilant) and gave it an S sound. The Greeks also adopted another Phoenician sibilant letter, which they called *san,* but it was later dropped.

The Romans included *sigma* in their alphabet and gave it its present shape. In the Middle Ages S was often written in a form resembling a small-letter F. This form persisted into the late 19th century, especially in handwriting for the first of two S's or an S preceding T.

In English S has sounds as in "sell," "choose," "sugar," and "measure." Common combinations of S with other letters are SH, as in "shall"; SC, pronounced as in "science" or "score"; SCH, as in "scheme" (skēm), "schist" (shĭst), or "schism" (sĭz'm or skĭz'm); and SION, pronounced as in "fission" or "fusion."

's Gravenhage. See HAGUE, THE.

Saadi. See SADI.

Saanen. See GOAT, subtitle *Domestic Goats.*

Saar, zär; sär, a historic region, now the state of Saarland in Germany. Located in the southwestern part of the country, it is bounded on the west and south by Luxembourg and France. It covers 992 square miles (2,570 km²), an area somewhat smaller than that of Rhode Island. The capital is Saarbrücken. For centuries, France and Germany disputed control of the Saar, first because of its strategic location and later because of its rich coal deposits and productive iron and steel industry.

The early inhabitants of the Saar region were Celts who came under the control of Rome in the first century B.C. In the fifth century A.D., the area was absorbed by the Frankish Empire. It became part of the Kingdom of Lotharingia when the empire was divided in 843. In 925 it passed to Germany. Despite this German connection, the Saar was strongly influenced by neighboring France during the Middle Ages.

The Saar was under French rule from 1797 to 1815. By the Treaty of Paris of 1815, it was divided between Prussia and Bavaria. It became a part of Germany after German unification in 1871. At the end of World War I, the Saar Territory, as it was called, was put under the administration of the League of Nations. France was allowed to operate the coal mines as payment for the wartime destruction of French coalfields by Germany. In 1935 the German-speaking Saarlanders voted overwhelmingly for reunion with Germany.

After World War II, the Saar was placed in the French military occupation zone. It was granted internal autonomy in 1947 but was linked with France in a monetary, customs, and economic union. In a 1955 plebiscite, the people again voted for a return to German rule. In 1957 the Saar became a state of West Germany; it remained a state after Germany was reunified in 1990.

Population: 1,084,000.

See also SAARBRÜCKEN.

Saarbrücken, zär'brük'ĕn, Germany, the capital of the Saarland. It lies on the Saar River near the French border, about 100 miles (160 km) southwest of Frankfurt am Main. Saarbrücken is the commercial, industrial, and transportation center for the coal-rich Saar Basin and produces iron and steel. Among the few buildings that survived the bombings of World War II are several 18th-century Baroque-style churches. The University of the Saarland is here.

Saarbrücken was chartered in 1321 and

The Deere & Company Administration Center in Moline, Illinois, designed by Eero Saarinen in 1957, is made of Cor-Ten steel.

from 1381 until 1793 was the seat of the House of Nassau-Saarbrücken. The French captured the city in 1793 and held it until 1815, when it was given to Prussia. As part of the Saar, the city has changed hands several times. (See SAAR.)

Population: 192,000.

Saarinen, sä′rĭ-nĕn, the family name of two Finnish-born United States architects and designers, father and son.

Eliel Saarinen (1873-1950), the father, helped establish a national Romantic school of Finnish architecture with his designs for the National Museum and Central Station in Helsinki. He emphasized simplicity of line and form and sparse ornamentation in his buildings and furniture designs. After winning second place in the 1922 Chicago Tribune Tower architectural competition, Saarinen settled in the United States. He designed the campus and buildings of the Cranbrook complex of schools in Bloomfield Hills, Michigan.

Eero Saarinen (1910-1961), the son, gained fame for his imaginative, varied designs. He experimented with new materials and construction techniques and designed buildings in various styles, ranging from rectangular steel-and-glass (Deere & Company, Moline, Illinois) to flowing masses of reinforced concrete (TWA Terminal at Kennedy Airport, New York City). He also produced innovative furniture designs. (For pictures, see DESIGN, INDUSTRIAL; FURNITURE, picture titled *Tulip Chair*.)

Saarinen studied in Paris and at Yale University before joining his father's firm in 1936. He first gained recognition in 1948 when his design of Gateway Arch for St.

Louis' Jefferson National Expansion Memorial won first prize in a national competition. The 630-foot (192-m) stainless steel arch was completed in 1965. (For picture, see ST. LOUIS.) Among Saarinen's other works are Kresge Auditorium, Massachusetts Institute of Technology; United States embassies in Oslo and London; General Motors Technical Center near Detroit; Dulles International Airport, the first planned for jet planes, near Washington, D.C.; University of Chicago Law School Center; and the CBS Building in New York City.

Saarland. See SAAR.

Saavedra Lamas, Carlos. See NOBEL PRIZES (Peace, 1936).

Sabah, a part of Malaysia on the island of Borneo. See BORNEO; MALAYSIA.

Sabatier, Paul. See NOBEL PRIZES (Chemistry, 1912).

Sabatini, sä-bä-tē′nĕ, **Rafael** (1875-1950), an Italian-born English author. He wrote more than 40 novels, biographies, histories, and plays, besides many short stories. His popularity became international with the publication in the United States of *Scaramouche* (1921) and *Captain Blood* (1922). These and other historical romances were made into motion pictures.

Sabatini was born in Italy of an English mother and an Italian father. He studied in Switzerland and Portugal. Sabatini became a British subject and in World War I served with the intelligence department of the British War Office.

Among his other books are: *The Sea Hawk* (1915); *Fortune's Fool* (1923); *Chivalry* (1935); *The Sword of Islam* (1938); *Turbulent Tales* (1946); and *The Gamester* (1949).

Atlantic Sailfish
Field Museum

Clapperton-Oudney group, by the Frenchman René Caillé, and by Heinrich Barth, a German.

Meanwhile, European colonization of North Africa had begun. France ultimately gained control of most of the Sahara, with the exception of Egypt, Libya, the Anglo-Egyptian Sudan, and the Spanish territories in the west. By the 1950's a wave of nationalism began to bring independence to Africa; within a decade all of the Saharan colonies except Spanish Sahara (which was later absorbed by Morocco) had been granted independence.

Since the early 1970's the Sahel—the transitional region between the Sahara and the agricultural regions to the south—has been periodically devastated by droughts. These droughts have brought famine and starvation to countless thousands of nomads and their livestock.

Sahel. See SAHARA, subtitle *History*.

Saigon. See HO CHI MINH CITY.

Sail. See SAILING, subtitle *Parts of a Sailboat* (and illustrations).

Sailfish, the common name for a genus of game fish found primarily in the Atlantic and Pacific oceans. The sailfish is a fast swimmer and a tenacious, vigorous fighter. It has a long, slender body; a swordlike beak formed by the bones of the upper jaw; and a large, spotted dorsal fin (the "sail" for which it is named). It is dark blue on top and white or silver on the underside. Although highly prized as a game fish, the sailfish is not considered a particularly good food fish.

The Atlantic sailfish, found off the coasts of North and South America, can grow to a length of 10 feet (3 m). Average weight is about 40 pounds (18 kg). In spring the Atlantic sailfish migrates northward to reach cooler waters and a better food supply.

The Pacific sailfish, found south of the California coast, can grow to a length of 11 feet (3.4 m). Average weight is about 100 pounds (45 kg).

Sailfish belong to the billfish family, *Istiophoridae*. In some classifications the Atlantic sailfish is *Istiophorus albicans* and the Pacific, *I. greyi;* in others, both are considered to belong to the same species, *I. platypterus*.

For record catches, see FISHING, table titled *Saltwater Fishing Records*.

For further information, see:

Countries

ALGERIA	MAURITANIA
CHAD	MOROCCO
EGYPT	NIGER
LIBYA	SUDAN
MALI	TUNISIA

Miscellaneous

DUNE	TANEZROUFT
LIBYAN DESERT	TÉNÉRÉ
OASIS	TUAREG
QATTARA DEPRESSION	

Books about the Sahara

Asher, Michael. *Two Against the Sahara: on Camelback from Nouakchott to the Nile* (Morrow, 1989).

Durou, Jean-Marc. *Sahara: the Magic Desert* (Arpel Graphics, 1987).

Plossu, Bernard. *The African Desert* (University of Arizona, 1987).

Porch, Douglas. *The Conquest of the Sahara* (Fromm, 1986).

For Younger Readers

Haliburton, Warren. *Nomads of the Sahara* (Crestwood House, 1992).

Sailing. Sailboats are used as pleasure craft on lakes, rivers, and oceans in many parts of the world. The sport of sailing, like the sport of boating in power-driven craft, is called yachting and includes racing and all kinds of cruising, from an afternoon's sail to a globe-circling voyage. In some countries, sailboats are also used for fishing, transporting goods, and training naval and merchant-marine officers. Before the age of steam, sailing vessels were the chief means of water transportation.

Modern pleasure sailboats range from one-person boats only 7 feet (2.1 m) long to luxury yachts accommodating 20 to 30 persons and measuring 150 feet (45.7 m) or more in length. They are divided into three basic types according to the activity for which they are designed. A *day-sailer* is a small boat (usually under 20 feet [6.1 m] in length) designed for comfortable sailing but without sleeping accommodations; it has a roomy cockpit, either open or partly covered. A *cruiser* is a medium-sized or large boat that has a cabin and, generally, an auxiliary motor. A *racer* is a boat designed for speed and ease of handling, often at the expense of comfort. Two styles popular in the United States are the *racer-day-sailer,* designed primarily for racing and secondarily for day sailing, and the *cruiser-racer,* designed mainly for overnight cruising and secondarily for racing.

Parts of a Sailboat

The Hull, which is commonly made of wood, fiberglass, or aluminum, has one of three basic shapes: flat bottom, round bottom, or V-shaped bottom. Multihull craft have two or more hulls joined by a deck or cross beams. Attached to the stern (aft part of the hull) is the rudder, which is controlled by the helm—a tiller or a wheel. The rudder is turned to starboard (right) or port (left) to steer the boat.

Extending down from the hull is a keel, a centerboard, a daggerboard, or, on a few craft, a pair of bilge boards or leeboards.

A keel is a fixed metal plate or a weighted extension of the hull. A centerboard is a plate, usually of metal, that is housed in a compartment (called a well or trunk) in the hull. The centerboard is pivoted at the front so it can be raised into and lowered out of the well. A daggerboard resembles a centerboard, except that it is not pivoted; it slides straight up and down in the well. Bilge boards resemble centerboards or daggerboards; they are set on opposite sides of the hull. Leeboards are plates pivoted to the outside of the hull.

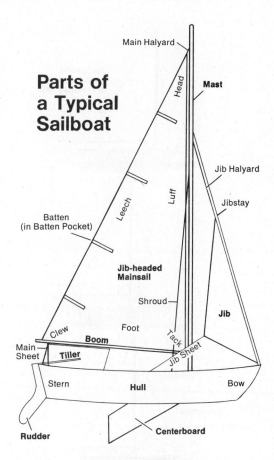

Parts of a Typical Sailboat

Main Halyard

Head

Mast

Jib Halyard

Luff

Jibstay

Leech

Batten (in Batten Pocket)

Jib-headed Mainsail

Shroud

Jib

Foot

Clew

Tack

Boom

Jib Sheet

Main Sheet

Tiller

Stern

Hull

Bow

Rudder

Centerboard

A Centerboard Sloop

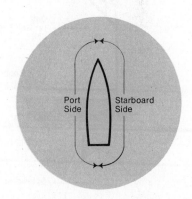

Port Side

Starboard Side

Common Sails

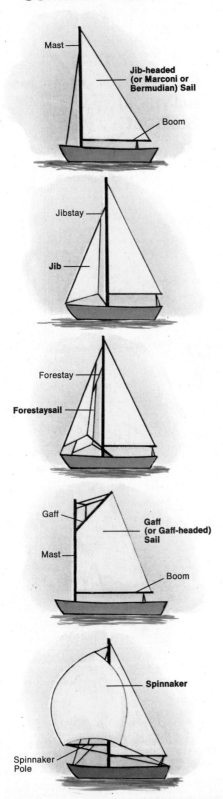

Mast

Jib-headed
(or Marconi or
Bermudian) Sail

Boom

Jibstay

Jib

Forestay

Forestaysail

Gaff

Gaff
(or Gaff-headed)
Sail

Mast

Boom

Spinnaker

Spinnaker
Pole

The purpose of any of these devices is to reduce the boat's tendency to move sideways under certain wind conditions. These devices also increase the boat's stability and aid in steering it.

The Spars are the masts, booms, and any other poles used to support the sails. They are usually made of wood or aluminum. On a four-masted ship, the masts are called (from bow to stern) the foremast, mainmast, mizzenmast, and jigger. A three-masted craft does not have a jigger. A two-master has a mainmast and either a foremast or a mizzenmast.

The Standing Rigging, which is usually wire rope, supports the masts. A *stay* runs from a mast toward the bow or stern; a *shroud* provides sideways support.

The Running Rigging, which is usually *line* (fiber rope), wire rope, or a combination, is used to manipulate the sails. A sail is pulled up by a *halyard*, out by an *outhaul*, and down by a *downhaul*. A *sheet* adjusts a sail's angle to the wind. A *topping lift* raises or lowers the outer end of a boom or pole. *Guys* control the fore-and-aft position of poles.

The Sails are made of pieces of cloth, usually Dacron or canvas, sewn together. (Exceptions are various experimental types.) Most cloth sails are of one of two types—the formerly common but now rare *square sail* or the widely used *fore-and-aft sail*. A square sail is a four-sided sail that has its top rigged to a horizontal spar called a *yard*. The yard is set at right angles to the fore-and-aft line (lengthwise axis) of the boat, but the yard and sail may be angled slightly fore and aft. Square sails on a square-rigged ship are named for their mast (fore-, main-, or mizzen-) and for their position on the mast (from bottom to top: course or sail, lower topsail, upper topsail, top-gallant sail, royal, and skysail).

A fore-and-aft sail is a triangular or four-sided sail that has its forward edge rigged to a spar or stay; its trailing edge can be moved across the fore-and-aft line of the boat. A fore-and-aft sail hoisted on a mast is normally named for the mast. (For example, a sail hoisted on a mainmast is called a mainsail.) A fore-and-aft sail hoisted on a stay is called a *staysail* or, before the first mast, a *headsail*.

A widely used racing sail that is neither a square sail nor a fore-and-aft sail is the triangular, parachutelike *spinnaker*. It floats before the first mast, held in place only at its three corners. The top corner hangs from a halyard; one lower corner is attached to a sheet; the other lower corner is attached to the end of a horizontal *spinnaker pole* extending from the mast. Both the sheet and the pole may be moved to control the position of the spinnaker. Spinnakers are usually made of nylon.

Sailing a Fore-and-aft-rigged Boat

A sailboat is moved by the force of the wind on its sail or sails. It can travel in any direction except directly into the wind. A boat is said to be sailing on a *starboard tack* when the wind is from anywhere on the starboard side. It is on a *port tack* when the wind is from the port side. A boat is said to be running, reaching, or beating, depending upon the angle of the wind.

Running is sailing away from the wind with the sail at an angle near 90 degrees to the lengthwise axis of the boat. The wind comes from directly astern (behind) or from astern and slightly to the side. It exerts a pushing force on the back of the sail, driving the craft forward. Running is also called sailing free, sailing downwind, sailing downhill, sailing off the wind, or sailing before the wind.

Reaching is sailing with the wind coming from the side and the sails set on the opposite side at an angle of about 45 degrees to the boat's lengthwise axis. The wind exerts both a pushing and a pulling force on the sail.

The force that pulls the sail is similar to the force that lifts the wing of an airplane. It is created as the wind hits the sail and divides into two flows, one on each side of the sail. The curved outer surface of the sail causes the outer flow to move farther and faster than the inner flow. This speedup lowers the air pressure on the outer side of the sail, creating a suction that pulls the sail outward.

A boat is on a *beam reach* when the wind blows from directly abeam (at right angles to the side of the boat). It is on a *close reach* when the wind blows from slightly ahead of abeam. When the wind comes from aft of abeam, the boat is on a *broad reach. Tacking downwind* is the maneuver of broad reaching or running on alternate tacks, or zigzagging away from the wind. This maneuver is sometimes used instead of running dead before the wind because it may be faster even though the distance covered is greater.

Beating is sailing as close as possible into the wind with the sail set almost parallel to the boat's lengthwise axis. (In practice, beating is sailing at an angle of about 45 degrees

Running, Reaching, and Beating

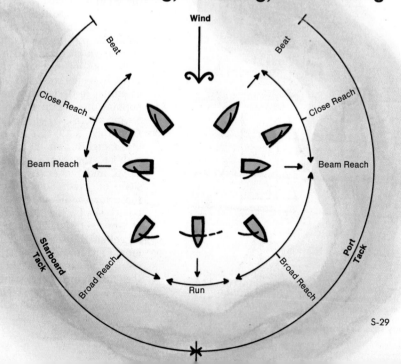

Main Types
of Fore-and-aft Rigs

A fore-and-aft rig has one or more masts; each mast carries fore-and-aft sails. The various rigs differ only in the height and placement of the mast or masts; each rig may carry a variety of sails. Most modern sailboats have fore-and-aft rigs.

Catboat. One mast, stepped (set) well forward.

Sloop. One mast, stepped farther back than the catboat's mast and farther forward than the cutter's. Most pleasure craft in the United States are sloops.

Cutter. One mast, stepped at a point about two-fifths of the waterline length from the bow.

Yawl. Two masts—a tall mainmast and a short mizzenmast stepped behind the rudder post.

Ketch. Two masts—a tall mainmast and a medium-height mizzenmast stepped in front of the rudder post.

Schooner. Two or more masts, the aftermast being as tall as or taller than the others. The foremast may carry square sails at its top.

to the wind with the sail set at an angle of 10 to 15 degrees off the lengthwise axis.) The wind exerts a pulling force on the outside of the sail, drawing the craft forward and sideways. The keel or centerboard-type device resists the sideways pressure, and the craft moves forward.

Beating is also called sailing to windward, sailing close-hauled, or sailing on the wind. Beating on alternate tacks, or zigzagging into the wind, is the only way to reach an upwind destination; this maneuver is commonly called *tacking*.

Changing Tacks. A boat may change from one tack to another by *coming about* (or *tacking*), or by *jibing*. In *coming about*, the bow of the boat is steered into and across the wind; the sail swings to the center of the boat, where it *luffs* (flaps back and forth), and then it fills on the other side. A *jibe* is used to change course when reaching and is made by steering the boat's stern into and across the direction of the wind, so that the sail swings from one side to the other. An unintentional jibe caused by a change in wind direction, or a jibe performed in strong winds, can be dangerous because the momentum of the swinging boom can damage or capsize the boat.

Stopping. A boat may be stopped by a fast turn, sheeting or *trimming* a sail on the wrong side, or luffing by either steering into the wind or releasing the sheets.

Sailboat Racing

Small racing sailboats are divided into hundreds of classes. Each class is either a *one-design class,* in which all the boats are built alike, or a *restricted* (or *development*) *class,* in which the boats vary slightly, within limits, in design and construction. Some popular one-design classes are those for the *Snipe,* a 15'6" (4.7-m) centerboard sloop; the *Lightning,* a 19' (5.8-m) centerboard sloop; the *Penguin,* an 11' (3.4-m) centerboard catboat; the *Star,* a 22'8½" (6.9-m) keel sloop; and the *Triton,* a 28'6" (8.7-m) keel sloop or yawl. Some restricted classes are those for the *Moth,* an 11' (3.4-m) centerboard sloop; the *International 14,* a 14' (4.3-m) centerboard sloop; and the *12-meter,* a keel sloop usually 60' to 70' (18 to 21 m) long. (The term "12-meter" does not refer to any particular dimension of the craft; it is the maximum permissible value derived from a formula that takes into account a variety of dimensions.)

S-30

SAILING

A *class race* is between sailboats of the same one-design or restricted class. A *handicap race* is between boats of different types; smaller vessels receive a time allowance. Most races use triangular courses to include reaches, runs, and beats. Some races—called distance races—are run on handicaps between two geographic points; they may last several days or longer.

Sailboat races—often called yacht races or regattas—are usually sponsored by a local yacht club or by a sailboat racing association. The most popular classes are represented by class associations that conduct local, regional, national, and, in some cases, international competitions.

The most highly prized international trophy is the *America's* Cup, named for the United States schooner *America,* which first won it at Cowes, England, in 1851. Originally, yachts of any tonnage and design could compete, but they had to sail from their home port to the race site. In the 1930, 1934, and 1937 races, J-class (135-foot, or 41.1-m) sloops competed. The requirement that yachts sail to the race site was dropped in 1956, and during 1958-88 competition was between the much smaller 12-meter class sloops. In 1988 a catamaran and a 133-foot (40.5-m) sloop were allowed to compete. In 1992 a new class of sloop, the International America's Cup Class, was introduced. Typically, these sloops measure 75 feet (22 m). Competition is between a challenger and a defender; normally, these are chosen in a series of elimination contests. For results of the *America's* Cup races, see the table on the next page.

Other international races held on closed courses include those for the One Ton Cup, the Scandinavian Gold Cup, and the International Catamaran Challenge Trophy, as well as the sailboat racing events in the Olympic Games. The North American Yacht Racing Union sponsors annual championships for the Mallory Cup (men's champion), the Adams Cup (women's champion), the Sears Cup (junior champion), the O'Day Trophy (single-handed champion), and the Prince of Wales Trophy (match-race champion).

Important regularly scheduled international distance races include the Bermuda Race, from Newport, Rhode Island, to Bermuda; the Fastnet Race, from the coast of England around Fastnet Rock off the Irish coast and back to England; the Trans-Pacific Race, from Los Angeles, California, to Hawaii; the Sydney-Hobart Race, from Australia to Tasmania; the Buenos Aires-Rio de Janeiro Race, from Argentina to Brazil; the Bayview-Mackinac Island Race, from Port Huron, Michigan, to Mackinac Island; and the Chicago-Mackinac Race.

History

For the early history of sailing, see SHIP.

Yachting originated in Holland. (The word yacht comes from the Dutch *jaght schip,* meaning "hunting ship"—a light, fast ship.) By the early 1600's, wealthy Dutch businessmen and members of royalty were staging nautical parades and mock naval

Main Types of Square Rigs

A square rig has two or more masts; at least one carries square sails. Square-riggers, once the masters of the high seas, are used today mainly for training naval and merchant-marine officers.

Full-rigged Ship. Three or more masts, all with square sails.

Bark. Three or more masts. All carry square sails except the aftermast, which carries fore-and-aft sails.

Barkentine. Three or more masts. The foremast carries square sails; the other masts all carry fore-and-aft sails.

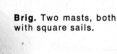

Brig. Two masts, both with square sails.

Brigantine (or Hermaphrodite Brig). Two masts. The foremast carries square sails; the mainmast, fore-and-aft sails. The mainmast may carry square sails at its top.

America's Cup Race

Countries of origin are indicated as follows: G—Great Britain; C—Canada; A—Australia; NZ—New Zealand; I—Italy. Country of origin is not indicated for United States yachts.

Year	Winner	Loser
1851	*America*	*Aurora* (G)*
1870	*Magic*	*Cambria* (G)†
1871	*Columbia; Sappho*‡	*Livonia* (G)
1876	*Madeleine*	*Countess of Dufferin* (C)
1881	*Mischief*	*Atalanta* (C)
1885	*Puritan*	*Genesta* (G)
1886	*Mayflower*	*Galatea* (G)
1887	*Volunteer*	*Thistle* (G)
1893	*Vigilant*	*Valkyrie II* (G)
1895	*Defender*	*Valkyrie III* (G)
1899	*Columbia*	*Shamrock I* (G)
1901	*Columbia*	*Shamrock II* (G)
1903	*Reliance*	*Shamrock III* (G)
1920	*Resolute*	*Shamrock IV* (G)
1930	*Enterprise*	*Shamrock V* (G)
1934	*Rainbow*	*Endeavor* (G)
1937	*Ranger*	*Endeavor II* (G)
1958	*Columbia*	*Sceptre* (G)
1962	*Weatherly*	*Gretel* (A)
1964	*Constellation*	*Sovereign* (G)
1967	*Intrepid*	*Dame Pattie* (A)
1970	*Intrepid*	*Gretel II* (A)
1974	*Courageous*	*Southern Cross* (A)
1977	*Courageous*	*Australia* (A)
1980	*Freedom*	*Australia* (A)
1983	*Australia II* (A)	*Liberty*
1987	*Stars & Stripes*§	*Kookaburra III* (A)
1988	*Stars & Stripes*§	*New Zealand* (NZ)
1992	*America³*	*Il Moro di Venezia* (I)
1995	*Black Magic 1* (NZ)	*Young America*

Aurora, one of 15 British yachts in the race, finished second.
†*Cambria*, the only British yacht in the race, faced 23 U.S. yachts and finished tenth.
‡*Columbia* won the first two races, but was disabled in the third; *Sappho* substituted, winning the fourth and fifth races.
§The 1987 *Stars & Stripes* was a 12-meter sloop, the 1988 vessel a catamaran.

battles in luxurious yachts manned by large professional crews. King Charles II of England brought yachting to his country in 1660, while Dutch settlers introduced it to the American colonies. The first yacht club was the Water Club of the Harbour of Cork (later the Cork Yacht Club), founded in Ireland in 1720. The first yacht races were held in England during the last half of the 18th century.

In the 19th century many yacht clubs were formed, including the New York Yacht Club (1844). Among the international races established were the *America*'s Cup Race (1851), the Trans-Atlantic Race (1866), the Sydney-Hobart Race (1879), and the Chicago-Mackinac Race (1898). Distance cruising became a popular activity for large yachts and, toward the end of the 19th

century, for smaller craft. The first solo sail around the world was made by an American, Joshua Slocum, during 1895–98.

In the early 1900's the first one-design-class sailboat—the *Star*—was designed and built. Its success led to the creation of hundreds of one-design craft, most of which were under 40 feet (12.2 m) in length. Important races founded early in the 20th century include the Bermuda Race (1906), the Trans-Pacific Race (1906), the Fastnet Race (1925), and the Bayview-Mackinac Island Race (1925). By the 1960's sailing had expanded to a sport for amateur sailors in relatively small craft and the great luxury yachts with mostly professional crews had largely disappeared.

International Yacht Racing Union (IYRU) is the world governing authority for yacht racing. It administers a number of one-design and restricted classes known as international classes. The IYRU was founded in 1907. Headquarters are in London.

U.S. Sailing is the governing body for sailboat racing in the United States. It interprets the IYRU racing rules, hears and decides appeals, sponsors annual championships, and publishes a yearbook. The organization was founded in 1897. Headquarters are in Newport, Rhode Island.

United States Sailing Foundation (USSF) provides support and assistance to United States sailing in international competition, particularly in the Olympic Games and the Pan-American Games. The USSF was founded in 1958. Headquarters are in Newport, Rhode Island.

Books about Sailing

Bond, Bob. *The Handbook of Sailing,* revised edition (McKay, 1993).

Conner, Dennis, and Michael Levitt. *Sail Like a Champion* (St. Martin's Press, 1992).

Hall, Major. *Sports Illustrated Boardsailing* (HarperCollins, 1985).

Pelly, David. *The Illustrated Encyclopedia to World Sailing* (Simon & Schuster, 1989).

Terry, John. *The Fundamentals of Sailing* (St. Martin's Press, 1991).

For Younger Readers

Bailey, Donna. *Sailing* (Raintree, 1990).

Burchard, Peter. *Venturing: an Introduction to Sailing* (Little, Brown, 1986).

Evans, Jeremy. *Windsurfing* (Crestwood House, 1992).

Sailplane. See GLIDER, subtitle *Types of Gliders* (The Performance-type Glider).

Sainfoin, sān′foin, a perennial herb native to the temperate regions of Europe and Asia. It is also called *holy clover.* The sainfoin grows to a height of about two feet (60 cm). It has many oval leaflets and small pale pink or white flowers. Sainfoin is used primarily for forage. It is grown for this purpose in parts of the United States.

The sainfoin is *Onobrychis viciaefolia* of the pea family, Leguminosae.

Saint, or **St.** *A note on alphabetization.*

Persons who bear the title "Saint" are listed in this encyclopedia under their first names; for example, ANDREW, Saint, and PAUL, Saint. In the few cases where a saint is better known by his last name, he is listed under that name; for example, AQUINAS, Saint THOMAS. In these cases there is a cross-reference entry under the first name: **Thomas Aquinas,** Saint. See AQUINAS, Saint THOMAS.

Surnames, place names, and names of things beginning with "St." are alphabetized as if spelled "Saint." Examples: ST. CLAIR, ARTHUR; ST. LOUIS, Missouri; ST. VITUS'S DANCE. Where a hyphen is used in such a name (as in SAINT-GAUDENS, AUGUSTUS), the hyphen is ignored for alphabetizing purposes. Thus SAINT-GAUDENS is alphabetized as if spelled SAINT GAUDENS.

Saint, a person honored for extraordinary religious qualities. The term is most commonly associated with the Roman Catholic and Eastern Orthodox branches of the Christian faith. Members of these churches believe that certain holy persons have special power, both on earth and after death, to perform miracles and to intercede with God on behalf of sinners. Most Protestants do not believe in saints with such special powers. However, they often refer to holy persons, particularly the disciples of Christ and other New Testament figures, as saints.

Non-Christians also sometimes refer to holy persons as saints. The practice of praying to saints for aid was adopted by some Muslim sects, although the founder of Islam, Mohammed, had regarded the Christian concept of sainthood as heretical.

Roman Catholics venerate as saints the Virgin Mary and many New Testament figures. (Some Old Testament personages, such as Moses and Daniel, are also considered saints, as are the archangels Michael, Gabriel, and Raphael.) Other saints are designated as *martyrs* (those who died for Christianity) and *confessors* (those who are considered to have testified as effectively for the Christian faith by the holiness of their lives as the martyrs did by dying for Christ).

Recognition of Saints

In modern Roman Catholic practice, holy persons are first recognized by *beatification* —a declaration by the pope that a person is in heaven and may be accorded limited veneration. Upon further evidence that the person was holy, but generally no less than 50 years after his or her death, the beatified person may be recognized as a saint by the pope in the ceremony of *canonization.* (See CANONIZATION.)

Canonized saints are publicly venerated by Roman Catholics throughout the world. Masses are said in their honor. Their relics are held in great esteem. Churches and schools may be named for them. The Church believes that many true saints have never been recognized by canonization, either because of the humbleness of their lives or because they lived so long ago that proper records of their deeds cannot be found. These unrecognized saints are venerated on All Saints' Day (November 1).

In the Eastern Orthodox faith, saints are proclaimed by the patriarch of Constantinople. Since the Eastern Orthodox and the Roman Catholic churches were not officially separated until 1054, many early saints are venerated by members of both churches.

© SuperStock

Castillo de San Marcos was built in St. Augustine, Florida, by the Spanish, 1672-96, of coquina (shellstone) blocks. It is a national monument.

Anglicans commemorate many notable Christians on special holy days, but they have no definite standards for sainthood and no procedure equivalent to canonization.

History

New Testament writers often referred to all good Christians collectively as "saints," meaning those who had sanctified their lives by dedication to Christ. In the latter part of the second century martyrs began to be referred to individually as saints. It became customary for Christians to observe a feast day on the anniversary of a saint's martyrdom, to preserve saints' relics, and to baptize persons with the names of saints. By the end of the fourth century confessors as well as martyrs came to be venerated as saints. During the Reformation of the 16th century

Protestants rejected as unbiblical the Catholic concept of sainthood.

Books about Saints

Attwater, Donald. *The Penguin Dictionary of Saints,* 2nd edition (Penguin Books, 1983).

Delaney, J. J. *Dictionary of Saints* (Doubleday, 1980).

Farmer, D. H. *The Oxford Dictionary of Saints,* 3rd edition (Oxford University, 1992).

Kieckhefer, Richard, and G. D. Bond, editors. *Sainthood: Its Manifestation in World Religions* (University of California, 1988).

Woodward, K. L. *Making Saints: How the Catholic Church Determines Who Becomes a Saint, Who Doesn't, and Why* (Simon & Schuster, 1991).

For Younger Readers

Clarke, Brenda. *Fighting for Their Faith* (Steck-Vaughn, 1990).

Young, John. *Heroes of Faith: Stories of Saints for Young and Old* (Light & Life, 1989).

For a list of Roman Catholic saints, see ROMAN CATHOLIC CHURCH (cross references titled *Saints*).

St. Albans, ôl′bănz, England, a city in Hertfordshire, 20 miles (32 km) northwest of London. It was named for Saint Alban, the first Christian martyr of England. Alban, a Roman soldier, was beheaded about 303 for aiding Christians. On the site of his martyrdom, a hill overlooking the ancient Roman town of Verulamium (now part of St. Albans), a Benedictine abbey was built about 793. It was rebuilt in the 11th century and became a center for historical writing. The abbey church was made an Anglican cathedral in 1877.

Population (district): 126,202.

St. Ambrose University. See UNIVERSITIES AND COLLEGES (table).

St. Andrew's Cross. See CROSS, illustration titled *Some Types of Crosses*.

St. Andrews Presbyterian College. See UNIVERSITIES AND COLLEGES (table).

St. Anselm College. See UNIVERSITIES AND COLLEGES (table).

St. Anthony's Cross. See CROSS, illustration titled *Some Types of Crosses*.

St. Anthony's Fire. See ERGOT; ERYSIPELAS.

St. Augustine, ô′gŭs-tēn, Florida, the oldest city in the United States. It was founded in 1565 by the Spanish. St. Augustine is the seat of St. Johns County. The city is in northeastern Florida on the Matanzas River, a saltwater lagoon, 35 miles (56 km) southeast of Jacksonville. Anastasia Island separates the city from the Atlantic Ocean.

The tourist trade is the mainstay of St. Augustine's economy; however, there is some shrimp fishing and boatbuilding.

The most notable among St. Augustine's many historic attractions is Castillo de San Marcos, a massive stone fort on Matanzas Bay. Begun in 1672, it is the oldest masonry fort in the United States.

Part of the city has been restored to its appearance during colonial days. In this section the streets are narrow and winding. Most of the old Spanish houses, made of native coquina stone, have patios, walled gardens, and overhanging balconies. The oldest house dates from the 1720's.

In the heart of the city is the Plaza de la Constitución. It was originally laid out as a military parade ground in 1598, and was named to commemorate Spain's adoption of a constitution in 1812. The public market on the plaza was built in 1824 and occasionally served as a slave market. The Cathedral of St. Augustine, surmounted by a Moorish bell tower, was completed in 1797.

St. Augustine has the council-manager form of government.

History

The Spanish explorer Juan Ponce de León discovered Florida in 1513 and made his first landing near what is now St. Augustine. The region was then inhabited by Timucua Indians. St. Augustine was founded in 1565 as a military outpost by Pedro Menéndez de Avilés, a Spanish admiral. The Spaniards repeatedly fought off attacks by the British and their Indian allies. As part of the settlement of the Seven Years' War, Spain was forced to cede Florida to Britain. A treaty returning it to Spain was signed in 1783.

In 1819 St. Augustine, with all of Spanish Florida, was ceded to the United States, which took possession in 1821. The Florida territorial legislature met there until 1824, when Tallahassee became the capital. Development was slow until the city was turned into a popular resort in the late 19th century. Many of the city's historic buildings were restored, and some reconstructed, during the 1960's and 1970's.

Population: 11,692.

See also MENÉNDEZ DE AVILÉS, PEDRO.

St. Augustine's College. See UNIVERSITIES AND COLLEGES (table).

St. Bartholomew's Day Massacre, bär-thŏl'ŏ-mūs (August 24, 1572), the slaying in France of thousands of Huguenots (French Protestants) during the religious conflict of the 16th century. The massacre, instigated by the queen mother Catherine de' Medici and sanctioned by the young king, Charles IX, was a severe blow to French Protestantism. However, its ultimate result was to strengthen the resistance of surviving Huguenots to Catholic pressures, and open religious warfare was soon renewed.

During the 16th century, Protestantism spread rapidly in France. Hostility between Catholics and Huguenots developed into civil war in 1562. The extreme Catholic party was led by members of the powerful ducal family of Guise. Prominent among Huguenot leaders was Gaspard de Coligny, Admiral of France. The queen mother, whose dominance over her son made her the true ruler of France, attempted to maintain a balance of power between the two factions so that neither would be strong enough to challenge her own position.

Showing favor to the Huguenots, in 1572 Catherine arranged a marriage between her daughter Margaret and Henry of Navarre (later Henry IV), a Huguenot. However, Catherine soon grew to resent the influence that the Huguenot leader Coligny was gaining over her son. She conspired with the Guises in a plot to murder Coligny. When the plot failed, the queen, fearful that her part in it would be revealed, told the king that the Huguenots planned to assassinate him. After hours of argument, she won his consent to the slaying of the Huguenot leaders gathered in Paris for the wedding of Margaret and Henry of Navarre.

Early on the morning of St. Bartholomew's Day (August 24), assassins murdered Coligny and most of the other leading Huguenots. Henry of Navarre was spared, but was forced to renounce his religion. (The renunciation was insincere, and Henry remained a Protestant until 1593.) Paris mobs, stirred by the leaders of the plot, slaughtered thousands of Huguenot men, women, and children. Similar massacres occurred in many other parts of France. No reliable figure is known for the total number of victims, but some authorities estimate it to have been at least 10,000.

St. Benedict, College of. See UNIVERSITIES AND COLLEGES (table).

St. Bernard. See DOG, subtitle *Breeds: Working Dogs.*

St. Bernard Passes, bĕr-närd', two passes in the Alps near Mont Blanc. Great St. Bernard Pass, 8,100 feet (2,469 m) above sea level, lies east of Mont Blanc on the Italian-Swiss border. Little St. Bernard, at 7,178 feet (2,188 m), is on the French-Italian border south of the peak. The two passes are about 20 miles (32 km) apart. Both are crossed by highways.

The passes were known to the Romans and Gauls well before the time of Christ. In the 11th century Saint Bernard of Menthon established a hospice on each pass to aid travelers. Augustinian monks still operate the hospice on the Great St. Bernard Pass, where the famed St. Bernard dogs were used to locate stranded travelers.

In 1800 Napoleon crossed Great St. Bernard in his invasion of Italy. Little St. Bernard is believed by some historians to be the pass used by Hannibal when he invaded Italy in 218 B.C. The passes have lost much of their importance since the opening of the Great St. Bernard Tunnel (1964) and the Mont Blanc Tunnel (1965).

See also ALPS (map).

St. Bonaventure University. See UNIVERSITIES AND COLLEGES (table).

St. Catharines, Ontario, Canada, a city on Lake Ontario and the Welland Canal, near Niagara Falls. It is an industrial city with a variety of manufacturing industries. A specialty is the processing of produce, mainly fruit, grown in the surrounding area. Brock University is here.

St. Catharines was founded in the 1790's, incorporated as a town in 1845, and chartered as a city in 1876. In 1961 the nearby towns of Port Dalhousie and Merritton and part of Grantham township were annexed. The city became part of the Regional Municipality of Niagara in the late 1960's.

Population: 129,300.

St. Catherine, College of. See UNIVERSITIES AND COLLEGES (table).

St. Charles, Missouri, the seat of St. Charles County. It is on the Missouri River, about 20 miles (32 km) northwest of downtown St. Louis. St. Charles is a local trade center and manufactures numerous agricultural and industrial products. Missouri's first capitol and Lindenwood College are here. The city has the mayor-council form of government.

Founded in 1769, St. Charles is one of the oldest settlements west of the Mississippi

Arthur St. Clair
by Charles Willson Peale

River. It was Missouri's capital, 1821-26. The city suffered extensive damage in 1993 when the lower Missouri River flooded.

Population: 54,555.

St. Christopher and Nevis. See ST. KITTS AND NEVIS.

St. Clair, Arthur (1736?-1818), an American Revolutionary War general and public official. His career was marked by a series of military and political controversies.

St. Clair was born in Scotland. After joining the British army in 1757, he fought in Canada against the French, at Louisbourg (1758) and at Quebec (1759). In 1762 he left the British army and settled on an estate in western Pennsylvania.

When the Revolutionary War began, St. Clair entered the Continental Army. He served under George Washington, 1776-77. In 1777 St. Clair, then a major general, was placed in command of strategically important Fort Ticonderoga on Lake Champlain. His evacuation of the fort before advancing British forces led to a court-martial in 1778. He was exonerated, but for the remainder of the war he held only minor posts.

St. Clair entered politics as a Federalist. He was a member of the Continental Congress, 1785-87, and its president in 1787. In 1788 he was appointed governor of the Northwest Territory. As commander of the frontier militia in the territory, he suffered a disastrous defeat at the hands of a smaller Indian force near Fort Wayne in 1791. Although Congress, which investigated the defeat, found him blameless, he resigned from the army. In 1802 he was removed as governor because his opposition to statehood for the territory conflicted with the views of President Jefferson. St. Clair then returned to his Pennsylvania estate. Through generous but unwise lending of his money, he lost most of his wealth. He spent his final years in poverty and political obscurity.

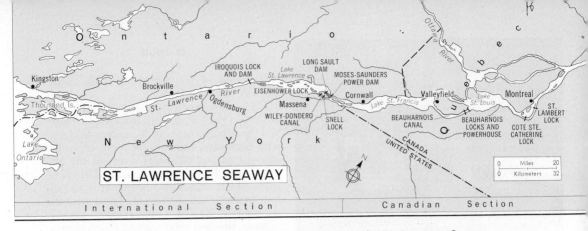
the St. Lawrence soon became a controversial issue in business and government circles of both countries. The railroads and representatives of Atlantic coast ports were strongly opposed to the seaway. They argued that the severe winters would limit the shipping season to seven or eight months of the year, and that the project would be far too costly to build. Midwesterners, generally in favor of the seaway, contended that business generated by shipping would offset winter shutdowns, and that tolls could be charged so that the seaway could pay for itself.

For nearly 60 years the seaway issue was debated. After Congress failed to approve a 1932 treaty and a 1941 agreement between Canada and the United States, Canada announced in 1952 that it would build the seaway alone.

Finally, in 1954, Congress passed the Wiley-Dondero Act, which created the St. Lawrence Seaway Development Corporation, an agency of the federal government. The corporation was made responsible for the planning and construction of the United States' share of navigation works in the seaway, in the area from Lake Ontario to near Cornwall, Ontario. The corporation also cooperated with Canada's St. Lawrence Seaway Authority in the control and operation of the seaway after it was completed in 1959.

Canada assumed full responsibility for building navigation facilities between Cornwall and Montreal, and for improving the Welland Canal. Power development on the seaway was carried out by agencies of the Ontario and New York governments. Much of the approximately $500,000,000 cost of the entire project was spent for canals, locks, and hydroelectric plants in the international section.

See also GREAT LAKES; ST. LAWRENCE RIVER; WELLAND CANAL.

Books about the St. Lawrence Seaway

Gillham, Skip, and Alfred Sagon-King. *The Changing Seaway* (Stonehouse, 1985).

LeStrang, Jacques. *Great Lakes/St. Lawrence System: the World's Richest Economic Region* (Harbor House, 1991).

Ray, D. K. *Water Works: a Survey of Great Lakes/St. Lawrence River Waterfront Development* (Harbor House, 1991).

For Younger Readers

Gibbons, Gail. *The Great St. Lawrence Seaway* (Morrow, 1992).

St. Lawrence University. See UNIVERSITIES AND COLLEGES (table).

St. Leo College. See UNIVERSITIES AND COLLEGES (table).

St. Lambert Lock in the St. Lawrence Seaway

St. Lawrence Seaway Authority

St. Louis Waterfront. The majestic Gateway Arch, 630 feet (192 m) high, rises from the Mississippi riverbank to dominate the St. Louis skyline. The arch commemorates the city's pioneer role as the "Gateway to the West."

St. Louis, loo′is, Missouri, the second largest city in the state. It adjoins, but is independent of, St. Louis County. The city lies on the west bank of the Mississippi River, just south of the river's junction with the Missouri River. With its metropolitan area, which includes adjacent parts of Missouri and Illinois, St. Louis is a major center of transportation, manufacturing, commerce, and education.

Because of its historic role in the nation's westward expansion, St. Louis is frequently called "Gateway to the West." The commemorative Gateway Arch, designed by Eero Saarinen, is the focal point of the Jefferson National Expansion Memorial on the downtown riverfront.

General Plan

St. Louis is roughly oval and lies in a large bend of the Mississippi. From the riverfront, some 19 miles (31 km) long and dotted with low bluffs, the city stretches westward as much as 7 miles (11 km). Elevations vary from about 400 feet (120 m) to more than 500 feet (150 m) above sea level.

Downtown St. Louis covers some 50 square blocks just west of the Gateway Arch. Midtown—a secondary center with office buildings, theaters, Powell Symphony Hall, and the campus of St. Louis Universi-

S-46

ty—is west of the downtown area about halfway to Forest Park.

From downtown St. Louis major thoroughfares radiate outward to the city's fringe and the suburbs beyond. Numerous bridges, with highways, railways, or both, cross the Mississippi and Missouri rivers in the St. Louis area. Eads Bridge, completed in 1874, is the oldest and most historic. It is one of four bridges that connect St. Louis with its sister-city of East St. Louis, Illinois.

Since the mid-1950's urban renewal projects have attempted to arrest urban blight brought on by the exodus of people and industry to the suburbs. Especially notable has been the redevelopment of downtown St. Louis and of Mill Creek Valley, a 454-acre (184-hectare) tract between downtown and midtown St. Louis.

The greatest suburban development has been in St. Louis County, which adjoins St. Louis on the north, west, and south. Among suburbs in Missouri are Florissant, University City, St. Charles, Kirkwood, Ferguson, Webster Groves, Overland, and Clayton. Nearby Illinois cities, in addition to East St. Louis, include Alton, Granite City, and Belleville.

Economy

The St. Louis metropolitan area, with abundant water, electric power, mineral resources, and transportation, and a large labor force, is a leading industrial area. Much of the manufacturing is concentrated near the river, in both Missouri and Illinois; much is in the suburbs.

Nearly half of the total labor force in the city is employed in manufacturing industries. The aerospace, brewing, and chemical industries are major employers. Large national firms with their headquarters in the area include the McDonnell Douglas Corporation, Anheuser-Busch, Inc., and the Monsanto Company. General Motors, Ford, and Chrysler have assembly plants here, making the St. Louis area one of the nation's foremost producers of automobiles. Other products include automobile parts, cement, electrical equipment, glass, grain foods, meat, petroleum products, printed and published matter, shoes, and steel and other metals.

St. Louis has long been a wholesale, insurance, and financial center for much of the central Mississippi Valley. In addition to many commercial banks, a Federal Reserve bank and a federal land bank are here.

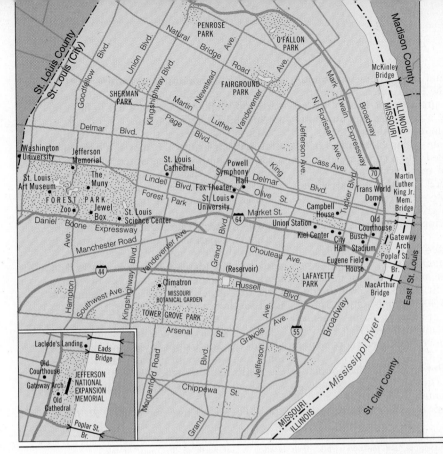

ST. LOUIS

State Boundary ...... ‑ ‑ ‑ ‑
County Boundary ... ‑ · ‑ · ‑
Park or Garden ......
Expressway ....
Major Street ....

0   Miles   1
0   Km   1

Stockyards on the Illinois side of the river make the St. Louis area a major market for livestock, especially hogs. It is also a significant grain market.

St. Louis is a leading railway hub and is also a trucking center. Four Interstate highways serve the city. Metrolink, a mass-transit rail line, serves the city and outlying areas. Numerous airlines use Lambert–St. Louis International Airport. St. Louis is also served by barge lines operating on the Mississippi.

Prominent Places

In the downtown area are many of the city's landmarks and historic buildings. Especially notable are the Old Cathedral, completed in 1834, and the Old Courthouse, where the Dred Scott slavery case was first tried. Both structures have been restored and are part of the Jefferson National Expansion Memorial. A panoramic view of the entire St. Louis area is provided from an observation room at the top of the Gateway Arch. Also downtown are the National Bowling Hall of Fame; Busch Stadium, home of the Cardinals (professional baseball); the Trans World Dome, home of the

Rams (professional football); and the Kiel Center, home of the Blues (professional hockey).

Around Memorial Plaza, just west of the business district, are the city hall, the main

Facts about St. Louis

Name—St. Louis was named in honor of the patron saint of Louis XV, the reigning king of France at the time the city was founded. (The patron was Louis IX, the "Crusader King.") It is nicknamed "Gateway to the West."

Location—Downtown St. Louis, 38° 38' N. and 90° 12' W.

Area—61.2 square miles (158.5 km²).

Climate—Average temperatures: January, 31° F. (-1° C.); July, 79° F. (26° C.). Annual precipitation: 36 inches (910 mm).

Government—Mayor and council.

Founding and Charter Dates—Founded in 1764 as a trading post by Pierre Laclède and his assistant René Auguste Chouteau. Incorporated as a town in 1808 and as a city in 1822 (effective 1823).

Further Information—St. Louis Convention and Visitors Commission, Suite 1000, 10 S. Broadway, St. Louis, MO 63102.

public library, and other municipal buildings. Nearby is the Kiel Center, home of the St. Louis Blues professional hockey team. Campbell House, a preserved and authentically furnished mansion of the 1850's, is nearby. The ornate Union Station has been restored and turned into a commercial complex consisting of restaurants, promenades, shops, and a hotel. In Aloe Plaza, at the entrance to Union Station, stands Carl Milles's fountain group of 14 statues, symbolizing the meeting of the Mississippi and Missouri rivers.

Forest Park, site of the 1904 Louisiana Purchase Exposition, is the largest of some 70 city parks. The most popular of its many attractions is the St. Louis Zoo, which contains more than 3,400 animals. Other Forest Park attractions are the St. Louis Science Center, Mark Steinberg Memorial Skating Rink, and the Jewel Box, which presents floral displays.

The Missouri Botanical Garden, popularly called Shaw's Garden (after its founder, Henry Shaw), contains one of the world's outstanding botanic collections. It maintains a suburban arboretum and features the Climatron, a geodesic dome greenhouse with rare tropical plants, and a 14-acre (6-hectare) traditional Japanese garden.

Also of interest are the St. Louis Cathedral, with its brilliantly colored tile mosaics; Laclede's Landing, a renovated 1850's riverfront district with specialty shops, restaurants, and nightclubs; St. Louis Centre, an enclosed shopping mall in the downtown business district; and several Mississippi excursion boats. Grant's Farm, just south of St. Louis, is part of the huge Busch estate. It includes the farm home of Ulysses S. Grant and is noted for its Clydesdale horses and herds of buffalo, deer, and elk. Six Flags Over Mid-America is a large entertainment park southwest of St. Louis.

Education and Culture

St. Louis University, the oldest university west of the Mississippi River, and Washington University—both private—are the leading institutions of higher learning. The University of Missouri and Southern Illinois University have branch campuses in the area. There are also more than 25 other

Meeting of the Waters, a fountain with 14 statues by Carl Milles, symbolizes the meeting of the Mississippi and Missouri rivers. Their junction is just north of St. Louis. In the background is Union Station.

Arteaga Photos

Gateway to the West. St. Louis, shown in this color lithograph as it appeared in 1832 from the east bank of the Mississippi, was a major starting point for traveling westward overland or by way of the Missouri River.

institutions of higher education, including Harris-Stowe State College.

The St. Louis Symphony Orchestra (founded in 1880) ranks next to the New York Philharmonic as the nation's oldest symphonic group. It presents both classical and pops concerts. Another major musical organization is the Opera Theatre of St. Louis. From June through August, the Muny, a 12,000-seat outdoor theater in Forest Park, presents musicals and light opera.

Museums of many kinds are among St. Louis' leading cultural attractions. The St. Louis Art Museum, atop Art Hill in Forest Park, has a permanent collection that includes works by many American and European masters. Beneath the Gateway Arch is the underground Museum of Westward Expansion with exhibits on the conquest of the West. In St. Louis County is the National Museum of Transport, which exhibits old locomotives, streetcars, buses, trucks, and horse-drawn equipment.

Jefferson Memorial, in Forest Park, is the home of the Missouri Historical Society. Among its exhibits are trophies of aviation pioneer Charles A. Lindbergh.

History

Early Developments. In 1762 the governor of French Louisiana, which included the entire Mississippi Valley, commissioned the New Orleans firm of Maxent, Laclède & Co. to establish a fur trade up the river. Pierre Laclède and a young assistant, René Au-

guste Chouteau, chose the site of present St. Louis the next year, and in 1764 a trading post was built and the first settlers arrived.

Meanwhile, in 1762, a preliminary treaty ending the Seven Years' War gave Spain control of New Orleans and Louisiana west of the Mississippi. A Spanish lieutenant governor took up residence in St. Louis in 1770, but the settlement retained its French character. In 1800 Spain returned the territory to France, which sold it to the United States in 1803.

The 19th Century. St. Louis had about 1,000 residents in 1804, when Lewis and Clark used it as a base for their expedition into the nation's new western lands. The expedition brought a great upsurge of interest in the Missouri River fur trade. The St. Louis Missouri Fur Company, formed in 1809, had William Clark himself as one of the partners. St. Louis became headquarters for a thriving fur industry, outfitting trappers and traders and merchandising furs. Old-time St. Louisans such as Manuel Lisa and the Chouteaus were leaders in the fur trade, but most of their associates were new residents from east of the river.

In 1817-19 steamboat routes were established down the Mississippi and up the Ohio and Missouri. A lucrative overland trade with Santa Fe began in 1821. German immigrants arrived in the late 1820's and in great numbers after 1848, bringing the city many industrial skills. Outfitting wagon trains bound for Oregon and California helped build industry.

The population, less than 17,000 in 1840, rose to nearly 78,000 by 1850. During the next decade St. Louis became a rail terminal as well as one of the major United States ports. The population more than doubled.

At the outbreak of the Civil War, there was strong Confederate sentiment in St. Louis. However, Congressman Francis P. Blair, Jr., had organized the Germans and other antislavery groups into Union clubs. These clubs protected the federal arsenal and the U.S. Treasury vaults, and the city was secured for the Union. In 1864 General Sterling Price directed a Confederate raid against St. Louis, but his forces were defeated by Union troops outside the city.

In the second half of the 19th century St. Louis was noted for its distinguished journalism. Carl Schurz, who later represented Missouri in the U.S. Senate, became editor of a German-language newspaper in 1867. In 1878 Joseph Pulitzer bought two local newspapers and merged them into the *Post-Dispatch*.

The 20th Century. St. Louis was the site of the 1904 Louisiana Purchase Exposition, popularly called the St. Louis World's Fair. In 1927 Charles A. Lindbergh, who flew a mail route between St. Louis and Chicago, was financed by a group of St. Louis businessmen on his historic solo transatlantic flight. By the mid-20th century the heart of the city had been overcome by urban blight. Joseph Pulitzer II began urging action in 1950. Two years later a group of leading citizens launched an urban renewal campaign, and a bond issue was passed in 1955. The waterfront area where the original village had stood became the 82-acre (33-hectare) Jefferson National Expansion Memorial, site of the Gateway Arch, completed in 1965. In the 1970's and 1980's, other redevelopment brought new commercial buildings and rehabilitation of many neighborhoods.

Population

Census figures since the city's incorporation in 1823 have been:

1830	4,977	1920	772,897
1840	16,469	1930	821,960
1850	77,860	1940	816,048
1860	160,773	1950	856,796
1870	310,864	1960	750,026
1880	350,518	1970	622,236
1890	451,770	1980	452,801
1900	575,238	1990	396,685
1910	687,029		

In 1870, at the close of the steamboat era, St. Louis was the nation's third largest city, surpassed only by New York and Philadelphia. In 1950, the year of its highest census population, it ranked eighth. It then declined both in population and in national rank: to 10th in 1960, 18th in 1970, 26th in 1980, and 34th in 1990.

St. Louis College of Pharmacy. See UNIVERSITIES AND COLLEGES (table).

St. Louis Park, Minnesota, a city in Hennepin County, adjoining Minneapolis on the west. It is primarily a residential suburb; there is some light industry. The city has the council-manager form of government. St. Louis Park was founded in 1854. Population: 43,787.

St. Louis University. See UNIVERSITIES AND COLLEGES (table).

St. Louis Zoological Park. See ZOO, subtitle *Famous Zoos.*

St. Lucia, lū'shá; lŭ-sē'à, an island country in the Caribbean Sea. It is one of the Windward Islands of the West Indies. St. Lucia is a mountainous, volcanic island, rising about 3,100 feet (945 m) above sea level. Its area is 238 square miles (616 km²). The economy is basically agricultural. Bananas, cacao, and coconuts are the chief crops. There is also a significant tourist industry. The population is 133,308; about half the people live in Castries, the capital. Most of the people are of African descent. Languages are English and a French patois, or dialect.

The earliest known inhabitants of St. Lucia were Arawak and Carib Indians. The British made several attempts to settle St. Lucia in the early 17th century, but failed because of the hostile Carib Indians. French colonists began arriving from Martinique in 1650. Britain and France contested ownership of the island until 1814, when it was

---

For further information, see:
LOUISIANA PURCHASE EXPOSITION
MISSOURI BOTANICAL GARDEN
Noted St. Louisans
BENTON, THOMAS
  HART (1782-1858)
BLAIR (Montgomery
  Blair; Francis
  P. Blair, Jr.)
CHOUTEAU (family)
CLARK, WILLIAM
FIELD, EUGENE
LACLÈDE, PIERRE
LISA, MANUEL
LYON, NATHANIEL
MUSIAL, STAN
PULITZER, JOSEPH
SCHURZ, CARL

ceded to Britain by the Treaty of Paris. In 1967 St. Lucia became a self-governing state associated with Great Britain. Independence was gained in 1979.

See also FLAG (color page).

St. Mark's, a basilica and cathedral in Venice, Italy. ("Basilica" is a title given in the Roman Catholic Church to certain historic or privileged churches.) It is often called the "golden church"—both interior and exterior are decorated with colored marble, gold and stone mosaics, and ancient columns and sculpture.

St. Mark's was built mainly between 1042 and 1085 over the ruins of an earlier church. Its Byzantine design was altered by many Gothic and Renaissance additions. A large central dome and four smaller domes roof the building, which has a floor plan in the shape of a Greek cross. The west facade, with its five large doorways, faces the great Piazza San Marco. St. Mark's originally was the chapel for the doge (chief magistrate); it was made the cathedral of Venice in 1807.

See also VENICE, subtitle *Places of Interest,* and picture.

St. Martin's College. See UNIVERSITIES AND COLLEGES (table).

St. Mary's College. See UNIVERSITIES AND COLLEGES (table).

Saint Mary's College of California. See UNIVERSITIES AND COLLEGES (table).

St. Marys River, the river connecting Lake Superior and Lake Huron. It is about 60 miles (97 km) long and forms part of the boundary between Michigan and Ontario. At the twin cities of Sault Ste. Marie (in Michigan and Ontario) the St. Marys drops 20 feet (6 m) in a distance of one mile (1,600 m), creating extensive rapids. These are bypassed for navigation by the Sault Ste. Marie (Soo) Canals. The river is part of the Great Lakes–St. Lawrence Seaway system. Below Sault Ste. Marie, islands divide the river into numerous lakes and channels.

See also MICHIGAN (map); SAULT STE. MARIE CANALS.

St. Mary's University. See UNIVERSITIES AND COLLEGES (table).

St. Mary's University of Minnesota. See UNIVERSITIES AND COLLEGES (table).

St. Michael's College. See UNIVERSITIES AND COLLEGES (table).

St. Mihiel, Battle of. See WORLD WAR I, section "The War in 1918," subtitle *The Western Front:* St. Mihiel Attack.

St. Moritz, mŏ-rĭts', Switzerland, one of the most fashionable and popular resorts in Europe. It lies in the Alps of southeastern Switzerland on the Lake of St. Moritz, more than 6,000 feet (1,800 m) above sea level. The resort's year-round activities center in two adjacent villages. St. Moritz-Dorf, site of the 1928 and 1948 Winter Olympic Games, offers winter sports. Mineral springs at St. Moritz-Bad are the chief attraction during the summer.

Saint-Nazaire Bridge. See BRIDGE, table *Some Notable Bridges.*

St. Nicholas Magazine. See LITERATURE FOR CHILDREN, subtitle *The Nineteenth Century.*

St. Norbert College. See UNIVERSITIES AND COLLEGES (table).

Saint Olaf College. See UNIVERSITIES AND COLLEGES (table).

St. Patrick's, the cathedral of the archdiocese of New York. It is on Fifth Avenue between 50th and 51st streets in New York City. St. Patrick's is one of the largest Roman Catholic cathedrals in the United States. The white marble structure, designed by James Renwick, is an outstanding example of the Gothic Revival style, blending elements of French and German Gothic. St. Patrick's was begun in 1858 and dedicated in 1879. The twin spires were completed eight years later.

St. Patrick's Day. See PATRICK, Saint.

St. Paul, Minnesota, the capital and second largest city of the state, and the seat of Ramsey County. It is in southeastern Minnesota on the Mississippi River near the mouth of the Minnesota River. St. Paul and the adjoining city of Minneapolis are known as the Twin Cities. St. Paul lies chiefly on the north side of the Mississippi and rises from 700 feet (210 m) to almost 1,100 feet (335 m) above sea level.

St. Paul's central business district, nine miles (14 km) east of downtown Minneapolis, fronts on the north bank of the Mississippi. Industrial areas and railroad yards along the river flank downtown St. Paul. Most of the city's residential areas are on higher ground, some distance from the river.

St. Paul is an important center for shipping and commerce. It also has industries that produce such diverse items as adhesives, abrasives, electronic equipment, autos, and printed and published materials. St. Paul also has refineries, chemical plants, and breweries. St. Paul's various attractions make the tourist industry an important part of the city's economy.

St. Paul is served by a network of railways, and by highways that include Interstate routes 35 and 94. On the Mississippi, barges carry coal, grain, and petroleum between the Twin Cities and downstream points. Minneapolis–St. Paul International Airport is eight miles (13 km) southwest of downtown St. Paul.

On Kellogg Boulevard, on the downtown riverfront, are several prominent buildings, including the 20-story city hall and courthouse, the main public library, the Science Museum of Minnesota, and Union Depot. The state capitol overlooks downtown St. Paul from a hill about one mile (1.6 km) from the river. A zoo, a conservatory, and picnic and boating facilities are located in Como Park, which surrounds one of the city's several lakes. Notable annual events include the state fair, usually held in late August, and the winter carnival.

A number of cultural organizations, including the St. Paul Chamber Orchestra and the Minnesota Opera, perform at the Ord-way Center for the Performing Arts. Institutions of higher learning include Macalester College, Hamline University, and the University of Minnesota's Institute of Agriculture.

St. Paul has the mayor-council form of government. A Metropolitan Council supervises certain regional functions in the Minneapolis–St. Paul metropolitan area.

History

Father Louis Hennepin, a Franciscan friar and explorer of the late 1600's, was probably the first European to visit the St. Paul area. The U.S. Army established Fort St. Anthony (later Fort Snelling) in 1819 at the junction of the Minnesota and Mississippi rivers to protect river commerce and the fur trade. In 1840 several squatter families, evicted from Indian land near the fort, crossed the Mississippi and moved eastward a short distance. Their new settlement, on the present site of downtown St. Paul, was called Pigs Eye after the nickname of a local trader.

The community was renamed the following year when a chapel was built here and dedicated to Saint Paul. It was incorporated as a town and made the capital of Minnesota Territory in 1849.

Downtown St. Paul, Minnesota, as seen from across the Mississippi River

© Conrad Bloomquist/Scenic Photo Imagery

By the time regular steamboat service was established on the river around 1847, bringing more settlers and traders, the town was well on its way to becoming one of the most important centers on the upper Mississippi. More than 10,000 people lived here when the first railroad came through in 1862. Thirty years later, when rail links to all parts of the nation had been built, St. Paul had more than 150,000 citizens.

Population: 272,235.

See also MINNEAPOLIS (map of Twin Cities area).

St. Paul's, the largest church in London and the cathedral of the Anglican Bishop of London. It is the masterpiece of Sir Christopher Wren. Standing on the top of Ludgate Hill in central London, St. Paul's, with its great Renaissance dome and twin Baroque towers, dominates the city skyline.

Description

The imposing building is of Portland stone, in the form of a Latin cross. Its exterior length, from the western facade to the eastern apse, is 514½ feet (157 m). A broad flight of steps leads to the west facade, which is 177 feet (54 m) wide and has a two-story portico. Steepled bell towers, 212½ feet (65 m) high, flank the portico. The church is surmounted by a great dome 112 feet (34 m) in diameter. Above the dome are a golden gallery and lantern (a towerlike decorative structure) topped by a ball and gilded cross, 366 feet (111.5 m) from the pavement.

The interior of St. Paul's is richly decorated. The dome, supported by eight piers, has scenes of the life of Saint Paul painted by Sir James Thornhill. Gringling Gibbons carved the choir stalls and organ case. Monuments to such noted persons as John Donne, Samuel Johnson, Lord Nelson, and Sir Joshua Reynolds are in the church. Buried in the crypt beneath the church are Wren, Benjamin West, the Duke of Wellington, Lord Nelson, and other famous persons.

History

The site of the present building was originally occupied by a church said to have been erected by Ethelbert, king of Kent, in the seventh century. This church was destroyed by fire in 1087, and another, later known as Old St. Paul's, was begun shortly afterward. Old St. Paul's was damaged by fire and lightning, and finally was destroyed by the great fire of 1666. Charles II commissioned Wren to design a new St. Paul's. Under

Ian Murphy/TSW—Click Chicago

St. Paul's Cathedral in London, England. The cathedral was designed by Sir Christopher Wren and completed in 1710.

Wren's direction, the cathedral was begun in 1675 and completed in 1710.

St. Paul's was partially obscured by other buildings until much of the surrounding area was leveled by bombs during World War II. During the 1940-41 air raids, the east end and north transept of St. Paul's were hit by bombs. A new high altar and the American Memorial Chapel in the apse behind it were dedicated in 1958. The chapel honors the 28,000 Americans who died in action while stationed in Great Britain during World War II. The north transept was reopened and dedicated in 1962.

See also LONDON, picture titled *The Blitz.*

Saint Paul's Church National Historic Site. See NATIONAL PARKS, section "United States."

Saint Paul's College. See UNIVERSITIES AND COLLEGES (table).

St. Peter's, a basilica in Vatican City. ("Basilica" is a title of honor conferred on certain historic or privileged churches by the Roman Catholic Church.) St. Peter's is the largest and most noted Christian church in the world. Its site is said to be that of Nero's

Circus, where many early Christians were put to death. St. Peter's was built between 1506 and 1626 to replace the fourth-century basilica erected by Constantine. A masterpiece of the Italian High Renaissance, St. Peter's is the work of a number of 16th-century architects. The form of the present church is due mainly to three men—Michelangelo, Carlo Maderna, and Giovanni Lorenzo Bernini.

The imposing entrance square, the Piazza di San Pietro, is partly encircled by two large colonnades. In the center an 82-foot (25-m) obelisk stands between two fountains. A triple flight of steps leads to the eastern facade, 375 feet (114 m) wide and 167 feet (51 m) high. Although the dome with its lantern and cross rises 452 feet (138 m), the facade cuts off its view from the piazza.

There are five entrances to the church. The central bronze doors were in the original St. Peter's. The Holy Door, on the far right, is opened by the pope only in Holy Years. On the extreme left are the Doors of Death, depicting such scenes as the Crucifixion, the

Interior of St. Peter's. St. Peter's Chair is seen in the background; the right foreground shows part of Bernini's *baldacchino.*
SCALA, Florence

stoning of Saint Stephen, and Cain killing Abel. These bronze doors, designed by the 20th-century sculptor Giacomo Manzù and completed in 1964, replaced oak doors that had been considered temporary for 500 years.

Inside St. Peter's
The church is in the form of a Latin cross. It is 613 (187 m) long and, at the transepts, 450 feet (137 m) wide. At the beginning of the nave a round slab of porphyry marks the spot where the Holy Roman emperors were crowned. The dome, 137½ feet (42 m) in diameter, rises 335 feet (102 m) from the floor. It is supported by four massive piers, each 240 feet (73 m) in circumference. A frieze below the drum of the dome bears a Latin inscription for "Thou art Peter, and on this rock I will build my church."

Beneath the dome Bernini's bronze *baldacchino,* or canopy, rises about 100 feet (30 m) over the high altar. Behind the altar, in the western apse, is St. Peter's Chair, also by Bernini. In front of the altar is the *confessione,* a sunken semicircular area. Stairs in it lead to the chamber below, containing the sarcophagus long revered as that of Saint Peter. Nearby is a bronze statue of Saint Peter seated. The toes of its extended foot are worn and shiny from the kisses of the faithful.

The side aisles contain many chapels, statues, and memorials to saints, popes, and others who have served the Roman Catholic Church. Among the numerous art works are Michelangelo's *Pietà,* Algardi's relief *The Encounter of Leo I and Attila,* and Canova's *Monument of Clement XIII.* (See MICHELANGELO, picture titled *Pietà.*)

History
An earlier basilica was built here by Constantine in the fourth century. Over the years the building deteriorated and in the 15th century Pope Nicholas V ordered St. Peter's repaired. His death in 1455 halted the work. About 50 years later Pope Julius II decided to build a new basilica. Donato Bramante won the competition to design it. Bramante planned a Greek-cross church, roofed by a vast central dome. The foundation was laid in 1506.

Bramante died in 1514 and Raphael was appointed architect by Pope Leo X. Leo's zeal to raise money for St. Peter's led to abuses in the use of indulgences in Germany; the abuses aroused Martin Luther, helping to spark the Reformation. (See REFORMA-TION, subtitle *Spread of the Reformation:* Luther in Germany.)

After Raphael's death in 1520, a number of architects continued to build and redesign St. Peter's, alternating between Latin-cross and Greek-cross plans. When Michelangelo was appointed architect in 1546, he returned to Bramante's plan but enlarged the dome and redesigned the chapels and apses. The dome was completed from his plans after his death in 1564.

About 1605 Pope Paul V ordered Carlo Maderna to extend the nave to form a Latin cross and to design a new facade. The church was dedicated in 1626. Bernini, appointed architect in 1629, designed the colonnaded entrance piazza and many of the interior monuments.

Excavations beneath St. Peter's were begun in the 1940's. In 1950 Pope Pius XII announced that archeologists had identified the tomb of Saint Peter. In 1968 Pope Paul VI announced that bones discovered in the 1953 excavations had been identified as those of Saint Peter. Many scholars, however, believe that there is insufficient evidence for firm identification of the tomb and remains as those of Saint Peter.

See also DOME; VATICAN CITY (picture).

St. Peter's College. See UNIVERSITIES AND COLLEGES (table).

St. Petersburg, Florida, a city in Pinellas County on the Gulf of Mexico. It lies at the southern end of Pinellas Peninsula between Tampa and Boca Ciega bays and is connected with the city of Tampa by two bridges. The Sunshine Skyway Bridge, 15 miles (24 km) long, links St. Petersburg with Bradenton to the south.

St. Petersburg, with bright, clear weather during much of the year, is primarily a residential and resort city. Its excellent climate attracts tourists and has led many retired people to make their homes here. The principal industries are the production of electronic equipment and engineering research and design. St. Petersburg is served by rail, an Interstate highway, and the international airport at Tampa.

Numerous parks, beaches, fishing piers and marinas are located along the city's more than 30 miles (48 km) of waterfront. Near Tampa Bay are the main cultural institutions—the Salvador Dali Museum, with the largest collection of the artist's work in the

Adrian Neal/TSW—Click Chicago

St. Peter's seen from the Piazza di San Pietro

world, the Museum of Fine Arts, the St. Petersburg Historical Society, and the Bayfront Center. The Florida International Museum opened in 1995.

The Pier is a commercial development extending into Tampa Bay that has restaurants and shops. Florida's Sunken Gardens houses tropical plants and birds. Fort De Soto Park, on an island in the gulf, is the site of Old Fort De Soto, built to protect the entrance to Tampa Bay during the Spanish-American War. Tropicana Field is the home of baseball's Tampa Bay Devil Rays.

St. Petersburg was founded in 1888, when a railway was completed linking Pinellas Peninsula with Florida's eastern coast. The Florida land boom that followed World War I contributed greatly to the city's growth. In the 1980's and 1990's much of the old downtown was renovated.

Population: 235,988.

St. Petersburg, Russia, a city in the northern part of the country. It was called Petrograd during 1914-24 and Leningrad during 1924-91. St. Petersburg was the capital of czarist Russia, 1712-1918, during which time it became one of Europe's most beautiful cities.

St. Petersburg, situated about 400 miles (640 km) northwest of Moscow, lies at the delta of the Neva River at the head of the Gulf of Finland. Of the world's great cities it is farthest north; the latitude is about

St. Petersburg, Russia. The Winter Palace, built 1754-62, contains more than 1,000 rooms and halls. It is the main building of the Hermitage Museum.
© John Lamb/Stone

that of Anchorage, Alaska. The climate is marked by extremely long, severely cold winters and short, cool summers.

Description

Built on both banks of the Neva River and on islands at the river's mouth, St. Petersburg has gained a distinctive character from its many canals, river branches, bridges, and embankments. The chief section of the city is along the river's south bank. Forming the heart of the city are three main streets intersected by three large canals. The busiest of these streets is Nevsky Prospekt. In this central area are many former palaces and sumptuous residences, and many museums, libraries, theaters, and institutes.

As the former capital of Russia and a cultural and educational center second only to Moscow, St. Petersburg has many outstanding public buildings. Some were built by the czars; others are Soviet restorations and new constructions. Some of the city's historic buildings have been neglected and are in disrepair.

The Peter and Paul Fortress, on the city's original island site, is St. Petersburg's oldest structure. In its basilica are buried many of the Romanov czars. Just across the Neva is the Admiralty, a long, spired building and a major St. Petersburg landmark. Nearby are a large statue of Peter the Great astride a horse and Decembrist Square, scene of an 1825 revolt.

St. Isaac's Cathedral, topped by a golden dome 330 feet (100 m) high, is one of the city's most beautiful churches. On the outskirts of St. Petersburg is Petrodvorets, a summer palace built by Peter the Great in the early 18th century.

Culture and Education

The State Hermitage Museum, one of the world's great art museums, is made up of five buildings, including the Winter Palace, the winter residence of the czars until the October Revolution in 1917. The Russian Museum, made up of several palaces, displays an enormous collection of Russian art. The city has many other museums, including ones devoted to history, science, music, and famous Russian writers.

Preeminent among St. Petersburg's many performing-arts groups is the Mariinsky, or Kirov, Ballet, one of the world's foremost ballet companies. The city also has a symphony orchestra, an opera company, and several theater companies.

Educational institutions include St. Petersburg University and the St. Petersburg State Technical University. The Saltykov-Shchedrin Library is one of Russia's largest public libraries.

Industry and Commerce

St. Petersburg ranks second only to Moscow as the country's largest manufacturing center. Of particular importance is the manufacturing of complex machinery, especially electrical machinery such as turbines, generators, and motors. The city produces specialty steels, chemicals, rubber goods, textiles, and foods, and is a large shipbuilding center.

Favored by its location in respect to western Europe and the Baltic Sea, St. Petersburg has one of Russia's best ports. It is a principal railway and air center and is connected to the interior of the country by canals. The city has an extensive subway system.

History

St. Petersburg was founded in 1703 by Peter the Great on land won in his war with Sweden. It was built to give Russia a "window on Europe." The city was planned as a modern capital in the Western European style and was built of stone set on pilings driven into the marshy land. In 1712 it replaced Moscow as capital, and gradually it became one of the world's most beautiful cities.

When Germany declared war on Russia in 1914, the city's Germanic name was changed to Petrograd (Peter's city). With the overthrow of the czar in 1917, Moscow again became the capital, and Petrograd lost much of its previous significance. In 1924 the city was renamed Leningrad, in honor of the revolutionary leader who died that year.

During World War II, Leningrad was besieged by the Germans from September, 1941, to January, 1944. The city withstood the 900-day attack, but was left in almost total wreckage and with 649,000 dead. Reconstruction was rapid after the war. In 1991 the city's original name, St. Petersburg, was restored. Population: 5,020,000.

St. Pierre and Miquelon, pēr; mĭk′ĕ-lŏn, an overseas *collectivité territoriale* (territorial community) of France, consisting of several barren, rocky islands about 15 miles (24 km) off the southern coast of Newfoundland. It is the only remaining possession outside the Caribbean of the once great French empire in North America. The chief islands are St. Pierre, Miquelon, and Langlade (or Little Miquelon), which account for virtually all of the total area of 93 square miles (242 km²). Fishing, especially for cod, is the mainstay of the economy; tourism is also important. Most of the people live in St. Pierre, the capital and chief port. A French fishing settlement was founded here as early as 1604. French sovereignty over the islands was permanently established by the Treaty of Paris, 1814. Population: 6,041.

Saint Rose, College of. See UNIVERSITIES AND COLLEGES (table).

Saint-Saëns, săN′säNs′ (Charles) **Camille** (1835-1921), a French composer and organist. Versatile and prolific, he composed more than 200 works, in almost every musical form. Although he used Romantic elements, Saint-Saëns believed emotion and imagery should be used with restraint. Much of his music, such as the symphonic poem *Danse Macabre* (1875), *Symphony No. 3* (1886), and *Piano Concerto No. 2 in G Minor* (1868), is marked by mastery of form

Camille Saint-Saëns
Culver Pictures

and orchestration. The instrumental suite *Carnival of the Animals* (composed 1886; first performed 1922) reveals his keen wit and sense of musical characterization. Of his 12 operas, only *Samson and Delilah* (1877) is performed regularly.

At a time when opera was preferred, Saint-Saëns helped popularize French instrumental music. He was one of the founders of the Société Nationale de Musique, established in 1871 to help French composers have their works performed. Saint-Saëns was a virtuoso on both the piano and the organ and a master of improvisation. He was organist at the Church of the Madeleine for 19 years.

Saint-Saëns was born in Paris. A child prodigy, he gave his first piano performance before the age of five. At 10 he made his debut as a professional pianist in Paris. In 1848 he entered the Paris Conservatory.

Saint-Saëns became organist of the church of Saint-Merry, Paris, in 1853, the year his first symphony was performed. He remained there until the end of 1857, when he was appointed organist of the Madeleine. He taught piano at the École Niedermeyer, 1861-65. Saint-Saëns traveled widely in Europe, North Africa, and the Americas, conducting and performing his own works.

His other works include: *Le Rouet d'Omphale* (1872), a symphonic poem; *Concerto in A Minor for Cello and Orchestra* (1873); and the piano concertos in *C minor* (1875) and *F* (1896).

See also DANCE OF DEATH.

St. Scholastica, College of. See UNIVERSITIES AND COLLEGES (table).

Saint-Simon, săN′ sē′môN′, Claude Henri de Rouvroy, **Comte de** (1760-1825), a French social philosopher and reformer. He is considered the father of French socialism. Saint-Simon believed that society should be reorganized and ruled by an aristocracy of merit (particularly, by scientists and indus-

Robert Glander/Shostal Associates
Marina near Kingstown, captial of St. Vincent and the Grenadines

trialists) rather than by an aristocracy of inherited power or wealth. Society's guiding principle would be association for the good of all. His philosophy, expressed in a series of essays, was put into systematic form (later known as Saint-Simonianism) by his followers. Saint-Simon was born in Paris. He served with the French army in the American Revolution and supported the French Revolution. He made a fortune in land speculation but lost it in various ventures.

Saint Sophia. See HAGIA SOPHIA.

St. Thomas. See VIRGIN ISLANDS.

St. Thomas, University of. See UNIVERSITIES AND COLLEGES (table).

St. Thomas Aquinas College. See UNIVERSITIES AND COLLEGES (table).

St. Thomas University. See UNIVERSITIES AND COLLEGES (table).

St. Valentine's Day. See VALENTINE.

St. Valentine's Day Massacre. See CAPONE, AL.

St. Vincent and the Grenadines, a country in the Windward Islands of the West Indies. It consists of the island of St. Vincent and most of the Grenadines, to the south. St. Vincent is mountainous, with peaks rising as much as 4,000 feet (1,220 m); the Grenadines are somewhat less rugged. The country's total area is 150 square miles (388 km²). The economy of St. Vincent and the Grenadines is based largely on the growing and export of bananas and arrowroot. Tourism is also important. Most of the people are of African descent. English is the principal language. Kingstown is the capital and largest city.

St. Vincent and the Grenadines is a constitutional monarchy. The head of state is the British monarch, who appoints a governor-general to represent the Crown. The head of government is the prime minister. Legisla-

tive power is vested in the House of Assembly. The country is a member of the Commonwealth of Nations.

In pre-Columbian times St. Vincent and the Grenadines were inhabited by the Arawak and Carib Indians. In 1498 Columbus became the first European to reach the islands. During the 17th and 18th centuries St. Vincent changed hands between Great Britain and France several times, until British sovereignty was established by the Treaty of Paris in 1783. In 1969 St. Vincent, with most of the Grenadines, became a self-governing state in association with Great Britain. Independence was gained in 1979. In the 1990's the country pursued the creation of a limited economic and political union with other English-speaking Windward Islands.

Population: 114,221.

See also FLAG (color page).

St. Vincent College. See UNIVERSITIES AND COLLEGES (table).

St. Vitus's Dance, also called **Sydenham's Chorea, Rheumatic Chorea,** or **Chorea Minor,** a disease of the central nervous system. It occurs primarily in children as a complication of a streptococcus, or "strep," infection, most frequently rheumatic fever. The "strep" bacteria invade the motor centers of the brain, disrupting the transmission of nerve impulses to the muscles, causing in involuntary, purposeless movements, clumsiness, and grimacing. The disease lasts about 10 to 12 weeks and does not usually cause permanent damage to the nervous system. Treatment includes the use of barbiturates or tranquilizers as sedatives.

The name St. Vitus's dance originated in medieval Europe when persons afflicted with apparently hysterical maladies called *dance manias* prayed to Saint Vitus, patron of actors and dancers, to be cured of their dance-like movements. The name *chorea* is from the Greek for "dance."

St. Xavier University. See UNIVERSITIES AND COLLEGES (table).

Alphabetizing Note

Names beginning with "Saint" followed by a hyphen (as SAINT-GAUDENS, AUGUSTUS) are alphabetized as if the hyphen were not there. Thus, SAINT-GAUDENS is alphabetized as if spelled SAINT GAUDENS.

Sainte-Anne-de-Beaupré, dû bō-prā', Quebec, a town on the St. Lawrence River 20 miles (32 km) northeast of the city of Quebec. It is famous for its shrine, contained in the town's basilica, honoring Saint Anne, mother of the Virgin Mary. Miraculous cures have been reported by persons visiting the shrine, and hundreds of thousands of pilgrims come here annually. The first cure here was reported in 1658.

Population: 3,162.

Sainte-Beuve, săNt'bûv', **Charles Augustin** (1804-1869), a French literary critic. He is credited with being the first to employ the biographical method of literary criticism. He believed that knowledge of an author's personality and environment is essential to a full understanding of his or her writing. Sainte-Beuve applied this theory in his most important works, which include *Literary Portraits* (1844), *Contemporary Portraits* (1846), *Monday Chats* (1851-62), and *New Mondays* (1863-70). A champion of the Romantic movement, Sainte-Beuve himself wrote poems and a novel in the Romantic style.

Sainte-Beuve studied medicine in Paris, but soon turned his attention to literature. He contributed to several journals and lectured at various universities. He was elected to the French Academy in 1844 and was appointed to the French Senate in 1865.

Saintpaulia. See AFRICAN VIOLET.

Saints Peter and Paul, Cathedral of. See WASHINGTON, D.C., subtitle *Churches*.

Saintsbury, George (George Edward Bateman Saintsbury) (1845-1933), an English literary historian and critic. He was a leading critic of French as well as of English literature. Among his most important works are *History of Criticism and Literary Taste in Europe* (3 volumes, 1900-04), *History of English Prosody from the Twelfth Century*

(3 volumes, 1906-10), and *History of the French Novel* (2 volumes, 1917-19). He also wrote biographies of John Dryden, Sir Walter Scott, and Matthew Arnold. His *Collected Essays and Papers* (1924) appeared in four volumes.

After attending Oxford, Saintsbury was a schoolteacher and later a journalist. From 1895 to 1915 he was professor of rhetoric and English literature at Edinburgh University.

Saipan. See NORTHERN MARIANAS.

Sakai, sä-kī, Japan, a city in Osaka prefecture in southern Honshu. It lies on Osaka Bay, separated from the city of Osaka by the Yamato River. Sakai is a port and industrial center, producing iron, steel, machinery, and chemicals. From the 1460's until the mid-1600's it was a major trading port. Then foreign trade was banned, and the city began to decline. When trade was reopened in the 1850's, Sakai was eclipsed by Osaka and failed to regain its former importance. Since World War II, however, it has become one of Osaka's most industrialized suburbs.

Population: 807,765.

Sakakawea. See SACAJAWEA.

Sake, sä'kē, an alcoholic beverage made from fermented rice. It is considered the national drink of Japan. Because sake resembles wine in appearance and has a dry, sherrylike taste, it is commonly called rice wine. It is colorless or pale yellow and contains 12 to 18 per cent alcohol by volume. The beverage is usually served warm.

Sakhalin, săk'ä-lēn, a Russian island off the northeastern coast of Asia. It lies between the Sea of Okhotsk and the Sea of Japan, separated from Siberia by Tatar Strait and from Hokkaido, Japan, by La Perouse Strait. About 590 miles (950 km) long and 15 to 100 miles (24 to 160 km) wide, Sakhalin has an area of 28,597 square miles (74,066 km²). Mountain ranges, reaching nearly 5,300 feet (1,615 m), run the length of the island.

Many of the people live by fishing; the island is not well suited to farming, and only a few hardy crops are grown. Other economic activities include lumbering, coal-mining, and petroleum extracting. Yuzhno Sakhalinsk, the administrative center, and Aleksandrovsk Sakhalinskiy are the principal cities.

Sakhalin was explored by Russians in the 17th century and colonized by Russia and

Japan in the 18th and 19th centuries. In 1875 Russia gained the entire island and established a penal colony on it. The southern part, called Karafuto by the Japanese, was granted to Japan in 1905 as a concession following the Russo-Japanese War. It was returned to Russia in 1947, after Japan's defeat in World War II.

Population: 660,000.

Sakharov, säk'*a*-rôf', **Andrei** (1921-1989), a Soviet physicist, author, and Nobel laureate. His work on the principles of nuclear fusion was instrumental in developing the Soviet hydrogen bomb. He later became a political dissident and a protestor against nuclear weaponry.

Sakharov first gained international attention as a social activist with his essay *Progress, Coexistence, and Intellectual Freedom* (1968), discussing world problems such as the nuclear arms race, hunger, and the loss of individual freedom. He proposed political and humanitarian cooperation between the Soviet Union and the United States as the one hope for preventing universal destruction. He received the Nobel Peace Prize in 1975 for his promotion of liberty.

From 1980 to 1986 Sakharov was internally exiled in the city of Gorkiy (Nizhniy Novgorod). After his release, he continued to be an outspoken critic of injustice and a defender of human rights.

Other writings include: *Sakharov Speaks* (1974), *My Country and the World* (1975), *Alarm and Hope* (1978), and *Memoirs* (1990).

Saki, sä'kĭ, the pen name of Hector Hugh Munro (1870-1916), a British writer. Saki is best known for his polished and witty short stories, in which he satirized British life. Among the best collections of his stories are *Reginald* (1904), *Reginald in Russia* (1910), *The Chronicles of Clovis* (1911), and *Beasts and Super-Beasts* (1914). *The Westminster Alice* (1902) is a collection of whimsical political sketches. Saki was killed in action in World War I.

Saki. See MONKEY, subtitle *Kinds of Monkeys*.

Sal Ammoniac. See AMMONIA, subtitle *Ammonium Salts*.

Saladin, sal'*a*-dĭn (*Arabic:* **Salah al-Din**) (1137?-1193), a sultan of Egypt and Syria. He united the Saracens (Muslims) against the Crusaders and restored Jerusalem to Muslim rule. Though ruthless in battle, Saladin was gallant and honorable in his

dealings with the Crusaders, who admired and respected him.

Saladin was the son and nephew of Kurdish generals in the service of Nureddin, the Turkish Muslim sultan of Syria. Sent to Egypt with his uncle to establish Nureddin's authority there, Saladin became vizier (governor) of Egypt in 1169 and deposed the hereditary ruler in 1171. After the death of Nureddin in 1174, the caliph of Baghdad permitted Saladin to proclaim himself monarch of Egypt and Syria.

Meanwhile, Saladin had joined the holy war begun by Nureddin to drive the Crusaders out of the Holy Land. After many smaller victories, in 1187 Saladin inflicted a crushing defeat on the Christians at the Battle of Hattin; a few months later he took Jerusalem. The Third Crusade was organized to rescue the Holy City. Richard the Lion-Hearted, one of the leaders, defeated Saladin in several engagements. In a peace treaty, 1192, Saladin granted Christians the right to visit Jerusalem.

Saladin's empire was ruled by his family, the Ayyubids, until 1250.

Salam, Abdus. See NOBEL PRIZES (Physics, 1979).

Salamanca, säl'*a*-măng'k*a*, Spain, the capital of Salamanca province. The city is on the Tormes River about 105 miles (170 km) northwest of Madrid. There is some manufacturing of textiles here. Among many tourist attractions are an ancient Roman bridge, 12th-century Romanesque and 16th-century Gothic cathedrals, and many Renaissance buildings.

Salamanca, an important city of the ancient Celtiberians, was captured for Carthage by Hannibal in the third century B.C. It then fell in turn to the Romans, Goths, and Moors. Salamanca was incorporated into the Christian kingdom of León about 1055. The University of Salamanca, founded in the 13th century, rivaled the universities at Bologna, Paris, Oxford, and Cambridge as a center of learning. The university still functions and some 16th-century buildings are still in use.

Population: 162,544.

Salamander, săl'*a*-măn'dĕr, a tailed amphibian. Salamanders are cold-blooded animals (their temperature changes with that of their surroundings). They have soft skin that is usually moist and must have a humid if not wet environment. Most species are found on land; a few are strictly aquatic. Like other amphibians, salamanders are never found in seawater. Land salamanders are often found under stones and logs. Salamanders are found in North America, Asia, Europe, North Africa, and northern South America.

Salamanders of most species have four limbs; members of a few species have only two. Most salamanders are from 3 to 8 inches (7.5 to 20 cm) long. The largest species, the giant salamander, grows to about 5½ feet (1.7 m); the smallest is a Mexican species that measures 1½ inches (4 cm). Some species are brightly colored; others are quite dull.

Salamanders are active mainly at night. They feed primarily on insects, spiders, and worms. All salamanders respire to some extent through their skin. Some may also respire through gills, lungs, or the lining of their mouths. Almost all salamanders lay eggs.

Salamanders are often used in laboratory experiments. In some parts of the world, certain species are eaten. Salamanders are sometimes kept as pets. In ancient times it was believed that salamanders could withstand fire and live in flames.

There are about 55 genera of salamanders and more than 300 species, grouped into the following 8 families:

Hynobiidae. Asiatic land salamanders. These are among the most primitive salamanders. They are found only in eastern Asia.

Cryptobranchidae. Giant salamanders. Included in this family are the giant salamander (*Megalobatrachus japonicus*) of Japan and the hellbender (*Cryptobranchus alleganiensis*) of North America. The hellbender, which inhabits rivers and streams, can reach a length of more than 25 inches (64 cm).

Ambystomidae. Mole salamanders. Members of this family are found throughout North America. Included in this family are the marbled salamander of the eastern half of the United States and the axolotl. The marbled salamander (*Ambystoma opacum*) is black with white or grayish markings; it grows to about 5 inches (13 cm). (See also AXOLOTL.)

Salamandridae. Fire salamanders and newts. The fire salamanders are found in Europe and are of the genus *Salamandra*. For newts, see NEWT.

Amphiumidae. Amphiumas. There are only two species, found in the southeastern United States. One species (*Amphiuma means*) grows up to 36 inches (90 cm), the other (*A. tridactylum*) to about 40 inches (1 m).

Plethodontidae. Lungless salamanders. It is the largest family, with 180 species. All but two species are found in the Western Hemisphere; the two exceptions are European. Members of this family are from 1½ to 8½ inches (4 to 22 cm) long. Included in this

Dr. Robert S. Simmons

Marbled Salamander. These salamanders grow from 3½ to 5 inches (9 to 13 cm) long.

family is the red-backed salamander (*Plethodon cinereus*).

Proteidae. Olm and mud puppies. The olm (*Proteus anguinus*), found in Croatia and Montenegro, is a white salamander that reaches a length of about 12 inches (30 cm). For information about the mud puppy, see MUD PUPPY.

Sirenidae. Sirens. The three species in this family are also permanently larval forms. They are the only salamanders without hind limbs. All three are aquatic and are found in the eastern United States.

Salamanders make up the order Urodela.

For color pictures, see AMPHIBIAN.

Salamis, Battle of, săl'ȧ-mĭs, 480 B.C., the decisive naval battle of the Persian Wars, fought in the strait between the island of Salamis and the Greek mainland. The Greek victory ended the threat of Persian domination of the Mediterranean world.

Persia's first attempt at expansion into Greek lands, under King Darius, had been stopped at Marathon in 490 B.C. Ten years later Xerxes marched his huge army into Greece, with his fleet positioned offshore. The Persians overcame a Greek force at Thermopylae and moved on to Athens. The Athenian leader Themistocles had long realized that the Greeks could best defend themselves against the Persians at sea and had been building up Athens' fleet. In accordance with his plan, the city was abandoned to the Persians.

Athens and its allies assembled their ships in protected waters between Salamis and the mainland. Some of the Greeks wanted to withdraw. Themistocles sent a message to Xerxes informing him of this fact; Xerxes, as Themistocles had hoped, responded by sending his ships to block the ends of the strait, forcing the Greeks to fight. This action on the part of Xerxes was a serious blunder because in the narrow strait the Persians' numerical superiority gave them no advantage against the Greeks. There was no room for maneuver and the battle was fought primarily by soldiers over decks. The Greek soldiers were more heavily armed, and the Persians were routed. Accounts of the num-

Salem Maritime NHS

Salem Custom House (1819), where Nathaniel Hawthorne worked during 1846-49, is part of Salem Maritime National Historic Site in Massachusetts.

ber of ships lost vary, but hundreds of vessels were involved. Persia's losses are believed to have been far heavier than the Greeks'.

With his fleet shattered, Xerxes could no longer supply his land forces and returned to Persia with most of the army. The next year the Greeks defeated the Persian rear guard at Plataea and destroyed the remainder of the Persian navy at Mycale. Persia never again attacked Greece.

Salazar, să-lá-zàr′, **Antonio de Oliveira** (1889-1970), a Portuguese statesman. As minister of finance, 1928-40, and premier, 1932-68, Salazar ruled Portugal as a dictator for 40 years. His conservative administration brought financial and governmental stability to Portugal, but permitted little political freedom and achieved only limited economic progress.

Salazar was born into a peasant family near Coimbra, Portugal. He received a bachelor's degree (1914) and a doctorate (1918) from the University of Coimbra. He served briefly in the Portuguese legislature, but soon retired in disgust at the chaotic state of the republican government. A mili-

tary group took over Portugal in 1926 and Salazar became minister of finance for this government during a severe financial crisis. Granted extremely broad powers, he successfully dealt with the crisis and gradually extended his authority. In 1933, as premier, Salazar sponsored a new constitution that created an authoritarian, centralized government, which he dominated.

Salazar maintained close relations with the Spanish dictator Francisco Franco. Although Portugal was technically neutral in World War II, Salazar at first sympathized with the Axis powers; toward the end of the war, however, he aided the Allied powers. In 1949 he brought Portugal into the North Atlantic Treaty Organization.

In the 1960's Salazar's regime was repeatedly troubled by native uprisings in Portugal's African territories and by the liberals' discontent at home. Illness forced him to retire from office.

Salem, sā′lĕm, Massachusetts, the seat of Essex County. It is one of the oldest and most historic cities in the United States. Salem is located on an arm of Massachusetts Bay, 16 miles (26 km) northeast of Boston.

Electronic components, leather goods, and machinery are manufactured in Salem.

Many of Salem's historic structures have been preserved. One of the oldest is the Witch House (1642), so called because several persons accused of witchcraft in the 17th century were questioned there. Also of note is the House of Seven Gables (1668), the setting for Nathaniel Hawthorne's novel of the same name. (Hawthorne was born and grew up in Salem.) In the days of Salem's maritime glory, wealthy merchants and shipmasters built palatial homes. A number of these homes remain; many are outstanding examples of Federal architecture.

Salem Maritime National Historic Site includes Derby House and Derby Wharf (built in the 1760's) and the Custom House (1819) where Hawthorne once worked as port surveyor. The Peabody and Essex Museum has notable historical exhibits and reference libraries.

Salem has the mayor-council form of government.

History

Roger Conant led a group of Puritans from Cape Ann to the site in 1626. The settlement was called by its Indian name, Naumkeag, until 1630, when it was chartered as Salem. That year it became the first settlement of the newly established Massachusetts Bay Colony. From the beginning, fishing and shipping were the chief industries. In the late 17th century, Salem and nearby Salem Village (now Danvers) became the center of a witchcraft hysteria that swept New England. (See WITCHCRAFT, subtitle *Witchcraft in the Past*: In America.)

In the 18th century, overseas trade developed, first with the West Indies, later with China and India. By the end of the Revolutionary War, Salem was an important world port, headquarters for many prosperous merchants and shipmasters. It was incorporated as a city in 1836. When its shipping trade began to decline in the mid-19th century, Salem turned to manufacturing.

Population: 38,091.

See also MASSACHUSETTS, picture *House of Seven Gables*.

Salem, Oregon, the state capital and the seat of Marion County. It lies on the Willamette River in northwestern Oregon and is a trade center for the central Willamette Valley. The manufacturing of paper and other wood products and the processing of fruits and vegetables are major industries. An airport and an Interstate highway serve the city.

The focal point of Salem is the Capitol Mall, which is adjoined by the white marble capitol, several office buildings, and the state library. Willamette University, a Methodist school established as the Oregon Institute in 1842, is the oldest university in Oregon. The Oregon State Fair is held in Salem. The city has the council-manager form of government.

Salem was founded by Jason Lee as a Methodist mission in 1840. The townsite was laid out four years later. Salem was made the capital of the Oregon Territory in 1851 and became the state capital after Oregon was admitted to the Union in 1859. The city was incorporated in 1860.

Population: 107,786.

Salem, Virginia, the seat of Roanoke County. The city is on the Roanoke River near the Blue Ridge Mountains in the Appalachians. Salem's products include processed foods and machinery. Roanoke College, established in 1842, is here. The city was founded in 1802. It has the council-manager form of government.

Population: 23,756.

Salem College. See UNIVERSITIES AND COLLEGES (table).

Salem Maritime National Historic Site. See NATIONAL PARKS, section "United States"; SALEM, Massachusetts.

Salem State College. See UNIVERSITIES AND COLLEGES (table).

Salerno, sȧ-lûr′nō, Italy, a city in Campania region and the capital of Salerno province. It lies on the Gulf of Salerno, an inlet of the Tyrrhenian Sea, about 30 miles (48 km) southeast of Naples. Salerno is situated in an agricultural area. Its products are mainly canned vegetables and fruits. Among the city's landmarks are a castle built in the eighth century and the Cathedral of St. Matthew. The cathedral was consecrated in 1085 and is especially noted for its elaborate pulpit and the tomb of Pope Gregory VII.

Salerno was founded by either the Greeks or the Etruscans. It was captured by the Romans late in the second century B.C. In the sixth century A.D. it was made part of the Lombard duchy of Benevento. Salerno became an independent principality in the 800's. The Norman leader Robert Guiscard, duke of Apulia, captured the city in 1076. From 1130 until 1861, when Italy was unified, Salerno was part of the Kingdom of the Two Sicilies.

During medieval times Salerno was famous for its medical school, said to have been the first in Europe. In World War II a major battle of the Italian Campaign was fought at Salerno in September, 1943.

Population: 143,751.

Sales, Saint **Francis de.** See FRANCIS OF SALES, Saint.

Sales Promotion, an attempt, by means other than personal selling and normal advertising methods, to persuade the consumer to buy a product or service. Sales promotions and advertising are closely related and a clear distinction is not easily made. In general, sales promotion is a more direct process than advertising—that is, it is aimed more specifically at getting customers into the store or making the sale.

Promotions are part of the marketing process and may be undertaken by the producer, wholesaler, or retailer. The producer's or wholesaler's efforts may be designed to motivate the retailer or to suggest to the retailer ways of selling the product.

Perhaps the most familiar sales promotion is the offering of merchandise at a lower-than-normal price. Other common forms of promotion are store displays, the giving of free samples, contests and sweepstakes, premiums, and the use of trading stamps. (See PREMIUM; TRADING STAMPS.) For certain products demonstrations are widely used—a person in a retail store shows how a hair dryer is used, for example, or prepares and serves a food product. Common printed promotional materials are booklets and brochures, which are either mailed to persons who request literature (often by clipping a coupon from a printed advertisement) or are made available in the store or showroom. Promotional materials are also available at many company sites on the Internet.

Some sales promotional efforts are continued indefinitely, while others are used to introduce new products, to boost lagging sales, or to boost sales during a traditionally "slow" season. Special promotions are often publicized in advertisements and are generally coordinated with an advertising campaign.

Sales Tax. See TAXATION, subtitle *Sales Tax.*

Salesmanship. See SELLING.

Salic (or **Salique**) **Law,** săl′ĭk; să′lĭk, a principle of royal succession holding that a throne might not be inherited by a daughter or her heirs. According to tradition the principle originated with a code of laws—also called Salic Law—drawn up by the Salian Franks, founders of the Frankish kingdom; this origin, however, is doubted by most historians. The principle was observed mainly among descendants of the Franks.

Invocation of the Salic Law of inheritance played a part in several wars. It was used in the 14th century by Philip VI of France in rejecting the claim of Edward III of England to the French throne. Edward invaded France, starting the Hundred Years' War. In the 18th century Charles VI of Austria issued his Pragmatic Sanction (1713) to ensure inheritance of the Hapsburg domains by a daughter, should he leave no son. Although Charles later specified his daughter Maria Theresa as his heir, his death in 1740 brought claims based on the Salic Law from several male contenders and resulted in the War of the Austrian Succession.

Salicylate. See SALICYLIC ACID.

Salicylic Acid, săl′ĭ-sĭl′ĭk, a white, crystalline solid that is a strong organic acid. It occurs in small amounts in the roots, leaves, flowers, and fruits of many plants. Salicylic acid is used in the manufacture of dyes and as a preservative for hides and glues. Because it has antiseptic properties, it is used in ointments for treating skin diseases such as eczema and ringworm. It is also used for removing calluses and warts. Commercial salicylic acid is made from phenol by chemical processes.

Salicylic acid combines with metals and organic compounds to form derivatives called *salicylates,* many of which are drugs. The commercially important salicylates are *acetylsalicylic acid* (aspirin), *methyl salicylate* (chief component of oil of wintergreen), and *phenyl salicylate* (salol). Used in moderation, salicylate drugs are relatively safe. Large doses, however, are poisonous and can cause severe acidosis. (See ACIDOSIS AND ALKALOSIS.)

Chemical formula: $HOC_6H_4CO_2H$.

See also ASPIRIN; WINTERGREEN.

Salina, să-lī′nà, Kansas, the seat of Saline County, about 160 miles (257 km) west of Kansas City. Located in a large cattle- and wheat-producing area, Salina is a prominent livestock market and a flour-milling and grain-storage center. It produces light aircraft, lamps, and feeds. Kansas Wesleyan University and Marymount College are here. Salina was founded in 1856 by Preston B. Plumb and incorporated three years later.

Population: 42,303.

Salinas, sȧ-lē′nȧs, California, the seat of Monterey County. It lies on the Salinas River, about 85 miles (137 km) southeast of San Francisco. The city is the shipping and processing center for a rich agricultural area, which produces lettuce and other vegetables, sugar beets, fruits, and dairy products. A rodeo is held here each July. Salinas was founded in 1856 and incorporated in 1874. It is the birthplace of the novelist John Steinbeck.

Population: 108,777.

Salinas Pueblo Missions National Monument. See NATIONAL PARKS, section "United States."

Salinger, săl′ĭn-jēr, **J. D.** (Jerome David Salinger) (1919-   ), a United States author. His first book, the novel *The Catcher in the Rye* (1951), won critical acclaim for its style, satiric humor, and faithful reflection of the thought and speech of the upper-middle-class adolescent. It was popular especially with young people, who felt that its 16-year-old hero, Holden Caulfield, personified the sensitivity and honesty of youth as opposed to the hypocrisy of adult society. This theme is restated in many of Salinger's stories.

Franny and Zooey (1961) and *Raise High the Roof Beam, Carpenters* (1963)—each containing two long stories—deal with the brilliant, eccentric Glass family who were introduced in *Nine Stories* (1953), a collection.

Salinger was born in New York City. He attended three colleges, but did not graduate. He served with the U.S. Army during World War II. His first published short story appeared in *Story* magazine in 1940. Many of his later stories appeared in *The New Yorker* magazine. Salinger became a recluse in the early 1960's; his last published work appeared in 1965.

Salinity. See OCEAN, subtitle *Properties of Seawater.*

Salique Law. See SALIC LAW.

Salisbury, sôlz′bēr-ĭ; sôlz′brĭ, Robert Cecil, 1st **Earl of** (1563?-1612), an English statesman, chief minister of Elizabeth I and

James I. As secretary of state (1596-1612) and lord treasurer (1608-12), the shrewd and skillful Salisbury wielded immense influence over the foreign, domestic, and financial policies of England. He was responsible for bringing James VI of Scotland to the English throne as James I, having secretly arranged for the accession prior to Queen Elizabeth's death in 1603. He also negotiated an end to England's long war with Spain, 1604. For his services, King James made him Baron Cecil in 1603, Viscount Cranborne in 1604, and Earl of Salisbury in 1605.

Robert Cecil was the son of Lord Burghley (William Cecil), Elizabeth's chief minister until his death in 1598. The younger Cecil was educated by his father, who groomed him as his successor. In 1584 Cecil became a member of Parliament. He was knighted in 1591 and assumed the duties of secretary of state, although he was not officially appointed to that post until 1596. After his father's death, he became Elizabeth's principal adviser, winning a power struggle with Robert Devereux, Earl of Essex.

Salisbury, Robert Arthur Talbot Gascoyne-Cecil, Third **Marquess of** (1830-1903), a British statesman. Salisbury, a Conservative, was three times prime minister, 1885-86, 1886-92, 1895-1902, and during most of his time in office served as his own foreign secretary. He was a champion of imperialism and the policy of maintaining a strong naval establishment. He expanded the British Empire in Asia and Africa, but kept Britain out of the power struggles between European states. He strongly opposed the rising tide of democracy in Britain. After successfully concluding the Boer War in 1902, he retired from public life.

Robert Gascoyne-Cecil attended Eton College and Oxford University. He was elected to the House of Commons in 1853. In 1868 he succeeded his father as marquess, taking his seat in the House of Lords. He held the posts of secretary of state for India, 1866-67 and 1874-78, and foreign secretary, 1878-80, before succeeding Benjamin Disraeli as leader of the Conservative party.

Salisbury, North Carolina, the seat of Rowan County, about 40 miles (64 km) northeast of Charlotte. It is the trade center for an agricultural area and produces textiles, furniture, and processed foods. A national cemetery here contains the graves of some 12,000 Union soldiers who died in a

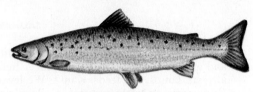

Atlantic Salmon

Confederate prison at Salisbury during the Civil War. The Rowan Museum houses 18th- and 19th-century furnishings and other items from the county's past. Catawba College and Livingstone College are here. Salisbury was settled in 1753.

Population: 23,087.

Salisbury, Zimbabwe. See HARARE.

Salisbury State University. See UNIVERSITIES AND COLLEGES (table).

Salish Indians. See FLATHEAD INDIANS.

Saliva. See DIGESTION.

Salk, sôlk, **Jonas E.** (Edward) (1914-1995), a United States physician and medical researcher. In the early 1950's, using techniques originated by the American scientists

Jonas E. Salk
The Salk Institute

John F. Enders, Thomas H. Weller, and Frederick C. Robbins, Salk developed the first successful polio vaccine. His work, which was supported by the National Foundation for Infantile Paralysis (now the National Foundation), greatly reduced polio as a public health threat. (See also POLIOMYELITIS, subtitle *Treatment and Control.*) Salk also helped develop influenza vaccines and worked toward finding a vaccine for AIDS.

Salk was born in New York City and received an M.D. degree from New York University in 1939. He served on the faculty of the University of Michigan School of Public Health, 1944-47, and the University of Pittsburgh School of Medicine, 1947-63. In 1963 he became director and fellow of the Salk Institute for Biological Studies, a research center named for him in the La Jolla area of San Diego, California.

His writings include: *Man Unfolding* (1972); *The Survival of the Wisest* (1973).

Salmon, săm′ ŭn, a valuable food and game fish. Salmon are normally found in temperate or Arctic waters of the Northern Hemisphere. There are seven species of salmon—one found in the Atlantic Ocean and six in the Pacific.

Most salmon are *anadromous*—that is, the adults migrate into freshwater rivers or lakes to breed. Salmon are famous for the runs they make as they return to their place of birth to spawn. Leaping high into the air to surmount obstacles, the fish fight their way upstream to the headwaters of their native rivers. It is at this time, when the fish are in prime condition, that the catch is taken by sport and commercial fishermen. (For record catches, see FISHING, table of freshwater fishing records.)

Atlantic Salmon

The Atlantic salmon is found on both sides of the North Atlantic as far north as the Arctic Circle. The adult is blue-black above with silvery sides. During the long journey to spawn, the male becomes dirty red on the sides and develops a hook-shaped lower jaw. The sides of the female become black. The adult fish ordinarily is 2 to 4 feet (60 to 120 cm) long and averages 8 to 12 pounds (3.6 to 5.4 kg).

At one time this fish was plentiful in North America as far south as the Hudson

Sockeye Salmon Leaping a Waterfall. Swimming upstream to their spawning grounds, salmon overcome such obstacles as rapids and waterfalls.
©John Shaw/Tom Stack & Assoc.

Sockeye Salmon
(spawning color)

Chinook Salmon

River, but the principal fisheries are now in Canada. Atlantic salmon are also found in a few freshwater lakes, where they remain throughout their lives. These fish are called *landlocked salmon.* They are caught as game fish in Maine, New York, New Hampshire, and the Maritime Provinces of Canada.

Pacific Salmon

Five species of Pacific salmon are found in North American waters, from Alaska to southern California. They are the chinook salmon (also called king, or spring, salmon); the sockeye, or red, salmon; the coho, or silver, salmon; the chum salmon (also called dog, or keta, salmon); and the pink, or humpback, salmon.

Chinook and coho are the most important sport species. Commercially the pink salmon holds first place in quantity caught, the sockeye in value of the catch. A few populations of certain species of Pacific salmon are landlocked, spending their entire lives in freshwater.

Pacific salmon are silvery with bluish backs that are spotted with black. As the fish mature and reach spawning time, their color changes to shades of red, yellow, or black, depending on species and sex. The males also develop a hook at the tip of both jaws.

The *chinook salmon* is the largest of the Pacific species, weighing about 20 to 25 pounds (9 to 11.3 kg). An average mature fish is about 4 feet (120 cm) long. The flesh is red, pink, or white.

The *sockeye salmon* weighs about 5 pounds (2.3 kg) and is about 2 feet (60 cm) long. It is highly prized for its firm, red flesh and excellent flavor.

The *chum salmon* usually weighs 8 to 18 pounds (3.6 to 8.2 kg) and reaches a length of 3 feet (90 cm). The flesh is whitish.

The *pink salmon* is the smallest of the Pacific species. It weighs about 3 to 5 pounds (1.4 to 2.3 kg) and is about 2 feet (60 cm) long. The flesh is pink. An unusual feature of the pink salmon is that on its way to spawn the male develops a large hump on its back.

The *coho salmon* attains a length of about 3 feet (90 cm) and usually weighs 6 to 15 pounds (2.7 to 6.8 kg). The flesh ranges from pink to red.

Spawning

Salmon that survive to maturity in the oceans return to the freshwater river of their origin to spawn, although some may stray to other streams. Scientists cannot fully explain why salmon are able to return to their native rivers to spawn, but it is known that in the final stages of their migration, the fish are guided largely by their sense of smell.

The migration to the spawning grounds begins at the same time for all the salmon in any one population. Depending on the particular population, the migration may begin any time from May to December, and spawning takes place from about June to January. The trip may be 200 miles (320 km) or more upstream. At the start of the run the fish are in prime condition; during the migration they eat nothing.

Once the spawning grounds are reached, the female, by using her tail, makes a nest (called a *redd*) in the gravel. She deposits her eggs, and the male releases sperm to fertilize the eggs. Salmon lay several thousand eggs. After spawning, the adults of the Pacific species die. Adult Atlantic salmon slowly make their way downstream to reenter the sea. The Atlantic salmon may spawn several times before dying.

The eggs hatch the following spring. Attached to the underside of a baby salmon (called an *alevin* or *fry*) is a yolk sac that will nourish the young fish for a few weeks. After the food material in the yolk sac is used up, the fish is called a *parr* or *fingerling*. At this time the young fish may immediately make its way to saltwater, or it may remain in freshwater for up to four years, depending on the habits of its population. At all times, salmon are prey to other animals, and only a small percentage of them live to reach the ocean. The salmon remain in the ocean from two to eight years before they are ready to spawn.

Fish Ladder. Fish ladders permit salmon to bypass dams as they swim upstream to their spawning grounds. The one shown here, on the Snake River near the Oregon-Washington border, has two long segments connected by a turn not visible in the photograph. In the background is Lower Monumental Dam.
© Gary Braasch/Woodfin Camp & Associates, Inc.

Commercial Fisheries

Most of the commercial catch is made at or near the mouths of rivers as the fish approach the coast. The fish are generally caught with gill nets or purse seines, or by trolling. Most of the Atlantic salmon catch is marketed fresh or frozen; small quantities are canned, pickled, or smoked. About half of the Pacific catch is canned. In modern canneries, nearly all the salmon are cleaned and canned by machinery. In some smaller canneries the cutting and several other operations are done by hand. Some floating canneries are also in operation. Salmon eggs are used to make red caviar. They are also used for bait.

Salmon are among the most valuable fish caught, although the size of the catch by weight is relatively small. They are used almost exclusively for human food, and much of the world catch is canned or otherwise processed. The Atlantic salmon normally provides 8 to 16 per cent of the total world salmon catch, with Norway, Great Britain, Denmark, and Canada the leading nations. The Pacific salmon catch is taken by the United States, Japan, Russia, and Canada.

Conservation

Overfishing and water pollution have caused a decrease in the number of salmon. In addition, dams, particularly hydroelectric dams on the Columbia and Snake rivers, block salmon from upstream spawning grounds. Many young salmon are killed in turbines at hydroelectric plants. A number of conservation measures are used to protect salmon populations. One of the major conservation measures is the artificial propagation of salmon. Millions of salmon eggs are hatched in hatcheries maintained by state and federal organizations. (See also FISH CULTURE.) Fish ladders (series of pools arranged like steps) allow adult salmon to swim upstream over or around dams. At some hydroelectric plants, there are underwater screens that divert young salmon away from turbines and into bypass channels. Despite these and other conservation measures, some species, especially the chinook and the sockeye salmon, continue to decline in numbers.

Salmon belong to the family Salmonidae. The Atlantic salmon is *Salmo salar*. It is of the same genus as true trout. Pacific salmon belong to the genus *Oncorhynchus*. The chinook is *O. tshawytscha;* the sockeye, *O. nerka;* the coho, *O. kisutch;* the pink, *O. gorbuscha;* the chum, *O. keta;* the cherry, *O. masou*.

Salmon River, a major river of central Idaho. The Salmon River flows from the Sawtooth Range generally northeastward to the town of North Fork, then westward to Riggins; from there it winds northwestward to the Idaho-Oregon border, where it flows into the Snake River. The total length of the river is 425 miles (685 km). The Salmon flows through several spectacular gorges and has long stretches of rapids.

Salmon River Mountains, a mountain range in central Idaho. The range is bounded on the north and east by the Salmon River and on the west by the South Fork of the Salmon River. In the south, the range reaches the headwaters of the Middle Fork of the Salmon River. Several peaks exceed 9,000 feet (2,700 m); the highest, Twin Peaks, reaches 10,328 feet (3,148 m).

Salmonella, a genus of bacteria. Various species cause diseases in humans and other animals. See FOOD POISONING; TYPHOID FEVER.

Salome, sȧ-lō′mē̆, the young woman who, according to Biblical accounts, was responsible for the death of the prophet John the Baptist. She was the stepdaughter of Herod Antipas, ruler of Galilee and Perea, and the daughter of Herodias. In the Bible (Matthew 14:3-11 and Mark 6:17-28) she is referred to only as "Herodias' daughter," but she is mentioned by name in *Antiquities of the Jews,* written by the first-century historian Flavius Josephus. Salome's dancing so pleased Herod that he promised to grant any favor that she asked. Prompted by her mother, who hated John the Baptist for denouncing her immoral conduct, Salome asked for the head of the prophet.

The story of Salome has been the subject of many works of art, notably Jules Massenet's opera *Hérodiade* (1881), Oscar Wilde's poetic drama *Salomé* (1893), and Richard Strauss's opera *Salome* (1905).

Salomon, săl′ō̆-mŭn, **Haym** (1740-1785), a Polish-American financier and Revolutionary War patriot. During the American Revolution, he helped to save the government from bankruptcy by lending his own money and by securing loans from others.

Salomon was born in Poland of Jewish-Portuguese ancestry. He came to New York City in 1772 and founded a successful brokerage business. Salomon allied himself with the patriot cause and was twice imprisoned by the British, 1776 and 1778. He escaped to Philadelphia in 1778. There he established a brokerage house and resumed his efforts on behalf of the Continental government. Salomon obtained more than $650,000 in aid. He was never repaid and died almost penniless.

Salonica, or **Salonika,** sȧ-lŏn′ĭ-kȧ; săl′ō̆-nē̆′kȧ (*modern Greek:* **Thessaloníki,** thâ′sä-lô-nyē̆′kyĕ), Greece, the nation's second largest city and the chief city of the Macedonia region of Greece. Salonica lies at the head of the Gulf of Therma, an inlet of the Aegean Sea, and is a major port. It is also the commercial, industrial, and transportation center of northern Greece.

Salonica has numerous historical landmarks, including a 2nd-century Roman forum, a 4th-century Roman arch, and many early Christian churches. The White Tower, the last remnant of the city's 15th-century fortifications, stands on the waterfront. The old Turkish quarter was the birthplace of Kemal Atatürk, founder of modern Turkey. Salonica has two universities and an archeological museum, which houses treasures of the ancient kingdom of Macedonia.

The Dance of Salome, by Benozzo Gozzoli in 1461-62; tempera on wood, 9¾ × 13½″ (24.8 × 34.3 cm)
National Gallery of Art, Samuel H. Kress Collection

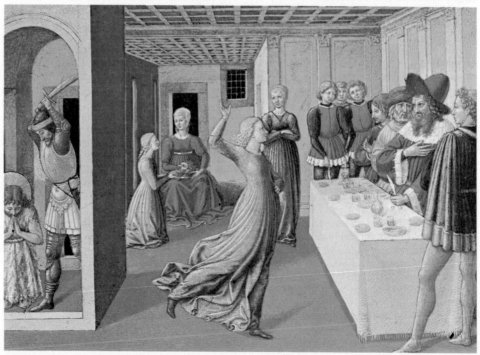

Salonica was founded about 315 B.C. on the site of ancient Therma by Cassander, king of Macedonia. The city later became the capital of the Roman province of Macedonia. It steadily gained in importance and under Byzantine rule was second only to Constantinople. It was the capital of the Kingdom of Thessalonica, part of the Latin Empire established by Franks of the Fourth Crusade, from 1204 until 1222. The city was restored to the Byzantine Empire by the Nicaeans in 1261, after a struggle with the Greeks. Salonica fell to the Turks in 1430 and remained part of the Ottoman Empire until the Balkan War of 1912, when it became part of Greece. Population: 377,951.

Salpiglossis, săl'pĭ-glŏs'ĭs, a genus of about eight species of annual or perennial herbs native to Chile. The plants can grow to a height of three feet (90 cm). Their leaves are pale green and are covered with short, sticky hairs. The large, funnel-shaped flowers can be purple, blue, red, yellow, or white, and may be veined in gold. One species, called *painted tongue,* is commonly cultivated as an ornamental garden flower.

Painted tongue is *Salpiglossis sinuata* of the nightshade family, Solanaceae.

Salsify, săl'sĭ-fĭ, a biennial root vegetable native to southern Europe. It is also called *oyster plant* and *vegetable oyster.* The thick root is about 12 inches (30 cm) long and 2 inches (5 cm) in diameter and is grayish white in color. The plant can grow to a height of about 4 feet (120 cm). The light purple flower heads are large, and the leaves are long and grasslike. Salsify is eaten as a vegetable and used as a relish. It grows wild in southern and central Europe; it is also grown in England, Spain, the United States, and Canada.

Salsify is *Tragopogon porrifolius* of the composite family, Compositae.

Salt, in chemistry. A salt is usually defined as a compound formed by the reaction of an acid with a base, but salts are formed also by other reactions. A salt can be formed, for example, by the reaction of two other salts; an acid with another salt; and an acid with a metal or its oxide. This article deals with salts in general. For *common salt,* or *table salt,* see SALT, COMMON.

Salts vary greatly in their physical and chemical properties. At ordinary temperature, most salts are crystalline solids. Many are soluble in water. Salts generally have a relatively high melting point. When melted or dissolved, salts can conduct electricity.

Salts are classified as either inorganic or organic. Inorganic salts, which are of mineral origin, make up a large percentage of the rocks and minerals of the earth's crust. Organic salts occur in, or can be produced from, animal and vegetable matter.

Common inorganic salts include sodium chloride, calcium carbonate (the chief component of limestone), sodium bicarbonate (baking soda), potassium nitrate (saltpeter), hydrated magnesium sulfate (epsom salts), and ammonium chloride (sal ammoniac). Sodium chloride is essential in the diet of humans and other animals, and is the most widely used substance in the chemical industry. Calcium phosphate, magnesium sulfate, and other inorganic salts are essential nutrients for plants and animals. Inorganic salts are used in making glass, cement, fertilizers, paper, explosives, dyes, photographic films, matches, and many other products.

Organic salts always contain carbon. Bile salts, which occur in bile (the secretion of the liver), aid in the absorption of fats from the intestine. Other important organic salts are calcium propionate, used in bread and drugs to prevent the formation of mold; lead acetate, used as a mordant (fixing agent) in dyeing; and sodium citrate, used as a flavoring in medicines and soft drinks. Organic salts are also used in tanning hides and in the manufacture of baking powders, printing inks, paints, and insecticides.

How Salts Are Formed

Salts, like acids and bases, consist of positive and negative ions. (An ion is an electrically charged atom or *radical*–a group of atoms that acts as a single atom.) Many salts can be derived from acids. A salt is derived from an acid when one or more hydrogen atoms of the acid are replaced by one or more metal ions or positively charged radicals. For example, zinc reacts with sulfuric acid to form zinc sulfate and free hydrogen.

$$Zn + H_2SO_4 \rightarrow ZnSO_4 + H_2$$

Some salts can be regarded as compounds derived from hydrogens—inorganic bases that contain the hydroxyl radicals (OH^-). Such a salt is formed when one or more hydroxyl radicals of a hydroxide are replaced by one of more nonmetal ions or negatively charged radicals. For example, calcium hydroxide reacts with sulfuric acid to form calcium sulfate and water.

$$Ca(OH)_2 + H_2SO_4 \rightarrow CaSO_4 + 2H_2O$$

In this reaction the sulfate radical ($SO_4^=$) replaces two hydroxyl radicals. Water is produced in all reactions between acids and hydroxides.

Normal salts, as those produced by the reactions shown, contain no replaceable hydrogen atoms or hydroxyl radicals. *Acid salts* result when the hydrogen of an acid is only partially replaced. For example, sodium hydroxide can react with sulfuric acid to form sodium bisulfate and water.

$$NaOH + H_2SO_4 \rightarrow NaHSO_4 + H_2O$$

The same acid and the same base can also react to form the normal salt sodium sulfate and water.

$$2NaOH + H_2SO_4 \rightarrow Na_2SO_4 + 2H_2O$$

Basic salts result when the hydroxyl of a hydroxide is only partially replaced. For example, bismuth hydroxide reacts with nitric acid to form basic bismuth nitrate and water. (The reaction is reversible.)

$$Bi(OH)_3 + HNO_3 \rightleftharpoons Bi(OH)_2NO_3 + H_2O$$

SALT, in international diplomacy, the common name for negotiations and treaties between the United States and the Soviet Union intended to limit strategic nuclear weapon strength of each nation. (SALT refers to both "Strategic Arms Limitations Talks" and "Strategic Arms Limitations Treaty.") Strategic weapons include (1) land- and submarine-based offensive ballistic missiles, (2) land-based anti-ballistic interceptor missiles (ABM's), (3) long-range bombers armed with nuclear bombs, and (4) cruise missiles (small, unmanned airplanes with nuclear warheads) launched from bombers or submarines.

The first series of negotiations, SALT I, resulted in a treaty and an interim agreement in 1972. The treaty provided that each country could deploy up to 200 ABM's, but limited to two sites with no more than 100 missiles on each. In 1974 the two nations agreed to limit ABM's to just one site. The United States dismantled its ABM's in 1976; the Soviet Union chose Moscow as its single site. (Russia, after the Soviet Union broke up in 1991, continued to deploy the ABM's there.) The interim agreement limited for five years the number of each nation's offensive ballistic missiles.

Negotiations for SALT II were held during 1972-79, and a treaty was signed placing limitations on all kinds of strategic weapons and weapon systems. Opponents of SALT II in the United States contended that the nature of the limitations left the Soviets with an advantage and blocked ratification in the U.S. Senate. Nevertheless, at first both the United States and the Soviet Union adhered to the arms-limitations provisions of SALT II. In 1987, however, President Reagan authorized the building of more launch vehicles than allowed by the treaty.

Salt, Common, the chemical compound sodium chloride, a substance known chiefly for its use as a food seasoning. It is also called *table salt.* Common salt is essential to humans and other animals. It is widely used in the chemical industry and has important uses in medicine, in agriculture, and in various industrial processes.

Salt occurs in nature as a solid and in solution, mainly in seawater. It is also found in the body fluids of humans and other animals and in many plants. As a solid, salt is colorless or white, and is usually in the form of cube-shaped crystals. It has a glass-like luster and is transparent or translucent. It is easily soluble in water. When melted or dissolved, salt can conduct electricity. With water, it forms a solution that has a lower freezing point than pure water. Because of this property, salt can melt ice or snow. Salt accelerates corrosion of most metals. It has antiseptic properties.

Salt provides the body with sodium and chlorine, which are essential elements in the blood, lymph, and other body fluids. They serve chiefly to regulate the balance of water and dissolved substances outside the cells and to regulate the balance of acids and bases within the cells. They also have a role in maintaining proper blood volume, in regulating blood pressure, and in conducting nerve impulses. Chlorine is used by certain stomach glands to make the hydrochloric acid needed for digestion.

Maintenance of the proper salt level in the body fluids is essential to health. Because small amounts of salt are normally lost when the body eliminates water, some salt must be included in the diet. Adults need 230 mg of salt per day, or approximately one-tenth of a teaspoon, in order for the body to function properly. In humans, most salt is lost through perspiration; in extreme heat, if the lost salt is not replaced, water cannot be used effectively and salt deficiency can

Silvio Fiore/SuperStock
Solar Evaporation of Salt in Mauritius

occur. Symptoms include muscle cramps, nausea, vomiting, and confusion. The reduced concentration of salt in the blood can cause a decrease in blood volume that can strain the heart. To avoid salt deficiency, persons who are active in hot weather should take salt tablets.

Too high a level of salt is also dangerous; it can cause violent illness and even death through dehydration (drying out of the body tissues). Normally, the body can excrete a small excess of salt, but only if enough water is taken in. It is for this reason that a person should never drink seawater. (A given volume of seawater contains much more salt than the body can eliminate in that volume of water, so that drinking seawater raises the salt level.) The consumption of excessive amounts of salt has been linked with *hypertension,* or high blood pressure. People with hypertension should restrict their salt intake by following a low-sodium diet.

Humans and other animals get salt from food or natural deposits. People who eat meat or fish do not usually require more salt than is already in these foods. People who eat mainly vegetables or cereal grains, such as wheat and rice, need additional salt because these foods have a low salt content. Plant-eating animals such as horses and deer also need additional salt, but flesh-eating animals, such as lions and wolves, do not. Wild animals obtain salt from surface deposits called *salt licks*. Cattle and other livestock are usually given feed that contains salt, and often blocks of salt are placed in pastures and feed lots.

Uses of Salt

Most commercially produced salt is used by the chemical industry in the manufacture of chlorine, caustic soda, and other chemi-

S-72

cals. Large quantities of salt are used in livestock feeding. Salt is widely used on highways, roads, and streets in winter to help keep them clear of ice and snow. In the food industry salt is used to improve food flavors, to control the growth of bacteria in yeast and cheese, and to cure and preserve certain foods. Farmers use salt as a preservative for hay.

Salt is used in steelmaking to remove rust and to harden certain types of steel. Salt is also used in tanning hides, in dyeing textile fibers, in softening water, in refining oil, and in the manufacture of soap, glass, paper, rubber, ceramics, and many other substances. *Brine,* a strong salt solution, is often used as a refrigerant in ice making. Transparent crystals of salt are used as prisms and lenses in spectroscopes to study ultraviolet and infrared radiation.

In medicine, substances to be injected into the body are often suspended in a *physiological salt solution* (a solution composed of water and 0.75 to 0.90 per cent salt by weight) to make the injected substances acceptable to the tissues. Salt is also used in the treatment of sore throat and inflammation of the eye. *Iodized salt* is table salt that contains trace amounts of iodine, which is essential for preventing goiter.

Where Salt Is Found

Salt is commonly found in nature as the mineral *rock salt,* or *halite,* and in solution in seawater, in salt lakes, and in salt springs. (For illustration of halite, see MINERAL.) It is also found in some underground waters and in small amounts in rivers and streams. The salt in water comes from sodium compounds and chlorine compounds that are dissolved from rocks; in water these compounds react chemically to produce dissolved salt. Much of the dissolved salt is ultimately carried to the sea or to salt lakes by rivers and streams.

The amount of salt found in water varies from place to place. Seawater contains sodium chloride in an average concentration of 2.7 per cent by weight. In some bodies of water, where there is little rain and evaporation of water is high, the salt concentration is greater than in the oceans.

Rock salt is widely distributed in the earth's crust. Deposits were formed by the evaporation of ancient seas and other bodies of saltwater. Rock salt usually occurs in layers and is commonly found associated with gypsum, anhydrite, calcite, clay, and sand. *Salt domes* are large, vertical columns of salt, often more than 1,000 feet (300 m) in height, that were forced upward toward the surface from deeply buried salt beds by pressures within the earth. Petroleum is often found associated with salt domes. (See PETROLEUM, illustration titled *Oil Traps.*)

Production of Salt

Salt is obtained commercially by mining and by the evaporation of seawater, water from salt lakes, and natural or artificial brine. Seawater or water from salt lakes is usually evaporated by the sun's heat, brine by artificial heat.

Natural brine is formed when underground water flows into salt deposits. Artificial brine is produced by drilling wells into salt deposits and injecting fresh water under pressure to dissolve the salt. The resulting brine is about 25 per cent salt by weight.

In the United States most salt is obtained by mining and by the evaporation of artificial brine. The greater part of the brine produced in the United States, however, is not used for salt production, but is used as brine in the chemical industry for such purposes as the making of soda ash by the Solvay process and the manufacture of chlorine and caustic soda.

The United States and China are the world's leading producers of salt. Louisiana, Texas, New York, and Ohio are the major producing states. Other important salt-producing countries include Germany, Canada, India, Great Britain, Mexico, and Australia.

Salt from Mines. Rock salt is usually mined by the room-and-pillar method. This method consists of removing salt to form a series of large rooms or chambers, leaving pillars of salt to support the roof. In removing the salt, standard mining procedures are used.

If the mined salt is relatively pure, it is crushed and then graded according to the size of the particles. The salt is then packaged for market or shipped in bulk. If the mined salt contains a high percentage of impurities, it is purified by chemical processes before being marketed. Most rock salt is used for industrial purposes and to melt ice and snow. Some is pressed into blocks for livestock feeding.

Brine Evaporation. The brine from salt wells is usually pumped into large settling tanks. Chemicals are added to the brine to remove impurities, which settle to the bottom of the tank. The purified brine is then evaporated. The two most common methods of evaporating brine are the vacuum pan process and the grainer, or open, pan process.

Vacuum Pan Process. In this process brine is evaporated under a partial vacuum in large closed vessels. When the pressure is reduced, the brine boils at a lower temperature than is needed at atmospheric pressure. For greater fuel economy, vacuum pans are operated in series, usually three or four, with the steam generated by the boiling brine in one vacuum pan being used to boil the brine in the next.

The brine is boiled vigorously. As the water evaporates, small cube-shaped crystals of salt are formed. The salt settles to the bottom of the pan, and is drawn off as a slurry, a mixture of solid salt and brine. The slurry is filtered to remove the brine. The salt is dried in kilns and then graded. It may be packaged, or it is blended with other substances to obtain salt products for special purposes. For example, table salt is mixed with a material that coats the crystals to prevent caking in damp weather. The salt produced by the vacuum pan process is between 99.5 and 99.9 per cent pure. It is called *granulated salt, evaporated salt,* or *vacuum pan salt.*

Grainer, or *Open, Pan Process.* In this process brine is evaporated in open tanks. Salt crystals, usually in the shape of flakes, are formed on the surface of the brine where evaporation takes place. After the crystals reach a certain size, they settle to the bottom of the tank. The salt is usually scraped from the tanks by rakes. It is then dried, graded, and packaged. This type of salt, called *grainer salt,* or *flake salt,* is about 99.8 per cent pure. It is used on crackers and in producing cheese, butter, and other foods.

Solar Evaporation. In this process, seawater or salt lake water is evaporated by the sun's heat in a series of large, shallow ponds. The salt water is first pumped into concentrating ponds, where the water is partially evaporated until the remaining solution becomes saturated with salt. In the early stages of evaporation, suspended impurities and the less soluble compounds in the salt water are deposited on the bottom of the ponds. The saturated salt solution is then run into cyrstallizing ponds, where it is further concentrated. As more water evaporates, large crystals of salt are deposited on the bottom of the ponds. The remaining solution, called *bittern,* is drawn off; it is sometimes used as a source of magnesium, bromine, potassium, or sodium compounds.

After the ponds are drained, the salt is removed by machines. It is then dried, crushed, and graded. A portion of the salt is usually dissolved in water to form brine, which is used to make granulated salt. The rest is used mainly for industrial purposes and for livestock feeding. The salt produced by solar evaporation is between 99.4 and 99.8 per cent pure. It is called *solar salt.*

History

As early as Neolithic times (beginning about 9000 B.C.) some primitive people in western Europe were evaporating salt water. During this period salt was quarried near the Dead Sea, in Asia Minor, and in South America. Quarrying led to attempts to mine salt at deeper levels. Remains of such mines, dating from about 2000 B.C., have been found in central Europe.

Salt has been an important commodity for thousands of years. No one knows who first discovered its preservative quality, but the practice of using salt or brine to preserve fish and meat was already widespread in ancient times. Among some ancient peoples, salt was commonly used in religious offerings. Because salt was so highly valued, it was even used as money in ancient Ethiopia and China. Roman soldiers were given a ration of salt as part of their wages, and later a sum of money to buy salt; the word *salary* is derived from the Latin *salarium,* "salt money."

The chemical formula is NaCl. Melting point: 1,473.8° F. (801° C.). Specific gravity: 2.165.

Books about Common Salt

Adshead, S. A. M. *Salt and Civilization* (St. Martin's Press, 1992).

For Younger Readers

Joly, Dominique. *Grains of Salt* (Young Discovery, 1988).

Salt Lake. See GREAT SALT LAKE.

Salt Lake City, Utah, the capital and largest city of the state, and the seat of Salt Lake County. It lies between 4,200 and 5,200 feet (1,280 and 1,585 m) above sea level on a plain between Great Salt Lake and the Wasatch Range. The Jordan River, on its way to Great Salt Lake, flows through the city's west side. As one of the few large cities between the Rocky Mountains and the west coast, Salt Lake City is an important commercial and industrial center. It is also a

Mormon Temple faces Temple Square in Salt Lake City. The square is enclosed by a wall, part of which is visible in the foreground.
© Phil Degginger/Color-Pic, Inc.

religious center—the headquarters of the Church of Jesus Christ of Latter-day Saints, or Mormon Church.

The city's wide streets, many of them tree-lined, form an orderly grid. Toward the northern end of town lies the central business district. The eastern and northern sections of Salt Lake City are built on a series of terraces, locally called "benches," on the slopes of the Wasatch Range. Most of the manufacturing districts are outside the city limits to the west and south.

Located in the heart of Utah's richest agricultural and mining area, Salt Lake City, with its metropolitan area, is a major processing and marketing center. Major industries are food processing, the smelting of metallic ores, oil refining, and the manufacture of steel products, paper and printed matter, electronic and missile components, and chemicals. Interstate routes 15 and 80 and several railroads and airlines serve the city.

Temple Square, a walled city block in the downtown area, encloses the Mormon Temple, the Tabernacle, and the Assembly Hall. The six-spired Temple, completed in 1893, is open only to persons of the Mormon faith. The adjacent Tabernacle is an oval, domed structure; it is the home of the renowned Mormon Tabernacle Choir. Nearby are the Mormon Church administration building, the Museum of Church History and Art, and the Salt Palace Center, a complex of buildings that includes a convention center, a concert hall, and an art museum. Also nearby are the Pioneer Memorial Museum, the state capitol, and the Family History Library, the largest genealogical library in the world.

Near the mouth of Emigration Canyon at the eastern edge of the city stands the "This is the Place" monument. From a vantage point here Brigham Young's party of Mormons first viewed the site of the present city. The University of Utah and Westminster College are in Salt Lake city. The city is home to the Utah Jazz and Utah Starzz professional basketball teams.

History

The region that includes what is now Salt Lake City was inhabited by Ute Indians when the first white men arrived. During the winter of 1824-25, two trappers, James Bridger and Étienne Provost, independently discovered the Great Salt Lake.

The first white settlement in the Great

Salt Lake Valley was made by the Mormons, led by Brigham Young, in 1847. They were seeking a place "to colonize in peace and safety," having long suffered persecution. Young laid out plans for the city. The land, chosen for its isolation, was in Mexican territory. (It became part of the United States at the end of the Mexican War.) Crops were planted, and City Creek was dammed to supply water to the dry land—the first irrigation project by white settlers in the Americs. In 1848 the crops were threatened by swarms of crickets, but gulls from the Great Salt Lake islands devoured the insects and saved the settlement.

The settlement, which originally consisted of 143 men, 3 women, and 2 children, grew rapidly as immigrants came from the East and from Europe. In late 1848, there were about 3,700 Mormons in Salt Lake City. The settlement was run as a cooperative venture with most activities under church control. In 1849 the city's isolation was ended by the California gold rush. A measure of prosperity came from supplying prospectors with provisions and fresh horses. In 1851 the city was chartered as Great Salt Lake City ("Great" was dropped in 1868). It served as the capital of Utah Territory for most of the period before statehood was achieved.

As headquarters for the Mormon Church, Salt Lake City acted as the parent colony for other Mormon settlements. It also was a way station for pioneers traveling farther westward. By the 1880's, it had rail links to all parts of the country. New settlers arrived; many, however, were not Mormons, and friction arose.

In 1896 Salt Lake City was made the capital of the new state of Utah. With the 20th century came accommodation between Mormons and non-Mormons, substantial growth, and industrial development. In 1995 Salt Lake City was chosen as the site of the 2002 Winter Olympics.

Population: 159,936.

See also UTAH (illustrations).

Salt River, a river in southern Arizona. It is formed by the junction of the Black and White rivers in the White Mountains. Its course runs westward for 200 miles (320 km) to the Gila River near Phoenix. Because of damming and water diversion upstream, the westernmost portion of the riverbed is usually dry. The lower Salt valley is the most populated part of the state and an important irrigated area, producing cotton, hay, citrus fruits, and other crops. Water for irrigation, urban use, and hydroelectric power is provided by the Salt River Project, which includes five dams on the Salt and two on the Verde.

See also ROOSEVELT DAM.

Salt Sea. See DEAD SEA.

Salta, Argentina, the capital of Salta province. It lies in northwestern Argentina near the foothills of the Andes. Sugar refining and meat packing are among the principal industries. Salta is one of Argentina's best-preserved colonial cities. Prominent buildings in the colonial style include the Cabildo (city hall), the cathedral, and the Church of San Francisco. Salta was founded by the Spanish in 1582.

Population: 367,099.

Saltbox House. See AMERICAN COLONIAL LIFE, picture *Colonial Houses*.

Salten, zäl'tĕn, **Felix** (1869-1945), an Austrian writer. His international fame rests on *Bambi* (1923), a story about a wild deer. Like the animals in Salten's other books for children, Bambi is given human emotions and characteristics. Among Salten's other animal stories are *The Hound of Florence* (1921), *Fifteen Rabbits* (1929), *Florian, the Emperor's Stallion* (1933), and *Bambi's Children* (1939).

Salten was born in Hungary but went to Austria as a child. He was an influential journalist and drama critic, but his plays and novels for adult readers were unsuccessful. In 1939 he went to Switzerland as a refugee from the Nazi regime.

Saltillo, säl-tē'yŏ, Mexico, the capital of Coahuila state, about 440 miles (710 km) north-northwest of Mexico City. Saltillo lies about a mile (1,600 m) above sea level in an agricultural and mining area. The city has some manufacturing, and is especially noted for brightly colored serapes. It is a popular summer resort. Among prominent buildings are the 18th-century cathedral, one of the finest in northern Mexico, and the Palacio del Gobierno, the state capitol.

Saltillo was founded by the Spanish late in the 1500's and soon became the headquarters for northward exploration. From 1824 until 1836 it was the capital of a territory that included Texas and Coahuila. The Battle of Buena Vista in the Mexican War was fought nearby in 1847.

Population: 440,845.

Salt-marsh Caterpillar. See BUTTER-FLIES AND MOTHS, subtitle *Kinds of Moths:* Tiger Moths (Acrea) and illustration.

Salton Sea, sôl′t′n; sôl′tŭn, a lake in the Imperial Valley of southern California, 235 feet (72 m) below sea level. It is about 30 miles (48 km) long and 8 to 14 miles (13 to 23 km) wide, and covers some 350 square miles (900 km²). Maximum depth is 46 feet (14 m). Until the early 1900's the area was known as the Salton Sink. During 1905-07 a succession of floods on the Colorado River inundated the depression, creating the lake. For nearly 40 years evaporation slowly reduced the area of the lake, increasing the saltiness of the water. Overflow from irrigation canals now offsets the evaporation, keeping the size fairly constant.

Saltpeter, the common name for potassium nitrate, a white, crystalline solid composed of potassium, nitrogen, and oxygen. It is also called *niter*. Saltpeter commonly occurs as a crust on the soil and on the surface of rocks in dry climates and in the soil of limestone caves. Its name is derived from the Latin *sal petrae,* "salt of the rock." Naturally occurring saltpeter is found in very limited quantities. Most saltpeter is produced commercially by the reaction of potassium chloride with sodium nitrate.

Saltpeter is used as an oxidizer in explosives, matches, fireworks, and rocket propellants. It is also used as a source of potassium and nitrogen in fertilizers and as a meat preservative.

Chile saltpeter is a form of sodium nitrate. It resembles saltpeter in appearance, and sometimes occurs in the same deposits as saltpeter. The largest deposits of Chile saltpeter are found in the desert regions of northern Chile and Bolivia. Chile saltpeter is used in fertilizers, in explosives, and in the manufacture of nitric acid. After World War I synthetic processes were developed for producing large quantities of sodium nitrate, so the demand for the natural form has declined.

The formula for saltpeter is KNO_3; for Chile saltpeter, $NaNO_3$.

Saltwater. See OCEAN, subtitle *Properties of Seawater.*

Saluki. See DOG, subtitle *Breeds of Dogs:* Hounds.

Salute, a formal gesture of respect and recognition for a high-ranking person, a national flag or anthem, or a nation. The most

Civilian Salute

Hand Salute

Sword Salute

Rifle Salute
(Present Arms)   Rifle Salute
(at *Order Arms*)   Rifle Salute
(at *Right Shoulder Arms*)

common type of salute is the armed forces *hand salute,* made by bringing the right hand to the head so that the forefinger touches the hat or the forehead. In general, this salute is exchanged between officers and between enlisted personnel and officers upon meeting, with the lower-ranking person saluting first. The other major occasions for the hand salute are during honors to the national flag and the playing of the national anthem. Variations of this salute are used by some organizations. For example, Boy Scouts use a three-fingered salute. Civilians salute by placing the right hand (or, for men who are not bareheaded, the hat held in the right hand) over the heart.

A *sword salute* or a *rifle salute* is generally substituted for the hand salute by armed forces personnel under arms. A salute with a sword is made by raising it to the face. A rifle salute is made in one of three ways—*present* (prē-zĕnt') *arms,* at *order arms,* or at *shoulder arms* (see illustration), depending upon the person's activity.

A *gun salute* is made by firing one or more guns a certain number of times. For example, an 11-gun salute consists of 11 successive rounds of gunfire. Salutes for persons range up to 21 guns for the head of a nation. A nation may be honored by a 21-gun salute on such occasions as patriotic holidays. In the United States, a 50-gun salute is fired on Independence Day to honor the 50 states.

A *flag salute* is a dip of a flag. On land, the United States flag is never dipped, but other flags, such as regimental flags, may be dipped. At sea, a ship may salute another by dipping the national ensign.

The salute dates at least to the days of chivalry in the Middle Ages. At that time, knights in armor raised their visors to be identified as friends; other displayed an empty sword hand to show that they were not hostile. Common soldiers saluted their superiors by removing their headgear. From these various gestures came the modern hand salute.

Several other types of salute derive from disarming to show loyalty, friendship, submission, or peaceful intentions. Presenting arms, for example, was originally an act of submission to the monarch. The salute by gunfire had its origins in a custom practiced on the approach of dignitaries to a ship or military installation. To assure the visitors of their safety, the largest guns were fired be-

Salvador, Brazil, is built on two levels, one 200 feet (60 m) above the other. The tall structure at the far left is an elevator tower linking the two levels.

© Jose Azel/Woodfin Camp & Associates, Inc.

fore their arrival. When England was the strongest naval power in the world, foreign ships in English waters lowered their sails to acknowledge the authority of an English ship; from this practice evolved dipping the ensign.

Salvador, săl′vȧ-dôr, Brazil, the capital of Bahía state and one of Brazil's largest cities. The city is known locally as Bahía, but Salvador is the official name. Salvador lies at the entrance to Todos os Santos Bay, an inlet of the Atlantic Ocean, about 750 miles (1,200 km) northeast of Rio de Janeiro. It is the commercial, industrial, and transportation center for an agricultural area that produces tobacco, sugarcane, and cacao. Manufactured products include cigars, cigarettes, and cocoa. The city has an excellent port.

Salvador is built on two levels, connected by elevators and roads. The Baixa, along the bay, is the shipping and commercial section. The Alta, some 200 feet (60 m) above the Baixa, is the site of government buildings, hotels, residences, and the main shopping district. Here also are numerous 17th- and 18th-century fortifications and buildings. The city is the seat of the state university, founded in 1946.

Salvador, founded in 1549, is one of Brazil's oldest cities. It soon became the capital and leading city of Portuguese America. Rio de Janeiro was made the capital of Brazil in 1763, but Salvador continued to be an important commercial center and port.

Population: 2,211,539.

Salvador, El. See EL SALVADOR.

Salvage, in maritime law, money paid to persons who save a ship and its cargo from peril at sea, or rescue such property when it is wrecked on the coast. In the United States, salvage laws apply also to vessels on rivers and lakes. The amount of salvage is determined by an admiralty court and is based on the value of the property saved, the effort and danger involved, and other factors.

An important point in a salvage case is whether the ship was truly in peril. Often when a ship is disabled, its captain and some of the crew will stay aboard in hopes of bringing it in safely themselves and so avoiding salvage costs. If assistance is given by an official agency, such as the Coast Guard, there is no salvage.

Salvation Army, a Christian denomination that is also an international social welfare organization. It is operated along military lines, with uniforms, bands, and a distinctive flag. The Salvation Army has an estimated membership of about 1,500,000. Membership in the United States is about 450,000.

Beliefs and Activities

Salvation Army doctrines are based on the Bible. They emphasize human salvation

Cabrillo, the first explorer to visit the west coast of what is now the United States.

Near the mouth of the San Diego River is Mission Bay, once an area of sand bars and tidal flats. Reclaimed and turned into a spacious park, it features swimming, boating, water skiing, and Sea World, known for its whale and dolphin shows. Beaches dot San Diego's shoreline; mountain and desert recreation areas are nearby. Qualcomm Stadium is the home of the San Diego Chargers, a professional football team, and of the Padres of baseball's National League.

Music and dance organizations include the San Diego Symphony Orchestra, the San Diego Opera, and the California Ballet. There are numerous institutions of higher education, the largest of which is San Diego State University. A campus of the University of California is near the city's La Jolla area. The nearby Scripps Institution of Oceanography, long one of the leading schools of its type, is associated with the university. Other institutions of higher learning include the University of San Diego, the United States International University, and Point Loma Nazarene College.

History

In 1542 Spanish explorers under Juan Rodríguez Cabrillo sailed into the waters of San Diego Bay. The bay area was not colonized, however, until 1769. In that year a Franciscan mission was founded by Father Junípero Serra on the order of Gaspar de Portolá, the Spanish governor of California. The mission, San Diego de Alcalá, was the first of California's 21 Franciscan missions. Portolá established a presidio (military post) at San Diego at about the same time.

The settlement grew very little before 1822, when California became part of newly independent Mexico. After the Mexican War began in 1846 U.S. Marines under Commodore R. F. Stockton seized the presidio at San Diego. They were driven out by Mexican forces a few weeks later but soon recaptured the post. The rest of the town was occupied by troops under General Stephen W. Kearny, and American rule was permanently established.

In 1867 A. E. Horton, a merchant and prospector, laid out a new city nearby. It was incorporated in 1872 and eventually absorbed the old city. After a brief period of prosperity because of a nearby gold strike in the 1870's, there was a slow growth in tuna

processing, shipping, and other industries. Glenn Curtiss's flight here in 1911 in the first seaplane stimulated establishment of an aircraft industry. Naval installations were built in the 1920's, eventually forming one of the largest naval complexes in the United States.

During the 1940's and 1950's the city became heavily dependent on the aerospace industry, and it was hit hard by recession in this industry in the 1960's. Industrial diversification and massive building projects, including convention and tourist facilities, were undertaken and contributed to the city's increased prosperity during the 1970's. In 1981 a trolley line linking San Diego with Tijuana, Mexico, was opened. In the 1980's, San Diego was one of the fastest-growing major cities in the nation.

Population

The city's population by census years has been as follows:

1860	731	1930	147,995
1870	2,300	1940	203,341
1880	2,637	1950	334,387
1890	16,159	1960	573,224
1900	17,700	1970	697,027
1910	39,578	1980	875,538
1920	74,361	1990	1,110,549

San Diego, University of. See UNIVERSITIES AND COLLEGES (table).

San Diego State University. See UNIVERSITIES AND COLLEGES (table).

San Diego Zoo. See ZOO, subtitle *Famous Zoos.*

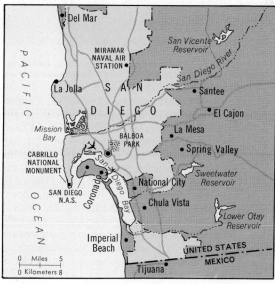

© D. C. Lowe/TSW—Click Chicago

San Francisco. Shown here, linking the downtown section of the city and Yerba Buena Island, is the double-decked suspension section of the San Francisco–Oakland Bay Bridge.

San Francisco, săn′ frăn-sĭs′kō, California, the fourth most populous city in the state. It occupies all of San Francisco County. The city lies on the tip of the San Francisco Peninsula, overlooking the Pacific Ocean on the west, San Francisco Bay on the east, and the Golden Gate (the entrance to the bay) on the north. With a magnificent natural setting and architecturally distinctive buildings, San Francisco is generally regarded as one of the nation's most beautiful cities. It is also a hub of commerce, a cultural and educational center, and a city of diverse nationalities.

S-90

General Plan

San Francisco is roughly square in shape. Much of the land is extremely hilly, reaching a height of more than 920 feet (280 m) above sea level at Mount Davidson and Twin Peaks, in the central part of the city. In these and other high hilly areas, roads are laid out in a circular manner; elsewhere they form a rectangular pattern, aligned mainly north-south and east-west. The chief limited-access highways are the James Lick, Southern, and Bayshore freeways.

Downtown San Francisco, with its tall buildings, steep hills, and clanging cable cars, occupies the northeastern corner of the city. Here, Market Street runs diagonally southwestward from the Ferry Building past the financial district and the Civic Center to the base of Twin Peaks. Along the Embarcadero, a broad semicircular street skirting the downtown waterfront, are many of the city's piers, wharves, and warehouses. Nearby are Telegraph Hill, Russian Hill, and Nob Hill.

Outside the downtown area, San Francisco is primarily residential. Large tracts, however, are occupied by Golden Gate Park, John McLaren Park, and the Golden Gate National Recreation Area, which includes the Presidio, a former army base covering nearly 1,500 acres (600 hectares). Industrial areas are mainly in the southeast along the bay shore flats.

San Francisco has fixed boundaries and can expand no farther. It is, however, part of a vast and rapidly growing urban complex called the Bay Area, which adjoins San Francisco Bay. (See CALIFORNIA, full-color map and inset titled *San Francisco and Vicinity*.) Cities in this area include Oakland, San Jose, Fremont, Sunnyvale, Concord, Berkeley, Hayward, and Santa Clara.

Five bridges cross the bay in the metropolitan area; two of them serve San Francisco. The Golden Gate Bridge, one of the world's longest suspension bridges (main span 4,200 feet [1,280 m]), connects the city with the Marin Peninsula to the north. The San Francisco–Oakland Bay Bridge, with suspension, cantilever, and truss sections, joins San Francisco and Oakland.

Economy

To a large extent San Francisco is a commercial and maritime city. Much of its economic vitality stems from shipping and the business it creates in such fields as finance, insurance, wholesaling, and processing.

Several of the nation's largest commercial banks, including the Bank of America and the Wells Fargo Bank, are here, as well as a Federal Reserve bank, a major stock exchange, and numerous foreign banks. San Francisco is the headquarters of many large corporations, including insurance, utility, transportation, and engineering companies.

In wholesale trade, San Francisco is among the leaders on the West Coast. Goods from all parts of the nation are shipped here for regional distribution and for ex-

port. Much of the foreign trade is with the Far East.

Manufacturing, though important, is relatively less significant in San Francisco than in most major American cities. Because land values are high, light manufacturing industries—which require less space than heavy industries—prevail. Among them are food processing; printing and publishing; and the making of clothing, small metal articles, and machinery.

Hyde Street Cable Car reaching the top of a hill. Alcatraz and Angel islands are in the background. Cable cars, pulled by moving underground cables, were developed in the 1870's to overcome the city's steep hills. The city's cable car system was made a National Historic Landmark in 1964.

© David Frazier

The Bay Area as a whole has widespread and diversified industries. In addition to those of the city, they include petroleum refining; automobile and truck assembly; and the making of steel, heavy machinery, chemicals, space and electronic equipment, paper, and stone, clay, and glass products.

A cosmopolitan city with outstanding hotels and restaurants, entertainment, and cultural attractions, San Francisco draws many tourists and conventioneers. Tourism

San Francisco's Chinatown, viewed here along Grant Avenue, is the largest Chinese community outside Asia. Its narrow, congested streets are lined with a wide variety of shops and many restaurants.
© Cathlyn Melloan/TSW—Click Chicago

and the convention industry are two of the city's chief sources of revenue. For conventions San Francisco has several major facilities, including the Moscone Convention Center, the Civic Auditorium, and, in nearby Daly City, the Cow Palace.

Besides being a major center for ocean shipping, the San Francisco area, including Oakland, is a leading air and land transportation center. San Francisco International Airport, south of the city, ranks among the nation's busiest. The city is also served by Oakland International Airport, several railways, and numerous bus and truck lines. The rapid transit system, BART (Bay Area Rapid Transit), completed in 1972, is a 75-mile (121-km) system of high-speed subways and surface and elevated lines linking San Francisco and the major outlying cities.

Prominent Places

Union Square, which is adjoined by the St. Francis Hotel and many fine shops and stores, is the focus of downtown San Francisco. To the north, centered on Grant Avenue, is Chinatown, home to one of the largest Chinese communities outside the Far East. In the neighborhood are clustered hundreds of restaurants, food stores, and shops featuring Oriental wares.

On nearby Nob Hill, where the mansions of San Francisco's wealthiest families once stood, are Grace Cathedral and several of the city's finest hotels. Farther north is Russian Hill, capped by high-rise apartment buildings; to the east is Telegraph Hill, with its 210-foot (64-m) Coit Memorial Tower. Between the two hills lies the North Beach district, a predominantly Italian area and one of the chief centers of the city's nightlife.

On San Francisco's north shore stands the restored Palace of the Legion of Honor, a fine arts museum in the only remaining building of the Panama-Pacific International Exposition of 1915. To the east are a yacht harbor, several small parks, Ghirardelli Square, the Cannery, and Fisherman's Wharf. Ghirardelli Square (a former chocolate factory) and the Cannery (a former fruit-canning plant) house a wide variety of restaurants and specialty shops. At Fisherman's Wharf, seafood is featured in numerous restaurants and sidewalk stalls. Nearby at the Hyde Street Pier the three-masted sailing ship *Balclutha* is permanently moored. A short distance offshore is Alcatraz Island, site of a former federal prison.

About midway along Market Street is the

Civic Center, a complex of government and public buildings built largely in Italian Renaissance style. The city hall, main public library, civic auditorium, symphony hall, and opera house are here.

One of San Francisco's outstanding features is Golden Gate Park, more than three miles (5 km) long and with an area of some 1,000 acres (400 hectares). It contains a great variety of attractions, including two museums of fine art, a planetarium, an aquarium, an arboretum, and a conservatory.

Most of the northern and western coastal areas of San Francisco are part of the Golden Gate National Recreation Area, a unit of the National Park System. Included in the recreational area are several long beaches, a promenade, and such historic places as Fort Point, Fort Mason, and Alcatraz Island. Seal Rocks, also a part of the recreational area, is a gathering place for hundreds of California sea lions.

Mission Dolores, in the Mission District northeast of Twin Peaks, is an adobe structure built by the Spanish as the Mission San Francisco de Asís shortly after they estab-

lished their presidio (military post) in 1776. In the city's southeast is 3Com Park, home of two professional sports team—the San Francisco Giants (baseball) and the San Francisco Forty-Niners (football).

Education and Culture

About a dozen universities and colleges are in San Francisco. They include San Francisco State University, the University of San Francisco, Golden Gate University, and a medical branch of the University of California. Scattered throughout the Bay Area are more than 40 other four-year institutions of higher learning, including the University of California at Berkeley and Stanford University at Palo Alto.

San Francisco has several museums of fine arts. These include the California Palace of the Legion of Honor, the M. H. deYoung Memorial Museum, the Asian Art Museum of San Francisco, and the San Francisco Museum of Modern Art.

Items relating to the history of the city are exhibited in the California Historical Society's Whittier Mansion. The National Maritime Museum, in Aquatic Park, has models

Fisherman's Wharf is the home of many of the city's finest seafood restaurants. The pointed building in the background (right center) is the Transamerica Pyramid. The round structure (left) is the Coit Memorial Tower.

of old ships and various relics from the city's early years as a port. The museum also maintains several permanently moored historic ships that can be boarded by the public. At the Palace of Fine Arts is the Exploratorium, a science museum with more than 600 hands-on exhibits.

Other collections are exhibited at the Cable Car Museum, the Old Mint, and the Navy/Marine Corps/Coast Guard Museum.

Among the several musical organizations are the San Francisco Symphony Orchestra and the San Francisco Opera. There are also a number of dance companies, including the San Francisco Ballet. Chief among the many professional theatrical groups is the American Conservatory Theatre. Japan Center, which includes shops and restaurants, a kabuki theater, and the Japanese consulate, reflects the heritage of San Francisco's thousands of Japanese-Americans.

History

Although Spain claimed California in the mid-16th century, colonization did not begin until the 18th. An overland expedition from Mexico discovered San Francisco Bay in

1769, and in 1776 Spanish settlers arrived at the site of the present city. A presidio (military post) was built near the entrance to the bay. A Franciscan mission, San Francisco de Asís, was established about three miles (5 km) southeast, on a stream called Nuestra Señora de los Dolores (Our Lady of Sorrows). The mission came to be known as Dolores. The fine harbor soon attracted ships of various nations to the bay.

After Mexico gained its independence in 1821, the presidio was gradually abandoned, and in 1834 the mission was transferred from religious to civil authority. In 1835 a port administration was set up, with William A. Richardson, who had arrived in 1822 on a British whaler, in charge of it. A new port community, Yerba Buena, was laid out on a cove of the eastern shore. It was centered in what is now Chinatown; present Montgomery Street was part of the shoreline road.

In 1846, after the beginning of the Mexican War, Yerba Buena was occupied for the United States by a naval detachment under Commander John B. Montgomery. Three

Facts about San Francisco

Name—San Francisco was originally called Yerba Buena, meaning "good herb." The city took its present name from the Mission San Francisco de Asís, honoring Saint Francis of Assisi. It is sometimes called the "City by the Golden Gate." The nickname "Frisco," often used by persons in other parts of the country, is unpopular with San Franciscans.

Location—Downtown San Francisco: 37° 47' N. and 122° 25' W.

Land Area—45.4 square miles (117.6 km²).

Climate—Downtown average temperatures: January, 51° F. (11° C.); July, 59° F. (15° C.); September (the warmest month), 62° F. (17° C.). Annual precipitation, 21 inches (530 mm); most of it falls from December through February.

Government—A consolidated city and county government, with a mayor and an 11-member board of supervisors.

Founding and Charter Dates—Founded in 1776, when the Spanish built a presidio (military post) and a mission here. Incorporated as a city in 1850. New charters granted in 1856, 1861, 1898, and 1932.

For Further Information—San Francisco Convention and Visitors Bureau, PO Box 6977, San Francisco, California 94101.

---

weeks later a party of about 240 Mormons, fleeing the United States, sailed into the harbor and decided to stay. In 1847 the town changed its name to San Francisco. The population was less than 500, not including residents of Mission Dolores and its surrounding community and the American garrison at the presidio.

From Gold Rush to Earthquake. The discovery of gold near Sutter's Mill (Coloma) in 1848 nearly emptied San Francisco, as residents rushed off to the diggings. The news spread quickly to Latin America, Pacific islands, and the Far East, and the harbor was soon filled with foreign ships.

In 1849 the Gold Rush from the eastern United States began. San Francisco became a vast tent city, with large numbers of transients to be fed and outfitted. Merchants, gambling-house proprietors, and real-estate speculators made fortunes. With the population sometimes doubling in 10 days, the city soon reached almost halfway across the peninsula. More land was gained by taking sand from the hills and filling in the areas around Yerba Buena cove, Mission Bay, and North Beach inlet.

Lawlessness was a serious problem and was met at various times by formation of citizens' committees. In 1851 a group calling itself the Vigilance Committee hanged four men during its 10 weeks' existence. The Second Vigilance Committee, formed in 1856, hanged four more.

By 1856 the first economic boom had ended, but prosperity and growth resumed

Golden Gate Park extends inland from the Pacific Ocean. The Conservatory of Flowers, shown here, was built in 1879.

© Arthur Threadgill

San Francisco in Ruins, as the result of the earthquake and fire in April, 1906. This view of Market (left) and Sacramento streets was taken from the Ferry Building tower while smoke still hung over the city.

after the 1859 Comstock Lode silver strike in Nevada. San Francisco, again the supply center, became the home of the "bonanza kings," who made the city known for luxury and elegance. Meanwhile, near the waterfront an area known as the Barbary Coast became notorious for vice.

A transcontinental railroad was completed in 1869, and the builders of the Central Pacific Railroad joined the bonanza kings in San Francisco's hierarchy of wealth. The city's shipping trade dropped drastically because of railroad competition, worsening the economic depression that had followed the Civil War. Thousands of Chinese coolies, imported to help build the railroad, glutted the city's labor market. In 1876 Chinatown had an estimated population of about 47,000. Anti-Chinese hostility was intense; riots and legislation forced many Chinese to leave. Tong wars—feuds between rival Chinese associations over control of vice—gave Chinatown an unsavory reputation.

San Francisco's reputation suffered from political corruption that developed under dominance of the railroad interests. Labor unionism, especially among maritime workers, brought strikes and violence.

On April 18, 1906, San Francisco experienced a severe earthquake, followed by fires that destroyed 28,000 buildings in the heart of the city and caused some 500 deaths. San Franciscans rushed to rebuild their city.

Modern Development. In 1908 Abe Ruef, San Francisco's political boss, was convicted on charges of graft, and a period of civic improvement began. A world's fair, the Panama-Pacific International Exposition, was held in 1915 to celebrate completion of the Panama Canal. Violent labor troubles broke out in 1916. After a bomb was thrown among spectators at a "Preparedness Day" parade (favoring national military strength), two labor leaders—Tom Mooney and Warren K. Billings—were convicted on what later proved to be perjured testimony.

World War I brought an influx of workers to San Francisco's shipyards and war industries of the metropolitan area. An increased water supply was urgently needed, and in 1934 a system that brought water from reservoirs 150 miles (240 km) away was completed. Two great bridges were built—the Bay Bridge to Oakland (completed in 1936) and the Golden Gate Bridge to Marin County (1937). The Golden Gate International Exposition was held in 1939-40.

During World War II there was another vast increase in population, as local industry expanded to meet wartime needs. The conference at which the United Nations was founded took place in 1945 in San Francisco. Beginning in the 1950's, the city undertook a far-reaching rehabilitation program. Major waterfront projects included the Golden Gateway Center and the Embarcadero Center. Several skyscrapers were built, among them the Transamerica Pyramid and the Bank of America building.

In 1978 Mayor George Moscone was shot to death by a disgruntled former member of the city board of supervisors. His successor was Dianne Feinstein, who became the city's first woman mayor.

In the 1990s, numerous Internet and multimedia companies started up in the San Francisco Bay area. This created many new jobs, which helped boost the city's economy yet also contributed to a severe housing shortage that sent real estate prices skyrocketing.

Population

San Francisco ranks fourth among California cities. Until 1920, when Los Angeles surpassed it, San Francisco was the largest city in California. The population by census years has been as follows:

1850	34,776	1930	634,394
1860	58,802	1940	634,536
1870	149,473	1950	775,357
1880	233,959	1960	740,316
1890	298,997	1970	715,674
1900	342,782	1980	678,974
1910	416,912	1990	723,959
1920	506,676		

For further information, see:
ALCATRAZ
BANK OF AMERICA NATIONAL TRUST
 AND SAVINGS ASSOCIATION
GOLDEN GATE
GOLDEN GATE BRIDGE
GOLDEN GATE INTERNATIONAL EXPOSITION
PANAMA-PACIFIC INTERNATIONAL EXPOSITION
SAN FRANCISCO BAY
SAN FRANCISCO CONFERENCE
UNITED STATES, section "The Economy," picture
 titled *Golden Gate Bridge*
History
ANZA, JUAN BAUTISTA DE
PORTOLÁ, GASPAR DE
SERRA, JUNIPERO
Noted San Franciscans

ATHERTON, GERTRUDE	LONDON, JACK
GEORGE, HENRY	STANFORD, LELAND
HEARST (William	WIGGIN, KATE
Randolph Hearst)	DOUGLAS
HUNTINGTON,	
COLLIS P.	

Books about San Francisco

Gayot, Andre. *The Best of San Francisco and Northern California,* 3rd edition (Gault Millau, 1993).

Hansen, Gladys. *Denial of Disaster: the Untold Story and Unpublished Photographs of the San Francisco Earthquake and Fire of 1906* (Cameron, 1989).

Mcgrew, Patrick. *Landmarks of San Francisco* (Abrams, 1991).

Olmstead, Marty. *San Francisco and the Bay Area: California Gateway to the Future* (Windsor, 1992).

For Younger Readers

Climo, Shirley. *City! San Francisco* (Macmillan, 1990).

Haddock, Patricia. *San Francisco* (Macmillan, 1988).

Wilson, Kate. *Earthquake! San Francisco, 1906* (Raintree, 1992).

San Francisco, University of. See UNIVERSITIES AND COLLEGES (table).

San Francisco Bay, an arm of the Pacific Ocean in California and one of the world's finest deepwater harbors. It is nearly landlocked, being connected to the Pacific only by the narrow strait called the Golden Gate. Including San Pablo Bay, its northern arm, San Francisco Bay is about 50 miles (80 km) long and up to 13 miles (21 km) wide. Maximum depth in the bay proper is about 140 feet (43 m), in the Golden Gate about 350 feet (107 m). Ports accommodating large ocean-going vessels are located at San Francisco, Oakland, and Richmond. There are several islands in the bay, including Alcatraz and Yerba Buena.

The Bay Area—especially the eastern side, called East Bay—is a rapidly growing commercial and industrial region. Five major bridges, including the Golden Gate and San Francisco–Oakland Bay bridges, span the bay. The Transbay Tube, a sub-

© John Elk III

Winchester Mystery House, San Jose, California. Built by an eccentric heiress, the house contains 160 rooms and intricate winding hallways, many leading to blank walls.

way tunnel beneath the bay, is between San Francisco and Oakland.

San Francisco Bay may have been entered by Sir Francis Drake in 1579, but most scholars believe he entered another bay, farther north. Actual discovery of San Francisco Bay is attributed to a Spanish land expedition under Don Gaspar de Portolá in 1769. Six years later Don Juan Manuel Ayala sailed into the bay through the Golden Gate.

See also ALCATRAZ; CALIFORNIA (opening photo and two-page map, inset titled *San Francisco and Vicinity*); GOLDEN GATE; GOLDEN GATE BRIDGE; SAN FRANCISCO (opening photo); YERBA BUENA ISLAND.

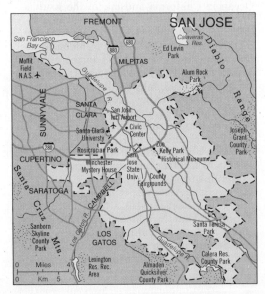

San Francisco Conference, April 25 to June 26, 1945, the international conference at which the United Nations was organized. It was officially called the United Nations Conference on International Organization. Some 800 representatives from 50 nations met in San Francisco to draw up a charter for an international organization designed to maintain world peace. The charter that was agreed upon became effective on October 24, 1945.

San Francisco State University. See UNIVERSITIES AND COLLEGES (table).

San Jacinto, Battle of. See HOUSTON, SAM, subtitle *Hero of Texas Independence*.

San Joaquin River, săn'wŏ-kēn', a major river in the Central Valley of California. It begins in the Sierra Nevada near Yosemite National Park and flows southwestward and then northwestward for a total of 350 miles (563 km). The San Joaquin merges with the Sacramento River and empties into San Pablo Bay, the northern arm of San Francisco Bay. Tributaries include the Mokelumne, Stanislaus, Tuolumne, and Merced rivers. The extensively irrigated San Joaquin Valley is one of the nation's most productive agricultural areas. Fresno, Stockton, and Modesto are the principal cities on or near the river. Dams on the San Joaquin and its tributaries are important for irrigation, flood control, and hydroelectric power.

San Jose, săn' [h]ŏ-zā', California, the seat of Santa Clara County. The city lies near the southern end of San Francisco Bay in the broad Santa Clara Valley. Its center stands about 80 feet (24 m) above sea level, but elevations increase to the east and west toward the nearby Diablo Range and the Santa Cruz Mountains. The city of Santa Clara adjoins San Jose on the west.

San Jose is situated in what is often called Silicon Valley, one of the world's chief centers of high-technology industries. Manufacturing, especially of processed foods and electronic items such as computers and semiconductors, provides the largest share of the city's jobs. Also important are services and wholesale and retail trade. San Jose is a major distribution center for one of the state's richest agricultural areas. Railways, freeways, and Interstate highways provide excellent transportation. Air service is available at the municipal airport and at nearby San Francisco International Airport.

Kelley Park, with a zoo, a Japanese garden, and a historical museum, and Alum Rock Park offer varied recreational facilities. In Rosicrucian Park are an Egyptian museum, a science museum, and a planetarium.

Near Rosicrucian Park is the Winchester Mystery House, a Victorian mansion built from 1884 to 1922. The Lick Observatory, in the Diablo Range, houses one of the world's largest refracting telescopes. San Jose has a symphony orchestra, an opera company, and a theater company. The Tech Museum of Innovation, located downtown, has approximately 250 interactive exhibits, most focusing on applications of technology in daily living. The city's professional hockey team, the Sharks, plays at the San Jose Arena. San Jose State University (1857) is the oldest state institution of higher learning in California.

History

San Jose was founded in 1777 by a Spanish colonist from Mexico, José Joaquin Morago. It was the first settlement other than a mission in what is now the state of California. The community had only some 500 residents in 1831, but grew fairly rapidly after California became a United States territory in 1848 and the Gold Rush began. San Jose was the seat of the California territorial legislature in 1849 and the first state capital, 1850-51. In 1850 San Jose was incorporated as a city. After the arrival of the first railway in 1864 and as gold prospecting declined, residents turned increasingly to agriculture.

Between 1900 and World War II San Jose, stimulated by the development of agriculture, developed as a food-processing center. Extremely rapid growth came with land annexations and the influx of manufacturing industries after 1950, when the population was roughly 95,000. By 2000, most of the largest electronic firms in the United States had offices in San Jose, creating one of the highest concentrations of high-technology companies in the world.

Population: 782,248.

San José, săn [h]ō-zā', Costa Rica, the nation's capital and largest city and the seat of San José province. It lies about 3,900 feet (1,190 m) above sea level on the Meseta Central (central plateau), surrounded by mountains with prominent volcanoes. San José is the commercial, cultural, and transportation center of Costa Rica. Coffee, the country's chief export crop, is shipped here from the

surrounding area for distribution to coastal ports. San José's manufactured products include consumer goods such as beverages, textiles, and processed foods. Several railways, an international airport, and the Inter-American Highway serve the city.

San José's architecture is a mixture of traditional Spanish and modern. The city has wide avenues flanked by parks and flower gardens, as well as narrow streets suitable only for one-way traffic. Most impressive of the pre-20th-century structures are the National Theater, modeled after the Paris Opera House, and the National Museum, a former fortress. Government buildings include the National Palace, where the legislature meets, and the Municipal Palace, or city hall. The National University has campuses in San José and in the neighboring suburb of San Pedro.

San José was founded in 1737 as a trading center for coffee plantations. It became the national capital in 1823, two years after Costa Rica declared its independence from Spain.

Population: 296,625.

San Jose Scale. See SCALE INSECTS.

San Jose State University. See UNIVERSITIES AND COLLEGES (table).

San Juan, săn wŏn', Argentina, the capital of San Juan province. It lies in the foothills of the Andes, about 620 miles (1,000 km) northwest of Buenos Aires. San Juan is the trading center for an area producing wine grapes, other fruits, and cattle. The main industry is the making of wine. Spaniards from Chile founded San Juan in 1562.

Population: 119,492.

San Juan, Puerto Rico, the commonwealth's capital and largest city. It lies on the northeastern coast along the Atlantic Ocean, some 1,025 miles (1,650 km) southeast of Miami. The center and oldest part of the city, including the section called Old San Juan, is on a small island at the entrance to San Juan Bay. Several bridges connect this island with the rest of the city.

San Juan is the commercial, financial, and industrial center of Puerto Rico. The tourist and convention trade, which has greatly increased since the early 1960's, is one of the mainstays of the city's economy. Industries include rum distilling, sugar refining, and the manufacturing of metal products, electrical goods, drugs, and chemicals. San

San Juan. Old Fort San Geronimo, completed about 1771, contrasts sharply with the modern luxury hotels in the city's Condado Beach section. The fort is now a military museum.

Juan's well-equipped port handles much of Puerto Rico's overseas trade. Railways, ocean liners, modern highways, and an international airport serve the city.

Much of San Juan has modern commercial and residential buildings and wide avenues. In contrast is historic Old San Juan with its narrow streets and Spanish colonial buildings. The most imposing landmarks here are the fortresses of El Morro (16th century) and San Cristóbal (17th century). Casa Blanca and the Church of San José, built in the early 1500's, are among the oldest buildings in continuous use in the Americas. La Fortaleza, the residence of Puerto Rico's governors for more than 400 years, dates to 1533. In San Juan Cathedral is the tomb of Ponce de León.

Other attractions in San Juan include the Plaza de Colón, with an imposing statue of Columbus; the white marble capitol building; and numerous art and historical museums. Two campuses of the University of Puerto Rico are in or near the city.

San Juan was founded in 1521 after Ponce de León's original settlement across San Juan Bay was abandoned. The city was quickly fortified to resist attacks by privateers. It was occupied briefly by the English in 1598 and by the Dutch in 1624. San Juan stagnated under restrictive colonial policies from the early 1600's until 1815, when Spain permitted free trade with foreign ports and opened Puerto Rico to immigration and settlement. In 1898, during the Spanish-American War, United States troops captured the city. San

Juan's modern development began in the 1940's with "Operation Bootstrap," a program to diversify and strengthen the Puerto Rican economy.

Population: 437,745.

For other pictures of San Juan, see PUERTO RICO.

San Juan Hill. See SPANISH-AMERICAN WAR.

San Juan Island National Historical Park. See NATIONAL PARKS, section "United States."

San Juan Mountains, a range of the Rocky Mountains in southwestern Colorado and northern New Mexico. It extends southeastward for about 150 miles (240 km) from Uncompahgre Plateau to the junction of the Rio Chama and the Rio Grande. The mountains form part of the Continental Divide. Several peaks exceed 14,000 feet (4,267 m) in height; Uncompahgre, at 14,309 feet (4,361 m), is the highest. Near the source of the Rio Grande is Silverton, one of the best preserved of Colorado's old silver-mining towns.

San Juan National Historic Site. See NATIONAL PARKS, section "United States."

San Leandro, săn′ lē-ăn′drō, California, a city in Alameda County. It lies on the east side of San Francisco Bay, eight miles (13 km) south of downtown Oakland. Like many of the communities in the East Bay area that once were largely residential, San Leandro is now a sizable industrial and commercial city. Products include processed foods, trucks and tractors, wood products,

scientific instruments, metal goods, and paper items. Cherries and cut flowers are notable commercial crops in the area. The city has the council-manager form of government.

The first settler at San Leandro was José Joaquin Estudillo in 1837. A village was established in 1849, and the town was laid out six years later. From 1854 until 1871 San Leandro was the seat of Alameda County. The city was incorporated in 1872.

Population: 68,223.

San Lorenzo, Treaty of. See PINCK-NEY'S TREATY.

San Luis Dam. See DAM (table).

San Luis Obispo, săn loo'ĭs ō-bĭs'pō, California, the seat of San Luis Obispo County, about 160 miles (260 km) northwest of Los Angeles. Tourism, retail trade, food processing, and light manufacturing are the mainstays of the local economy. California Polytechnic State University is here. San Luis Obispo grew up around the Mission San Luis Obispo de Tolosa, founded in 1772. The settlement was incorporated in 1856. The restored mission is a leading attraction.

Population: 41,958.

San Luis Potosí, sän lwēs' pō' tōsē', Mexico, the capital of San Luis Potosí state. It lies some 6,100 feet (1,860 m) above sea level on the Central Plateau, about 225 miles (362 km) northwest of Mexico City. San Luis Potosí is the industrial, commercial, and transportation center for a mining and agricultural area. Industries include tanning, flour milling, smelting, brewing, and furniture manufacturing. San Luis Potosí's notable buildings include the state capitol, the cathedral, and the churches of San Francisco and El Carmen. Part of the city has narrow cobbled streets and Spanish-style buildings with colored tile roofs. The state university, founded in 1804, is here.

San Luis Potosí was founded by the Spanish in the 1580's as a silver-mining center and soon became a seat of colonial administration. For more than 100 years after Mexico won its independence in 1821 the city was involved periodically in political disorders. In 1863 it was briefly the seat of the government of Benito Juárez.

Population: 525,819.

San Marino, săn' ma-rē'nō, or **Republic of San Marino,** the world's smallest republic. It lies in the foothills of the Apennines about 10 miles (16 km) from the Adriatic Sea, surrounded by Italy. Mount Titano (2,425 feet [769 m] high) accounts for most of the republic's area of 24 square miles (62 km²).

Farming and livestock raising on the mountain's lower slopes are the principal occupations. However, most of the republic's revenue comes from tourists and the sale of postage stamps to collectors. San Marino's basic currency unit is the Italian lira. Manufactured products include textiles, ceramics, and wine. Transportation is entirely by road, except for summer helicopter service to Rimini, Italy, 15 miles (24 km) northeastward on the Adriatic coast.

The Town of San Marino, capital of the world's smallest republic. Guaita, or Rocca, Tower (11th century), part of the town's medieval fortifications, is at top right.

Cecil Ferguson

The people of San Marino, called San Marinesi, are of Italian origin. They speak Italian and virtually all are literate. Roman Catholicism is the state religion. The chief towns are San Marino, the capital, near the summit of Mount Titano, and Serravalle. The republic is governed by the Great and General Council, whose 60 members are elected for five-year terms. The executive branch consists of two captains regent (chief executives), elected by the council from its members and changed every six months, and the 10-member Congress of State, also elected from the council.

San Marino's early history is unknown. According to local tradition, the republic was founded in the fourth century by Marinus, a Christian stonecutter from Dalmatia, who established a haven here for persecuted Christians. By 885 a monastery had been built. Outside powers have seldom invaded San Marino or threatened its independence. The republic has maintained close ties with Italy since 1862, when a treaty of friendship was signed and a customs union formed. The treaty was renewed in 1939 and 1971.

The population of the republic in 1994 was about 25,000; that of the capital, 4,335 in 1993.

See also FLAG (color page).

San Martín, sän' mär-tēn', **José de** (1778-1850), a South American revolutionary leader and statesman. A professional soldier with an exceptional talent for leadership and military organization, he helped to liberate Argentina, Chile, and Peru from Spanish rule. He is considered Argentina's national hero.

José
de San Martín
OAS

San Martín was born at Yapeyú in La Plata (now Argentina), the son of a Spanish colonial official. At an early age, he was taken to Spain by his parents. He began his military career in the Spanish army, fighting in wars against Great Britain, Portugal, and France.

After hearing of the independence movement in South America, San Martín returned to his native land in 1812. He helped the Argentine revolutionaries win their independence, becoming commander in chief of the army of liberation in 1814.

After it was decided to carry the war of liberation to Chile and Peru, San Martín recruited and trained the Army of the Andes, 1814-17. Early in 1817, he led his troops in the perilous crossing of the Andes. He won decisive victories at Chacabuco (1817), with the aid of General Bernardo O'Higgins, and at Maipú (1818), and gained independence for Chile. San Martín then marched on Peru. His army occupied Lima in 1821. He declared Peru independent and was given the title of protector of Peru. The country's independence from Spain, however, was not yet guaranteed.

In 1822 San Martín met with Simón Bolívar, liberator of the northern Spanish colonies, whose armies were advancing toward Peru. Their conversations were private, but it is believed that the two great revolutionary leaders failed to agree on the future direction of the independence movement. Soon after, San Martín resigned his command. He returned to Europe, remaining there the rest of his life.

San Mateo, săn' ma-tā'ō, California, a city in San Mateo County. It lies on San Francisco Bay, 19 miles (31 km) south of downtown San Francisco. San Mateo is a large residential community and a center of commercial flower growing. It has little manufacturing. The San Mateo-Hayward Bridge, completed in 1967, links the city with the east side of the bay. San Mateo was laid out in 1863.

Population: 85,486.

San Rafael, săn' ra-fĕl', California, the seat of Marin County. It is on San Francisco Bay and is 13 miles (21 km) north of downtown San Francisco. San Rafael is primarily a residential community, with some light manufacturing. The Richmond–San Rafael Bridge spans the bay and links the city with Richmond. The city grew up around the Mission San Rafael Arcangel, founded in 1817, and was incorporated in 1874.

Population: 48,404.

San Salvador, săn săl'va-dôr, the capital and largest city of the Central American republic of El Salvador. It lies on a plateau about 2,240 feet (683 m) above sea level, surrounded by low, volcanic mountains. San Salvador is the commercial, industrial, and cultural center of El Salvador. Coffee and other agricultural products are shipped here from the surrounding area for processing and distribution. Manufactured products include processed foods and beverages. The Inter-American Highway (part of the Pan American system), several railways, and an international airport serve the city.

San Salvador is a relatively modern city with several wide avenues and many parks. Most of the prominent public buildings, including the National Palace, the Archbishop's Palace, and the National Theater, are in the center of the city near the main plaza. The National Museum and the National University of El Salvador are in the city.

San Salvador was founded by the Spaniard Pedro de Alvarado in 1525. It soon became the administrative center of El Salvador province. The city grew in importance after the collapse of Spanish rule in 1821 and the formation of the United Provinces of Central America in 1823. From 1831 until 1838 it was the federation's capital. San Salvador has been El Salvador's capital since the republic was proclaimed in 1841. An earthquake virtually destroyed the city in 1854 and another serious one occurred in 1986.

Population: 422,570.

San Salvador. See BAHAMAS; COLUMBUS, CHRISTOPHER, subtitle *First Voyage.*

San Sebastián, săn sĕ-băs'chăn, Spain, the capital of Guipúzcoa province. It lies on the Bay of Biscay, 12 miles (19 km) from the French border. San Sebastián is a popular summer resort, noted for its parks, beaches, and promenades. Industries include paper manufacturing, flour milling, and commercial fishing. Among historical buildings is the former royal summer residence.

Although San Sebastián is an old city, very little of it dates back beyond the 19th century; the old city was virtually destroyed in 1813 during the Napoleonic Wars.

Population: 169,933.

San Simeon. See CALIFORNIA, section "Interesting Places."

Sana, sŏn-ä', the capital of Yemen. It lies on a plateau about 7,200 feet (2,200 m) above sea level in one of the best farming areas on the Arabian Peninsula. Sana is an ancient walled city with multistory buildings of sun-dried brick and dirt streets. There is virtually no industry except that of the handicraft type. Sana has a jet airport and is linked by a highway to Aden, the country's chief port and commercial center.

Sana was a flourishing city before the time of Christ. It came under Ethiopian control in the sixth century A.D. Following the spread of Islam in the seventh century, it became the seat of a small Islamic state. The Ottoman Turks ruled Sana from the early 16th century until 1918, but except for brief periods, exercised little control.

Population: 926,595.

Sancho Panza. See DON QUIXOTE.

Sanction, in international law, a punitive action taken by one or more nations to prevent or to punish aggression by another nation. Usually, a sanction is a collective action involving diplomatic, economic, or military measures. Sanctions may include severance of diplomatic relations, economic embargo, or military intervention. Under the United Nations Charter, sanctions can be invoked against a nation when there is a "threat to the peace, breach of the peace, or act of aggression."

Sanctions have been employed through the years with varying degrees of success. The League of Nations imposed an economic boycott against Italy after the Italians invaded Ethiopia in 1935, but most nations did not comply and the boycott failed. The UN succeeded in halting North Korean aggression against South Korea through the use of military force, 1950-53. The UN imposed severe economic sanctions against Iraq after the Iraqis invaded Kuwait in 1990.

Many nations, including the United States, applied economic sanctions against South Africa in protest of its racial policies. The United States has employed sanctions against certain Communist countries, such as Cuba, and against nations believed to promote terrorism or commit human-rights abuses, such as Libya.

Sanctuary. See ASYLUM; CHURCH, subtitles *Roman Catholic, Anglican, and East*

George Sand
International Museum
of Photography at
George Eastman House

ern Orthodox Churches: Parts of the Church, and *Protestant Churches.*

Sand, sănd, **George** (1804-1876), the pen name of Amandine Lucile Aurore Dupin Dudevant, a French novelist. She rebelled against social conventions, especially those that restricted women, and often wore men's clothing. She won the friendship of leading thinkers and artists, and her literary reputation was excellent among her contemporaries. Today she is remembered chiefly because of her personality.

Critics consider George Sand's novels of rural life, written in her middle years, to be her best writing. In them she describes country scenes vividly and poetically, and portrays country people with warmth and understanding. *The Haunted Pool* (1846), *Fadette* (1849), and *Francis the Waif* (1850) are generally regarded as her best novels.

Such early novels as *Indiana* (1832), *Lélia* (1833), and *Mauprat* (1836) express George Sand's romantic and unconventional ideas about love. Her interest in social reforms is shown in a group of novels that includes *Consuelo* (1842), *The Mosaic Workers* (1845), and *The Miller of Angibault* (1845).

George Sand was born in Paris and brought up in a country home at Nohant. At 18 she was married to Casimir (later Baron) Dudevant. In 1831 she left her husband and went to Paris, later taking her two children to live with her. She had love affairs with a number of well-known men, including the novelist Jules Sandeau, the poet Alfred de Musset, and the composer Frédéric Chopin. Her first novel, *Pink and White* (1831), was written in collaboration with Sandeau; she adapted her pen name from his last name.

See also CHOPIN, FRÉDÉRIC FRANÇOIS; MUSSET, ALFRED DE.

Sand, small particles of rock and minerals or other materials, such as coral or slag. The term *sand* refers to the size of the particles, not to their composition. There

are, however, no universally accepted limits for the size of sand particles. Geologists define sand as those particles between .0025 inch and .079 inch (.064 mm and 2 mm) in diameter. Sand for industrial use is defined as particles between .0029 inch and .25 inch (.074 mm and 6.35 mm) in diameter. In everyday usage, sand is considered to consist of particles just large enough to be seen individually with the unaided eye.

Sand is used for many purposes. Quartz sand is melted down to make glass. Various types of sand are used in cement and concrete for building materials and paving. Sand is a natural abrasive and is used for cleaning, etching, stonecutting, and smoothing in sandblasting and is also used in making sandpaper. (See SANDBLASTING.) Water and other liquids are filtered through sand to remove suspended matter. In gardening, sand is sometimes added to clay soils to improve their aeration and drainage.

Sand is found over much of the earth—in soils, on ocean floors, on beaches, in deserts, and along streambeds. Most sand consists of quartz (silicon dioxide). Few deposits, however, contain pure quartz sand. Usually other minerals, such as feldspar, mica, magnetite, and garnet, are mixed with the quartz; they account for the particular color of any given sample of sand. There are some places where the sand contains no quartz. The white sand of White Sands National Monument, in New Mexico, is pure gypsum. Some beaches in Florida and on some of the Caribbean islands are made up of coral sands.

Sand can be manufactured by pulverizing any sufficiently hard material such as rock or slag. Naturally occurring sand is the product of wind and other agents of erosion. Weathering breaks down the parent material into particles of various sizes, including sand. Wind and water carry the particles to new locations, where deposits build up.

The texture of the sand in a particular deposit depends on the way in which the sand particles were transported. The ability of water to carry suspended particles, such as sand, depends on its rate of flow. A swiftly moving stream, for example, may pick up particles of assorted sizes, carry them downstream, and then drop them at a point where a bend in the stream or an obstruction slows the water. At such points, deposits of mixed texture tend to build up.

Wind of moderate velocity sorts out the particles by size. Particles larger than sand are generally not moved, while dust particles (smaller than sand) are lifted high in the air and carried for great distances. Sand particles, on the other hand, skip along the ground and build up in front of almost any obstacle. In areas of prevailing winds sand builds up into dunes, such as those at Great Sand Dunes National Park, in Colorado. (See COLORADO, color picture titled *Great Sand Dunes National Monument*.)

Sand deposits may be laid down, compressed, and cemented together to form rock, usually sandstone. (See SANDSTONE.) If it does not become rock, sand may be continually moved about, worn down, and finally become so small that it ceases to be sand and becomes dust.

Sand Dollar, a small disc-shaped marine animal closely related to the sea urchin. Sand dollars live on the sandy ocean floor. Their grayish-white skeletal remains are often found washed up on coastal beaches.

Sand dollars are usually about 3 inches (7.5 cm) in diameter and ⅜ inch (1 cm) thick. Most sand dollars are purple or blue. They have a dense velvety covering of short spines and tiny muscular projections called tube feet. The spines and tube feet are used for locomotion and for burrowing into sand. Sand dollars creep about the ocean floor, mouth side down, feeding on minute organic particles.

Sand dollars are of the class Echinoidea of the phylum Echinodermata.

Sand Dune. See DUNE.

Sand Eel. See SAND LANCE.

Sand Grouse, the common name for a family of birds found in Africa, Asia, and Europe. There are 2 genera and 16 species. One genus consists of two species, found in arid or semiarid regions of Asia. The other genus has 14 species, found throughout Africa except in forested areas. Some of the African species are also found in Asia and Europe. Some species of sand grouse are hunted as game.

Sand grouse are about the size of small pigeons. They have short, feathered legs and are sandy brown in color. They feed mainly on seeds. The female lays two or three gray or yellow eggs on bare ground. Sand grouse are gregarious birds, gathering in large flocks at watering holes.

Sand grouse belong to the family Pteroclidae. The Asian species make up the genus *Syrrhaptes;* the African species the genus *Pterocles.*

Sand Lance, or **Sand Eel,** a small marine fish found in schools in shallow waters of northern seas. The sand lance has an elongated body, a pointed head, and a prominent lower jaw. It is metallic bluish-green above and silver below and grows to eight inches (20 cm) long. It burrows in the sand to escape predators. Of the 12 species, 3 are found in the United States—the American, northern, and Pacific sand lances.

Sand lances make up the sand lance family, Ammodytidae. The American sand lance is *Ammodytes americanus;* the northern sand lance, *A. dubius;* the Pacific sand lance, *A. hexapterus.*

Sand Myrtle. See MYRTLE.

Mick Church
Sand Dollars

Sandalwood, the common name for several species of evergreen trees found from India east through Polynesia. The mature sandalwood tree is a partial parasite, its roots drawing some nourishment from the roots of other trees. The sandalwood seedling can live independently. Sandalwood trees grow slowly, reaching a height of about 50 feet (15 m) at maturity, in about 40 years.

The *white sandalwood,* a tree found in southern India, Hawaii, and other tropical areas, is valued for its white sapwood, used in making cabinets and for carvings. *Sandalwood oil,* distilled from the yellow heartwood, is used for incense and in the manufacture of perfume.

The white sandalwood is *Santalum album* of the sandalwood family, Santalaceae.

Sandblasting, the use of sand and other abrasives to etch or clean hard materials such as glass and stone. The abrasive is forced by compressed air or steam through a jet or nozzle. When a design is to be etched, the part of the surface that is not to be cut is masked by some material, such as rubber, tape, or wax, which resists the cutting action of the blast. The abrasive cuts into the unshielded portions to form the pattern. Glass may be frosted in this way. Sandblasting often is used to clean the outside of stone buildings and to clean castings.

A sandblast process for shaping objects made of hard, brittle material was developed in the 19th century by Benjamin and Richard Tilghman, American chemists.

Sandburg, Carl (1878-1967), a United States poet, biographer, and journalist. Acclaimed as a poet of the people, he was especially interested in expressing the optimism and democratic spirit of the Midwest. He used colloquial language and the rhythms of ordinary speech to portray with crude and powerful realism the pioneer days and expanding industrialism of America. An example is "Chicago," one of his early poems. He also wrote delicate lyrics, such as "Fog," that are concentrated and precise in the Imagist manner. (See IMAGISM.)

Sandburg was awarded the 1940 Pulitzer Prize for history for *Abraham Lincoln: the War Years* (4 volumes, 1939). In 1951, he won the Pulitzer Prize for poetry for *Complete Poems* (1950).

Early Life

Sandburg was born in Galesburg, Illinois, the son of Swedish immigrants. Carl's schooling was irregular, and he worked at various jobs to help support the family. When he was 17 he became a migratory laborer, riding freight trains in search of work. In 1898, he enlisted for service in the Spanish-American War. His first published writing was the war correspondence he sent

Carl Sandburg

Editta Sherman

from Puerto Rico to the Galesburg *Evening Mail. Always the Young Strangers* (1952) is his account of his boyhood.

After the war, Sandburg entered Lombard College in Galesburg, where he worked his way for four years. He did not graduate, leaving the college in 1902 to travel about the country taking temporary jobs. In 1904 and 1905, one of his college professors privately printed three small books of Sandburg's prose and poetry.

In 1907 Sandburg settled in Milwaukee, where he wrote for several newspapers and became active in the Social-Democratic party. In 1908 he married Lillian Paula Steichen, sister of the photographer Edward Steichen. They had three daughters. From 1910 to 1912 Sandburg was secretary to Milwaukee's first Socialist mayor.

Poet and Biographer

Sandburg moved to Chicago in 1912 and resumed his career as a journalist. He joined the staff of the Chicago *Daily News* in 1917. His first wide recognition came with publication of his poems in *Poetry* magazine in 1914. *Chicago Poems* (1916) and *Cornhuskers* (1918) established Sandburg as a leader in Chicago's vigorous new literary group.

In the 1920's and 1930's Sandburg wrote for newspapers and traveled over the country lecturing, giving readings of his poems, and singing folk songs to his own accompaniment on a guitar. It was during this period that he completed and published his biography of Lincoln. It consisted of *Abraham Lincoln: the Prairie Years* (2 volumes, 1926), and the four volumes concerning the war years. He also published several books of poems, including *Smoke and Steel* (1920); *Good Morning, America* (1928); and *The People, Yes* (1936); and such children's books as *Rootabaga Stories* (1922) and *Potato Face* (1930).

During World War II, Sandburg made foreign broadcasts for the U.S. Office of War Information and wrote for a number of other government projects. Sandburg and his family lived in Michigan for several years. In 1945, they moved to a farm near Flat Rock, North Carolina. The property is a national historic site.

His other books include: Poetry—*Slabs of the Sunburnt West* (1922); *Honey and Salt* (1963); and the posthumous *Breathing Tokens* (1978). Novel—*Remembrance Rock* (1948). Biography—*Steichen the Photographer* (1929); *Mary Lincoln: Wife and Widow* (with Paul M. Angle, 1932). *The American*

Songbag (1927) and *The New American Songbag* (1950) are collections of American folk songs and ballads. A one-volume condensation of the Lincoln biography was published in 1954.

Sanderling, a shorebird. It is one of the sandpipers, but differs from the others in that it lacks a hind toe. The sanderling grows from about seven to nine inches (18-23 cm) long. Its bill and legs are black. In winter its plumage is white below and pale gray above. During the breeding season head and breast are a light chestnut. The sanderling breeds along the Arctic Circle and winters south as far as the Southern Hemisphere.

The sanderling is *Calidris alba* of the family Scolopacidae.

Sandglass. See HOURGLASS.

Sandhill Crane. See CRANE (bird).

Sandia National Laboratories. See NUCLEAR ENERGY, section "Research and Development," subtitle *Important Installations*.

Sandoz, săn-dōz', **Mari** (1901-1966), a United States author. She wrote biographies, histories, and novels dealing mainly with inhabitants of the Great Plains in the 19th century. Her first book, *Old Jules* (1935), a biography of her Swiss immigrant father, won her critical praise and wide recognition. Miss Sandoz was born in Sheridan County, Nebraska, and attended the University of Nebraska.

Other nonfiction: *Crazy Horse* (1942); *Cheyenne Autumn* (1953); *The Buffalo Hunters* (1954); *The Cattlemen* (1958); *Love Song to the Plains* (1961); and *The Battle of the Little Bighorn* (1966). Among her novels are *Slogum House* (1937); *The Tom-Walker* (1947); and *The Horsecatcher* (1957). *Sandhill Sundays and Other Recollections* (1970) contains autobiographical sketches.

Sandpiper, any one of a large group of shorebirds. Sandpipers breed in the northern parts of the Northern Hemisphere. For the winter they migrate far south of their breeding grounds. Some species winter in the Southern Hemisphere. They are from 5 to 15 inches (13-38 cm) long, depending on the species, and have rather long legs and bills. Sandpipers are mostly brown and gray with light underparts. Their coloring blends with that of the shore where they live in large flocks. These birds receive their name from the piping sound they make as they run along beaches in search of food. They eat mostly insects and other small invertebrates.

Most species make their nests in grass-

Don Riepe/Vista Images
Pectoral Sandpiper

lined hollows on the ground. In general, four eggs are laid. The eggs vary in color, depending on the species, but most are speckled with brown.

The *spotted sandpiper,* the most widespread North American species, is also called "teeter-tail" from its habit of wagging its tail and rump while walking along the water's edge. Other North American species include the least sandpiper, the pectoral sandpiper, the upland sandpiper (also called upland plover), and the sanderling. (See SANDERLING.)

Sandpipers are of the family Scolopacidae. The spotted sandpiper is *Actitis macularia;* the least sandpiper, *Calidris minutilla;* the pectoral sandpiper, *C. melanotos;* the upland sandpiper, *Bartramia longicauda.*

Sandstone, a porous sedimentary rock composed of grains of sand usually held together by a natural cement, such as lime. Various minerals in sandstone, such as feldspar, garnet, or magnetite, may color it yellow, brown, red, or gray. Sandstone is sometimes marked with animal tracks and may contain fossilized plants and animals.

Depending on the degree of cementation, sandstone may be hard and durable or fragile and easily crumbled. Durable forms, such as brownstone, are frequently used as a building material. In underground formations, sandstone often acts as a natural reservoir for water, oil, or natural gas.

Sandusky, săn-dŭs'kĭ, Ohio, the seat of Erie County. It lies on Sandusky Bay, an arm of Lake Erie, 55 miles (89 km) west of Cleveland. Sandusky is primarily an industrial center, producing a wide range of manufactured goods. It is one of the largest coal-shipping ports on the Great Lakes. Nearby are a campus of Bowling Green State University, Cedar Point (a large resort and amusement park), and Perry's Victory and International Peace Memorial. The city was settled in 1816.

Population: 29,764.

Sandwich, John Montagu, Fourth **Earl of** (1718-1792), a British statesman. He is said to have invented the sandwich so that he could eat without leaving the gambling table. He was first lord of the Admiralty, 1748-51 and 1777-82. The Sandwich Islands (now Hawaiian Islands) were given his name because the explorer James Cook discovered them while Lord Sandwich headed the Admiralty. Sandwich is traditionally blamed for Britain's naval weakness at the start of the American Revolution, but there is evidence that his superiors hampered his efforts to strengthen the fleet.

Sandwich Islands. See HAWAII, subtitle *History.*

Sandys, săndz, the name of two English officials prominent in the history of the colony of Virginia. They were brothers.

Sir Edwin Sandys (1561-1629) was a leader in the House of Commons and a prime mover in the founding of Virginia. He served as a member of the original Council for Virginia, 1607, and later was joint manager, 1617, and treasurer (manager), 1619-20, of the Virginia Company of London. He promoted the prosperity of the colony and granted the colonists representative government. Sandys, the son of an archbishop, was educated at Oxford. He first entered the House of Commons in 1586.

George Sandys (1578-1644) was a colonist and poet. After becoming treasurer of the Virginia Company in 1621, he went to Virginia and remained there several years. His translation of the last 10 books of Ovid's *Metamorphoses* into English verse was the first translation of a classic made in the English colonies.

Sanger, Frederick. See NOBEL PRIZES (Chemistry, 1958 and 1980).

Sanger, Margaret (1883-1966), a United States leader of the birth control movement. Her efforts for birth control—for which she coined the name—helped win support for family planning in the United States and most of the world. Mrs. Sanger was born Margaret Higgins in Corning, New York. As a young maternity nurse among the poor of New York City, she became convinced that parents should have the right to limit the size of their families.

Although it was then illegal to distribute birth control information in the United States, Mrs. Sanger in 1914 founded a magazine, *Woman Rebel,* to advocate family planning. She was indicted and made liable to a 45-year prison term for sending birth control advice through the mails. (The indictment was later dropped.) In 1916 she was arrested for opening a birth control clinic—the nation's first—in Brooklyn, New York. Mrs. Sanger served 30 days in jail, but her appeal of the case led to a 1918 court decision that opened the way for doctors to give birth control advice.

Mrs. Sanger founded the National Birth Control League (now known as Planned Parenthood Federation of America) in 1921 and organized the first international birth control conference in 1925. She helped establish birth control clinics in many foreign countries. In 1952 Mrs. Sanger founded and became the first president of the International Planned Parenthood Federation. Among her books is *Margaret Sanger: an Autobiography* (1938).

Sangre de Cristo Mountains, săng'grě dě krĭs'tō, a range of the Rocky Mountains in southern Colorado and northern New Mexico. It extends generally southward for about 220 miles (350 km) from the Arkansas River to Santa Fe, New Mexico. Numerous peaks exceed 13,000 feet (3,960 m) in height; Blanca Peak, in Colorado, at 14,345 feet (4,372 m), is the highest. Lumber and minerals, especially metals, are important products of the range. Ski resorts, particularly around Taos, New Mexico, are popular tourist attractions.

Sanhedrin, săn-hē'drĭn; săn-hĕd'rĭn, the supreme civil and religious court of the Jews from the third century B.C. or earlier until the destruction of Jerusalem by the Romans in 70 A.D. Even after the Romans gained control over Judah in 63 B.C., the Sanhedrin retained a great deal of independent authority. However, sessions could not be held without the consent of the Roman procurator, nor could a death sentence be carried out without his approval.

According to the Talmud (a compilation of writings that supplement the Hebrew Bible) the court had 71 members. The sources that describe the Sanhedrin are often contradictory, and many of the details of its origin and workings are uncertain. Although the Sanhedrin is never named in the New

an expressway make the steep descent to the port, 35 miles (56 km) to the southeast. Two major airports serve São Paulo. The city has a subway system.

São Paulo's parks and squares are among its chief attractions. At one corner of the Triângulo is Patriarch Plaza, surrounded by banks, offices, and shops. Several blocks to the west beyond the broad, tree-lined Avenida Anhangabaú is the large Plaza of the Republic, in the heart of a major shopping district. South of the Triângulo is Avenida Paulista, lined with postmodern skyscrapers and the site of the São Paulo Art Museum, which has one of the continent's finest collections of western art. Further to the south lies Ibirapuéra Park. In the park are a planetarium, a sports stadium, and several museums; one, the Museum of Contemporary Art, is the site of the internationally important Bienal art competition.

The University of São Paulo, Mackenzie University, and Pontifical Catholic University are the principal institutions of higher learning. The Butantan Institute conducts research on snake venom and produces antidotes.

History

For more than three centuries after its founding in 1554, São Paulo remained a small city. About 1885, the introduction of coffee cultivation to nearby areas, together with a heavy influx of Italian, Portuguese, Spanish, German, Japanese, and other immigrants, began a period of rapid expansion. Within 15 years the population grew from 35,000 to almost 250,000 as the city became a major industrial center. Considerable population growth continued well into the 20th century.

Population: 9,839,066.

São Tomé and Príncipe, souNn tōō-má; prēN'sĕ-pĕ, a country consisting of two islands in the Gulf of Guinea about 150 miles (240 km) off the west African coast. São Tomé accounts for most of the country's 372 square miles (964 km²). Agriculture, especially the plantation cultivation of cacao, is the chief economic activity. Most of the people are of African, Portuguese, or mixed descent and live on São Tomé, particularly in the capital city, São Tomé. Their language is Portuguese. The country is governed under the constitution of 1990. The head of state is the president; the legislature is the 55-member National Assembly. The

Portuguese were the first Europeans to land on the islands, in 1471. Except for a century of Dutch control (1641-1740), Portugal ruled the islands until 1975, when independence was granted.

In 1991 the population was 117,504.

See also FLAG (color page).

Sap, the watery juice of plants. Sap is mostly water in which minerals and certain foods are dissolved. It is present in most parts of living plants. Sap that occurs in the rounded structures known as *vacuoles* of ordinary cells is called *cell sap.* Sap is also present in the cavities of specialized conducting cells in certain plants. Plants with conducting cells are called *vascular plants;* ferns, conifers, and flowering plants are examples.

The water in sap may come from the soil, and in most vascular plants the water and dissolved minerals are absorbed through the roots. Plants that live in water (water lilies and seaweeds, for example) absorb water directly through their outer layers. Some algae, fungi, and bacteria absorb water directly from the moisture in the air. Epiphytes—plants that grow attached to the surfaces of living or dead trees or other plants, to rock, or even to buildings—also get their water from the moisture of the air. Plants that are parasitic on other plants absorb sap directly from their hosts.

In vascular plants, sap is carried in special conducting tissues called *xylem* and *phloem,* besides occurring in the vacuoles and in other parts of the plant. Xylem and phloem usually contain many specialized conducting cells, permitting the rapid movement of sap throughout the plant. For example, the xylem carries water and dissolved minerals absorbed from the soil through the roots and stems to the green leaves. Here the water from the sap is used in the manufacture of food. The phloem carries the food to parts of the plant where it is needed for growth or where it can be stored for future use.

Some commercially important products are made from sap—sugar and molasses from the sap of sugarcane, maple syrup from the sap of the sugar maple, and sorghum syrup from the sap of the sweet sorghum.

Sapajou. See CAPUCHIN.

Sapir, sȧ-pǐr', **Edward** (1884-1939), a United States anthropologist and linguist. He made pioneering studies on North American Indian languages and on the relation-

Red-breasted Sapsucker

ship between culture and personality. Sapir was born in Germany and brought to the United States as a boy. He received a Ph.D. degree from Columbia University in 1909. After serving as chief of the anthropology division of the Canadian National Museum, 1910-25, Sapir taught at the University of Chicago and Yale University.

Sapodilla. See CHICLE.

Saponification. See DETERGENTS AND SOAPS, subtitle *Soaps;* ESTER.

Saponins. See SOAP PLANT.

Sapphire, săf'ĭr, a form of gem-quality corundum (aluminum oxide). The name "sapphire" usually refers to blue varieties of corundum, but the gems also occur in green, yellow, purple, and pink varieties. (Gemstones of red corundum are called *rubies*.) A sapphire's color is produced by traces of iron, titanium, chromium, or other metals. A *star sapphire* contains particles of the mineral rutile; when such a sapphire is cut and polished, light reflected by the rutile produces a star-shaped pattern.

The major producers of natural sapphires are Thailand, Sri Lanka, and Australia; India and Burma were formerly important sources. Synthetic sapphires are made commercially in several countries by a number of different processes. Sapphires are used primarily as gemstones in rings and other jewelry. Sapphire is the birthstone for September, and represents wisdom and clear thinking. Sapphires are also used as bearings in high-quality meters, compasses, and watches.

Chemical formula: Al_2O_3. Specific gravity: 4.00. Hardness: 9.0.

See also GEM (color page).

Sappho, săf'ō, a Greek poet who lived about 600 B.C. She was held in high esteem by her contemporaries, and by such Roman poets as Catullus and Ovid, who were influenced by her. Plato called her the "Tenth Muse." Most modern critics consider her love lyrics among the finest ever written. She wrote in conversational rather than literary language, producing an effect of simplicity and intense passion. Only fragments remain of her eight or nine books of poems.

Little is known of Sappho's life. She was born on the island of Lesbos, probably in Mytilene, where she spent most of her life.

Sapporo, säp-pô-rô, Japan, the capital and largest city of Hokkaido, Japan's northernmost island and prefecture. The city lies in western Hokkaido near the Sea of Japan, about 520 miles (840 km) north of Tokyo. Sapporo is a commercial and industrial center, producing wood products, textiles, processed foods, beer, and machinery.

The heart of the city is the Odori, a long, tree-lined and landscaped mall flanked by modern buildings. Notable institutions include the Batchelor Museum, with exhibits on Ainu culture, and Hokkaido University, founded in 1876. An elaborate Snow Festival is held here each February; in nearby mountains are some of Japan's best ski areas and spas.

Sapporo was originally an Ainu village. It was laid out as a city in 1871 and in 1886 replaced Hakodate as the capital of Hokkaido. Unlike many other Japanese cities, Sapporo was not damaged during World War II. Sapporo was the site of the 1972 Winter Olympic Games.

Population: 1,671,742.

Saprophyte. See DECAY.

Sapsucker, a woodpecker that drinks the sap of trees. Sapsuckers also eat insects that come to feed on the sap.

The *yellow-bellied,* or *common, sapsucker,* which is found throughout most of North America, is blackish above and yellowish below. The forehead is crimson in both sexes and the throat of the male is also crimson. Both sexes have long white wing markings. The yellow-bellied sapsucker is from eight to nine inches (20 to 23 cm) long. It nests in holes in trees.

The *red-naped sapsucker* and the *red-breasted sapsucker* are subspecies of the yellow-bellied sapsucker. The red-naped sapsucker has patches of red on the nape, forehead, and throat. It is found from western Canada to western Mexico. The red-breasted sapsucker is solid red from the head to the breast. It is found from southeastern Alaska to western Oregon. Both subspecies have a black chest band.

Williamson's sapsucker, which is found primarily west of the Rocky Mountains, grows to about nine inches (23 cm) long. The male resembles the common sapsucker but does not have the crimson patch on the forehead. The female, which is brownish with white stripes on the sides, nests in a hole in a stump or tree.

The yellow-bellied sapsucker is *Sphyrapicus varius; red-naped, S. v. nuchalis;* red-breasted, *S. v. ruber;* Williamson's, *S. thyroideus.* Sapsuckers belong to the family Picidae.

Saraband. See MUSIC, subtitle *Musical Form* (Saraband).

Saracens, săr′á-sĕz, the name by which Muslims were generally known to Christians during the time of the Crusades. (The Muslims who invaded Spain from Morocco, however, were known as Moors.) Based on a word meaning "easterners," the term Saracens had long been used in the Byzantine Empire for the Arabian nomads of the Syrian desert. After the founding of Islam, the name was extended to the Muslim forces that attacked Bzantine territory.

Saragossa. See ZARAGOZA.

Sarah, sâr′á; sä′rá, or **Sarai,** sä′rī, in the Bible, the wife of Abraham and mother of Isaac. She is revered as the first Hebrew matriarch. According to Genesis 17:17 and 21, Sarah bore Isaac at the age of 90 in fulfillment of God's promise of a son to her and Abraham. Sarah then had Abraham send his concubine Hagar and their son Ishmael into the desert.

Sarah Lawrence College. See UNIVERSITIES AND COLLEGES (table).

Sarajevo, sä′rä-yĕ′vŏ, the capital of Bosnia-Herzegovina. It is in the southeastern part of the country. Sarajevo is the country's chief industrial, commercial, and transportation center. The city has an old Turkish quarter, with many mosques and a bazaar.

Sarajevo was founded in the mid-13th century. It was conquered in 1429 by the Ottoman Turks, who ruled for nearly 450 years. Along with the rest of Bosnia-Herzegovina, the city was occupied by Austria-Hungary in 1878 and annexed in 1908.

The assassination in Sarajevo of the Austrian Archduke Francis Ferdinand on June 28, 1914, touched off World War I. After the war Sarajevo became part of the newly created Kingdom of the Serbs, Croats, and Slovenes (later Yugoslavia). Sarajevo was the site of the 1984 Winter Olympics. In 1992 it became the capital of newly independent Bosnia-Herzegovina. From 1992 to 1995 Sarajevo suffered severe damage during a civil war between Bosnian government forces (led by Bosnian Muslims) and Bosnian Serbs. Throughout the war the city remained under government control but some of the surrounding suburbs came under Serb control. In 1996, in accordance with the treaty ending the war, the Serbs gave control of the suburbs they were holding to the Bosnian government.

Population: 415,631.

Saran. See PLASTICS, subtitle *Thermoplastics:* Vinyls.

Sarasate, sä′rä-sä′tä, **Pablo de,** the professional name of Pablo Martín Melitón Sarasate y Navascuez (1844-1908), a Spanish violinist and composer. He was praised as one of the most technically skilled violinists of the 19th century. His best known compositions—*Zigeunerweisen, Navarra,* and several sets of *Spanish Dances*—are favorites in the violin repertoire.

Sarasota, săr′á-sō′tá, Florida, the seat of Sarasota County. It lies on the Gulf of Mexico, some 30 miles (48 km) south of Tampa. Sarasota is primarily a residential and resort community with excellent beaches and marinas. There is some processing of foods, especially vegetables and citrus fruits. Until 1959 Sarasota was the winter headquarters of the Ringling Brothers and Barnum & Bailey Circus. Probably the city's greatest attraction is the Ringling Museums, a complex that includes the John and Mable Ringling Museum of Art and the Ringling Museum of the Circus. Nearby Sarasota Jungle Gardens features tropical plants and birds. Sarasota was settled in the mid-1880's.

Population: 50,961.

Saratoga Campaign, an important series of engagements in the American Revolutionary War. The campaign, sometimes called the turning point of the war, secured

Surrender at Saratoga, by John Trumbull. General Burgoyne is offering his sword to General Gates. The officer in white frontier garb is Daniel Morgan. Philip Schuyler, for whom Saratoga was renamed, is third from right in a light coat.

upper New York state for the revolutionists and induced France to make an alliance with the United States. The field of the two final battles, between Schuylerville and Stillwater, New York, is a national historical park.

Early in 1777 the British planned to divide the rebellious colonies by converging three armies on Albany, New York. Lord William Howe's army was to proceed northward from New York City, but it failed to do so because of a delay in orders, caused by the failure of Lord George Germain, Britain's secretary of state for colonies, to coordinate the campaign. General John Burgoyne moved southward from Canada and in July captured Fort Ticonderoga, between Lakes George and Champlain.

Colonel Barry St. Leger's men marched eastward from Fort Oswego and in August besieged Fort Stanwix (then called Fort Schuyler) on the Mohawk River. His forces were beaten back by the fort's defenders, and he abandoned efforts to subdue it on the approach of an American army led by General Benedict Arnold. Meanwhile, General Philip Schuyler's Continental troops destroyed crops along Burgoyne's route, creating an acute supply problem for the British commander. In mid-August, units of Bur-

S-120

goyne's forces went on a foraging expedition near Bennington, Vermont, where they were decisively defeated in the Battle of Bennington. (See BENNINGTON, BATTLE OF.)

In September Burgoyne, 10 miles (16 km) south of the village of Saratoga (now Schuylerville), New York, met a force led by General Horatio Gates. On September 19, at the battle of Freeman's Farm, Burgoyne's men succeeded in gaining control of the battlefield, but they failed to dislodge Gates's forces from their hilltop position on Bemis Heights.

Burgoyne, after waiting in vain for aid from Howe, was forced by lack of supplies to make some kind of move. On October 7 he ordered a detachment of his forces to advance. American units also advanced, and in the ensuing battle of Bemis Heights the Americans, partly due to the bold leadership of Arnold, routed the British. The British army retreated to Saratoga. There, on October 17, 1777, Burgoyne surrendered his army of some 5,000 men to Gates's army of some 15,000 men.

See also REVOLUTIONARY WAR, AMERICAN, map titled *Saratoga Campaign, 1777.*

Saratoga National Historical Park. See NATIONAL PARKS, section "United States."

sentimental attitude toward human nature. Many of his works are autobiographical or semiautobiographical. Saroyan rejected the Pulitzer Prize for drama in 1940 for his play *The Time of Your Life* (1939), saying art should not be patronized by commerce.

Saroyan was born in Fresno, California, of Armenian-American parents. "The Daring Young Man on the Flying Trapeze," a short story published in *Story* magazine in 1934, won him critical acclaim and public notice. He lived in France for several years.

His other works include: Novels—*The Human Comedy* (1943); *One Day in the Afternoon of the World* (1964). Story collections—*Inhale and Exhale* (1936); *My Name is Aram* (1940); *The Whole Voyald* (1956). Plays—*My Heart's in the Highlands* (1939); *The Beautiful People* (1941). Autobiography—*Here Comes, There Goes, You Know Who* (1961); *Not Dying* (1963); *Days of Life and Death and Escape to the Moon* (1970); *Places Where I've Done My Time* (1972); *Sons Come and Go, Mothers Hang in Forever* (1976); *Chance Meetings* (1978). Miscellany—*I Used to Believe I Had It Forever Now I'm Not So Sure* (1968); *Obituaries* (1979).

Sarsaparilla. See SMILAX.

Sarto, sär'tṓ, **Andrea del** (1486-1530), an Italian painter of the High Renaissance. He was a superb craftsman with a fine sense of color harmony and did much to advance *chiaroscuro* (the treatment of light and shade in painting) as in his *Portrait of a Young Man* and other works. Many of his paintings, such as *Madonna del Sacco,* foreshadow Mannerism, the 16th-century movement that was a revolt against the classicism of the Renaissance.

Andrea was born in Florence. His nickname del Sarto ("of the tailor") was a reference to his father's trade. Del Sarto spent most of his life in Florence, where Pontormo and Vasari were among his pupils. He was named court painter to Francis I of France in 1518, but gave up that position the next year and returned to Italy. Robert Browning's poem *Andrea del Sarto* (1855) tells of his great love for his wife.

His other works include *Madonna of the Harpies, Charity,* and *Sacrifice of Isaac.*

Sartor Resartus. See CARLYLE, THOMAS.

Sartre, sär'tr', **Jean-Paul** (1905-1980), a French author and philosopher. He was considered to be the leading French Existentialist. A versatile writer, he presented his philosophical theories in novels, plays, short stories, treatises, and essays. According to Sartre, the mind has no contents; it is an

Jean-Paul Sartre
French Embassy

activity, a projection onto things. Existentialism uses phenomenology as a way of studying this activity. Sartre extended his concept of mind to the total person: a person must project him- or herself into existence by making a choice or taking a side. People are free because they can do this; they are in anguish because they must. (See EXISTENTIALISM; PHENOMENOLOGY.)

Sartre's philosophical ideas are elaborated in such treatises as *Being and Nothingness* (1943) and *Existentialism Is a Humanism* (1946). Among his best works from a literary standpoint are his first novel, *Nausea* (1938); a play, *The Flies* (1943); and *The Words* (1963), an autobiography.

Sartre refused the Nobel Prize for literature in 1964. He said that he always refused official honors because he wished his writings to stand alone and not carry the prestige and influence of institutions granting the honors. He also objected to what he termed the anti-Communist bias of the Nobel awards.

Sartre was born in Paris. He studied philosophy in France and Germany, and taught philosophy in France for several years. He fought in World War II, was captured by the Germans in 1940, and was released nine months later. He returned to France and joined the resistance movement. In 1964, he declared himself "converted" to Marxism, but he criticized the Communists' suppression of individual freedom.

His other works include: Plays—*No Exit* (1944); *The Respectful Prostitute* (1946); *The Devil and the Good Lord* (1951); *The Condemned of Altona* (1960). Collections of essays—*Between Existentialism and Marxism* (1975); *Life/Situations* (1977). *The Age of Reason* (1945), *Reprieve* (1945), and *Troubled Sleep* (1949) are parts of an unfinished novel, *Roads to Freedom.*

Sasebo, sä-sĕ-bṓ, Japan, a city in Nagasaki prefecture on the island of Kyushu. It lies on an inlet of the East China Sea about 600 miles (965 km) southwest of Tokyo. Sasebo is an industrial center and a port and has both Japanese and United States naval bases. Population: 244,677.

Saskatchewan Coat of Arms

Saskatchewan, săs-kăch'ĕ-wŏn, one of the Prairie Provinces of Canada. It is bordered by Alberta and Manitoba, the Northwest Territories, and the states of Montana and North Dakota. Its northeast corner meets the southwest corner of Nunavut. Saskatchewan has an area of 251,866 square miles (652,330 km²). Nearly one-eighth of the province is covered by lakes and streams. Maximum dimensions are about 760 miles (1,220 km) north-south and 390 miles (630 km) east-west.

Physical Geography

Land. Saskatchewan lies within three major physiographic regions of North America: the Canadian Shield, the Central Lowlands, and the Great Plains. The entire area now occupied by the province was glaciated during the last Ice Age, when enormous glaciers moved southward, scouring and eroding the land. On retreating, the glaciers left thick coverings of glacial debris in many areas, especially in the south.

The Canadian Shield, or Laurentian Plateau, extends across most of Saskatchewan's northern half. It is a rolling, forested area, about 700 to 1,600 feet (210 to 490 m) above sea level, with thousands of lakes and muskegs (bogs). There are frequent outcroppings of the ancient crystalline rock underlying the entire region.

The Central Lowlands section consists of fertile prairies in the central and southeastern parts of the province. Here are found

most of the people and the richest farms. Like the prairies of the north-central and midwestern United States, it is an area of level-to-rolling terrain crossed by broad river valleys. Except for a few isolated ranges of hills, the surface lies at elevations of 1,000 to 2,000 feet (300 to 600 m).

The Great Plains section rises fairly abruptly from the Central Lowlands along the Missouri Coteau, a hilly belt extending northwestward from North Dakota. The highest point in the province, 4,816 feet (1,468 m), is in the Cypress Hills, near the Alberta border in the extreme southwest.

Water. Most of the rivers crossing Saskatchewan drain eastward to Hudson Bay; the major ones originate either in the Rocky Mountains or on the Great Plains. The largest is the Saskatchewan, formed by the union of the North and South Saskatchewan rivers near Prince Albert. Many rivers of the Canadian Shield region follow intricate courses marked by frequent rapids and falls. The Assiniboine and the Qu'Appelle are major rivers in the southeast.

Northern Saskatchewan has thousands of lakes, many of which lie in basins gouged by glaciers during the last Ice Age. Lake Athabasca, which lies partly in Alberta, is the largest lake. It is part of the vast Mackenzie River system and receives the waters of the province's northernmost streams. Other large lakes are Reindeer Lake, Wollaston Lake, Lac la Ronge, and Cree Lake.

A Sea of Wheat Surrounds a Farm Village near Saskatoon

Climate. Situated near the center of North America, Saskatchewan has a continental climate, with great extremes between winter and summer temperatures. Winters are very cold, averaging near 0° F. (–18° C.) in the south during January and as low as –20° F. (–29° C.) in the north. Temperatures of –50° F. (–46° C.) and lower have been recorded throughout the province. Summers are warm and somewhat humid, much like those of the north-central United States. Average July temperatures range from 60° to 70° F. (16° to 21° C.). Many weather stations have recorded highs of more than 100° F. (38° C.).

Average yearly precipitation is 10 to 20 inches (250 to 500 mm), the lower amounts occurring in the far north and in the southwest. Most of the rain falls in the summer, when it is most needed for growing crops. Rainfall varies considerably from year to year, however, and occasionally droughts cause severe losses of crops. Snow falls between late October and the end of April, totaling 40 to 50 inches (1,000 to 1,270 mm) in most places.

Natural Vegetation. Evergreen forests spread across the Canadian Shield region of Saskatchewan; spruce, pine, and fir are the predominant species. Broadleaved trees, such as poplar and birch, become common toward the south as the forest gives way to a zone of scattered wooded areas. Grassland covers most of southern Saskatchewan.

Economy

A combination of favorable climate and rich prairie soils helps make Saskatchewan one of the world's great grain producers. The province's economy is based largely on agriculture, especially the growing of wheat, but it is slowly becoming less dependent on farming. Manufacturing, services and the production of minerals and fuels account for a growing share of the province's income.

Agriculture. Saskatchewan is one of Canada's leading agricultural provinces. It leads all provinces in agricultural acreage and ranks third in cash receipts. Large farms are typical in Saskatchewan, averaging about 1,100 acres (445 hectares). Most of the cultivated land lies in the southern half of the province, where hard red spring wheat is by far the most important crop. Saskatchewan is Canada's leading producer of wheat.

Many farmers in Saskatchewan engage in mixed farming, raising livestock and such crops as barley, oats, rye, canola (rapeseed), and flaxseed. Cattle ranching prevails on the drier plains of the southwest. As a producer of beef cattle, Saskatchewan ranks second only to Alberta.

Mining. Saskatchewan's mineral resources are among the most important in Canada.

Government of Saskatchewan—Photographic Svcs.
Minerals. Saskatchewan's mineral resources are of major importance to its economy. *Top,* an oil well near Estevan. *Bottom,* workers in a potash mine.

University of Saskatchewan, at Saskatoon, was founded in 1907. Shown is the Agriculture Building.
Thomas Kitchin/Tom Stack & Associates

Fuels—petroleum, uranium, lignite, and natural gas—account for most of the province's output by value. Petroleum is the leader. Production amounts to roughly one-sixth of Canada's total output and is surpassed only by that of Alberta. Uranium ranks second to petroleum among the fuels. Lignite, or brown coal, is mined in large amounts and is used primarily for generating electric power. Except for uranium, all the fuels are produced in central and southern Saskatchewan, south of the Canadian Shield.

One of the largest mineral finds in Canada's history was the discovery of huge potash deposits beneath the southern Saskatchewan prairies. Production of the mineral, which is used as a fertilizer, began in the late 1950's, and it has been estimated that the reserves are among the world's largest. Other minerals mined in Saskatchewan include gold, silver, and salt.

Manufacturing. The leading industries are those of the food-processing type, principally flour milling, meat-packing, and the production of dairy goods. A number of activities have developed in association with the mineral industry. Since the discovery of oil and gas in the late 1940's a network of pipelines has been built and there are refineries at such cities as Regina, Saskatoon, and Moose Jaw.

The forested north has pulp and paper mills and other plants specializing in wood products. Saskatchewan's other industries include printing and publishing, and the production of chemicals and electrical and electronic equipment.

Forestry. Although much of Saskatchewan's 111,200 square miles (288,000 km²) of forest is commercially valuable, only the small area penetrated by roads is actually used for cutting timber. The producing area is largely mixed forest and yields both hard and soft woods. Spruce, pine, and poplar are the main species cut. Prince Albert is the industry's center.

Fishing. Saskatchewan's larger rivers and lakes, especially those in the north, support a small but active commercial fishing industry. Whitefish, trout, and pike make up most of the catch.

Transportation. A network of railways serves the heavily agricultural southern half of Saskatchewan. One route extends to Churchill, Manitoba, the grain-shipping port on Hudson Bay. There are no rail lines in the northern half of Saskatchewan.

The highway system is also confined mainly to the southern half of the province, although there are roads extending into the far north. The chief commercial airports are at Regina and Saskatoon.

The People

More than 40 per cent of Saskatchewan's population is of British ancestry. About 50 per cent is of European descent, mainly German, Norwegian, Ukrainian, Polish, and French. Most of the remaining people are native Indians—principally Crees, Assiniboins, and Chipewyans.

According to the 1996 census, Saskatchewan had a population of 990,237. Some 60 per cent of the people live in cities and towns. The percentage of people living on farms is much higher than it is for Canada as a whole, but it is slowly declining.

Saskatchewan's Largest Cities

Saskatoon 193,647	Moose Jaw 32,973
Regina, the	Yorkton 15,154
capital 180,400	Swift Current ..14,890
Prince Albert .. 34,777	North Battleford 14,051

Religion. About 30 per cent of the people are members of the United Church of Canada; about 25 per cent belong to the Roman Catholic Church. Other principal denominations are Anglican, Lutheran, Ukrainian Catholic, Greek Orthodox, Mennonite, Baptist, and Presbyterian.

Education. Education in Saskatchewan is free and compulsory from age 7 to age 16. Public elementary and secondary schools are under the direction of the provincial department of education. The department of continuing education handles post-secondary education. There are also a few Roman Catholic and Protestant schools. In addition, there are schools for technical, vocational, and teacher training.

The University of Saskatchewan, the provincial university, was established in 1907 at Saskatoon. It includes colleges or schools of agriculture, arts and sciences, commerce, dentistry, education, engineering, graduate studies and research, law, medicine, nursing, pharmacy, physical education, and veterinary medicine. The University of Regina (founded in 1974), also under provincial control, has colleges or schools of the arts, education, engineering, administration, fine arts, physical activity studies, social work, science, and graduate studies.

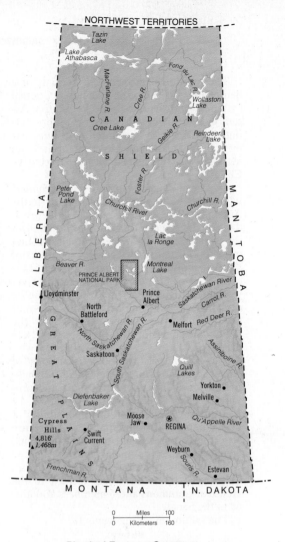

Physical Features Summary

AREA: Land, 220,349 square miles (570,700 km²); water, 31,517 square miles (81,630 km²)

GREATEST DIMENSIONS: north-south, 760 miles (1,220 km); east-west, 390 miles (630 km)

ELEVATIONS: highest, 4,816 feet (1,468 m), Cypress Hills; lowest, 699 feet (213 m), surface of Lake Athabasca

Facts about Saskatchewan

Origin of Name—From the Saskatchewan River; the river's name is Cree Indian for "swift flowing."

Total Area—251,866 square miles (652,330 km²); rank, 5th among provinces; almost as large as Texas

Population (1996)—990,237; rank, 6th among provinces

Capital—Regina

Largest City—Saskatoon

Became a Province—September 1, 1905

Government

The provincial government consists of a lieutenant governor, the Executive Council (cabinet), and the one-house Legislative Assembly. The lieutenant governor, representing the Crown, is appointed to a five-year term by the Canadian government and can act only on the advice of the Executive Council.

The head of government is the premier, who is the leader of the majority party in the Assembly. The premier serves as the president of the Executive Council and chooses the other members of the Council (cabinet ministers) from majority-party members of the Assembly. The Legislative Assembly is composed of 66 members, elected to five-year terms. However, the Assembly can be dissolved at any time during the five-year period and a new election called by the lieutenant governor upon the advice of the premier.

The judiciary is headed by the Court of Appeal and the Court of the Queen's Bench. Lesser courts include family court and provincial courts. Judges are appointed.

Local government is the responsibility of urban and rural municipalities. There are also unincorporated improvement districts, which are under provincial control.

Saskatchewan is represented in Canada's Parliament by 14 members elected to the House of Commons and 6 members appointed to the Senate.

The minimum voting age is 18.

History

Long before Europeans began to explore Canada, nomadic Indians roamed the plains of what is now Saskatchewan hunting buffalo. They remained undisturbed until the late 17th century, when the first Europeans came to the area in search of furs. The principal inhabitants at that time were the Chipewyans, the Blackfeet, the Assiniboin, and the Cree.

Fur Traders and Settlers. In 1670 the Hudson's Bay Company received a charter from Charles II of England, giving it both governing power and a trade monopoly in the region that was the drainage basin of Hudson Bay. Rupert's Land, as the region was called, included much of present-day Saskatchewan. An employee of the company, Henry Kelsey, was probably the first European to see Saskatchewan. From 1690 to 1692 he explored the area between Hudson Bay and the Saskatchewan River.

The trade monopoly of the Hudson's Bay Company was soon threatened by French-Canadian fur traders. Rivalry became intense and ended only when France withdrew from North America after its defeat in the French and Indian War (1756-63). The Hudson's Bay Company then began to build trading posts in the interior of Rupert's Land. The first of these posts was Cumberland House, established near the Saskatchewan River by Samuel Hearne in 1774. It was the first permanent British settlement in Saskatchewan.

For much of the 19th century, fur trading remained the main occupation in the region. However, the buffalo herds, which were the principal source of furs, were rapidly being depleted. From 1857 to 1860, a British expedition under John Palliser explored the

Saskatchewan's Legislative Building, Regina

© Thomas Kitchin/Tom Stack & Associates

Saskatchewan Rebellion. After a bloody four-day struggle, federal militia captured the stronghold of Batoche, May 12, 1885, decisively defeating the rebelling métis.

vast prairie lands to determine whether they would be suitable for farming. In 1869 Rupert's Land was purchased from the Hudson's Bay Company by the Dominion of Canada (established 1867) and in 1870 it was made a part of Canada's Northwest Territories. Free land was offered to attract new settlers. To protect the settlers, the North West Mounted Police was organized in 1873. The first Mounted Police post in Saskatchewan was established in 1874.

The districts of Saskatchewan, Alberta, Athabaska, and Assiniboia were created within the Northwest Territories in 1882. That year the Canadian Pacific Railway reached as far west as Moose Jaw, with new settlements being founded along its route. The influx of settlers angered the *métis* (persons of mixed French and Indian ancestry), who had migrated to Saskatchewan from Manitoba after an unsuccessful revolt against the government. (See RED RIVER REBELLION.) Once more the métis felt that the whites were taking away their lands. In 1885, under the leadership of Louis Riel, the métis rebelled for a second time, but again they failed. (See SASKATCHEWAN REBELLION.) In the aftermath of the uprising, the Northwest Territories were given represen-

tation in the Dominion Parliament, and a territorial legislature was established.

Province. In 1905 the province of Saskatchewan was formed, with Regina as its capital. Walter Scott, a Liberal party leader, was chosen the first premier. Now settlers came

---

For further information, see:

Physical Features
ATHABASCA, LAKE
CHURCHILL RIVER

REINDEER LAKE
SASKATCHEWAN RIVER

Cities
MOOSE JAW
PRINCE ALBERT

REGINA
SASKATOON

History
ASSINIBOIN INDIANS
BLACKFEET INDIANS
CO-OPERATIVE COMMONWEALTH
FEDERATION
CREE INDIANS
DIEFENBAKER, J. G.
HEARNE, SAMUEL

HUDSON'S BAY
COMPANY
NORTHWEST TERRITORIES
RIEL, LOUIS
RUPERT'S LAND
SASKATCHEWAN
REBELLION

Books about Saskatchewan

Christiansen, Deanna. *Historic Saskatchewan* (Douglas & McIntyre, 1990).
Smith, D. E. *Building a Province: a History of Saskatchewan in Documents* (Fifth House, 1992).
For Younger Readers
Richardson, Gillian. *Saskatchewan* (Lerner, 1995).

Interesting Places in Saskatchewan

Batoche National Historic Site, near Duck Lake, is the site of the decisive battle of the Saskatchewan Rebellion of 1885. Here are battle trenches, graves of those killed, and a museum of métis history and culture.

Cypress Hills Interprovincial Park, southwestern Saskatchewan and northeastern Alberta, is a heavily wooded area noted for its plants and its wildlife, including antelope, deer, elk, and beaver.

Fort Battleford National Historic Site, near Battleford, is a restored North West Mounted Police post dating from 1876.

Grasslands National Park, southern Saskatchewan, preserves a section of Saskatchewan's virgin prairie land.

Lac la Ronge Provincial Park, northern Saskatchewan, is a rocky wooded lakeland renowned for its sport fishing, canoeing, and cross-country skiing.

Moose Jaw, south-central Saskatchewan, is the site of the Saskatchewan Air Show, held each June, and the Kinsmen International Band Festival, the largest gathering of marching bands in North America, in May. Also here are the Moose Jaw Zoo and the Western Development Museum/ History of Transportation.

Prince Albert National Park, covering 1,496 square miles (3,875 km²) in central Saskatchewan, contains woodlands, lakes, rivers, and white sand beaches.

© Ray F. Hillstrom

Prince Albert National Park

Qu'Appelle Valley, southeastern Saskatchewan, is a picturesque region with numerous lakes.

Regina, southeastern Saskatchewan, is the province's capital. See REGINA.

Saskatoon, west-central Saskatchewan, is a major distribution, transportation, and industrial center. Among its points of interest are the University of Saskatchewan, Western Development Museum/1910 Boomtown, Mendel Art Gallery, Ukrainian Museum of Canada, and Wanuskewin Heritage Park.

See also NATIONAL PARKS, section "Canada."

Further tourist information is available from: Tourism Saskatchewan, 500-1900 Albert Street, Regina, Saskatchewan, Canada, S4P 4L9.

---

in even greater numbers—from Europe, eastern Canada, and the United States. Between 1901 and 1910, the population rose from 91,279 to 492,432. Agricultural development followed, and farmer cooperatives were started. Progress continued until the worldwide depression of the 1930's. The economy of Saskatchewan was especially hard hit, as the price of wheat and other farm products dropped sharply. Economic recovery took more than a decade.

During and after World War II, there was considerable industrial development, particularly in the mining industry. Additional cooperative associations were organized. For much of the period, the province has been governed by socialist parties—the Co-operative Commonwealth Federation (CCF) from 1944 to 1964 and the New Democratic party (NDP), successor to the CCF, from 1971 to 1982. Under these parties, several social-welfare measures were enacted and the government took control of natural resources. In 1982 the Progressive Conservative party came to power. It reversed some socialist policies and sold several government-owned corporations to private investors. The NDP was returned to power in 1991 and retained control of the government in elections held in 1995.

Saskatchewan Rebellion, 1885, the second and last uprising in Canada of the *métis* (persons of mixed French and Indian ancestry), led by Louis Riel. It is sometimes called the Northwest Rebellion.

The métis living in the Saskatchewan River valley felt their lands were threatened by the coming of the railroad and large numbers of settlers. They demanded recognition of their claims to the land by the Canadian government. When no action was taken, Louis Riel set up a provisional government in March, 1885. A Mounted Police force sent to put down the rebellion was defeated at Duck Lake. In April, some Cree Indians allied with the métis massacred most of the white settlers at Frog Lake. This incident aroused eastern Canada, and more than 4,000 militiamen were sent to Saskatchewan. In May, the militia decisively defeated the métis at Batoche. By July, the Indians had also been subdued. Riel was tried and hanged with eight others.

Although the uprising failed, the métis were given titles to their land. Also, representation in the Canadian Parliament was granted to the Northwest Territories (in which Saskatchewan was one of four districts), and a territorial legislature was established.

See also RED RIVER REBELLION; RIEL, LOUIS; SASKATCHEWAN, picture *Saskatchewan Rebellion*.

Saskatchewan River, a river of southwestern Canada, formed by the union of the North and South Saskatchewan rivers. From their headwaters, close together in the Rocky Mountains along the British Columbia–Alberta border, these two rivers flow eastward and join near Prince Albert, Saskatchewan. From there the Saskatchewan River continues eastward some 340 miles (547 km) to its outlet at Lake Winnipeg in Manitoba. The distance from the head of the Bow River (principal headstream of the South Saskatchewan) to Lake Winnipeg is 1,205 miles (1,939 km).

The Saskatchewan River drains a large part of Canada's Prairie Provinces. With the Nelson River, which flows out of Lake Winnipeg, it forms one of North America's longest river systems. Once valuable as a fur-trading route, the river now furnishes hydroelectric power and irrigation water.

Saskatoon, săs'kȧ-tōōn', Saskatchewan, Canada, the province's largest city. It lies on the South Saskatchewan River, about 150 miles (240 km) northwest of Regina, the provincial capital. Saskatoon is the pro-

cessing and distribution center for a large agricultural region. Flour milling, meat packing, and potash mining are the principal industries in and near the city.

The University of Saskatchewan, opened here in 1909, is the leading institution of higher learning in the province. At the Western Development Museum are displayed old farm machinery, vintage automobiles, and house furnishings and other items used by early settlers of Saskatchewan. The province's early history is the theme of the annual Pioneer Days Exhibition.

Saskatoon was founded in 1882 by members of the Ontario Temperance Society.

Population: 186,058.

Sasquatch. See YETI.

Sassafras, săs'ȧ-frăs, an ornamental tree native to the eastern half of North America. The sassafras usually grows to a height of 30 to 60 feet (9 to 18 m) but may be as tall as 90 feet (27 m). It has small, fragrant, greenish-yellow flowers that appear before the leaves unfold in the spring. The smooth-edged leaves have from one to three lobes. In autumn, the leaves turn a bright scarlet color, and red, fleshy stalks bear the bluish-black fruit.

The wood is moderately hard, fragrant, and durable. It is used in making boats, oars, fence posts, and boxes. The root bark is dried and used to make sassafras tea and a fragrance for soaps and perfumes. Sassafras oil is used in many floor and polishing oils. The oil is sometimes used as a food and beverage flavoring, although its use as such is prohibited in the United States because of a possible connection with liver cancer.

The sassafras of eastern North America is *Sassafras albidum*. A second species, *S. tzumu*, is native to China and Taiwan. Both belong to the laurel family, Lauraceae.

Sassetta, sä-sĕt'ä, the name given to Stefano di Giovanni (1392?-1450?), an Italian painter. One of the leading painters of

Sassafras Leaves
Grant Heilman

The Metropolitan Museum of Art: bequest of Maitland F. Griggs

Journey of the Magi, by Sassetta, about 1430; tempera on wood, 8¹/₂ x 11⁵/₈ inches (21.6 x 29.5 cm)

Siena, he continued the International Gothic style in his altarpieces and frescoes. The slender figures, delicate colors, and rhythmic line seen in *Journey of the Magi* are typical of his work. Little is known of Sassetta's life. His earliest known work is an altarpiece painted in 1423-26.

Sassoon, să-soon', **Siegfried** (1886-1967), an English author. His best-known works are poems dealing with the horror and senselessness of war. They range in treatment from bitter satire to brutal realism. *Counter-Attack* (1918) is an outstanding volume of his war poems. His fictionalized memoirs are collected in *The Memoirs of George Sherston* (1937). Sassoon was born in London and attended Cambridge University. He served as an infantry officer in World War I and was wounded several times.

His other books include: Poetry—*The Old Huntsman* (1917); *The Heart's Journey* (1928); *Vigils* (1935); *Collected Poems, 1908-1956* (1961). Autobiography—*The Weald of Youth* (1942); *Siegfried's Journey* (1945). Biography—*Meredith* (1948).

Satan. See DEVIL.

Satellite, in astronomy and astronautics, a natural or artificial object that travels around a celestial body under the influence of gravitational attraction. The earth's moon is a satellite of the earth; the earth and other

planets of the solar system are satellites of the sun. Most artificial satellites are in orbit around the earth; some have been placed in orbit around another planet, the sun, or the moon. For information about some specific satellites, see MOON; PLANET; SATELLITE, ARTIFICIAL.

The path of a satellite is called its orbit, and the body around which the satellite travels is called its primary. The motion of satellites is described by Johannes Kepler's laws of planetary motion and explained by Sir Isaac Newton's law of gravitation and his laws of motion. (See GRAVITATION; PLANET, subtitle *Planetary Motion.*)

Why a Satellite Stays in Orbit

There are two principal factors to be considered in analyzing the motion of a satellite in orbit: (1) the satellite's *inertia*—that is, its tendency to keep moving at a constant velocity unless acted upon by some outside force; and (2) gravitational attraction between the satellite and its primary. In the absence of gravitational attraction an artificial satellite would travel along a straight line in the direction in which it was launched, at its launching speed. Gravitational attraction pulls the satellite toward the center of its primary. The orbital motion of the satellite is due to the combination of these effects.

Figure 1 shows a satellite in a circular orbit. The velocity of the satellite and the gravitational attraction acting on the satellite are *vectors* (quantities having both magnitude and direction) and are represented by arrows. (See VECTOR.) With a circular orbit, the gravitational attraction (G) is always at right angles to the velocity (V). The speed of the satellite does not change, but the direction of the satellite's motion changes continuously.

Figure 2 shows the more complicated case of a satellite in an elliptical orbit. The distance from the primary, and therefore the magnitude of G, changes from each point in the orbit to the next. The angle between G and V also keeps changing. The satellite's speed decreases as the satellite moves away from its primary and increases as the satellite approaches the primary. To help understand why the speed changes, vector G can be considered to be made up of two component vectors, D and M, as shown in Figure 2a. Component vector D, at right angles to V, causes the change in direction that makes the satellite stay in orbit. Component vector M, parallel to V, increases the speed of the satellite when pointing in the direction of the satellite's motion (see red arrows) and slows down the satellite when pointing in the direction opposite to that of the satellite's motion (see blue arrows).

The orbits of both natural and artificial satellites are subject to perturbations—irregularities caused by gravitational attraction between the satellite and some celestial body other than the primary. Over a long period of time, perturbations can cause major changes in an orbit.

An artificial satellite's orbit can also be changed by other external means, such as the firing of a small rocket to produce a change either in the satellite's speed or in its direction. If the orbit of an artificial satellite of the earth passes through the earth's upper atmosphere, the satellite will be slowed by air friction and its orbit will gradually decay (that is, the satellite will gradually lose altitude). When the speed of a satellite is increased by firing a rocket, the average distance between the orbiting satellite and the center of its primary increases. If the satellite's velocity exceeds a certain value, called its escape velocity, gravitational attraction can no longer keep the satellite in orbit, and it flies off into space.

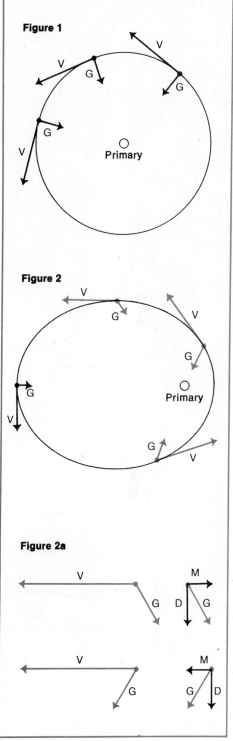

Figure 1

Primary

Figure 2

Primary

Figure 2a

NASA

A Satellite Is Launched. This Juno II rocket carries a research satellite inside its nose cone.

Note

This article concerns unmanned satellites. For a discussion of manned spaceflight, see SPACE EXPLORATION.

Satellite, Artificial, a man-made object that orbits the earth, the moon, the sun, or any other celestial body. On October 4, 1957, the Soviet Union's Sputnik I became the first man-made object to be placed in orbit—an event that ushered in the space age.

The advent of the space age had a profound influence on education in the United States. The science content of high school curricula was modernized, and advanced study in engineering and the sciences received new emphasis. Later, there was a widening exploration into the methods and principles of teaching, to enable students to cope with the rapidly changing and expanding technological aspects of society. Politically, the ability to orbit ever heavier and more complex satellites immediately became a matter of prestige among nations, particularly the United States and the Soviet Union. The concepts of international law were extended to space, and many political questions were raised. Some of these questions, such as the banning of nuclear weapons in space, were settled, but other issues, such as the development of weapons to destroy satellites in space, remain unresolved.

Satellites have important applications in communications and meteorology. Satellites are also important in the study of some of the most challenging problems of pure science, such as the origin of the earth and, indeed, of the whole universe.

The developments of space science have also provided society with direct benefits in the form of what has been called technological fallout—that is, inventions and processes that were originally developed for the space program (or in an unsuccessful attempt to solve a problem for the space program) and later became useful in other applications. For example, metallized plastic film developed for an early artificial satellite called Echo later found use as a material for camping equipment, food packaging, and winter clothing. One unique application is as a lightweight emergency blanket that can protect a person against freezing temperatures, yet when folded is small enough to fit in a shirt pocket.

How a Satellite Is Launched

Satellites are launched into space by various types of rockets, called *launch vehicles*. A single launch vehicle can be used to place two or more satellites into orbit at one time. Some launch vehicles are expendable—they are designed to be used only once. The *space shuttle*, a type of manned spacecraft, serves as a reusable launch vehicle. A few satellites have been launched from high-flying airplanes.

A major consideration in the choice of a launch vehicle for a particular flight, or *mission*, is the amount of thrust generated by the vehicle. The greater the *payload* to be lifted and the higher the orbit, the greater the thrust must be. (The payload consists of the satellite, its protective coverings, and any other hardware, such as separation devices, and sometimes a rocket engine that boosts the satellite into its proper orbit.)

The launch vehicle may be a single-stage rocket (having one main set of rocket engines) with or without auxiliary boosters, or it may have two or three stages stacked one on top of another. (See MISSILES AND ROCKETS.)

Preparation for a mission begins months in advance of the anticipated launch date. The launch vehicle must be assembled and its various parts—including pumps, fuel tanks, engines, and steering mechanisms—tested. The satellite is checked to determine, as completely as possible, if it will function as planned in space. In this check the satellite is subjected to, among other things, intense vibration (simulating rocket flight), near vacuum, and extremes of heat and cold.

In the hours prior to a launch, many preparations and checks must be made. Launch vehicles that use liquid propellants must be fueled during this time. The sequence of events leading up to the launch is referred to as the *countdown*.

For a few seconds after the rocket engines of the launch vehicle are ignited, the vehicle is held down by restraints to permit the engines' thrust to build. The restraints are then released and lift-off occurs. The launch vehicle rises slowly at first, but rapidly gains speed as it gains altitude.

With a multistage launch vehicle, only the engines of the first stage are ignited for lift-off. After its fuel is exhausted, the first

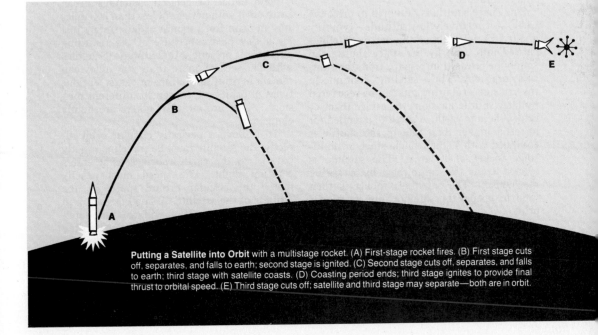

Putting a Satellite into Orbit with a multistage rocket. (A) First-stage rocket fires. (B) First stage cuts off, separates, and falls to earth; second stage is ignited. (C) Second stage cuts off, separates, and falls to earth; third stage with satellite coasts. (D) Coasting period ends; third stage ignites to provide final thrust to orbital speed. (E) Third stage cuts off; satellite and third stage may separate—both are in orbit.

stage is jettisoned and the second stage is fired. Each stage is fired and jettisoned in turn. The space shuttle is a single-stage launch vehicle with three liquid-fuel rocket engines and two solid-fuel rocket boosters. The liquid-fuel engines are supplied with fuel from a large external tank. The boosters and the liquid-fuel tank are jettisoned before the shuttle reaches orbit.

A launch vehicle travels straight up only for the first few seconds of its flight. To enter earth orbit, the satellite must be traveling parallel or nearly parallel to the earth's surface at the end of powered flight. Shortly after lift-off, therefore, the launch vehicle begins to tilt over, entering a long curved path that will bring it to orbital altitude in a nearly horizontal position.

In addition to carrying a satellite to a given altitude, a launch vehicle must impart to the satellite enough horizontal speed to keep it in orbit. The speed required depends on the satellite's altitude; the lower the satellite, the faster it must travel to stay in orbit. For example, a satellite must travel at 17,253 miles per hour (27,766 km/h) to stay in a circular orbit at an altitude of 200 miles (322 km) and it must travel 15,802 miles per hour (25,431 km/h) to stay in a circular orbit at an altitude of 1,000 miles (1,609 km). In the lower orbit the satellite will circle the earth in 90.96 minutes; in the higher orbit, in 118.41 minutes.

The space shuttle is designed to orbit the earth at a relatively low altitude—typically about 200 miles above the earth. Satellites carried into orbit by the space shuttle can simply be released into space from the shuttle's cargo bay. These satellites continue in the same general orbit and can be recovered by later shuttle missions to service them or return them to earth. A satellite intended for an orbit higher than that of the shuttle is equipped with a small single-stage or multi-stage rocket of its own. The satellite is ejected from the cargo bay by a spring mechanism. The satellite's rocket is then fired to propel the satellite into its proper orbit.

Virtually all United States satellites are launched from either Cape Canaveral on the eastern coast of Florida or from Vandenberg Air Force Base on the southern coast of California. The Cape Canaveral launch site is used for launching satellites into orbits that circle the earth above or nearly above the Equator. They are launched eastward, across the Atlantic Ocean. Launching a satellite eastward takes advantage of the speed imparted to it by the earth's rotation. At the latitude of the cape, this speed is 900 miles per hour (1,448 km/h). The Vandenberg launch site is used for launching satellites southward into polar or near-polar orbits. Most United States military satellites are launched from Vandenberg.

The Commonwealth of Independent States also has two major launch sites. Most of the commonwealth's satellites with general west-to-east orbits are launched from a site in Kazakhstan east of the Aral Sea. Most satellites placed in polar or near-polar orbits are launched from a site in Russia south of Archangel, a city near the White Sea.

Other launch sites include one built by France near Kourou, French Guiana, and a Japanese launch site on Tanega Island in southern Japan.

The Orbit

Once a satellite enters coasting flight in orbit, it behaves according to the same rules that govern natural satellites. (See SATELLITE.) The low point of an elliptical earth orbit is called *perigee,* the high point is *apogee.* In a lunar orbit, the low point is *perilune,* the high point is *apolune.* In a solar orbit, the corresponding points are *perihelion* and *aphelion.*

Earth Orbit. In general, satellites in an earth orbit with perigee of less than 200 miles stay in orbit for a month or less, many just for a day or so, because of the retarding effect of air present at that altitude. Satellites with perigees of more than 200 miles can remain in orbit for months or years. Various types of orbits are chosen for different missions. Some are circular; others are highly elongated.

To achieve a perfectly circular orbit directly, the satellite must be traveling exactly parallel to the earth's surface as it enters coasting flight. The speed must exactly match the circular orbital speed for the altitude of the satellite. A small deviation in either speed or direction will cause the satellite to enter an elliptical orbit; the greater the deviation, the more elongated the ellipse.

To make an orbit more circular, rocket engines—either in the final stage of the launch vehicle or built into the satellite itself—are fired to accelerate the satellite along a tangent to the orbit at apogee. This

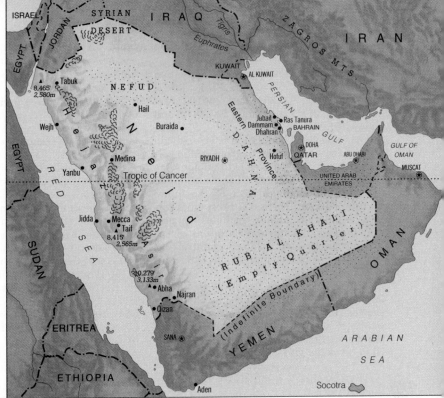

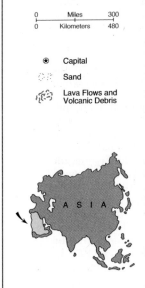

SAUDI ARABIA

| 0 | Miles | 300 |
| 0 | Kilometers | 480 |

⊛ Capital

🔅 Sand

🔆 Lava Flows and
Volcanic Debris

To a large extent the oil is exported un-refined, mostly through the Persian Gulf terminal at Ras Tanura but also via pipeline to the Red Sea port of Yanbu. However, crude oil is increasingly being refined within Saudi Arabia, mainly at Ras Tanura, Jidda, and Yanbu.

Most of Saudi Arabia's natural gas is produced as a by-product of the oil industry. Liquefied petroleum gas (LP gas) is the chief product of the natural gas industry, and the country is a major exporter of this product.

Agriculture. A large, but declining, number of Saudi Arabians still rely on a traditional kind of agriculture or nomadic herding for a living. The tilled area, which amounts to less than 2 per cent of the total area, consists mainly of irrigated oasis land and tracts in Asir. Wheat, sorghum, tomatoes, watermelons, and dates are significant crops. Many foods must be imported. The raising of livestock for milk, meat, and wool is particularly important, especially to the Bedouins, who roam the deserts with their herds and flocks. Chickens, sheep, and goats are the chief animals raised.

Manufacturing and Mining. The expansion of manufacturing is one of the chief goals set by the Saudi government to lessen the country's dependence on petroleum exports. Heavy industry is emphasized. Petroleum refining, truck assembly, and the making of steel pipe, petrochemicals, fertilizer, and cement are among the manufacturing industries established so far. The east coast, especially around Jubail and Dammam, is the chief area where industrial development is taking place. Yanbu is the main center of industrial development on the west coast. There is also some small-scale, local production of processed foods and consumer goods. Mining is a small but growing industry.

Transportation. Vast areas of Saudi Arabia have no transportation facilities and are accessible only by camel or helicopter. Outside of these areas modern transportation is being developed. The building of asphalt roads is a major priority, and many have been completed, mainly in coastal areas and inland to Riyadh, the capital. Riyadh is linked by rail to Dammam and Hofuf.

The country's chief cargo ports are Jidda, Dammam, Jubail, and Yanbu. A causeway links Saudi Arabia to Bahrain. International airports are located at Riyadh, Jidda, and Dhahran. Saudia is the national airline.

The People

According to the 1992 census, Saudi Arabia has a population of 16,929,294. The largest cities are Riyadh, the capital, with a population of 666,840 in 1974; Jidda, 561,104; Mecca, 336,801; Taif, 204,857; Medina, 198,186; Dammam, 127,844; and Hofuf, 101,271.

The indigenous population is virtually all Arab, except for some Negroid groups. A small minority of Arabs called Bedouins live a nomadic tribal life. Most Saudis belong to the orthodox Wahhabi sect of the Sunni branch of Islam. There is a substantial foreign population, which includes persons from the United States and Europe as well as persons from such Islamic countries as Egypt, Iran, and Pakistan. Arabic is the official language.

Education in Saudi Arabia is free at all levels, but it is not compulsory. There is a shortage of schools and teachers. Illiteracy is estimated at about 75 per cent and is highest among the Bedouins. Universities are located in the major cities.

Government

Saudi Arabia is a monarchy ruled by a king. Under three royal decrees of 1992, called "The Basic System of Government," the king serves as prime minister and appoints his cabinet. The cabinet enacts all laws. The king also appoints a 60-member consultative council, which advises the cabinet and may propose new laws and review existing ones. Most of the important positions in the government are held by members of the royal family.

For administrative purposes, the country is divided into 14 regions, called *amirates,* headed by governors. The nation's court system is based on Islamic law.

History

Saudi Arabia traces its origins to the 1700's. For the earlier history of the region, see ARABIA.

In 1744 Emir Muhammad Ibn Saud, aided by the Muslim Wahhabi sect, began expanding his holdings in central Arabia. Saud's descendants continued expansion and conquered the Hejaz during the first decade of the 19th century. During 1812-18, however, Egyptian forces of the Ottoman Empire retook the Hejaz. From that time until the early 20th century, the Saud family fought Ottoman forces and rival families for control of central Arabia. By the mid-1920's Ibn Saud ruled the Nejd and Hejaz. In 1932 he renamed the entire region the Kingdom of Saudi Arabia.

In 1933 an American company was permitted to explore for oil. Huge reserves were discovered in 1938, and after World War II the oil fields were developed, bringing the country vast wealth. Saudi Arabia supported other Arab nations against Israel but remained friendly with the United States.

Under King Faisal, who took the throne in

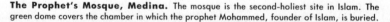

The Prophet's Mosque, Medina. The mosque is the second-holiest site in Islam. The green dome covers the chamber in which the prophet Mohammed, founder of Islam, is buried.

Royal Embassy of Saudi Arabia

1964, a program was begun to raise the standard of living and to industrialize so that eventual depletion of oil reserves would not weaken the economy. Faisal was assassinated in 1975 by one of his nephews. One of Faisal's half brothers, Khalid, became king, and another, Fahd, became crown prince and responsible for the day-to-day administration of the country. Upon Khalid's death in 1982, Fahd was chosen king.

Following the revolution that overthrew the shah of Iran in 1979, relations between Iran and Saudi Arabia deteriorated, largely because of Iran's attempts to impose its fundamentalist religious views on its neighbors. In 1987 a clash between Iranian pilgrims and Saudi security forces in Mecca resulted in the death of more than 400 persons, mostly Iranians.

Following the invasion and seizure of neighboring Kuwait by Iraq in August, 1990, Saudi Arabia joined 36 other nations—principally the United States, Great Britain, France, Egypt, and Syria—in a coalition against Iraq. During January-February, 1991, the coalition forces, operating out of Saudi Arabia, freed Kuwait of the Iraqi occupation.

U.S. military forces remained in the country throughout the 1990's and became a target of Islamists who considered their presence a religious affront. In 1996, Islamic terrorists attacked a U.S. military barracks at Khobar with a truck bomb, killing 19 servicemen.

See also BEDOUINS; FLAG (color page); IBN SAUD, ABDUL AZIZ; JIDDA; MECCA; MEDINA; RIYADH; SYRIAN DESERT.

Books about Saudi Arabia

Alireza, Marianne. *At the Drop of a Veil* (Houghton Mifflin, 1991).
Graham, D. F. *Saudi Arabia Unveiled* (Kendall/Hunt, 1991).
Lindsey, Gene. *Saudi Arabia* (Hippocrene Books, 1991).
Mackey, Sandra. *The Saudis: Inside the Desert Kingdom* (Houghton Mifflin, 1987).
For Younger Readers
Foster, L. M. *Saudi Arabia* (Childrens Press, 1993).
Janin, Hunt. *Saudi Arabia* (Marshall Cavendish, 1992).

Sauger. See PERCH.

Saugus, sô′gŭs, Massachusetts, a town in Essex County. It is a residential community on the Saugus River, eight miles (13 km) northeast of downtown Boston. America's first successful ironworks was established here in 1646 and is commemorated by Saugus Iron Works National Historic Site. The

Royal Embassy of Saudi Arabia
King Saud University, Riyadh. Saudi Arabia's oldest and largest university was established in 1957. It has an enrollment of about 50,000 students and a teaching staff of about 1,500.

area was settled about 1630. It was originally part of Lynn (which was called Saugus until 1637). It became a separate town in 1815 and took Lynn's original name. Population: 25,549.

Saugus Iron Works National Historic Site. See NATIONAL PARKS, section "United States."

Sauk Indians. See SAC INDIANS.

Saul, sôl, the first king of ancient Israel. His reign began about 1020 B.C. According to I Samuel, Saul, after being anointed by the prophet Samuel, was chosen by the Israelites to be their king and unite them against their enemies. Throughout his reign, Saul fought valiantly against the Philistines and other foes. Saul lost favor with God after disobeying his command to destroy an enemy tribe and its possessions. As foretold by the Witch of Endor, Saul died in battle against the Philistines at Mount Gilboa; he took his life by his own sword to avoid capture.

See also DAVID; SAMUEL.

Saul of Tarsus. See PAUL, Saint.

Sault Ste. Marie, sōō′ sȧnt mȧ-rē′, Michigan, the seat of Chippewa County. It is the oldest permanent European settlement in Michigan, and one of the oldest cities in the United States. The city lies on the St. Marys River between Lakes Superior and Huron, opposite Sault Ste. Marie, Ontario. The United States Sault Ste. Marie Canal and Locks are on the river here.

Sault Ste. Marie grew out of a mission founded in 1668 by Fathers Jacques Marquette and Claude Dablon, who came west from French-controlled Quebec. American possession of Sault Ste. Marie was established in 1820 after the site had been held successively by the French and British.

Population: 14,689.

Sault Ste. Marie, Ontario, Canada, a city on the St. Marys River and the Canadian Soo Canal. It is linked by the International Bridge with Sault Ste. Marie, Michigan. Sault Ste. Marie is a commercial, industrial, and shipping center and one of Canada's major steel producers. Several railways, an airport, and the Trans-Canada Highway serve the city.

French explorers visited the site of Sault Ste. Marie as early as 1622. Settlement began when a fur-trading post was established here in 1783. The first canal lock was built in the 1790's. Sault Ste. Marie was incorporated as a town in 1887 and as a city in 1912.

Population: 80,905.

See also SAULT STE. MARIE CANALS.

Sault Ste. Marie Canals, or **Soo Canals,** two waterways between Lake Superior and Lake Huron. The St. Marys River, the natural link between the two lakes, drops some 20 feet (6 m) in shallow rapids near the twin cities of Sault Ste. Marie in Michigan and Ontario. Here the river has been canalized and locks have been built to bypass the rapids and allow ships to sail between the two lakes. One of the canals is on the Michigan side; the other is within Ontario. Since 1987 the Canadian canal has not been operational because of cracks in its walls.

The United States canal, properly known as the St. Marys Falls Ship Canal, is just under 2 miles (3.2 km) long and has four locks side by side. Across the rapids is the Sault Ste. Marie Canal, which is 1.4 miles (2.3 km) long and has only one lock. This canal is administered by the Canadian Park Service as a national historic site.

The United States canal is one of the world's busiest waterways. During the eight-month-long shipping season some 10,000 ships pass through the canal. (The canal is closed from mid-December to early April.) Iron ore and wheat are the chief commodities moving out of Lake Superior; coal is the principal inbound cargo.

History

The first canal to bypass the rapids, with a lock for small boats, was built on the Canadian side in the 1790's. It was destroyed by American troops during the War of 1812. Soon after Michigan's admission to the Union in 1837, state leaders urged the building of a canal. After many delays the project was begun by the state, and the first ship canal, with a single lock, was opened in 1855. By permitting easy shipment of the Lake Superior region's vast iron, copper, and lumber resources, the canal played an important part in the industrial development of the United States.

In 1881 a second, larger lock was built by the United States, and the old original lock was replaced in 1896, one year after the present Canadian canal was opened. Additional locks were built in 1914, 1919, and 1943. The 1896 lock was replaced in 1969 with a larger one.

Sauna. See BATH.

Saunders, Richard, the pen name of Benjamin Franklin. See FRANKLIN, BENJAMIN.

Saurischian. See DINOSAUR, subtitle *Kinds of Dinosaurs: Saurischians.*

Sausage, a processed food made of chopped or ground meat blended with seasonings and usually stuffed in a casing. Certain cereals, such as rice flour or corn flour, are sometimes mixed in with the meat. Pork, beef, and veal are the meats generally used. The casing is usually made of hog, sheep, or cattle intestines; cellulose; plastic; or fabric.

There are more than 200 varieties of sausage, divided into six general groups. *Fresh sausage,* made from fresh, uncured meat, includes such varieties as fresh pork sausage and bratwurst. *Uncooked smoked sausage,* made from smoked meat, includes Polish pork sausage and Italian pork sausage. *Cooked smoked sausage* is made from cured meats and includes frankfurters and bologna. *Cooked sausages,* such as liver sausage and blood sausage, are usually prepared from fresh meats and are then thoroughly cooked. *Cooked meat sausages,* such

Jeanne Benoit Sauvé
Proulx Brothers, Inc.
Ottawa

as luncheon meat and veal loaf, are cooked or baked and are ready to serve. *Dry sausages,* including salami and summer sausage, are air dried and are usually more highly seasoned than other sausages.

Sausages have been eaten at least since the time of the ancient Greeks. Many sausages, such as bologna, frankfurters, and braunschweiger, are named for their city of origin.

Sauvé, sō-vā′, **Jeanne Benoit** (1922-1993), a Canadian journalist and public official. She was Canada's first woman governor general, serving 1984-90. She previously had been the first woman to be speaker of the House of Commons, 1980-83.

Jeanne Benoit was born in Prud'homme, Saskatchewan. After attending the universities of Ottawa and Paris, she began working as a journalist in Quebec. In 1948 she married Maurice Sauvé, a Liberal party politician. She was first elected to the House of Commons, as a Liberal, in 1972. She served as minister of state for science and technology, 1972-74; minister of the environment, 1974-75; and minister of communications, 1975-79.

Sava I Bridge. See BRIDGE, table *Some Notable Bridges*.

Sava River, sä′vä, a river in the Balkan Peninsula. It is a principal tributary of the Danube. From its source in the Julian Alps in Slovenia, the Sava flows southeastward for about 585 miles (940 km); through northern Croatia, along part of Bosnia-Herzegovina's northern border, and into Serbia, where it joins the Danube at Belgrade. The Sava is navigable for about two-thirds of its course. Its main tributaries are the Kupa, Una, Vrbas, Bosna, and Drina rivers.

Savanna. See GRASSLAND, subtitle *Kinds of Grasslands*.

Savannah, sȧ-văn′ȧ, Georgia, the seat of Chatham County. Savannah lies on the Savannah River at the South Carolina boundary, about 10 miles (16 km) from the Atlantic Ocean. It is one of Georgia's chief commercial and industrial centers and a leading port. Produced here are lumber, transportation equipment, fabricated metals, chemicals, processed foods, fertilizers, petroleum products, and paper. Shipping is the major industry, and naval stores, such as turpentine and rosin, are a major export. The city is also a popular tourist center. Several railways, an airport, a network of highways, and the Intracoastal Waterway serve Savannah.

Savannah is noted for its pre-Civil War mansions; broad, tree-lined streets; and numerous squares, parks, and gardens. The Low Mansion, one of Savannah's most prominent buildings, was the birthplace of Juliette Gordon Low, founder of the Girl Scouts of America. On the riverfront is Factors' Row, a group of restored 19th-century warehouses and offices; it is named for the cotton factors (ships' agents) who once worked here. Savannah's notable churches include the Cathedral of St. John the Baptist, Wesley Monumental Methodist Church, and Christ Episcopal Church, where John Wesley, founder of Methodism, was once the minister. The Telfair Academy of Arts and Sciences displays paintings, sculpture, and antique furnishings.

Armstrong State College and Savannah State College are here. Nearby are several historic forts, including Fort Pulaski, now a national monument. The city has the council-manager form of government.

History

Savannah was founded by General James Oglethorpe in 1733 and was the first permanent settlement in Georgia. It was made the colonial capital when Georgia became a royal colony in 1754. During the Revolutionary War, when Savannah was the state capital, the city was held by the British from 1778 until 1782. It was chartered as a city seven years later. Eli Whitney invented the cotton gin here in 1793; thereafter, Savannah grew steadily as a cotton center and port. The first sailing ship to cross the Atlantic using some steam power, the *Savannah,* sailed from here to Liverpool, England, in 1819.

Savannah was an important Confederate supply depot during the Civil War. It resisted Union attacks until December, 1864, when General Sherman captured it, ending his March to the Sea.

Population: 137,560.

Savannah River, a river in the southeastern United States, forming most of the Georgia–South Carolina boundary. From Hartwell Lake it flows southeastward for about 314 miles (505 km) to the Atlantic Ocean. Savannah and Augusta, both in Georgia, are the principal cities on the river. J. Strom Thurmond Dam, upstream from Augusta, impounds a second large reservoir. Both Hartwell and J. Strom Thurmond dams are important for flood control and the generation of hydroelectric power. The river is navigable for oceangoing vessels to Savannah and for small craft to Augusta.

Savannah River Plant and Laboratory. See NUCLEAR ENERGY, section "Research and Development," subtitle *Important Installations*.

Savannah State College. See UNIVERSITIES AND COLLEGES (table).

Savings Account. See BANKS AND BANKING, section "Banking Services," subtitle *Receiving Money*.

Savings and Loan Association, a financial institution that accepts savings deposits from the public and invests primarily in residential mortgages and home-improvement loans. In some states a savings and loan association may be called a homestead association (primarily in Louisiana) or a cooperative bank (in New England). Savings and loan associations are a major private source of funds for financing the building and purchasing of homes.

Deposits in savings and loan associations originally were legally considered investments in the association by the depositor. They were unlike bank deposits, which are debts of the bank to the depositor. Since the late 1960's, several changes have taken place. Savings and loan associations have been allowed to accept bank-type savings deposits and to provide savings accounts with check-writing privileges, referred to as NOW (negotiable order of withdrawal) accounts. Most also offer regular checking accounts.

Organization and Regulation

Approximately half of the 2,000 savings and loan associations in the United States are organized as mutual firms—corporations that do not issue stock. The election of the board of directors and other important issues are voted upon by the savers. Savers are given a number of votes according to the size of their deposits, but most sign proxies when

opening their accounts, so that comparatively few actually vote.

An increasing number of savings and loan associations now are organized as ordinary corporations. They are controlled by shareholders, who are not necessarily depositors.

Savings and loan associations must be either federally or state chartered. Federally chartered associations are regulated by the Office of Thrift Supervision of the U.S. Treasury Department. They must join the Federal Deposit Insurance Corporation (FDIC), which insures deposits in savings and loans up to $100,000 through its Savings Association Insurance Fund (SAIF). State-chartered savings and loans are regulated by both the states and the federal government, and deposits are insured by SAIF.

History

During the last half of the 18th century English workingmen formed *building societies* to provide homes for themselves. They paid a fixed sum to the society periodically. Homes were built one at a time until all of the members were housed. These associations terminated when all of the homes were completed. Soon associations began to accept deposits by persons who merely wanted to save. These associations were nonterminating, or permanent. The first terminating association in the United States was founded near Philadelphia in 1831; by 1850 most associations in the United States were of the permanent type.

Savings and loan associations were found throughout the country by 1890. Major growth in accounts and loans occurred after World War II, when there was an enormous increase in the demand for homes and home financing. The Depository Institutions Deregulation Act of 1980 removed interest-rate ceilings and minimum-balance requirements from savings institutions. The Garn–St. Germain Depository Institutions Act of 1982 allowed them to offer commercial checking accounts and a greater variety of consumer and commercial loans, to invest in a wider range of business activities, and to convert easily into savings banks.

The new laws spurred tremendous growth in the savings and loan industry. Much of the growth, however, was built on reckless, often fraudulent, banking practices. In the absence of strong state and federal regulations many savings and loans built deposits by offering excessively high interest rates and loaned money on unsound real estate ventures. At the same time, savings and loans faced greater competition from banks and other institutions in the home mortgage market.

By the late 1980's, the savings and loan industry was in severe economic distress, with more than a third of the institutions losing money and hundreds of others having closed after becoming insolvent. In 1989 Congress passed the Financial Institutions Reform, Recovery and Enforcement Act, which restructured the industry and replaced the existing regulatory agencies— the Federal Savings and Loan Insurance Corporation (created in 1934) and the Federal Home Loan Bank Board (created in 1932)—with new ones. The law also empowered the federal government to liquidate insolvent institutions and to impose tighter control on savings and loans.

America's Community Bankers is the national trade association for savings and loans. It was formed in 1992 by the merger of the United States League of Savings Institutions and the National Council of Community Bankers. Headquarters are in Washington, D.C.

Savings Bank. See BANKS AND BANKING, box titled *Kinds of Banking Institutions:* Savings Bank.

Savings Bond. See BOND, subtitle *Types of Bonds:* Savings Bonds.

Savings Institutions. See BANKS AND BANKING; CREDIT UNION; SAVINGS AND LOAN ASSOCIATION.

Savonarola, săv′ō-nȧ-rō′lȧ, **Girolamo** (1452-1498), an Italian religious and political reformer. One of the most controversial religious figures in history, he has been venerated as a saint and martyr by some and condemned as a fanatic and heretic by others.

Savonarola was born of a minor noble family in Ferrara. He had some training in medicine and philosophy at the court of the d'Este family, where his grandfather was a physician. At 22 he entered a Dominican monastery at Bologna. He was assigned to Florence in 1482 and settled there permanently in 1489. He began to preach at the Monestary of St. Mark and became its prior in 1491.

Savonarola was horrified by the immorality among the people and the corruption among public officials and the clergy. He attacked these evils and rebuked evildoers in his sermons, gaining many adherents among

The New-York Historical Society; bequest of Mr. Louis Durr
Girolamo Savonarola, by Fra Bartolommeo, early 16th century; oil on panel, 28½ x 22½ inches (72.4 x 57.2 cm)

the Florentines. At first he had the support of Lorenzo de' Medici, dictator of Florence, but his attacks on the vices of the aristocracy and his growing influence made the two adversaries.

Dictator of Florence

When Lorenzo died in 1492 and leadership fell to his less capable son Piero, Savonarola's importance increased further. In 1493 he won papal approval for his plan to reform the Dominican order in Tuscany. In 1494, when a French army under Charles VIII threatened Florence, Savonarola helped to negotiate its withdrawal. In the meantime, his followers expelled the Medici faction and assumed power.

Savonarola's personal prominence made him virtual dictator under the new government. A new constitution was adopted at his urging, establishing a republic. He was uncompromising in his pursuit of moral purity and social righteousness. Twice he required the citizens to cast upon a "bonfire of vanities" what he considered their profane possessions, including jewelry, books, and paintings.

Savonarola's impassioned sermons kept the people under his influence for a time, but many Florentines eventually tired of the puritanical restrictions he tried to impose and turned against him. His zeal led him to denounce Pope Alexander VI, and he was excommunicated by the pope in 1497. Meanwhile, the Medici faction had regained control of the government. Savonarola was seized, convicted of heresy and sedition, and hanged.

Savory, sā′vẽr-ĭ, the common name for several aromatic herbs and low shrubs native to the warm regions of Europe and North Africa. The plants usually grow to a height of five inches to three feet (13 to 90 cm) or more and have a square stem. The flowers may be pink, purple, or white. Two species commonly cultivated in the United States are *summer savory* and *winter savory*. They are grown chiefly for their leaves, which are used as a flavoring. Occasionally they are cultivated as border plants.

Summer savory is *Satureja hortensis;* winter savory is *S. montana.* Both belong to the mint family, Labiatae.

Savoy, så-voi′, a historical region of southeastern France. It consists approximately of the present French departments of Haute-Savoie and Savoie. The region adjoins Italy and Switzerland on the east; its northern boundary is formed by Lake Geneva. Principal cities are Chambéry and Annecy. In the Middle Ages Savoy was a feudal domain in the Kingdom of Arles. It became a duchy in the 15th century. The duchy's ruling house, which also held Piedmont and Nice, acquired Sardinia in 1720 and combined the four domains into the Kingdom of Sardinia. France had control of Savoy from 1792 until 1815, when the Kingdom of Sardinia regained control. In 1860 Savoy was ceded to France.

Savoy, House of, the ruling family of Italy, 1861-1946. The line was founded by Count Humbert the Whitehanded, who became ruler of Savoy about 1034. The domain was soon extended by marriage to include Piedmont; in 1388 Nice was added.

Through the War of the Spanish Succession, 1701-14, Duke Victor Amadeus of Savoy acquired Sicily. In 1720 he gave Sicily to Austria in exchange for Sardinia and founded the Kingdom of Sardinia, consisting of Savoy, Piedmont, Nice, and Sardinia. After 1831 the Sardinian monarch Charles Albert and his successor, Victor Emmanuel II, led a movement to free Italy of foreign sovereignty and unite the various states into a single nation. Their efforts resulted in the unification of Italy in 1861 and Victor Emmanuel II's accession to its throne. The House of Savoy ruled Italy until 1946, when

King Humbert II abdicated and a republic was established.

See also VICTOR EMMANUEL II; VICTOR EMMANUEL III.

Saw, a cutting tool. Most saws have metal blades with teeth along the edge; in one type, however, the teeth are attached to a chain, and in another, abrasive particles are used instead of teeth. Saws are used to cut wood, metal, stone, plastic, bone, and other substances. The saw is a basic tool used in lumbering, in stonecutting, in carpentry and other woodworking crafts, and in many metalworking industries.

Most saws use detachable blades that can be replaced when damaged or worn. Certain special-purpose saws have removable teeth that make replacement of the entire blade unnecessary. Some saws used for cutting metal and wood have tungsten carbide tips on the teeth to provide a sharper, longer-lasting cutting edge. Stonecutting saws often have diamonds set in the teeth.

Saw blades are designed to make as thin a cut as possible to avoid waste. The shape, size, and spacing of the teeth vary according to the intended use of the tool. In sawing, the tooth edge of the blade is moved across the work. Action of the teeth produces a cut, or *kerf,* of uniform width through the material. To prevent the blade from becoming wedged in the cut, the tooth edge is made slightly wider than the rest of the blade. This is done by either tapering the sides of the blade or bending the teeth, either singly or in groups, alternately outward from the sides of the blade. The amount of bending is called the *set* of the teeth.

The earliest saws were small, thick flakes of flint with irregular notches along one edge. The first metal saws were made of copper and bronze. The ancient Egyptians developed stonecutting saws of bronze with gems set in the teeth. Most handsaws had developed into their present forms by the end of the 18th century. Machine saws—saws using the power of treadmills, windmills, and waterwheels—were used as early as late Roman times, and some are known to have been used in sawmills as early as the 13th century. However, power-driven saws did not become important until the early 19th century, when steam-powered saws came into use. By the early 20th century electric saws began to hold the dominance they maintain today.

SAW

Kinds of Saws

Saws have either reciprocating or continuous cutting action, and are either handsaws or power saws. *Reciprocating saws* include those that cut on a forward or backward stroke, or both. Most reciprocating saws are handsaws, but many are power-driven (electric or pneumatic). *Continuous-action saws* have revolving blades, usually in the form of circular disks or endless bands, that cut continuously in one direction. All continuous-action saws are power-driven.

Handsaws. The two most common handsaws are the carpenter's *crosscut saw,* used for cutting wood across the grain, and *ripsaw,* used to cut wood along the grain. The two types are similar in appearance, consisting of a wide, slightly tapered blade fitted into a handle at its widest end, and differ only in the shape of the teeth. Crosscut saw teeth are shaped like sharp-pointed knives; ripsaw teeth are shaped like tiny chisels.

The *coping saw,* a thin, fine-toothed blade held under tension in a metal frame, is used to cut curved and irregular shapes in various materials. The *hacksaw,* used chiefly for cutting metals, has a narrow, fine-toothed blade set in an adjustable metal frame.

The *backsaw* has a wide, fine-toothed blade reinforced with a metal strip along its back edge. It is used mainly with a miter box for cutting angles in wood. The *keyhole saw* is used to cut openings in various materials. It has a narrow, fine-toothed blade tapered to a point at one end. To use the saw, a small hole is first drilled into the material to admit the blade. Other special-purpose saws include the *bow saw,* used chiefly for cutting small logs and trimming trees and bushes; the *bucksaw,* used to cut firewood; and the *two-handed crosscut saw,* used to cut down trees.

Power Saws. Many power saws are stationary units that either have their own floor stands or are used on a work table; others are held in the hand. Most types are driven by electric motors. Power saws usually include various types of guides to assist in making accurate cuts, and many accept accessory equipment, such as dado (groove-cutting) blades and planers.

Circular saws are the most widely used power saws in woodworking, metal cutting, and stonecutting. Two common types of circular saws are the bench saw and the radial-arm saw. The *bench saw* consists of a

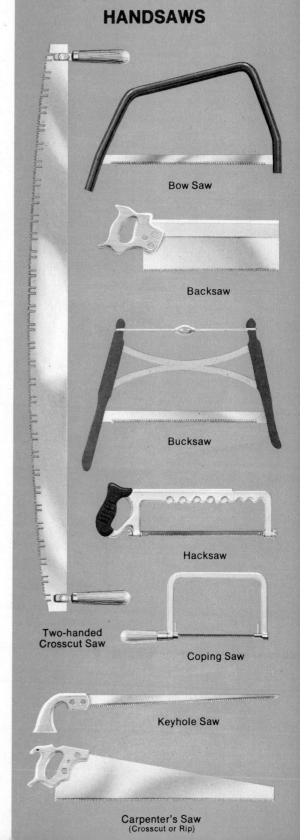

HANDSAWS

Bow Saw

Backsaw

Bucksaw

Hacksaw

Two-handed Crosscut Saw

Coping Saw

Keyhole Saw

Carpenter's Saw
(Crosscut or Rip)

POWER SAWS

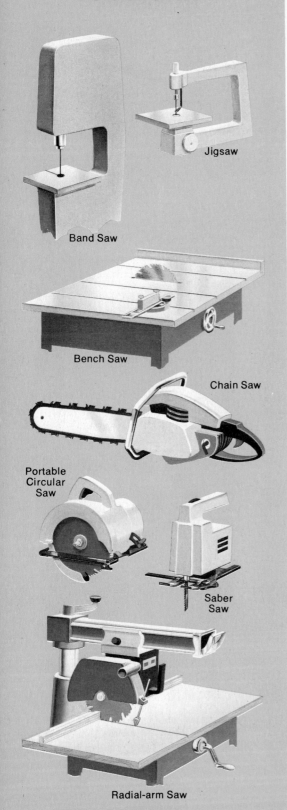

Band Saw

Jigsaw

Bench Saw

Chain Saw

Portable Circular Saw

Saber Saw

Radial-arm Saw

circular blade that is aligned vertically and projects through an opening in a saw table; in most models, the blade can be raised or lowered to vary the depth of cut and tilted for cutting on an angle. The *radial-arm saw* has its circular blade and motor mounted above the saw table on a movable arm that permits a wide range of saw cuts. The *portable circular saw* is especially useful on construction sites and farms, and for general-purpose work in the home.

The *band saw* has a narrow blade in the form of an endless belt that travels over two rotating pulleys. Band saws are used for straight, curved, or irregular cuts in wood, metal, and other substances. The *jigsaw* has a thin, vertically reciprocating blade. Like the coping saw, the jigsaw is used for cutting curves and irregular shapes in various materials. The *saber saw,* which is either portable or a stationary unit, has a narrow, vertically reciprocating blade attached at one end. This saw is used for straight, curved, or irregular cuts in various materials.

The *chain saw,* which is hand-held, is used chiefly for trimming and cutting down trees. Its teeth are set on an endless chain that revolves around a rigid frame. Chain saws are powered by gasoline engines or electric motors.

Sawatch Range, så-wŏch′, a range of the Rocky Mountains in central Colorado. It extends north-south for about 100 miles (160 km) and forms part of the Continental Divide. The Arkansas River runs along its eastern edge. Within the range is the highest peak in the Rockies—14,433-foot (4,399-m) Mount Elbert. Other summits exceeding 14,000 feet (4,267 m) include Mount Massive and the Collegiate Peaks—Mounts Harvard, Yale, Princeton, Columbia, and Oxford.

Sawfish. See SKATES AND RAYS.

Sawfly, any of a group of four-winged insects. The name sawfly comes from the shape of the *ovipositor* (the egg-laying organ of the female). The ovipositor usually has rows of toothlike ridges and somewhat resembles a saw. The female uses the ovipositor to make slits in various plant parts where she lays her eggs.

Sawflies range from ¼ inch to two inches (6 mm to 5 cm) in length. Many species have bodies of red, green, or yellow. Although the adult sawfly is relatively harmless, the caterpillarlike larvae of some species cause much destruction, especially to forests and cultivated plants. Spraying with various insecticides is usually an effective means of control.

Sawflies make up several families of the order Hymenoptera. The majority of sawflies are of the family Tenthredinidae.

Sawmill. See LUMBERING, subtitle *How Lumber Is Produced*.

Sax, Adolphe. See SAXHORN; SAXOPHONE.

Saxhorn, a valved brass wind instrument. Adolphe Sax of Belgium developed a set of seven saxhorns in 1842-45. A saxhorn has a long, winding conical tube with a bell-shaped opening at one end and a cup-shaped mouthpiece at the other. Saxhorns range from sopranino to contrabass and have a full, mellow tone. Most are held upright when played, like the tuba. Some soprano saxhorns, however, are made to be played in a horizontal position, like the trumpet. Saxhorns are used in European military and brass bands. In the United States the baritone horn, euphonium, and other instruments developed from the saxhorn are more popular.

Saxifrage, săk′sĭ-frĭj, the common name for a large family of herbs, shrubs, woody vines, and trees, as well as for a genus of this family. The family consists of about 80 genera and more than 1,000 species, found in temperate climates. Most of the genera under cultivation serve chiefly as ornamentals. Only the genus to which the currant and gooseberry belong is cultivated for its fruit. Plants of the saxifrage genus are grown primarily in rock gardens.

The saxifrage family is Saxifragaceae. The saxifrage genus is *Saxifraga*.

For members of the saxifrage family, see CURRANT; DEUTZIA; GOOSEBERRY; HYDRANGEA; MOCK ORANGE.

Saxons. See ANGLO-SAXONS; SAXONY.

Saxony, săk′s'n-ĭ (*German:* **Sachsen,** zäk′sĕn), the name of two historic regions in Germany.

The original Saxony was an area in northwest Germany that roughly approximates the state of Lower Saxony. It was settled by the Saxons, a Germanic people, about 400 A.D. In the eighth century, they were conquered by Charlemagne, king of the Franks. Saxony became one of the five original duchies of the kingdom of Germany. In 919 a Saxon duke assumed the German throne as Henry I; in 962 Henry's son Otto I founded the

Holy Roman Empire, which was ruled by his line until 1024. In 1180 Emperor Frederick I seized Saxony from its duke, Henry the Lion, and divided the duchy into several smaller states. The area remained divided until 1946, when it became the state of Lower Saxony.

The second Saxony lay to the southeast. It was often referred to as Upper Saxony, to distinguish it from the earlier duchy. The domain, established by a new line of dukes of Saxony, in 1356 became an electorate—a state whose ruler helped elect the German monarch.

In 1485 the electorate was split between two heirs, Albert and Ernest. The Albertine domain lay in the east, around Dresden and Leipzig, while the Ernestine domain, to the west, included Wittenberg and the historic region of Thuringia. During the Thirty Years' War (1618-48), the Ernestine heirs lost Wittenberg. As a result of the treaty ending that war, the rest of the domain was split into five domains—Saxe-Weimar, Saxe-Gotha, Saxe-Altenburg, Saxe-Coburg, and Saxe-Meiningen—which became known as the Thuringian states.

An ally of France in the Napoleonic Wars, the Albertine domain in the east was made a kingdom by Napoleon in 1806. At the Congress of Vienna (1815) the northern half of the kingdom was awarded to Prussia and became the province of Saxony. The rest of the kingdom of Saxony became part of the German Empire in 1871.

During 1945-46, Upper Saxony was organized into three states: Thuringia, Saxony, and Saxony-Anhalt. Shortly after the creation of East Germany in 1949, these states were dissolved and broken up into several districts. In 1990 Germany was reunited and Thuringia, Saxony, and Saxony-Anhalt were reconstituted as states.

See also HENRY, subtitle *Germany* (I and II); OTTO (I, II, and III).

Saxophone, săk′sō-fōn, a wind instrument that combines the features of brass and woodwind instruments. It consists of a conical metal tube with 18 to 21 keyed sound holes. A single-reed mouthpiece is at one end and in some types an upturned bell-shaped opening is at the lower end. The saxophone is made in eight sizes. The most common, ranging from highest to lowest sounding, are soprano in B-flat, alto in E-flat, tenor in B-flat, and baritone in E-flat. The instru-

The Saxophone is a major jazz instrument. John Coltrane, in this picture shown playing the tenor sax, introduced improvisational techniques that influenced many jazzmen.
ABC Records

ment has a range of nearly three octaves and a soft, rich tone that blends well with woodwinds and brass instruments. Saxophones are used regularly in jazz and dance bands and are often heard in military bands. They are seldom used in a symphony orchestra.

The saxophone was invented in the 1840's by Adolphe Sax of Belgium.

Say, Thomas (1787-1834), a United States naturalist. He wrote the first major American works on insects (*American Entomology*, 3 volumes, 1824-28) and shells (*American Conchology*, 2 volumes, 1830-34). Say was born in Philadelphia. He served as zoologist on the United States government expeditions, led by Stephen H. Long, to the Rocky Mountains (1819-20) and the source of the Minnesota River (1823). Say was curator of the American Philosophical Society, 1821-27, and professor of natural history at the University of Pennsylvania, 1822-28. He was a founding member of the Academy of Natural Sciences in Philadelphia.

Scab, in medicine, the protective crust over a wound. It consists of a dried blood clot. (See BLOOD, subtitle *Clotting of the Blood*.) The scab drops off when the injured tissue underneath has healed. If the scab is removed before the tissue has healed, there is risk of introducing infection and deepening the wound. As a result, the healing processes may be slowed and the possibility of scarring is increased. Occasionally, however, a physician will remove a scab prematurely to apply medication to the wound.

Scab, a plant disease; also, the roughened crustlike area on the plant surface resulting from the disease. The disease is caused by various parasitic fungi, each of which usually infects only one kind of plant. Agricultural commodities susceptible to the disease include apples, avocados, barley, cucumbers, peaches, pecans, potatoes, and wheat. Spraying with fungicides and the use of disease-resistant varieties are common methods of prevention and control, but scab is difficult to control once it has taken hold.

Scabies. See MANGE.

Scabiosa, skā′bĭ-ō′så; skăb′ĭ-ō′så, a genus of about 100 species of annual and perennial herbaceous plants native to Europe, Africa, and Asia. Scabiosas are bushy plants that grow from slightly less than one foot (30 cm) up to about four feet (120 cm) in height. Their ball-shaped flower heads are up to 3 inches (7.5 cm) wide. The long, thin stamens projecting outward from the flower head give it the appearance of a pincushion. Scabiosas are also known as *pincushion flowers* and *mourning brides*.

Because they are colorful and easily grown, scabiosas are popular garden flowers. They bloom in white and yellow and in shades of red, blue, and lavender. A popular garden species is the *sweet scabiosa*.

Scabiosas belong to the teasel family, Dipsacaceae. The sweet scabiosa is *Scabiosa atropurpurea*.

Scalare. See ANGELFISH.

Scalawags. See CARPETBAGGERS.

Scald. See BURN.

Scald. See SKALD.

Scale, of fish. See FISH, subtitle *The Body of Fish*: Scales.

Scale, a weighing device. See BALANCES AND SCALES.

Scale, of maps. See MAP, subtitle *Reading a Map*: Scale.

Scale, in music. See MUSIC, subtitle *Elements of Music*: Melody (Scales).

Scale Insects, a family of insects that feed on plants. The name refers to a secretion of waxy scales that serve as a protective covering. Scale insects attack almost any part of a plant and feed by sucking out the juices. They inhabit almost all parts of the world. Many species are serious agricultural pests.

They range in size from $\frac{1}{16}$ inch (1.5 mm) to one inch (25 mm) in length.

Scale insects are classified by the type of scale they secrete. *Armored scale insects* secrete a hard, crusty covering. The scales differ in shape and color in each species. Adult males develop wings and legs and shed the protective covering before mating. Adult females have no legs, antennae, or wings. They remain under the protective covering for life. They lay 40 to 100 oval white eggs on the underside of the covering. The newly hatched young, or *crawlers,* attach themselves to the host plant with their tubular mouths. Among the most destructive species are the *San Jose scale* and the *oyster shell scale.* The San Jose scale is gray and about $\frac{1}{16}$ inch (1.5 mm) in length. It attacks such fruit trees as apple, pear, and peach. The oyster shell scale is brownish and about $\frac{1}{8}$ inch (3 mm) long. It attacks many kinds of trees and shrubs, such as lilac, ash, poplar, and maple.

Unarmored, or *soft, scale insects* secrete a small amount of powdery or mealy wax that adheres to the insect. The most destructive species are the *black scale* and *citricola scale.* Both feed on fruit trees. *Mealybugs* are pests of citrus trees and of ornamental and house plants. (See MEALYBUG.) Scale insects are controlled by introducing natural predators, such as beetles and parasitic wasps.

A few species of scale insects are beneficial to humans. For example, the cochineal insect yields a dye and the lac insect is a source of shellac. (See COCHINEAL; LAC.) The manna of the Bible is believed by some persons to have been the secretion of certain species of scale insects.

Scale insects belong to the superfamily Coccoidea of the order Homoptera. The San Jose scale is *Quadraspidiotus perniciosus;* the oyster shell scale, *Lepidosaphes ulmi.* Both are of the family Diaspididae. The black scale is *Saissetia oleae;* the citricola scale, *Coccus pseudomagnolarium.* Both are of the family Coccidae.

Scallion. See ONION.

Scallop, skŏl'ŭp; skăl'ŭp, an edible mollusk related to the oyster and the clam. There are more than 200 species of scallops. They live in colonies on the ocean floor, some in shallow coastal areas and others at great depths.

The scallop has a bivalve shell (one composed of two parts). The shell is ribbed and rounded, with wavy edges. Depending on species, scallops are from three to eight inches (7.5 to 20 cm) wide. A common North American species, the *Atlantic bay scallop,* is about three inches wide. Scallop shells are used as plates and as decorative pieces.

The scallop's soft body is surrounded by a thin fold of tissue called a mantle, which lines the inside of the shell. The body, as in other mollusks, has a nervous system, a circulatory system, and a digestive system. Scallops feed on tiny plants and animals. Two rows of well-developed eyes are set into the edge of the mantle. A scallop has one large, round muscle that opens and closes its shell. This muscle is the part of the scallop that is eaten. The scallop moves through water by clapping the two parts of its shell together.

The Atlantic bay scallop is *Argopecten irradians.* Scallops are of the family Pectinidae.

See also SHELL (picture).

Scalp. See HEAD.

Scaly Anteater. See PANGOLIN.

Scanderbeg. See ALBANIA, subtitle *History:* Turkish Conquest.

Scandinavia, skăn'dĭ-nā'vĭ-à, the part of northern Europe occupied by Norway, Sweden, and Denmark. In a narrower sense, the term refers only to the peninsula occupied by Norway and Sweden; in a broader sense, it is sometimes taken to include Finland. Iceland, because of its cultural heritage and the Scandinavian origin of its population, is also often considered part of Scandinavia.

Scandinavian Drama. See DRAMA, subtitle *Scandinavian Drama.*

Scandinavian Languages. See LANGUAGE, section "Major Languages of the World" (Scandinavian).

Scandinavian Literature. See LITERATURE, DANISH; LITERATURE, ICELANDIC; LITERATURE, NORWEGIAN; LITERATURE, SWEDISH.

Scandinavian Mythology. See MYTHS AND LEGENDS, subtitle *Germanic Myths and Legends;* SAGA; SNORRI STURLUSON.

Scandium. See RARE EARTHS, subtitle *Related Elements.*

Scanner, in computer science, a device that converts an image, point by point, into computer data. A computer can then interpret, modify, store, reproduce, or transmit the image electronically. Scanners commonly referred to as *optical scanners* are used for "reading" bar codes such the Universal

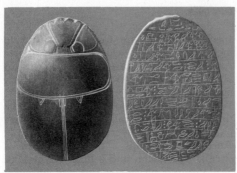

The Oriental Institute of the University of Chicago
Egyptian Scarab Amulet from about 1500 B.C. It is of greenish-black slate, has carved hieroglyphics, and is about three inches (7.6 cm) long.

Product Code, which identifies merchandise. *Color scanners* are widely used in preparing color photographs for printing. Scanners in an optical character recognition (OCR) system are used to produce image data of a page of text; a computer changes the image of the text into text that can be edited with a word-processing program.

The typical scanner works by directing a beam of light across the image being scanned. As it does so, it measures the amount of light that is reflected from (or, in the case of a slide, the light transmitted through) individual small areas of the image. Most scanners produce digital data that represent the scanned image as an array of small individual picture elements, or *pixels,* each having a specific level of brightness.

Scanners vary in the amount of detail and the number of brightness levels they can detect. The simplest scanners are small handheld devices that are drawn over the image to be scanned. The highest-quality scanners are drum scanners; the image is placed on a drum that rotates rapidly as a narrow beam of light slowly sweeps along the length of the cylinder.

Scanning Electron Microscope. See MICROSCOPE, subtitle *Kinds of Microscopes.*

Scapa Flow, skăp′*à* flō′, a sheltered body of water in Scotland's Orkney Islands. This stretch of sea, about 15 miles (24 km) long and 8 miles (13 km) wide, was a major British naval base in World Wars I and II. After the armistice in 1918 a large part of the German fleet, consisting of 77 surface vessels and 102 submarines, was interned at Scapa Flow by the victorious Allies. In June, 1919, caretaker German crews sank the vessels to prevent them from being divided among the Allied nations. In World War II, a German

submarine penetrated British defenses at Scapa Flow in 1939 and sank the battleship *Royal Oak.*

Scapegoat, one of the two goats used in the ancient Hebrew ritual of the Day of Atonement (Yom Kippur). The other was sacrificed to God, but the scapegoat, after being loaded symbolically with the sins of the people, was driven into the wilderness, where apparently it was expected to join a demon called Azazel. The name Azazel is sometimes used to designate the scapegoat in the Old Testament. The ceremony is described in Leviticus 16. In New Testament times, the scapegoat was forced over a cliff to its death. The word scapegoat is now used to mean a person who is blamed for the misconduct or mistakes of others.

Scarab, a black beetle. It is also called the Egyptian sacred scarab because it is believed to be the beetle held sacred by the ancient Egyptians. The scarab is little more than one inch (2.5 cm) long. It feeds primarily on cow dung, which it rolls with a tumbling motion into a ball much larger than itself. For these reasons it is also called a tumblebug or dung beetle.

The beetle digs a burrow in the ground, buries itself and the ball, and feeds. After mating, the female deposits each of her two to four eggs in a mass of dung. The eggs hatch into larvae that are surrounded by their own food supply. When the larva becomes an adult beetle, it digs its way up out of the ground.

To the ancient Egyptians, the scarab symbolized the sun god Khepera. The sharp projections on the scarab's head represented the rays of the sun. The beetle's habit of disappearing into the earth and later reappearing symbolized immortality and resurrection.

The Egyptians carved scarab forms out of metal and stones to use as seals for documents and as charms and amulets. They inscribed the undersides with words, images, and symbols to keep away evil. Scarab amulets were placed upon mummies to ensure the rebirth of the souls of the dead.

The scarab is *Scarabaeus sacer* of the scarab family, Scarabaeidae, of the order Coleoptera.

Scarlatti, skär-lät′tĕ, the family name of two Italian composers, father and son.

Alessandro Scarlatti (1660-1725), the father, was a leader of the Neapolitan School of opera. He helped establish the *da capo* (three-part) aria, Italian overture, and other traditions that dominated 18th-century opera. Scarlatti was born in Palermo and studied in Rome. He worked in Rome and Naples, serving in church posts and as musical director to the former Swedish queen Christina in Rome and to the Spanish viceroy of Naples. None of his more than 115 operas is well known today. He is said to have composed 14 oratorios, 600 cantatas (said to be his best music), 200 masses, 12 concertos for small orchestras, and compositions for keyboard instruments.

Domenico Scarlatti (1685-1757), the son, was the most important Italian keyboard composer of the 18th century. He wrote more than 500 one-movement sonatas for harpsichord, many of which are still performed. A virtuoso harpsichordist, he introduced arpeggio passages and the crossing of hands to obtain special effects. He is often called the founder of modern piano techniques. Scarlatti studied with his father in his native Naples. He was organist and composer to the court there at the age of 16. From about 1719 until his death, he was composer and teacher for the Portuguese Princess Maria Barbara.

Scarlet Fever, or **Scarlatina,** an acute, highly contagious disease caused by certain strains of bacteria called streptococci. The bacteria enter the body mainly through the mouth and nose. Most cases of scarlet fever occur in children between the ages of two and eight. The disease is spread primarily by airborne bacteria, released when an infected person coughs or sneezes.

Symptoms of scarlet fever, which develop about three to five days after infection, include fever, sore throat, and a thick, whitish coating on the tongue. About a day later, a bright red rash appears on the face. On the third day, the rash spreads to other parts of the body, the fever subsides, and the tongue appears bright strawberry-red in color.

In rare cases, scarlet fever is fatal, and in other cases it can cause such complications as ear infections, kidney disease, meningitis, or rheumatic fever. With prompt treatment, however, most victims recover completely within five weeks. Treatment of the disease includes the administration of antibiotic drugs, typically penicillin, erythromycin, or clindamycin, for 10 days.

Scarlet fever is most frequently caused by the bacterium *Streptococcus scarlatinae*.

Scarlet Letter, The, a novel by Nathaniel Hawthorne, published in 1850. It is a powerful study of the destructive effects of hidden guilt and hate. The scene is Puritan Boston of the mid-1600's. The title refers to the letter "A" (for "adulteress") that the heroine, Hester Prynne, is sentenced to wear.

Hester, a young wife unavoidably separated for a while from her elderly husband, bears an illegitimate daughter. Hester is condemned by the authorities and shunned by the townspeople, but refuses to name the child's father. Her husband suspects Arthur Dimmesdale, a young clergyman, and becomes obsessed by a vengefulness that ruins his own life. After years of persecution by the husband and torment by his own conscience, Dimmesdale publicly confesses and then dies. Hester, who has accepted her punishment, finds strength and peace in her love for her daughter and in helping others.

See also LITERATURE, AMERICAN, picture titled *The Scarlet Letter*.

Scarlet Oak. See OAK, subtitle *Types of Oaks:* The Black Oak Group (Scarlet Oak).

Scarlet Tanager. See TANAGER.

Scaup. See DUCK, subtitle *Wild Ducks*.

Schally, Andrew V. See NOBEL PRIZES (Physiology or Medicine, 1977).

Schawlow, Arthur. See NOBEL PRIZES (Physics, 1981).

Scheele, shā'lĕ, **Karl Wilhelm** (1742-1786), a Swedish chemist. He discovered the element oxygen in the early 1770's, independently of and prior to Joseph Priestley. (However, Priestley is often credited with the discovery because his findings were published first.) In 1774 Scheele discovered chlorine, but he thought (incorrectly) that it was an oxgyen-containing compound. He was the first to isolate glycerin, as well as a number of acids, including tartaric acid, lactic acid, uric acid, citric acid, and prussic (hydrocyanic) acid. He contributed to the discovery of the elements manganese, molybdenum, barium, and tungsten. *Scheele's green* (copper arsenite) and *scheelite*, a tungsten ore, are named for him.

Scheele was born in western Pomerania (then part of Sweden, now part of Germany). He was apprenticed to a pharmacist who taught him chemistry. Scheele worked as a pharmacist in Malmö, Stockholm, Uppsala, and Köping, doing chemical experiments in his spare time.

Scheelite. See TUNGSTEN.

Scheherazade. See ARABIAN NIGHTS.

Schelde River, skĕl'dĕ (also **Scheldt,** skĕlt; *French:* **Escaut,** ĕs'kō'), a river in northwestern Europe. From its source in France it flows generally northeastward across Belgium to the Netherlands. There it empties into the North Sea through a wide estuary, called the Wester Schelde. Tributaries include the Leie, Dender, and Rupel rivers. The Schelde is about 270 miles (435 km) long and is navigable by barge for most of its length. Oceangoing vessels travel as far as Antwerp. Ghent is the only other important city on the river. Numerous canals, including the Albert, Ghent, and Schelde-Maas canals, link the Schelde to major cities and industrial areas and to other waterways in the area.

Schelling, shĕl'ĭng, **Friedrich Wilhelm Joseph von** (1775-1854), a German philosopher. Schelling was one of the chief idealists of the 19th century. His early writings on nature influenced German Romanticism and the philosophy of Georg Wilhelm Friedrich Hegel. Schelling agreed with Johann Gottlieb Fichte's view that the world of nature is a creation of the mind, but he also believed that the reverse is true—that nature gives birth to the world of mind. He viewed nature and mind as parallel expressions of a single absolute, nature being visible mind and mind being invisible nature. He stressed the supreme value of art, regarding the work of art as that phenomenon in which nature and mind are perfectly united and the absolute is revealed.

In the 20th century, Schelling has been best known for his later writings, in which he dealt briefly with some of the ideas that have become important in existentialism.

Schelling was born in Leonberg, Württemberg, and studied at the University of Tübingen. He taught at the universities of Jena, Würzburg, Erlangen, Munich, and Berlin. *System of Transcendental Idealism* (1800) is one of his major works.

Schenectady, skĕ-nĕk'tȧ-dĭ, New York, the seat of Schenectady County. It lies on the Mohawk River, 15 miles (24 km) northwest of Albany, the state capital. Schenectady is an industrial center, producing primarily electrical goods, equipment for nuclear power plants, and jet engines. The General Electric Company is the city's main employer. Schenectady is served by rail, the New

York State Thruway, the New York State Barge Canal, and Albany County Airport. Among notable buildings are several early-18th-century homes, St. George's Episcopal Church (dating from 1759), and the Schenectady Museum. Union College is here. The city has the council-manager form of government.

Schenectady was founded in 1661 by Arendt Van Curler, a Dutchman. Schenectady was incorporated as a city in 1798. It became a trade center for settlers moving westward through the Mohawk Valley and by the mid-1800's was a transportation hub on the Erie Canal and the Mohawk and Hudson Railroad. The city's electrical industry was established in 1886 by Thomas A. Edison, who built a plant here to manufacture electrical machinery.

Population: 65,566.

Schiaparelli, skyä'pä-rĕl'lĕ, **Giovanni Virginio** (1835-1910), an Italian astronomer. He is best known for his studies of Mars, begun in 1877, in which he described in detail the Martian "canals." (Space probes in the 1960's proved that the canals—lines that Schiaparelli and others saw through telescopes—were an illusion caused by discolorations on Mars's surface.) Schiaparelli was among the first to observe that some meteor swarms travel in the same orbits as known comets. He was the first to suggest the long-held but now discredited theory that Mercury always keeps the same side toward the sun. Schiaparelli was director of the Brera Observatory in Milan, 1862-1900.

Schick, shĭk, **Béla** (1877-1967), a Hungarian-American pediatrician. In 1913 Schick developed a test for determining susceptibility to diphtheria. He also contributed to the understanding of allergy and of various diseases that afflict children.

Schick was born in Boglár, Hungary. After receiving an M.D. degree (1900) from Karl Franz University in Graz, Austria, he taught pediatrics at the University of Vienna. In 1923 Schick settled in the United States, and in 1929 he became a citizen. He served on the pediatric faculty of Columbia University, 1936-43, and on the pediatric staffs of a number of New York City hospitals.

Schick Test. See SCHICK, BÉLA.

Schiller, shĭl'ẽr, **Johann Christoph Friedrich von** (1759-1805), a German dramatist, poet, philosopher, and historian.

Some critics rank him as the greatest German playwright, and he was the first to become well known outside his own country. Perhaps the greatest of his plays is the tragedy *Wallenstein* (1798-99), a trilogy based on the military career and downfall of the Bohemian general Count Albrecht von Wallenstein during the Thirty Years' War. Schiller's most popular play is *William Tell* (1804), inspired by the legend of the Swiss liberator. (See TELL, WILLIAM.)

Schiller is also famous for his ballads and philosophical poems, most of which were written in the late 1790's. His best ballads include "The Diver," "The Glove," and "The Cranes of Ibycus." One of his finest philosophical poems is "Song of the Bell." Parts of Schiller's "Ode to Joy" form the choral finale of Beethoven's *Ninth Symphony* (1824).

As a philosopher, Schiller was an idealist. He believed that absolute freedom—moral and artistic as well as political—would help man to achieve harmony and unity within himself. Man could then establish a society based on the highest moral and esthetic standards. Because of these and related theories, some thinkers consider Schiller to be the originator of the concept of alienation with which much 20th-century philosophy and sociology are concerned. According to this concept, the individual in a highly specialized society is alienated (estranged) from certain aspects of himself (such as his creativity) and from other human beings.

Schiller's Life

Schiller was born at Marbach near Stuttgart in southwestern Germany, the son of an army surgeon. Young Schiller intended to study theology, but in 1773 the duke of Württemberg ordered him to enroll as a law student in the duke's military academy. Later, Schiller was allowed to switch to medicine.

The youth's revulsion against the duke's domination and the school's military discipline found expression in a play, *The Robbers,* written in 1777. Schiller received a degree from the academy in 1780 and became an army surgeon. *The Robbers* was produced in Mannheim in 1782 and was enthusiastically received. Its theme of rebellion against tyranny angered the duke and he forbade Schiller to write any more plays.

Unable to endure such coercion, Schiller left his army post and fled to Mannheim. Ill

Chicago Public Library

Friedrich von Schiller

health and poverty caused him to accept for several years the hospitality of friends in various places, including Leipzig and Dresden. *The Conspiracy of Fiesco* (1782), the first of his historical dramas, and *Love and Intrigue* (1784), a domestic tragedy, were written during this time. In his second historical tragedy, *Don Carlos* (1787), Schiller showed a growing maturity in his emphasis on the universal rather than on the personal aspects of human freedom.

His first important historical work, *The Revolt of the Netherlands* (1788), and a recommendation from Germany's leading literary figure, Johann Wolfgang von Goethe, secured for Schiller the post of professor of history at the University of Jena in 1789. In the same year, he married Charlotte von Lengefeld.

His historical research led Schiller to an increasing interest in the underlying meaning of human events. He turned to a study of the German philosopher Immanuel Kant, and to the development of his own ideas of freedom and esthetics. Among his most important prose philosophical writings, revealing this interest, are *Grace and Dignity* (1793), *Letters on the Esthetic Education of Man* (1795), and *Naïve and Sentimental Poetry* (1795-96).

A close friendship between Goethe and Schiller began in 1794, and the two became leaders of the classical movement in German literature. In 1799, Schiller moved to Weimar, not far from Jena, to be near Goethe, whom he helped in directing the court theater of the duke of Weimar. Here Schiller wrote two plays modeled in some respects after the ancient Greek tragedies: *Mary Stuart* (1800) and *The Bride of Messina* (1803). His *Maid of Orleans* (1801) is a romantic drama based on the life of Joan of Arc. Schiller was working on another classical tragedy, *Demetrius*, when he died of tuberculosis.

Schipa, skē'pä, **Tito** (1889-1965), an Italian lyric tenor. He became famous on the concert and operatic stage for his ability to sustain a long melodic phrase and for his interpretations of such leading roles as Alfredo in *La Traviata,* Mario in *Tosca,* and Don Ottavio in *Don Giovanni.* Schipa studied in his native Lecce and made his debut in 1911 in *La Traviata.* He sang with the Chicago Civic Opera, 1919-32, and with the Metropolitan Opera, 1932-35. Schipa sang regularly with opera companies in Italy, Spain, and South America, and made extensive concert tours.

Schipperke. See DOG, subtitle *Breeds of Dogs:* Non-Sporting Breeds.

Schism, Great, sĭz'm; skĭz'm, a term used for two historic cleavages in the medieval Christian church. The first was the separation of the Roman Catholic and Eastern Orthodox churches, usually dated from 1054. The second was a division of the papacy, 1378-1417, into rival lines.

The Great Schism of 1054—called also the Great Eastern Schism, Schism of the East, and Schism of the East and West—grew out of centuries of conflict between the church of the Latin rite, governed from Rome, and the church of the Greek rite, governed from Constantinople. The Greek, or Eastern, patriarch acknowledged the higher spiritual rank of the Roman pope, but resisted being ruled by him. Doctrinal disagreements arose, and different customs developed. A preliminary break came in 867, but was mended in 920. (See PHOTIUS.)

The beginning of the final break occurred in 1054 when Patriarch Michael Cerularius renounced the authority of Pope Leo IX. The Crusades intensified the hostility between Latins and Greeks, especially after the Crusaders sacked Constantinople in 1204. Reunions in the 13th and 15th centuries did not last. In 1472 the schism became permanent when the Ottoman Turks, conquerors of the Byzantine Empire, made the patriarch at Constantinople head of all Christians

in their domains. (For further details, see EASTERN ORTHODOX CHURCH, subtitle *History.*)

The Great Schism of 1378-1417 is also called the Great Western Schism, Schism of the West, and Papal Schism. It followed the so-called Babylonian Captivity of the Church, 1309-77, during which the popes lived at Avignon, France. At the first papal election back in Rome, in 1378, a group of cardinals withdrew and elected a second pope, who reestablished the papal seat at Avignon. The Council of Pisa in 1409 attempted unsuccessfully to depose both; it added a third pope, at Pisa. The schism was ended by the Council of Constance in 1417.

Schist, shĭst, a common metamorphic rock. Schist consists mainly of silicate minerals, chiefly mica, hornblende, talc, or chlorite. Quartz is also usually present. The minerals in schist are arranged in fairly parallel and often wavy layers. Because of its layered structure, schist can be easily split into sheets; the sheets are not smooth, but have an uneven surface. (Its name is derived from a Greek word meaning "to split.") The color of schist—varying with its mineral composition—is usually gray, yellow, light or dark green, brown, or black. Most forms of schist are named for the abundant minerals in them. *Mica schist,* the most common form, is rich in mica and quartz and frequently contains large crystals of garnet or kyanite.

Schist is formed from various igneous or sedimentary rocks under great pressure and heat. It is widely distributed in the earth's crust, but is most common in mountain ranges. Many forms of schist are used as flagstone for fireplaces and patios. Some schists are used as building stone.

Schistosomiasis, shĭs'tŏ-sŏ-mī'*a*-sĭs, or **Bilharziasis,** bĭl'här-zī'*a*-sĭs, a tropical disease caused by parasitic flukes called *schistosomes.* There are three main forms of schistosomiasis, each caused by a different species of fluke. One form occurs in South America and the Caribbean islands, another in Africa and the Mediterranean regions, and the third in Japan, China, and the Philippines. After malaria, schistosomiasis is the most common parasitic disease.

The schistosome spends part of its life cycle in certain freshwater snails. It emerges from the snail as a free-swimming larva. When a person wades or bathes in water infested with these larvae, the larvae penetrate the skin and are carried by the blood to the liver, where they develop into young worms. The young worms then enter the bloodstream and settle in small veins of the body, usually in the large or small intestine or in the bladder. There the adult females lay their eggs, which are expelled in the feces or urine of the infected person. When the contaminated waste is discharged into a body of water, the eggs hatch, and the larvae must find freshwater snails.

Symptoms of schistosomiasis include fever, diarrhea, high blood pressure, loss of appetite, and bloody urine. A rash usually develops at the site where the larvae entered the body. Treatment consists of administering such drugs as praziquantel, oxamniquine, or metrifonate to kill the adult worms and their eggs. If left untreated, schistosomiasis can cause fibrosis of the liver, chronic urinary tract infections, bladder cancer, or heart and kidney disorders.

Preventive measures consist largely of sanitary disposal of feces and urine and elimination of the snails without which the schistosomes could not complete their life cycle.

Schistosomiasis is caused by the flukes *Schistosoma mansoni*, *S. haemotobium*, and *S. japonicum*. Schistosomes belong to the family Schistosomatidae of the class Trematoda.

Schizophrenia. See PSYCHIATRY, subtitle *Psychiatric Disorders* (Psychotic Disorders).

Schlegel, shlā′gĕl, the family name of two German critics and writers who were brothers. Leaders of the Romantic movement in German literature, they founded and edited *Athenaeum* (1798-1800), the journal of the Romantic school of German writers. Both brothers studied Sanskrit and pioneered in the field of comparative philology.

Karl Wilhelm Friedrich von Schlegel (1772-1829) originated most of the critical and philosophical theories of Romanticism. He defined romantic poetry as "progressive universal poetry," free and infinite, contrasting it with the fixed and limited poetry of the ancient classical world. Friedrich believed that a literary work should be evaluated on its own terms rather than judged according to preconceived standards. Among his many philosophical writings are *A History of Modern and Ancient Literature* (1815) and *Philosophy of History* (1829). He also wrote a novel, *Lucinde* (1799), and a tragedy, *Alarcos* (1802). Friedrich was born in Hannover and attended the universities of Göttingen and Leipzig.

August Wilhelm von Schlegel (1767-1845) was primarily a linguist and an interpreter of his brother's ideas. One of his most important critical works is *On Dramatic Art and Literature* (1809-11). Perhaps his greatest literary contribution, however, was his translation of 17 of Shakespeare's plays (1797-1810). These translations—and the translations of the rest of Shakespeare's plays by Dorothea Tieck and Count Wolf von Baudissin, who were influenced by him—were responsible for the great popularity of Shakespeare's works in Germany. August was born in Hannover and attended the University of Göttingen.

Schleiden, shlī′dĕn, **Matthias Jakob** (1804-1881), a German botanist. He and Theodor Schwann established the fact that all living organisms are made up of cells. Schleiden published his conclusions, which applied only to plants, in 1838; Schwann extended Schleiden's concept to include animals. Schleiden was born in Hamburg. After a brief career as a lawyer he obtained a degree as a doctor of philosophy and medicine. He taught botany at the universities of Jena and Dorpat.

Schleiermacher, shlī′ĕr-mä′kĕr, **Friedrich Daniel Ernst** (1768-1834), a German Protestant theologian and philosopher. He is generally regarded as the most influential Protestant thinker of the 19th century. Schleiermacher rejected dogma as a basis for religion and the traditional view that theology should be the study of sacred texts and the nature of God. He believed rather that the basis of religion is a unique feeling—an attitude of dependence upon God. In his view, theology should be the study and interpretation of the beliefs of Christianity in the light of this experience of absolute dependence.

Schleiermacher was born in Breslau and studied at the University of Halle. He was ordained a Reformed minister in 1794. After 1807 he lived in Berlin, preaching, teaching theology, and writing. His chief book is *The Christian Faith* (1821-22).

Schlesinger, shlā′zĭng-ĕr, the name of two United States historians, father and son.

Arthur M. (Meier) Schlesinger, Sr. (1888-1965), the father, was a leading authority on the colonial history of the United States and on American social history. His major writings on these subjects include *The Colonial Merchants and the American Revolution* (1918), *New Viewpoints in American History* (1922), and *The Rise of the City* (1933).

Schlesinger was born in Xenia, Ohio. He graduated from Ohio State University in 1910 and received a Ph.D. from Columbia in 1917. He taught at Ohio State, 1912-19; the State University of Iowa, 1919-24; and Harvard, 1924-54.

His other works include: *A History of American Life* (12 volumes, 1929-44), edited with Dixon Ryan Fox; and the autobiographical *In Retrospect: the History of an Historian* (1963).

Arthur M. (Meier) Schlesinger, Jr. (1917-), the son, became influential both as a historian and as a political adviser. He was twice awarded the Pulitzer Prize—for history in 1946, for *The Age of Jackson;* and for biography in 1966, for *A Thousand Days: John F. Kennedy in the White House*. Active in liberal politics, he helped to found the Americans for Democratic Action (1947). He served as adviser to prominent Democrats and was an assistant to President Kennedy, 1961-63.

Schlesinger was born in Columbus, Ohio. He graduated from Harvard in 1938 and taught there, 1946-61. In 1966 he joined the faculty of the City University of New York.

His other books include: *The Age of Roosevelt* (3 volumes, 1957-60); *The Bitter Heritage* (1967); *The Imperial Presidency* (1973); *Robert Kennedy and His Times* (1978); *The Cycles of American History* (1986); *A Life in the Twentieth Century: Innocent Beginnings, 1917-1950* (2000).

Schleswig-Holstein, a historic region located on the southern Jutland Peninsula. It now comprises the German state of Schleswig-Holstein and the area of Denmark called Sonderjylland or North Slesvig. For centuries, the Danes and the Germans vied for possession of the region.

During the Middle Ages, the separate duchies of Schleswig (in the north) and Holstein (in the south) developed. In Holstein, the population was predominantly German; in Schleswig, German in the south and Danish in the north. In 1460 the duchies were united as a domain of the Danish king, although not as a part of Denmark.

In 1815 the Congress of Vienna made Holstein a state of the German Confederation, while also continuing the union of Schleswig and Holstein under the Danish crown. This relationship proved unworkable as nationalist feelings rose among the Danes and the Germans. There was a brief rebellion by Germans in the duchies in 1848. Then in 1864, following repeated Danish demands for annexation of Schleswig, war broke out between Denmark and the German states. As a result of the war, Prussia and Austria gained joint control of the duchies. Prussia took sole possession in 1866, when it defeated Austria in the Seven Weeks' War.

After World War I, a plebiscite was held. The people in northern Schleswig voted to join Denmark; the rest of Schleswig-Holstein remained German.

Schlieffen Plan. See WORLD WAR I, section "Historical Introduction," subtitle *The Plan of Campaign*.

Schliemann, shlē'män, **Heinrich** (1822-1890), a German amateur archeologist. He made two of the most spectacular archeological finds of the 19th century—the ruins of Troy, which was the site of the Trojan War described by the Greek poet Homer, and the first evidence of the Mycenaean civilization of ancient Greece. His work proved that the tales of Homer, widely regarded as myths, were at least partly true; it also stimulated popular interest in archeology. As one of the first archeologists to make detailed notes and drawings of the objects he excavated, Schliemann contributed to the development of archeological technique. However, Schliemann aroused controversy among scholars because he tended to make hasty—and often erroneous—interpretations and datings.

Schliemann was born in Mecklenburg-Schwerin (now part of Germany), the son of a clergyman. As a boy, Heinrich listened to his father relate the stories of Homer and resolved to find Troy. After amassing a huge fortune—chiefly through business investments in Russia and the United States—

Heinrich Schliemann
Newberry Library

religious affiliation. Special scholarships are often available to students who qualify as outstanding athletes.

Fellowships, like scholarships, vary in value from those that cover only tuition to those that cover all expenses. They usually are given to gifted students or faculty members to do advanced study or to engage in research. Such awards are also made to artists or writers to enable them to work on creative projects. The person receiving the grant is generally called a *fellow.* Fellows who are graduate students are sometimes required to do part-time teaching or give other academic service.

Information on scholarship, fellowship, and loan opportunities and requirements can be obtained from high school teachers, counselors, and principals; college scholarship committees; state departments of education; and professional guidance agencies or placement bureaus, such as the College Scholarship Service (Princeton, New Jersey, and Los Angeles, California).

For information on some specific awards, see FULBRIGHT SCHOLARSHIP; GUGGEN-HEIM MEMORIAL FOUNDATION; NATIONAL MERIT SCHOLARSHIP CORPORATION; RHODES SCHOLARSHIPS; ROCKEFELLER FOUNDATION.

Books about Scholarships and Fellowships

Blum, Laurie. *Free Money for College* (Facts on File, 1990).

Cassidy, D. J. *The International Scholarship Book,* 2nd edition (Prentice Hall, 1990).

Darby, Anthony. *The Great American National Scholarships and Grants Guide* (National Scholarships and Grants Services, 1993).

Keeslar, Oreon. *Financial Aids for Higher Education,* 15th edition (Brown, 1992).

Leider, Robert and Anna. *Lovejoy's Guide to Financial Aid,* 3rd edition (Simon & Schuster, 1989).

Scholasticism, the theology and philosophy of Christian Europe during the second half of the Middle Ages. The term comes from the Latin *scholasticus* (pertaining to a school), for Scholasticism originated in the medieval church schools.

The role of the *Scholastics,* or *Schoolmen,* in the history of intellectual development has been subject to controversy. They brought order and clarity to Christian theology and stimulated enthusiasm for learning among multitudes of students. The Scholastics' emphasis on logic gave European thought a new precision. However, the later Scholastics were accused (especially by Humanists of the Renaissance) of being led by this love

of logic to meaningless distinctions. It has also been argued that the Scholastics' largely uncritical acceptance of Aristotle hindered the progress of natural science. Modern scholarship, however, has tended to establish the importance of medieval contributions to the history of science.

The Scholastics tried to gain a rational understanding of Christian doctrines. Their method was to state the arguments on each side of a question and then resolve it, often by applying principles of logic. The early Scholastics used the principles of Aristotle's logic. (The logic of Aristotle was all that the early Scholastics knew of his writings, which had been largely lost to the Western world after the fall of the Roman Empire.) From the 12th century on, medieval logicians, typical of whom is Peter of Spain, developed logic far beyond what they had received from Aristotle. Experiment and independent observation were unimportant to the Scholastics; they relied on the authority of the Bible, Christian tradition, and—after all of Aristotle's works became known in the 13th century—the teachings of Aristotle and his Muslim interpreters, especially Avicenna and Averroës.

Scholasticism arose between the 9th and the 12th century through the work of such thinkers as Johannes Scotus Erigena, (Saint) Anselm of Canterbury, Peter Abelard, and Peter Lombard. An important early problem was how far the methods and assumptions of reason should be used in interpreting such topics of Christian dogma as the Holy Trinity. The 12th century was marked by a controversy over universals. A universal is a general term, such as *woman,* that applies to a group of particulars (in this case, to every adult female person). The controversy was whether or not universals are real—that is, whether they have a reality of their own (not as particulars) in the realm of being. The *Realist* position was that universals are real. *Nominalists* denied that universals were real: some nominalists held that universals are only names, others held that universals are concepts in the mind.

The 13th century has been called the golden age of Scholasticism. After the recovery of Aristotle's writings, at first through contact with Muslim scholars, the Scholastics discovered that Aristotle had opinions on many scientific and philosophical questions as well as on logic. Enraptured by his learning, the Scholastics began to study the bearing of Aristotle's teaching on Christianity, especially on matters where Aristotle and Christianity were apparently in disagreement. (For example, Christianity regards the world as having been created, whereas Aristotle tried to prove that it must be eternal.)

The study of Aristotle divided the Scholastics roughly into three groups. The *Augustinians,* typified by the Franciscan theologian (Saint) Bonaventura, accepted much of Aristotle's terminology. However, they rejected whatever disagreed with traditional Christianity, which was then dominated by the theology of Saint Augustine. The Augustinians were strongly influenced by *Neoplatonism* as well as by Aristotle's philosophy.

The *Integral Aristotelians* (or *Latin Averroists,* as they are sometimes called), typified by the secular scholar Siger de Brabant, accepted Aristotle's doctrines and paid special attention to the interpretations of those doctrines by Averroës. Where Aristotle conflicted with Christianity, the Integral Aristotelians accepted the truth of the Christian position, but claimed that the rational position was the one proven by Aristotle. The Christian position was sometimes said to be miraculously true.

An alternative approach was developed by the *Aristotelians,* typified by the Dominican scholars (Saint) Albertus Magnus and (Saint) Thomas Aquinas. They tried to harmonize Aristotelian philosophy with Christian theology. The system of Thomas Aquinas, called *Thomism,* is regarded by many as the outstanding achievement of Scholasticism. Thomism is based on the idea that reason and faith are two separate sources of knowledge that must be harmonious because they both ultimately come from a single God. Aquinas maintained that some Christian doctrines (for example, the existence of God) are provable by reason alone; in the case of others (for example, the creation of the world), it can be shown that reason cannot *disprove* them. Though these doctrines are accepted on faith, they may be clarified by reason.

Toward the end of the 13th century, Thomism was challenged by *Scotism,* the theological system of the Franciscan John Duns Scotus. Duns Scotus accused Thomists of an inadequate understanding of the nature and nobility of the will. In the 14th

century, a nominalism was revived by the Franciscan scholar William of Ockham, who applied the logical analysis of terms to all kinds of scientific, philosophical, and theological problems. Duns Scotus and William of Ockham claimed that many Christian doctrines that had been regarded as provable by reason could only be shown to be probable, a conclusion that stressed the role of faith in Christian belief.

Scholasticism declined in the 14th and 15th centuries as it became increasingly preoccupied with formalistic disputes over trivial matters. There was a brief revival in Paris in the 16th century under the influence of the Counter Reformation.

Neo-Scholasticism

Neo-Scholasticism (or *Neo-Thomism*), a movement to apply the principles of Scholasticism to modern problems, began among Italian Roman Catholic scholars in the mid-19th century. Pope Leo XIII furthered the movement by recommending in 1879 that all Roman Catholic priests and scholars study the works of Saint Thomas Aquinas. Neo-Scholasticism has since flourished among Roman Catholics and even gained some Protestant and non-Christian followers. Leading Neo-Scholastics have been Désiré Joseph Cardinal Mercier of Belgium, Jacques Maritain and Étienne Gilson of

---

For further information, see:

Scholastics

ABELARD, PETER	AQUINAS, Saint
ALBERTUS MAGNUS,	THOMAS
Saint	BACON, ROGER
ANSELM OF CANTER-	BONAVENTURA, Saint
BURY, Saint	DUNS SCOTUS, JOHN

Neo-Scholastics

ADLER, MORTIMER	MERCIER, DÉSIRÉ
MARITAIN,	JOSEPH CARDINAL
JACQUES	

Books about Scholasticism

Baldwin, J. W. *The Scholastic Culture of the Middle Ages, 1000-1300* (Heath, 1990).

Fairweather, E. R., editor. *A Scholastic Miscellany: Anselm to Ockham* (Westminster Press, 1982).

Gallagher, D. A., editor. *Thomas Aquinas and His Legacy* (Catholic University of America, 1994).

Kretzmann, Norman. *The Cambridge History of Later Medieval Philosophy: from the Rediscovery of Aristotle to the Disintegration of Scholasticism, 1100-1600* (Cambridge University, 1988).

Southern, R. W. *The Rise of Scholastic Humanism* (Blackwell, 1994).

France, Martin Grabmann of Germany, and Mortimer Adler of the United States.

Schönberg, Arnold. See SCHOENBERG, ARNOLD.

Schongauer, shōn′gou′ẽr, **Martin** (1430?-1491), a German engraver and painter. He was the first engraver to be known internationally. His more than 100 signed prints greatly advanced the art of engraving and influenced Albrecht Dürer and other artists. Schongauer's prints, such as *The Temptation of St. Anthony* and *Flight into Egypt,* are marked by great detail and a carefully balanced complex design. Only a few of the paintings ascribed to Schongauer are known to be his; they include *Madonna in a Rose Bower* and the frescoes *The Last Judgment.* Schongauer spent most of his life in his native Kolmar (now Colmar, France). His first artistic training was under his father, a goldsmith.

School, an institution for instruction; also, the building in which it is housed. The term "school" is used for educational institutions below the college level—elementary, grammar, or grade, school and secondary, or high, school. It is also used for special programs of instruction, such as night schools or summer schools, and may designate a professional division of a university, such as a school of engineering. Other establishments called schools include various nonacademic bodies, such as nursery schools and Sunday schools; training institutions for the disabled, such as schools for the blind; and vocational training institutions, such as art schools and secretarial schools. For articles on schools, see EDUCATION and cross references.

The term "school" is also used to describe a group of persons engaged in artistic and intellectual pursuits who show a similarity of style, method, or attitude. For examples, see ALEXANDRIAN SCHOOL; ASHCAN SCHOOL.

School Employees, American Association of Classified. See LABOR UNION (table).

School Lunch Program, a national food-assistance program for schoolchildren in the United States. It provides lunches at cost, at less than cost, and free—depending on the economic need of the children involved. The program covers pupils in public and nonprofit private elementary and secondary schools and children living in institutions such as detention centers, orphanages, and

National Gallery of Art, Rosenwald Collection
The Temptation of St. Anthony
by Martin Schongauer
about 1471-73
engraving

homes for the mentally retarded. Upon application of parents or other authorized persons, local officials determine eligibility for the lower-cost or free lunches. The program is supported by federal, state, and local funds. It is administered nationally by the U.S. Department of Agriculture.

Government distribution of surplus farm products to schools began in the 1930's, during the Depression. In 1946 Congress passed the National School Lunch Act, which established the lunch program.

Related Programs

In 1954 the Special Milk Program began subsidizing milk for all public and nonprofit private schools that requested it, to be given pupils at reduced prices or free. The Child Nutrition Act of 1966 authorized federal aid to equip schools for food service. It also established a School Breakfast Program. In 1968 the Child Care Program was established, extending federal food assistance to children in day camps and day-care centers. The Summer Food Service Program for Children, established in 1975, provides food in summer camps. The U.S. Department of Agriculture administers these programs.

School of Visual Arts. See UNIVERSITIES
AND COLLEGES (table).

Schoolcraft, skool′krȧft, **Henry Rowe**
(1793-1864), a United States explorer and
ethnologist. He was noted for his studies of
American Indians. During a 19-year period,
he was a federal Indian agent and a superintendent of Indian Affairs. He had jurisdiction over tribes, mainly Algonquian, along
the southern shore of Lake Superior and in
the Sault Ste. Marie-Mackinac area of Michigan. He published several works describing
Indian culture.

Schoolcraft was born in Albany County,
New York, and attended Union and Middle-
bury colleges. He began geological explora-
tions in Missouri and Arkansas, 1817-18,
and was with the Lewis Cass expedition to
the Lake Superior region in 1820. He began
his ethnological studies after his appointment to the Indian Affairs post in 1822.
While on an expedition in northern Minnesota about 1832, he discovered Lake Itasca,
which he identified as the source of the
Mississippi River. Schoolcraft negotiated
several land treaties with the Chippewa
Indians.

Schoolcraft's major study on Indian culture was
*Historical and Statistical Information Respecting
the History, Condition, and Prospects of the Indian
Tribes of the United States,* published in six volumes
between 1851 and 1857. Other works include *Algic
Researches* (1839), concerning Indian mental characteristics, and *Oneota* (1844-45), an Indian history.

Schoolmen. See SCHOLASTICISM.

Schooner. See SAILING, illustration titled
Main Types of Fore-and-aft Rigs.

Schopenhauer, shō′pĕn-hou′ēr, **Arthur**
(1788-1860), a German philosopher. He is
regarded as one of the foremost advocates of
voluntarism, the view that will is prior to or
superior to intellect. His voluntarism began
an increased emphasis on will in modern
philosophy. Schopenhauer is also noted for
his pessimism, which contrasted with the

optimism of most of his European contemporaries. Although his writings received little recognition at first, they began to be
widely known toward the end of his life.
Among persons Schopenhauer influenced
were Richard Wagner, Friedrich Nietzsche,
and Thomas Mann.

Schopenhauer himself was influenced by
the ideas of Plato and Immanuel Kant, as
well as by oriental philosophy. In his major
work, *The World as Will and Idea* (published 1818 but dated 1819), he contends
that the only reality is the will to live—a
blind, purposeless striving. In Schopenhauer's view, life flows from willing to attaining.
Because man's desires are infinite and can
never be satisfied, life consists mainly of
suffering. Pleasure is only a temporary absence of pain. For Schopenhauer, the only
escape from suffering is denial of all desire
and achievement of a state of complete indif-
ference to life similar to the Buddhist Nirva-
na. Temporary relief from suffering may be
obtained through sympathy for others and
contemplation of works of art.

Schopenhauer was born in Danzig
(Gdańsk), the son of a wealthy merchant. He
studied philosophy at the universities of
Göttingen, Berlin, and Jena, receiving a
Ph.D. degree from Jena in 1813. In 1820
Schopenhauer lectured at the University of
Berlin, but he failed to attract many students. Disappointed and bitter, he left university life and eventually settled alone in
Frankfurt am Main. He spent his later years
developing his philosophy and writing
sharply critical essays on such varied topics
as women, noise, and university philosophers.

Schreyer, Edward R. (Richard) (1935-
   ), a Canadian statesman. He was Canada's 22nd governor general, serving from
1979 to 1984. The grandson of an Austrian
immigrant, Schreyer was the first Canadian
of neither French nor British ancestry appointed to that office. He had been leader of
Manitoba's New Democratic party since
1969 and premier of the province from 1969
to 1977.

Schreyer was born in Beauséjour, Manitoba, and graduated from the University of
Manitoba. He was first elected to the provincial legislature in 1958 and served until 1965
when he was elected to the Canadian House
of Commons. He resigned in 1969 to return
to Manitoba to head the New Democratic

Arthur
Schopenhauer
Newberry Library

party. In 1984 he was appointed high commissioner (ambassador) to Australia.

Schrieffer, John Robert. See NOBEL PRIZES (Physics, 1972).

Schrödinger, shrû'dĭng-ēr, **Erwin** (1897-1961), the Austrian physicist who founded wave mechanics, a form of quantum mechanics. Following the suggestion made by the French physicist Louis de Broglie in 1924 that all particles have wave properties, Schrödinger in 1926 developed the *Schrödinger wave equation*. It is the basic equation in wave mechanics, used to calculate the amplitude of the wave associated with a particle. Schrödinger shared the 1933 Nobel Prize in physics with the British physicist Paul Dirac for the discovery of new forms of atomic theory, which were based on wave mechanics. (See also ATOM, subtitle *Atomic Theories:* Atomic Theory Becomes Complex.)

Schrödinger was born in Vienna and attended the University of Vienna. He taught physics at a number of European universities, including Zurich, Berlin, and Oxford.

Schubert, shoo'bĕrt, **Franz** (Peter) (1797-1828), an Austrian composer. He is credited with creating the 19th-century German *lied,* an art song in which melody, accompaniment, and words are perfectly united. He composed more than 600 lieder, many of them set to poems by Goethe, Heine, and Schiller. Schubert has been called the supreme master of melody because his instrumental works, such as *Moments Musicaux* (composed 1823-27) and *Phantasie in C for Violin and Piano* (1827), have a lyrical, songlike quality.

Schubert was born in Lichtenthal, then a suburb of Vienna. The son of a schoolmaster and cellist, he was taught to play the violin, piano, and organ before he was 10. Schubert joined the Vienna court choir in 1808 and studied theory and composition at the choir's music school. He completed his first symphony in 1813, the same year he left the choir. He taught music at his father's school, 1814-17. While there he composed prolifically—operettas, church music, and lieder. By the time he was 19, Schubert had composed more than 250 lieder, including his famous "Gretchen at the Spinning Wheel" and "Erlkönig," both set to Goethe's verse.

During the final 10 years of his short life Schubert lived in poverty in Vienna. Except

Oesterreichische Nationalbibliothek
Franz Schubert

for the summers of 1818 and 1824, which he spent in Hungary teaching music, he devoted all his time to composing. Much of his music was sold and performed but he was greatly underpaid by his publishers. Loyal friends gave him food and shelter and arranged concerts of his works. Schubert was unsuccessful in his several attempts to obtain a salaried court position. A public concert of his works was given successfully in 1828. Schubert died later that year of typhus or typhoid fever. At his request, he was buried near the grave of Beethoven, whose works he greatly admired.

Symphony No. 8 in B (nicknamed "Unfinished" because it contains only two movements, 1822) and *Symphony No. 9 in C* ("The Great," 1828) are among his frequently performed symphonies. Other works include 7 overtures, 15 string quartets and many other chamber works, and numerous short piano pieces. He wrote about 15 operas and operettas, more than 70 choral works, and much church music.

Books about Franz Schubert

Hartling, Peter. *Schubert* (Holmes & Meier, 1995).

Kramer, Richard. *Distant Cycles: Schubert and the Conceiving of Song* (University of Chicago, 1994).

Woodford, Peggy. *Schubert* (Omnibus Press, 1987).

For Younger Readers

Thompson, Wendy. *Franz Schubert* (Viking Books, 1991).

Charles Schulz's Charlie Brown and Snoopy

Schuller, Gunther (1925-   ), a United States composer, conductor, French horn player, and educator. He became known internationally for composing works that combine elements of jazz, traditional music, and atonal music. Schuller introduced the term "third stream" to describe works, such as his *String Quartet* (1957) and *Spectra* (1960), that blend jazz and classical music.

Schuller was born in New York City and attended the Manhattan School of Music. He played horn in the Cincinnati Symphony Orchestra (1943-45) and the Metropolitan Opera Orchestra (1945-59), and conducted major American and European orchestras. He was president of the New England Conservatory of Music, 1967-77, and artistic director of the Berkshire Music Center, 1970-84. In 1994 he was awarded the Pulitzer Prize in music for the orchestral piece *Of Reminiscences and Reflections*.

His other works include *Variants* (1960), a ballet; the opera *The Visitation* (1966); the orchestral piece *Triplum* (1967); *Concerto for Double Bass and Chamber Orchestra* (1968); *The Fisherman and His Wife* (1970), an opera for children; *Concerto No. 2* (1976), for orchestra; *Concerto for Contrabassoon and Orchestra* (1979); *In Praise of Winds* (1981), for orchestra; *A Question of Taste* (1989), an opera; *Violin Concerto* (1991). He wrote the books *Horn Technique* (1962), *Early Jazz* (1968), *Musings: The Musical Worlds of Gunther Schuller* (1986), *The Swing Era* (1988), and *The Compleat Conductor* (1997).

Schultz, Theodore W. See NOBEL PRIZES (Economic Science, 1979).

Schulz, shŏŏlts, **Charles** (1922-2000), a United States cartoonist, creator of *Peanuts*, a comic strip appealing to young and old alike. Its child characters—including Charlie Brown, the losing hero; Lucy, his chief antagonist; and security-loving Linus, Lucy's brother—combine traits of children and adults. Another main character is Snoopy, Charlie Brown's thinking dog.

Schulz was born in Minneapolis, Minnesota. He took his first drawing lessons in the early 1940's and after army service became a cartoonist. By 1950 he had created the *Pea-*

nuts strip, which eventually appeared in more than 1,000 newspapers in North America and some 40 foreign countries, in a dozen different languages. Schulz also published many books portraying the comic-strip characters. A musical, *You're a Good Man, Charlie Brown* (1967), and a number of television specials were based on *Peanuts*.

Schuman, shōō'män', **Robert** (1886-1963), a French statesman. He originated the Schuman Plan by which the coal and steel resources of western European nations were pooled under a common authority. In 1947-48 he was premier of France.

Schuman was born in Luxembourg. He became a lawyer and was a member of the French Chamber of Deputies from 1919 to 1940, when he was imprisoned by the Nazis. He escaped and became active in the Resistance movement. Between 1946 and 1953 Schuman was at various times minister of finance and minister of foreign affairs as well as premier. His austerity programs hastened France's postwar recovery. In 1950 he proposed his economic plan; it was used as a guide in establishing the European Coal and Steel Community two years later.

Schuman, shōō'măn, **William** (Howard) (1910-1992), a United States composer and educator. *Symphony for Strings* (5th symphony, 1943) and other works are marked by rhythmic variety, fluid melody, and dramatic expression. The cantata *A Free Song* brought him the first Pulitzer Prize in music (1943). Schuman studied in his native New York City. He taught at Sarah Lawrence College, 1935-45, and was president of the Juilliard School, 1945-62, and of the Lincoln Center for the Performing Arts, 1962-69.

Other works include: *New England Triptych* (1956); *Song of Orpheus* (1962); *In Praise of Shahn* (1970); *Symphony No. 10* ("American Muse," 1976); *American Hymn: Orchestral Variations on an Original Melody* (1982); *Dances* (1985); *On Freedom's Ground* (1986).

Schumann, shōō'män, **Robert** (Alexander) (1810-1856), a German composer. Much of his music was inspired by the Romantic literature of his time. His descriptive piano pieces and *lieder* (art songs) are often considered his best works. *Papillons* (composed 1832), *Carnaval* (1834-35), and other piano works are marked by lyricism and personal expression.

Like Schubert, Schumann was a master of the art song. Among the poems of Heine that he set to music are "Die Beiden Grenadiere" ("The Two Grenadiers," 1840) and "Dichterliebe" ("Poet's Love," 1840). Schumann's music, however, was not well accepted in his lifetime; he was better known as a music critic than as a composer.

His Life

Schumann was born in Zwickau, Saxony. At the age of seven he was already composing songs. His father, a bookseller, encouraged his interest in music and literature. After his father died in 1826, Schumann's mother induced him to study law at the universities of Leipzig and Heidelberg. He did poorly and in 1830 began studying piano with Friedrich Wieck in Leipzig.

About 1832 his right hand was injured. Some scholars believe the injury was caused by a mechanical device he had been using to strengthen his fingers; others believe the damage was caused by the then-common mercury treatment for syphilis. Forced to give up a concert career, he turned to composition and writing. In 1834 he founded a journal to advocate Romantic music. It became one of the most influential music journals in Europe.

His marriage, in 1840, to his teacher's daughter, Clara Wieck (1819-1896), was a happy one. She was an internationally known pianist and often played her husband's music at her concerts. The year 1840 is called Schumann's "song year" for he composed more than 120 songs. During the next few years he composed symphonies, concertos, and chamber music. Not all were successful.

Mendelssohn appointed Schumann to the faculty of the new Leipzig Conservatory in 1843, but he was a poor teacher and soon resigned. He did not have much success as musical director at Düsseldorf, 1850-53. Schumann often had worked himself to the point of exhaustion and suffered periods of depression. His mind began to fail, and in 1854 he attempted to drown himself in the Rhine. At his own request he was placed in a mental institution, where he died.

Schumann's other works include *Symphonic Études* (1843); *Fantasia in C* (1836); *Concerto in A for Piano and Orchestra* (1841-45); *Quintet in E flat for Piano and Strings* (1842); many pieces for solo piano, including *Scenes from Childhood* (1838) and *Album for the Young* (1848); three piano sonatas; and four symphonies.

Schumann-Heink, shōō′măn-hīngk′, **Ernestine** (Rössler) (1861-1936), an Austrian-

American opera and concert singer. The power and extraordinarily wide range of her contralto voice brought her fame, especially in Wagnerian roles. She made her concert debut at the age of 15. Two years later she made her operatic debut as Azucena in *Il Trovatore* at Dresden. She performed in the Bayreuth festivals, 1896-1903 and 1905-06. In 1898 Madame Schumann-Heink made her American debut in Chicago, and the next year she joined the Metropolitan Opera in New York City. She made her last operatic appearance, at the Metropolitan in *Siegfried,* when she was 71 years old.

Schurz, shŏŏrts, **Carl** (1829-1906), a German-born American reformer, public official, and journalist. He is regarded as one of the great American statesmen of foreign birth. During an age when corruption was commonplace, he was an influential champion of social and political reform.

Schurz was born in Liblar, near Cologne, Germany. While at the University of Bonn, he took part in the unsuccessful Revolution of 1848 and was forced to flee Germany. He came to the United States in 1852, settling in Watertown, Wisconsin, in 1856. Schurz soon became active as an opponent of slavery and joined the newly organized Republican party. In 1860 he campaigned extensively for Abraham Lincoln, who named him United States minister to Spain. Schurz held this post, 1861-62, resigning to become a brigadier general in the Union Army. He commanded German-American troops at Second Bull Run, Chancellorsville, and Gettysburg.

After the war, Schurz became a journal-

Clara and Robert Schumann
Robert-Schumann-Haus, Zwickau

Carl Schurz
NEW STANDARD
Collection

ist. While joint editor of the St. Louis *Westliche Post* in 1868, he was elected to the U.S. Senate from Missouri. There he led the anti-Grant Republicans and helped organize the reform Liberal Republican party. (See LIBERAL REPUBLICAN PARTY.) Schurz advocated civil service reform and a moderate policy toward the South. As secretary of the interior under President Hayes, 1877-81, he initiated reforms in the treatment of the Indians. He spent most of his later years lecturing and writing.

Schütz, shüts, **Heinrich** (1585-1672), a German composer. He influenced the development of German church music by introducing the Italian dramatic Baroque style. In the *St. Matthew Passion,* the oratorio *Seven Words from the Cross,* and other works, he used Italian forms and techniques to convey the deep feeling characteristic of German music. He composed the first German opera, *Dafne* (1627), set to a German translation of an Italian libretto. The music, however, is lost.

Schütz began his career as a choirboy in the court chapel at Kassel in 1599. He continued his music studies in Venice, 1609-12. About 1615 he settled in Dresden as court conductor, but he continued to visit Italy.

Schuyler, skī′lẽr, **Philip John** (1733-1804), a United States army officer and statesman. He was commander of the Continental army in northern New York during the American Revolution and, as a Federalist, was one of the state's first two United States senators.

Schuyler was born in Albany, New York, a member of one of New York's wealthiest and most influential families. After serving in the French and Indian War, 1755-60, he devoted his time to developing his vast landholdings in the Mohawk Valley. In 1775 he was a delegate to the Continental Congress, which appointed him one of four major generals under George Washington in the newly created Continental Army.

Schuyler supervised the recruiting and provisioning of the northern Continental army. He organized the invasion of Canada, 1775-76, but did not take part because of ill health. Following the fall of Fort Ticonderoga to the British in 1777, he was replaced by General Horatio Gates. He demanded a court-martial to clear himself of blame for the fort's loss, and was exonerated. He resigned from the army in 1779 but continued to advise Washington. Schuyler served in the Continental Congress, 1779-80, and in the U.S. Senate, 1789-91 and 1797-98. In his later years, he was a political ally of his son-in-law, Alexander Hamilton.

Schwab, shwŏb, **Charles Michael** (1862-1939), a United States industrialist. During a time when the steel industry was expanding rapidly, he was president successively of three of the nation's largest steel companies. In World War I, he directed the government's shipbuilding program.

Schwab was born in Williamsburg, Pennsylvania. He began his career as a laborer at the Carnegie-owned steel plant in Braddock, Pennsylvania. Displaying a genius for dealing with people, he rapidly advanced, and in 1897 he was named president of the Carnegie Steel Company. When the Carnegie properties became part of the newly formed United States Steel Corporation in 1901, he was picked to be president of the new company. Schwab resigned in 1903 to become head of Bethlehem Steel Company, a small firm he had purchased in 1902, and made it one of the nation's leading steel producers.

Schwann, shvän, **Theodor** (1810-1882), a German physiologist and anatomist. Schwann and the German botanist Matthias Schleiden established one of the basic ideas in modern biology—the theory that all living organisms are made up of cells and cell products. Schleiden developed the cell theory for plants in 1838, while Schwann extended the theory to animals and elaborated it in 1839. Schwann also discovered the digestive enzyme pepsin and made important contributions to the study of fermentation and putrefaction.

Schwann was born in Neuss. He studied under Johannes Müller at the universities of Bonn and Berlin, receiving his medical degree from Berlin in 1834. Schwann taught anatomy at the universities of Louvain and Liège, and in 1858 he became professor of physiology at Liège.

Schwartz, shwôrts, **Delmore** (1913-1966), a United States author, critic, and editor. He is best known for his brilliant and ironic poetry, but some critics prefer his short stories and critical essays. Schwartz was born in Brooklyn, New York, and graduated from New York University in 1935. He won recognition with *In Dreams Begin Responsibilities* (1938), a volume containing poems, a play, and a story. He was editor, then associate editor, of *Partisan Review* (1943-55) and poetry editor of *The New Republic* (1955-57).

His other works include the verse play *Shenandoah* (1941); poetry, *Genesis, Book I* (1943), *Vaudeville for a Princess* (1950), *Summer Knowledge* (1959), and *The Last Poems of Delmore Schwartz* (1979); a story collection, *Successful Love* (1961); and literary criticism, *Selected Essays* (1970).

Schwartz, Melvin. See NOBEL PRIZES (Physics, 1988).

Schwarzkopf, shwärts'kŏpf, Dame **Elisabeth** (1915-   ), a German operatic and concert soprano. She became known for the flexibility of her lyric voice and for her interpretation of *lieder* (art songs) by Hugo Wolf and Franz Schubert. The Marschallin in *Der Rosenkavalier* and the Countess in *The Marriage of Figaro* are among her varied operatic roles. Schwarzkopf made her operatic debut in Berlin in 1938. She then sang with the Vienna State Opera and other leading opera companies in Europe and the United States. She married Walter Legge, a British record producer, in 1953. She was made a Dame Commander of the British Empire in 1992.

Schwarzkopf, shwôrts'kŏpf, **H.** (Herbert) **Norman** (1934-   ), a United States army officer. He commanded the coalition forces in the Persian Gulf War of 1991. His battle plan, which called for a massive flanking maneuver around the enemy, was given credit for the quick defeat of the Iraqi army and the small number of casualties among the coalition forces.

Schwarzkopf was born in Trenton, New Jersey. After graduating from the U.S. Military Academy in 1956, he was commissioned a second lieutenant in the infantry. Schwarzkopf served in Vietnam, 1964-65 and 1969-70. During the 1970's and 1980's, he held various command posts, including deputy commander of United States forces in the Grenada invasion of 1983. He was promoted to four-star general in 1988 and retired in 1991. *It Doesn't Take a Hero* (1992) is his autobiography.

Schwarzschild Observatory. See OBSERVATORY (table).

Schwarzwald. See BLACK FOREST.

Schweitzer, shvī'tsēr, **Albert** (1875-1965), a German medical missionary, theo-

Dr. Albert Schweitzer visits the outdoor schoolroom of young patients at his hospital.

Erica Anderson; Albert Schweitzer Friendship House, Great Barrington, Mass.

logian, philosopher, and musician famed for his life of dedication to humanity and his many scholarly accomplishments. Schweitzer received the 1952 Nobel Peace Prize for his work as a medical missionary in Africa.

Schweitzer was a noted concert organist and an authority on organ construction. He wrote a definitive work on Johann Sebastian Bach, *J. S. Bach* (1905; English translation, 1911), and an influential historical criticism of the New Testament, *The Quest of the Historical Jesus* (1906; English translation, 1910). In his *Philosophy of Civilization* (two volumes, 1923), Schweitzer developed a profound ethical system based on a "reverence for life" that applies to every living thing. Its fundamental principle is: it is good to help life and evil to harm life. Schweitzer earnestly tried to live by his philosophy, even refusing, for example, to kill insect pests in his African hospital.

Schweitzer's dedicated life made him one of the world's most admired men. However, his patronizing attitude toward Africans and his refusal to modernize his hospital aroused controversy in his later years.

A Dedicated Life

Albert Schweitzer was born in Kaysersberg, Upper Alsace (then part of Germany, now part of France). He grew up in the nearby village of Günsbach, where his father was pastor of a Lutheran church. Albert showed an early interest in music and by the age of nine was able to substitute for the organist at church services. He studied at the universities of Strasbourg, Paris, and Berlin, receiving a doctorate in philosophy (1899) and a licentiate in theology (1900) from Strasbourg.

During his university years, Schweitzer resolved to live for science and art until he was 30 and then devote himself to the service of humanity. He was appointed preacher at St. Nicholas Church in Strasbourg in 1899, lecturer in theology at the university there in 1902, and principal of the university's theological college in 1903. By his 30th year—1905—Schweitzer was distinguished as a theologian, scholar, organist, and authority on Bach.

Schweitzer spent the next seven years studying medicine in preparation for a new life as a medical missionary. In 1912 he married Hélène Bresslau, a trained nurse. After receiving an M.D. degree from the University of Strasbourg in 1913, he sailed

for Africa with his wife. They established a hospital at Lambaréné, a village in French Equatorial Africa (now Gabon). Their work was halted by World War I, when they were interned as enemy aliens and then sent to France.

In 1924 Schweitzer returned to Lambaréné. He remained there for the rest of his life, except for lecture and concert tours to raise funds for his work. Although hospitals were at that time unfamiliar institutions to most Africans, Schweitzer's hospital attracted thousands of patients. He patterned the hospital compound after a native village and encouraged patients to bring relatives to cook for them and help nurse them. At Schweitzer's death, the compound contained more than 70 buildings, 350 beds, and a leprosarium with space for 200 patients.

Schweitzer's autobiographical works include *On the Edge of the Primeval Forest* (1921; English translation, 1922); *Memoirs of Childhood and Youth* (1924); and *Out of My Life and Thought* (1931; English translation, 1933).

Schwenkfelder Church, shvĕngk'feltĕr, a small group of American Protestant churches. All are located within 50 miles (80 km) of Philadelphia, Pennsylvania. Schwenkfelders deny the presence of Christ in Holy Communion and accept the Scriptures only when confirmed by an inner conviction of divine truth. Each church is independent and there is no liturgy. The denomination was founded by German Protestant leader Kaspar Schwenkfeld (1489-1561), who broke with Martin Luther over doctrine. The American churches, the only ones surviving, stem from a group of Schwenkfeld's disciples who migrated to Pennsylvania in 1734. Membership is about 2,500.

Schwinger, Julian. See NOBEL PRIZES (Physics, 1965).

Schwitters, shvĭt'ĕrs, **Kurt** (1887-1948), a German painter, sculptor, and writer. He was a leader of German Dadaism, which he called *Merz.* He was known especially for his fanciful collages, such as *Opened by Customs,* and for his assemblages called *Merzbau.* Many of his poems and stories appeared in the magazine *Der Sturm.* He also published his own magazine, *Merz,* 1923-32. Schwitters studied in his native Hanover and in Dresden. He left Germany in 1937 and settled in England in 1940.

Sciatica. See BACKACHE; NEURITIS.

Science, the systematic and unbiased study of the world, including everything that can be seen or detected in nature, man, and society, together with the knowledge that grows out of such study. The word *science* comes from the Latin *scientia,* meaning "knowledge."

Scientists try to understand, explain, and predict the way in which everything in the world behaves or acts. In pursuing this goal, they study objects, forces, and events as varied as stars, atoms, microorganisms, earthquakes, climate, chemical reactions, magnetic forces, social groups, and human attitudes.

Science has had a profound impact on daily life. The knowledge scientists accumulate about nature, or the physical world, is used to produce tools and machines and to develop technology for agriculture, medicine, manufacturing, communication, transportation, construction, mining, lumbering, and fishing. Scientific findings about human society and behavior influence the methods used in rearing children, teaching students, and treating the mentally ill.

The scientist's method of inquiry, called the *scientific method,* is what most distinguishes science from other fields of learning, such as philosophy, literature, and the fine arts. In general, the scientific method involves the following steps: state a problem to be solved; collect pertinent *data* (information) in an objective way; form one or more *hypotheses* (trial interpretations or explanations); test the most likely hypotheses through objective observation and experimentation; and form a conclusion. The scientific method is discussed in more detail later in this article.

The scientific method is somewhat harder to follow in the study of human society and behavior than in the study of nature. For example, it is generally more difficult to be unbiased in studying social phenomena, such as marriage or suicide, than in studying physical phenomena, such as rocks or plant diseases. Also, it is usually more difficult to perform experiments involving human beings than experiments involving animals, plants, or nonliving matter.

The difficulties involved in following the scientific method in studying human society and behavior have led some scholars to believe that such studies are less scientific than the study of the physical world. How-

AT&T Technologies Inc.

Product of Science. This photograph was taken through the optical system of a laser being used in the manufacture of miniaturized electronic components. Lasers were created during the course of scientific research, and the first lasers were little more than devices that demonstrated scientific principles. Like many such devices, they were soon given practical applications by engineers and technicians, and today are widely used in business, science, and industry. One of the most familiar uses of lasers is in a consumer product—the compact disk player.

ever, other scholars believe that these difficulties can be overcome and that both areas of study are equally scientific.

Classifications

Classification by Subject Matter. The sciences are divided into two main groups—the *natural sciences,* which deal with nature, or the physical world; and the *social sciences,* which study human society and behavior, or the social world. The natural sciences, in turn, can be subdivided into the *physical sciences,* studies concerned with nonliving matter; and the *biological,* or *life, sciences,* studies dealing with living matter. Each of these subdivisions is in turn divided into various branches with a number of specialized areas of study.

The physical sciences include such areas of study as physics, chemistry, engineering, astronomy, geology, oceanography, and meteorology. A grouping within the physical sciences, the *earth sciences,* is made up of geology, oceanography, meteorology, and those parts of astronomy, engineering, and other fields that deal with the earth as a physical object. (Mathematics was formerly regarded as a physical science but is now usually regarded as a tool of science, rather than a science.)

The biological sciences include such fields as botany, zoology, physiology, medicine, forestry, genetics, agronomy, and animal husbandry.

Included within the social sciences are sociology, economics, education, and political science. History is sometimes classed as a social science, sometimes as one of the humanities.

Anthropology, geography, and psychology deal with both physical and social facts. Physical anthropology, physical geography, and physiological psychology are usually called natural sciences. Cultural anthropology, human geography, and the nonphysiological fields of psychology are classed as social sciences.

Another grouping, the *behavioral sciences,* is made up of major portions of sociology, anthropology, and psychology, and the areas of political science, economics, geography, biology, law, and other fields specifically concerned with human behavior.

Classification by Purpose. When scientists attempt to solve specific problems in order to discover facts of practical use, they are practicing *applied science.* Examples of applied

sciences are engineering, medicine, forestry, and animal husbandry.

Studies that are undertaken to discover facts without regard to their immediate usefulness or value are called *pure,* or *basic, science.* Examples of pure sciences are physics, physiology, botany, and zoology. Much of pure science is motivated by scientific curiosity alone. However useless or unrelated to immediate problems pure scientific research may seem to be, scientists recognize that all scientific development is ultimately based on such far-reaching and imaginative studies.

Scientific Method

The scientific method is not a specific set of rules for discovering new scientific knowledge. Rather, it is the general procedure that scientists usually follow.

Stating a Problem. The first step in scientific inquiry is to state a problem, usually by asking a clear, answerable question about physical or social events. The more specific the question, the better the chance of finding an answer. For example, it may be difficult, if not impossible, to answer a broad question such as "What causes juvenile delinquency?" because delinquent behavior seems to be produced by many interacting factors (for example, family relationships, attitudes of friends, level of education, age, social class, size of community). However, it may be possible to answer a narrower question such as "Does the size of a community affect its rate of juvenile delinquency?"

Collecting Data. The second step in scientific inquiry is to collect pertinent data through observation or measurement, or both. Whenever possible, the scientist observes and measures things directly. Such instruments as magnifying glasses or electron microscopes assist scientists in making observations. Many times, however, scientists wish to study things that cannot be seen, such as sound, electricity, atmospheric pressure, human opinions, or attitudes. They then must use instruments that detect the presence of the phenomenon and measure its strength. A physicist, for example, can measure atmospheric pressure with a barometer. A sociologist can gauge public opinion on a subject by asking people carefully worded questions.

Forming Hypotheses. After collecting data, scientists analyze it and form one or more hypotheses about the problem. (In practice, they may be forming hypotheses while they are collecting data.) A hypothesis may be extremely simple and limited. For example, a botany student may measure the length of 100 pin oak leaves and form the hypothesis that all pin oak leaves are three to five inches (8 to 13 cm) in length. A hypothesis may also be broad and complex. For example, the hypothesis that the earth's surface is divided into sections that move in relation to each other helps explain earthquakes, volcanoes, and many other geological phenomena.

In forming a hypothesis, the scientist uses inductive reasoning. Induction is the process of deriving a general, all-encompassing statement from a limited number of particular facts. There is no set procedure for reasoning inductively, and persons vary greatly in their ability to construct useful inductive statements. Successful induction depends upon creative individual insight.

Testing Hypotheses. After a hypothesis is formed, scientists test it. First they determine the consequences of the hypothesis by deductive reasoning. Deduction is the process of drawing particular conclusions from a general, all-encompassing statement. For example, from the hypothesis "All contagious diseases are caused by microorganisms" it might be deduced that "Chicken pox is caused by a microorganism." Scientists test such a hypothesis by making observations or conducting experiments.

Scientists usually follow one of two basic approaches. In one approach, they form deductions about what events should occur and then see if they actually do occur. The occurrence of a deduced consequence provides support for the hypothesis; however, if a supposed consequence does not occur, either the deduction or the hypothesis is incorrect, and has to be changed or rejected.

In the second approach, scientists form deductions about what events should *not* occur and then see if such events actually do occur. If a deduced impossibility occurs, either the deduction or the hypothesis is incorrect. Repeated failures to disprove a hypothesis, however, only serve to strengthen that hypothesis.

To determine whether or not a supposed event occurs, the scientist uses observation or, more often, *experimentation,* deliberately manipulating conditions in order to observe what happens. Designing a valid experiment is often the most difficult part of testing a hypothesis. Most experiments are based on the so-called classic experimental design. At the start of a classic experiment, two groups of subjects as identical as possible are set up, and the members of each group are measured for some characteristic. Then one group, called the *experimental group,* receives the chosen treatment. The other group, called the *control group,* is left untreated. Afterwards, both groups are remeasured. Any difference in measurement between the experimental and control groups can be attributed to the effect of the chosen treatment.

For example, to determine the effect of fertilizer on plant growth by a classic experiment, scientists might use two groups of seedlings sprouted from the same kind of seeds. First, they would measure the height of each plant. Then they fertilize the seedlings of only one group, while keeping other conditions for both groups constant—that is, making certain each group received the same amount of light, water, etc. After a period of time, they would again measure the height of each plant. The scientists could then attribute differences in height between the plants of one group and the plants of the other group to the application of the fertilizer.

Forming a Conclusion. Depending on the results of observations and experiments, scientists accept, reject, or change their hypotheses. When they believe they have developed a valid new hypothesis, they report it to scientific colleagues through scientific journals. Other scientists, in turn, can perform the same experiments to test their validity and can develop new experiments to further test the hypothesis.

Once adequately tested by the scientific community, the hypothesis may be accepted as a *theory,* a probable explanation or interpretation. Theories that have stood extensive tests are sometimes referred to as *laws.* Because of the complexity of natural and social phenomena, and the inductive nature of science, scientific laws are not regarded as absolutely true statements. Rather, they are viewed as approximations of the truth or limited representations of reality that will be changed, extended, and improved as more scientific knowledge is discovered.

History

This section traces the changes in the outlook and method of science. For information on the growth of scientific knowledge itself, see the history sections of articles on the individual sciences.

In ancient and medieval times, people sought scientific knowledge by two different methods that were only partly scientific.

Craftsmen and artisans used trial-and-error experimentation to find out about natural events and objects. For example, in ancient Egypt they learned through trial and error how to form a right angle. They divided a rope into 12 equal units and then laid out the rope in the shape of a triangle with sides of 3, 4, and 5 units; the angle between the 3-unit side and the 4-unit side was then a right angle. Craftsmen and artisans used their knowledge for such practical purposes as surveying fields or designing tools, but they did not try to form general conclusions that could be used to solve new problems.

Philosophers, on the other hand, sought general knowledge about the world and the human race. Although philosophers sometimes observed nature and experimented, they generally formed their conclusions by reasoning deductively from assumed premises—by speculation alone. The ancient Greek philosopher Aristotle, for example, made observations in biology, but he used the deductive method of inquiry in physics and astronomy. Like other philosophers who used deduction, Aristotle arrived at many false conclusions because many of his premises were wrong. For example, he accepted the false premise that a heavy object always falls faster than a light object. The quest of philosophers for an understanding of nature was called *natural philosophy*.

During the Middle Ages, craftsmen and artisans continued to seek knowledge by trial-and-error experimentation. Muslim scholars continued to speculate about nature, frequently combining speculation with observation and experimentation. By contrast, scholars in Christian Europe devoted themselves to theology and largely neglected natural philosophy. In the 13th century, Aristotle's writings, including those on nature, gained acceptance and Christian scholars settled questions about nature by relying on the authority of Aristotle instead of by looking at nature.

Beginning of Modern Science. Modern science developed when the two methods of pursuing scientific knowledge—trial-and-error experimentation and speculation—were combined and systematized to form the scientific method. As early as the 13th century, the Englishman Roger Bacon stressed the need for observation and experimentation in natural philosophy, but he had little influence on his contemporaries. The scientific

method did not fully emerge until the late 16th and early 17th centuries during the Renaissance when natural scientists combined observation and induction with deduction tested by experiment. The chief founders of the scientific method were Galileo Galilei and Isaac Newton. The changes in methods and outlook were so great they are often referred to as the scientific revolution.

Two 17th-century scholars who were eloquent spokesmen for the scientific approach —although they made no major scientific discoveries—were the Englishman Francis Bacon and the Frenchman René Descartes. Bacon stressed the importance of inductive reasoning in scientific study. Descartes emphasized the need for a critical spirit—an attitude of doubting everything that has not been logically proved.

Scientific investigation in the late 16th and the 17th century was greatly aided by the invention of various instruments for studying nature. Among these instruments were the microscope and telescope, which extended the range of human vision; the pendulum clock, which improved the measurement of time; and the air pump and mercury barometer, useful in the study of the properties of air. Through newly formed scientific societies, such as the Royal Society of England and the French Academy of Science, scholars began to exchange information and cooperate in solving problems.

Science in the 18th and 19th Centuries. Natural philosophy—or science, as it commonly came to be called in the 19th century—began to separate into various branches. First physics and chemistry, then biology, geology, and psychology emerged as distinct sciences. Unable to master the entire field, scientists began to specialize.

As scientific instrumentation and mathematics advanced, science became less qualitative and more quantitative. For example, the use of thermometers enabled scientists to replace vague words such as "hot" and "cold" with precise numbers on a temperature scale. The development of probability theory and statistics helped scientists analyze their observations and experiments.

Throughout the 18th and most of the 19th century, scientists held certain basic assumptions about nature and science. They believed that nature behaves according to the principle of cause and effect—every event in nature has a cause, and a given cause always produces the same effect. The task of science, they believed, is to establish theories that explain the causes of events. Scientific laws, such as Newton's law of universal gravitation, were regarded as true statements about nature. Scientists were confident that in time they would be able to grasp the complete truth about nature.

Late in the 19th century, this outlook began to change. Mathematics, which had been regarded as a collection of true statements about nature, was shown to be a collection of artificial logical systems. For example, Euclid's basic assumptions in geometry were regarded as truths until Nicholas I. Lobachevsky, John Bolyai, Karl Friedrich Gauss, and Georg F. B. Riemann invented *non-Euclidean geometries,* systems of geometry based on sets of assumptions other than Euclid's. Each non-Euclidean system was internally consistent but contradicted Euclid's system. The discovery of contradictory but internally consistent systems in geometry and other branches of mathematics showed that mathematics by itself revealed no truths about nature.

Another change in outlook was initiated by the Austrian scholar Ernst Mach. He challenged the view that scientific theories should explain the causes of natural events. Instead, he advocated the now widely held view that scientific theories should describe nature in a way that will enable scientists to make accurate predictions.

Science in the 20th Century. A revolutionary discovery early in the 20th century overturned the view that nature proceeds from cause to effect. Physicists discovered that the behavior of subatomic particles of matter—those within the atom—cannot be described with certainty. They found that an event within an atom cannot be described as the certain consequence, but only as the probable consequence, of another event. This discovery led many scientists to believe that the universe consists of complex, uncertain phenomena that will never be fully understood. Scientific theories and laws came to be regarded as statements that are approximately, but not absolutely, true.

Another new view, which became important through the efforts of the American physicist Percy Williams Bridgman, was *operationalism.* Operationalists tried to rid scientific theories of meaningless terms—

"smooth" and "rough," for example—by insisting that each scientific term can be *operationally defined,* described in terms of the operations that can be performed to measure it. For example, the surface texture of an object might be measured by drawing a phonograph needle and pickup across the object's surface and measuring the electrical signal produced by the needle's vibration. In this example, surface texture could be operationally defined as the magnitude of the electrical signal produced. Most scientists eventually rejected the completely operational approach.

Science in the 20th century has been marked by an increased rate of scientific

Books about Science

Allaby, Michael, editor. *Illustrated Dictionary of Science,* revised edition (Facts on File, 1995).

Asimov, Isaac. *Asimov's Chronology of Science and Discovery,* revised edition (HarperCollins, 1994).

Flaste, Richard, editor. *The New York Times Book of Science Literacy* (Random House, 1991).

Hann, Judith. *How Science Works: 100 Ways Parents and Kids Can Share the Secrets of Science* (Reader's Digest Association, 1991).

Hellemans, Alexander, and Bryan Bunch. *The Timetables of Science: a Chronology of the Most Important People and Events in the History of Science* (Simon & Schuster, 1991).

McGraw-Hill Encyclopedia of Science and Technology, 7th edition (20 volumes; McGraw-Hill, 1992).

Ronan, C. A., editor. *Science Explained: the World of Science in Everyday Life* (Holt, 1996).

Spangenburg, Ray, and D. K. Moser. *The History of Science* (5 volumes; Facts on File, 1993-94).

Wellnitz, W. R. *Science in Your Backyard* (McGraw-Hill, 1992).

Williams, T. I. *Science: a History of Discovery in the Twentieth Century* (Oxford University, 1990).

For Younger Readers

Busch, P. S. *Backyard Safaris: 52 Year-Round Science Adventures* (Simon & Schuster, 1995).

Coulter, George. *Science in History* (Rourke, 1995).

Gallant, R. A. *A Young Person's Guide to Science: Ideas That Change the World* (Simon & Schuster, 1993).

Hirschfeld, Robert, and Nancy White. *The Kids' Science Book: Creative Experiences for Hands-on Fun* (Williamson, 1995).

Markham, Lois. *Discoveries That Changed Science* (Raintree, 1994).

Ruchlis, Hy. *How Do You Know It's True?: Discovering the Difference Between Science and Superstition* (Prometheus Books, 1991).

Sherrow, Victoria. *Great Scientists* (Facts on File, 1992).

discovery and the birth of hundreds of specialized fields of scientific study. Many new instruments and techniques have been developed, making possible new kinds of experiments and scientific discoveries. Increasingly, scientists work in teams rather than individually, largely because of the expense and complexity of the equipment required for their experiments. The development of electronics and of the digital computer has greatly assisted scientists in collecting and analyzing data in a large variety of scientific fields. Major new fields of scientific study include the study of the earth with artificial satellites and of outer space with satellites and space probes; the study of nuclear energy and of the interaction of subatomic particles; and the study of the chemical processes within living cells.

See also AMERICAN ASSOCIATION FOR THE ADVANCEMENT OF SCIENCE; INTERNATIONAL COUNCIL OF SCIENTIFIC UNIONS; RESEARCH (and cross references).

Science Fiction, a form of fiction in which real or imaginary scientific discoveries, principles, or technological advancements are integral to the story. A number of inventions and developments—including submarines, spaceflight, robots, nuclear weapons, and television—were written about in science fiction before they existed in real life. Horror and fantasy stories often contain elements of science fiction, and the distinctions between these genres are frequently unclear.

The events in science fiction adhere to natural laws—although not necessarily the natural laws with which we are familiar. Typically these stories deal with such events as space travel, time travel, or cosmic disasters. Science fiction stories are often set in the future, although some are set in the past or the present. Science fiction has played a large part in popularizing science, and a number of science fiction authors have a background in science.

Stories with science fiction elements have existed since ancient times, but science fiction as a distinct genre did not begin to develop until the 19th century. Mary Shelley's *Frankenstein* (1818) is often considered one of the first works of science fiction. Jules Verne, noted as the first science fiction writer to pay close attention to scientific detail, described space travel in the novel *From the Earth to the Moon* (1865). H. G.

Wells, who was influenced by Verne, wrote of the invasion of the earth by aliens in *The War of the Worlds* (1898).

In the 20th century, Hugo Gernsback popularized the term "science fiction" and in 1926 founded *Amazing Stories,* a magazine devoted to publishing the works of science fiction writers. Important writers of the early 20th century include Edgar Rice Burroughs, whose novel *A Princess of Mars* (1917) was the first in his series about adventure on another planet; Olaf Stapledon, whose *Last and First Men* (1930) follows the progress of humanity for billions of years; and Aldous Huxley, whose *Brave New World* (1932) depicts emotionally barren life in a technologically controlled society.

Writers who achieved prominence in the 1940's include Isaac Asimov, Robert Heinlein, and A. E. van Vogt. In the 1950's Arthur C. Clarke, Frederik Pohl, John Wyndham, Theodore Sturgeon, and Ray Bradbury gained attention. By the 1960's science fiction stories increasingly focused on social issues—for example, Philip Dick's novel *The Three Stigmata of Palmer Eldritch* (1965) explores the effects of drug use; Frank Herbert's *Dune* (1965) emphasizes ecology; Kurt Vonnegut's *Slaughterhouse Five* (1969) deals with the horrors of war; and Ursula Le Guin's *The Left Hand of Darkness* (1969) portrays a society without sexual discrimination. Other authors who became well known in the 1960's and 1970's were Brian Aldiss, Samuel Delany, and Thomas Disch. They continued to write into the 1980's and 1990's.

A variety of authors who do not primarily write science fiction have also contributed to this genre. They include Karel Čapek, George Orwell, Don DeLillo, Margaret Atwood, and Doris Lessing.

See also ASIMOV, ISAAC; BRADBURY, RAY; APEK, KAREL; HEINLEIN, ROBERT A.; HUXLEY, ALDOUS; ORWELL, GEORGE; VERNE, JULES; WELLS, H. G.

Scientific Creationism. See CREATIONISM.

Scientific Management. See TAYLOR, FREDERICK W.; TIME AND MOTION STUDY.

Scientific Method. See SCIENCE, subtitle *Scientific Method.*

Scientology, Church of, a religious and mental-health organization. Scientology combines beliefs and practices found in Christianity, Buddhism, Taoism, and Hinduism. The term "Scientology" is a registered trademark of the church. Members work to attain spiritual peace by eliminating *engrams* (unhappy memories) from the mind. To achieve this goal, a member attends *auditing* (counseling) sessions with a Scientologist minister. The sessions consist of interviews using a device called an E-meter, which Scientologists believe measures the mental state of an individual. Ministers are trained in the organization's own schools.

The basic principles of Scientology were first advanced by L. Ron Hubbard in the book *Dianetics: The Modern Science of Mental Health* (1950). To put his views into practice, Hubbard founded the Scientology movement in 1952. The Church of Scientology was incorporated as a religious body in 1954. Scientologists count as members all persons who have participated in auditing sessions; no figures for the number of regularly participating members are available. Headquarters are in Los Angeles.

Scilla, s(k)ĭl′a or **Squill,** a large genus of perennial herbs native to the temperate regions of Africa, Asia, and Europe. The genus is made up of about 80 species. Scillas grow from bulbs planted in the early fall. The plant may reach a height of 36 inches (90 cm). Long, narrow, grasslike leaves surround stalks that bear blue, white, or purple bell-shaped flowers. One species of scilla is the English bluebell. (See BLUEBELL.)

The genus *Scilla* belongs to the lily family, Liliaceae.

Scilly, Isles of, sĭl′ĭ, a group of about 140 small British islands and reefs off Cornwall, England. They are some 28 miles (45 km) southwest of Land's End, at the entrance to the English Channel. The Scillies are noted for production of flowers, some 50,000,000 blooms a year. The island reefs are a notorious ships' graveyard. Tourists to the five inhabited islands can see ruins of a medieval abbey, burial chambers, and figureheads from wrecked ships.

Scholars believe that the ancient Phoenicians may have gotten their tin from the Scillies. King Athelstan of England (925-940) allowed Benedictine monks to settle there in the 10th century A.D. The islands have belonged to the Duchy of Cornwall since the 14th century.

Population: 2,938.

Scimitar. See SWORD (illustration).

Scintillation Counter. See RADIOACTIVITY, subtitle *Studying Particles and Rays*.

Scion. See GRAFTING.

Scipio, sĭp′ĭ-ō, the family name of several ancient Roman military and political leaders. The two most famous were Publius Cornelius Scipio Africanus (called Scipio the Elder, or Scipio Major) and Publius Cornelius Scipio Aemilianus Africanus Numantinus (called Scipio the Younger, or Scipio Minor). Each defeated the Carthaginians in one of the Punic Wars.

Scipio the Elder (236?-183? B.C.) represented the fourth generation of his family to gain fame on the battlefield. He fought in Spain, against the Carthaginian brothers Hannibal and Hasdrubal, under his father and uncle. After they died about 211 B.C., Scipio was given command of the army in Spain. He was so successful that he was made consul in 205. The next year he took an army to Africa and won a series of victories, defeating Hannibal at the battle of Zama (202) and ending the Second Punic War. The Romans gave him the honorary surname Africanus.

In the next decade Scipio held several major public offices. In 190 B.C. he went with his brother Lucius to Asia, where Lucius defeated Antiochus III of Syria at the battle of Magnesia. Rival forces in the Roman Senate, led by Cato the Elder, attacked the brothers with various accusations, and in the mid-180's the Scipios retired from public life.

Scipio the Younger (185?-129 B.C.) was the adopted son of Publius Cornelius Scipio, who was the son of Scipio the Elder. After serving in Spain and Africa, the young man was elected consul in 147 B.C. (by special dispensation, because of his youth). The Romans were engaged in the Third Punic War. Scipio Aemilianus went to Africa and took command of the army there. In 146 B.C. his forces destroyed Carthage and occupied North Africa for Rome, gaining for him the surname Africanus. He was made consul again in 134, during a war with natives in Spain. Taking command of the Roman forces there, he captured and destroyed the stronghold of Numantia (133), after which he was called Numantinus.

Scissorbill. See SKIMMER.

Scissors. See SHEARS.

Sclera. See EYE, subtitle *Parts of the Eye*, and illustration.

Scoke. See POKEWEED.

Scoliosis, skō'lē-ō'sĭs, a physical deformity in which the spine curves sideways. In the early stages of scoliosis, the spine curves in one direction only; later, it may curve in the opposite direction as well. Some cases are caused by poor posture, muscle paralysis, or other known factors, but for most cases the cause is uncertain.

Scoliosis typically develops during childhood or adolescence. The first sign of scoliosis is usually that one shoulder is higher than the other. If scoliosis is not treated promptly, it may lead to difficulty in breathing, recurrent infections of the chest, and severe deformity. Depending on the case, the curvature can be corrected through physical therapy, the wearing of a metal brace or plaster cast, or surgery.

Scone, Stone of, skōōn, also called the Stone of Destiny, the traditional coronation seat of Scottish kings. It rests in Edinburgh Castle in Scotland. According to a favorite Scottish legend, the stone was brought to Scotland by Gaythelus, mythical ancestor of the Gaels (Celts). Kenneth MacAlpine, king of the Scots, supposedly placed the stone at Scone (on the outskirts of Perth) in the ninth century when he established his capital there. The stone was carried off to England in 1296 by Edward I, who claimed sovereignty over Scotland. It remained in England, beneath the coronation chair in Westminster Abbey, until 1996, when it was returned to Scotland. A prophecy that wherever the stone rested a king of Scots would reign was fulfilled in 1603 when the Scottish Stuarts came to the English throne.

Scopas, skō'păs, a Greek sculptor of the fourth century B.C. He was noted for expressing intense emotion in his work, and influenced many later sculptors. No work remains that can be definitely attributed to him. Scopas was one of four sculptors involved in decorating the Mausoleum of Halicarnassus. Some scholars believe that the parts of the frieze that are marked by violent action were done by Scopas. He was the architect of the temple of Athena Alea at Tegea and may have done some of the sculpture.

Scopes Trial, the trial of John T. Scopes in Dayton, Tennessee, in July, 1925, for violating a state law that forbade the teaching of evolution in the Tennessee public schools. The "monkey trial," as it is sometimes called (fundamentalists ridiculed the theory of evolution by claiming that it held that humans were descended from apes), attracted worldwide attention.

The Scopes case was arranged to test the constitutionality of the law. Tennessee's was not the only such law; the fundamentalist movement, with William Jennings Bryan as its popular leader, had for some years been mounting an attack against the theory of evolution. (See FUNDAMENTALISM.) Among more liberal persons, there was growing concern over the idea that a religious group could control public education to the extent of banning teachings with which it did not agree.

The high point of the trial was the examination of Bryan (who was an attorney for the prosecution and took the stand as an expert witness on the Bible) by Clarence Darrow, chief counsel for the defense. Bryan's rigid fundamentalism was exposed to worldwide ridicule. Although Bryan's testimony was stricken from the trial record, it had appeared in the press; although Scopes was convicted, the fundamentalist movement's drive was blunted.

An appeal was made to the state supreme court, which overturned the verdict on a technicality but upheld the antievolution statute. The law was finally repealed in 1967.

The trial was dramatized in *Inherit the Wind,* a play by Jerome Lawrence and Robert E. Lee (1955) and a motion picture (1960). With James Presley, Scopes wrote *Center of the Storm* (1967), a personal account of the controversy.

Score, in music. See ORCHESTRA, subtitle *The Conductor,* and illustration.

Scorpio. See SCORPIUS.

Scorpion, skôr'pĭ-ŭn, an animal related to spiders, mites, and ticks. The scorpion lives in warm, dry regions and in the tropics. It is most commonly found in southern Eu-

Scorpion
© Doug Sokell/Visuals Unlimited

Field Museum of Natural History; Mick Church

Scorpion Fish. The picture at right shows how the fish blends into its environment.

rope, Africa, the western and southwestern United States, and the tropical regions of the Western Hemisphere. There are about 1,500 species of scorpions, ranging from about ½ inch to 10 inches (1.3 to 25 cm) in length. About 70 species are found in the United States. These scorpions are usually about 1 to 3 inches (2.5 to 7.5 cm) in length.

A scorpion's long, slender body consists of a cephalothorax (joined head and thorax) with six pairs of appendages and an abdomen. The first two pairs of appendages are used for catching and mashing prey and for transferring it to the mouth; the last four pairs are legs. The abdomen is a flexible structure made up of 12 segments; it ends in a sharp, hollow, venom-injecting sting.

During the day, the scorpion rests in an underground burrow. It emerges at night to feed on insects and spiders, which it immobilizes and kills with the sting. The sting is also used when the scorpion is threatened; the venom of some species is deadly to many large animals, including humans.

Most scorpions are solitary and will attempt to kill and eat other scorpions that invade their territory. Prior to mating, the male and female grasp each other's claws and perform a courtship dance. Several months after mating, the female gives birth to 6 to 90 young, which are born live one at a time over a period of weeks. They climb upon the mother's back and cling there for about a month before molting and going off on their own. A scorpion reaches maturity in one to five years.

According to fossil records, the scorpion has been in existence for about 400 million years. Fossil remains reveal very little change between the ancient and the present-day scorpion.

Scorpions make up the order Scorpionida of the class Arachnida.

Scorpion Fish, a family of marine fish. Scorpion fish are named for the venomous spines on their fins. They have large heads covered with ridges and spines. In most species, the skin is brightly colored and mottled to blend in with the ocean bottom, where they dwell. Scorpion fish have teeth, and feed primarily on shrimp and other crustaceans. They are a valuable food fish in North America. The commercially most important species are the *Pacific ocean perch,* found along the coast of California, and the *redfish,* found along the Atlantic coast. (See REDFISH.) Many Pacific species are known as *rockfishes* because they inhabit rocky crevices.

Scorpion fish make up the family Scorpaenidae. The Pacific ocean perch is *Sebastes alutus;* the redfish, *S. marinus.*

Scorpius, skôr′pĭ-ŭs, a constellation in the Southern Hemisphere and the eighth sign of the zodiac. (The sign of the zodiac is known as *Scorpio.*) From the mid-north latitudes the constellation can be seen in the south during summer. The bright, reddish star Antares is the brightest star in Scorpius. (See ANTARES.)

For location, see ASTRONOMY (Index to Star Maps). See also ZODIAC.

Scotch Pine. See PINE, subtitle *Old World Pines:* Scotch Pine.

Scotch Whisky. See WHISKEY, subtitle *Kinds of Whiskeys:* Scotch Whisky.

Scoter. See DUCK, subtitle *Wild Ducks.*

Scotism. See DUNS SCOTUS, JOHN.

SCOTLAND

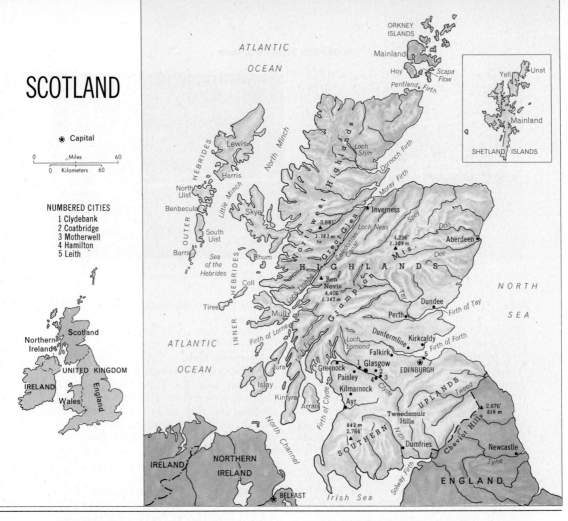

Capital ✪

Miles 0 _____ 60
Kilometers 0 _____ 60

NUMBERED CITIES
1 Clydebank
2 Coatbridge
3 Motherwell
4 Hamilton
5 Leith

ATLANTIC OCEAN

ORKNEY ISLANDS

Mainland
Hoy
Scapa Flow
Pentland Firth

Yell
Unst
Mainland
SHETLAND ISLANDS

HEBRIDES
Lewis
Harris
North Uist
Benbecula
South Uist
Barra
Skye
Rhum
Coll
Tiree
Mull
OUTER
Little Minch
North Minch
INNER HEBRIDES
Sea of the Hebrides
ATLANTIC OCEAN
Jura
Islay
Kintyre
Arran
North Channel

NORTHWEST Highlands
Loch Shin
Dornoch Firth
Moray Firth
3,881'
1,183 m
Loch Ness
Inverness
Spey
4,296'
1,309 m
Mts.
Don
Aberdeen
Dee
Caledonian Canal
Great Glen
HIGHLANDS
Ben Nevis
4,406'
1,343 m
Grampian
Tay
Dundee
Perth
Firth of Tay
NORTH SEA
Loch Linnhe
Loch Fyne
Firth of Lorne
Loch Lomond
Dunfermline
Kirkcaldy
5 Firth of Forth
Falkirk
1 Glasgow
Greenock
2
Paisley 4 3
EDINBURGH
Kilmarnock
Clyde
Ayr
Firth of Clyde
Tweedsmuir Hills
UPLANDS
Tweed
2,676'
816 m
842 m
2,764'
SOUTHERN
Dumfries
Nith
Cheviot Hills
Newcastle
Tyne
Solway Firth
ENGLAND

IRELAND
NORTHERN IRELAND
BELFAST
Irish Sea

Northern Ireland
Scotland
UNITED KINGDOM
IRELAND
Wales
England

Scotland, a political division of the United Kingdom of Great Britain and Northern Ireland. It consists primarily of the northern part of the island of Great Britain and three offshore island groups: the Hebrides and the Orkney and Shetland islands. On the south Scotland adjoins England; elsewhere it is bordered by the Atlantic Ocean and such arms of the Atlantic as the North Sea and Irish Sea. Northern Ireland lies 13 miles (21 km) southwest of the peninsula of Kintyre. The area of Scotland is 30,418 square miles (78,781 km²). Maximum dimensions on the mainland are about 275 miles (440 km) north-south and 150 miles (240 km) east-west.

Physical Geography

Land. Scotland is usually divided into three regions: the Highlands, the Central Lowlands, and the Southern Uplands.

The Highlands, occupying the northern part of the country, consist largely of two

S-192

mountain ranges running roughly northeast-southwest: the Grampian Mountains and the Northwest Highlands. Both these ranges are extremely eroded and rounded; their appearance is largely the result of the scouring action of glaciers during the last ice age. The roughest terrain lies along the west coast, where numerous mountains reach elevations of 3,000 to 4,000 feet (900 to 1,200 m). Great Britain's highest peak, 4,406-foot (1,343-m) Ben Nevis, is here. The east coast is comparatively level.

Throughout the Highlands there are innumerable valleys, called *glens* where narrow and *straths* where broad. The Great Glen, known also as Glen Mor, is a narrow, lake-studded valley stretching from coast to coast. Most of the highland region, especially its treeless, heather-covered moors, is thinly populated; some areas are virtually uninhabited.

The Central Lowlands, a depression 40

miles (64 km) wide just south of the Highlands, run northeast-southwest from coast to coast. Part of the land is relatively level, but much of it is rolling and dotted by hills. Concentrated here are the vast majority of Scotland's people, almost all of its large cities and mineral resources, and much of its best cropland.

The Southern Uplands, situated between the lowlands and the English border, center on an old eroded plateau and consist mainly of gently rounded hills. Elevations in several locations exceed 2,500 feet (760 m). Grassy moors, used extensively for grazing, cover much of the land. There are numerous valleys, called *dales* in this part of Scotland.

Water. The Clyde, which flows through Glasgow to the Atlantic Ocean, is Scotland's chief river, for it provides a major waterway through the industrial heart of the country. Almost all the other principal rivers flow to the North Sea, mainly from the Highlands. Among them are the Spey, Dee, Tay, Forth, and Tweed rivers. Lakes, known as *lochs,* abound in the Highlands. Some of them, especially Loch Lomond, have been made famous by Scottish literature and legend. Loch Ness, a deep, narrow lake in the Great Glen, is reputedly the home of a sea monster.

Numerous bays, sounds, and long, narrow arms of the sea, also called lochs, indent the Scottish coast, particularly the island-studded west coast. There are also broad river estuaries, or *firths;* the most notable are the Firth of Clyde, Firth of Forth, Firth of Tay, Moray Firth, and Solway Firth.

Climate. Scotland lies some 370 to 800 miles (600 to 1,300 km) farther north than the most northerly point in the United States, excluding Alaska. Its climate, however, is moderate because of the tempering influence of the ocean. Except in the high mountains, temperatures average about 35° to 40° F. (2° to 4° C.) in January and 55° to 60° F. (13° to 16° C.) in July. Rarely is the weather either very hot or cold.

Rains, drizzles, mists, and long cloudy periods make Scotland one of the most humid and overcast parts of Britain. In general, precipitation increases from east to west—from less than 25 inches (635 mm) annually on some parts of the east coast to more than 150 inches (3,810 mm) in the high western mountains. Most of the country, however, receives from 35 to 65 inches (890

British Travel Association
Scotland's Loch Lomond, the largest lake on the island of Great Britain. Sparkling clear water, a mountainous setting, and numerous songs and stories have brought it worldwide fame.

to 1,650 mm), depending on location. Except in the loftiest parts of the Highlands, snows are light and infrequent.

The Economy

Scotland has a predominantly industrial economy, the origins of which go back to the Industrial Revolution. During the 19th century, the economy was led by coal and iron-ore mining; steel, engineering, and textile industries; and shipping. Many Scottish products, especially ships, received worldwide acclaim for their excellence. After World War I there was a drastic industrial decline, brought on partly by dwindling resources, outdated production methods, and increased foreign competition.

The economy was revived by World War II. After the war, however, many industries, especially the traditional ones dating from the 19th century, were either unstable or in serious decline. At the same time many people left Scotland for England and overseas lands. To revitalize the economy and reduce unemployment, a government program of industrial development was begun. As a result of this program many new industries have been established, including the electronics industry, which is one of Scotland's most rapidly growing industries.

Oil exploration and exploitation in Britain's section of the North Sea since the early 1970's has brought a boom to some parts of Scotland, especially along the east coast and to the city of Aberdeen.

Manufacturing. Scottish manufacturing is heavily concentrated in the Central Lowlands. Along the Clyde River, in and near Glasgow, is the area called Clydeside, center of Scotland's iron and steel, shipbuilding, and marine-engineering industries. Many of the world's largest ships have been built here. Clydeside also has a great variety of other industries, such as the manufacturing of locomotives, chemicals, Scotch whisky, and textiles. Few of these industries, however, are thriving; Clydeside has long been among the most economically depressed areas in Britain.

Cities in the east, particularly the coastal cities from Dundee to Edinburgh, have some

Brian Seed: CLICK/Chicago
Robert Harding Associates, London
Prominent Industries—the making of whisky and textiles. *Top,* cask of whisky being sealed to undergo aging. *Bottom,* worker in a carpet factory. Scotch whisky and Scottish woolens have worldwide markets.

Croft, or small farm, in the Scottish highlands. Much of Scotland's agricultural land is devoted to raising livestock, especially sheep and cattle.
© Buddy Mays/Travel Stock

North Sea Oil Rig. Almost all of Britain's oil is produced off Scotland's east coast, in the North Sea.
© Arnulf Husmo/Tony Stone Images

heavy industries such as shipbuilding and petroleum refining, but they are primarily centers of light manufacturing. Food processing, textile-making, printing, publishing, brewing, and the distilling of whisky are traditional activities. Here, too, are many of Scotland's new industries, including the manufacturing of electronic equipment, business machines, electrical appliances, and plastics.

Aberdeen, the leading city on the northeast coast, has both heavy and light industries and is the operational center for companies developing Britain's North Sea oil and gas. With few exceptions, there is little or no manufacturing elsewhere in Scotland.

Agriculture. Livestock has long played a prominent role in Scottish agriculture. Some of the world's best breeds, including the Aberdeen Angus and Galloway beef cattle

and Ayrshire dairy cattle; Clydesdale horses; and Cheviot and Black-faced Highland sheep, were developed in Scotland.

Only about a fifth of the land is suitable for crops or permanent pasture; the rest is classed mainly as rough grazing land suitable only for sheep. The chief crop area is the eastern part of the lowlands. Production here is the most varied in Scotland and includes wheat, barley, oats, potatoes, turnips, sugar beets, hardy fruits, and berries. Dairying dominates in the western part of the lowlands and along the southwest coast; the raising of beef cattle leads along the northeast coast. Elsewhere, the rearing of sheep prevails. In the Highlands, most of the sheep are raised on *crofts*—small farms that provide a bare subsistence.

Fishing and Forestry. Fishing has long provided a livelihood for thousands of Scots

S-195

living in the cities and villages along the coast. The chief fishing ports are along the east coast in or near Edinburgh and Aberdeen. Many of the fishing ports, especially those on the north and west coasts, are small. The catch, obtained mainly from coastal waters and nearby seas, includes cod, haddock, plaice, herring, turbot, pilchard, mackerel, and such shellfish as lobsters and crabs. About 15 per cent of Scotland is forested, mainly by conifers. Scotland accounts for about a third of Britain's timber production.

Mineral Resources. Scotland's chief mineral resource is oil, obtained from the North Sea. Production began in the early 1970's; by the early 1980's Scotland's output was largely responsible for making Britain one of the leading oil-producing countries in the world. The only mineral obtained in quantity from the mainland is coal, which comes chiefly from the lowlands.

Transportation. General cargo port facilities are mainly on the Clyde River below Glasgow and at Leith and Aberdeen. There are large petroleum ports on the east coast and in the Orkney and Shetland islands that handle oil from the North Sea. Scheduled domestic and international air service is provided by a number of carriers, mainly through international airports near Glasgow, Edinburgh, and Aberdeen.

The main railway and highway routes connect the cities of the lowlands and extend southward into England. Except along the east coast, relatively few roads or railways penetrate the Highlands. Much of the northwest coast is rather isolated; here coastal shipping is important. Most canals, including those in the lowlands that were once of great economic value, are either little used or abandoned.

The People

The people of Scotland are a blend mainly of Celtic, Anglo-Saxon, and Norse strains. The Celtic heritage has been dominant. Of the three Celtic peoples of ancient Scotland—the Picts, Scots, and Britons—the Scots gave the Scottish people not only their name but also the Gaelic tongue and Gaelic legends.

Population. In 1991 Scotland had a population of 4,998,567, about 2.5 per cent fewer than in 1981. The population density was about 163 persons per square mile (63 per km²). The vast majority of the Scots live in lowland cities and towns.

Scotland's Largest Cities*

Glasgow	662,853	West Lothian	144,137
Edinburgh,		Motherwell	142,632
the capital	418,914	Falkirk	140,980
Aberdeen	204,885	Cunninghame	136,875
Dundee	165,873	Dunfermline	127,258
Kirkcaldy	147,053		

*District Council Areas (County Districts).

Oban, a port and summer resort on the Firth of Lorne

Michele Burgess/Photobank, Inc.

Melrose Abbey, *left,* is an outstanding example of Gothic architecture. It was founded by David I in 1136 and was heavily damaged by English invaders during the 14th and 16th centuries. A heart reputed to be that of Robert Bruce is buried here.
NEW STANDARD photo

© Mike Roessler/Photobank, Inc.
Piper, *below,* in traditional dress, which includes a plaid (a tartan cloak worn over the left shoulder) and kilts. The bagpipe is the national instrument of Scotland.

Language and Religion. English is used throughout Scotland; less than 2 per cent of the people, mainly in the Highlands and western islands, also speak Gaelic. In 1968 the British government launched a program to increase the knowledge of Gaelic and its use, especially in literature.

The Church of Scotland, the legally established (state) church, is Presbyterian. About a fourth of the population belongs to the established church. Roman Catholics make up the second largest group, followed by Episcopalians, Congregationalists, Presbyterians unaffiliated with the established church ("Free Presbyterians"), Baptists, and Methodists.

Education. Scotland's primary and secondary educational system, entirely separate from England's, is under the direction of the Scottish Education Department. Education is compulsory between the ages of 5 and 16, and schooling is largely free. In addition to public schools, there are both state-aided and independent private schools. Elementary education lasts seven years and is followed by either academic or vocational secondary education.

Universities include St. Andrews, founded in 1410; Glasgow, 1451; Aberdeen, 1494; Edinburgh, 1583; and several institutions chartered since 1960. Universities are self-governing, although four-fifths of their funds come from the government.

Other institutions of higher learning in-

Ministry of Public Building and Works, Edinburgh
Rock Carving at Dunadd, the fifth-century fort that was capital of the kingdom of Dalriada. The boar is carved in outline, as sketched here, on a rock where the Scots probably crowned their kings.

clude junior colleges (known as *further education institutions*) and colleges (known as *central institutions*) that give courses in various professional and vocational fields. Scholarships and grants are available for advanced study.

Culture, Sports, and Recreation. Writers and poets are paramount in Scotland's cultural heritage. Outstanding Scottish literary figures include Robert Burns, Sir Walter Scott, William Dunbar, J. M. Barrie, Robert Louis Stevenson, and Edwin Muir. Major playwrights include C.P. Taylor, Osborne Henry Mavor (who wrote under the pseudonym James Bridie), Robert McLellan, Joe Corrie, and Robert Kemp. Other important writers include the biographer James Boswell, the essayist and critic Thomas Carlyle, and the philosopher and historian David Hume.

Scottish contributions in art and music have also been important. Leading Scottish painters include Henry Raeburn, David Wilkie, and Allan Ramsay. Scottish ballads and bagpipe music are well-known. The Scottish National Orchestra, in Glasgow, is internationally acclaimed. The National Gallery of Scotland, in Edinburgh, is Scotland's premier art museum.

The Scots share the general British enthusiasm for soccer as a spectator sport; rugby also has an immense following. The favorite participant sports, however, are of Scottish origin—in summer, golf; in winter, curling and shinty, or shinny, a Highlands version of field hockey. The annual Braemar Gathering is the best known of a number of Highland games, in which contestants vie in field events such as tossing the caber (a tree trunk), putting the weight, and throwing the hammer, as well as in traditional Scottish dancing and playing the bagpipes.

Government

As part of Great Britain, Scotland is governed by the United Kingdom Parliament and the British cabinet. Under a 1948 act of Parliament, Scotland is represented in the House of Commons by no fewer than 71 members. (See GREAT BRITAIN, subtitle *Government*.) Scotland's separate 129-member Parliament, its first since Scotland and England joined in 1707, opened in 1999 in Edinburgh. The Scottish Parliament controls taxes and legislates on a wide variety of domestic issues, including health, education, and local government. For administrative purposes, Scotland is divided into 29 regions on the mainland and three island areas (Orkney, Shetland, and the Western Islands).

In the Scottish judicial system, both civil and criminal cases may be heard in sheriff courts. The supreme civil court in Scotland is the Court of Session; action may originate in its Outer House, and appeals are heard in its Inner House. Further appeal may be made to the British House of Lords. The High Court of Justiciary is a trial court and the highest appeal court for criminal cases.

History

Ancient Scotland was settled by various peoples who arrived by a number of routes from southern, central, and northern Europe. When the Romans came to the British Isles in the first century B.C., they found in the Scottish Highlands a Celtic-speaking people whom they called Caledonians (later known as Picts). In the Lowlands and Southern Uplands were Britons, the Celtic people who had settled present England, called Britain after them.

The boundary of Roman Britain was considered to be as far inside Caledonia as the Roman legions could protect themselves against the fierce natives. Under Agricola, the Romans crushed the Caledonian forces at the battle of Mons Graupius in 84 A.D. Two Roman walls were built to protect Britain—Hadrian's Wall, 122?-28, south of the Cheviot Hills, and the Wall of Antoninus, about 142, between the firths of Forth and Clyde.

See also CELTS.

Formation of the Scottish Kingdom. Early in the fifth century the Roman legions were withdrawn. At the end of the century the Scots, a Gaelic branch of Celts in Ireland, migrated to the coastal region of Scotland northwest of the Firth of Clyde. They established a kingdom named Dalriada; the region became known as Argyll (from "coast land of the Gael").

In the seventh century the Anglo-Saxons, a Germanic people who had conquered central Britain, extended their rule to the Firth of Forth. In the Highlands, the Picts (Caledonians) grew in strength and gradually imposed overlordship on the Scots.

Early in the ninth century Norsemen—mainly Norwegians—began raiding Scot-

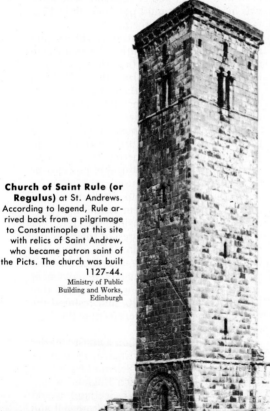

Church of Saint Rule (or Regulus) at St. Andrews. According to legend, Rule arrived back from a pilgrimage to Constantinople at this site with relics of Saint Andrew, who became patron saint of the Picts. The church was built 1127-44.
Ministry of Public Building and Works, Edinburgh

land in the north and down the west coast. Kenneth MacAlpine, king of Scots, gained the Pict throne about 843 and united the Picts and Scots in the kingdom of Albany (or Alba), consolidating resistance to the Norsemen. However, many Norse coastal settlements were founded in the 10th century. The Picts and Scots (whose country soon took the name of Scotland) fought the Anglo-Saxons (English), but were defeated by them in 937. About 1016, however, Malcolm II, king of Scotland, won a victory over the English north of the Tweed River, extending Scotland's southern boundary to its approximate present location.

There was constant rivalry for the Scottish throne. Malcolm II killed all the rivals of his grandson Duncan, who succeeded him in 1034. Macbeth, whose wife was the heir of one of Duncan's slain rivals (possibly Kenneth III), murdered Duncan in 1040. In 1057 Macbeth was slain by Duncan's son Malcolm (III) Canmore, whose house then ruled Scotland for the next 200 years.

See also IONA; MACBETH; MACBETH (drama); MALCOLM III; PICTS; SCONE, STONE OF.

Conflict with England. The Normans who conquered England in 1066 were soon in conflict with Malcolm, whose wife Margaret was of the Anglo-Saxon royal house (see MARGARET, Saint). However, numerous marriages between the Anglo-Norman and Scottish royal families brought a period of peace. This was shattered in 1173 when Henry II of England reneged on an earlier promise to transfer certain domains to Scotland. War broke out between Scotland and England. William I of Scotland was captured at Alnwick, England, in 1174 and forced to acknowledge Henry as his overlord. He was released from this obligation by Richard I in 1189.

Meanwhile, the Norsemen were being driven out of Scotland. Their last Scottish domains, except the Orkney and Shetland islands, were relinquished by treaty in 1266.

The Canmore line died out in 1290, and Edward I of England was invited to arbitrate between the competitors for the Scottish throne. Although the Scots preferred Robert Bruce, Edward's arbitration council chose John de Baliol, who did homage to Edward. The Scots soon rebelled against English domination. In 1296 Edward marched north, defeated the Scots, carried the Stone of Scone (the Scottish coronation seat) back to England, and declared Scotland his.

A Scottish revolt led by William Wallace collapsed in 1304. Two years later Robert Bruce, grandson of John de Baliol's rival, had himself crowned king of Scots. His progress against the English was slow, but his victory at Bannockburn in 1314 was decisive, although fighting continued until 1323. In 1328 England conceded Scotland's independence.

David II, Bruce's son, succeeded to the throne in 1329. In 1332 Edward de Baliol, son of John de Baliol, seized the throne and, after receiving much-needed English support, did homage to Edward III of England. The majority of Scots refused to accept Baliol. In 1356 Edward removed him and the next year restored David to the throne. In 1371 David was succeeded by his nephew Robert Stewart.

See also ALEXANDER (rulers), subtitle *Scotland;* BALIOL (family); BANNOCKBURN, BATTLE OF; BRUCE, ROBERT; DAVID (kings of Scotland); DOUGLAS (family); STUART (family); WALLACE, Sir WILLIAM; WILLIAM, subtitle *Scotland.*

Scotland under the Stuarts. For more than 150 years, Scotland, although independent and for the most part free of English aggression, was torn by clan feuds and stormy resistance to the authority of the Stewart (or Stuart, as the name eventually came to be spelled) rulers. James I (reigned 1406-37) was murdered by a resentful baron. James III (1460-88) met his death fighting rebellious subjects. His son James IV (1488-1513) was a gallant and popular king who brought order to much of Scotland, although the Highlands were not altogether subdued. In 1503 James married the English princess Margaret Tudor. When Margaret's brother, Henry VIII, went to war against Scotland's ally France, James invaded England and was killed at the battle of Flodden Field.

Mary Stuart, queen of Scots, was reared in France, married the dauphin (the heir to the French throne), became queen of France in 1559, and was widowed the next year. Catholics considered her—rather than her Protestant cousin Elizabeth I—the rightful claimant to the English throne, through her grandmother Margaret Tudor.

In 1561 Mary returned to Scotland, where under the leadership of John Knox Catholicism had been rejected and Calvinism made the official religion. Mary did not oppose the new kirk (church), but lost the support of the Scots in 1567 when she was suspected of being involved in the mysterious death of her second husband, Lord Darnley. Upon her marriage to Darnley's presumed murderer, the Earl of Bothwell, the Scots rose against her and proclaimed her infant son, James (VI), king. Mary fled to England, where she was held prisoner until put to death in 1587 for plots against Elizabeth.

James, godson of Queen Elizabeth and next in line (after the death of his mother) to the English throne, was brought up a Protestant and succeeded Elizabeth in 1603 (as James I), uniting Scotland and England under a single monarch, although they remained separate countries.

The Scottish Parliament established a presbyterian form of church government in 1592. Parliament's enactments, however, left the king with a great deal of power over the church, which he used in 1598-99 to reintroduce bishops into Parliament and then to superimpose them on the kirk government. In 1638, during the reign of Charles I, the Scots expressed their discontent with royal policy in a document, the National Covenant. The issuing of this document was the beginning of a movement that eventually overthrew the bishops (the Bishops' Wars of 1639-40) and restored the presbyterian form of government to the Scottish church.

After the Great Rebellion against Charles broke out in 1642, the English Parliament and the Scots signed the Solemn League and Covenant (1643), by which England would become Presbyterian and Scotland would support the rebellion. Oliver Cromwell and the Independents (Congregationalists) opposed the Scots and prevented the implementation of the covenant. The beheading of Charles in 1649 horrified the Scots, who proclaimed his son Charles (II) to be their king. Thereafter the Covenanters were allied with the royalists against the Puritans, who conquered Scotland, 1650-52.

When the monarchy was restored in 1660, Charles II reestablished episcopacy in Scotland. His brother James, a Catholic, was made commissioner for Scotland in 1680, and persecution of Convenanters became intense. After his succession to the throne in 1685, James (VII of Scotland and II of England) quickly antagonized his subjects in both countries and was deposed in the Glorious Revolution of 1688. Under his daughter Mary and her husband, William of Orange, Presbyterianism was reestablished in Scotland (1690). Mary's sister Anne came to the throne in 1702 and recommended the union of England and Scotland under a single Parliament. The Act of Union in 1707 joined the countries into the nation of Great Britain.

See also:

ANNE (queens), subtitle *Great Britain*
BOTHWELL, EARL OF
CHARLES, subtitle *England*
COVENANTER
FLODDEN FIELD, BATTLE OF
GREAT REBELLION
JAMES (kings)
KNOX, JOHN
MARGARET TUDOR
MARY (English queens), subtitle *Mary II*
MARY, QUEEN OF SCOTS
MORAY, EARL OF
WILLIAM, subtitle *England and Great Britain:* William III

Scotland in the Union. Many Scots wished to restore James to the throne and to continue the Stuart line. These people were known as Jacobites. When Anne was succeeded in 1714 by George I, a German, the Jacobites rose in rebellion. James Stuart, son of the late king and later known as the Old Pretender, landed in Scotland in 1715 but, finding his local forces ineffectual, departed.

In 1745 James's son Charles Edward Stuart (Bonnie Prince Charlie), the Young Pretender, raised the Highland clans in rebellion. He soon won most of Scotland and proclaimed his father king (as James VIII); Charles then moved into England but was forced by his clan chiefs to withdraw. A few months later Charles was defeated at Culloden, and the rebellion ended.

As part of Great Britain, Scotland developed economically. Agriculture improved, textile mills flourished, fisheries thrived, and an iron industry developed. Meanwhile, dissension arose in the Presbyterian church

AP/Wide World Photos

Queen Elizabeth conducts the official opening of Scotland's parliament in Edinburgh in 1999. The 129-member assembly is Scotland's first Parliament in nearly 300 years.

following the Act of Union, which had made it the official Church of Scotland. Various factions within the church vied for control in the 18th and 19th centuries, with the result that many groups seceded and founded nonestablishment churches.

A feeling of being treated politically as inferior to England created periodic discontent. A growing national consciousness led to a demand for home rule in the 1880's that gained support from the Liberal party, but no legislation was passed. In the 1920's a movement for independence developed and led to the formation of the Scottish National party (SNP). The SNP had its first election successes in 1945. Its strength began growing in the late 1950's and increased in the early 1970's. In 1975 the British government announced plans to give Scotland limited home rule. In a 1979 referendum, however, the proposal failed to win approval by a required 40 per cent of the Scottish voters. In a 1997 referendum voters approved the restoration of Scotland's Parliament in 1999.

Meanwhile, in the late 1960's oil and natural gas were discovered in the North Sea off the Scottish coast. These fields were developed extensively in the 1970's and still yield enormous amounts of oil and natural gas. In 1993 a massive oil spill occurred off the Shetland Islands when a tanker ran aground.

See also CHARLES EDWARD STUART; JAMES FRANCIS EDWARD STUART; MACDONALD, FLORA; ROB ROY.

For further information, see:

Geography

CHEVIOT HILLS	HEBRIDES
CLYDE RIVER	LOCH LOMOND
FIRTH	LOCH NESS
FORTH RIVER	MORAY FIRTH
GALLOWAY	ORKNEY ISLANDS
GRAMPIAN	SHETLAND ISLANDS
MOUNTAINS	TAY RIVER

Cities

ABERDEEN	INVERNESS
DUNDEE	STIRLING
EDINBURGH	
GLASGOW	

Some Noted Scotsmen

BARRIE, J. M.	PARK, MUNGO
BOSWELL, JAMES	RAEBURN, Sir HENRY
BURNS, ROBERT	RAMSAY, ALLAN
CARLYLE, THOMAS	SCOTT, Sir WALTER
DOUGLAS, DAVID	SELKIRK,
DUNBAR, WILLIAM	ALEXANDER
HUME, DAVID	SELKIRK, EARL OF
LANG, ANDREW	SMITH, ADAM
LAUDER, Sir HARRY	STEVENSON, ROBERT
MACDONALD,	LOUIS
RAMSAY	WATT, JAMES
NAPIER, JOHN	

Miscellaneous

BAGPIPE	ROYAL COLLEGE OF
CLAN	PHYSICIANS
HAGGIS	ROYAL SOCIETY OF
LITERATURE,	EDINBURGH
SCOTTISH	TARTAN
MAC	

Books about Scotland

Burke, John. *A Traveller's History of Scotland* (Trafalgar Square, 1991).
Connachie, Ian, and George Hewitt. *A Companion to Scottish History: from the Reformation to the Present* (Facts on File, 1990).
Maclean, Fitzroy. *A Concise History of Scotland* (Thames & Hudson, 1983).
Michelin Green Guide to Scotland, 2nd edition (Michelin, 1990).

For Younger Readers

Campbell, D. G. *Scotland in Pictures,* revised edition (Lerner, 1991).
MacVicar, Angus. *Scotland* (Chelsea House, 1988).
Meek, James. *The Land and People of Scotland* (Lippincott, 1990).

Scotland, Church of. See SCOTLAND, subtitle *The People.*

Scotland Yard, the common name for the headquarters of the London Metropolitan Police Force and, especially, its Criminal Investigation Department (CID). The CID is responsible for criminal investigations throughout Greater London. It is known the world over for its effectiveness. The primary concern of the Metropolitan Police Force is the policing of London. Special activities include protection of royalty, cabinet ministers, and distinguished foreign visitors; keep-

ing fingerprints and criminal records for all persons convicted in England and Wales; and assisting other police forces outside its jurisdiction when asked.

The Metropolitan Police Force was established by Robert Peel in 1829. Its headquarters was situated in an area where visiting Scottish kings had traditionally been housed. The name Scotland Yard comes from this location. A new headquarters building near the Houses of Parliament was occupied in 1890 and named New Scotland Yard. In 1967 New Scotland Yard was moved to a location near Westminster Abbey.

Scott, Dred. See DRED SCOTT DECISION.

Scott, James. See MONMOUTH, DUKE OF.

Scott, Robert Falcon (1868-1912), a British naval officer and explorer. He commanded two expeditions to Antarctica, reaching the South Pole on the second journey. Among important discoveries of the first expedition were the Ross Ice Shelf and King Edward VII Land (now called Edward VII Peninsula).

Scott was born at Devonport, England, and entered the navy at the age of 14. He became a naval officer in 1889 and a commander in 1900. He led the Royal Society and Royal Geographical Antarctic expedition of 1901-04, which made magnetic surveys of the continent, studied its topography, and determined routes to the interior. Scott was promoted to captain on his return and served in the navy until 1909.

In 1910 Scott headed a second Royal Society expedition to the Antarctic, this one to the South Pole. He hoped to reach the Pole before an expedition led by the Norwegian explorer Roald Amundsen. After using dogs and ponies to move supplies into the interior, Scott and four companions pulled sledges to the final supply camp on the polar route. He and his four-man team reached the Pole about January 18, 1912, but found that Amundsen's expedition had preceded them by more than a month.

Blizzards, cold, and illness brought disaster on the return trip to the base camp. The entire party perished; Scott and two others pushed to within 11 miles (18 km) of the safety of their supply camp before dying of hunger and exposure. Their bodies were found in November by a search party. Scott's diary, with the final entry dated

March 29, was published as *Scott's Last Expedition* (2 volumes, 1913).

Scott, Sir **Walter** (1771-1832), a Scottish novelist, poet, historian, and critic. He was for many years one of the most widely read authors in Europe and America. His stirring tales of adventure brought to life for millions of readers the history of Scotland and England from the 12th through the 18th century. *The Lady of the Lake* (1810), a story of the Scottish Highlands in the 16th century, was the most popular of Scott's long narrative poems, and has been the most often reprinted. Critics consider *The Heart of Midlothian* (1818), a novel set in 18th-century Scotland and England, the best of all Scott's works.

Scott's popularity rested largely upon his descriptions of scenes and manners unfamiliar to his readers, and upon lively action and romantic episodes. He did not plot carefully, and he wrote hastily and without revising. As a result, his novels and narrative poems lack unity and forcefulness. Most of his heroes and heroines are unrealistic, and their speech is stilted and trite. Except for some of the short lyrics incorporated in his narrative poems, his verse is second-rate.

Scott's importance is based on several valuable contributions to literary development. He created the historical novel and gave prestige to the novel in general. Among writers he influenced were Robert Louis Stevenson, Charles Dickens, William Thackeray, Honoré de Balzac, Dumas the Elder, Leo Tolstoy, Aleksander Pushkin, and James Fenimore Cooper. Scott was the first novelist to present people of the lower classes as real human beings rather than as comic or sentimentally idealized figures. He was also the first novelist to use regional dialects in a serious instead of a mocking manner.

Scott's Life

Walter Scott was born in Edinburgh. At the age of two he had an attack of poliomyelitis that left him permanently lame in the right leg. To restore his general health after his illness, Walter was sent to his grandfather's farm near the border of Scotland and England. Here his interest in Scottish history was stimulated as he listened to exciting tales and ballads of the past.

Scott studied law at the University of Edinburgh, served in his father's law office, and in 1792 was admitted to the bar. He was

National Portrait Gallery, London
Sir Walter Scott, painted by Sir Edwin Landseer

married in 1797. In 1799 he was made deputy sheriff of Selkirkshire, and some years later was appointed court clerk in addition. His duties in these offices left him time for the historical and literary interests that had occupied him since childhood.

In 1802-03 Scott published *The Minstrelsy of the Scottish Border,* a three-volume collection of ballads with critical and historical commentary. *The Lay of the Last Minstrel* (1805), the first of his long narrative poems, made Scott famous. His next two narrative poems, *Marmion* (1808) and *Lady of the Lake,* brought him to the peak of his poetic career. During these years he also edited the complete works of John Dryden, which he prefaced with a biography; and contributed critical articles to *The Edinburgh Review* and *The Quarterly Review.*

Rokeby (1813), another narrative poem, was not well received, and the demand for Scott's poetry declined sharply. He had long been interested in writing a novel and had begun work on one some years earlier. This novel, *Waverley, or 'Tis Sixty Years Since* (1814), was published anonymously. It was an immediate success.

During the next 16 years Scott published 23 novels, most of them historical. In addition to those already mentioned, the more famous include: *Guy Mannering* (1815), *The Antiquary* (1816), *Old Mortality* (1816), *Rob Roy* (1818), *The Bride of Lammermoor* (1819), *Ivanhoe* (1820), *Kenilworth* (1821), and *Quentin Durward* (1823). In this time he

Winfield Scott
National Archives

also wrote short stories, plays, histories, biographies, and poems, and edited the complete works of Jonathan Swift. In 1820, Scott was created a baronet in recognition of his literary work.

In 1812 Scott had bought Abbotsford, an estate near Selkirk, and through the years he had spent large amounts of money on it. In 1826 a firm of publishers of which he was a partner failed. Scott would not ask the courts to declare him bankrupt, and accepted the firm's indebtedness. In spite of ill health he worked constantly to pay off the heavy load of debts and thought he had done so before his death. However, the debts were not wiped out until his copyrights were sold in 1847.

Scott, Winfield (1786-1866), a United States army officer. He was commanding general of the U.S. Army for more than 20 years; during this period the Mexican War was fought and the Civil War began. Scott's men referred to him as "Old Fuss and Feathers" because he insisted on strictness in dress and manners and was fond of military pomp and ceremony.

Scott was born near Petersburg, Virginia, and briefly attended the College of William and Mary. In 1807 he enlisted in the Petersburg cavalry troop, and the next year he was commissioned an artillery captain in the U.S. Army. He was suspended in 1809 for insulting a superior officer, but was reinstated at the outbreak of the War of 1812. Scott distinguished himself in some of the fiercest fighting of the war, at Chippewa and Lundy's Lane, and was promoted to the rank of brevet major general. After the war, he helped write the first standard set of American military drill regulations. Later he revised and enlarged a manual on infantry tactics; it was a standard guide until the Civil War.

During the South Carolina nullification crisis in 1832-33, Scott's mediation efforts helped prevent armed conflict between state and federal forces. In 1838 troops under his command began the task of moving more than 15,000 Cherokee Indians from Georgia

to land west of the Mississippi. Despite Scott's attempts to alleviate the Cherokees' hardships in the journey, their suffering was great and the journey became known as the Trail of Tears.

Scott was made commander of the U.S. Army in 1841. After American forces fought a series of inconclusive battles in the Mexican War, Scott in 1847 took personal command. His troops captured Veracruz and fought their way on to final victory at Mexico City.

A popular hero after the war, Scott was the Whig candidate for President in 1852, but he was defeated by Franklin Pierce. Scott was made a lieutenant general in 1855. He was in command of the Union Army when the Civil War began and planned the defenses of Washington, D.C. Illness forced him to retire in October, 1861.

Scottish Deerhound. See DOG, subtitle *Breeds of Dogs:* Hounds.

Scottish Literature. See LITERATURE, SCOTTISH.

Scottish Rite. See MASONS, subtitle *Concordant Degrees*.

Scottish Terrier. See DOG, subtitle *Breeds of Dogs:* Terriers (Scottish Terrier).

Scottish Topaz. See CAIRNGORM.

Scotts Bluff National Monument. See NATIONAL PARKS, section "United States."

Scottsboro Case. In 1931, nine young black men were accused of raping two white women aboard a train near Scottsboro, Alabama. The court decisions that followed helped to establish some of the most important civil rights precedents of the 20th century.

Haywood Patterson, Clarence Norris, Charley Weems, Andrew Wright, Ozie Powell, Willie Robinson, Olen Montgomery, Eugene Williams, and Leroy Wright—who became known as the "Scottsboro boys"—were homeless black youths, who ranged in age from 12 to 19. They had been riding a freight train on which several whites were also traveling when a fight ensued. Authorities were alerted and stopped the train. A white woman who had also been on board told police that she and a companion had been raped by the black youths.

Local public outrage was so great that the youths were nearly lynched before they could stand trial. Within three weeks of their arrest, the nine had been tried and convicted, and all but the youngest, Leroy Wright, had been sentenced to death in the electric chair.

The Communist Party of the U.S.A., through the International Labor Defense (ILD), appealed the case on behalf of the young men. In 1932 the U.S. Supreme Court ruled in *Powell* v. *Alabama* that the youths had not had adequate legal counsel and ordered a new trial.

The state of Alabama began trying the defendants again in 1933. Norris was the first to be tried and, despite medical evidence and testimony that contradicted the alleged victims' claim, was found guilty. His conviction was appealed. In 1935 the Supreme Court ruled in *Norris* v. *Alabama* that Norris had been denied due process of law because blacks had been systematically excluded from jury service in Alabama. The conviction was overturned.

Patterson, Norris, Weems, Andrew Wright, and Powell were again tried and found guilty, receiving sentences ranging from 20 years to life; charges against the remaining four were dropped. Patterson escaped to Michigan in 1948; the others were paroled during 1943-50.

In 1966 the judge who had presided over the 1933 Norris trial admitted that he had information at the time that would have exonerated each of the accused. In 1976 Norris, the last defendant known to be still alive, was granted a pardon by Governor George Wallace of Alabama.

Scottsdale, Arizona, a city in Maricopa County, just east of Phoenix. Scottsdale is mainly a residential community with popular winter resorts. There is some light manufacturing.

Among the city's attractions is Rawhide, a replica of an 1880's Western town. The Scottsdale Center for the Arts offers music and dance events and art exhibits. Scottsdale's annual rodeo and Arabian horse show, both in February, are major events.

The population of Scottsdale has increased dramatically since the city's incorporation in 1951. Many new residents are attracted by the dry, sunny climate.

Population: 130,069.

Scotus, Duns. See DUNS SCOTUS, JOHN.

Scouring Rush. See HORSETAIL.

Scouts. See BOY SCOUTS; GIRL SCOUTS; GIRL GUIDES.

Scranton, Pennsylvania, the seat of Lackawanna County. It is on the Lack-

awanna River in the northeastern part of the state. Scranton is a commercial and industrial center with industries producing such products as plastics, heavy machinery, and tools. Steamtown National Historic Site, which includes a collection of steam locomotives and a museum, is here. Educational institutions include the University of Scranton and Marywood College.

Scranton was founded in 1786. Rich anthracite deposits in the area led to economic growth, which began in the 1840's when George and Seldon Scranton established several iron furnaces here. The city soon became a center for coal mining and iron production. Industrial decline began in the 1920's, severely depressing Scranton's economy. Recovery began after World War II when city leaders established an economic redevelopment plan that attracted new industries and strengthened old ones.

Population: 81,805.

Scranton, University of. See UNIVERSITIES AND COLLEGES (table).

Scrap Iron. See IRON AND STEEL, section "Steelmaking and Steel Products" (introduction).

Scrapie. See PRION, subtitle *Prion Diseases.*

Screech Owl. See OWL, subtitle *Kinds of Owls:* Typical Owls, and picture.

Screen Actors Guild. See ACTING (end of article).

Screw, in physics, a simple machine, usually consisting of a cylindrical body with one or more spiral ribs, or ridges, around it. (For the basic principles of simple machines, see MACHINE.) The screw is a modification of the inclined plane—it is the equivalent of an inclined plane wrapped around a cylin-

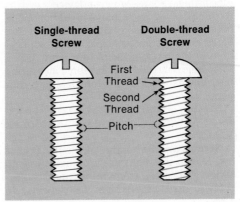

Single-thread Screw   Double-thread Screw

First Thread

Second Thread

Pitch

Screws and Bolts

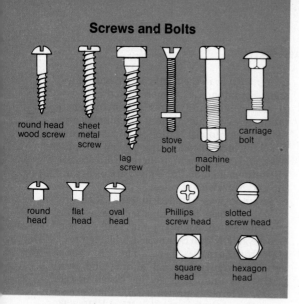

round head wood screw

sheet metal screw

lag screw

stove bolt

machine bolt

carriage bolt

round head

flat head

oval head

Phillips screw head

slotted screw head

square head

hexagon head

der. The ribs are called *threads*. A screw may have one thread or several wound around it many times.

The *pitch* of a screw is the distance between two adjacent corresponding points, such as between crest and crest, of the threads. On a single-thread screw, when a rotational force is applied through one complete turn, the screw advances, or moves along its long axis, a distance equal to the pitch. The smaller the pitch, the greater the holding or biting power the screw has, but the less it advances with each turn. Multiple-thread screws combine much of the holding power of a screw with small pitch and the relatively rapid advance of a screw with a large pitch. With a double thread, the screw advances a distance equal to twice the pitch for each full turn; triple-thread screws advance three times the pitch for each full turn.

Screws are useful in many applications. Screw fasteners include screws, bolts, and pipe fittings. Some conveyor devices, such as Archimedes' screws, move material along between the threads. Ship propellers are based on the screw principle. Other applications of the screw principle are screw jacks, some kinds of drill bits, and some measuring instruments, such as micrometers and calipers.

See also ARCHIMEDES' SCREW; CALIPER; JACK; MICROMETER; SCREWS AND BOLTS; VALVE.

Screws and Bolts, threaded metal fasteners. Screws and bolts are produced in many styles and sizes, from miniature headless screws, used in precision instruments, to

giant bolts, as much as 12 inches (30 cm) in diameter, used in bridges and other large structures. The terms *screw* and *bolt* are often used interchangeably. In this article, however—and in the screw and bolt industry generally—a bolt is a fastener secured by a *nut* (a small piece of metal with a threaded hole); a screw uses no nut.

Screws and bolts are formed from lengths of rod or wire. The threads are usually made by rolling the screw or bolt stock under pressure between a fixed and a moving die. In a less common method—machining—grooves are cut in the screw or bolt stock.

A screw or bolt of a given type is typically identified by indicating the diameter, thread spacing (threads per inch, for example), and length. Sizes of screws commonly used in the United States have been assigned whole numbers related to the gauge (size) of the rod or wire from which the screws are made. Numbers used for wood screws range from 0 (1/16 inch diameter) to 24 (3/8 inch diameter). Metric screws and bolts have sizes and thread spacing based on metric units and are not interchangeable with non-metric screws and bolts.

Self-tapping Screws

Self-tapping screws cut their own threads as they are driven into the material being fastened. Examples of this type include wood screws, sheet metal screws, and lag screws (which are used in wood and masonry). In practice, a pilot hole is usually drilled for these screws; the screws then cut threads as they are driven into the hole. Self-tapping screws have conical tips to enable the screws to start cutting the threads.

The most common head shapes for wood screws are flat, oval, and round. Some sheet metal screws are made in the same styles. The heads of flat-headed screws are designed to be countersunk (set flush with the surface of the wood). Oval heads are partially countersunk. In materials that are soft enough, a flat-headed screw can be driven with a screwdriver until the head has been forced into the material. In harder materials, a small conical hole must be drilled to accommodate the head of the screw.

Most wood and sheet metal screws have either a single straight slot or a small X-shaped slot. A screw with an X-shaped slot, called a Phillips screw, requires a special screwdriver. Because the shape of the slot tends to prevent the screwdriver from slipping, Phillips screws are often used on finished surfaces and with power-driven screwdrivers. Lag screws usually have square, unslotted heads and are turned with a wrench.

The threads on sheet metal screws are usually hardened and are deeper than those on wood screws because the sheet metal screws must cut metal. Wood and sheet metal screws are commonly made of brass or plated steel.

Bolts and Machine Screws

Bolts and machine screws, unlike self-tapping screws, do not have conical tips. Machine screws require threaded holes in the material into which they are turned; bolts use smooth-drilled holes, since they are secured with nuts. Among the common varieties of bolts are stove bolts, carriage bolts, and machine bolts.

Bolts and machine screws function best when tightened to a limit based on the properties of both the fastener and the material in which it is used. Proper tightening ensures that the maximum amount of force is exerted on the fastened parts without placing undue stress on either the parts or the fastener. A bolt can be tightened the desired amount by using a torque wrench, which indicates the amount of twisting force being applied.

Screwworm, the larva of a species of blowfly. Female screwworm flies lay their eggs in wounds of warm-blooded animals, especially cattle. When the screwworms hatch, they feed on the animal's flesh. Up to 400 screwworms may infest a single wound. Mass infestation with screwworms can kill an animal.

Full-grown screwworms, about ⅔ inch (17 mm) long, drop to the ground and enter the pupal stage. In about 8 to 60 days, depending on the temperature, the adult flies emerge from the pupal stage. In a few days, they mate and the female seeks out a wound in which to lay her eggs.

In the past, screwworms have caused millions of dollars of damage to livestock in the United States. Since the late 1950's, however, a program in which sterile male flies are reared in the laboratory and then released to mate has resulted in female flies laying unfertilized eggs. This program has been successful in controlling screwworms in most parts of the United States, but occasional outbreaks still occur.

The screwworm is the larva of *Cochliomyia hominivorax* of the order Diptera, family Calliphoridae.

Scriabin, skryȧ′byĭn, **Alexander** (1872-1915), a Russian composer and pianist. His experimentation in harmony, in *Poem of Ecstasy* (1908) and other works, in many ways foreshadowed the polytonality and atonality of 20th-century music. Scriabin was born in Moscow. He attended the Moscow Conservatory and taught there, 1898-1903. He made many concert tours, including one to the United States in 1906.

His other works include *Prometheus (The Poem of Fire)* (1911), which combines music and color through lights flashed on a screen as the work is played; 3 symphonies; 10 piano sonatas; and many smaller works for the piano.

Scribe, skrēb, **Augustin Eugène** (1791-1861), a French playwright. He was the chief exponent of the "well-made play"—a type of play, written according to a strict formula, in which all the complications of the plot are tidily resolved in the final outcome. Scribe's plays set the pattern for European drama during the first half of the 19th century. They owed their popularity and influence to their suspenseful plots, but they were superficial, with dull and unrealistic characters. *The Glass of Water* (1842), a historical comedy, is typical of the "well-made play."

Scribe wrote more than 400 dramatic works, most of them with the help of collaborators. *Adrienne Lecouvreur* (1849), based on the life of a famous 18th-century actress, was his most successful play. He wrote librettos for operas by Auber, Weber, Meyerbeer, Donizetti, Verdi, and Gounod. Scribe was born in Paris, where his first play was produced when he was 21.

Scribe. See HANDWRITING, subtitle *Development of Handwriting.*

Scrimshaw. See WHALE, illustration titled *Scrimshaw, or Whaleman's Art.*

Scrip, a document used to pay debts. It temporarily substitutes for money or whatever the payee is entitled to. The United States government issued scrip redeemable in land on many occasions as a means of paying its debts. During the depression of the 1930's some cities paid their employees in scrip that could only be redeemed for merchandise at specified establishments.

The federal government sometimes issues scrip, called Military Payment Certificates, to its armed forces in foreign countries as a means of limiting the circulation of United States currency abroad.

Scripps, skrĭps, **Edward Wyllis** (1854-1926), a United States newspaper publisher. He formed the first chain of daily newspapers in the United States with assistance from his brothers James and George. Scripps then founded the Newspaper Enterprise Association (NEA), the first newspaper syndicate operated in conjunction with a chain of daily papers. He also organized the United Press Association, now known as United Press International.

Scripps was born near Rushville, Illinois. With his brother James, he entered newspaper work in Detroit in 1873. After forming the newspaper chain in the 1880's, Scripps broke with James and took Milton McRae as a partner. Scripps formed the NEA in 1902 and in 1907 organized the United Press Association. A son, Robert Paine Scripps, and Roy W. Howard formed the Scripps-Howard newspaper chain in the 1920's.

Scripps College. See UNIVERSITIES AND COLLEGES (table).

Script. See HANDWRITING.

Scriptures. See BIBLE.

Scrub Oak. See OAK, subtitle *Types of Oaks:* The White Oak Group (Scrub Oak).

Scrub Pine. See PINE, subtitle *American Hard Pines:* Two-needled Hard Pines (Lodgepole Pine).

Scruple, a unit of weight. See WEIGHTS AND MEASURES, *Tables of Weights and Measures:* The U.S. Customary System (U.S. Weight).

Scuba Diving. See DIVING, subtitle *Diving with Breathing Apparatus:* Scuba Diving.

Scull. See ROWING, subtitle *Competitive Rowing.*

Sculpin, skŭl′pĭn, a family of mostly bottom-dwelling fish. Sculpins live mainly in cold seas, although some species live in fresh water. There are about 300 species. Sculpins have large, spiny heads, wide mouths, and large fins. They usually have no scales. Sculpins vary in length from 2 to 30 inches (5-75 cm), depending on the species. One of the largest sculpins is the crab-eating *cabezon,* found along the west coast of North America. Sculpins are sometimes used for food and many species are used by fishermen for bait.

Sculpins make up the family Cottidae. The cabezon is *Scorpaenichthys marmoratus.*

Sculpture, the art of shaping materials such as wood, stone, and metal into three-dimensional forms by carving, modeling, casting, and constructing. Sculpture also refers to the object produced, such as a statue or a monument.

Although sculpture may have specific uses —to commemorate an event or person, to decorate a building, or to inspire worship— it is primarily concerned with beauty and traditionally is classed as one of the fine arts. Ceramics, metalwork, and other crafts are related to sculpture in that they share some of sculpture's basic techniques. The objects they produce, however, while often of high artistic quality, are mainly utilitarian and generally are not considered sculpture.

Sculpture is often called a tangible art; it has a sense of reality. Unlike painting, sculpture may be appreciated through the sense of touch as well as the sense of sight. A sculpture has mass and weight, absorbs light and casts shadows, and occupies space. Without actually touching a sculpture a person may be aware of its texture.

Sculpture that may be viewed from all sides is called *freestanding* sculpture, or sculpture *in the round.* Sculpture that projects from or recesses into a flat surface is called *relief* sculpture. Recessed relief sculpture is sometimes called *intaglio.* (See RELIEF.)

Sculpture is an art that expresses in material form the visions and ideals of man. As in the other arts, sculpture reflects not only its creator's personal idea or feeling, but also the general character of the time and place in which he lived. Throughout history each civilization has emphasized different ideals —and sculptors have chosen forms which, to them, had the most meaning and beauty. Ancient Egyptian sculptors, for example, emphasized mass, or three-dimensional solidity, in their blocklike forms. Sculptors of the 17th-century Baroque period emphasized movement in their twisting open forms.

Until the 20th century, most sculpture was *representational,* or *figurative,* always having clearly recognizable objects or figures for subject matter. Many 20th-century sculptors

Venus de Milo (detail), *right*
marble, about 150 B.C.
6 feet 8¼ inches (204 cm) high
Louvre Museum

Carving. *Left,* standing on a scaffold, British sculptor Barbara Hepworth uses an iron mallet and chisel to carve her stone figures. *Right,* sculptor Henry Moore of Britain uses a wooden mallet and gouge to carve an abstract sculpture from wood.

have distorted the subject in their *abstract* works; others have made no direct reference to a subject in their *nonobjective* works.

Methods and Materials of Sculpture

Sculpture can be made of almost any material and fashioned by virtually any method. The materials are innumerable, for any solid material may be shaped into some kind of three-dimensional design. Stone, wood, clay, and bronze are the traditional materials of sculpture. Technological developments in the 20th century have added aluminum, steel, various plastics, polyester resins, and a wide range of other synthetic industrial materials as sculptural media. To sculpture's traditional methods of carving, modeling, and casting have been added welding, brazing, laminating, and other techniques.

The material that is available to the sculptor greatly influences his ideas. Sculptural forms are often determined by the material. Generally, stone and wood limit the sculpture to a compact design—one without large projections, for example. Clay allows more freedom of design and a greater opportunity to portray movement. Many excellent sculptors, however, have produced stone carvings that have the liveliness and spontaneity usually associated with the modeling technique.

Carving is a slow, painstaking technique. It consists of removing excess material until the desired form is achieved. The materials used usually are hard, heavy, and durable.

Stone is often considered the classic sculptural material. The tools and methods used in carving stone have changed little since ancient times. The type of stone determines the way it is to be carved. Soft stones, such as alabaster and sandstone, are often pounded to break down the surface and then *abraded,* or rubbed into shape, with files and rasps, and with other stones. Marble, limestone, and other hard stones are carved with a mallet and various pointed, flat, and toothed chisels. A bushhammer or boucharde, a flat-headed toothed hammer, is used to wear down the rough stone surface. Hand-held air hammers with various points are sometimes used by modern sculptors to rough in stone sculpture. The final carving is done with smaller chisels and with such abrasives as rifflers and pumice stone.

There are two principal methods of carving stone—the direct, or *taille directe,* and the indirect. A sculptor carving directly on the stone may make a preliminary model, or *maquette,* by carving roughly in plaster or by modeling in wax or clay. The maquette, usually a rough sketch, helps him visualize the projected sculpture. The general forms are then blocked out on the stone, and the large unwanted sections are removed until a rough image emerges. After refining the form with various chisels, the sculptor finishes the work with files and abrasive stones.

The indirect method, especially popular in the 19th century, is a mechanical process called *pointing*. From a large plaster model the design is transferred to a block of stone by a pointing machine that indicates the main projections of the sculpture and the depth at which the carving should be done. A professional stonecutter then carves the work, while the sculptor adds the finishing touches. Many 20th-century sculptors reject this method as unoriginal and work directly on the stone.

Wood is also a difficult medium. The sculptor must consider the natural contours of the wood and the direction of the grain, for he cannot cut against it. The kinds of wood used in sculpture range from such soft woods as pine, spruce, and cedar to such hard woods as walnut, oak, and ebony. The wood, regardless of what kind, must be well seasoned, for green (unseasoned) wood will crack and split after it dries.

In carving a block of wood, the sculptor first sketches his design directly on the wood. Large sections of waste material are then removed with a saw and ax. After roughing out the image, the sculptor does more detailed carving with various mallets, chisels, and gouges. Rasps and sandpaper are commonly used for finishing a wood sculpture. The completed sculpture is often waxed and polished to emphasize the grain.

Various other materials are suitable for carving. Ivory, horn, and bone have been used by sculptors since ancient times. Relief sculptures have been carved in brick to decorate buildings. Plaster of Paris is often cast into blocks to be carved. Soap, wax blocks, rigid polystyrene foam such as Styrofoam, and other plastics also may be carved.

Modeling is a building-up, or additive, process. A pliable material, such as clay, is built up, layer by layer, until the design or image is completed. Modeling gives the sculptor greater freedom and flexibility than does carving. Changes can be made easily as the sculptor's fingers push, pull, and smooth the material into shape.

Of the many materials that can be modeled, clay is used most often. Although any clay can be used for modeling, the sculptor ordinarily uses a clay that is pliable and will not break easily. Three kinds of clay are used most often. A moist, natural earth clay is used when the sculpture is to be fired, or made into terra-cotta. Natural earth clay is also used as a modeling material for one of the casting processes. Self-hardening clays

Art Reference Bureau

Preliminary Model and Finished Sculpture. *Top,* Michelangelo made a rough sketch in wax (the preliminary model, or *maquette*) to help him establish his ideas before cutting into the block of marble. *Bottom,* the finished carving, *Twilight,* is part of the Tomb of Lorenzo de' Medici in the Church of San Lorenzo, Florence.

Some Terms Used in Sculpture

This list contains some of the technical terms used in sculpture. Others are defined in the text.

Bronzing, the process of coloring a plaster cast in imitation of bronze.

Bust, a sculpture of the upper part of a person, usually the chest, shoulders, and head.

Caryatid, a sculptured female figure that takes the place of a column in architecture. Male figures so used are called *Atlantes*. See CARYATID.

Cast, a work of sculpture that has been produced from a mold. See CASTING.

Cast Stone, a mixture of cement or concrete and stone that is cast from a mold.

Colossal. See LIFE-SIZE, in this list.

Dry Lacquering, a technique in which a modeled clay form is covered with many layers of lacquer-soaked cloth. When the cloth is dry, the clay is removed and the hollow form is finished with gesso (a fine plaster) and painted.

Equestrian Statue, a sculpture of a person, usually a soldier or ruler, seated on a horse.

Figurine, a small modeled or carved figure; it may also be called a *statuette*.

Glyptic. See PLASTIC, in this list.

Heroic. See LIFE-SIZE, in this list.

Life-size, a term referring to a sculpture that is equal to the height of an average man. When the sculpture is slightly larger than life-size, it is called *heroic*. A sculpture more than twice life-size is called *colossal*.

Medium, in general, the material used by a sculptor, such as stone and clay; the term may also refer to the instrument or tool a sculptor uses. *Mixed media* is a combination of materials.

Mobile, a sculpture designed to move in balanced patterns. See MOBILE.

Mold, the shell-like impression into which a casting material is poured or pressed. A *piece mold* is made in several sections, or pieces; it can easily be pulled off the cast and used again. A *waste mold* has to be broken, or "wasted," to remove the cast.

Monumental, a term used for sculptures, whatever their size, that convey a sense of grandeur, stability, and timelessness.

Patina, the colors, usually green, formed on copper and bronze sculptures by the action of the atmosphere, or by applying chemicals. The term is sometimes used for the coloring, artificial or natural, found on any sculpture.

Piece Mold. See MOLD, in this list.

Pietà, a sculpture of the Virgin Mary mourning over the dead body of Jesus.

Plastic, a sculpture that was produced by the modeling technique; it is the opposite of *glyptic*, a sculpture that was produced by carving. Any material that can be shaped by modeling is also referred to as plastic.

Polychrome Sculpture, sculpture that is painted in many colors.

Repoussé, a term used in sculpture to describe a sculpture that has been hammered, or beaten, from a sheet of metal into the desired shape.

Slip, clay mixed with water until it has a creamy consistency. It is sometimes used in casting.

Stabile, an abstract metal, wire, and wood sculpture that remains motionless; the opposite of mobile.

Statuette. See FIGURINE, in this list.

Stele, a stone pillar, carved with reliefs and inscriptions, usually used to mark a site.

Stucco, a blend of gypsum or cement and pulverized marble used as a medium for relief sculpture.

Tooling, the decoration or finishing of bronze or metalwork.

Waste Mold. See MOLD, in this list.

---

dry hard without firing or baking. An oil-base clay that is permanently semi-soft is often used to create sculptures intended for casting.

Other modeling materials that can be used by the sculptor include plaster of Paris, papier-mâché, and wax. Most modeling materials will not retain a stretched shape without support. Before he begins to model, the sculptor first makes an *armature,* a framework arranged in the basic form of the proposed sculpture. Depending on the weight of the modeling material and the size of the sculpture, the armature may be made of wire, wood, pipe, or welded steel bars.

Casting. Objects modeled in clay or wax are often reproduced, or *cast,* in another material. Casting materials include bronze, lead, aluminum, stainless steel, plaster of Paris, concrete and cement, and various plastics. The metallic materials are used in liquid form, being poured into a mold. The nonmetallic materials may also be poured, or they may be used in paste form and packed, pressed, or otherwise applied to the mold surface.

Bronze is the traditional casting material. The two standard methods of casting bronze are the lost-wax technique and the sand-mold process. The *lost-wax technique,* or *cire perdue technique,* is quite complex. Two molds are used—an outer *investment* and an inner *core.* They are separated by a coating of wax the exact shape and thickness of the finished sculpture. The wax is melted and replaced by molten metal; to accomplish this, a complex plumbing system is built into the investment mold.

In the sand-mold process, a full-sized model of the sculpture is embedded in damp sand to form a mold. The model is removed and a core is fixed in place with pins. The space between the core and the outer mold is then filled with molten metal.

Lost-wax and hollow sand castings are costly to produce, and many sculptors have adopted simpler casting techniques. In the ceramic-shell method, a hollow wax sculpture is alternately dipped into a ceramic slurry mixture and sprinkled with a refractory sand called stucco. When the shell is about one-half inch (13 mm) thick, it is placed in a kiln to melt the wax. Molten metal is then poured through ducts into the hollow shell. When the metal cools and hardens, the shell is broken to reveal the cast sculpture. In another technique, the sculptor makes his original model in a polystyrene foam, such as Styrofoam, and presses it into a bed of sand. The molten metal vaporizes the foam and fills the mold. This method produces a solid cast and, because of the weight involved, is used only for small objects.

All of the casting methods described are also used in industry, and often the sculptor will have the casting done in an industrial foundry. In all of these methods, the casting as it comes from the mold is rough and must be *chased,* or finished, with hammer and chisel, files, and scrapers.

Constructing and Assembling are among the many names given to various sculptural techniques developed in the 20th century. These techniques differ from carving and modeling in that the sculpture is built up or constructed of separate pieces of material. Usually the sculptor is concerned more with space, movement, and abstract design than with mass and representational form.

The tools and materials a sculptor may use are diverse. Working directly in metal he may cut or hammer flat sheets of tin, lead, or copper into shape. Or he may weld or braze iron, steel, and nickel into shape with an oxyacetylene torch. Various plastics lend themselves to numerous techniques. Polystyrene foam, such as Styrofoam, and acrylics, such as Plexiglas, may be cut, carved, filed, and glued. Polyester resins may be used alone or combined with metal powder and cast in a mold. Alternate layers of fiberglass and polyester resin may be laminated in a mold.

Scrap material (such as discarded machine parts and automobile bumpers), fluorescent lights, and electric motors are among other materials the sculptor may use. No standard techniques for using these new sculptural materials have been devised.

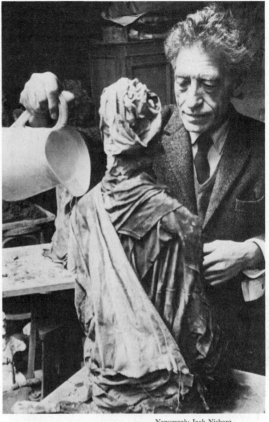

Newsweek: Jack Nisberg

Modeling. *Top,* Swiss-born sculptor Alberto Giacometti is shown in his Paris studio wetting a clay figure to keep the clay moist and pliable.

Constructing and Assembling. *Bottom,* David Smith, one of the first Americans to create direct metal welded sculpture, uses an oxyacetylene torch in his studio.

Dan Budnik

SCULPTURE

Prehistoric Sculpture

Prehistoric peoples modeled and carved animal and human figures, both in the round and in relief. Stone, ivory, and bone carvings may have been carried by hunters as magic charms. Reliefs carved on weapons and tools may have been marks of ownership. Especially common are carved ivory and stone statuettes of women whose features suggest fertility; these figures, called Venuses, have been found in a wide area of Europe. (See illustration, *Venus of Willendorf*.)

These sculptures date from the late Old Stone Age, from about 30,000 to 15,000 B.C., which is the era of the cave paintings. In the New Stone Age, about 9000 to 3000 B.C., Neolithic man continued to make sculpture in stone, ivory, and clay, and began to work with copper.

Sculpture in the Ancient World

Egypt. Sculpture in ancient Egypt was dominated by a religion that stressed a belief in life after death. Both relief and freestanding sculpture played a prominent part in burial customs. Each tomb of an important person contained statuettes of servants at various tasks and reliefs showing scenes of the dead person's life. It was believed that the figures and reliefs, through magical

means, would serve the deceased in the afterlife. Each tomb also contained portrait sculptures of the deceased to house the spirit or soul of the dead person should the mummy be destroyed.

Portrait sculpture came to a peak in the Old Kingdom period (about 2686-2181 B.C.). Stone was the major medium, and Egyptian sculptors created standing and seated figures with highly polished surfaces. The statues have lifelike facial features and idealized bodies in a rigid pose—the head faces forward and the arms are set close to the body. (See illustration, *Mycerinus and His Queen*.) The Sphinx of Giza, carved in the 26th century B.C., is thought to be a portrait sculpture; although it has the body of a lion, its head is that of a man, probably Pharaoh Khafre. (See SPHINX.)

By the New Kingdom (about 1570-1085 B.C.) sculpture had become less formal and more individualistic. Colossal stone figures of kings were placed at the entrances to temples. (For picture, see ASWAN DAM.) Other sculptures, such as the portrait bust of Queen Nefertiti, are more personal in style and use color as an effective element. (For picture, see NEFERTITI.) Although the Egyptians knew of bronze they rarely used it as a sculptural medium.

Mesopotamia. Several civilizations developed in the region of the Tigris and Euphrates rivers. The Sumerians established a civilization before 3500 B.C. and developed a style of art that influenced successive Mesopotamian cultures. Sumerian sculptors carved small freestanding statues of men and women that were placed in temples to offer prayers to the gods. Large expressive eyes and beak noses dominate this type of Sumerian statuette.

Sculptors of the Akkadian period (about 2400-2200 B.C.) introduced a more naturalistic concept of the human figure. A masterly sense of composition can be seen in the few surviving Akkadian reliefs, such as the Stele of Naram-Sin. The barbaric Guti overthrew the Akkadians, but the city of Lagash (modern Telloh) became a center of art under its ruler Gudea. The many surviving statues of Gudea, most of them carved out of diorite, an extremely hard stone, are remarkable for their rounded, polished surfaces.

Sculpture in the round was less common at the height of Assyrian rule (about 884-612 B.C.). The Assyrians skillfully carved reliefs of battles, hunts, and ceremonies on great stone slabs to decorate the palace walls. Colossal human-headed winged bulls or lions guarded the entrances to Assyrian pal-

Left to right:
Mycerinus and His Queen
2599-2571 B.C., Egyptian
Old Kingdom, 4th Dynasty;
slate, 4 feet 6½ inches
(138 cm) high
Museum of Fine Arts, Boston

Venus of Willendorf
about 21,000 B.C., Prehistoric;
limestone, 4½ inches (11.4 cm) high
Naturhistorisches Museum, Vienna

The Adorer
2700-2600 B.C., Sumerian;
alabaster, 9 inches (22.9 cm) high
The University Museum
University of Pennsylvania

Top to bottom:
Lion from the Palace of Ishtar
6th century B.C., Babylonian;
glazed terra-cotta bricks
3 feet 5 inches (104.1 cm) high
7 feet 6 inches (228.6 cm) long
Museum of Art
Rhode Island School of Design

Seated Man
8th century B.C., Greek Geometric;
bronze, 2⅞ inches (7.3 cm) high
The Walters Art Gallery, Baltimore

Statuette of Snake Goddess
16th century B.C., Minoan;
ivory and gold, 6½ inches (16.5 cm) high
Museum of Fine Arts, Boston
Gift of Mrs. W. Scott Fitz

aces. The bulls were carved in extremely high relief and could be seen from three sides. They were given five legs so that when the sculpture was viewed directly from the side, four legs were seen; when it was viewed directly from the front, two legs were seen. (See ASSYRIA, picture.)

Sculptors in the second Babylonian (or Chaldean) empire (about 612-539 B.C.) introduced the brick relief. The walls of palaces and gates, such as the Ishtar Gate, were decorated with brick relief animals, glazed in brilliant colors.

When the Persians conquered Babylon in 539 B.C. they borrowed many elements of Mesopotamian sculpture. The reliefs and winged bulls of Persepolis, for example, resemble those of Assyria. The palace of Darius at Susa was decorated with glazed brick reliefs more elaborate than those in Mesopotamia. Other influences came from eastern Iran and from the Scythians, and eventually Persian sculpture took on an opulence suggestive of central and eastern Asia. Persian sculpture ranged from huge stone cliff carvings to delicate work on jewelry. It reached its peak in the Sassanid period, 226-641 A.D.

It was the Persian decorative style, with its intertwining motifs, that led to the Islamic low-relief stone and stucco architectural sculpture. The Persians were adept also in the design and cutting of cylinder seals, a miniature low-relief art form that had flourished in all the Mesopotamian lands from earliest Sumeria to the end of the second Babylonian empire.

Crete and Mycenae. About 1500 B.C. the Minoan civilization was flourishing on Crete in the eastern Mediterranean. The Minoans

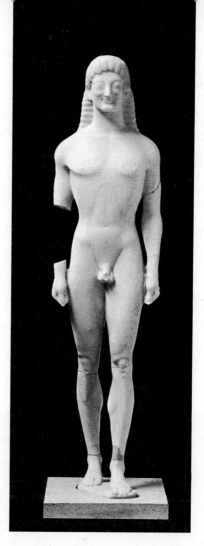

Top to bottom:
Kouros from Tenea
about 550 B.C., Greek Archaic;
Parian marble, 5 feet (1.5 m) high
Staatliche Antikensammlungen und Glyptothek
Munich

Zeus from Artemision
about 460 B.C., Greek Classic;
bronze, 6 feet 10 inches (2 m) high
National Archaeological Museum, Athens

excelled in modeling and carving statuettes and small reliefs. Numerous figurines of goddesses and athletes in terra-cotta, bronze, and ivory have been found. The female figures—perhaps priestesses—usually hold snakes and are shown wearing tight-waisted, long flounced skirts.

About 1400 B.C. the center of Aegean civilization shifted from Crete to the fortified city of Mycenae in southern Greece. Little sculpture has been found among its relics. The Lion Gate, with two lions carved in high relief, is the earliest known example of monumental sculpture in Greece.

Classical Sculpture

Greece. Early Greek sculpture was mainly religious. Small bronze statuettes of gods and animals are among the many works known from the Geometric Period (about 11th to eighth century B.C.). These statuettes, such as *Seated Man,* have elongated, almost abstract stylization and show the barest essentials of natural form. Life-size stone sculpture became common in the Archaic Period (about seventh and sixth centuries). Some of the earliest statues are of young men, or *kouroi.* The nude kouroi, with arms and hands at sides and left foot slightly forward, are similar to the rigidly posed Egyptian sculpture of the Old Kingdom. Statues of clothed young women, or *korai,* have the same frontal pose. Many of these kouroi and korai have the corners of the mouth turned up in a fixed expression known as the Archaic smile.

Greek sculpture reached its full development in the fifth century B.C. Relief sculptures and freestanding figures adorned temples and other public places.

The first half of the century was a transi-

tional period. Physical proportions were rendered more naturally but the pose remained stiff, as in the bronze *Charioteer of Delphi*. By mid-century Myron captured the movement of athletes in his *Discobolus* (The Discus Thrower). (See DISCUS, picture.) The second half of the fifth century, often called the Golden Age, was dominated by the sculptors Phidias and Polyclitus. Both were concerned with ideal forms and monumental dignity; both sculpted secular as well as religious works. The most famous sculptor of his day, Phidias was admired especially for his colossal statues *Athena* and *Zeus*. Polyclitus was known for his theories, or *canons,* of ideal proportion based on parts of the body. His *Doryphorus* (Spearbearer), with its balanced, harmonious proportions, was his most famous and influential work.

In the fourth century B.C. there was no longer a demand for monumental religious sculpture. Idealized proportions were al-

tered and statues were more naturalistic. Praxiteles' *Hermes* represents the softer modeling and gracefulness of fourth-century sculpture. (See HERMES, picture.) Scopas expressed vigor and animation in many of his works. Lysippus introduced taller, slimmer figures and more movement.

The expressive realistic sculpture made between the death of Alexander the Great in 323 B.C. and the Roman conquest of Greece in 146 B.C. is called *Hellenistic*. Strong emotion dramatically depicted and restless movement are characteristics of such well-known Hellenistic works as the *Nike* (or *Winged Victory*) *of Samothrace* and the *Laocoön* group. (For pictures, see NIKE; LAOCOÖN.) The famous *Venus de Milo,* with her graceful, sensuous body and ideal classic face is considered a late Hellenistic work. Hellenistic sculptors introduced genre (everyday life) figures and portraiture. Best known are the figurines from Tanagra, a

town in Boeotia, and those from Myrina in Asia Minor.

Etruria and Rome. The earliest known major civilization on Italian soil flourished in Etruria. Etruscan sculptors worked mainly in terra-cotta and bronze. Realism and great technical skill mark Etruscan sculpture, such as the sarcophagus (coffin) from Cerveteri and the Apollo of Veii. (For picture, see TERRA-COTTA.)

The Romans took hundreds of Greek statues to Rome and made numerous copies of Greek originals. Roman sculptors on their own developed portrait sculpture and the historical relief. Many sculptors combined the idealistic and realistic elements of earlier Greek sculpture. Naturalism, however, is more characteristic of Roman portraits. Historical reliefs, carved on triumphal arches and commemorative columns, depicted specific events with detailed figures and backgrounds.

Left to right:
Two Women Talking
3rd century B.C., Greek Hellenistic;
painted terra-cotta, 7¼ inches (18.4 cm) high
The British Museum, London

Bust of Emperor Philip the Arabian
244-249 A.D., Roman portraiture;
marble, 2 feet 4 inches (71.1 cm) high
Chiaramonti Musuem, The Vatican

Arch of Constantine
315 A.D., Roman relief;
stone, detail upper left corner
Scala
Sculpture located in Rome

Early Christian and Byzantine Sculpture

The Biblical prohibition of graven images caused the decline of large sculpture in the round. One of the few known religious freestanding sculptures produced by the early Christians is *The Good Shepherd*. The Roman emperors and high government officals, however, continued having themselves portrayed in busts and statues. Elaborately carved marble sarcophagi are the most numerous examples of early Christian sculpture. Reliefs of Biblical scenes decorated the sarcophagus of Junius Bassus and others.

Large freestanding sculpture was also rare in the Byzantine Empire. Byzantine sculpture is best known through the sarcophagi and through the ivory carving that decorated furniture, jewelry, boxes, and book covers, although independent ivory relief panels, especially those used as altar pieces, are common.

See also BYZANTINE ART.

Sculpture in Primitive Societies

For untold generations the art of sculpture flourished among the peoples of Africa, the Americas, and the South Pacific Islands. African sculpture—fetish figures, statues of kings, and ceremonial masks—was closely linked to religion and court life. Natural forms were stylized and simplified in line, plane, and mass to emphasize their significant characteristics. The bronzes of the West African kingdoms of Ife and Benin, cast by the lost-wax method, are ranked among the great achievements of world art.

The Mayas and Toltecs of Mexico and Central America excelled in architecture,

and architectural sculpture was important. (See MEXICO, illustration *Toltec Pillars*.) Reliefs were either carved in stone or modeled in stucco on the facades of temples. Large freestanding sculptures, such as the gigantic Olmec basalt heads, were rare. (For pictures, see OLMEC INDIANS.) Countless statuettes were modeled and carved and may have been used in funeral and sacrificial rites. With the Incas and other cultures of the South American west coast, the art of sculpture played its greatest part in the arts of pottery and metalwork. Gold and silver were cast as well as beaten and hammered into shape. The Mochica culture excelled in modeling realistic portrait jugs or vases.

The Maori of New Zealand developed one of the most elaborate wood-carving styles in the South Pacific. Gables, doors, and window frames were covered with intricately carved designs. The peoples of Polynesia used wood and shells in their masks and figurines for ceremonies and dances. The peoples of Easter Island carved colossal stone heads; their purpose and significance are unknown. (For picture, see EASTER IS-LAND.)

The Indians of North America carved impressive totem poles and masks in wood, and practiced a wide range of minor sculpture in ivory, clay, and whalebone. Their small carved pipes, bannerstones, and birdstones are carved realistically and are often decorated with geometric designs. (Bannerstones and birdstones are weights used on throwing sticks.) The Eskimos created styles of their own; for many years their realistic

Left to right:
The Good Shepherd
3rd century A.D., early Christian; stone, 3 feet 3 inches (99 cm) high (with base)
Lateran Museum, The Vatican

Portrait Jug
400-700 A.D., Pre-Columbian, Peru; terra-cotta, 14 inches (35.5 cm) high
The Art Institute of Chicago
Buckingham Fund

Oni, King of Ife
12th-14th centuries, West African; bronze, 14½ inches (36.8 cm) high
The British Museum, London

small carvings in ivory, traded to the white man, have been widely known and favored. (See ESKIMO; TOTEM.)

Eastern Sculpture

India and Southeast Asia. The development of early Indian sculpture is linked with Buddhism. Reliefs of scenes of Buddha's life decorated many shrines. The earliest known freestanding sculptures of Buddha as a human being were made in Gandhara (a region now shared by India and Afghanistan) during the first several centuries A.D. Gandharan sculptors established the two most common types of Buddha images—the standing, or teaching, Buddha, and the seated cross-legged, or meditating, Buddha. Sculptors in the Gupta period (about 320-600) perfected the two Buddha images and set the standards for all later Buddhist sculpture.

The revival of Hinduism at the end of the sixth century ushered in a great era of temple building and sculptural decoration. While Buddhist sculpture was marked by serenity and repose, Hindu sculpture is marked by vitality and movement. Hindu sculptors glorified and often sensuously portrayed the body. Shiva, or Siva, represented as Lord of the Dance, was a favorite subject. Hindu sculptors worked in bronze, using the lost-wax method, as well as in stone.

Buddhism and its sculpture spread throughout Southeast Asia. In Cambodia, Hinduism and Buddhism flourished side by side. The sculptures of the shrines at Angkor Wat and Angkor Thom have a light, youthful quality, sometimes decorative, sometimes spiritual, that distinguishes them from other Asian religious sculpture. Siam (Thailand) and the Indonesian island of Java added notable contributions to Eastern Buddhist sculpture.

China. The cast bronze vessels and jade carvings made during the Shang Dynasty (about 1523-1028 B.C.) and the Chou Dynasty (about 1028-222 B.C.) are considered the beginnings of Chinese art. (See ORIENTAL ART, pictures titled *Chinese Bronze* and *Chinese Jade*.) These objects, used in ceremonies and rituals, often had low-relief decorations of fantastic dragons. Terra-cotta figures to be placed in tombs, small bronze animals, and jade pieces both in the round and in relief were the principal sculptures made in the Han Dynasty (about 206 B.C.-220 A.D.). Large freestanding sculptures of

the human figure were introduced with Buddhism in the fourth century.

Buddhist sculpture developed and flourished during the Tang Dynasty (618-907), often called the Golden Age of Chinese art. Stone became an important medium and the dried-lacquer technique was introduced. Colossal stone figures of men and animals guarding the entrances to tombs and palaces were made during the Sung Dynasty (960-1279) and the Yuan Dynasty (1279-1368). The art of sculpture began its decline in the 15th and 16th centuries.

Japan. The earliest Japanese sculptures are primitive works that date from the period known as Jomon (about 3000-300 B.C.). In the fourth and fifth centuries A.D. sculptors produced small clay figures, called *Haniwa*, that were placed outside burial mounds. (For an example, see ORIENTAL ART, picture titled *Japanese Terra-cotta*.) Large sculpture in the round was introduced to Japan with Buddhism in the sixth century. The lack of workable stone made bronze and wood the favored medium of Japanese sculptors. The dry lacquering technique was also used.

In the Kamakura era (12th-14th centuries)

Left to right:
Nataraja—Dancing Siva
about 12th century, India, Hindu;
bronze, 3 feet 10½ inches (118.1 cm) high
Museum of Art
Rhode Island School of Design

Bust of Buddha
about 8th-10th century, China,
Tang or Liao Dynasty;
dry lacquer, 14½ inches (36.8 cm) high
Seattle Art Museum
Eugene Fuller Memorial Collection

Guardian Figure
1185-1392, Japan, Kamakura era;
wood, 7 feet 8 inches (2.3 m) high
Freer Gallery of Art, Washington, D.C.

an influential school of wood carving developed. Unkei and Kaikei are among the sculptors who were especially skilled in following the grain of the wood and in incorporating knife marks in the designs they carved. Sculptors of the Kamakura era were also skilled in bronze work. The colossal *Daibutsu* ("Great Buddha") of the city of Kamakura was cast in the mid-13th century. (For picture, see BUDDHA.) Japanese sculpture, like Chinese and Indian sculpture, declined after the 15th century.

Western Sculpture in the Middle Ages

From about the sixth century until the rise of Romanesque art in the 11th century, few large-scale sculptures were produced. In the British Isles, especially Ireland, elaborately carved tall stone crosses were erected. During the Viking era Scandinavians excelled in wood carving. Patterns of intertwining animal figures decorated their long ships, chariots, sleighs, and other articles in a style related to that of Ireland and Saxon Britain.

The Romanesque Period brought a revival of large-scale stone sculpture to western Europe. This revival was caused largely by the widespread construction of churches and cathedrals. In these structures sculpture formed an essential, but subordinate, part of the architectural design. Most Romanesque sculpture is found above and around doorways and on column capitals. Human figures, animals, and plant motifs—many twisted and elongated to fit the architectural frame—project in high relief. Although Romanesque sculpture had many regional variations, common qualities include intense expression and the use of fantastic demons. The Last Judgment was the subject most often carved in the tympanum, the semicircular area over the main doors of a church.

In Italy and southern France, where the traditions of ancient Roman art were strong, sculpture was more massive and independent of the architecture than in northern France and England. Bronze was a favored medium in Germany. The doors of the cathedral at Hildesheim and the 11th-century Werden Crucifix are typical examples of German Romanesque sculpture.

The Romanesque period also brought the beginnings of individual artistic styles. Gis-

lebertus carved the imaginative figures on the Cathedral of St. Lazare in Autun, Burgundy. Benedetto Antelami carved the west facade of the cathedral at Fidenza, near Parma, Italy.

Gothic Sculpture, like Gothic architecture, developed from the Romanesque and began in northern France in the 13th century. Sculpture remained an integral part of architecture, but the exaggerated movement of Romanesque figures gave way to calm, graceful, and often idealized figures of kings and saints. Less dignified figures, such as grotesque monkeys and devils, are found in unexpected places on a Gothic cathedral. Gargoyles, open-mouthed heads of fantastic animals, served as waterspouts. (For picture, see GARGOYLE.)

In the 14th century the smiling Virgin became a favorite subject, and small free-standing devotional statues were carved in stone, wood, and ivory. Another kind of figure sculpture, effigies on tombs, developed in the 14th century. Many Gothic figure sculptures were painted in natural colors.

Left:
The Last Judgment
by Gislebertus
12th-century Romanesque
Cathedral of St. Lazare, Autun;
stone, detail of tympanum
Art Reference Bureau

Right:
Madonna and Child
1385-90, French Gothic;
limestone, with traces of paint
4 feet 5 inches (134.6 cm) high
The Cleveland Museum of Art
Purchase from the J. H. Wade Fund

The Dutch sculptor Claus Sluter, working in France in the late 14th century, introduced a new liveliness and realistic detail to sculpture. Naturalism dominated 15th-century sculpture, especially in Germany. Tilman Riemenschneider and Adam Kraft are among the German sculptors whose carvings foreshadow the Renaissance.

In Italy, sculptors combined Gothic and Classical elements in their works. Nicola Pisano and his son Giovanni, Lorenzo Maitani, and Andrea Pisano are among the 13th- and 14th-century sculptors whose works reflect the transition from Gothic to Renaissance styles.

Renaissance Sculpture

The 15th century brought a revival of interest in the art and philosophy of ancient Greece and Rome. During the Renaissance the importance of the individual was emphasized. Interest in man—in his character as well as in his physique—led to broad stylistic changes in sculpture. Medieval sculptures had always been placed against a wall or in a niche as part of a building. Renaissance sculptors freed statues from this architectural background and produced the first life-size freestanding sculptures in Europe since Roman times.

Sculpture became a major form of artistic expression. Sculptors were commissioned to design equestrian monuments and fountains to decorate city squares. They reintroduced the portrait bust. The individual sculptor gained recognition as an artist, in contrast to the medieval sculptor who was largely an unknown craftsman.

Italy. Florence was the center of early Renaissance sculpture. Lorenzo Ghiberti combined graceful Gothic elements with elaborate perspective in his bronze doors for the Baptistery at Florence. The della Robbia family introduced glazed and polychromed terra-cotta sculpture. Jacopo della Quercia of Sienna, in his use of simplified forms, developed a powerful style that may have influenced Michelangelo.

It was Donatello, however, who was the

outstanding 15th-century sculptor. He revived the Greek concept of the beauty of the nude male figure in his bronze *David*. His *Gattamelata Monument*, in Padua, set the style for future equestrian statues.

Antonio Pollaiuolo and Andrea del Verrocchio were among the Renaissance masters who were painters and goldsmiths as well as sculptors. Verrocchio's equestrian *Bartolommeo Colleoni* in Venice is imbued with strength and vigor. In *Hercules and Antaeus* Pollaiuolo introduced melodramatic action into sculpture. Desiderio da Settignano, Donatello's follower, carved graceful, appealing portrait busts.

Michelangelo dominated 16th-century, or High Renaissance, sculpture. With immense technical skill, he expressed power, energy, and emotion through the human figure. His monumental *David*, an early work, reveals his mastery of anatomy. *Night, Day, Dawn,* and *Twilight*—reclining figures on the Medici tombs—express power and contained movement.

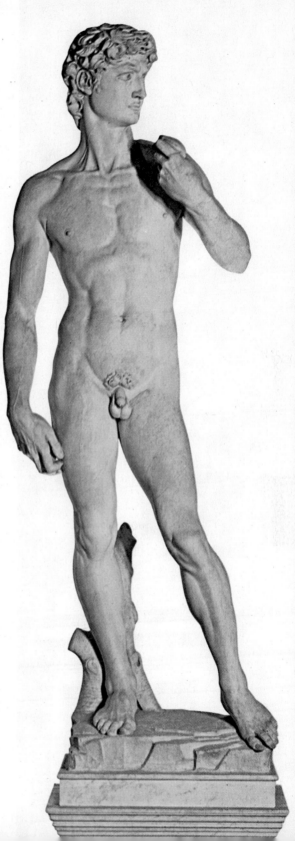

Left:
Gattamelata Monument
by Donatello
about 1450, early Renaissance;
bronze, about 11½ feet (3.5 m) high
Art Reference Bureau
Sculpture located in Padua

Right:
David
by Michelangelo
1501-03, High Renaissance;
marble, 13 feet 5 inches (4 m) high
Art Reference Bureau
Accademia, Florence

Left:
Rape of the Sabine Women
by Giovanni da Bologna
1579-83, Mannerist;
marble, 13 feet 5 inches (4 m) high
Art Reference Bureau
Loggia dei Lanzi, Florence

Right:
The Ecstasy of St. Theresa
by Giovanni Lorenzo Bernini
1645-52, Baroque;
marble; metal rays, life-size figures
Art Reference Bureau
Santa Maria della Vittoria, Rome

Restless movement, a tendency to exaggerate, and elegance were the main features of *Mannerism*, a style that developed in late-16th-century Renaissance sculpture. Benvenuto Cellini, Giovanni da Bologna, and Adrien de Vries are among the Mannerist sculptors whose works inspired the 17th-century Baroque sculptors.

Other Countries gradually adopted Italian Renaissance style. Jean Goujon and Germain Pilon were the outstanding French sculptors. In Germany the intermingling of Gothic and Renaissance styles can be seen in the works of Veit Stoss. Peter Vischer the Elder and his sons produced sculpture that is marked by simplicity and classical details. The leading Spanish sculptor, Alonso Berruguete, used Italian forms and ideas in a more animated, even agitated manner that came to be a mark of the Baroque style.

Baroque and Rococo Sculpture

Rome replaced Florence as the artistic center of Italy in the 17th century. Roman sculpture in this period was dominated by the sculptor and architect Giovanni Lorenzo Bernini. The characteristic features of Baroque style—the use of deep indentations to create strong contrasts of light and shade, dramatic movement, and a naturalistic quality—are found in Bernini's *Ecstasy of St. Theresa* and *Louis XIV*. Alessandro Algardi's works were more restrained.

Bernini influenced the France of Louis XIV. Pierre Puget and Antoine Coysevox adapted the Baroque style to convey the pomp and authority of the court. François Girardon's statues in the Versailles gardens are less dramatic. The Baroque style spread to Germany and Austria, where an enormous amount of sculpture decorated palaces and churches. Spanish sculpture was mainly

religious; altars and statues of saints were carved in wood and, in many instances, painted in vivid colors. Holland, England, and other Protestant countries produced little sculpture during this period.

The Rococo style developed from the Baroque in the 18th century and was centered in France. Graceful and decorative, Rococo sculpture emphasized elegance and reflected the frivolous character of the French court. Étienne Maurice Falconet, Jean Baptiste Pigalle, and Clodion produced many charming, decorative figures. Jean Antoine Houdon, hardly touched by Rococo influence, was one of the greatest portrait sculptors of all time. Emphasizing their most characteristic traits, Houdon brought out the humanity of his subjects.

Sculpture in the 19th Century

Sculpture as a major art form began to decline and lose prestige in the 19th century. After the French Revolution and the Industrial Revolution, fewer sculptures were commissioned. The sculptor either created forms

that pleased himself or he created sculpture he thought the public would buy. The sculptors who imitated past styles were most successful financially. As a result much 19th-century sculpture was academic and uncreative.

Europe. Many of the stylistic movements of painting and the other arts have their counterparts in sculpture. The discovery of ancient Greek and Roman statues in the late 18th century and dislike of the frivolity of the Rococo style brought about Neoclassicism, a revival of classical style. Antonio Canova of Italy, John Flaxman of England, and Bertel Thorvaldsen of Denmark were leading exponents of Neoclassic sculpture. Most of their works were imitative and tended to have a cold and artificial effect.

Romanticism in sculpture is marked by a return to the movement found in the Baroque style and to a new realism and emotionalism. The French sculptor François Rude, for example, rejected the Roman style of dress favored by the Neoclassic sculptors

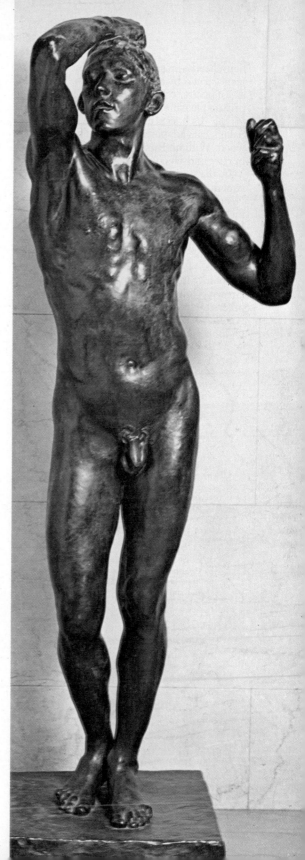

Left to right:
Madame de Serilly
by Jean Antoine Houdon in 1782
marble, 2 feet ½ inch (62.2 cm) high
The Wallace Collection, London

Marshal Ney
by François Rude in 1853
French Romantic
bronze, 8 feet 9 inches (2.6 m) high
Jean Roubier
Sculpture located in Paris

The Age of Bronze
by Auguste Rodin in 1877
bronze, 5 feet 11 inches (1.8 m) high
The Minneapolis Institute of Arts

and used contemporary dress in his *Marshal Ney*. Antoine Louis Barye's sculptures of animals convey energy and violence. Jean Baptiste Carpeaux combined complex movement with realistic details in *The Dance,* on the facade of the Paris Opera.

Toward the end of the century Auguste Rodin tried to free sculpture from its academic formality and make it the expression of the individual artist. His distortions, slurred details, and emphasis on emotions formed the bridge between the sculpture of the past and the sculpture of the 20th century. Rodin's works range in style from the naturalistic *The Age of Bronze* to the distorted *Balzac*.

An interesting feature of 19th-century sculpture is the work of a number of artists who were successful painters. Honoré Daumier and Edgar Degas are among those painters who produced many small-scale expressive sculptures.

United States. America's earliest sculptures —gravestones, weathervanes, and ship figureheads—were ritual or functional objects carved by artisan craftsmen. Sculpture as a fine art, created primarily for public or private pleasure, began to develop at the end of the 18th century. Samuel McIntire of Salem carved portrait busts and reliefs in wood. William Rush of Philadelphia worked in clay and wood.

In the early decades of the 19th century America's sculptors discovered Europe's Neoclassic movement. Most of them, including Horatio Greenough and Hiram Powers, went to Italy to study. Thomas Crawford used Neoclassic elements in his sculptural decorations of the United States Capitol.

Soon after mid-century Henry Kirke Brown, John Quincy Adams Ward, and others added a greater realism to sculpture. Another realistic trend is found in the works of John Rogers. His small sculpture groups depicting literary themes, Civil War subjects, and genre (everyday life) scenes were highly popular.

William Rimmer was one of the most talented but least appreciated sculptors of the period. His *The Falling Gladiator* reveals a sense of movement and expressive power unique in 19th-century American sculpture.

Sculpture of the last quarter of the century, often called the American Renaissance, was dominated by Augustus Saint-Gaudens. Other prominent sculptors of the period were Daniel Chester French, Frederick MacMonnies, and Lorado Taft.

Sculpture in the 20th Century

Complexity, experimentation, and diversity mark the sculpture of the 20th century. In the early years of the century many French sculptors rejected the rough surfaces and expressive movement in Rodin's works.

Left to right:
Ruth Mather Gravestone
about 1791, early American;
sandstone, 2 feet 5½ inches (74.9 cm) high
Windsor Historical Society, Windsor, Connecticut

The Greek Slave
by Hiram Powers in 1843
Neoclassic American
marble, 5 feet 2 inches (157.4 cm) high
The Corcoran Gallery of Art, Washington, D.C.

Woman Doing Her Hair
by Alexander Archipenko in 1916.
Cubist
terra-cotta, 22 inches (55.8 cm) high
Düsseldorf Kunstmuseum

Bird in Space
by Constantin Brancusi in 1925
polished bronze 4 feet 1⅔ inches
(126.1 cm) high
Philadelphia Museum of Art
Louise and Walter Arensberg Collection

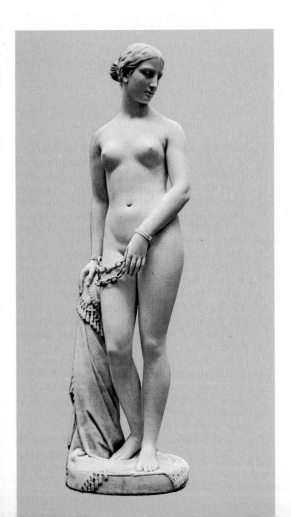

Antoine Bourdelle and Aristide Maillol turned to the classical ideal of serene beauty. The discovery of African art influenced many sculptors to depart from traditional concepts and to experiment with new ways of using traditional materials.

Various movements in painting, such as Cubism, Futurism, and Expressionism, also influenced sculpture. Raymond Duchamp-Villon, Alexander Archipenko, and Henri Laurens are among the Cubist sculptors; like the Cubist painters, they emphasized planes and geometric shapes. The influence of Cubism can be seen in the early works of Jacques Lipchitz and Ossip Zadkine. Related to Cubism in their simplification of form are the near-abstract works of Constantin Brancusi. Futurist sculptors, such as Umberto Boccioni, were concerned with the energy of movement and how it could be rendered in sculpture. The Expressionist

Wilhelm Lehmbruck modeled slender, elongated figures that combine vitality with a serene spiritual quality. Ernst Barlach continued the German tradition of wood carving and used blocklike masses in his Expressionist works. In England Jacob Epstein carved in the Expressionist tradition, although he is most famous for his later, realistic bronze portraits.

Between World Wars. The Russian-born brothers Antoine Pevsner and Naum Gabo led the Constructivist movement. Their works represent a complete break with traditional materials and techniques. Using transparent plastic, stretched wire, and other materials, they strove for a new formal beauty in their geometric abstract works. Another Constructivist, the Hungarian László Moholy-Nagy, foreshadowed the Kinetic and Luminist sculpture of the 1960's in his *Light-Space Modulator*.

Dadaism rejected all formal discipline in sculpture. Marcel Duchamp is said to have established Ready-Mades, or Found Objects (discarded everyday objects), as the sculpture of Dada. Kurt Schwitters and other Dadaists often combined many found objects, and their constructions are like three-dimensional collages. This technique was revived in the 1960's under the name Assemblage.

Surrealism's influence on sculpture can be seen in Jean Arp's organic shapes and in many of Alberto Giacometti's works. Henry Moore's simplified forms usually retain a suggestion of the human figure. His many reclining figures, with pierced openings and scooped-out hollows, convey a feeling of mass, repose, and monumental power. Barbara Hepworth's free forms suggest the unity of form and material found in living organisms.

In the 1930's the Spaniard Julio González introduced welding to sculpture and established wrought iron as a medium. His countryman Pablo Picasso also created welded sculptures, as well as Cubist and Dadaist works.

Alexander Calder, through his creation of the mobile, was one of the few Americans to

Left:
Light-Space Modulator
by László Moholy-Nagy
1923-30, Constructivist
chrome-plated metal, plastic
(set on a motorized base)
4 feet 11½ inches (1.51 m) high
Busch-Reisinger Museum, Harvard University
Gift of Mrs. Sibyl Moholy-Nagy

Below:
Recumbent Figure
by Henry Moore in 1938
stone, 4 feet 6 inches (1.37 m) high
The Tate Gallery, London

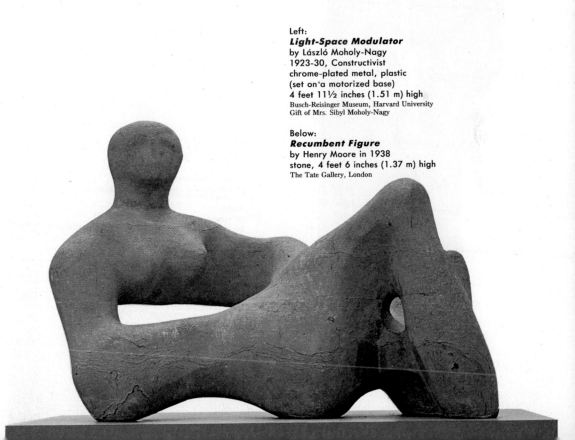

gain international attention. (For an illustration of one of his mobiles, see CALDER, ALEXANDER.)

Most American sculptors in the first half of the 20th century were conservative and their works academic. Realism dominated the works of George Grey Barnard, Gutzon Borglum, and Malvina Hoffman. William Zorach and John B. Flannagan led a revival of direct stone carving. Prominent wood carvers included Robert Laurent and Chaim Gross. Important European sculptors who settled in the United States included Alexander Archipenko, Jacques Lipchitz, and José de Creeft. Their influence was rather limited at first.

Sculpture since World War II. Much of the sculpture produced in the 1940's reflects despair. Germaine Richier of France used Surrealistic forms to convey feelings of terror or the fear of death. Related to the Surrealists in their quest for spontaneity are the

Left:
Montserrat
by Julio Gonzáles in 1937
sheet iron
5 feet 4 inches (1.63 m) high
Stedelijk Museum, Amsterdam

Right:
Women and Dog
by Marisol in 1964
wood, plaster, synthetic
polymer paint, miscellaneous items
6 feet (1.83 m) high,
6 feet 10 inches (2.08 m) wide,
1 foot 4 inches (41 cm) deep
Whitney Museum of American Art
New York City

English sculptors Lynn Chadwick, Kenneth Armitage, and Reg Butler.

Among American sculptors concerned with the human figure were Reuben Nakian and Leonard Baskin. Other Americans such as Richard Lippold, Isamu Noguchi, and Louise Nevelson created geometric and abstract works. Theodore Roszak and David Smith were among the first Americans to create direct metal sculpture. Marino Marini and Giacomo Manzù of Italy became widely known for their figure sculptures.

Until the middle of the century, sculpture was of less interest to the public than painting. In the 1960's sculpture emerged as the leader of artistic innovation. Electric lights, magnets, moving water, air currents, molded plastics, and polystyrene foam are among the many untraditional materials used by sculptors. Sculpture gained in prestige and once again became a monumental art as many cities and private corporations com-

missioned work to be displayed outdoors. Pop Art sculpture, sometimes called neo-Dada, used common objects assembled in various ways. (See POP ART, illustration.) The Americans George Segal and Marisol became known for their Assemblages based on the human figure. Claes Oldenburg introduced "soft" sculpture, sculpture made of stuffed and sewn canvas or vinyl.

Anthony Caro of England and the American Robert Morris are among the sculptors who emphasized huge, simple shapes. These works have been called Minimal Art, ABC Art, and Primary Structures. Other sculptors have based their works on technology, combining mechanics and art. Sculpture that uses motorized movement, flashing lights, and sound has been called Kinetic. When light is the dominating element, the sculpture is called Luminist. Jean Tinguely of Switzerland and Pol Bury of Belgium are among the leading Kinetic sculptors. In the

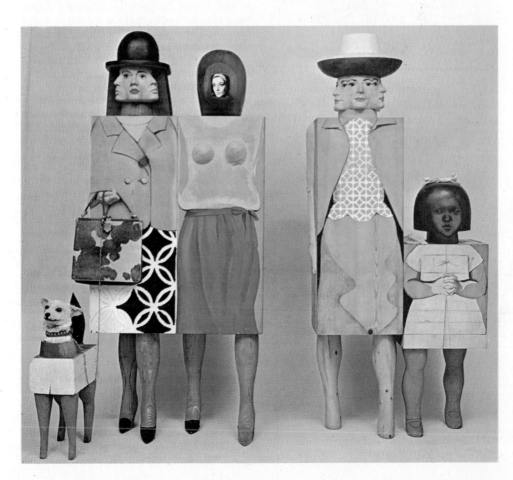

Opposite:
Spiral Jetty
by Robert Smithson in 1970
black basalt, limestone, earth, red algae
160 feet (49 m) in diameter
in Utah's Great Salt Lake
Gianfranco Gorgoni/Woodfin Camp & Assoc.

Left, top:
Mid-day
by Anthony Caro in 1960
painted steel
12 feet (3.66 m) long
Kasmin Gallery, London
Collection of I. M. and P. G. Caro

Left, bottom:
Zaga
by Nancy Graves in 1983
cast bronze with polychrome patination
72 inches (183 cm) high
The Nelson-Atkins Museum of Art, Kansas City, MO.
(Gift of the Friends of Art)

United States Red Grooms in *City of Chicago* and Lucas Samaras in *Mirrored Room No. 2* created works that the spectator walks through. These works are often called Environments, or Environmental Art.

In the 1970's many sculptors abandoned the traditional ways of making and selling art and created works that are called Earth Art or Earthworks. In this type of sculpture the landscape itself is made into a large-scale work of art that is often impermanent. Examples include *Spiral Jetty,* designed by Robert Smithson and constructed in the Great Salt Lake, and *Valley Curtain,* set up in Colorado by Christo (Christo Javacheff). Other sculptors returned to the representational tradition. Duane Hanson, for example, made realistic, life-size fiberglass and polyester sculptures depicting ordinary people in everyday situations.

Sculptors continued working in diverse styles and with a variety of materials in the last decades of the 20th century. In the United States Mark di Suvero and Richard Serra constructed large outdoor metal sculptures. Michael Heizer created Earthworks and Luis Jiminez used fiberglass in colorful, realistic public sculptures. Nancy Graves and Martin Puryear were among the many sculptors using the traditional materials of bronze and wood in untraditional ways. The English sculptors Tony Cragg and Bill Woodrow constructed sculptures from junk and found objects. Rebecca Horn of Germany created Kinetic sculptures.

ed through faulty observation or deliberate exaggeration. For example, 20th-century scientists believe that the legend of the *kraken,* a many-armed beast that could wreck the largest ships, was based on reports about the giant squid, an animal that was not reliably observed and classified until the 19th century. Some scientists believe that certain other accounts of sea monsters may describe real but as yet unknown large sea animals.

Sea serpents are the most frequently reported sea monsters. They are described as being 20 to 250 feet (6 to 76 m) long with large horselike or reptilelike heads. There are many species of real sea snakes, but they average only about four feet (1.2 m) in length and do not resemble sea serpents as they are traditionally described. Among known marine animals that have been mistaken for sea serpents are the giant squid, which is sometimes more than 60 feet (18 m) long, the basking shark, which is about 25 feet (8 m) long, and the oarfish, which reaches a length of 40 feet (12 m).

The Loch Ness monster, first reported in 1933, is perhaps the most widely publicized sea serpent. It supposedly inhabits Loch Ness, a deep lake in Scotland. Some people believe that a large marine animal may be in the lake, having entered through the Caledonian Canal.

Sea of . . . . See under specific name, as JAPAN, SEA OF.

Sea Otter. See OTTER.

Sea Parrot. See PUFFIN.

Sea Serpent. See SEA MONSTER.

Sea Slug. See SLUG.

Sea Snake. See SNAKE, subtitle *Kinds of Snakes:* Hydrophiidae.

Sea Spider, a sea-dwelling animal that looks somewhat like a spider. There are about 500 species. Sea spiders are found in all oceans. Species found in coastal waters are usually small and have a leg span of about 1 inch (2.5 cm); those living at great depths, up to 24 inches (60 cm).

The sea spider has a small, narrow body. It usually has four pairs of long, thin legs attached to the abdomen. Attached to the head there are usually three other pairs of appendages—a pair called *chelicerae,* used for grasping food; a pair of sensory projections called *palps;* and a pair of egg-carrying legs (sometimes underdeveloped or absent in the female). The female lays round masses of

Sea Squirts

eggs upon the egg-carrying legs of the male, which carries the eggs until they hatch.

On top of its head, the sea spider has a knobby projection bearing two, three, or four simple eyes. The head ends in a snout with a sucking mouth. Sea spiders feed by sucking the body juices of such marine animals as sea anemones, sponges, and sea squirts.

Sea spiders belong to the class Pycnogonida of the phylum Arthropoda.

Sea Squirt, a marine animal usually found in coastal areas. Most sea squirts live permanently attached to such objects as rocks, shells, and wharves. They are often brilliant in color and usually globular or cylindrical in shape. The soft body is surrounded by a transparent, flexible outer covering called a tunic. Sea squirts range from 1/100 inch to seven inches (0.025 to 18 cm) in diameter.

The adult sea squirt has two structures, called siphons, at the top of its body. One siphon draws in water and the other expels it. The sea squirt feeds on plankton, which it filters out of the water with its pharynx. When disturbed, the sea squirt contracts its siphons, expelling two streams of water—a habit from which it gets its name.

Many sea squirts reproduce asexually by means of budding as well as sexually by means of eggs and sperm. In budding, a new sea squirt develops as an outgrowth of the parent's body. In sexual reproduction, fertilized eggs develop into tiny tadpole-shaped,

Mick Church

Sea Urchin

free-swimming larvae. The larvae have a *notochord,* a backbone-like structure that eventually disappears when they mature. The larvae swim about for a few weeks before they develop into their adult form.

Sea squirts make up the class Ascidiacea of the phylum Chordata.

Sea Star. See STARFISH.

Sea Swallow. See TERN.

Sea Urchin, a prickly-looking marine animal, spherical in shape and covered with long movable spines. It somewhat resembles a hedgehog and is sometimes called the "hedgehog of the sea." Sea urchins are found on the ocean bottom, usually near rocky shores. Sea urchins may be brown, black, purple, green, white, or red. Most are about two to four inches (5 to 10 cm) in diameter, including the spines.

In addition to its spines, the sea urchin also has pedicellariae (three-jawed pincers atop slender stalks) and tiny tube feet projecting from its body surface. The movable spines (which in some species are solid and in others hollow and filled with poison) are used for locomotion and protection. The pedicellariae (which in some species contain poison glands) are used for defense and for cleaning the body by removing larval animals and small crustaceans. The tube feet are hollow, muscular projections ending in suckers. They are flexible and can be extended beyond the spines to grip objects on the ocean floor.

The sea urchin feeds on seaweed and other organic matter. On its undersurface is a mouth with five strong teeth used in feeding. Some sea urchins bore holes with their teeth in rocks along the shore and then use the

rocks as hiding places. Sea urchins reproduce sexually by means of eggs and sperm. The eggs are used as food in many European and Asian countries.

Sea urchins belong to the class Echinoidea of the phylum Echinodermata.

Seabees. See NAVY, UNITED STATES, subtitle *Organization:* Line and Staff Corps.

Seaborg, sē'bôrg, Glenn Theodore (1912-1999), a United States chemist. Early in his career he helped discover nine chemical elements—the 2nd through 10th transuranium elements (elements heavier than uranium). For his work, Seaborg shared the 1951 Nobel Prize in chemistry with the American physicist Edwin M. McMillan, who helped discover the first two transuranium elements. Seaborg was chairman of the U.S. Atomic Energy Commission (AEC), 1961-71, the first scientist to direct the nation's atomic energy program.

Seaborg was born in Ishpeming, Michigan. After receiving a Ph.D. degree from the University of California (Berkeley) in 1937, he joined its faculty. In 1940-41 Seaborg and his associates discovered the element plutonium and the isotope plutonium 239, which is a source of nuclear energy.

During World War II, Seaborg worked at the University of Chicago on the creation of the atomic bomb. After returning to the University of California, he directed nuclear chemical research at the Lawrence Radiation Laboratory, 1946-58, and served as university chancellor, 1958-61. During 1944-58, he helped discover eight more elements—americium, curium, berkelium, californium, einsteinium, fermium, mendelevium, and nobelium. In 1959 he received the Fermi Award. Seaborg served for 10 years as chairman of AEC beginning in 1961. He was awarded the 1991 Medal of Science, and in 1997, element 106 was named seaborgium in his honor.

Seabury, sē'ber-ĭ, **Samuel** (1729-1796), a United States clergyman, the first bishop

Glenn Seaborg
AEC

of the Episcopal Church in America. Seabury was born in Groton, Connecticut. After attending Yale and Edinburgh (Scotland) universities, he was ordained as an Anglican priest in 1753. In the American Revolution he served as a chaplain with the British army. Nevertheless, in 1783 the Connecticut clergy chose Seabury to be bishop of the independent American branch of the church. When the Church of England refused to consecrate Seabury without his taking an oath of allegiance to the British monarchy, the separatist Episcopal Church of Scotland consecrated him, in 1784. In 1789 Seabury became presiding bishop of the Protestant Episcopal Church.

Seal, a meat-eating mammal found in all oceans of the world, but most abundant in Arctic and Antarctic waters. Some seals swim up rivers, and a few are found only in freshwater lakes. Probably the best-known seal species is the Californian sea lion, which is often trained to perform tricks. It is the species most often found in zoos.

Some species of seals are hunted commercially—more for their blubber (fat) and pelts than for their flesh. The fur of some species is popular for fashionable wearing apparel; the hide of other species is used for leather. Oil rendered from the blubber goes mainly into soap. Seal flesh is eaten by Aleuts and was once a welcome food for seafarers. In some localities the flesh is utilized for fertilizer and animal feed. Eskimos have traditionally depended largely on seal, which they hunt with harpoons, for food, clothing, and hides for tents and boats.

Seals along with the walrus make up the taxonomic group Pinnipedia. Some authorities use the term "seal" in referring to all members of the group. For information on the walrus, see WALRUS.

Description

Seals are divided into two families—the *eared seals* (the sea lions and fur seals), and the *earless seals* (also called true, or hair, seals). Eared seals have small, protruding earflaps on the side of the head. Earless seals have no earflaps. (All seals have internal ears.)

A seal's body tapers from the chest towards the tail, which is very short or nearly absent. The digits of a seal's four limbs are modified into *flippers*—the digits of the "hands" and "feet" are webbed and resemble paddles. Flippers are very useful in steering

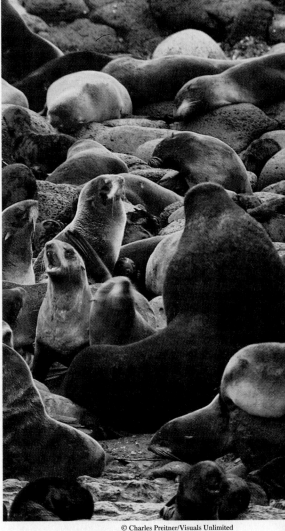

© Charles Preitner/Visuals Unlimited
Northern Fur Seal Rookery. The bellowing males and bleating females can be heard for great distances. Other kinds of seals may make barking or trumpeting sounds.

and maneuvering in water. Earless seals have fur-covered flippers; eared seals have flippers covered only with thick skin.

Seals are warm-blooded animals—that is, their body temperature remains constant regardless of the outside temperature. All seals have a layer of blubber under the skin that acts as an insulator against the cold. Sea lions, which are generally found in warmer climates than other seals, have little additional protection. Earless seals, on the other

Common Seal

hand, have a circulatory system that limits the quantity of blood that flows through the skin and thus reduces the amount of body heat lost from the skin. The fur seals, in addition to blubber, have a two-layer covering of fur. The upper layer consists of coarse guard hairs; the dense lower layer is made up of short, fine hairs and acts as an additional insulator.

Seals have large, roundish eyes that in some species are huge in proportion to the size of the skull. The eyes have thick, spherical lenses that enable the seals to see well under water. Unlike most other mammals, seals do not have tear ducts. Thus when seals are observed on land they look as though they are crying because their tears run out of the eye onto the face. Seals have rather long whiskers around the mouth.

Adult seals weigh from about 130 pounds (60 kg) to more than 8,000 pounds (3,600 kg), depending on the species and individual. They range in length from less than 4½ feet (1.4 m), for the Baikal seal, to 20 feet (6 m), for the southern elephant seal. The bulls

(males) are usually larger than the cows (females), except in some species of earless seals. The lifespan of some species is up to 40 years.

In many species, the male has a thick layer of fur, resembling a mane, around the neck. Seals vary in color depending on the species, and sometimes members of the same species have different coloration. In general, they are brownish or grayish, often with various shadings, blotches, or stripes.

Habits

Seals are skillful swimmers and divers. They can swim up to 15 to 18 miles per hour (24 to 29 km/h) and are very agile in the water. The eared seals get their swimming thrust mainly from the forelimbs. The earless seals get most of their thrust from their hind limbs. Seals can dive to great depths— 160 to 600 feet (50 to 180 m) is common, but some northern elephant seals have been recorded diving to depths of more than 2,000 feet (610 m). Many species are capable of remaining submerged for 20 minutes, some for more than 30 minutes.

On land, seals are rather clumsy. Eared seals, which can bring their hind limbs under their body, can stand on all fours and manage to move with a kind of gallop. Earless seals cannot move their hind limbs forward; they move on land by using their forelimbs and wriggling their body. Some seals, such as the common, or harbor, seal, spend much of their time on land; others, such as the northern fur seal, may spend up to eight months at sea. Many species spend their time out of the water exclusively on ice (rather than land).

Southern Elephant Seal

Seals eat fish, crustaceans, squid, and occasionally, birds and other seals. They catch their food primarily with their mouths.

Most species of seals return year after year to the same area—often the place of their birth—for breeding. These breeding grounds are called rookeries. Some species travel great distances each year from their feeding grounds to their rookery. Most seals have well-defined and short breeding seasons so that all the seals of a colony come together at the same time.

All eared and some earless seals are polygamous. The mature bulls attempt to gather a harem of females, and those who succeed are called harem bulls. The size of the harem, ranging from 3 to 40 females, depends on the species and on the strength and ferocity of the bull. Except for the gray and elephant seals, the earless seals are believed to be monogamous.

In polygamous species, the mature bulls are the first to arrive on the breeding grounds, where they attempt to establish definite territories. The females, pregnant from last year's mating, arrive two weeks later. A single pup is born within one week. After the birth, mating takes place. The gestation period is 250 to 365 days. Immature bulls arrive at the rookeries a few weeks after the mature males and remain on the fringes of the colony. A young bull is not sexually mature until four years of age and does not attempt to establish a harem until five to seven years of age.

Most pups (baby seals) are *precocial* (born in an advanced state of development) and are able to swim soon after bith. A newborn pup is thin, though it appears to be fat because it has a thick coat of fur. The pup grows quickly and, because the mother's milk is 45 per cent fat, it soon develops a thick layer of blubber.

Earless Seals

Earless seals make up the family Phocidae.

The Common, or Harbor, Seal is found in oceans—and sometimes large rivers—of the Northern Hemisphere. Some populations inhabit freshwater lakes. Both sexes are dark gray above and lighter below. The entire body is marked with brown or gray spots. Males grow up to 6 feet (1.8 m) in length and weigh up to 550 pounds (250 kg). Females are about 12 inches (30 cm) shorter and less than half the weight. The common seal is *Phoca vitulina.*

The Elephant Seals, or Sea Elephants. There are two species—the *southern elephant seal*, which is the largest of all seals, and the *northern elephant seal.*

The name is derived from the male's trunklike proboscis, an overdeveloped nose. The southern species is found around Antarctica. The male may be up to 20 feet (6 m) long and weigh 8,000 pounds (3,600 kg). Females are smaller. Bulls are bluish-gray above and pale gray beneath. Females are brownish-gray with lighter necks and underparts. The northern elephant seal resembles the southern, except that it is smaller and has a larger proboscis. In an adult male northern elephant seal, the proboscis may extend downward for 12 inches (30 cm) or more.

By 1900, elephant seals were almost exterminated for their blubber. They have been protected by international agreements since the 1930's, and their population is increasing.

The southern elephant seal is *Mirounga leonina;* the northern elephant seal, *M. angustirostris.*

The Gray Seal is found in the North Atlantic. Males grow to more than 9 feet (2.7 m) and females up to 7 feet (2.1 m). Weights are up to 630 and 550 pounds (285 and 250 kg), respectively. The color varies in different individuals from dark to light gray, brown, and silver. Underparts are usually lighter and the whole body surface is marked with spots.

The gray seal is *Halichoerus grypus.*

The Harp Seal is found in the Arctic and northern Atlantic oceans. Both sexes reach a length of about 6 feet (1.8 m) and a weight of about 400 pounds (180 kg). Harp seals are grayish-yellow with a broad dark band starting at the shoulders and continuing along the sides. These seals are migratory and breed on drifting pack ice. The pups were formerly killed in large numbers for their white, woolly pelts.

The harp seal is *Pagophilus groenlandicus.*

The Leopard Seal is usually found around Antarctica. The adult bull is up to 10 feet (3 m) long, the female as much as 2 feet (60 cm) longer. The head of the leopard seal somewhat resembles that of a reptile. Body color is dark gray on the back, shading to light gray on the underparts. The entire body is marked with spots. The leopard seal is the only seal to feed on penguins and other seabirds.

The leopard seal is *Hydrurga leptonyx.*

The Ringed Seal is one of the most abundant seals. It lives primarily in the Arctic Ocean and adjoining seas, but also in certain freshwater lakes. It averages four feet (1.2 m) in length and 140 pounds (65 kg) in weight. Ringed seals are grayish-black with light-colored oval rings above. Many are killed for skins, fur, oil, and meat.

Related species are the *Baikal seal,* of Lake Baikal in Siberia, and the *Caspian seal,* of the Caspian Sea, between Europe and Asia.

The ringed seal is *Pusa hispida;* the Baikal, *P. sibirica;* the Caspian, *P. caspica.*

The Weddell Seal generally lives within sight of the Antarctic mainland. Males measure up to 10 feet (3 m), females up to 11 feet (3.4 m). Both sexes weigh up to about 900 pounds (410 kg). The Weddell seal is dark gray above, lighter gray below. The entire body is marked with blotches and streaks.

The Weddell seal is *Leptonychotes weddelli.*

Other Earless Seals include the hooded, or bladder-nose, seal (*Cystophora cristata*); bearded seal (*Erignathus barbatus*); ribbon seal (*Histriophoca fasciata*); crabeater seal (*Lobodon carcinophagus*); Ross seal (*Omnatophoca rossi*); Mediterranean monk seal (*Monachus monachus*); Hawaiian monk seal (*M. schauinslandi*); and Caribbean monk seal (*M. tropicalis*). The Mediterranean and Hawaiian monk

Zoological Society of San Diego
Californian Sea Lions are popular zoo animals.

seals are endangered. The Caribbean monk seal is probably extinct; the last recorded sighting of one was in 1962.

Eared Seals

The fur seals and sea lions make up the family Otariidae.

The Californian Sea Lion is found in the Galápagos Islands, along the coast of California, and in parts of Japan. Males attain a length of 7 feet (2.1 m), females 6 feet (1.8 m). Weight is up to 600 pounds (270 kg) for the male, 200 pounds (90 kg) for the female. Body color is some shade of chocolate brown, and the top of the head becomes lighter with age.

The Californian sea lion is *Zalophus californianus*.

The Northern Fur Seal was formerly one of the most hunted seals. These seals are known for their seasonal migrations. They spend the winter and spring dispersed through the southern regions of the North Pacific Ocean. They breed in the Pribilof, Komandorskiye, Kuril, and Robben islands of the North Pacific. Adult bulls are about 7 feet (2.1 m) long and weigh about 600 pounds (270 kg). Females are about 5 feet (1.5 m) long and weigh up to 130 pounds (60 kg). Males have dark brown fur except for the mane, which has a grayish tinge. Females are slate gray above and reddish-gray below. Both sexes have a patch of lighter fur on the chest.

The northern fur seal is *Callorhinus ursinus*.

Southern Fur Seals live in seas near Baja California, South America, South Africa, Australia, and Antarctica. There are eight species. One of the most numerous is the *South African*, or *cape, fur seal*. It is the largest fur seal, reaching a length of 7.5 feet (2.3 m) and a weight greater than 660 pounds (300 kg). It is commercially hunted; a subspecies, the *Australian fur seal*, is protected.

The South African fur seal is *Artocephalus pusillus;* the Australian, *A. p. doriferus*.

The other southern fur seals are the South American fur seal (*A. australis*); New Zealand fur seal (*A. fosteri*); Galapagos fur seal (*A. galapagoensis*); Ant-

arctic fur seal (*A. gazella*); Philippi, or Juan Fernandez, fur seal (*A. philippi*); Guadalupe fur seal (*A. townsendi*); and Kerguelen, or subantarctic, fur seal (*A. tropicalis*).

The Steller's, or Northern, Sea Lion is found throughout the North Pacific and the Arctic Ocean. It is the largest of the eared seals. Bulls are up to 11 feet (3.4 m) long and weigh up to 2,000 pounds (900 kg). Females rarely exceed 8½ feet (2.6 m) and a weight of about 600 pounds (270 kg). The color is variable but is usually a yellowish shade of buff. The male has a thick, muscular neck with a mane of coarse, long hairs.

The Steller's sea lion is *Eumetopias jubatus*.

Other Eared Seals include the Australian sea lion (*Neophoca cinerea*), the southern sea lion (*Otaria byronia*), and Hooker's sea lion (*Phocarctos hookeri*).

Sealing

The commercial hunting of seals is controlled in many parts of the world by law and international treaty for purposes of conservation. Many species may not be hunted at all; others are protected except for an occasional period of culling (selective hunting). In the case of thriving species, hunting is generally confined to killing bachelor bulls, yearlings, and pups, so as not to interfere with breeding.

Pelagic sealing—the killing of seals at sea, where it is impossible to distinguish between bulls and cows—has been largely eliminated. Seals are usually hunted at their rookeries, where bachelor bulls occupy a territory separate from the harem bulls and their families. The seals are commonly clubbed or shot to death and the carcasses dressed on the spot, in order to take the blubber, the skin, or both.

Ringed seals, Caspian seals, and South African fur seals are among the most commonly hunted species today. Harp seals were killed in large numbers until 1983, when what is now the European Union banned the import of their pelts.

History. The earliest known instance of organized sealing occurred along the Barbary Coast of Africa, where the Mediterranean monk seal was hunted for its skin in the 15th century. By the end of the 18th century, explorers had discovered most of the major seal herds in the world, and sealing, for blubber and skins, grew into an important industry. In the early 19th century the slaughter reached such proportions that one species, the Philippi fur seal, became extinct. When seals had grown so scarce that the industry itself almost died, protective measures began to be taken.

In 1911 an international treaty outlawed

pelagic sealing of northern fur seals, which had almost become extinct. Large numbers of northern fur seals continued to be hunted on the Pribilof Islands until 1985. Since then, they have been hunted only by the Aleuts, for their own food supply.

Other species, including the elephant seals and some southern fur seals, have also received protection from international treaties. In the United States, the Marine Mammal Protection Act of 1972 prohibited most hunting of seals.

Books about Seals

Bonner, Nigel. *Seals and Sea Lions of the World* (Facts on File, 1994).

Riedman, Marianne. *The Pinnipeds: Seals, Sea Lions, and Walruses* (University of California, 1991).

For Younger Readers

Bare, C. S. *Elephants on the Beach* (Dutton, 1990).

Barrett, Norman. *Seals and Walruses* (Watts, 1991).

Bruemmer, Fred. *Seasons of the Seal* (Outlet, 1991).

Patent, C. H. *Seals, Sea Lions and Walruses* (Holiday House, 1990).

Petty, Kate. *Seals* (Watts, 1991).

Seal, a symbol used on a document to validate the identity of the person or agency issuing it. The term "seal" is used for the design of the symbol; an incised surface that will produce an impression of the symbol, such as a die stamp or a signet ring; and the impression itself or the wafer of paper or piece of wax carrying the impression. The official seal of a government may also be known as the great seal.

The term "seal" is used also to mean a piece of material such as sealing wax, paper, tape, or lead placed on an envelope, folded document, container, or door so that it cannot be opened without the seal being broken.

In ancient Mesopotamia, jars of grain or wine were sealed with clay, and an impression was made in the clay with a bead or gem bearing an engraved design identifying the owner. This practice was the origin of the identifying seal, used in place of a signature, to validate a signature, or to indicate the signer's official capacity. In the Middle Ages seals were impressed in warm beeswax. A sealing wax with a resin base was developed in modern times.

The Seal of the United States

The Seal of the United States, or the Great Seal, is a symbol of the nation's sover-

eignty. On the obverse, or face, side is an eagle clutching an olive branch and arrows, representing the nation's dedication to peace and the power to defend itself. The 13 stars, shield with 13 stripes, and Latin motto *E Pluribus Unum* (Out of Many, One) represent the union of the 13 original states. On the reverse side of the seal is an unfinished pyramid of 13 tiers, signifying strength and duration. Above it is the eye of Providence and the Latin words *Annuit Coeptis* (He [God] has favored our undertaking) and below it, *Novus Ordo Seclorum* (A New Order of the Ages). On the pyramid's base is the year of independence, 1776.

The Department of State has custody of the steel die incised with the design of the obverse side of the seal. (There is no die of the reverse side.) Embossed on paper wafers, seal impressions are affixed to government documents such as ambassadorial commissions and treaty ratifications with the authority of the President. Both sides of the seal design are pictured on the back of a one-dollar bill. The face design serves as the nation's coat of arms and is widely used for decorative as well as official purposes.

Creation of the Seal of the United States was authorized by the Continental Congress. William Barton, an authority on heraldry, and Charles Thomson, secretary of the Congress, designed the seal, which was approved in 1782. The seal design was redrawn in 1841, differing in some details from the original. The present die, which adheres strictly to the design adopted by the Continental Congress in 1782, came into use in 1904.

Sealyham Terrier. See Dog, subtitle *Breeds of Dogs:* Terriers (Sealyham Terrier).

Seaman, Elizabeth Cochrane. See BLY, NELLIE.

Great Seal

Obverse   Reverse

Séance. See SPIRITUALISM.

Seaplane. See AIRPLANE, section "Types of Airplanes," subtitle *Classification by Landing Gear:* Seaplane.

Seaport. See PORT.

Search, Right of, in international law, the right of ships of a warring nation to stop and search a neutral merchant vessel on the high seas. It is also known as right of visit, or right of visit (or visitation) and search. The purpose of the search is to determine if the merchant vessel is carrying contraband of war or is acting on behalf of the enemy. A vessel found to be doing either may be seized—that is, brought into a port of the search vessel's country, where an admiralty court known as a prize court judges the case and determines if the cargo or vessel is liable to confiscation. The right of search is sometimes claimed in peacetime when a nation is attempting to enforce revenue laws, control piracy, or protect other interests.

Interpretations of what the right includes are defined from time to time by international agreement. Extension of the right of search beyond its defined scope infringes on freedom of the seas. However, a nation with superior naval strength may refuse to recognize the defined restrictions.

In the early 19th century, during the Napoleonic Wars, Great Britain interpreted the right of search as covering the removal of seamen suspected of being British subjects from ships of neutral nations. American resentment against this practice helped cause the War of 1812. During the Civil War a United States warship stopped the British vessel *Trent* and took into custody two Confederate commissioners. The incident outraged Britain, which considered entering the war. President Lincoln eventually ordered the commissioners released. (See TRENT AFFAIR.)

Search Warrant, in United States law, a document signed by a judge that permits officers of the law to search the home or other premises of a specified person for evidence relating to a crime.

For the warrant to be valid, it must specify where police officers may search and what they may seize. A search warrant is issued only after officers have demonstrated that there is reason to believe that a crime has been committed. Warrants issued on suspicion alone, without a presentation of facts indicating that a crime has occurred,

have been held by the U.S. Supreme Court to violate the Fourth Amendment to the Constitution, which prohibits "unreasonable searches and seizures."

A warrant of arrest gives the arresting officers the right to examine the suspect and the suspect's immediate surroundings, but not to search the premises. A search without warrant may be made if the person in charge of the premises consents, but if he or she objects the search is held to be unconstitutional. However, premises may be inspected for compliance with safety and health regulations without a warrant.

The requirement for a search warrant is an important civil liberty. In totalitarian countries, officials may enter a home at will and without explanation.

The prohibition against "unreasonable searches and seizures" in the American Bill of Rights resulted from a particular colonial grievance. A general warrant known as a writ of assistance gave British customs officers the right to search any home or ship as they saw fit for evidence of smuggling. (See WRITS OF ASSISTANCE.)

Sears, Roebuck and Co., a United States retail company. It is one of the world's largest retailers, selling a wide range of merchandise. Sears has stores in every state and in Canada, Mexico, and Puerto Rico.

Sears was founded as a mail-order watch company by Richard W. Sears in 1886. Alvah C. Roebuck, a watchmaker, joined the firm the next year. The partnership of Sears and Roebuck was established in 1893, and expanded into other lines of merchandise.

Sears expanded enormously under the leadership of Julius Rosenwald, a clothing manufacturer who joined the firm in 1895. The following year, the company began publishing its general merchandise catalog. In 1925, under the direction of Robert E. Wood, the firm opened its first retail store. Catalog operations were discontinued in 1992. Headquarters are in Hoffman Estates, Illinois, a suburb of Chicago.

See also MAIL-ORDER BUSINESS, picture titled *Sears Mail-order Catalog;* ROSENWALD, JULIUS; WOOD, ROBERT E.

Sears Tower. See CHICAGO, subtitle *Interesting Places:* Prominent Buildings, and photograph titled *Downtown and the Lakefront.*

Seasickness. See MOTION SICKNESS.

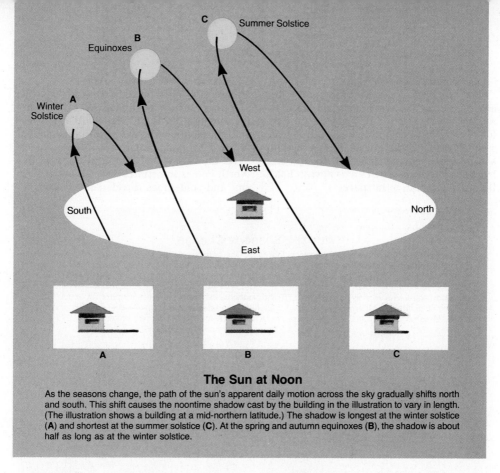

C Summer Solstice

B
Equinoxes

A
Winter Solstice

West

South

North

East

A   B   C

The Sun at Noon

As the seasons change, the path of the sun's apparent daily motion across the sky gradually shifts north and south. This shift causes the noontime shadow cast by the building in the illustration to vary in length. (The illustration shows a building at a mid-northern latitude.) The shadow is longest at the winter solstice (**A**) and shortest at the summer solstice (**C**). At the spring and autumn equinoxes (**B**), the shadow is about half as long as at the winter solstice.

Seasons, the four divisions of the year, called spring, summer, autumn (or fall), and winter. North and south of the tropics, summer is the warmest season, winter the coolest. Spring and autumn are transitions between the two extremes. In the tropics, little temperature variation occurs with the seasons. For conditions in the tropics and their causes, see TROPICS.

Like the day and the year, the seasons are based on astronomical occurrences. The seasons, however, are related only to the year itself and not to any other units of time.

In the Northern Hemisphere, spring begins about March 21, summer about June 21, autumn about September 23, and winter about December 22. In the Southern Hemisphere, it is autumn that begins in March and spring that begins in September. Winter in the Southern Hemisphere begins about June 21 and summer about December 22, so Christmas comes in summer.

Year after year, the seasons form a never-ending cycle. The sun is farthest south (lowest) in the sky and the period of daylight shortest in the Northern Hemisphere about December 22, the day of the *winter solstice*. From then on, each day the sun reaches a little higher (farther to the north) in the noon sky and each day the period of daylight is a little longer. About March 21, on the date of the *vernal equinox,* the sun reaches halfway on its northward journey in the sky; it crosses the Equator. On that day, daylight and darkness are the same length.

The days continue to get longer north of the tropics and the sun farther north in the noon sky until June 21, the date of the northern *summer solstice.* The sun is then directly overhead at 23°27′ north of the Equator—the Tropic of Cancer. After the summer solstice, the sun begins to move southward again. Each day in the area north of the tropics, the period of daylight is a little shorter and the night is a little longer. Each day the sun is a little farther south in the sky at noon. In September comes the *autumnal equinox,* when day and night are again the same length. The sun continues southward until the winter solstice is reached, when the sun is directly over the Tropic of Capricorn (23°27′ south of the Equator).

S-251

Causes of the Seasons

The earth's axis—the imaginary line around which the earth turns in its daily rotation—is not at right angles to the path followed by the earth in its orbit around the sun; instead, it is slightly tilted. The seasons as we know them are caused by this tilt and by the fact that the earth's axis always holds the same orientation in space.

The tilt of the earth's axis is $23°27'$, or almost $23\frac{1}{2}°$. If the axis were not tilted, the sun would always be directly over the Equator and the Northern and Southern hemispheres would both have constant, similar weather the year round.

As the earth travels around the sun, the North Pole is sometimes directed toward the sun and sometimes directed away from it.

Why the Seasons Change

The light bulb represents the sun, the globe the earth. The earth's axis always points toward the same direction in space. Because the axis is tilted, the amount of sunlight reaching the Northern and Southern hemispheres changes during the course of the year. The illuminated portion of the globe at each of the four positions around the light bulb is shown at bottom: on March 21 (**A**) the Northern and Southern hemispheres receive an equal amount of light; on June 21 (**B**) the Northern Hemisphere receives its maximum amount of light, the Southern its minimum; on September 23 (**C**) both hemispheres again receive equal amounts of light; and on December 22 (**D**) the Southern Hemisphere receives a maximum and the Northern Hemisphere a minimum amount of light.

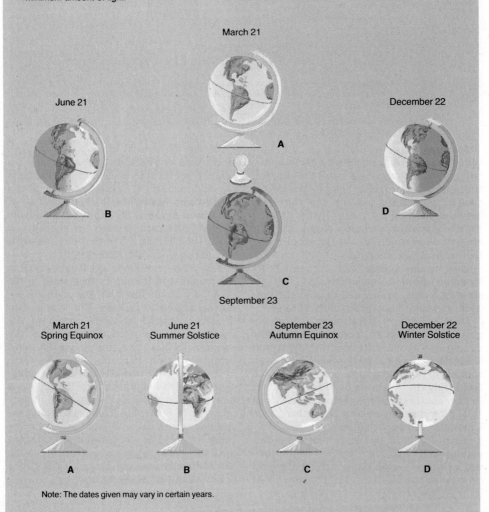

March 21

June 21

December 22

A

B

D

C

September 23

March 21 Spring Equinox	June 21 Summer Solstice	September 23 Autumn Equinox	December 22 Winter Solstice
A	B	C	D

Note: The dates given may vary in certain years.

When the North Pole is directed toward the sun, the sun's rays strike most directly on the Northern Hemisphere. The more directly the rays strike, the closer to vertical they are. Vertical rays of sunlight are more effective in producing light and heat than are slanting rays. There are two reasons: (1) slanting rays must pass through a greater thickness of atmosphere than vertical rays and thus lose more of their heat; and (2) slanting rays are spread out over a greater area than vertical rays, and are therefore less concentrated. Thus when the North Pole is directed toward the sun, summer is produced in the Northern Hemisphere; the Southern Hemisphere has winter. When the South Pole is directed toward the sun, the Southern Hemisphere receives the most heat and has summer.

The greater efficiency of the sun's rays is one reason summer is warmer than winter. A second reason is that the days are longer. While the sun is shining, the land and air heat up. When the sun goes down, they begin to lose heat. From the vernal equinox to the autumnal equinox, each day in the Northern Hemisphere is longer than the night and more heat is gained from the sun during the day than is lost at night.

The reverse is true as winter approaches and the northern half of the earth begins to cool. Not only does the sun move lower in the sky and become less effective in providing heat, but it shines for a shorter time each day, and heat is lost for a longer time than it is gained.

The earth's orbit is slightly elliptical, or elongated, so the earth is farther from the sun at some times than at other times. The earth is closest to the sun and moving most rapidly in January. In early July, when the earth is farthest from the sun, it is moving more slowly. The earth takes 186 days to go from the vernal to the autumnal equinox, but only 179 days to return from the autumnal to the vernal equinox.

There is also a small difference in the amount of heat received by the earth—less heat in July than in January. The total effect of this variation in time and heat is that the seasons in the Northern Hemisphere are a little milder than those in the Southern Hemisphere. The northern winter is shorter and warmer than the southern winter. The northern summer is longer and cooler than the southern summer.

Seasons and Weather

Although the seasons are based on astronomical events, the weather changes that are experienced during the seasons do not occur with the mathematical precision usual for most astronomical events. The day of the winter solstice—about December 22—has the shortest period of daylight and the least effective solar rays of the whole year in the Northern Hemisphere. It is rarely the coldest day of the year, however; the coldest days usually occur sometime in late January or in February. It takes time for the land and the oceans to cool after summer, and until they do, they warm the air somewhat, thus tempering the winter weather.

Similarly, the warmest weather usually occurs more than a month after the summer solstice—June 21—when the land and the oceans have been warmed to the maximums.

Around the time of the equinoxes, the hemisphere that has been cold begins to warm and the hemisphere that has been warm begins to cool. The atmosphere becomes somewhat unstable and the weather begins to fluctuate with great frequency. Thus during the spring and autumn, rains, high winds, and generally changeable weather conditions are common in many areas. The characteristic conditions of spring tend to move outward from the Equator as the sun does. Spring weather, therefore, may occur in some areas before the official opening of spring and later in other areas. Autumn weather may also begin before or after the autumnal equinox.

See also AUTUMN; EQUINOX; INDIAN SUMMER; SOLSTICE; SPRING; SUMMER; WINTER.

Books about the Seasons

O'Brien, Margaret. *Nature Notes: a Notebook Companion to the Seasons* (Fulcrum, 1990).
Teale, E. W. *Circle of the Seasons: the Journal of a Naturalist's Year* (Dodd, Mead, 1987).
For Younger Readers
Berger, Melvin. *Seasons* (Doubleday, 1990).
Bordon, Louise. *Caps, Hats, Socks, and Mittens: a Book About the Four Seasons* (Scholastic, 1992).
Borland, Hal. *The Golden Circle: a Book of Months* (Crowell, 1977).
Crawford, Sue. *The Seasons* (Watts, 1988).
Harlow, Rosie, and Gareth Morgan. *Cycles and Seasons* (Watts, 1991).
Sabin, Francine. *The Seasons* (Troll, 1985).

SEATO. See SOUTHEAST ASIA TREATY ORGANIZATION.

Cliff Hollenbeck/TSW—Click Chicago

Seattle's Space Needle, the tall structure at left, is a prominent landmark. Snowcapped Mount Rainier, about 60 miles (100 km) to the southeast, is visible on the horizon.

Seattle, sē-ăt''l, Washington, the state's largest city and the seat of King County. It is in western Washington on hilly land between Puget Sound and Lake Washington. Across the sound rise the snowcapped peaks of the Olympic Mountains. To the southeast, Mount Rainier's 14,410-foot (4,392-m) peak looms prominently above the Cascade Range.

Downtown Seattle faces Elliott Bay, an excellent natural harbor and the city's principal port area. There are other port facilities around Lake Union and along the Duwamish River. A short distance from the business district stands a major landmark, the 607-foot (185-m) Space Needle built for

the 1962 World's Fair. Residential areas cover the city's hills, which reach heights of 500 feet (150 m) or more.

Economy

Seattle is the largest city in the Pacific Northwest. Although nearly 150 miles (240 km) from the open sea, it is an important port and gateway to Alaska and Asia; it is closer to Asia than is any other major port on the United States West Coast. Grain, lumber, and wood products make up the largest share of the cargo shipped. Seattle is also the trade and business center for much of western Washington, an area heavily dependent on forest resources.

From its earliest days, the city has been a

lumber milling and shipping center. Numerous plants make a variety of wood products, including plywood and furniture. Aircraft manufacture is a major industry; the Boeing Company's plants in Seattle and nearby cities produce commercial and military aircraft, as well as missile and satellite parts. Other important activities are commercial fishing and associated canning and freezing, ship repairing, and the manufacture of machinery and paper.

Seattle is served by all principal means of transportation. A network of railroads and highways, including two Interstate routes, provides service to all parts of the country and to Canada. Seattle-Tacoma International Airport, a short distance south of the city, is a major terminus for overseas flights. The Port of Seattle includes the Lake Washington Ship Canal, linking Puget Sound, Lake Union, and Lake Washington; locks in the canal raise ships 26 feet (8 m) to the lakes. Ferries link Seattle with Canadian and Alaskan ports and serve cities on Puget Sound. Floating bridges carry highway traffic over Lake Washington.

Main Attractions

With water bordering much of Seattle, outdoor activities such as boating and fishing are extremely popular. Hydroplane races are a highlight of the annual Seafair held on Lake Washington. Beaches, parks, and other recreation areas dot the shores of Seattle and much of the Puget Sound region. Woodland Park, home of the Seattle Zoo, is one of the most popular attractions.

On a hill near the central business district stands the Seattle Center, occupying the site of the 1962 World's Fair. The Center's attractions include the Space Needle, science and art exhibits, shops, and restaurants. Seattle Aquarium, on the downtown waterfront, is a popular attraction. Also popular is the Museum of Flight, at Boeing Field, which displays vintage aircraft and has exhibits on aviation technology.

Seattle has three professional sports teams: the Seahawks (football), the Mariners (baseball), and the Supersonics and the Seattle Storm (basketball). Husky Stadium hosts the Seahawks, the Mariners play at SafeCo Field, and Key Arena, at the Seattle Center, hosts the Supersonics and the Seattle Storm.

Seattle Art Museum has a notable collection of Oriental art. Seattle is home to a sym-

© Esther Thompson

Containership being loaded near the mouth of the Duwamish River on Elliot Bay. Seattle is closer to Asia than any other United States port.

phony orchestra, an opera company, and a ballet company. Seattle also has a repertory theater. Institutions of higher learning include the University of Washington, the largest university in the state; Seattle University; and Seattle Pacific University.

History

A small group of pioneers from Illinois settled on the site of Seattle in 1851, at a place

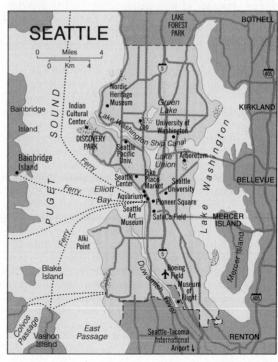

Facts about Seattle

Name—Named in honor of Chief Seattle, an Indian leader friendly to early settlers.

Location—Downtown Seattle, 47° 36′ N. and 122° 20′ W.

Land Area—83.6 square miles (216.5 km²).

Climate—Average temperatures: January, 40° F. (4° C.); July, 66° F. (19° C.). Average annual precipitation is 36 inches (914 mm), falling mostly as rain during winter months; snowfall is light.

Government—Mayor-council.

Founding and Charter Dates—Founded in 1851 and incorporated as a town in 1865.

Further Information—Seattle-King County Convention & Visitors Bureau, 8th and Pine Streets, Seattle, Washington, 98101.

now called Alki Point. At that time, the region was inhabited by various tribes of Salishan Indians. The settlement was named in honor of Chief Seattle (properly Seathl) of the Suquamish and Duwamish tribes, who had aided the settlers.

Lumbering soon became the main activity. In 1853 Henry L. Yesler, a lumberman from the Midwest, built a steam-powered sawmill in Seattle, the first on Puget Sound. In the 1860's, Asa S. Mercer, president of the Washington territorial university, brought a number of women from the East to provide wives for Seattle's loggers. Seattle was incorporated as a town in 1865 and as a city in 1869, but remained a small mill town for some years.

The coming of the first major railway early in the 1880's marked the beginning of Seattle's growth. The city developed rapidly despite bitter labor disputes, riots against Chinese workers in 1886, and a disastrous fire in 1889. Population increased twelve-fold, 1880-90. In 1893 Seattle became the western terminus of the Great Northern Railway. At about the same time, it became a port of entry for ships from the Far East.

The discovery of gold in Canada's Yukon Territory in 1896 brought prosperity to Seattle, which served as supply center for the gold miners. Expansion continued into the 20th century. In 1909 the Alaska-Yukon-Pacific Exposition was held in Seattle. The opening of the Panama Canal in 1914 led to an increase in the city's maritime trade. In 1916 Lakes Washington and Union were connected to Puget Sound by the Lake Washington Ship Canal.

During World War I, Seattle led the country in shipbuilding. At the same time, William Boeing began manufacturing airplanes there. World War II generated new industrial growth, particulary in the shipbuilding and aircraft industries. In 1962 the city was the site of a world's fair, the Century 21 Exposition. During 1966-71, Seattle's economy was hard hit by temporary cutbacks in production by the Boeing Company. By the late 1970's, industrial diversification had helped the city's economy to rebound. In 1989 voters approved limits on new construction in the downtown area and elected the city's first black mayor, Norman B. Rice. He was reelected in 1993.

Population

Seattle's population by census years has been:

1870	1,107	1940	368,302
1880	3,533	1950	467,591
1890	42,837	1960	557,087
1900	80,671	1970	530,831
1910	237,194	1980	493,846
1920	315,312	1990	516,259
1930	365,583		

Seattle Pacific University. See UNIVERSITIES AND COLLEGES (table).

Seattle University. See UNIVERSITIES AND COLLEGES (table).

Seaweed, the common name for many kinds of marine algae. Although the name is sometimes used for all of the marine algae, most botanists restrict the term to the larger algae that are attached or have been attached to the sea bottom. The brown algae, including the kelps, and the red algae are most commonly called seaweeds. Kelp is used as food and as fertilizer in the Far East. Kelp and red algae are frequently used as animal feed in Europe.

See also ALGAE; KELP.

Sebaceous Gland. See SKIN.

Sebastian, sĕ-băs′chăn, Saint, a martyr presumed to have lived in the third century A.D. All that is known with certainty about him is that he was venerated in Rome and Milan in the fourth century. According to legend he was an officer in the Roman army. When he was found to be a Christian, he was tied to a tree and used as a target by Roman archers and finally clubbed to death. His feast day is January 20 in the Roman Catholic Church and December 18 in the Eastern Orthodox.

Sebastopol. See SEVASTOPOL.

Secession, the withdrawal of part of a country or state from the central government's control. The withdrawal may be carried out peacefully or violently. Political conflicts that lead to secession are usually based on economic, cultural, or religious differences.

In United States history the question of secession arose several times before the Civil War, but the term generally refers to the withdrawal of the Southern states from the Union in 1860-61. Secession has also been an issue in other countries. Panama in 1903 seceded from Colombia partly because of Colombian opposition to plans by the United States to construct the Panama Canal. In 1967 the Ibo tribe of Nigeria, unwilling to be ruled by other tribes of that African country, tried to set up the Eastern Region as the separate nation of Biafra. Some French Canadians urge that the Province of Quebec secede from Canada on the grounds of political and cultural discrimination.

In the United States

From the time the U.S. Constitution was adopted, supporters of the doctrine of states' rights regarded secession as a right belonging to the states under the 10th Amendment. The Kentucky and Virginia Resolutions of 1798, though they did not use the word secession, stressed the sovereignty of the individual states.

In 1803-04 a small number of New England Federalists, facing decreased political power as a result of the admission of Southern states to the Union, proposed a separate nation to be called the Northeastern Confederacy. The idea did not gain support and was abandoned. Other Federalists hinted at secession in the Hartford Convention, 1814-15, called to protest the War of 1812, but they were disregarded. In 1832 South Carolina raised the threat of secession in the nullification crisis. (See NULLIFICATION.)

To many Southerners the election to the Presidency in 1860 of Abraham Lincoln, who won with exclusively Northern support, placed in jeopardy both slavery and states' rights. Southerners knew that abolition of slavery, the basis of the cotton economy, would be financially disastrous. Even if slavery were retained, the South feared political domination by the North, which was attempting to bar extension of slavery into all future new states.

Although there were groups in each state that were strongly opposed to secession, in 1860-61 seven states in what was known as

the Lower South seceded. On February 4, 1861, they formed the Confederate States of America. After Lincoln's call in April for a militia to enforce federal authority, four border, or Upper South, states seceded and joined the Confederacy. (In one of these states, Virginia, the western counties refused to secede from the Union. They set up their own government and in 1863 became the state of West Virginia.)

Lincoln rejected the argument put forth in the Confederacy that secession was constitutional and treated the secessionist states as groups in rebellion. The South's attempt to secede was thwarted by force of arms, and the constitutionality of secession has never been determined.

See also CONFEDERATE STATES OF AMERICA.

Second. See ANGLE, subtitle *Size of Angles;* TIME, subtitle *Units and Systems of Time Measurement.*

Second Manassas. See BULL RUN, SECOND BATTLE OF.

Secondary Education, in the United States, the schooling that follows elementary education, up to the college level. Secondary schooling, or high school, may begin at varying grade levels. For many years secondary schooling was considered to encompass the high school years—grades 9, 10, 11, and 12. Many school districts, however, no longer follow the traditional pattern of offering 8 years of elementary school followed by 4 of high school; instead, they have a 6-2-4 or a 6-3-3 system of elementary school, junior high, and high school as distinct levels. A few systems provide five years of secondary school, beginning with grade 8. Many substitute a middle school (grades 5 or 6 through grades 8 or 9) for a junior high school. Junior highs and middle schools are a bridge between elementary and secondary education but usually operate more like high schools than elementary schools; for example, the pupils have different teachers for each subject.

Some high schools use the grade system for designating class level (9th grade, 10th grade, etc.) but most, at least informally, use the college designations of freshman, sophomore, junior, and senior. Preparatory schools (private schools emphasizing preparation for college) often use the British term *form,* with 7th graders being in the first form and seniors in the sixth.

In the majority of states, school attendance is compulsory until age 16, by which time a pupil has usually completed only 9 or 10 grades. Because of increasing need in business and industry for highly trained persons, all students are being urged to complete their secondary schooling. Graduation from high school is a minimum requirement for most employment opportunities.

About nine-tenths of the country's high school pupils are enrolled in free public schools. The rest attend some type of private school, mainly parochial schools.

A secondary school that meets the academic standards of its regional association of colleges and secondary schools is designated as "accredited"—its graduates are not required to take examinations in high school subjects in order to be admitted to college. Most colleges, however, require that certain aptitude tests (such as the Scholastic Assessment Test, or SAT) be taken prior to admission.

Curriculum

Comprehensive high schools provide a variety of programs to meet the special interests and talents of youth. They generally offer at least two basic curriculums. One, often called an academic program, is designed to prepare pupils for college. The other, a general education program, is designed for pupils not continuing beyond high school. Many high schools, in addition, offer home-making, commercial, and industrial arts curriculums. In rural areas an agriculture curriculum is usually available.

A large city may have one or more secondary schools specializing in vocational training; in many cases such courses are included in comprehensive high schools. In each curriculum there are general subjects required of pupils in all curriculums for graduation, special subjects required in that particular curriculum, and elective subjects chosen by the pupils. Many states have *mandated* courses—courses, such as driver education or citizenship, required by state law of all pupils. Some high schools offer advanced placement (AP) courses; students who successfully complete such courses may be granted academic credit for them after they have been admitted to college.

Educators believe that secondary schooling should prepare young men and women for the responsibilities of citizenship, for the rewarding use of leisure time, and for the maintenance of good physical and mental health, as well as for earning a living or entering college. Many educators consider that the out-of-classroom programs, or student activity programs, offered by a school are as valuable educationally as the more formal courses.

Local and state authorities usually have considerable control over the courses offered. Curriculums are often modified to accommodate parental demands, school-board preferences, and governmental emphases. A local school board generally relies upon the professional judgments provided it by a superintendent and a staff.

The School Environment

The design of school buildings has changed radically in recent decades in an effort to put the student at ease and create an environment that is conducive to learning. Some large high schools are divided for administrative purposes into two or more schools-within-the-school—in effect, separate high schools within the same building—to provide a closer relationship between teachers and pupils. Some communities house freshmen and sophomores in one building and juniors and seniors in another.

Many secondary schools have expanded their libraries to include not only books but also video and audio tapes, maps, art reproductions, films, slides, and various other non-print media. Science and language laboratories, industrial arts shops, and other specially equipped rooms are generally found in the comprehensive high school. Classrooms of flexible size are desirable to assemble students in a large group to hear a lecture, for example, or in small groups for discussion or special study. Many schools provide several individual learning stations, or carrels, for independent study.

History and Trends

The earliest secondary schools in the United States were the Latin grammar schools, which were developed in the 1600's. They served boys who expected to attend college, and the curriculum emphasized classical languages and literature. The schools were financed through tuition payments, donations, and taxes. After the mid-1700's, academies largely replaced the Latin grammar schools. The academies were tuition-supported secondary schools that offered a broader, more practical, curriculum and often admitted girls as well as boys.

The first free public high school, the English Classical School, opened in Boston in 1821. Many communities, especially in the midwestern states, followed Boston's example in the next 50 years. Chicago established the first coeducational public high school in 1856. Preparation for college, however, was still recognized as the major purpose of secondary education, and children from middle- and working-class families rarely attended high school.

Beginning in 1890, high school enrollment doubled every decade until 1930. Reorganization of secondary education from the single high school into junior and senior high schools was introduced in 1909. The concept of universal education, which meant that all boys and girls could benefit from additional schooling, grew steadily. Comprehensive high schools developed, with curriculums expanded to include more nonacademic and vocational subjects. Extracurricular activities were expanded also and guidance services added.

A number of refinements were introduced in the American secondary school during the 1960's and early 1970's, including team teaching; the use of nonprofessional aides to reduce the teacher's clerical burden; and a variety of plans to individualize instruction.

During the same period, in response to student protests and criticism by educational reformers, many high schools began relaxing discipline, reducing the number of required courses, and broadening the curriculum to include such subjects as film study and science fiction literature. By the late 1970's, however, it became clear that college-admission test scores were trending downward and that a number of schools, especially those in inner-city neighborhoods, were graduating students who were functionally illiterate.

Many public school administrators face serious financial problems, especially in impoverished inner-city areas where real estate taxes (a principal source of school funding) are low due to low property values. In many school districts parents have chosen to send their children to private schools, where they believe there are fewer discipline problems and higher academic standards. During the 1970's and 1980's many private secondary schools were established by Protestant evangelical groups.

Because of a decrease in the school-age population, secondary school enrollment began decreasing in the 1970's. In the early 1990's, however, the number of secondary school students began to increase.

See also JUNIOR HIGH SCHOOL; VOCATIONAL EDUCATION.

___

Books about Secondary Education

Adams, D. M., and M. E. Hamm. *New Designs for Teaching and Learning in Tomorrow's Schools* (Jossey-Bass, 1994).

Armstrong, D. G., and others. *Secondary Education: an Introduction,* 3rd edition (Macmillan, 1993).

Dunnahoo, Terry. *How to Survive High School: a Student's Guide* (Watts, 1993).

French, Thomas. *South of Heaven: a Year in the Life of an American High School at the End of the 20th Century* (Doubleday, 1993).

Kim, E. C., and R. D. Kellough. *A Resource Guide for Secondary School Teaching,* 6th edition (Macmillan, 1994).

Meyer, Barbara. *How to Succeed in High School* (National Textbook Company, 1992).

Secondat, Charles Louis de. See MONTESQUIEU, BARON DE LA BRÈDE ET DE.

Secord, sē'kôrd, **Laura** (1775-1868), a Canadian heroine in the War of 1812. According to legend, she was responsible for the British victory over the Americans at the Battle of Beaver Dams, near the Niagara River in what is now Ontario, in 1813. From American troops billeted in her house, Mrs. Secord learned of plans for a surprise attack on the British encampment. Driving a cow before her to avoid suspicion, she carried the information some 20 miles (32 km) past enemy lines, to the camp. Actually, the British had already been warned. They and their Mohawk allies were prepared for the attack and won the battle.

Secret Agent. See ESPIONAGE.

Secret Police, police who operate secretly and are used for political purposes. They are also called secret political police. Secret police may wear uniforms or be a plainclothes force. It is their task to control or suppress political opponents of the government. They often use intimidation to create a climate of fear, so that most people will conform.

Secret police are characteristic of police states, in which a totalitarian government or a dictator uses police to control almost every aspect of life. In these societies, secret police often act as judges, jailers, and executioners. When power struggles develop within these police states, the secret police are often used by one faction against the other. In democratic societies law and custom severely limit the power of police and of secret internal-security agents (such as those of the Federal Bureau of Investigation and U.S. Secret Service). See BILL OF RIGHTS; HABEAS CORPUS; PRIVACY, RIGHT OF.

Secret police have been common wherever an oppressive minority government has sought to control a restless majority. The secret police of Sparta, in ancient Greece, were used to control the Helots (peasant serfs). Rulers of large empires such as the Roman Empire, the Inca Empire of South America, and the Mogul Empire of India often used secret police as political spies. Secret police were used as ruthless security agents by early European monarchs, Russian czars (especially Ivan IV and Nicholas I), and the leaders of the French Revolution. Napoleon I's secret police, created by Joseph Fouché, helped him control his European empire.

Notorious secret police of the 20th century have included Mussolini's secret police in Fascist Italy; the "Thought Police" of imperial Japan; and Nazi Germany's Gestapo, closely linked with the SS (Nazi party police) and SD (Security Service). Many Communist regimes and Third World dictatorships have also used secret police to prevent and suppress opposition.

The Soviet Union's secret police began with the Cheka, created by the Bolsheviks in 1917. The Cheka was reorganized under various names and agencies, including the OGPU, NKVD, NKGB, MGB, and MVD. In the 1930's, under Stalin, prisoners of the OGPU and NKVD were used as forced labor. After Stalin's death in 1953 the power of his police chief, Lavrenti P. Beria, momentarily rivaled that of the army and the Communist party itself. In 1954 the secret police were included in the KGB (Committee of State Security), an intelligence and internal security agency. In 1992, shortly after the collapse of the Soviet Union, the KGB was dissolved.

See also ANDROPOV, YURI; BERIA, LAVRENTI P.; GESTAPO; POLITICAL PRISONER.

Secret Service, United States, a law-enforcement bureau of the Treasury Department. A principal duty of the Secret Service is to protect the President of the United States (along with the President's immediate family) and other high officials. Another major duty is to catch counterfeiters and others who violate currency laws. Enforcement authority extends to offenses concerning bonds and other securities of the United States and of foreign governments. The bureau supervises the White House Police Force and the Treasury Guard Force.

The Secret Service also protects the major Presidential and Vice-Presidential candidates before an election and the winning candidates afterward. Upon request the service provides protection for a deceased President's spouse until that person remarries, and for the President's minor children to age 16. Former Presidents may also be guarded.

The Secret Service was established in 1865. Its force of agents was completely male until 1971.

Secret Societies, associations whose members are required to keep secret from nonmembers such information about their organizations as its purpose, its rituals, or the identity of its members. Secret passwords, special handshakes, and symbols are often used by members to identify themselves to each other.

In ancient cultures secret societies had primarily religious functions, as they do in some cultures today. Most modern secret societies are fraternal organizations that, apart from their secret activities, function publicly as social, benevolent, or patriotic groups. The oldest, largest, and most widely distributed secret fraternal society is the Masonic order, whose rituals have been imitated by many other societies. Other secret societies include revolutionary groups, such as the Irish Republican Army in Ireland, and criminal organizations, such as the Mafia in Sicily.

For further information, see:

ASSASSINS	KU KLUX KLAN
BOXER REBELLION	MAFIA
CAMORRA	MASONS
CARBONARI	MYSTERY
DRUIDS	NIHILISM
FENIANS	ROSICRUCIANS
FRATERNAL	THUGS
ORGANIZATIONS	TONG
FRATERNITIES AND	VOODOO
SORORITIES	
IRISH REPUBLICAN ARMY	

Secretary, in business, a person who handles correspondence and routine office duties for a superior. A secretary's duties vary according to the nature of the employer's business. In many offices, secretaries generate letters, memos, and other official documents from handwritten or recorded material provided by a superior. In some offices such work is done by a staff in a word processing department, allowing secretaries to spend more time on such duties as receiving visitors, answering telephones, filing, or answering letters. An *executive secretary* has greater responsibility, usually managing a variety of administrative tasks for the employer. Some secretaries supervise clerical workers or other secretaries.

Courses in secretarial subjects are offered in high schools, private secretarial schools, technical schools, and community or junior colleges.

Professional Secretaries International, founded in 1942, has about 41,000 members. Headquarters are in Kansas City, Missouri.

Secretary, in government. See CABINET.

Secretary, of an organization, the officer who maintains official records of the organization's activities and handles notices, reports, and correspondence. The secretary may also certify or sign all official documents. In some organizations the duties are divided between two persons. The *recording secretary* keeps the *minutes* (summary of proceedings) of meetings. The *corresponding secretary* is responsible for notices and other correspondence.

Secretary Bird, an African bird of prey. It is a long-legged bird about four feet (1.2 m) in height with a head and hooked beak similar to a hawk's. Its plumage is blue-gray except for black wing tips, thighs, tail, and crest. The bird derives its name from its long crest feathers, which stick out from the back of its head somewhat like the quill pens that office workers once carried behind their ears.

The secretary bird is famous as a hunter of snakes but also eats rodents, large insects, small birds, and eggs. It hunts on foot in open, sparsely wooded grasslands south of the Sahara. It is believed that secretary birds mate for life. The pair builds a nest of sticks on top of small trees. Usually two eggs, white with reddish-brown streaks, are laid in the nest.

The secretary bird is *Sagittarius serpentarius,* the only member of the family Sagittariidae.

Secretion. See GLAND.

Section, in surveying in the United States, a unit of land measurement equal to one square mile (2.6 km²). There are 36 sec-

© Will Troyer/Visuals Unlimited
Secretary Bird

tions to a township. (A township in this sense is a surveyor's term, not a political one.) The section and the township were established by the Ordinance of 1785 to provide a means of surveying the public lands in what later became the Northwest Territory.

Secular Humanism. See HUMANISM.

Securities, documents that represent an ownership or creditorship interest in a business concern or government. Such documents include stock certificates, stock rights and warrants, bonds, bond coupons, mortgages, options notes, and scrip.

See BOND; MORTGAGE; OPTION; PROMISSORY NOTE; SCRIP; STOCK.

Securities and Exchange Commission (SEC), an independent agency of the United States government. With the purpose of protecting investors, the SEC regulates certain financial activities—particularly transactions in securities (stocks and bonds)—involving interstate commerce and the use of the mails. It was formed in 1934 at a time when public confidence in securities was shaken by disclosures of fraudulent and careless practices following the stock market crash of 1929.

The SEC's major powers are provided by two federal laws, the Securities Act of 1933 and the Securities Exchange Act of 1934. The 1933 act provides, with some exceptions, that corporations issuing securities must register them with a federal agency prior to their offer for sale and must disclose financial and certain other information to potential investors. The act also prohibits fraudulent practices in the offer and sale of securities.

The Securities Exchange Act provided for the creation of the SEC and extended the disclosure doctrine of investor protection to securities listed on national securities exchanges. In 1964 the act was amended to further extend the disclosure principle to many companies whose securities are traded over-the-counter. In addition, the act provides for the registration and regulation of national securities exchanges and brokers and dealers in over-the-counter securities. The SEC also administers federal laws regulating public utility holding companies.

The SEC is empowered to make rules and regulations to further its goals of providing investors with adequate and truthful information about companies issuing securities and maintaining an honest securities market. The SEC enforces the laws administered by it through its power to review registrations, conduct administrative proceedings, and institute civil actions in the federal courts.

The SEC has five members, appointed by the President and approved by the Senate. Members serve five-year terms.

Securities Investor Protection Corporation (SIPC), a nonprofit federally chartered corporation that protects investors against losses in their accounts resulting from brokerage firm insolvency. Investors are protected against losses of up to $100,000 in their cash accounts and of up to $500,000 in their cash and securities accounts combined. Most brokerage houses are members and contribute to the insurance fund. The SIPC, created by Congress in 1970, operates under the Securities and Exchange Commission.

Security Council. See UNITED NATIONS, subtitle *UN's Major Organs.*

Sedalia, sḗ-dāl'yȧ, Missouri, the seat of Pettis County. It lies in west-central Missouri, about 60 miles (97 km) southeast of Kansas City. Sedalia is the trade center for a prosperous agricultural area and has railway repair shops and varied light industries. The Missouri State Fair is held here each August. Sedalia was founded in 1860. It has the mayor-council form of government.

Population: 19,800.

Sedan, Battle of, a decisive French defeat in the Franco-Prussian War (1870-71).

Before this battle, France had suffered a series of reverses along its eastern and northeastern frontiers. In August, 1870, one French army was trapped by the Prussians at the fortified city of Metz. A second army, led by Emperor Napoleon III, moved into the town of Sedan on the Meuse River, about 140 miles (225 km) northeast of Paris. There it was encircled by Prussian forces under the personal direction of King (later German Emperor) William I.

In a day-long battle at Sedan on September 1, 1870, Prussian artillery devastated French defenses. French infantry and cavalry suffered heavy losses in unsuccessful attempts to break through the Prussian lines; some 3,000 French troops were killed and 14,000 wounded. The next day, with all hope of victory lost, Napoleon surrendered himself and his army of more than 100,000 men to the Prussian king. The defeat had a profound effect on France; revolution broke out in Paris and within a week the Second Empire was overthrown.

Sedative, a drug that promotes relaxation of the body and mind by depressing activity in the central nervous system. In most cases, the person who takes the sedative remains awake, but is calm. In large doses most sedatives act as hypnotics (drugs that produce sleep). Sedatives are similar to tranquilizers, but are more likely to dull the mind and induce drowsiness. Among the drugs used as sedatives are barbiturates, chloral hydrate, and paraldehyde. Sedatives are often prescribed for such conditions as hypertension (high blood pressure) and hyperemotional states. Sedatives should be used only under medical supervision since many are habit-forming.

See also BARBITURATES.

Seder. See PASSOVER.

Sedge, sĕj, the common name of a large family of plants related to the grasses. The sedge family consists of about 90 genera and some 4,000 species. Sedges are found throughout the world, often in wet places such as swamps and bogs. They have narrow leaves and solid stems that, in cross-section, may be three-sided, cylindrical, or flattened. Sedges typically have small tan or green flowers arranged spirally on a stalk.

Carex, the largest genus of the sedge family, has more than 1,500 species. Various species of this genus are used in making matting and grass rugs. Other well-known sedges are the bulrush and the papyrus. Sedges are often confused with rushes. (See RUSH.)

The sedge family is Cyperaceae.

See also BULRUSH; PAPYRUS.

Sedimentary Rock. See ROCK, subtitle *How Rocks Are Formed:* Sedimentary Rocks.

Sedition, speech, writing, or other action that promotes disrespect for or resistance to the government. Sedition falls short of open acts of disloyalty, which are classified as treason. Unlike treason, sedition is not specifically defined in the U.S. Constitution, and Congress, therefore, may decide what is seditious. In 1798 Congress passed a sedition act making it a crime to criticize the government and its officials. A controversial law, it was allowed to expire in 1801. (See ALIEN AND SEDITION ACTS.) During World War I, antisedition legislation was enacted to control groups that might interfere with the war effort. The first peacetime sedition law since 1798 was the Alien Registration Act (Smith Act) of 1940.

Sedition legislation was also enacted after World War II to regulate the activities of Communists and other advocates of the forceful overthrow of the government. Two such laws were passed: the Internal Security Act (McCarran Act), in 1950, and the Communist Control Act, in 1954.

Sedum, sē'dŭm, a genus of about 600 species of succulent plants, mostly perennial. The sedums are found in the temperate region of the Northern Hemisphere. They store water in their thick, fleshy leaves. Sedums grow well in full sunlight and sandy soil. They are mostly cultivated in rock gardens and as border plants. Most species are low and creeping; some, however, grow upright. The flowers, borne in terminal clusters on the stem, may be white, yellow, blue, pink, or red.

Two of the most commonly cultivated species are the *wall pepper,* or *goldmoss stonecrop,* and the *live-forever,* or *orpine.* The wall pepper is a creeping plant up to five inches (13 cm) tall. It has small, triangular leaves and bright yellow flowers. The live-forever is an upright plant that grows to about 18 inches (45 cm). It has oval leaves with toothed edges and reddish-purple flowers.

The genus *Sedum* belongs to the orpine family, Crassulaceae. The wall pepper is *S. acre;* the live-forever, *S. telephium.*

Seed, a reproductive structure produced by plants as a means of giving rise to new plants similar to the parents. Not all plants produce seeds—only those that bear flowers or cones. And even some of these plants can reproduce by other means, such as by bulbs and runners.

USDA Photos

Sunflower Seeds
2½ x actual size

Cotton Seeds
2½ x actual size

Lettuce Seeds
6 x actual size

Soybean Seeds
2½ x actual size

Castor Bean Seeds
2¼ x actual size

Seeds vary greatly in size, shape, and color. Orchid seeds are scarcely larger than specks of dust, while a coconut seed can weigh as much as 50 pounds (23 kg). The size of a seed does not indicate the size of the plant that will grow from it. For example, a redwood that is 300 feet (90 m) tall grows from a seed that is only 1/6 of an inch (4 mm) long, but a lima bean seed that is one inch (2.5 cm) long produces a plant only two feet (60 cm) tall.

Some seeds are round, some are flat, and some are irregularly shaped. Some have a ridged surface; others are smooth. Seed color varies from species to species, as well as among plants of the same species. Some seeds have a characteristic shading or patterning. It is often possible to identify the species of plant from which the seed comes by the external appearance of the seed.

Economic Importance

Various seeds are rich in fats, proteins, or carbohydrates (chiefly starch and sugar). The grains of wheat, rice, corn, rye, and barley are important sources of food. (Botanically, a *grain,* also called a *kernel,* is a one-seeded fruit consisting almost entirely of the seed.) Coffee beans and cacao beans are seeds used to make beverages and flavorings. Cardamom, nutmeg, and mustard seed are used as spices in cooking. Many nuts are rich in calcium and iron. (A nut is a fruit consisting of a seed covered with a hard shell.) Some seeds, however, are harmful to humans and may be fatal if eaten in suffi-

cient quantity. For example, the seeds of apples and cherries contain a poisonous substance containing cyanide.

Many useful oils are obtained from seeds. The seed of the flax plant yields an oil used in making paints, varnishes, soft soap, and printer's ink. Soybean oil, extracted from the seed and then refined, is used in many different food products, chiefly margarines and shortenings. Corn kernels furnish an oil used in cooking. Cellulose fibers on the surface of the cotton seed are used in making cotton cloth.

Seeds are raised commercially for use by farmers in planting crops and by gardeners in planting fruits, vegetables, flowers, and lawns. In the United States, seeds marketed in interstate commerce must meet certain requirements set by the U.S. Department of Agriculture. Each package of seeds must be labeled with the percentage guaranteed to germinate (sprout) and the amount of weed seeds and other impurities.

The federal government and the large seed companies have extensive research facilities where new plant varieties are developed, and existing ones are improved. Such research often results in the development of seeds that give rise to crop plants better able to resist such conditions as drought and disease. To help them grow and develop these resistant crops, researchers often obtain seeds from *plant gene banks,* facilities throughout the world where seeds of almost every plant species are stored.

Structure

A seed consists of three parts: the embryo, the food-storage tissue, and one or two protective coverings.

Embryo. The embryo, the young plant in the early period of development, consists of one or more cotyledons, the epicotyl, and the hypocotyl. The *cotyledon,* also called the *seed leaf,* is a modified leaflike structure that digests and stores food. The *epicotyl* gives rise to the *plumule,* which becomes the stem and leaves of the mature plant. The *hypocotyl* gives rise to the *radicle,* or *root tip,* from which the roots of the mature plant develop.

Botanists classify angiosperms (flowering plants) according to the number of cotyledons present. If only one cotyledon appears in the embryo, as in corn, the plant is called a *monocotyledon,* or *monocot.* If two cotyledons are present, as in beans, the plant is called a *dicotyledon,* or *dicot.* Monocots and dicots differ in structure. For example, monocots usually have parallel veins in their leaves; dicots usually

Seed Structure. These cutaway views show a corn seed (a monocotyledon seed), *left,* and a bean seed (a dicotyledon seed), *right.*

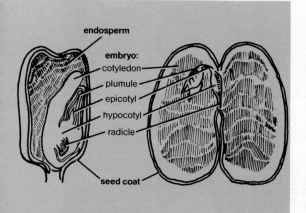

endosperm

embryo:
cotyledon
plumule
epicotyl
hypocotyl
radicle

seed coat

Germination of a Dicot Seed (bean)

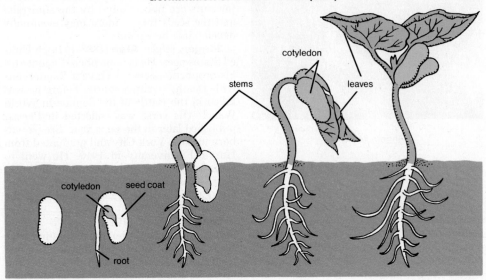

have branching veins. Gymnosperms (nonflowering plants that typically bear cones), such as pines and spruces, usually have several cotyledons. They are not classified according to the number of cotyledons because the seeds of all gymnosperms develop into structurally similar plants, regardless of the number of cotyledons present.

Food-storage Tissue. In plants with one cotyledon and in gymnosperms, the food-storage tissue is a specialized structure, the *endosperm*. In plants with two cotyledons, the cotyledons absorb the endosperm before the seed germinates (see subtitle *Dormancy and Germination*). The cotyledons then serve as the food-storage tissue.

Protective Covering. In gymnosperms and a few angiosperms, the protective covering consists of only the *seed coat* (or *testa*), which protects the embryo from excessive moisture, rapid changes in temperature, and injury. In most angiosperms, a second protective covering, the *tegmen,* forms on the inside of the seed coat.

Development

In angiosperms, sperm carried in pollen grains fertilizes the egg contained in the part of the flower called an *ovule*. (Ovules are enclosed in the part of the flower called an *ovary*.) After fertilization, the ovule develops into a seed and the ovary grows and matures. The mature ovary is commonly known as a *fruit*. (See FLOWER, subtitle *Seed and Fruit Development*.)

The seeds of gymnosperms also develop when sperm fertilize the eggs contained in the ovules. These ovules, however, are not inside ovaries; instead, they are typically borne on the scales of a cone. Because the seeds of gymnosperms are not enclosed in an ovary, these seeds are sometimes called *naked seeds*. (See CONIFER.)

Dormancy and Germination

A seed remains in a dormant, or resting, stage before the plant embryo begins to develop into a *seedling,* a young plant. This dormancy may last only a few days, or it may last several years, depending on the species of plant. During this time, the embryo uses little or no oxygen, and its life processes are considerably reduced. Some seeds remain dormant until environmental conditions enable them to resume growth. Other seeds remain dormant because the embryo has not developed fully enough to germinate; the resting stage allows the embryo to mature completely. Seeds hundreds of years old are occasionally found that will germinate when provided with proper conditions, such as heat and moisture.

Seed germination is the resuming of growth of the plant embryo. Many factors, such as water, oxygen, and light, influence the time at which the seed will germinate. A specific temperature range and a suitable soil acidity are also necessary. Auxins and other plant hormones must be produced inside the seed to stimulate growth. Finally, food must

Dr. I. W. Schmidt, F.P.S.A.
Andrés Segovia

be available for the embryo to grow and develop.

If the foregoing conditions are present, the seed will absorb water and begin digesting available food for the energy it needs to resume growth. The embryo grows through a continuous process of cell division and cell enlargement. Soon the seed coat ruptures because of the absorption of water and the pressure of the expanding embryo, and the seedling breaks through the ground. As soon as the seedling is able to make its own food by photosynthesis, germination is complete. The seedling continues to grow into the mature plant. A mature plant is capable of reproduction—that is, of producing a new generation of seeds.

Dispersal

Seeds are scattered widely by wind, water, and animals. Tumbleweeds break off near the ground in the autumn when their seeds are ripe. Their seeds are then scattered when the wind tumbles the plant along the ground. Some seeds are buoyant and are carried by water currents from place to place. Some weeds are covered with hooks, spines, or barbs that enable them to adhere to clothing and animal fur and feathers. Birds and other animals eat many kinds of fleshy fruits; in many cases the seeds pass through their digestive tracts unchanged and are deposited far from where the fruit was consumed. Squirrels often bury nuts some distance

Books about Seeds

Copeland, L. O., and M. B. McDonald. *Principles of Seed Science and Technology* (Chapman & Hall, 1995).

Loewer, P. H. *Seeds: the Definitive Guide to Growing, History, and Lore* (Macmillan, 1996).

Turner, C. B. *Seed Sowing and Saving* (Storey, 1997).

For Younger Readers

Pascoe, Elaine. *Seeds and Seedlings* (Blackbirch, 1996).

away from the tree that bore them. Many of the nuts are never found by the squirrels, and the seeds they contain may eventually develop into new plants.

Seeger, sē'gēr, **Alan** (1888-1916), a United States poet. He is remembered mainly for his prophetic poem, "I Have a Rendezvous with Death," written shortly before he was killed in the Battle of the Somme in World War I. His verse was collected in *Poems,* published later in the same year. Seeger was born in New York City and graduated from Harvard University in 1910. He went to Paris in 1912 and at the beginning of World War I enlisted in the French Foreign Legion. His *Letters and Diary* was published the year after his death.

Seeger, Pete (1919-   ), a United States folksinger who helped popularize American folk music. He became known for his songs of brotherhood, peace, and love. He also became noted as an advocate for social justice, freedom of speech, and environmental protection.

Seeger was born in New York City. He attended Harvard, 1936-38. He then traveled about the country, gathering and singing folk songs. In 1940 Seeger formed a folk group called the Almanac Singers. After serving in World War II, he helped found the Weavers, the group that led the folk music revival in the 1950's. (For photo, see FOLK MUSIC.)

Seeger wrote *How to Play the Five-String Banjo* (1948) and *The Incompleat Folksinger* (1973). His songs include "Where Have All the Flowers Gone" and "Turn, Turn, Turn."

Seeing Eye Dog. See BLINDNESS, subtitle *Mobility Aids:* Guide Dogs.

Seersucker. See TEXTILE (table).

Seferiades, Giorgos. See NOBEL PRIZES (Literature, 1963).

Sego Lily. See MARIPOSA LILY.

Segovia, sĕ-gô'vyä, **Andrés** (1893-1987), a Spanish virtuoso guitarist. His masterful technique and artistic expression helped make the guitar a solo concert instrument. Internationally famed for more than 50 years, Segovia inspired such contemporary composers as de Falla and Villa Lobos to write for the guitar. His performances also led many music schools throughout the world to establish courses in classical guitar. Segovia was largely self-taught as a guitarist. He made his debut in Granada at age 16. His debut in Paris (1924) marked the beginning of his international fame. Segovia transcribed many works by Bach and other composers, enriching the guitar repertoire.

Segré, Emilio. See NOBEL PRIZES (Physics, 1959).

Segregation, the setting apart of people on the basis of such differences as race, religion, culture, and sex. In modern history racial segregation has been practiced especially in nations where dominant whites have wished to keep blacks subservient. South Africa, for example, followed such a policy, known as apartheid, from 1948 to 1991. (See APARTHEID.) In the United States racial segregation developed after the Civil War when whites were unwilling to give former slaves equal social and economic opportunity. Desegregation (or integration) of schools, public transportation facilities and eating places, and residential areas was a primary goal in the civil rights movement. (See BLACK AMERICANS; CIVIL RIGHTS MOVEMENT.)

Religious differences caused the segregation of Jews, who through centuries of Christian history were forced to live in a separate section of the city known as the ghetto. In India the population has long been divided on the basis of cultural differences; in ancient times the "untouchables," a native people, were excluded by the conquering Aryans from any participation in the mainstream of Indian life. Although discrimination against untouchables has been outlawed, segregation practices still exist. Segregation by sex is the basis of separate religious orders for men and women.

See also GHETTO.

Sei Whale. See WHALE, subtitle *Baleen, or Whalebone, Whales:* Rorquals (and picture page).

Seiche, sāsh, a temporary rising and falling of water that occurs occasionally in lakes and certain coastal waters. The phenomenon may last from a few minutes to a few hours, with the change in water level varying from one or two inches (2.5 to 5 cm) to two feet (60 cm) or more. Seiches have long been known in Europe and were observed scientifically on Switzerland's lakes as early as the 16th century. They have since been found to occur throughout much of the world. They are seldom destructive.

The causes of seiches include storms, winds, and earthquakes. Probably the most common cause is a rapid change in barometric pressure, usually as a result of a storm passing over the body of water. The sudden drop in air pressure over one part of a lake, for example, causes the water level there to rise temporarily, with a corresponding lowering of the water elsewhere in the lake.

Seidl, Anton (1850-1898), a Hungarian conductor noted for Wagnerian opera. As leading conductor of the Metropolitan Opera (1885-92) and the New York Philharmonic (1891-98), he greatly influenced American musical life. He conducted the American premieres of many of Wagner's operas and introduced the works of many composers then considered modern. Seidl was born in Budapest and attended the Leipzig Conservatory. He worked with Wagner at Bayreuth, 1872-79.

Seifert, Jaroslav. See NOBEL PRIZES (Literature, 1984).

Seignorial System. See FEUDALISM, subtitle *Features of Feudalism:* The Manorial System.

Seikan Tunnel, an undersea railway tunnel between the Japanese islands of Honshu and Hokkaido. With a length of 33.5 miles (53.9 km), it is the world's longest tunnel. It contains two tracks, allowing trains to run in both directions through the tunnel at the same time. Seikan Tunnel was completed in 1988 after 24 years of construction. It was bored largely through volcanic rock and reaches a depth of 790 feet (240 m) below sea level, some 325 feet (100 m) below the seabed of the Tsugaru Strait.

Seine River, sān, a river in France. From its source on the Plateau de Langres near Dijon it flows northwestward for 482 miles (776 km), emptying into the English Channel through a wide estuary. Tributaries include the Aube, Yonne, Loing, Marne, Oise, and Eure rivers.

The Seine is one of the main arteries of France's inland waterway system and is navigable by barge for much of its length. Oceangoing vessels travel upstream as far as Rouen. Canals link the Seine and its tributaries with other major rivers, including the Rhine, Meuse, Rhône, and Loire.

Paris is the largest and most important city on the river; Le Havre, a principal seaport for northern France, lies at its estuary. The Seine basin is one of France's most productive agricultural areas. Historic cities along the river include Saint-Denis and Fontainebleau.

Seining. See FISHING INDUSTRY, subtitle *Fishing Techniques.*

Seismograph, sīz'mō-gràf, an instrument designed to measure and record vibrations in the earth. Seismographs are used to study earthquakes, to detect and measure the intensity of nuclear explosions, and to analyze vibrations caused by detonations used in prospecting for oil. Most seismographs can measure vibrations in one direction only, so at least three (one for up-and-down motion, one for east-west, and one for north-south) are required to describe completely the earth's motion during an earthquake or following a nuclear blast.

To measure a vibration of any kind, it is necessary to have a stationary reference against which to make the measurement. In most seismographs an *inertial mass,* such as a pendulum bob, serves as the reference. The frame of the seismograph is securely mounted on the earth and vibrates with it. The bob tends to remain motionless, and the resulting relative motion between the frame and the bob is recorded. In the simplest form of pendulum seismograph, there is a writing instrument, such as a pen or stylus, attached to the pendulum bob. The writing tool marks a revolving drum on the frame. Most seismometers today use various electrical measuring devices. With one such device, vibrations of the earth cause a magnet attached to the frame to move with respect to a coil attached to the bob. The motion of the magnet generates in the coil an electric current whose strength is proportional to the intensity of the vibrations.

Seismographs that measure up-and-down motion usually consist of an inertial mass suspended by a spring from a horizontal arm. The relative motion of the frame and the mass is the measurement actually made.

For the use of seismographs in oil prospecting, see PETROLEUM, subtitle *Hunting for Petroleum* (Seismograph).

Seismology. See EARTHQUAKE, subtitle *Detecting and Predicting Earthquakes.*

Selcraig, Alexander. See SELKIRK, ALEXANDER.

Selden, George Baldwin (1846-1922), a United States inventor and lawyer. He developed a gasoline engine for which he designed a so-called road locomotive. A patent applied for in 1879 was granted in 1895; it was the first American patent for an automobile propelled by a gasoline engine. Selden sold rights to his patent to auto manufacturers on a royalty basis. In 1911 his royalties ended as a result of a lawsuit won on appeal by Ford Motor Company; it was ruled that

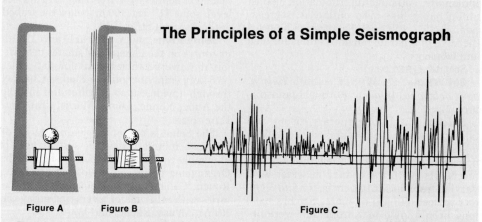

The Principles of a Simple Seismograph

Figure A   Figure B   Figure C

Figure A, a simple seismograph when the earth is calm. A pen, attached to the pendulum bob, draws a continuous line on a revolving drum that moves from right to left. **Figure B,** a simple seismograph when there is an earthquake. The frame and the revolving drum attached to it vibrate with the earth. The pendulum bob remains still. The jagged line is a permanent record of the relative motion between the drum and the pendulum bob. **Figure C,** a seismograph recording of an earthquake. The two bottom lines were made before the earthquake began.

Selden's patent did not cover the type of engine used by Ford and most other manufacturers.

Selden was born in Clarkson, New York. He studied law and began to practice in Rochester in 1871, specializing in patent law.

Selection, Natural. See EVOLUTION, subtitle *How Evolution Takes Place*.

Selective Service System, an independent agency of the United States government. Its purpose is to conduct, when specifically authorized to do so, compulsory registration of all men and to select from the registrants a pool of manpower for induction into the armed forces. It existed during both World Wars and was made permanent in 1951. The agency inducted (drafted) men into the armed forces until 1973, when conscription was ended. However, the Selective Service continues to exist, being maintained at a minimal level of organization with the capacity to expand quickly if military needs require reinstitution of the draft.

History

The draft was first used in the United States during the Civil War. Both sides originally relied on volunteers, but when these proved to be insufficient, conscription was authorized. The South adopted a draft law in 1862. From its beginning, it was highly unpopular. The poor felt it to be unfair, resenting the provision that men could hire a substitute, which allowed the wealthy to avoid the draft.

The North instituted its first national conscription law in 1863. There was widespread opposition to it, most seriously in New York, which underwent several days of near-anarchy during the Draft Riots of July, 1863. (See DRAFT RIOTS.) A person could avoid the draft by hiring a substitute or purchasing an exemption for 300 dollars.

The present Selective Service System dates back to the entrance of the United States into World War I. Congress passed the Selective Service Act of 1917, authorizing the "selective service" of men 21 through 30 years of age for the duration of the war. Avoiding the mistakes of the Civil War, it prohibited substitutions and the purchase of exemptions. The draft had popular support, partly because it involved the citizenry by making them responsible for conscription through local selective service boards.

Within three weeks of the passage of the Selective Service Act, more than 10 million

Wide World

Draft Lottery Drawing, 1969. A member of the Selective Service's Youth Advisory Committee makes a V sign for peace as he reaches for a capsule.

men were registered, and an army of 700,000 was raised within months. The 1917 draft terminated with the end of the war in November, 1918.

Under the National Defense Act of 1926, the Joint Army and Navy Selective Service Committee was set up to plan for a national draft in the event of another war emergency. When the Selective Training and Service Act of 1940 was passed by Congress, the committee had already developed a nationwide selective service system that was ready to go into operation within days after the law took effect.

The 1940 law was the country's first peacetime draft. The first registration involved more than 16 million men 21 through 35 years of age.

The 1940 law was repeatedly renewed by Congress during World War II, but was allowed to expire in 1947. By the following year, however, it had become evident that the manpower needs of the armed forces were not being met through voluntary enlistment, and Congress passed the Selective Service Act of 1948. The first registration included more than 8 million men aged 18 through 26. Subsequently, registration became a continual process, requiring all men to register as they reached 18.

Under 1951 amendments, the Selective Service System was made a permanent agency, but its authority to induct men was granted only for specific periods of time by Congress. For the first time, the induction of students was deferred until completion of their studies.

Congress renewed the Selective Service's authority to induct in 1955, 1959, 1963, and 1967 with little change in law. The 1967 act extended such authority to 1971. During the late 1960's the system came under intense criticism by some of the public. Many persons felt the system was unjust, because student deferments tended to permit men from prosperous families to avoid military service through continual deferment. Some opposed Selective Service because it sent men into service at a time when the United States was fighting in the Vietnamese War, a conflict in which many thought the country was wrongfully involved.

In 1969 the period of draft eligibility for registrants was reduced from seven years to one year. Previously, men could be conscripted anytime after their 18th birthday up to the age of 26 (35 if they received deferments), but the new law limited the period of eligibility to a 12-month period beginning (in most cases) with the 19th birthday. There was no need to draft everyone who was eligible each year, so a lottery was used to select the men to be drafted.

Under the Selective Service Act of 1971, most student deferments were eliminated. In 1973, the draft was abolished. Registration was discontinued in 1976 but reestablished in 1980.

Selene, sĕ-lē′nē, in Greek mythology, the moon goddess. She was generally described as a daughter of the Titan Hyperion and a sister of Helios, the sun god. The best-known legend of Selene was her romance with the mortal Endymion. She gradually came to be identified with the goddess Artemis—the Roman Diana.

Selenite. See GYPSUM.

Selenium, sĕ-lē′nĭ-ŭm, a chemical element. Selenium exists in four forms, one metallic and three nonmetallic. All four forms, and all selenium compounds, are poisonous. The metallic form, known as *gray selenium,* is the most stable form at ordinary temperatures. It is a fair conductor of heat

S-270

and has a metallic luster. The metal conducts electricity more readily on exposure to light than in the dark; its electrical conductivity varies with the amount of illumination.

The three nonmetallic forms slowly change into gray selenium when heated. *Monoclinic selenium* is a dark red crystalline form that is chemically stable below about 338° F. (170° C.). *Red amorphous selenium* is a red powder. *Vitreous selenium,* a black glassy solid, is formed when molten selenium is rapidly cooled. It is a poor conductor of heat and electricity. Both vitreous selenium and red amorphous selenium are chemically stable below about 140° F. (60° C.).

All forms except monoclinic selenium are commercially important. Most commercial selenium is used by the electronics industry in the manufacture of rectifiers and photoelectric cells. It is used as a decolorizer in the manufacture of clear glass and as a semiconductor in xerography. Selenium is also used in the manufacture of vulcanized rubber, pigments, red glass, deodorants, cortisone, and niacin.

Selenium forms many useful chemical compounds. *Selenium oxychloride,* an extremely corrosive liquid, is used as a solvent in paint and varnish removers. *Selenium dioxide* is used as an antioxidant in lubricating oils and in the manufacture of organic chemicals. *Sodium selenate* is used in medicine to treat certain animal diseases. Other selenium compounds are used in photographic toning baths, in insecticides and fungicides, and as solid lubricants in various aerospace devices.

Selenium was discovered by the Swedish chemist Jöns J. Berzelius in 1817. The element is widely distributed in the earth's crust, but deposits are small. It sometimes occurs free (chemically uncombined) in nature, but is usually found combined with a metal (most commonly copper, lead, or silver) in compounds called *selenides.* It also occurs as an impurity in various sulfide minerals. In some semiarid regions certain plants, commonly called locoweeds, concentrate selenium from the soil and sometimes poison grazing animals that feed on them.

Most commercial selenium, either in the form of gray selenium or red amorphous selenium, is recovered as a by-product in the refining of copper sulfide ores. The leading selenium-producing countries are Japan, Canada, and the United States.

Symbol: Se. Atomic number: 34. Atomic weight: 78.96. Specific gravity (gray selenium): 4.79. Melting point (gray selenium): 422.6° F. (217° C.). Boiling point (gray selenium): 1,265° F. (685° C.). Selenium has six stable isotopes: Se-74, Se-76, Se-77, Se-78, Se-80, and Se-82. It belongs to Group VIA of the Periodic Table and can have a valence of –2, +4, or +6.

Seleucid Kingdom, sē-lū′sĭd, an ancient realm that centered mainly in Syria. It was founded by Seleucus, one of the Diadochi (Successors), the group of generals in the army of Alexander the Great to whom control of Alexander's empire fell after his death in 323 B.C. Within a year the Diadochi were fighting each other for supreme control. In 312 B.C. Seleucus seized control of Babylonia. As Seleucus I, later called the Conqueror, he created an empire by annexing Syria, Asia Minor, and areas eastward to India. He founded as his capitals Seleucia-on-the-Tigris, near Babylon, and Antioch, in northern Syria. (See ANTIOCH.) Both cities became major trade centers.

The civilization of the Seleucid Kingdom was Hellenistic, or Greek, influenced by native Asian traditions. The kings, for example, spoke Greek, but they ruled in the Oriental manner—as absolute monarchs.

Seleucus I was murdered by a rival in Macedonia in 280 B.C. His descendants included five other kings named Seleucus and 12 kings named Antiochus. The most notable among them were Antiochus III (reigned 223-187 B.C.) and Antiochus IV (reigned 175-163 B.C.). (See ANTIOCHUS.) The empire gradually disintegrated under the later kings. The chief rivals were the Ptolemies of Egypt, with whom a succession of wars was fought. The Parthians, a native group in Persia, declared their independence from Seleucid rule and began to found their own empire in about 248 B.C. By 129 B.C. the Seleucid Kingdom had been reduced to a small area in northern Syria. It ended in 64 B.C. when Pompey made Syria a Roman province.

Self-defense, protecting oneself against attack. In law, the right of self-defense permits a person to defend himself or herself and family members against physical injury even to the point of taking the attacker's life. (See HOMICIDE, subtitle *Other Forms of Homicide*.) Use of a firearm or other weapon as a means of self-defense is controlled by law. Knowing some of the principles of defending oneself without weapons is considered desirable for persons living in urban areas where street crime is prevalent. Judo and karate are highly developed systems of self-defense.

See also MARTIAL ARTS.

Self-hypnosis. See HYPNOTISM.

Seljuks. See TURKS, subtitle *The Turks in History*.

Selkirk (or **Selcraig**), **Alexander** (1676-1721), a Scottish sailor. His adventures as a castaway inspired the plots of many tales, of which the best known is Daniel Defoe's *Robinson Crusoe* (1719).

Selkirk, who first went to sea as a youth, joined a privateering expedition to the South Pacific in 1703. A year later Selkirk was marooned on one of the Juan Fernández Islands. The circumstances are not entirely clear. According to one account, the crew deserted ship but later reboarded, except for Selkirk. According to another story, Selkirk quarreled with the captain and asked to be put ashore. Both accounts agree that Selkirk changed his mind and begged to be taken aboard again but was left behind. He spent more than four years alone on the island before being rescued. Selkirk died at sea, struck by tropical fever while serving as an officer in the Royal Navy.

Selkirk, Thomas Douglas, Fifth **Earl of** (1771-1820), a Scottish colonizer who helped settle landless Scottish and Irish farmers in Canada. He founded a successful colony on Prince Edward Island in 1803. In 1811 he obtained from the Hudson's Bay Company a tract of land called Assiniboia (in what is now Manitoba). A settlement was established in the Red River Valley the following year. When its existence was threatened by rivalry between the Hudson's Bay Company and the North West Company, he spent much of his fortune and his energies to preserve the settlement.

Selkirk was born in Scotland. He succeeded his father as earl in 1799.

Selling, exchanging a product, service, or property for money. Selling includes the efforts on the salesperson's part to persuade the buyer to make the purchase. *Salesmanship* is the art of persuasion used by the salesperson.

Men and women who sell goods and services are essential to an industrial economy based largely on free enterprise. With certain types of products or services—life insurance, for example—or an entirely new type of product, it is necessary to create in

Don & Pat Valenti/Hillstrom Stock Photo

Successful Selling depends in part on the salesperson's attitude and manner. Friendliness and interest do much to close sales and, equally important, to win repeat business.

the public a desire to buy. Where competition exists, each producer must convince potential customers that his product or service is better suited to their needs than that of a competitor. Even monopolies, such as public utilities, strive to increase the use of their product or service, to earn additional income for future development or greater profits. All of these efforts involve selling. The producer without an effective sales force, with rare exceptions, has few customers.

Salespersons are employed by manufacturers and other producers, by wholesalers, and by retailers. Services are often sold directly to the consumer; such is the case with a babysitter, a boy mowing lawns, or a barber. Most producers of goods prefer to deal in quantities greater than individual consumers wish to buy. A cannery, for example, prefers to sell boxcar loads rather than individual cans or even cases of cans. Therefore, products are generally sold first to either a wholesaler or a retailer. A wholesaler resells the product to a retailer, a professional or industrial user, or another wholesaler. A retailer sells the product to individual consumers.

Personal Selling

Most selling is personal, involving face-to-face contact between seller and buyer. There are two methods of personal selling—inside and outside.

In *inside selling* the customer comes to the seller, as in a store or shop. It is the usual method at the retail level. Some wholesalers maintain showrooms or sales offices for inside selling. The retail clerk is often thought of as being an order taker rather than a salesperson. However, a friendly clerk who takes an interest in the customers and in the merchandise is often able to sell them additional items and, at the very least, create the kind of goodwill that brings repeat business.

In *outside selling* the salesperson goes to prospective customers. A door-to-door salesperson, for example, is an outside retail salesperson. Wholesalers do most of their selling through representatives who call on potential customers. Outside selling is especially important for products whose need or importance might not be fully understood without a demonstration or sales talk.

The Salesperson and Salesmanship. A salesperson's job is to influence others to make a particular decision, to act in a particular way; he tries to get them to buy whatever he has to sell. Thus, the ability to influence people is the key to successful salesmanship. (In this sense, the art of salesmanship is useful in many other fields. The person seeking a job uses salesmanship to persuade an employer to hire him. The politician running for office, the lawyer addressing a jury, and the teacher trying to motivate or inspire pupils—all are trying to "sell" their services or ideas.)

It is important for the salesperson to present a pleasing appearance and have a pleasant, courteous manner. If the customer finds a salesperson annoying or disagreeable, he may not buy the product or service even though he wants it.

The salesperson needs to understand people—why they do what they do, and especially, why they buy what they buy. A knowledge of psychology can help the salesperson understand human motivations. Knowing what motivations create a desire for his product enables the salesperson to emphasize the product's appealing aspects. An automobile salesman, for example, might emphasize power and performance to a customer in his 20's, but safety and economy to a middle-aged couple.

The salesperson should have a thorough knowledge of his product or service. To convince a prospect of its value, he must know and be able to explain its advantages.

Salespeople must know how to demonstrate the product and how to display it so that it looks attractive. They must also know what competitors can offer.

Many high schools and colleges offer a general course in selling. Firms often provide special training for their sales personnel. This training is centered on the firm's product or service and may include demonstrations of actual selling. A set speech or sales talk, which the salesperson may alter to fit the circumstances, is a selling aid used with many types of products.

To sell products of a technical nature, a person may need a technical education. For example, a background in electrical engineering is necessary for a person selling electrical equipment to power companies.

Some salespeople are paid only a salary, but a combination of salary and commission (a percentage of sales made by the salesperson) is more common. Selling can be useful experience for a person intending eventually to hold a management or executive position.

Nonpersonal Selling

Nonpersonal selling does not involve direct contact between seller and buyer. Non-personal selling techniques generally work best when buyers already know and want the product. The reputation of the seller is also important.

Common types of nonpersonal selling include selling by mail, by catalog, and from vending machines. Telephone solicitation, or telemarketing, is considered nonpersonal because the salesperson and the customer do not meet face-to-face. Other selling techniques sometimes considered to be nonpersonal (although they are also often used in connection with personal selling efforts) are advertising flyers, coupons, sample products, and sales promotions, which aid in persuading the buyers that they want a product.

History

Throughout history, people have engaged in trade—that is, they have bartered one thing for another or bought and sold goods with some form of money. Before modern times, however, there was little need for salesmanship. Goods and services offered for sale were usually scarce and sought after; little persuasion was needed to convince a potential customer to buy. A seller's greatest asset was the ability to haggle.

In colonial America, salespeople often carried goods to customers. Seafaring merchants worked up and down the east coast. Itinerant peddlers traveled throughout the countryside. Criers offered their wares in the streets of the towns. In the eastern towns, craftsmen often sold their goods at their workshops, which in many cases were in their homes. Trading posts and, later, general stores served the frontier. Specialty shops selling a single line of goods spread with the growth of towns and cities in the 19th century.

Shopkeepers were generally impatient with casual inquiries; thus it was difficult to shop—that is, to look and consider—without feeling forced to buy. Price was decided by haggling. If a customer discovered his purchased goods to be of poor quality, he had little recourse. "Let the buyer beware" expressed the general attitude.

In the second half of the 19th century, following the example of a French merchant in Paris, the department stores of R. H. Macy in New York City, John Wanamaker in Philadelphia, and Marshall Field in Chicago introduced several changes in retail selling. Merchandise was displayed and customers were invited to browse without obligation to buy. Moreover, the quality of the merchan-

---

Steps in a Sale

The process of making a sale is divided into four basic steps, often summarized by the letters AIDA (attention, interest, desire, and action).

Getting the Prospect's Attention. Without attention it is obvious that the next steps cannot take place. Here the salesperson's appearance and method of approach are important in setting the stage for what is to follow.

Arousing Interest. Displaying the article, perhaps letting the prospect handle it, and stating what it will do for him or her—these are some effective ways of arousing interest. Interest must be secured early in the demonstration or the prospect may not be willing to listen further.

Creating Desire. The sales talk should attempt to show how important the article or service is to the prospect. Some leading buying motives are desire for comfort, for enjoyment, for gain, for self-improvement, for attention, for health, or for beauty.

Obtaining Action, or Closing the Sale. The salesperson must help the prospect decide to buy and overcome any reasons for delay. Although success in getting the order depends largely upon the effectiveness of the previous steps, many orders are lost because the salesperson is a weak "closer."

dise was backed by the store and an item could be returned for replacement or refund if it was unsatisfactory. "The customer is always right" was the slogan of these merchants.

Selling through direct marketing was a widespread practice in the mid-1900's. In direct marketing a seller uses one or more communications media—mail, television or print ads, catalogs, the telephone, or the Internet—to reach a potential buyer. Direct marketing pitches generally make an offer and provide a potential buyer with the means to respond—for example, a coupon, a response form, or a toll-free phone number.

The 1990's saw an increase in the use of promotions, such as product samples, contests, and coupons, to make sales. Trade shows and expositions, in which businesses gather to show and sell their products and services, attracted millions of visitors.

Another trend in the 1990's was for salespeople to seek professional certification. Professional sales and marketing associations in the United States and Canada offered certification to candidates who could demonstrate education, experience, and expertise in the field.

See also ADVERTISING; SALES PROMOTION.

Books about Selling

Frisch, Carlienne. *A Career Inside the World of Sales* (Rosen, 1998).
Gitomer, J. H. *The Sales Bible: the Ultimate Sales Resource* (Morrow, 1994).
Koller, John. *Encyclopedia of Sales and Selling: the Salesperson's Essential Handbook of Information* (Performance Consulting, 1996).
Russ, Fred, and Francis Nottuno. *Effective Selling*, 8th edition (South-Western, 1991).
Tracy, Brian. *Superior Selling: the Proven System of Selling Strategies Practiced by Salespeople Everywhere* (Simon & Schuster, 1995).

Selma, Alabama, the seat of Dallas County. It lies on the Alabama River about 45 miles (72 km) west of Montgomery, the state capital. Selma is a trading and processing center for an agricultural area and has varied light industries. Nearby is Old Cahawba, the site of Alabama's first capital, now an archeological park. Selma has a mayor-council form of government.

Selma was settled in about 1816 and soon became the shipping point for locally grown cotton. During the Civil War it was a Confederate armament center and was ravaged by Union forces in 1865. Selma was incorpo-

rated as a city in 1883. In 1965 civil rights demonstrations here, climaxed by a five-day march from Selma to Montgomery, helped to attain passage of the Voting Rights Act of 1965.

Population: 23,755.

Selten, Reinhard. See NOBEL PRIZES (Economic Science, 1994).

Selznick, David O. (Oliver) (1902-1965), a United States motion-picture producer. He is noted for his tasteful adaptations of literary works, particularly the epic *Gone with the Wind* (1939). Selznick was born in Pittsburgh, Pennsylvania. He entered the motion-picture industry in 1926 and worked for various studios, including Paramount, R.K.O.-Radio, and Metro-Goldwyn-Mayer, until 1935, when he organized his own enterprises.

His other films include *Little Women* (1933), *King Kong* (1933), *David Copperfield* (1935), *The Prisoner of Zenda* (1937), *Rebecca* (1940), *Spellbound* (1945), *Duel in the Sun* (1946), and *A Farewell to Arms* (1957).

Semantics, sĭ-măn'tĭks, the study of word meanings. It is one of the main divisions of linguistics. Sometimes the term semantics is used more broadly to include the study of all symbols—speech, writing, gestures, signs, or anything that conveys meaning. In this article, however, the discussion is limited to that study which concerns itself with determining what a word or another unit of language—such as a suffix, inflection, phrase, clause, or sentence—means and the changes in meaning that may occur over the course of time.

Semantics comes from the Greek *semaino*, "to signify." The term was introduced by the French philologist Michel Bréal in 1883. Another name for the study of meanings is semasiology.

Principles of Semantics

What Meaning Is. Meaning is defined as the symbolic value of a language unit used singly or, more commonly, with other language units; that is, in context. The basic language units are sounds, grammatical forms, words, phrases, clauses, and sentences. The central unit of meaning is the word. It is defined as a sound or series of sounds capable of standing on its own and communicating a certain meaning. Its function is to arouse in the hearer or reader a response similar to that which the speaker or writer intends. When a hearer or reader responds in a predictable way, it is said that the speaker or writer has been understood. This process is known as the transfer of meaning.

Several elements are involved in the transfer of meaning. A word in its dictionary sense has only potential meaning. It takes on actual meaning when used in a particular context or situation. For example, the word *play* has several potential meanings, including to engage in sport or recreation, to perform music, and to act on a stage. In context, it has actual meaning, as in "After school let's go outside and play." Its actual meaning is the sum total of all the relevant factors involved in the situation.

In a speaking situation, these factors may include the speaker's intention and past association with the word; the word's typical use in the language; the hearer's attitude and past experience with the word; the phenomenon to which the word refers; and the accessory words or grammatical forms that might be used to complete the meaning of what was said. Because no two situations are exactly alike, definiteness of meaning will vary.

In linguistic terms, to determine meaning one must consider the relation of the *symbol* (the word) to the *referent* (the phenomenon to which it refers) and to the *reference* (the information that it conveys).

How Meaning Changes. The generally accepted meaning of a word may change over a period of time because of a variety of factors. This process is called semantic change. How, why, or even when a particular change in word meaning occurs is, however, often obscure.

A semantic change may begin with a deliberate or accidental innovation that, through varying circumstances, becomes accepted as the meaning of the word. For example, the term *undertaker* once meant "one who undertakes a task or enterprise." One of the contexts in which it was used was that of funeral undertaker. Over the course of time, the word funeral was dropped and "one who arranges funerals" came to be the accepted meaning of undertaker.

A semantic change might also be the result of a nonlinguistic change, such as a cultural innovation. For example, the word *acre* originally meant a cultivated field. As land became more economically significant and the need for its accurate measurement more important, acre came to mean a field small enough to be plowed by a man and a yoke of oxen in one day, and eventually, a unit of area equal to 4,840 square yards.

After a semantic change, the old meaning of a word may be lost or old and new meanings may exist side by side.

Other Types of Semantic Inquiry

Logical Positivism is a philosophical movement that approaches truth and logic through the study of language. It holds that thoughts, ideas, and concepts are dependent on the structure of language. The movement originated in the 1920's with the work of Ludwig Wittgenstein and a group of philosophers at the University of Vienna known as the Vienna Group. (See WITTGENSTEIN, LUDWIG.)

General Semantics is an educational discipline that concerns itself with the relationship between symbols and behavior. Its purpose is to make language and thinking more logical and thus to improve human habits of response to the environment. It originated in the 1930's with the work of the Polish-American philosopher Alfred Korzybski. (See HAYAKAWA, S. I.; KORZYBSKI, ALFRED.)

See also RICHARDS, I. A.

Books about Semantics

Jay, Martin. *Cultural Semantics: Keywords of Our Time* (University of Massachusetts, 1998).
Lappin, Shalom, editor. *The Handbook of Contemporary Semantic Theory* (Blackwell, 1997).
Lyons, John. *Linguistic Semantics: an Introduction* (Cambridge University, 1996).
Muskens, Reinhard. *Meaning and Partiality* (Cambridge University, 1996).
Van Valin, R. D., and R. J. LaPolla. *Syntax: Structure, Meaning, and Function* (Cambridge University, 1998).

Semaphore, sĕm'ȧ-fōr, a system of signaling based on two movable arms, either human or mechanical. A person using it may hold a flag or lantern in each hand for greater visibility; or a mechanical system may have lights at the ends of the arms. Various positions of the arms stand for letters, words, and phrases. Semaphore is the fastest visual signaling system. Before wireless telegraphy it was widely used at sea for messages between ships and was used on railroads for communication between trainmen and for traffic signals.

Sembrich, Marcella (1858-1935), the stage name of Praxede Marcelline Kochanska, a Polish operatic and concert soprano. She was internationally known for the wide range and unusual beauty and brilliance of her coloratura voice. With superb technique and great emotional conviction she sang such roles as Violetta (*La Traviata*) and Gilda (*Rigoletto*). Sembrich made her operatic debut in 1877 in Athens as Elvira in *I Puritani* and her American debut in 1883 at the Metropolitan Opera in the title role of *Lucia di Lammermoor*.

Semenov, Nikolai N. See NOBEL PRIZES (Chemistry, 1956).

Semey, sĕm′ē, formerly **Semipalatinsk,** Kazakhstan, a city on the Irtysh River in the northeastern part of the country, near the Russian border. It is a railway center and a river port. Industries include meat packing, flour milling, tanning, ship repairing, and metalworking.

The city was founded by Russians in 1718 as a military outpost. Most of its growth and economic development came during the 20th century, following the construction of railways. The Turkestan-Siberia Railway, reached the city in 1906, linking it to Siberia in the north and to Central Asia in the south.

Population: 330,000.

Semicircular Canals. See EAR, subtitle *Parts of the Ear:* The Inner Ear.

Semicolon. See PUNCTUATION, subtitle *Punctuation Marks*.

Semiconductor, a material whose electrical conductivity is intermediate between that of a good conductor (such as copper) and that of an insulator (such as rubber). Most technologically important semiconductors are crystalline solids. They may be elements or compounds, either inorganic or organic. Examples are the elements silicon, germanium, tellurium, and selenium; the inorganic compounds lead sulfide, cadmium sulfide, and indium antimonide; and the organic compounds anthracene, naphthacene, and phthalocyanine.

The semiconductor that is most important commercially is silicon. It is used in such solid-state devices as transistors and rectifiers. Miniature solid-state devices formed with silicon are essential components of *integrated circuits* (complex electronic circuits manufactured as a unit) that are used in a wide variety of electronic equipment. Silicon is also used in solar cells, which produce an electric current when exposed to light. Other important semiconductors are gallium arsenide, used in LED's (light-emitting diodes), and

S-276

selenium sulfide and cadmium sulfide, which are used in photographic exposure meters.

Electrical Behavior

The usefulness of semiconductors lies chiefly in the nature of their electrical conductivity: to varying degrees, the conductivity increases with (1) an increase in temperature; (2) exposure to electromagnetic radiation; and (3) the addition of small amounts of certain impurities called dopants. The sensitivity of semiconductors to temperature, radiation, and impurities is a consequence of the semiconductors' atomic structure.

In this discussion silicon and germanium, being typical semiconductors, are used as examples. Atoms of both silicon and germanium have four valence electrons; each atom therefore requires four additional electrons to complete its outermost electron shell. (An atom with a filled outer shell is particularly stable, and atoms tend to combine in such a way as to achieve complete outer shells.)

A model of a small portion of a silicon or germanium crystal is shown in the illustration. Each atom is at the center of a regular tetrahedron of four other atoms, which are called its nearest neighbors. This structure permits each atom to share one of its valence electrons with each of its nearest neighbors, and vice versa. Thus each atom has a complete outer shell of electrons, even though they are all shared, and each is bound to each of its nearest neighbors by a two-electron bond (the shared pair of electrons).

Sensitivity to Temperature. At all temperatures above absolute zero there is some heat energy, which causes the atoms of a silicon or germanium crystal to vibrate about their average positions and also causes some of the valence electrons (which are only weakly bound to the atoms) to escape. The higher the temperature, the more frequently such escapes will occur.

When an electron escapes, two charge carriers are formed—the electron itself (called a free electron) and a positively charged vacancy (called a hole) left in one of the two-electron bonds. Since the hole is positive, it can attract electrons (which are negatively charged) from a neighboring two-electron bond. If an electron in a neighboring two-electron bond has enough thermal energy, it can shift from its original bond to the hole. This action creates a new hole in the neigh-

Semiconductor Structure

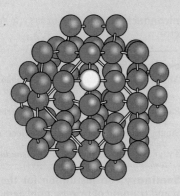 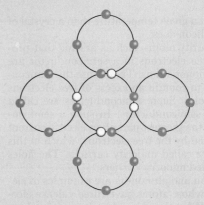

A Portion of the Structure of a Silicon or Germanium Crystal. *Left,* each sphere represents an atom. The four colored atoms are joined with a fifth atom (white) to form a tetrahedron. Except for the outermost atoms in the crystal, each atom is similarly joined to four others. (In an actual crystal there are millions of atoms, only a tiny fraction of which are on the outer surface. Also, the atoms are in constant motion; the positions shown here are called their *average* positions.)

Electron Sharing. *Right,* each large circle represents the outer electron shell of a silicon or germanium atom. The small spheres represent electrons. The small white spheres are electrons belonging to the central atom. The small colored spheres are electrons belonging to the central atom's four nearest neighbors. Thus, the central atom has its full complement of eight electrons. Each pair of shared electrons is a two-electron bond. In an actual crystal each of the central atom's nearest neighbors is similarly joined to its nearest neighbors, and also has eight electrons.

boring bond. This process can be repeated any number of times. Thus a hole can migrate through the crystal.

A hole and a free electron can recombine or unite whenever they meet to form a normal two-electron bond. In pure silicon or germanium this is the only mechanism by which a free electron or a hole can disappear.

The holes and the free electrons are the current carriers in silicon and germanium. Because the number of holes and free electrons increases with an increase in temperature, the electrical conductivity is greater at high temperatures than at low temperatures. At very low temperatures silicon and germanium behave like insulators, and at very high temperatures, like conductors.

Sensitivity to Radiation. Electromagnetic radiation can also cause an electron to be ejected from a two-electron bond. If a photon of electromagnetic radiation has sufficient energy and passes in the vicinity of a two-electron bond in a crystal of silicon or germanium, it may be absorbed and an electron simultaneously ejected from the bond. The result is the creation of a free electron and a hole. Electromagnetic radiation thus

increases the number of free electrons and holes (and therefore the electrical conductivity) in a crystal of silicon or germanium.

Sensitivity to Impurities. Two types of impurity atoms that have a profound effect upon the conductivity of silicon and germanium are those having either five valence electrons or three valence electrons.

Arsenic and phosphorus are examples of impurity atoms with five valence electrons. In a crystal of silicon containing a small amount of arsenic, the arsenic atoms randomly replace silicon atoms. Because the concentration of the arsenic is very small, the four nearest neighbors of any arsenic atom are silicon atoms. The arsenic atom forms four two-electron bonds with its four nearest neighbors exactly as a silicon atom would. Its fifth electron, however, cannot be part of a two-electron bond and the arsenic atom has a complete outer shell without it. Consequently this electron is much more easily removed from the atom than are any of the electrons in the two-electron bonds between arsenic and silicon atoms or between two silicon atoms. Thus, a silicon crystal containing arsenic contains many more free electrons at a given temperature than a crystal of pure silicon does.

Impurity atoms such as arsenic that provide free electrons in a semiconductor are called donor atoms. They cause the semiconductor to contain an excess of free electrons over holes. Such semiconductors are called *n*-type semiconductors. In such a semiconductor the greatest part of an electric current is carried by the free electrons, which in this case are called majority carriers. The holes are called minority carriers.

Boron and aluminum are examples of elements whose atoms have three valence electrons. When introduced as impurities they, too, greatly increase the electrical conductivity of silicon or germanium, but the mechanism of conduction is very different from that in the case just discussed. In a crystal of silicon containing a small amount of boron, the boron atoms substitute randomly for silicon atoms. Because a boron atom has only three valence electrons, it cannot form four two-electron bonds with its four nearest neighbors (which are silicon atoms because of the very low concentration of boron). Thus, one of the four bonds lacks a second electron. Although this structure is electrically neutral, there is a pronounced tendency to form four complete two-electron bonds. Consequently, the neutral boron atom tends to acquire an electron—either a free electron or an electron from a neighboring bond whose thermal energy is sufficient to allow it to jump. In either case the final result is a hole, which, as described before, is free to migrate through the crystal. Hence once again the presence of an impurity greatly increases the likelihood of the formation of charge carriers—in this case, predominantly holes.

Impurity atoms in semiconductors behave like boron in silicon are called acceptor atoms. They cause the semiconductor to contain an excess of holes over free electrons. Such semiconductors are called *p*-type semiconductors. In such semiconductors the greatest part of an electric current is carried by the positively charged holes. In this instance, the holes are called majority carriers and the free electrons, minority carriers.

If acceptor and donor impurity atoms are simultaneously present in a semiconductor such as silicon or germanium, then whichever one is present in the greatest concentration will determine whether the impure

semiconductor is a *p*-type or *n*-type semiconductor.

Books about Semiconductors

Angel, D. P. *Restructuring for Innovation: the Remaking of the U.S. Semiconductor Industry* (Guilford, 1994).

Parker, G. J. *Introductory Semiconductor Device Physics* (Prentice Hall, 1994).

Singh, Jasprit. *Semiconductor Devices: an Introduction* (McGraw-Hill, 1994).

Tyagi, M. S. *Introduction to Semiconductor Materials and Devices* (Wiley, 1991).

Seminary, an institution for the education and training of priests, ministers, or rabbis. (The term was widely used in the past for other types of educational institutions as well. Women's colleges, for example, were once called female seminaries.) The educational program of a seminary may begin at the high school, college, or graduate level. Roman Catholics, for example, have *preparatory seminaries* for high school students. Seminaries that offer graduate degrees in theology, leading directly to ordination (conferring of spiritual authority), are called theological seminaries, theological schools, or divinity schools.

A seminary is usually supported by a particular church, but some seminaries have programs that are nondenominational. A student enrolled in a seminary is generally called a *seminarian.*

A seminary curriculum includes biblical, theological, and doctrinal studies, as well as courses in religion and ethics. Training in practical areas, such as preaching and counseling, is also provided. A seminarian may be ordained upon completion of a graduate degree, such as the B.D. (Bachelor of Divinity), the S.T.B. (Bachelor of Sacred Theology), or the D.Mn. (Doctor of Ministry). The D.D. (Doctor of Divinity) is granted as an honorary degree.

Roman Catholic law, since the Council of Trent (1545-63), requires that there be a seminary in every diocese. The first Protestant theological seminary in the United States was founded by the Dutch Reformed Church in New York City in 1784.

Seminole Indians, sĕm'ĭ-nōl, a North American Indian tribe whose language belongs to the Muskhogean language family. The tribe came into being in the 18th century as bands of southern Indians, principally Creeks, moved into the Florida peninsula and assimilated Indians already living there.

(The name "Seminole," given the tribe by the Creek Nation, is Creek for "runaway" or "separatist.") Living among the Indians were a number of blacks. Some were slaves, purchased from white owners, and others were escaped slaves living as freemen. There was some intermarriage between blacks and the Seminoles.

By 1820 there were some 5,000 Seminoles in northern and central Spanish-held Florida. Like the Creeks, they were town dwellers who lived by farming, hunting, fishing and gathering wild plants. Their houses were thatched, open-sided huts called *chikees*.

The Seminoles were defeated in three wars (1817-18; 1835-42; 1855-58) with the United States. During the second war the majority were removed to Indian Territory (now Oklahoma), where they became one of the Five Civilized Tribes. (See also FIVE CIVILIZED TRIBES; SEMINOLE WARS.) Several hundred took refuge in the Everglades region, where reservations were later established.

In 1967 the U.S. Court of Claims ruled that the Seminoles were entitled to payment from the federal government for nearly 90 per cent of the land in Florida, which they once held. Payment of $12,347,500 was made in 1970.

There are about 4,000 Seminoles in Oklahoma, located mainly outside tribal lands. About 1,600 reside on or near four reservations in Florida.

Seminole Wars (1817-18; 1835-42; 1855-58), three wars fought between the United States and the Seminole Indians in Florida. The wars led to the removal of all but a handful of Seminoles to Indian Territory (now Oklahoma).

The First Seminole War resulted from raids into Spanish-owned Florida by state militias seeking escaped slaves who had been given sanctuary by the Seminoles. The opening battle was fought in late 1817 when United States troops clashed with Seminoles who had staged retaliatory raids into the United States. In 1818 General Andrew Jackson was ordered by President Monroe to end the conflict. Jackson, however, exceeded his orders by launching a full-scale invasion of Florida, burning every Seminole village he and his troops could find. Jackson not only subdued the Indians but also seized several Spanish towns and executed two British subjects—

Florida Development Commission
Seminole Artisan in Florida. The patchwork fabric she is sewing is of a traditional Seminole design. The fabric, popular with tourists, is an important source of income.

Alexander Arbuthnot and Robert Ambrister—whom he had accused of inciting the Seminoles.

In spite of public protest in Great Britain, the British government took no action. Spain initially demanded return of its territory but then, realizing that Florida could not be defended, reluctantly ceded it to the United States in the Adams-Onís Treaty, ratified in 1821.

After the war the Seminoles were forced to sign three treaties, the first (1823) restricting them to a reservation in central Florida and the other two (1832 and 1833) providing for their removal to west of the Mississippi River. The majority of the Indians resisted resettlement. In 1835 a few hundred warriors under the leadership of Osceola began fighting a guerrilla-style action against United States troops. After Osceola was seized and imprisoned in 1837, a succession of generals, including Zachary Taylor, slowly subdued most of the Seminoles, and about 4,000 Seminoles were sent west. The cost of the war to the United States was some 1,500 soldiers killed and more than $20,000,000 expended.

Several hundred undefeated Seminoles fell far back into the swamplands of the Florida Everglades. During 1855-58 a third war was fought, mainly a series of small engagements. The Seminoles were subdued, and all but about 125 then agreed to be removed to Indian Territory. Descendants of those that remained live in the Everglades today.

See also OSCEOLA.

Semipalatinsk. See SEMEY.

Semiramis, sĕ-mĭr′ȧ-mĭs, a legendary queen of Assyria. She was the daughter of a goddess and was acclaimed for her beauty and wisdom. After the death of her husband, King Ninus, the legendary founder of Nineveh, Semiramis reigned alone. She supposedly built the city of Babylon and led military campaigns against neighboring countries.

The historical figure behind the legend is believed to be Sammu-ramat, wife of King Shamshi-Adad V of Assyria. She reigned as regent for her son Adadnirari III for a short time late in the ninth century B.C.

Semites, people who speak languages of the Semitic branch of the Afro-Asiatic language family. Jews and Arabs are the major representatives of the Semites. There are many distinct physical types within this grouping. The term Semite comes from the name of Noah's son Shem, who, according to Hebrew legend, was the ancestor of the Semites.

The ancestral homeland of all Semites was the Arabian Peninsula. In about 3000 B.C. they began to migrate to more fertile areas and frequently intermarried with indigenous peoples. Among those who settled in Mesopotamia, Syria, and Palestine—the Fertile Crescent—were the Akkadians, Amorites (Babylonians, Canaanites, and Phoenicians), Hebrews, Assyrians, Aramaeans, and Chaldeans. Other groups crossed the Red Sea to Ethiopia. The Arab conquests of the early Middle Ages spread Arabic culture from Persia, across North Africa, to Spain. The Jews, persecuted since ancient times, dispersed all over the world. (The term anti-Semitism pertains to hostility specifically toward Jews.)

The Semites have contributed to civilization three major monotheistic religions: Judaism, Christianity, and Islam. The Semites also invented the alphabet.

See also ALPHABET, subtitle *History of the Alphabet;* LANGUAGE, section "Major Languages of the World" (Arabic; Hebrew).

Semitic Languages. See LANGUAGE, section "Major Languages of the World" (Arabic; Hebrew).

Semmelweis, zĕm′ĕl-vīs, **Ignaz Philipp** (1818-1865), a Hungarian obstetrician. He pioneered in introducing methods of *antisepsis* (killing or inhibiting the growth of disease-producing organisms). While on the maternity staff of Vienna General Hospital, 1846-49, Semmelweis drastically reduced the death rate from puerperal fever (childbed fever) by insisting that medical personnel wash their hands in a strong chemical solution before examining maternity patients. His hand-disinfecting procedure was ridiculed, however; it soon was abolished in Vienna and did not become common obstetric practice until about 1890.

Semmelweis received an M.D. degree from the University of Vienna in 1844. After his procedure was rejected in Vienna, he left that city to practice and teach obstetrics in Pest (Budapest).

Semmes, sĕmz, **Raphael** (1809-1877), a United States and Confederate naval officer. His daring as commander of the *Sumter* and *Alabama,* Confederate raiders that preyed on Union shipping, made him the naval hero of the Confederacy during the American Civil War.

Semmes was born in Charles County, Maryland. He was commissioned a midshipman in the U.S. Navy in 1826. During the Mexican War he served with distinction and rose to the rank of commander. At the outbreak of the Civil War in 1861, Semmes resigned and joined the Confederate navy. He was promoted to rear admiral in 1864. After the war he practiced law in Mobile, Alabama, and wrote about his wartime exploits.

See also ALABAMA CLAIMS.

Sempervivum. See HOUSELEEK.

Senate, in government, the upper house of a bicameral (two-chamber) legislature. In the United States, the upper house of the U.S. Congress and of each of the 49 bicameral state legislatures is called the senate. (Nebraska is the only state with a unicameral, or one-chamber, legislature.) Other countries, including Canada, France, Australia, and Argentina, have senates in their national legislatures. In some countries, there are also local, regional, state, or provincial senates. The word senate comes from the Latin *senatus* (a council of elders).

The role of the senate varies from country to country. Some senates wield considerable power, as in the United States; some play a lesser role, as in Canada. In general, however, the senate shares the lawmaking power with the lower house of the legislature. Usually the senate is the smaller body. It tends to be less representative than the lower house, its members in many cases being elected (or in some countries, appointed) on the basis of geographic area rather than population. In some legislatures, the senate may have special functions, such as confirming appointments made by the executive.

The original senate was that of ancient Rome. It began as an advisory body but gradually expanded its powers until it made all administrative decisions and laws. During the Middle Ages, similar bodies existed in some Italian city-states. In various countries in modern times, senates initially were established to act as a check on the popularly elected house of the legislature.

See also CONGRESS OF THE UNITED STATES, subtitle *The Senate;* ROME AND THE ROMAN EMPIRE, subtitle *Government.*

Sendai, sĕn-dī, Japan, the capital of Miyagi prefecture. It lies about 190 miles (306 km) north-northeast of Tokyo and is the economic and cultural center of northern Honshu. Manufactured products include processed foods, chemicals, lumber, machinery, and tools. One of the city's chief attractions is the Osaki Hachiman Shrine; its main building dates from 1607 and is an official national treasure. Tohoku University, founded in 1907, is Sendai's leading institution of higher learning. In the nearby mountains are several popular spas. Sendai originally developed around a castle built in 1602 by Masamune Date, a feudal lord.

Population: 918,398.

Sendak, sĕn'dăk, **Maurice** (1928-), a United States author and illustrator of children's books. His fanciful stories and imaginative drawings sensitively evoke the fears and joys of childhood. Sendak first established his reputation for creativity with illustrations for other authors' works, such as Ruth Krauss's *A Hole Is to Dig* (1952). *Kenny's Window* (1956) is the first book Sendak both wrote and illustrated. *Where the Wild Things Are* (1963), about a boy who rules an imaginary kingdom of monsters, won the 1964 Caldecott Medal. This book is the first in a trilogy including *In the Night Kitchen* (1970) and *Outside Over There* (1981). Sendak was born in Brooklyn, New York, and attended the Art Students League, 1949-51.

Other books he wrote and illustrated include *Nutshell Library* (1962); *Higglety Pigglety Pop!* (1967); *Seven Little Monsters* (1977); *We Are All in the Dumps with Jack and Guy* (1993). Among the many books he illustrated are *Seven Tales* (1959); *The Juniper Tree and Other Tales* (1973); *Dear Mili* (1988). *Caldecott & Co.: Notes on Books and Pictures* (1988) is a collection of essays. Sendak also designed sets for stage productions, including the opera *The Magic Flute.*

Seneca, sĕn'ē-kà, **Lucius Annaeus** (4?-B.C.-65 A.D.), a Roman philosopher and dramatist. Seneca's philosophical works are concerned with the wise conduct of life in the spirit of Stoicism. (See STOICISM.) As a teacher of ethics and morals he was noted for his practical advice rather than abstract speculation. The *Moral Letters,* for example, are informal instructions for his friend Lucilius. The *Naturales Quaestiones* ("Physical Problems"), a work in which he discussed morals and natural phenomena, became a popular science textbook in the Middle Ages.

Seneca is believed to have written nine tragedies; they are the only surviving dramas from the Roman Empire. They were based on Greek models and apparently were designed for dramatic reading rather than staging. They are characterized by gloom, horror, and bombastic style. Renaissance and Elizabethan dramatists regarded them as model tragedies and drew heavily from them.

Seneca was born in Corduba (now Córdoba), Spain, into a wealthy family. He studied in Rome. Seneca was the tutor of the young Nero and served as his adviser after Nero became emperor in 54 A.D. In 65 A.D. Seneca was accused of participation in a conspiracy to depose Nero and committed suicide at the emperor's demand.

Other philosophical treatises of Seneca are *On Clemency, On Anger, On the Brevity of Life, On the Happy Life,* and *On the Tranquillity of the Soul.* The nine tragedies are *Hercules Furens, Troades, Phoenissae, Medea, Phaedra, Oedipus, Agamemnon, Thyestes,* and *Hercules Oetaeus.*

Seneca Indians, sĕn'ē-kà, a North American tribe of the Iroquoian language family. The Senecas were the largest and the westernmost tribe of the Iroquois Confederacy, or Five Nations (later Six Nations). Originally living in what is now western New York, they expanded southwestward into what is now eastern Ohio in the late 1600's and early 1700's. At the height of their power, they numbered about 5,000.

After the Revolutionary War, in which many Senecas aided the British, part of the tribe moved to Canada. The rest eventually settled on reservations in Pennsylvania and New York. In 1848 many of the New York Senecas withdrew from the Iroquois Confederacy and formed a separate Seneca Nation. In the 1960's the Indians were forced to sell their Pennsylvania land and part of their New York land to the federal government for a dam project. Approximately 6,000 Senecas, most of whom belong to the Seneca Nation, live on or near New York reservations. About 300 Senecas reside on or near Indian reserves in Ontario, Canada.

Senefelder, Aloys. See LITHOGRAPHY.

Senegal, sĕn'ē-gôl', or **Republic of Senegal,** a country in western Africa. It faces the Atlantic Ocean at the westernmost part of the continent and extends 350 miles (560 km) inland. Bordering Senegal are Mauritania, Mali, Guinea, Guinea-Bissau, and Gambia. The area of Senegal is 75,750 square miles (196,192 km²).

Physical Geography

Most of Senegal is flat to gently rolling steppe or savanna grassland; there is forest only in the southwest. Nearly everywhere the land is only slightly above sea level. In the southeast, however, foothills of Guinea's Fouta Djallon highlands reach elevations of 1,640 feet (500 m). The coast, some 300 miles (480 km) long, varies from wide, sandy beaches north of Cape Verde to a maze of flat, swampy islands and meandering streams in the south.

Senegal's rivers, which drain westward to the Atlantic, include the Senegal and the Gambia. Both have year-round flows. Most other streams except the Casamance are dry for part of the year.

The climate throughout Senegal is tropical, with temperatures averaging about 70° F. (21° C.) to more than 80° F. (27° C.), depending on location and time of year. Most of the rain falls from June to October. The heaviest amounts, up to 65 inches (1,650 mm) annually, fall in the south. Northward, rainfall decreases gradually to about 12 inches (300 mm) a year. Devastating droughts occur periodically, especially in the northern half of Senegal, which is part of the Sahel, a transitional region bordering the Sahara.

Economy

Agriculture is the basis of the economy; manufacturing, commercial fishing, and tourism are growing steadily. Although Senegal is one of West Africa's more prosperous nations, it remains to a large extent underdeveloped. Poverty and illiteracy are widespread; unemployment is high; and a large foreign debt is owed. One of the most pressing problems is the country's inability to produce enough food for its own needs. Senegal's basic currency unit is the CFA franc.

Peanuts are by far the most important crop. They are grown as a cash crop on small farms in much of western Senegal. Peanuts and their products, especially peanut oil, are major exports. Cotton ranks second among cash crops and is also a leading export. Subsistence crops include rice, corn, millet, sorghum, tomatoes, onions, beans, mangoes, and oranges. Where water is abundant, as in the far south and in irrigated parts of the Senegal River valley, rice and sugarcane are cultivated. Livestock, especially cattle, sheep, and goats, are raised by many farmers and nomadic tribesmen but are of little commercial value.

Manufacturing and processing industries are better developed in Senegal than in most West African countries. The processing of foods and beverages is the nation's leading manufacturing activity. Also significant is the making of cotton textiles, shoes, chemicals and pharmaceuticals, refined petroleum products, cement, and metalwares and machinery. Most of the manufacturing is in the Dakar area.

Few mineral resources have been found in Senegal, and only one—phosphate rock—is

© Wolfgang Kaehler

Fishermen Near Dakar. Since the mid-1980's, fish and fish products have accounted for the largest share of Senegal's exports.

mined in large quantities. The phosphate is largely exported for use as fertilizer.

Fishing provides the chief livelihood in many villages along the coast and on the major rivers. Dakar is the base for a tuna-fishing fleet and has a number of modern fish canneries. Fish is a major export.

Most of Senegal's railways and roads center on Dakar, the capital and largest seaport. One rail line extends eastward into Mali, another northward to Saint-Louis. Most of the roads are unpaved, and many are impassable in the rainy season. Dakar is an important stopover on both sea and air routes between Europe, South America, and southern Africa. Kaolack, Saint-Louis, and Ziguinchor are lesser seaports.

The People

Senegal's population according to the 1988 census was 6,896,808. The average population density was about 91 persons per square mile (35 per km²). The majority of the people are concentrated in the west and in the Senegal River valley.

Senegal's Largest Cities

Dakar, the	Thiés 175,465
capital. . . .1,375,067	Kaolack 150,961

Most of the Senegalese belong to the Wolof, Serer, Diola, Toucouleur, and Fulani ethnic groups. Islam is the religion of more than 90 per cent of the people. There are small minorities of animists and Christians. The official language is French, but most Senegalese speak indigenous languages, which belong to the Niger-Congo linguistic family. Primary education begins at age seven and lasts six years; secondary education lasts seven years. Higher education is available at Cheikh Ant Diop University in Dakar and Gaston-Berger University in Saint-Louis. The literacy rate is about 40 per cent.

Government

Under the constitution of 1963 the chief executive is the president, elected for a seven-year term. The president appoints the prime minister. The legislature is called the National Assembly; its members are elected to five-year terms.

History

Little is known of the early history of Senegal. By the Middle Ages, such groups as the Wolof, Serer, and Toucouleur had entered the area from the north. In about the 11th century, North African traders brought the Islamic religion to the region. For many centuries, parts of Senegal were included in various African kingdoms.

European exploration of Senegalese lands was begun in the 15th century by the Portuguese. In the 17th century the French established trading settlements at the mouth of the Senegal River and on Gorée Island (off Dakar). During the 18th century France and Great Britain vied for control of the region around the Senegal and Gambia rivers known as Senegambia. French possession was confirmed by the Congress of Vienna in 1815. In the mid-19th century, the French extended their control to the interior of the region. In 1895 the colony of Senegal was officially established with its present borders and was made headquarters for the government of French West Africa.

Senegal became a republic within the French Community in 1958. In 1959 it joined the Sudanese Republic in forming the Federation of Mali. When the federation gained independence in 1960, Senegal withdrew and became an independent republic. Léopold S. Senghor, a leading African nationalist, was elected president. He was repeatedly reelected. Famine, resulting from persistent drought, marked the 1970's. At the end of 1980, Senghor resigned from the presidency and retired. In 1981 Senegal helped the president of Gambia put down a coup. The following year Senegal and Gambia united in a loose confederation called Senegambia; the confederation was dissolved in 1989.

In the early 1980's a separatist political movement arose in the southern province of Casamance. By the early 1990's the movement had grown into a guerrilla insurgency, which was engaged in intense fighting at the end of the decade.

See also DAKAR; FLAG (color page); FRENCH WEST AFRICA; SENEGAL RIVER; SENGHOR, LÉOPOLD SÉDAR.

Senegal River, a river in western Africa. It is formed by the junction of the Bafing and Bakoy rivers in Mali and flows generally northwestward along the Mauritania-Senegal boundary to the Atlantic Ocean near Saint-Louis, Senegal. The water level of the river fluctuates widely with the wet and the dry seasons. Virtually the entire 650-mile (1,050-km) course is navigable by small boats during high water, only the lower one-fourth during low water.

Senghor, sĕN-gôr′, **Léopold Sédar** (1906-   ), the first president of the Republic of Senegal. He also became noted as a poet and philosopher. Senghor helped Senegal gain independence from France and served as president, 1960-80. During his administration he maintained close ties with France and promoted socialism. In 1983 Senghor became the first black to be elected to the French Academy, France's most prestigious learned society.

Senghor was the son of a prosperous Senegalese planter. After graduation from the University of Paris in 1935, he taught school in France. Through his poems and essays he gained a reputation as a supporter of African nationalism. He served in the French National Assembly as a deputy from Senegal, 1946-58.

Senility. See BRAIN, subtitle *Disorders of the Brain:* Organic Disorders (Senility).

Senior Citizen. See RETIREMENT.

Senlac, Battle of. See HASTINGS, BATTLE OF.

Senna, a laxative made from the leaves of certain species of cassia plants. The chief sources are the *Alexandria senna,* native to Egypt, and the *Tinnevelly senna,* native to Arabia but widely grown in India.

Alexandria senna is *Cassia acutifolia;* Tinnevelly senna, *C. angustifolia.* They belong to the pea family, Leguminosae.

Sennacherib. See ASSYRIA, subtitle *History:* Formation of an Empire.

Sennett, Mack (1884-1960), a United States motion-picture producer and director. He made about 1,000 films, most of them short slapstick comedies featuring the Keystone Cops and the Mack Sennett Bathing Beauties. Pie throwing and wild chases were among his comedy devices.

Sennett, whose original name was Michael Sinnott, was born in Canada. He entered the film industry as an actor for D. W. Griffith's Biograph Company and in 1910 he began directing. In 1912 he formed his own Keystone Company, which made films until 1928. Sennett was given a special Academy Award in 1938 for his pioneering work in film comedy.

Senses. An animal receives information about its environment through its senses. Humans and most other mammals are traditionally said to have five senses—sight, hearing, taste, smell, and touch. However, they actually have many more senses, including the senses of hunger, thirst, pain, balance, heat, and cold.

Each sense is associated with a specialized cell or group of cells, called *receptors,* or *sense organs,* and each receptor responds to a special type of stimulus. Sense organs are usually classified into two groups. Sense organs receiving a stimulus from the external environment (a bird's call, for example) are called *exteroreceptors;* those receiving a stimulus from the internal environment (a hunger pang, for example) are called *interoreceptors.* When a receptor receives a stimulus from the environment, the stimulus is relayed through pathways of the nervous system to the brain, where it is registered as a sensation.

Taste, smell, hearing, balance, and vision are sometimes called *special senses.* Their receptors are structurally specialized and are located at specific places in the body rather than generally throughout the body, as are the receptors associated with the sense of touch.

For further information, see:

EAR		
EYE	PAIN	THIRST
NERVOUS	PERCEPTION	TONGUE
SYSTEM	SKIN	TOUCH
NOSE	TASTE	VERTIGO

Carolina Biological Supply Company

Sensitive Plant. *Left,* as it normally appears. *Right,* after being touched. After about 10 to 20 minutes the leaflets and stems resume their normal position.

Sensitive Plant, a perennial plant native to Brazil. It is a hairy plant with leaves made up of many individual oval leaflets. Its tiny, lavender flowers are clustered together in ball-shaped flower heads. The plant grows to about 15 inches (38 cm) high.

The sensitive plant is grown mostly as a curiosity. When touched, its leaflets fold together and the leafstalks droop. This response will often move from the area touched to other parts of the plant. A sudden change in temperature will bring about a similar reaction. The plant returns to normal within about 10 to 20 minutes.

The sensitive plant is *Mimosa pudica* of the pea family, Leguminosae.

Sensitivity Training, a type of group psychotherapy. Sensitivity training groups, also called T-groups or encounter groups, are intended to help persons cope with their emotional problems and get along better with others. The idea behind such therapy is that if persons talk openly to each other they will get to know each other—and themselves —better. Typically, a group consists of a leader and 8 to 15 individuals who meet regularly for a few hours a week or in a single session lasting up to 48 hours.

Psychiatrists generally have a cautious attitude toward sensitivity training. Few of them recommend it unless it is part of a broader program of treatment supervised by a person trained in all phases of psychiatry.

Sentence. See GRAMMAR, subtitle *Sentence Structure, or Syntax.*

Sentence, in law. See CRIME, subtitle *Treatment of Criminals:* Practice.

Seoul, sōl, South Korea, the nation's capital and one of the world's largest cities. It lies on the Han River in the northwestern part of the country, near the Yellow Sea and the North Korean border. Low mountains nearly surround the city.

Seoul is the commercial, industrial, cultural, and educational center of South Korea. Most of the nation's largest banks, manufacturing companies, and industrial organizations have headquarters in the city. Consumer and industrial goods are produced in great variety in and near Seoul.

High-rise buildings tower above the downtown area. Stately old palaces, tranquil gardens, and treasure-filled museums are found in several areas. Seoul is served by a network of railways, highways, and subway lines. Also serving Seoul are the port of Inchon, about 20 miles (30 km) west of the city, and Kimpo International Airport, about 10 miles (15 km) west of downtown.

Most of Seoul has been built since the Korean War (1950-53), when much of the city was destroyed. Remaining historic landmarks include former royal palaces, some built originally about the time of the city's founding late in the 14th century. Among them are Kyongbok, Changdok, and Toksu palaces. On the grounds of Kyongbok Palace is the National Museum, with exhibits pertaining to Korean history and culture; and the National Folklore Museum, a branch of the National Museum. Other museums include the National Museum of Science and the National Museum of Modern Art. There are three western-style symphony orchestras, a traditional Korean orchestra, three dance companies, and two opera companies. Grand Park is the site of a zoo and botanic garden.

More than 20 large universities and colleges are in Seoul, including Seoul National and Yonsei universities. Also in the city are the National Academy of Sciences and numerous research institutes and learned societies.

Seoul was founded in 1392 by Taejo, founder of the Yi Dynasty, and was the

South Gate, one of Seoul's oldest structures, stands amid modern high rises. It was built in the 1390's by Taejo, the city's founder.
© Dallas & John Heaton
TSW-Click/Chicago Ltd.

dynastic capital until Japan annexed Korea in 1910. The city, called Keijo by the Japanese, was the seat of the Japanese governor-general until the end of World War II, when it was occupied by United States troops. Seoul was made the capital of the newly formed Republic of Korea (South Korea) in 1948.

Seoul suffered tremendous damage during the Korean War. It was captured twice by North Korean forces (in 1950 and in 1951). The city underwent rapid economic and population growth during the 1960's and 1970's. In 1988 Seoul was the site of the Summer Olympic Games.

Population: 10,627,790.

Sepal. See FLOWER, subtitle *Parts of the Flower: The Sepals.*

Separation of Powers. See UNITED STATES, section "Government," subtitle *General Principles of Government:* 5. Separation of Powers.

Separatists. See CONGREGATIONALISTS, subtitle *History:* In England.

Sepia, Common. See CUTTLEFISH.

Sepiolite. See MEERSCHAUM.

Sepoy Mutiny. See INDIAN MUTINY.

September, the ninth month of the year in the Gregorian Calendar. It has 30 days. Autumn begins in the Northern Hemisphere about September 23, at the autumnal equinox, when day and night are of equal length. Spring begins in the Southern Hemisphere at the same time.

In the United States and Canada the first Monday in September is observed as Labor Day, a legal holiday in honor of working people. Rosh Hashana, the Jewish New Year's Day, usually occurs in September. September is harvest time in much of the Northern Hemisphere, and in many areas agricultural fairs are held to celebrate the gathering of crops.

September was the seventh month in the old Roman calendar. The name September stems from the Latin word *septem* (seven). In September the Romans held athletic games in honor of Jupiter, their supreme god. The Anglo-Saxons used the name *Gerst-monath* (Barley-month) for September because they harvested barley during this period.

The sapphire is September's gem. (See GEM for picture.) The aster and the morning glory are its flowers.

During September . . .

1 World War II began when Germany invaded Poland in 1939.

2 V-J Day, 1945—Japan's surrender, ending the fighting in World War II.

3 Treaty of Paris ending American Revolutionary War signed in 1783.

6 Jane Addams born in 1860.

7 Queen Elizabeth I of England born in 1533.

8 St. Augustine, Florida, first permanent European settlement in what is now the United States, founded by Spaniards in 1565.

10 Elias Howe patented the sewing machine in 1846.

13 Walter Reed born in 1851.

14 Francis Scott Key wrote the words to the "Star-Spangled Banner" in 1814.

15 William Howard Taft, 27th President, born in 1857.

16 Pilgrims sailed from England on the *Mayflower* in 1620.

17 Citizenship Day, commemorating signing of United States Constitution in 1787.

19 Washington delivered his Farewell Address in 1796.

25 Balboa discovered the Pacific Ocean in 1513.

Septic Tank. See SEWAGE, subtitle *Sewage Treatment and Disposal:* Septic Tank.

Septicemia. See BLOOD, subtitle *Diseases of the Blood.*

Septimius Severus (146-211 A.D.), a Roman emperor, ruled 193-211. He was the first emperor to rely solely on his own military authority as the basis for assuming imperial office. A distinguished soldier, Severus was proclaimed emperor by his legions after the death of Emperor Commodus. He forcibly put down rival claimants and rewarded his soldiers for their support with high government positions. The Senate was opened for the first time to members from Middle Eastern provinces and was made completely subservient to Severus.

Severus was born of Carthaginian ancestry in North Africa. He died in Britain while on a campaign against the Caledonians. His son Caracalla succeeded him.

Septuagint. See BIBLE, subtitle *The Christian Old Testament.*

Sequin. See DUCAT.

Sequoia, sĕ-kwoi'à, a genus of cone-bearing evergreen trees of the pine family. These trees were named after Sequoya, a Cherokee Indian leader and scholar. Sequoias are very tall, straight trees with furrowed reddish-brown bark. They surpass nearly all other plants in size and are among the oldest living things on earth. Sequoias were widely spread over the Northern Hemisphere before the Ice Age, which began about 2,000,000 years ago and continued to about 10,000 to 15,000 years ago. Fossil remains of sequoia trees have been found in many areas of Europe and the United States. Today the sequoia genus is represented by only two living species, found only in California and southwestern Oregon. These surviving sequoias are the redwood and the giant sequoia, which is also known as the *big tree.*

The redwood is a much taller tree than the giant sequoia. It grows to heights of about 275 to 350 feet (84 to 109 m), while the giant sequoia attains average heights of 250 to 280 feet (76 to 85 m). The giant sequoias, however, are much more massive and have longer life spans than the redwood. The oldest known giant sequoias are about 3,500 years old; the maximum life span of the redwoods is about 2,200 years. Both trees owe much of their remarkable life span to the facts that they are not easily destroyed by insects or

Eugene Memmler; Ralph Miller

Sequoias. *Top,* redwood, a species of sequoia. Redwoods are the world's tallest plants and grow along the Pacific coast of the United States. *Bottom,* a giant sequoia. This famous tree is named for General William Tecumseh Sherman.

disease and their bark is highly resistant to fire.

The Giant Sequoia

The giant sequoia grows in groves along the western slopes of the Sierra Nevadas at altitudes of about 4,500 to 8,000 feet (1,370 to 2,440 m). These trees grow at higher altitudes and in cooler areas than the redwoods. They have deep-green foliage and their leaves, which are small and scalelike, overlap one another. The woody oval cones are yellowish-brown and from two to three inches (5 to 7.5 cm) in length. The giant sequoia is not used as a timber tree; its wood is lightweight and brittle.

One of the most famous giant sequoia trees is the General Sherman tree in Sequoia National Park. Borings taken from the tree showed it to be about 3,500 years old. It is about 275 feet (84 m) tall and at ground level is 103 feet (31 m) in circumference. Some of the other national parks and national forests in which giant sequoia groves are preserved are Yosemite National Park, Kings Canyon National Park, and Sierra National Forest.

The Redwood

The redwood is the state tree of California. It requires a cool climate of high humidity, and is found only in the narrow fog belt along the Pacific coast from southern Oregon to Monterey, California.

Some of the tallest redwoods have been discovered in Redwood Creek Grove in Humboldt County, California. The tallest tree there measures about 370 feet (113 m) in height. Some areas have been established as state and national parks to preserve the largest and the most beautiful redwood groves. One of the most famous of these parks is Muir Woods National Monument.

Redwood trees have narrow, yellow-green leaves that are stiff, flat, and sharply pointed. The cones are egg-shaped and about one inch (2.5 cm) long. The redwoods are named for the reddish-brown lumber that is obtained from them. This lumber is very durable and is used for such things as shingles, fences, posts, and furniture. Redwood is heavier and stronger than the wood of the giant sequoia.

The redwood is *Sequoia sempervirens;* the giant sequoia, *S. gigantea.* The sequoia genus belongs to the pine family, Pinaceae. Some botanists classify the sequoia genus in the bald cypress family, Taxodiaceae.

Sequoia National Park. See NATIONAL PARKS, section "United States."

Sequoya, or **Sequoyah,** sĕ-kwoi'à (1770?-1843), a Cherokee Indian leader and scholar. In 12 years of work, 1809-21, he devised a syllabary (a system of writing in which characters represent the sound of syllables) for the Cherokee language, providing his tribe with a means to read and write what had been only a spoken language.

Sequoya was born near what is now Vonore, Tennessee, the son of a Cherokee mother and a white trader father. He was for a time known by the name of George Guess (also spelled Gist and Guest), which Sequoya believed to be that of his father. He worked as a trader and later as a silver craftsman. After his system of writing was adopted by the tribal council in 1821, Sequoya went to teach the Cherokee living west of the Mississippi River. In 1828 he represented the western Cherokee in Washington, D.C. He died in Mexico while searching for a missing Cherokee tribe.

A bust of Sequoya was placed in Statuary Hall in the U.S. Capitol by the state of Oklahoma. The sequoia tree was named in his memory.

Seraph (plural **Seraphim** or **Seraphs**), a six-winged angel. In the Old Testament

(Isaiah 6:2-7) seraphim adore God and use fire to purify the prophet Isaiah. In the Christian ranking of angels, seraphim belong to the highest of the nine orders, or choirs.

Serbia, sûr'bĭ-à, a region of the Balkan Peninsula. From 1946 to 1992, Serbia was one of the six republics of Yugoslavia. In 1992 Yugoslavia broke apart. Serbia and Montenegro formed a new Yugoslav state, which was not recognized internationally. Serbia is bordered by Hungary, Romania, Bulgaria, Macedonia, Albania, Montenegro, Bosnia-Herzegovina, and Croatia. It covers an area of 34,116 square miles (88,360 km^2), which includes two provinces: Vojvodina, and Kosovo and Methohija. (See YUGOSLAVIA, map.) Northern Serbia is made up mostly of plains and southern Serbia is generally mountainous. Crops grown in Serbia include wheat, corn, potatoes, plums, and wine grapes. Belgrade, Niš, and Kragujevac are the major industrial centers. Products manufactured in Serbia include steel, chemicals, cars, and textiles. Mining, especially of coal, copper, and zinc, is also important.

Serbo-Croatian, written in the Cyrillic alphabet, is the main language. Most Serbs are Orthodox Christians. In 1991 the population was 9,791,475; that of Belgrade, the capital, 1,554,826.

History

The Serbs, a South Slav people, moved from the area north of the Carpathian Mountains into the region of their present homeland during the 6th and 7th centuries. From the 8th to the 12th centuries the Serbs were under the nominal control of either Bulgar or Byzantine rulers. During this period, there were constant struggles for supremacy among the Serbian *županates* (clans). The Serbs were converted to Christianity in the 9th century.

By the 11th century two rudimentary states had emerged—Zeta (Montenegro) in the west and Raška in the east. When Zeta declined in the 12th century, Raška became the center of Serbian power. Stephen Nemanja, grand *župan* (chieftain) of Raška (1169-96), united the Serbians for the first time and founded a dynasty, the Nemanjid, that ruled for about 200 years.

The greatest period of the dynasty was the reign of Stephen Dušan, 1331-55. He conquered most of Macedonia, Albania, Epirus, and Thessaly and had himself crowned emperor of the Serbs, Greeks, Bulgars, and Albanians. During his rule, an independent church, the Serbian Orthodox Church, was established. After Dušan's death, misrule so weakened Serbia that it fell to the Turks at the battle of Kosovo in 1389 and became a vassal state of the Ottoman Empire.

Serbia remained under Turkish domination until the 19th century. In 1804 the Serbs rebelled under the leadership of Karageorge, but he was eventually driven into exile. In 1815 a rival Serbian leader, Miloš Obrenovic, began a revolt that won Serbia limited autonomy and himself the hereditary title of prince. Bitter rivalry for leadership between the Obrenovic and Karageorgevic families dominated Serbian politics for decades. In 1878 Serbia was granted full independence by the Treaty of Berlin. Its territory was more than doubled as a result of the Balkan Wars, 1912-13. (See BALKAN WARS.)

Conflict with Austria had existed for some time but reached a climax on June 28, 1914, when the Austrian Archduke Francis Ferdinand was assassinated while visiting Sarajevo. Austria blamed Serbia and declared war, beginning World War I. (See WORLD WAR I, section "Historical Introduction.") After the war, Serbia joined with Croatia and Slovenia to form a union of South Slavs called the Kingdom of the Serbs, Croats, and Slovenes (renamed Yugoslavia in 1929). Yugoslavia later became a federation of six republics.

During the 1970's and 1980's tensions mounted between the various national groups in Yugoslavia. In 1989 Slobodan Milošević, a Serb nationalist, was elected president of Serbia. In 1991, Yugoslavia collapsed, forming five separate nations. Serbia and Montenegro formed a new Yugoslav federation, and the other republics declared independence. Incited by Milošević, civil wars erupted in two of these newly independent nations—in Croatia and in Bosnia and Herzegovina. Serbs, who opposed independence, fought Croats and Bosnians, who favored independence.

In 1992 the United Nations imposed sanctions on Serbia for aiding Serb fighters in those wars. A cease-fire went into effect in Croatia in 1992 and in Bosnia and Herzegovina in 1995. All remaining sanctions on Serbia were lifted. Milošević assumed the presidency of Yugoslavia in 1997 and a short time later sent Yugoslav forces into the Serb province of Kosovo to supress a growing eth-

nic Albanian independence movement. He withdrew the Serb-led forces in 1999, after they had killed thousands of Kosovar civilians.

See also BELGRADE; MILOŠEVIĆ, SLOBODAN; NOVI SAN; YUGOSLAVIA, subtitle *History*.

Serbian Orthodox Church. See EASTERN ORTHODOX CHURCH.

Serbs, Croats, and Slovenes, Kingdom of the. See YUGOSLAVIA, subtitle *History*.

Sere. See ECOLOGY, subtitle *Scope and Principles*.

Seredy, Kate (1896-1975), a Hungarian-American author and illustrator of children's books. Her stories are lively and written with warmth and humor. There is often humor in her illustrations, too, and she is especially adept at portraying action. Seredy was born in Budapest. She came to the United States in 1922.

Serfdom. See FEUDALISM, subtitles *Features of Feudalism:* The Manorial System, and *Decline of Feudalism:* The Decline of Serfdom.

Serge. See TEXTILE (table).

Sergeant, an army, air force, or marine noncommissioned officer ranking above a corporal; also a police officer ranking above a patrolman but below a lieutenant. In the United States armed forces there are several grades of sergeants. (See RANK, MILITARY OR NAVAL.)

In the military, responsibilities and duties of sergeants vary according to a unit's function and the availability of sergeants. In general, sergeants in the lower grades have command over and train lower-ranking personnel while sergeants in the higher grades assist the officers in command. A *first sergeant* assists the company commander and sees that orders are carried out. Sergeants may also be technicians, holding such positions as communication specialist, computer operator, or maintenance-crew chief. Some sergeants have administrative positions, such as running a supply room or mess hall. A *sergeant major* is ordinarily the chief administrative assistant in a headquarters.

A *sergeant of the guard* is any enlisted person with the temporary assignment of supervising soldiers on guard duty.

A police sergeant supervises about eight officers and acts as a liaison between them and the higher-rank officers. Police sergeants have various jobs, including patrol duty and detective work. A *desk sergeant* is in charge of the receiving desk in a police station.

For pictures of sergeants' insignia, see AIR FORCE, UNITED STATES; ARMY, UNITED STATES; MARINE CORPS, UNITED STATES.

Sergeant at Arms, the officer of an organization who preserves order during its meetings. A sergeant at arms functions mainly at formal gatherings, where he enforces rules of procedure; in a legislative body he also enforces executive commands. Both houses of the U.S. Congress have a sergeant at arms, as do both houses of the British Parliament.

Sericulture, the raising of silkworms. See SILK.

Series, in mathematics, an indicated sum of numbers. An "indicated sum" is formed when the terms of a sequence of numbers are connected by the addition sign. Thus, for example, the series

$$2 + 5 + 8 + 11 + 14 + 17$$

is formed from the sequence

$$2, 5, 8, 11, 14, 17.$$

Series, like the sequences on which they are based, are either finite (that is, have a definite number of terms, as in the example) or infinite (unending). The *value* of the series is obtained by performing the addition indicated; in the example, the value is 57. Many series are based on the special kinds of sequences called *progressions*—sequences (finite or infinite) in which the terms are listed in some well-defined manner. (See PROGRESSION.) For some of these series, methods can be developed for finding the value without having to add each number individually.

Infinite series often occur in the calculus, and many mathematical situations can be expressed only as infinite series. For example, in elementary arithmetic an infinite series is obtained when the fraction 7/9 is changed to a decimal numeral by dividing 9 into 7 as follows:

$$
\begin{array}{r}
.7777 \\
9)\overline{7.0000} \\
\underline{6\ 3} \\
70 \\
\underline{63} \\
70 \\
\underline{63} \\
70 \text{ and so on without end.}
\end{array}
$$

So that

$7/9 = .7777 \ldots$

$= 7/10 + 7/100 + 7/1000 + 7/10{,}000 + \ldots$

where the three dots mean that the infinite

series is continued in the same manner; that is, in the example, each successive term in the sequence is obtained by multiplying the preceding term by 1/10. In elementary arithmetic it is assumed that this infinite sum is actually equal to 7/9. This equality can be shown as follows by methods of algebra:

$$
\begin{array}{r}
\text{Letting } x = .777 \ldots \\
10x = 7.777 \ldots \\
\underline{(-)\ x = \ \ .777 \ldots} \\
9x = 7 \\
x = 7/9
\end{array}
$$

By knowing the general form taken by each term of a sequence, it is possible to write down a particular term without actually writing out the entire sequence. For example, in the series

$$1/1 + 1/2 + 1/3 + 1/4 + \ldots + 1/n$$

each term has the general form $1/n$, so that the 3rd term is 1/3, the 7th term is 1/7, and the nth term is $1/n$. (This series is called a *harmonic* series because it is based on a harmonic progression; see PROGRESSION.)

In the series

$$1/2 + 1/2^2 + 1/2^3 + 1/2^4 + \ldots + 1/2^n$$

(also written

$$1/2 + 1/4 + 1/8 + 1/16 + \ldots + 1/2^n)$$

each term has the general form $1/2^n$. Thus, the 3rd term is $1/2^3$, the 4th term is $1/2^4$, and the nth term is $1/2^n$. (This series is called a *geometric* series because it is based on a geometric progression.)

Partial sums are finite series that form part of another series. For example, in the harmonic series above, the first three partial sums (written as S_1, S_2, and S_3) are

$$S_1 = 1/1$$
$$S_2 = 1/1 + 1/2$$
$$S_3 = 1/1 + 1/2 + 1/3$$

and the nth partial sum is

$$S_n = 1/1 + 1/2 + 1/3 + 1/4 + \ldots + 1/n$$

Thus, S_2 represents the sum of the first 2 terms, S_3 represents the sum of the first 3 terms, and S_n represents the sum of the first n terms of the sequence.

In the geometric series above, the first three partial sums are

$$S_1 = 1/2$$
$$S_2 = 1/2 + 1/2^2$$
$$S_3 = 1/2 + 1/2^2 + 1/2^3$$

and the nth partial sum is

$$S_n = 1/2 + 1/2^2 + 1/2^3 + \ldots + 1/2^n$$

These two examples can be used to illustrate the concept of divergence and convergence. The harmonic series in the example is said to be divergent because, given any

Finding the Value of a Series

In a series based on a progression such as the example used in the first paragraph of this article, where any two successive terms always have a constant difference, the sum can be found as follows:

Add the first term of the sequence to the last term.	$2 + 17 = 19$
Multiply this sum by the number of terms in the sequence (in this case, 6).	$6 \times 19 = 114$
Take one-half of this product. The answer is the sum of the terms in the sequence.	$1/2 \times 114 = 57$

For a way of finding the value of a series based on a geometric progression, see the article PROGRESSION.

arbitrary value (no matter how large), there is always some partial sum whose value is larger: that is, the value of the harmonic series can be made as large as desired by including more terms.

In contrast, the geometric series in the example is convergent because no matter how many terms are added, their sum is always less than 2. Another way of saying the same thing is "the limit of S_n as n approaches infinity is 2." Note that, strictly speaking, therefore, 7/9 is not equal to 7/10 + 7/100 + 7/1000 + 7/10,000 + . . . ; rather, 7/9 is the limit of this particular infinite series.

Serigraph. See SILK-SCREEN PRINTING.

Serkin, the family name of two American pianists, father and son.

Rudolph Serkin (1903-1991), the father, gained fame for his interpretations of German and Austrian composers, especially Beethoven, and for his virtuoso technique. He was born in Bohemia of Russian parents. After studying piano and composition in Vienna, he began his long concert career in 1920, in Berlin. His first American concert was in 1933. He joined the faculty of the Curtis Institute of Music, Philadelphia, in 1939 and served as director, 1968-76. In 1950 he helped found the summer Music School and Festival at Marlboro, Vermont.

Peter Serkin (1947-), the son, was born in New York City. He studied with his father privately and later attended the Curtis Institute. He first performed in public at the age of 10. His performances of both classical and 20th-century composers brought him wide acclaim.

Sermon on the Mount. See JESUS CHRIST, subtitle *Ministry and Teachings:* Teachings.

Serotonin. See BRAIN, subtitle *Chemistry of the Brain.*

Serpentine, sûr'pĕn-tēn, a common rock-forming mineral. Serpentine is a hydrous magnesium silicate, consisting of magnesium, silicon, oxygen, and hydrogen. It has a greasy feel, and is easily scratched with a knife. Serpentine is usually some shade of green, but may be red, yellow, white, brown, or black. It often has a mottled, or spotted, appearance because of impurities, and is translucent or opaque. (It was named for the serpentlike patterns of the green, mottled varieties.) Most forms of serpentine have a waxy luster. Some translucent varieties are used in jewelry and in making small ornamental objects. *Chrysotile,* a fibrous variety, has a silky luster and can be easily separated into fine fibers. It is the chief source of asbestos. (See ASBESTOS.)

The term "serpentine" is also applied to rocks composed chiefly of the mineral serpentine. When polished, some forms of serpentine rock resemble marble. They are widely used as ornamental building stone.

Serpentine is usually found associated with magnesium silicates such as olivine and various pyroxenes and amphiboles, and as grains in both igneous and metamorphic rocks. Most chrysotile is mined in Russia and Canada. Serpentine rock of great beauty is obtained from Great Britain, Ireland, Italy, France, and Greece.

Chemical formula: $Mg_6Si_4O_{10}(OH)_8$. Specific gravity: 2.2 to 2.65. Hardness: 2 to 5.

Serra, Junípero (1713-1784), a Spanish missionary. He was an important figure in the colonization of what is now the state of California. Serra established nine missions in California in order to bring Christianity to the Indians. He helped to found San Diego (1769), the first European settlement in California; its mission was San Diego de Alcalá.

Serra was born on the island of Mallorca. He became a Franciscan friar and taught philosophy in the university at Palma. In 1749 he sailed to Mexico to labor among the Indians. In 1769 he accompanied a Spanish expedition to California. In 1988 he was beatified by Pope John Paul II.

Serra Museum, San Diego
Junípero Serra. This statue, made shortly after his death, is thought to be a close likeness.

The other missions founded by Father Junípero Serra were San Carlos de Borroméo (Monterey; 1770); San Antonio de Padua (1771); San Gabriel Arcángel (1771); San Luís Obispo de Tolosa (1772); San Francisco de Asís (1776); San Juan Capistrano (1776); Santa Clara de Asís (1777); and San Buenaventura (Ventura; 1782).

Serum. See BLOOD, subtitle *Clotting of Blood*.

Serum Hepatitis. See HEPATITIS.

Serval, sûr′văl, an African wildcat of the grasslands and brush country south of the Sahara. It has yellowish-brown fur marked with dark brown or black spots and streaks. The serval has large, pointed ears and long legs. It is about 20 inches (50 cm) in height at the shoulders and about 40 inches (1 m) long, not including the tail, which is about 16 inches (40 cm) long. The serval is a fast distance runner and a good climber. It feeds on birds and small mammals. The female usually gives birth to one to four kittens.

The serval is *Felis serval* of the cat family, Felidae.

Servetus, sûr-vē′tŭs, **Michael** (*Spanish:* **Míguel Serveto**) (1511-1553), a Spanish physician and theologian. His medical researches led to his discovery of the pulmonary circulation of the blood—the passage of blood from the heart to the lungs and back again. Servetus' religious opinions infuriated both Catholics and Calvinists and led to his being put to death as a heretic. His views foreshadowed Unitarianism.

Servetus was born in Tudela, Spain. He studied law at Zaragoza and Toulouse, but soon became more interested in the religious disputes of the time. In 1531 he published a controversial pamphlet, *De Trinitatis erroribus,* attacking the doctrine of the Trinity. In 1536 he went to Paris, where he studied medicine. He settled down to practice in Vienne in southern France in 1541.

About 1546 Servetus began corresponding with John Calvin, and sent him the manuscript of a treatise he intended to publish, which set forth his religious views and described his medical discovery. Calvin denounced the work for its rejection of the divinity of Christ and of the doctrine of predestination. In 1553 Servetus published the work secretly as *Christianismi restitutio (The Restitution of Christianity).* The book caused a furor. Servetus was identified as the author, brought before the Inquisition, and condemned to death. He escaped from prison; while fleeing to Italy, however, he passed through Geneva, Switzerland, where he was seized on Calvin's order. Tried by the Calvinists, he was convicted of heresy and then burned at the stake.

Service, Robert (William) (1874?-1958), a Canadian author. He is best known for his vigorous poems of the Yukon during the period of the gold rush. "The Shooting of Dan McGrew," the most popular of these poems, has often been quoted and parodied. It appeared in Service's first book, *Songs of a*

Serval

Grant Heilman

Sourdough (1907), which was later reprinted as *The Spell of the Yukon*. Service also wrote novels.

Service was born in England and emigrated to British Columbia in 1894. He lived in France during his later years, except during World War II.

His volumes of verse include: *Ballads of a Cheechako* (1909); *Rhymes of a Rolling Stone* (1912); *Rhymes of a Red Cross Man* (1916); *Rhymes of a Roughneck* (1950); and *Rhymes for My Rags* (1956). *Ploughman of the Moon* (1945) is autobiographical.

Service Bureau. See COMPUTER, subtitle *The Computer Industry*.

Service Club. See BIG BROTHERS/BIG SISTERS; CIVITAN INTERNATIONAL; EXCHANGE CLUB, THE NATIONAL; JAYCEES; KIWANIS INTERNATIONAL; LIONS CLUBS INTERNATIONAL; OPTIMIST INTERNATIONAL; PILOT INTERNATIONAL; QUOTA INTERNATIONAL, INCORPORATED; ROTARY INTERNATIONAL; SOROPTIMIST INTERNATIONAL.

Service Employees International Union. See LABOR UNION (table).

Service Medals. See DECORATIONS AND MEDALS, subtitle *United States Awards:* Service Medals.

Servomechanism. See AUTOMATION, subtitle *Control Systems:* Closed-loop Systems.

Sesame, sĕs′ȧ-mē, an annual herb native to tropical Asia and Africa. There are about 30 species of sesame, but only one is cultivated, primarily for its seeds. Seeds of the cultivated sesame are small, soft, and usually straw-colored. They are used in baking as a topping for breads and cookies, and are a source of a nearly tasteless and odorless oil used in cooking, in medicine, and in industry. The cultivated sesame plant, which grows from one to two feet (30 to 60 cm) in height, has oblong leaves and pink or white flowers.

The cultivated species is *Sesamum indicum* of the pedalium family, Pedaliaceae.

Sessions, Roger (1896-1985), a United States composer and teacher. His highly complex music requires concentrated listening and was slow in gaining public acceptance. Various devices—polytonality, involved counterpoint, atonality—are found in his works, such as *Violin Concerto* (1940) and *Idyll of Theocritus* (1956). Sessions was born in Brooklyn, New York. He studied music at Harvard and Yale universities and with Ernest Bloch. Sessions began his teaching career in 1917 at Smith College. He later taught at Princeton University, the University of California at Berkeley, and the Juilliard School of Music. In 1974 he was awarded a special Pulitzer Prize in music for his life's work.

His other compositions include eight symphonies; the orchestral suite *The Black Maskers* (1930); *String Quartet No. 2* (1950); *Montezuma* (1964), an opera; *Six Pieces for Cello* (1968); *Three Choruses on Biblical Texts* (1975), for chamber orchestra and chorus. He wrote several books, including *The Musical Experience* (1950), *Harmonic Practice* (1951), and *Questions about Music* (1970).

Set. See OSIRIS.

Set Theory, the study of sets (aggregates or collections). Set theory is an important theoretical tool used in modern mathematics and logic. In fact, some mathematicians have sought to show that all the basic concepts in mathematics can be derived by beginning with the theory of sets. Practical applications for set theory have been found in computers and electrical circuits.

Modern set theory was founded by Georg Cantor late in the 19th century. An important aspect of Cantor's work was his treatment of infinite sets, that is, sets such as the natural numbers, in which there is no end to the listing of members. Although infinite sets had been known to the ancient Greeks and had been used by Leibniz and Newton in the development of calculus in the late 17th century, Cantor was the first to study infinite sets systematically and precisely. Cantor's work met with much opposition from some mathematicians of the time, but today set theory is widely accepted and some of its concepts and language are frequently taught at the elementary school level.

Basic Terms and Concepts

A *set* is any collection of objects, such as a flock of birds, the letters of the alphabet, or all the whole numbers. The objects in the set are called its members, or *elements*. The set of those things under consideration is called the *universe*. In mathematics, a set must be well-defined—that is, it must be possible to tell definitely from the description of the set whether a given object is or is not a member of the set.

The brackets { } are commonly used to designate a set, and members of that set are written within the brackets. Two methods are commonly used to describe the members of a set. By the *rule method*, an object is a member of a set if it fulfills certain general conditions, and these are usually stated with-

VENN DIAGRAMS

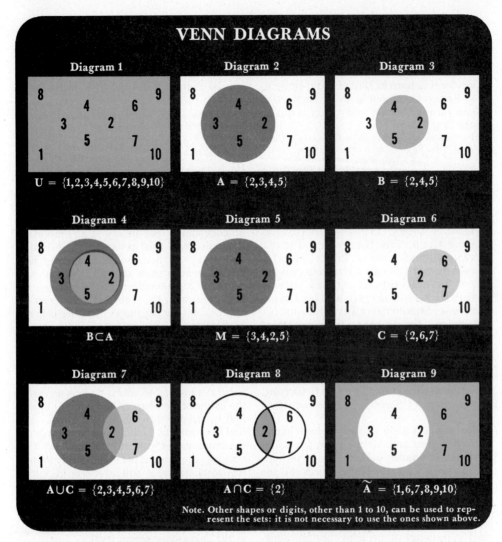

Diagram 1

U = {1,2,3,4,5,6,7,8,9,10}

Diagram 2

A = {2,3,4,5}

Diagram 3

B = {2,4,5}

Diagram 4

B⊂A

Diagram 5

M = {3,4,2,5}

Diagram 6

C = {2,6,7}

Diagram 7

A∪C = {2,3,4,5,6,7}

Diagram 8

A∩C = {2}

Diagram 9

Ã = {1,6,7,8,9,10}

Note. Other shapes or digits, other than 1 to 10, can be used to represent the sets: it is not necessary to use the ones shown above.

in the brackets. By the *listing method,* every member of the set is actually listed within the brackets. Sets are usually named by capital letters, elements by lower-case letters.

In the following discussion, the first ten natural numbers will be the universe:

U = {1, 2, 3, 4, 5, 6, 7, 8, 9, 10}

Venn diagrams, invented by and named for the English logician John Venn, will be used in illustrating the fundamental relations and operations in set theory. Diagram 1 shows the universe.

Relations. The most basic relation is that of membership in a set. For example, the set

A = {2, 3, 4, 5}

has the members 2, 3, 4, and 5. (See Diagram 2.) To indicate membership, the symbol ∈ is sometimes used. Thus, "3 ∈ A" is

read "3 is a member of the set A," and "1 ∉ A" is read "1 is not a member of the set A."

Subsets. The set

B = {2, 4, 5}

is called a *subset* of A because every element of B is also an element of A, and B is said to be contained in A. (See Diagram 3.) To indicate that B is a subset of A, the symbol ⊂ is used. Thus, "B ⊂ A" is read "B is a subset of A." Because there is an element in A that is not also an element of B, the set B is a *proper* subset of A. (See Diagram 4.) The set

M = {3, 4, 2, 5}

is an *improper* subset of A because A and M have the same elements. (See Diagram 5.) Every set is an improper subset of itself.

Equality. Two sets are equal if they have the same elements, as, for example, sets M and A. (To put it more precisely, two sets are equal if every element of the first set is also an element of the second and every element of the second is also an element of the first.) Equal sets are improper subsets of each other.

Equivalence. Two sets are equivalent if to each element in one set there corresponds one and only one element in the other set. The two sets are then said to be in *one-to-one correspondence* and to have the same *cardinality* (numerical size). For example, the set a, c, b, d, and the set A are equivalent (the arrows indicate the one-to-one correspondence):

$$\{a, \quad c, \quad b, \quad d\}$$
$$\updownarrow \quad \updownarrow \quad \updownarrow \quad \updownarrow$$
$$\{2, \quad 3, \quad 4, \quad 5\}$$

The two sets have the same cardinality, 4. They are not equal, however, because they do not have the same members.

Similarity. Two sets are said to be similar if (1) they are equivalent and (2) any two members of the first set are in the same order as their corresponding members in the second set. Thus,

$$\{5, 7, 8, 10\}$$

is similar to

$$\{2, 3, 4, 6\}$$

but not similar to

$$\{3, 2, 4, 5\}.$$

In this particular example, the first two sets are ordered in the same way because the smallest number in each is listed first, the second smallest second, etc. This is an example of ascending order. As the following examples show, the order may also be descending (Example 1) or both ascending and descending (Example 2):

(1) $\{9, 8, 7, 5\}$ (2) $\{3, 2, 4, 1\}$
    and   and
$\{6, 4, 3, 2\}$ $\{9, 8, 10, 7\}$

Operations. The three basic operations with sets are union, intersection, and complement.

Union. The union of two sets is defined as the set of all elements belonging to either or both of the sets. For example, if, as in Diagram 6,

$$C = \{2, 6, 7\}$$

the union of A and C (written $A \cup C$) is

$$\{2, 3, 4, 5, 6, 7\}.$$

(See Diagram 7.)

Intersection. The intersection of two sets is defined as the set of those elements that are common to both sets. Thus the intersection

of A and C (written $A \cap C$) is the set $\{2\}$. (See Diagram 8.) If the two sets have no element in common, their intersection is the empty set, represented by $\emptyset$ or sometimes $\{\ \}$.

Complement. The complement of a set is all those elements in the universe that are not members of the set. For example, as shown in Diagram 9, the complement of set A is the set

$$\bar{A} = \{1, 6, 7, 8, 9, 10\}.$$

The union of a set and its complement is the universe; the intersection of a set and its complement is the empty set.

Another important operation in set theory is the *cartesian product,* or *cross product,* of two sets. The cartesian product, or cross product, of sets A and C (written "A × C" and often read "A cross C") is the set of all possible pairs in which the first member is an element of A and the second an element of C. Such pairs of numbers are called ordered pairs. For example, the cartesian product of

$$A = \{2, 3, 4, 5\} \text{ and } C = \{2, 6, 7\}$$

is the set consisting of the following ordered pairs:

$$(2, 2)\ (2, 6)\ (2, 7)$$
$$(3, 2)\ (3, 6)\ (3, 7)$$
$$(4, 2)\ (4, 6)\ (4, 7)$$
$$(5, 2)\ (5, 6)\ (5, 7)$$

Infinite Sets. All the sets that have been discussed thus far are finite sets, but sets such as the set of natural numbers are *infinite* because the listing of their elements continues without end.

Infinite sets have some surprising properties. One of these properties is that any infinite set is equivalent to one or more of its *proper* subsets. For example, consider the set N of all natural numbers and the set E of all even numbers. It would seem that there are twice as many natural numbers as there are even numbers, but the two sets can be put into one-to-one correspondence:

$$N = \{1, \quad 2, \quad 3, \quad 4, \ldots\}$$
$$\updownarrow \quad \updownarrow \quad \updownarrow \quad \updownarrow$$
$$E = \{2, \quad 4, \quad 6, \quad 8, \ldots\}$$

For every number x in N there exists a number 2x in E, and the two sets are therefore equivalent.

Transfinite arithmetic is the study of the rules that govern infinite sets.

If an infinite set is equivalent to the set of natural numbers, it is *denumerable.* An infinite set that is not equivalent to the set of natural numbers (that is, is larger than the set of natural numbers) is *nondenumerable.*

Mother Seton Guild; Library of Congress

Elizabeth Seton and **Ernest Thompson Seton**

The irrational numbers (which include numbers such as the square root of 2) form a nondenumerable set.

A set is said to be *inductive* if (a) 1 is a member of the set and (b) when x is a member of the set, x + 1 is also a member of the set. The set of natural numbers is an example of an inductive set, but the set of numbers between 0 and 2, for example, is not an inductive set.

The systematic treatment of infinite sets has not been without difficulty. For instance, consider *Russell's paradox,* which shows that the notion "set of all sets" can lead to contradictions. Let S be "the set of all sets that are not elements of themselves." If S ∈ S, then it follows that S cannot be an element of itself, and S ∉ S. On the other hand, if S ∉ S, it follows that S is an element of itself, and S ∈ S. That is, S is an element of itself if and only if it is not an element of itself.

Seton, Saint **Elizabeth Bayley** (1774-1821), the first native-born American to become a saint of the Roman Catholic Church. She was canonized on September 14, 1975. Mother Seton, as she was known, founded the first Roman Catholic order of nuns organized in the United States. She also was a pioneer in Catholic education and social welfare.

Elizabeth Bayley was born into a prominent Episcopalian family in New York City. In 1794 she married William M. Seton, a wealthy merchant. She was active in charitable work and in 1797 helped found the first organized charity in New York City. When her husband died in 1803, she was left a widow with five children. After becoming a convert to Catholicism in 1805, Mrs. Seton moved to Baltimore, where she opened a school for Catholic girls. In 1809 she found-

ed the Sisters of St. Joseph (later called the Sisters of Charity of St. Vincent de Paul), and was mother superior of the order the rest of her life. Mother Seton established the first Catholic free school in the United States— the beginning of the American parochial school system.

Seton, Ernest Thompson (1860-1946), a Canadian-American naturalist, artist, and author. He wrote and illustrated more than 40 books about wildlife, of which the most popular is *Wild Animals I Have Known* (1898).

In 1902 Seton organized the Woodcraft Indians, one of the first youth organizations for outdoor and craft activities. When the Boy Scouts of America was formed in 1910, the Woodcraft Indians united with it. Seton was Chief Scout of the Boy Scouts, 1910-15. He adapted the English Scout Manual for use by Scouts in America.

Seton was born in South Shields, Durham, England. In 1866 he went with his parents to live in the backwoods in the southern part of what is now Ontario, Canada. He studied art at the Ontario College of Art, and from 1879 to 1896 continued his studies in London, Paris, and New York. Seton was one of the chief illustrators for *The Century Dictionary.* He went on extensive field trips, including an expedition to the Arctic (1907). Seton delivered more than 3,000 lectures about nature and wildlife. He spent most of his last years in Santa Fe, New Mexico, where he established the Seton Institute (1930), a children's school for studies in woodcraft and wildlife.

Other books by Seton are: *Lives of the Hunted* (1901); *Two Little Savages* (1903); *Lives of Game Animals* (1925-28); and *Trail of an Artist-Naturalist* (1940), his autobiography.

Seton Hall University. See UNIVERSITIES AND COLLEGES (table).

Seton Hill College. See UNIVERSITIES AND COLLEGES (table).

Setter. See DOG, subtitle *Breeds of Dogs:* Sporting Dogs (English Setter, Gordon Setter, and Irish Setter).

Settlement House. See SOCIAL WELFARE, subtitle *Social Service:* Social Work.

Seurat, sû-rà′, **Georges** (1859-1891), a French Postimpressionist painter. He developed a style of painting known variously as *pointillism, divisionism,* and *neo-impressionism.* His pointillist technique consisted of applying small, uniform brush strokes or

Bridge at Courbevoie, by Georges Seurat in 1886; oil on canvas, 18 x 21½ inches (45.7 x 54.6 cm)

dots of colors side by side so they partially blended when viewed from a distance. *Sunday Afternoon on the Island of La Grande Jatte,* generally considered his masterpiece, reveals the order and balance of his style. (For a color reproduction, see PAINTING.)

Seurat was born in Paris and attended the École des Beaux-Arts. When his first large painting, *The Bathers,* was rejected for the 1884 Salon exhibition, Seurat helped found the Société des Artistes Indépendants. Although he completed only seven large canvases, Seurat painted about 60 small scenes, including *Fishing Fleet at Port-en-Bessin, Bridge at Courbevoie,* and *The Eiffel Tower.* An excellent draftsman, he was also known for his conté crayon (a hard, chalk-base crayon) drawings, in which he used gradations of tone in place of lines. (See DRAWING, illustration titled *Conté Crayon.*)

Seuss, Dr. See GEISEL, THEODOR SEUSS.

Sevastopol (sometimes also **Sebastopol**), sě-văs′tȯ-pôl, Ukraine, a city on the Black Sea near the tip of the Crimean peninsula. It is a major naval base and has shipyards, food-processing plants, and woodworking factories. Sevastopol is the southern terminus of the Moscow-Crimea railway. The mild climate makes Sevastopol a popular resort. A history museum, an anthropology museum, and a marine biology station of the Ukrainian Academy of Sciences are here.

Sevastopol was founded in 1783 as a fortified town and port, following Russia's annexation of the Crimea. It served as a bastion against the Turks and its founding marked the end of Russia's struggle to gain access to the Black Sea. By the early 1800's Sevastopol was the principal base for the Black Sea fleet. During the Crimean War (1853-56) the city was besieged by English, French, Turkish, and Sardinian troops for 11 months before surrendering. The treaty ending the war closed the Black Sea to warships, and Sevastopol declined. After the ban was lifted in 1871, the city soon regained its importance. During World War II Sevastopol was virtually destroyed during a German siege that lasted 239 days (November, 1941-June, 1942). It was rebuilt after the war.

Population: 350,000.

Seven Cities of Cibola. See CORONADO, FRANCISCO VÁSQUEZ DE.

Seven Days' Battles, June 25-July 1, 1862, a series of battles in the American Civil War that took place near the city of Richmond, Virginia. The most important encounters were the battles of Mechanicsville, June 26; Gaines's Mill, June 27; and Malvern Hill, July 1. Despite huge losses suffered by the Confederate forces, the Union army withdrew because of overcaution by its generals, thus ending the Peninsular Campaign (the Union offensive against Richmond, the Confederate capital).

See also CIVIL WAR, AMERICAN, subtitle *1862: The East.*

Seven Last Words of Christ, in the Bible, the seven sentences spoken by Jesus while he was on the cross. Traditionally, they are the topics of sermons given on Good Friday, the day that commemorates the Crucifixion.

The Seven Last Words of Christ are:

1. "Father, forgive them; for they know not what they do" (Luke 23:34), said to God.
2. "Verily I say unto thee, Today shalt thou be with me in paradise" (Luke 23:43), said to the good thief.
3. "Woman, behold thy son! ... Behold thy mother!" (John 19:26-27), said to his mother and to the disciple John.
4. "My God, my God, why hast thou forsaken me?" (Matthew 27:46), said to God.
5. "I thirst" (John 19:28), a statement.
6. "It is finished" (John 19:30), a statement.
7. "Father, into thy hands I commend my spirit" (Luke 23:46), said to God.

A musical work by Joseph Haydn, *The Seven Words of the Saviour on the Cross,* includes a choral arrangement of the last words.

Seven Oaks Massacre. See MANITOBA, subtitle *History:* Traders and Settlers.

Seven Pines, Battle of. See FAIR OAKS, BATTLE OF.

Seven Weeks' War, or **Austro-Prussian War** (1866), a war between Prussia and Austria, the two most powerful members of the German Confederation. The war was brought on by the determination of Prussian statesman Otto von Bismarck to expel Austria from the confederation, a necessary step

in his plan to unify Germany under Prussian leadership.

In 1864 Prussia and Austria as allies in a war against Denmark had gained control of the duchies of Schleswig and Holstein. Though jointly held, Schleswig was administered by Prussia, and Austria governed Holstein. Intent upon annexing both duchies, Bismarck invaded Holstein in 1866, precipitating a war with Austria.

Italy, an ally of Prussia, was quickly defeated in its attempt to seize the province of Venetia. Prussian forces, led by General Hermuth K. B. von Moltke, quickly defeated Hanover, an Austrian ally. The decisive action of the war occurred in Bohemia, where on July 3 the Prussians scored an overwhelming victory against the Austrians at Sadowa near Königgrätz (what is now Hradec Králové, Czech Republic). A truce was signed before the end of the month.

By the Treaty of Prague (August, 1866), Austria agreed to the dissolution of the German Confederation and its replacement by a federation, to be under Prussian domination, of states north of the Main River. Austria also renounced its rights to Schleswig-Holstein and allowed Prussia to annex four German states. Italy received Venetia. The terms of the treaty were considered moderate since Prussia annexed no Austrian territory and demanded no indemnity. This leniency on the part of Bismarck paved the way for Austria's future cooperation with Prussia.

Seven Wonders of the Ancient World, a list of structures considered by Greco-Roman tourists to be outstanding for their size or beauty. The first known list was compiled by Antipater of Sidon in the second century B.C. and included:

Pyramids of Egypt. See PYRAMIDS.
Hanging Gardens of Babylon. See BABYLON.
Statue of Zeus (Jupiter). See OLYMPIA.
Temple of Diana (Artemis). See EPHESUS.
Mausoleum at Halicarnassus. See MAUSOLEUM.
Colossus of Rhodes. See COLOSSUS.
Pharos of Alexandria. See LIGHTHOUSE.

The pyramids are the only structures that are still standing.

Seven Years' War (1756-63), a power struggle in Europe, North America, and India that involved most of the nations of Europe. Prussia emerged from the war as a powerful state. Great Britain, victorious over France, became the world's greatest colonial power.

Background

Maria Theresa, ruler of Austria, resolved to check the rising power of Frederick II of Prussia. During the War of the Austrian Succession (1740-48) he had taken Silesia, a rich province, from her. To regain it, she formed against Frederick a very powerful coalition that included Austria, Russia, France, Saxony, and Sweden.

Great Britain signed a treaty with Frederick early in 1756. This treaty in effect loosely allied the two countries against their common enemy, France, and any other nation that might attack the German state of Hanover, which was ruled by George II, the British monarch.

See also FREDERICK, subtitle *Prussia* (Frederick II); MARIA THERESA; SILESIA.

Course of the War

Europe. Frederick invaded Saxony in 1756 and Bohemia in 1757. He was allied with four small German states, including Hanover. Frederick, with British financial aid, was victorious at first. In 1759 he suffered a major defeat by the Austrians and Russians at Kunersdorf, in Brandenburg. Prussia was reduced to fighting defensive battles for the remainder of the war. Meanwhile, in the Mediterranean, the French had taken Minorca from Britain. France began to prepare an invasion of England, but was thwarted when the British fleet blockaded French ports. In the fall of 1759 the British defeated the French decisively at Lagos Bay and at Quiberon Bay.

In 1762 Spain entered the conflict in support of France and joined in an attack on Portugal, which had refused to close its ports to British ships. Britain helped to repulse the attack. Busy with France and Spain, Britain could give little aid to Prussia, and Frederick seemed on the brink of defeat. He was saved by three unrelated events. Sweden failed in an attempt to conquer Pomerania and withdrew from the war. Peter III succeeded to the Russian throne and quickly made peace with Frederick, whom he had long admired. Then France, whose military resources were being exhausted fighting Britain in the colonies, deserted the Austrian cause. Austria then agreed to make peace with Prussia.

North America. The American phase of the war is called the French and Indian War. It started in 1754 when the British set out to expel the French from the Ohio Valley, where French forts were being built to link together Canada and Louisiana. Although unsuccessful at first, the British finally defeated the French both in what is now the United States and in Canada. The decisive event was the capture of Quebec in 1759. (See QUEBEC, BATTLE OF.)

See also FRENCH AND INDIAN WAR.

India. Britain and France competed for the rich Indian trade by supporting rival native puppet rulers. Robert Clive, in the service of the British East India Company, captured a French center at Chandernagor and gained control of Bengal at the battle of Plassey in 1757. The major French center of Pondichéry fell to the British in 1761.

See also CLIVE, ROBERT; EAST INDIA COMPANY.

Results

Austria and Prussia signed a treaty at Hubertusburg, in Saxony, in 1763. Prussia kept Silesia, and other boundaries were unchanged. Prussia had established itself as an important European power. By the Treaty of Paris in the same year, Great Britain was given France's mainland possessions in North America; Chandernagor and Pondichéry were returned to France, on condition they not be used for military purposes. And Spain, in exchange for the return of Havana and Manila, which had been taken in the war, ceded Florida to Great Britain. In a separate treaty, France gave Spain, its ally, territory west of the Mississippi.

See also PARIS, TREATIES OF, subtitle *Treaty of 1763*.

Seventeen-year Locust. See CICADA.

Seventh-day Adventist Church, a Protestant group that observes Saturday rather than Sunday as the Sabbath. It is the largest church of the Adventist faith, which centers on belief in the Second Advent, or second coming, of Christ in the near future. The Seventh-day Adventists believe that only the righteous will achieve immortality and that it is the function of their church to point the way to salvation. They adhere to the Ten Commandments, abstain from alcoholic beverages and tobacco, and support their church by tithing and offerings.

The Seventh-day Adventists maintain several thousand schools and operate hospitals and clinics throughout the world. An executive committee, elected at the world General Conference Session held every four years, serves as the administrative body of the church.

The Seventh-day Adventists developed from the Advent movement that began in the United States in the early 1840's. (See AD-VENTISTS.) They adopted their present name in 1860. World membership is about 6,000,000, including about 720,000 in the United States. Headquarters are in Silver Spring, Maryland.

Severn Bridge. See BRIDGE (table).

Severn River, sĕv'ẽrn, the longest river in Great Britain. From its source in west-central Wales, the river follows a roughly semicircular course, mostly in England, for 220 miles (355 km) to the Bristol Channel. Its mouth is a broad estuary, with tides reaching nearly to Gloucester. Tributaries include two Avon rivers and the Usk, Wye, and Teme rivers. The Severn is navigable by small barge for much of its length. Small ships travel as far as Gloucester by means of the Gloucester and Sharpness Canal. Other canals link the Severn with other parts of England. The Severn estuary is crossed by a railway tunnel and two long bridges.

Severnaya Zemlya, syä'vyĭr-nȧ-yȧ zyĭm-lyä', an island group in the Arctic Ocean belonging to Russia. The name means "north land." The group is located between the Kara and Laptev seas off the Siberian coast. There are four large islands and several small ones; the total area is some 14,300 square miles (37,000 km²). The islands are rugged, attain heights of more than 3,000 feet (900 m), and have extensive glaciers. There are no permanent settlements. Severnaya Zemlya was discovered in 1913.

Seversky, Alexander Procofieff de. See DE SEVERSKY, ALEXANDER PROCO-FIEFF.

Severus, the family name of a Roman dynasty of military monarchs (193-235 A.D.). See ALEXANDER SEVERUS; CARACALLA; SEPTIMIUS SEVERUS.

Sevier, sĕ-vēr', **John** (1745-1815), a Unit-ed States frontiersman, soldier, and political leader. He played an important role in the history of Tennessee prior to statehood and served as the first governor of the state of Tennessee.

Sevier was born near New Market, Vir-ginia. In 1773 he moved to the far western frontier of North Carolina (later included within the borders of Tennessee). There he helped direct the Wautauga Association, the local governing body in the region. During the Revolutionary War, he led frontiersmen

across the Great Smoky Mountains to defeat the British at Kings Mountain, South Caroli-na (1780), and he later led raids against the Cherokees. After the war, Sevier became involved in various land-speculation ven-tures.

In 1784 North Carolina turned its western frontier over to the central government. The settlers in the region rejected this move, however, and formed the separate state of Franklin, with Sevier as governor. Denied recognition and beset by rivalries, Franklin collapsed. Sevier was pardoned for his sepa-ratist activities and in 1789 was elected to the first U.S. Congress from North Caroli-na's western district. When the state of Tennessee was organized, he was chosen governor, serving 1796-1801 and 1803-09. He represented Tennessee in Congress, 1811-15.

For picture, see TENNESSEE.

Sévigné, sā'vē'nyā', **Madame de** (1626-1696), a French noblewoman noted for the letters she wrote to members of her family and to friends. Her full name was Marie de Rabutin-Chantal, Marquise de Sévigné. Her letters, written in a fresh, clear style, give a detailed and witty picture of court life and intimate accounts of various historical events. About 1,500 of the letters, most of them written to her daughter, have been published in numerous editions beginning a few years after her death.

Seville, sĕ-vĭl' (*Spanish:* **Sevilla,** sȧ-vē'[l]yä), Spain, the capital of Seville prov-ince and the fourth largest city in Spain. It is in Andalusia on the east bank of the Guadal-quivir River, about 245 miles (395 km) southwest of Madrid. Seville is the commer-cial, cultural, and transportation center of southwestern Spain. Although 50 miles (80 km) inland, it is also a seaport, connected with the Atlantic Ocean by the river and a canal. Industries produce a wide variety of goods, including wines and liqueurs, ceram-ics, chemicals, textiles, olive oil, cork, and tobacco and fish products.

Seville is one of Spain's most historic and colorful cities. The older sections are a maze of narrow, winding streets lined by white-washed houses with wrought-iron grillwork. Numerous plazas, parks, gardens, and foun-tains add to the city's charm.

Prominent buildings in Seville include several that are largely Moorish in architec-tural style. The Alcázar, begun in the late

Seville. This is a courtyard in the Alcázar, a castle-fortress that was the residence of Moorish and Christian kings. In the background rises the Giralda, the cathedral's bell tower and the symbol of the city.

Sèvres Porcelain

12th century by the Moors as a castle and fortress, was substantially rebuilt and enlarged during the reign of Pedro the Cruel (1350-69). The Giralda, which has come to be the symbol of Seville, was built in the 12th century as a minaret and is now the bell tower of the cathedral. The cathedral itself, built 1402-1519 on the site of a mosque, is of Gothic design, and is one of the largest Gothic buildings in the world. Paintings by El Greco, Goya, and other artists decorate its interior. Here, too, is what is thought by some to be the tomb of Christopher Columbus.

Among Seville's museums are the Archives of the Indies, containing exhibits and documents relating to Spain's colonies in America, and the Museum of Fine Arts, with works by Spanish masters. Seville's opera house, the Maestranza Theater, was built during 1986-91. The University of Seville dates from 1502.

History

Seville was an Iberian settlement called Hispalis before Julius Caesar conquered it in 45 B.C. After the decline of Rome, Seville was captured by Vandals about 420 A.D., by Visigoths in the sixth century, and by the Moors in 712. The city flourished as a Moorish commercial and cultural center until 1248, when it fell to Ferdinand III of Castile. With the subsequent departure of some 300,000 Muslims, the city declined.

Seville's greatest period followed the discovery of America, when the city was granted a virtual monopoly on trade with the New World. Closely associated with Seville, a center of art and culture, were several prominent painters, including Murillo, Velázquez, and Zurbáran. The golden age ended after the port of Cádiz was opened in 1717 to trade with America, and the city entered a long period of decline.

Seville was occupied by Napoleon's forces during the Peninsular War (1808-14). In the Spanish Civil War (1936-39) the city was captured early by the forces of Franco and served briefly as his headquarters. Seville was the site of the 1992 Universal Exposition, which commemorated the 500th anniversary of Columbus' first voyage to the Americas.

Population: 659,126.

Sèvres, sâ'vr', a French porcelain made at the national factory in Sèvres, near Paris. It became famous for its elegant decoration, lavish use of gold, and beautiful rich glazes, including *rose Pompadour, bleu de roi,* and *jaune jonquil.* The highly prized Sèvres biscuit (unglazed) figurines resemble marble.

Early Sèvres ware was a soft-paste porcelain, in contrast to hard-paste, or true, porcelain. French potters perfected the soft-paste technique, and Sèvres became the most sought-after European porcelain in the second half of the 18th century. After kaolin

S-301

was discovered in France in 1768, the Sèvres factory made both soft-paste and true porcelain until 1804, when soft-paste was abandoned.

Sèvres ware was first made in 1738 at Vincennes. Through the influence of Madame de Pompadour, Louis XV took an interest in the factory, and it was moved to Sèvres in 1756. Ownership passed to the crown in 1759. Since 1793 the factory has been controlled by the French government.

Sèvres, Treaty of, an agreement signed August 10, 1920, at Sèvres, France, by the victorious Allies of World War I and the defeated Ottoman (Turkish) Empire. The harsh provisions of the treaty, which called for surrendering parts of Turkey as well as giving up claims to all non-Turkish lands, were a factor leading to the overthrow of the government by Turkish nationalists. The nationalists under Mustafa Kemal refused to recognize the treaty. They drove Greek occupation forces from Turkish soil and succeeded in obtaining a treaty more favorable to Turkey, the treaty of Lausanne (1923).

See also LAUSANNE CONFERENCE.

Sewage, the mixture of water and waste products carried off through a drainage system of underground pipes, or *sewers.* The waste products consist of both organic and inorganic matter, including human wastes, mineral salts, and garbage. In most large cities sewage also contains liquid wastes from various industrial processes.

The organic matter in sewage decomposes rapidly, giving off foul-smelling and hazardous gases. Disease-causing organisms are passed into sewage through the feces and urine of infected persons. The wastes from industrial processes are often toxic. The safe disposal of sewage is therefore essential to the health of a community.

The collection and treatment of sewage is one of the most important municipal services. In the United States, most cities and towns have sewer systems that carry sewage to a sewage treatment plant. At the plant the sewage is treated to destroy disease organisms and to remove substances that can cause harmful or other undesirable effects in the water. The treated sewage is then discharged into nearby streams, lakes, or coastal waters. In rural areas, the treated sewage is usually disposed of in the soil.

The disposal of untreated or inadequately treated sewage directly into a stream or body of water can result in serious water pollution. Disease organisms endanger water supplies and swimming areas. Various chemicals may poison the water, killing fish and other wildlife, while certain nutrients in the sewage can cause an excessive growth of aquatic plants. As wastes decompose, they can deplete the oxygen supply in the water, making it unfit for all forms of aquatic life.

The facilities for collecting, treating, and disposing of sewage are called a *sewerage system.* In cities and towns, sewerage systems are designed to serve the entire community. Sewage from individual buildings flows into collecting sewers, which carry the waste to a central plant for treatment and disposal. Sewers that only carry domestic sewage— that is, sewage from residential and commercial buildings—are called *sanitary sewers. Storm sewers* are designed specifically for carrying runoff from rain and melted snow. In many systems, both domestic sewage and runoff water are carried in *combined sewers.* Combined sewers are generally undesirable, however, because overflow caused by heavy rains often makes it necessary to discharge untreated sewage from the sewage treatment plant.

Sewers are usually made of clay, concrete, or plastic. Sewerage systems are usually built so that gravity will carry the waste through the pipes. Where this is not possible, the sewage must be pumped.

In rural areas and in communities not served by municipal sewerage systems, sewage is disposed of through the use of septic tanks or, less commonly, cesspools. The *privy,* or outdoor toilet, is commonly used for disposing of human wastes where there is no indoor plumbing.

Sewage Treatment and Disposal

Municipal Sewage Treatment Plants. Raw sewage entering the plant is first passed through screens to remove coarse debris. This material may be buried, burned, or ground in disintegrators and returned to the flow. After screening, the sewage flows slowly through a grit chamber, a shallow tank in which sand and other heavy particles settle to the bottom. This material is periodically removed and usually disposed of in a landfill. The sewage is then pumped into primary settling tanks, where much of the remaining solid material settles out. Chemicals are sometimes added to the sewage to help remove suspended particles and reduce

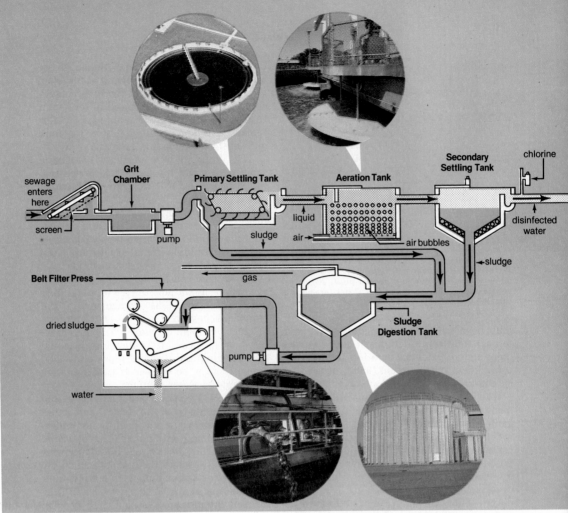

Top photos: © J. Edwards/TSI; © E. R. Berndt/Unicorn. Bottom: WMD; © David Frazier

Sewage Treatment Plant for a large city

foam caused by detergents. The settled material is called *sludge.*

The liquid portion is drawn off and is usually given further treatment. This treatment, called *secondary treatment,* removes most of the organic matter remaining in the sewage. The two most common methods of secondary treatment are the activated sludge process and the trickling filter process.

Activated Sludge Process. In this process the liquid from the primary settling tank passes into large, elongated tanks where it is mixed with sludge containing large numbers of bacteria. The bacteria decompose the organic matter, using it as food. Oxygen is dissolved in the mixture by bubbling either compressed air or pure oxygen gas through it, a process called *aeration.* Aeration provides the bacteria with the oxygen they need for respiration. The mixture is then transferred to settling tanks called final clarifiers. The activated sludge settles out and the clear liquid that remains is removed from the

tank. The liquid is then sometimes disinfected with chlorine before it is discharged into a body of water. Some of the activated sludge that settles out in the final clarifiers is recycled to the aeration tanks.

Trickling Filter Process. In this process the liquid is sprayed over a filtering material, typically a bed of crushed rock. As the liquid seeps through the crushed rock, bacteria and other organisms growing on the rock surfaces decompose most of the organic matter. The products of decomposition are simple compounds, such as nitrates and sulfates, and humuslike matter. The mixture then flows into secondary settling tanks, where the solids settle out as sludge. Chlorine is sometimes added to the clear liquid to disinfect it. The liquid, which contains various inorganic compounds, is then discharged into a body of water.

Very fine particles and such substances as nitrogen and phosphorus compounds usually remain in the sewage water even after secondary treatment. Therefore, when the water discharged from a sewage treatment plant

Everett Johnson/Leo de Wys, Inc.
Trickling Filter. Sewage is sprayed from distributor arms revolving around a central pivot. As the sewage trickles through the bed of stones, organic matter in the sewage is decomposed.

must be of especially high quality, it is given tertiary treatment. Methods of tertiary treatment include extended aeration and filtering using fine-meshed screens, sand, or activated charcoal.

The sludge formed in the various treatment stages contains both organic and inorganic solids. It flows by gravity or is pumped into large closed tanks. In the absence of air, certain types of bacteria in the sludge decompose much of the organic matter. This process is called *sludge digestion.* During this process, methane and other gases are produced. The gas mixture is usually used as fuel to provide heat and power for the sewage plant or sold commercially as fuel.

After digestion, the remaining sludge is often dried by air on large beds of sand or by various mechanical methods that use pressure to remove the water from the sludge. It is then buried, burned, or sold as a soil conditioner or filler for commercial fertilizers. In some areas, the sludge is dried by heat or incinerated to destroy the remaining organic substances before it is sold commercially.

Septic Tanks. Septic tanks are widely used on farms and in communities that do not have municipal sewage disposal systems. The septic tank, which is located underground, usually serves a single building. It is usually made of concrete or steel. The size of tank needed depends upon the number of occupants of the building.

Sewage from the building flows to the tank through the *building sewer.* Inside the

tank, heavy solids settle out as sludge; grease and fine particles rise to form a scum. Bacteria in the sewage digest the organic substances both in the sludge and in the scum, converting them to liquids and gases. The remaining sludge accumulates in the tank and must be removed at intervals.

The liquid portion, usually containing some solids, and the gases are carried into the surrounding soil through a system of distribution pipes. The gases escape to the surface. Liquid and solid wastes are absorbed by the soil, where bacteria decompose the organic matter. In heavy soils, two sets of distribution pipes usually are used alternately to insure proper absorption.

Any disease-causing organisms in the sewage ordinarily do not survive long in either the tank or soil. The sewage wastes and organisms, however, may be carried for long distances through the soil where it is fractured or creviced. It is therefore essential that the tank and disposal pipes be located where there is no danger of contaminating underground water supplies.

Cesspools. Cesspools are sometimes used for sewage disposal on farms and other isolated areas. The cesspool is an underground pit lined with either brick or stone, without mortar. The sewage liquids seep out into the soil through the open spaces in the lining. Solids accumulate as in a septic tank and must be removed at intervals. In time the soil around the cesspool may become clogged with solids, causing overflow. When they are poorly covered, cesspools allow foul-smelling gases to escape and often become breeding places for mosquitoes. Cesspools are not recommended by most health authorities.

History

In ancient cities, covered channels or pipes were often used for removing human wastes from dwellings. Rome, for example, had a system of sewers for disposing of wastes and rainwater. Most ancient sewers fell into disrepair during the Middle Ages. Refuse and human wastes were commonly thrown into the streets. By the late 1700's, many large cities had sewers for removing storm water, but cesspools were usually used for sewage disposal. Both cesspools and privies were widely used in cities and towns.

Modern sewage disposal systems were introduced in the 19th century. Existing storm sewers were usually enlarged to carry

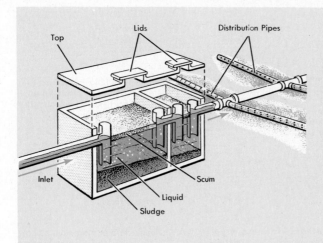

A Double-chamber Septic Tank. Inside the tank, heavy solids settle out as sludge; grease and fine particles form a scum. Bacteria in the sewage decompose the organic substances, changing them to liquids and gases. Sewage liquids, gases, and (usually) solids are carried into the surrounding soil. Gases escape to the surface; liquid and solid wastes are absorbed.

both rainwater and wastes. In the late 19th century, either combined sewers or sanitary sewers were used for disposing of sewage and industrial wastes. The wastes were usually discharged into nearby bodies of water.

Municipal sewage treatment was introduced in the early 20th century, but many cities and industrial plants were slow to adopt it. As the population increased, some existing sewage plants became inadequate. In cities with combined sewers, heavy rains periodically overloaded otherwise adequate disposal facilities. By the 1970's, water pollution caused by the discharge of untreated or inadequately treated sewage had become a major problem. In the United States, legislation was passed in the 1970's to help control and prevent water pollution. The legislation set standards for the quality of treated sewage discharged into streams and lakes and established funding to assist in the improvement and construction of sewage treatment facilities. Additional legislation passed in the 1980's set standards for storm water discharges.

Books about Sewage Disposal

Burks, B. D. *Onsite Wastewater Treatment Systems* (Hogarth House, 1994).

For Younger Readers

Asimov, Isaac. *What Happens When I Flush the Toilet?* (Gareth Stevens, 1992).

Sewall, sū'ăl, **Samuel** (1652-1730), an American colonial jurist. He was the only one of the presiding judges at the Salem witchcraft trials of 1692, which resulted in the death of 20 persons, later to confess that a tragic error had been made. Sewall was born in England and came to Boston with his parents in 1661. He graduated from Harvard in 1671. As a justice of the Massachusetts superior court, 1692-1718, and its chief justice, 1718-28, he became known for his liberal views.

The Diary of Samuel Sewall (3 volumes, 1878-82; revised edition, 2 volumes, 1974), written during 1674-1729, is considered the most vivid account of New England life of that period.

Sewall-Belmont House National Historic Site. See NATIONAL PARKS, section "United States."

Seward, William Henry (1801-1872), a United States statesman. For nearly half a century he was an influential figure in American political life. As secretary of state, 1861-69, Seward played an important role in the Civil War and in the postwar period. A skillful diplomat, he helped to prevent European intervention in the war; particularly adept was his handling of the *Trent* Affair. (See TRENT AFFAIR.) After the war, Seward's protest to the French led to their withdrawal of troops from Mexico and the

William Henry Seward, photo by Mathew Brady
NEW STANDARD Collection

An Illustrated Glossary

Facing—A finish for a raw edge of material, consisting of a band of material seamed to the edge and folded to the inside or outside surface, where it is tacked or stitched.

Pleat—A double fold of material, forward and back, from an upper horizontal edge, which gives hanging fullness.

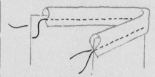

Binding—A finish for a raw edge of material, consisting of a tape, ribbon, or strip of material folded over the edge and stitched.

Gathers—Fullness created by drawing up the material along one or more threads in a line of stitching.

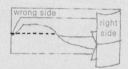

Seam—Two or more layers of material joined by stitching together near the edge.

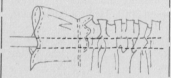

Casing—Two parallel rows of stitching through two layers of material, forming a channel through which cord, elastic, or a rod may be drawn.

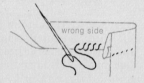

Hem—A finish for a raw edge of material, consisting of a folded edge stitched (or bonded) against the inside surface of the material.

Tacking—A stitch or several stitches in the same place to secure the positioning of material or to reinforce a point of stress; also, the loose joining of two surfaces of material by hand stitching.

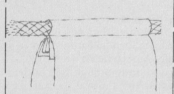

Cording—A seam or edge finish, consisting of a cord folded into a strip of material and stitched into the seam from the right side or along the raw edge.

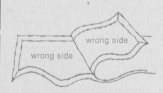

Lining—An inner layer of material shaped like the outer layer and attached to it.

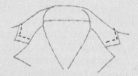

Top-stitching—A line of stitching on the outside surface of two or more layers of material for the purpose of joining them or holding them in position or for decorative effect.

Dart—A line of stitching from a folded edge of material diagonally to the outer edge or in a curve back to the folded edge, for shaping.

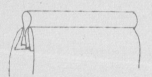

Piping—A finish similar to cording, but without a cord folded into the strip of material.

Tuck—A stitched fold of material, used for shortening, creating fullness, or decorative effect.

overthrow of their puppet emperor, Maximilian. An advocate of territorial expansion, Seward negotiated the purchase of Alaska from Russia for $7,200,000 in 1867. At the time, many considered it a bad bargain and called the new territory "Seward's Folly" or "Seward's Icebox."

Seward was born in Florida, New York. He graduated from Union College in 1820. Shortly afterward he began to practice law in Auburn, New York, and entered politics. Elected to the New York legislature in 1830, Seward became a leader of the Whigs. He was the first Whig governor of New York,

1839-43. In 1848 he was elected to the U.S. Senate as a Whig; he later became a Republican. Already known as an abolitionist, he vigorously fought against the extension of slavery. Seward was defeated by Abraham Lincoln for the Republican Presidential nomination in 1860. After the election, Lincoln made Seward secretary of state.

The night Lincoln was assassinated, Seward was attacked in his home by a fellow conspirator of John Wilkes Booth and stabbed, nearly fatally.

Sewellel. See MOUNTAIN BEAVER.

Sewer. See SEWAGE.

Sewing, joining pieces of flexible material together or attaching something to material by *stitching*—drawing a thread or filament through the material with a needle. Sewing may be done by hand or on a sewing machine. The material sewed is most often fabric, but it may be fur, leather, plastic, paper, or other substance that a threaded needle can penetrate. (For an alternate method of joining, without using thread, see STITCHLESS SEWING.)

The greatest single use of sewing is for making garments. Numerous other products are made wholly or in part by sewing—for example, draperies and other interior furnishings, luggage, tarpaulins, tents, bags, and conveyor belts. No matter what the article is, certain stitching constructions are used to form it and finish it. Some of these are shown in the Illustrated Glossary.

Making an article by sewing involves various procedures besides stitching. Any or all of the following may be required:

1. Designing the article.
2. Preparing a pattern of paper, fabric, or cardboard, so that there is a piece in the proper shape for each piece of material to be cut and stitched.
3. Cutting the material.
4. Basting (sewing temporarily), pinning pieces of material together, or temporarily gluing.

5. Fitting (in case of a garment or a cover for something, such as furniture).
6. Stitching (followed by removing pins or basting threads, if any).
7. Attaching fasteners—buttons, snaps, hooks and eyes, and zippers.
8. Pressing (smoothing the article with an iron or other device).

Sewing may be done at home, in a shop, or in a factory. In all three situations, most of it is done by machine. Certain kinds of sewing, however, are still done by hand. Some of the basic hand stitches are shown in the illustration on the next page. For machine stitches, see SEWING MACHINE, subtitle *Kinds of Machine Stitches* (and accompanying illustrations).

Garments

Home Sewing. Commercial pattern companies design garments and prepare paper patterns for them in a wide range of sizes. The person who sews at home, if very experienced, may design a garment and cut the pattern for it. Generally, however, the sewer selects a design from a pattern book or women's magazine and buys a pattern in the proper size.

The pattern may need adjustments to conform to the figure of the person for whom the garment is being made. It is advisable to pin the pieces of pattern together (forming half a garment) and try it on, matching the center of the pattern to the center of the body. Instructions for making the desired adjustments are included with the pattern.

After adjusting the pattern, the sewer lays the pieces on the fabric and, following printed directions, cuts out the garment. The pieces are pinned, glued, or basted together. The sewer next has the garment tried on by the person for whom it is being made or fits it on a dress form. Adjustments are completed as required to improve the fit. The garment then is stitched, according to directions on the pattern, with seams being pressed out as the sewing proceeds, until finished. Finally, the completed garment is pressed.

Commercial patterns are available also for

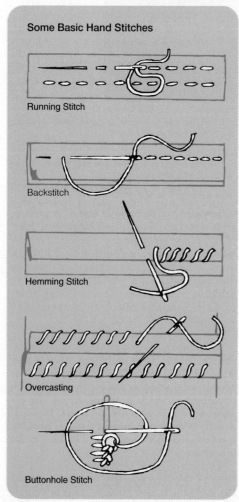

Some Basic Hand Stitches

Running Stitch

Backstitch

Hemming Stitch

Overcasting

Buttonhole Stitch

accessories such as scarves, ties, and handbags.

Sewing by Dressmakers and Tailors. A garment may be custom-made (made to order) by a professional dressmaker or tailor. Generally, such persons choose not to use commercial patterns. They may create a pattern of paper or cloth by measuring and shaping the pieces on the customer or on a dress form. Or they may cut the garment fabric itself by such a procedure, without using any pattern. Their procedures for sewing the garment are approximately the same as those who sew at home. A tailor shop, however, may have special sewing machines that eliminate some of the hand sewing usually required at home—for example, hemming, tacking, and sewing on buttons.

Custom-made garments are also available from *couturiers* (designers of fashionable apparel) and custom departments of apparel stores, although this service is becoming increasingly rare. The sewing may be done by several persons, each performing one or two operations, in much the same way that expensive ready-made garments are sewn, as described in the next section.

Sewing of Ready-made Garments. The manufacture of garments is discussed in the article GARMENT INDUSTRY. The procedures differ from those described here mainly in being organized on an assembly-line basis. Typically, one person performs only one or two operations on the garment, then passes it on to another operator. A further difference is in the amount of hand sewing; the lower the price of the garment, the less hand sewing is done on it.

Expensive ready-made garments are produced in relatively limited quantity and are not made by typical mass-production methods. Each garment is cut individually. Some makers of men's suits cut them to the customers' individual measurements as supplied by the stores placing the orders. Sewing is done mainly by a single operator, although certain details are handled by specialists. Men's suits in the higher price ranges are often semi-finished—certain seams are left open so the garment can be custom fitted by the store's tailor.

Other Applications of Sewing

Mending and Alterations. Mending is usually done at home. A hole in utilitarian wearing apparel or linen may be *patched* or *darned*. (In patching, the hole is covered with a piece of fabric stitched or bonded down around the edge; in darning, matching yarn is woven over the hole.) Most mending, however, consists of such procedures as reattaching buttons and snaps, resewing part of a hem, replacing trouser pockets, and turning in and tacking down frayed edges. Some tailor shops and dry cleaners do mending. Special sewing machines are available for the darning and patching of work clothes, bags, and other utilitarian articles.

Ready-made garments often need to be altered. Alterations may be made by a skilled sewer at home, by someone on the store staff, or by a dressmaker or tailor.

Household Furnishings. Articles such as draperies, bedspreads, and furniture slipcovers can also be sewn at home. Commercial patterns, sewing books, and women's magazines give explicit instructions with detailed illustrations for such articles. There are professionals who specialize in this type of work. They may be employed directly by the client or by an interior designer engaged by the client. Such articles are also produced industrially and sold ready-made.

Other Sewed Products. Many articles that are difficult or impossible to sew at home are sewed on industrial machines in factories. Examples are large items, such as parachutes and tents, and items such as shoes and leather handbags. Such products are made in the same manner as ready-made garments, except that they are not basted, fitted, or pressed.

History

Archeological evidence indicates that sewing developed in temperate climates in prehistoric times. People learned to sew animal pelts together to form close-fitting garments. Needles were made of bone; split tendons or long hair probably served as thread. In the eastern Mediterranean region, the site of several ancient civilizations, woven fabrics were formed into clothing generally by draping rather than by cutting and stitching. The women of Minoan Crete, however, wore fitted bodices and bell-shaped skirts that must have required skilled cutting and sewing.

In the Middle Ages clothing and other fabric articles were sewed at home. Members of the nobility had full-time seamsters and seamstresses on their domestic staffs. However, medieval craftsmen who sewed articles of leather, such as saddles and shoes, often had shops for making and selling their wares. Gradually some of the merchants who sold woolens and silks began to function as tailors (from the French for "one who cuts"), making to order the elaborate fitted garments of the Renaissance. The makers of the equally elaborate headwear were known as haberdashers.

By the early 19th century, most sewed articles other than clothing were made by tradesmen or in factories. An 1810 United States government report estimated that only one-third of the country's garment-making was done in tailor shops rather than at home.

As ready-made clothes were introduced, many tailors became manufacturers, hiring out the hand stitching to women who worked at home. Those who did industrial sewing were eager purchasers of the sewing machine, after it began to be produced in quantity in the 1850's. The purchase of machines for home sewing was vastly stimulated in the 1860's by the introduction of paper patterns in graded sizes for clothing.

Meanwhile, in the late 1850's, shoe manufacturers began using machine sewing, and gradually manufacturers of other products requiring sewing began doing likewise. By 1900 virtually all commercial stitching was done by machine. An important development in home sewing in the late 20th century was the introduction of the serger, or overlock machine, which cuts the fabric and stitches in the same operation.

See also EMBROIDERY; SEWING MACHINE; SHEARS; THREAD.

Books about Sewing

Blaxland, Kathleen. *Beginner's Guide to Using Sewing Patterns* (Seven Hills, 1994).

Parks, Carol. *Sewing the New Classics: Clothes with Easy Style* (Sterling, 1995).

Shepherd, Sandy, editor. *Complete Guide to Sewing: Step-by-Step Techniques for Making Clothes and Home Furnishings,* revised edition (Reader's Digest, 1995).

Smith, S. L. *The Art of Sewing Basics and Beyond,* revised edition (Sewing Arts, 1992).

Vogue & Butterick Step by Step Guide to Sewing Techniques (Simon & Schuster, 1994).

Zieman, Nancy. *501 Sewing Hints* (Oxmoor House, 1996).

For Younger Readers

Hoffman, Christine. *Sewing by Hand* (HarperCollins, 1994).

Smith, Nancy. *Sewing Machine Fun* (Possibilities, 1993).

Sewing Machine, a device for stitching or sewing mechanically. There are many types of sewing machines, from portable household machines for domestic sewing or mending to industrial machines that stitch luggage or home furnishings. Sewing machines are usually powered by an electric motor; hand- or treadle-operated machines are still common where electricity is not available.

Clothing and many other kinds of manufactured items can be produced faster, more uniformly, and more sturdily with a sewing machine than is possible by hand. Many forms of decorative stitching may also be done by machine.

The sewing machine is generally regarded as one of the most important inventions of the 19th century. It revolutionized the manufacture of ready-made clothing, shoes, and a host of other products. The sewing machine was the first consumer appliance to be widely advertised and the first to be sold on the installment plan. It introduced mechanization to many technologically underdeveloped regions of the world.

Kinds of Machine Stitches

There are five major types of machine stitches—the chain stitch, the lockstitch (also called the shuttle, or plain, stitch), the double-locked stitch (also called the multiple-thread chain stitch), the overlock stitch (also called the overedge stitch), and the flat-seam stitch (also called the covering stitch).

A stitch is formed by the simultaneous action of one or more needles and one or more stitch-forming devices. Each needle has an eye near its point for carrying thread. Some stitch-forming devices carry thread; others do not. The most common stitch-forming device in home sewing machines consists of a rotary hook attached to a stationary bobbin. (See illustration *How a Lockstitch Is Formed.*)

As each stitch is formed, a feeding mechanism moves the cloth along. Four-motion feeding is commonly used. In this method, a toothed plate called the *feed dog* moves forward after each stitch, carrying the cloth with it; the feed dog then drops away from the cloth, moves backward, and rises against the cloth to repeat the first step. The *presser foot* keeps the cloth against the feed dog.

The Chain Stitch, made with a single thread, is strong and stretchy, but it ravels easily. It is used primarily for basting and for other temporary stitching, such as closing the tops of filled bags.

The Lockstitch, formed with two or more threads, is firm, rather than stretchy, and

Industrial Sewing Machine being used by a textile worker in Texas. Industrial machines are specialized, designed to perform only one or two types of sewing operations.

©Oscar Williams/Journalism Services

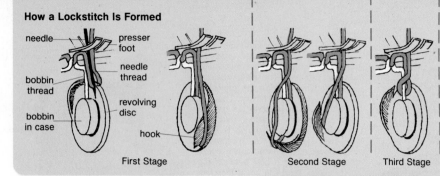

needle presser foot

needle thread

bobbin thread

revolving disc

bobbin in case

hook

First Stage — Second Stage — Third Stage — Fourth Stage

does not ravel easily. However, it is not as strong as a chain stitch or a double-locked stitch made with the same strength thread. The lockstitch is used for most types of household sewing, including zigzag stitching. In industrial sewing, the lockstitch is often used where appearance is more important than strength—as, for example, on shirt collars and blouse facings. It is also used industrially for such operations as tacking, making buttonholes, and sewing on buttons.

The Double-locked Stitch, made with two or more threads, is strong, stretchy, and nonraveling. However, it is bulkier than the lockstitch and requires more thread. The double-locked stitch is used primarily where strength and elasticity are more important than appearance—as, for example, on the main seams of trousers.

The Overlock Stitch, made with two to five threads, covers the edge of a piece of material. It is used to join two or more layers of material, as well as to decorate or protect the raw edge of a single piece of fabric.

The Flat-seam Stitch, made with three to nine threads, is strong, secure, stretchy, and decorative. It is widely used for joining layers of knitted material.

Household Sewing Machines

A household machine may be portable, weighing as little as 12 pounds (5.4 kg), or a console model complete with a furniture cabinet. The simplest type of household machine does a straight lockstitch. Machines that produce a zigzag lockstitch have one or more needles that swing back and forth. Zigzag stitching is used for such types of sewing as making decorative patterns, mending, and automatic button-holing. The sideward motion of the needle or needles in zigzag stitching is produced by rotating cams or, in most computerized machines, by a small, electronically controlled motor.

In addition to various forms of stitching, sewing machines can be made to do a variety of more complex jobs, such as producing

S-311

A *lockstitch* is formed by passing the bobbin thread (shown in white) through a loop of the needle thread (in color). Several methods are used, the one shown being common.

First Stage: As the needle reaches its lowest point and reverses direction, the needle thread forms a small loop, which is caught by a hook on a revolving disk set slightly behind the bobbin case. The bobbin case, containing the bobbin wound with thread, is not connected to this disk and does not revolve. It fits loosely in place, allowing the needle thread to pass between it and the disk.

Second Stage: The loop of needle thread has been carried by the hook to the bottom of the bobbin case. Tension on the thread causes it to become taut, so that it slips out of the hook and passes around the bobbin case.

Third Stage: The bobbin thread has been enclosed by the needle thread, which is being pulled up by a lever (not shown) and by the upward motion of the needle to tighten the stitch.

Fourth Stage: The two threads have been drawn into the middle of the fabric and are tightly locked.

Some Machine Stitches

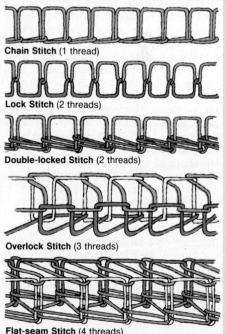

Chain Stitch (1 thread)

Lock Stitch (2 threads)

Double-locked Stitch (2 threads)

Overlock Stitch (3 threads)

Flat-seam Stitch (4 threads)

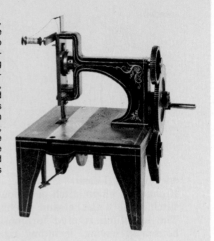

Early Sewing Machines. *Left,* Howe's machine, 1846, was the first workable lockstitch machine to be patented. The cloth was impaled by hand on the projecting pins (left) for stitching. The machine never reached the market, but other inventors adopted Howe's ideas. *Right,* in Singer's machine, 1851, a mechanism moved cloth forward continuously, but engaged it only beneath the needle. The cloth could therefore be turned for stitching in a curved line. The hand crank (right) was soon replaced by a foot treadle.
Smithsonian Institution Photos

ruffles and pleats. Special attachments are designed for inserting zippers and for hemming napkins and other flat items.

In using a household sewing machine it is important to maintain proper tension in the thread. When both threads of a lockstitch machine are at the proper tension, the stitch will lock in the middle of the fabric. Proper tension in the thread produces a regular, flat chain in the chain stitch. Too much tension can cause puckering of the fabric; too little can produce loose, uneven stitches.

Industrial Sewing Machines

There are several hundred kinds of industrial sewing machines, ranging greatly in size, weight, and appearance. Unlike household sewing machines, which can usually do a variety of jobs, most industrial machines are designed for a single purpose, such as attaching buttons or stitching cuffs.

Most industrial machines have 1 or 2 needles, although some have as many as 12. The needles may be straight or curved, and set vertically, horizontally, or on a slant. Most machines have a flat *bed* (sewing platform). However, machines used to sew tubular articles, such as sleeves, have a bed in the shape of a horizontal cylinder. Tubular and curved articles that are difficult to handle on a flat or cylinder bed are sewed on a machine with a bed that resembles a vertical post.

An industrial sewing machine is usually mounted on a table. However, some models used to sew the edges of large, heavy articles such as mattresses and carpets are mounted on a pedestal that travels along the edge of the article being sewed.

Industrial sewing machines can do two kinds of stitches that household sewing machines cannot—the double-locked stitch and the flat-seam stitch. The typical industrial machine is operated at a speed of between 6,000 and 10,000 stitches a minute, compared to the home machine's average speed of 800 to 1,000 stitches a minute. Computerized industrial sewing machines can be programmed to perform many sewing operations—such as positioning needles and trimming threads—automatically. At some modern facilities, sewing machines form part of a computer-controlled system that automatically positions material to be sewn and then removes the sewn articles and transfers them to a storage area.

History

The earliest known sewing machine was a chain-stitching device patented in 1790 by Thomas Saint, an English cabinetmaker. It is not known, however, whether Saint ever built a working model of his machine. The first person known to have put a sewing machine into commercial use was Barthelemy Thimonnier, a French tailor. Between 1830 and 1841, he patented a chain-stitch machine and put 80 of his machines into operation sewing army uniforms. The machines were destroyed by tailors who feared the invention would take their jobs.

The sewing machine as it is known today was largely the result of inventions made in the United States between 1830 and 1854. In the early 1830's Walter Hunt invented the first workable lockstitch machine, but he did not patent it. The machine could sew only short straight seams.

Elias Howe was the first to patent a workable lockstitch machine. Howe developed his machine during 1843-45 and patented it in 1846. (See picture.) Like Hunt's machine, it sewed only short straight seams. In 1849 John Bachelder patented the first machine able to sew a straight seam of any length.

In 1851 Isaac Merrit Singer patented the first successful lockstitch machine that could sew a curved seam of any length. Like the Hunt and Howe machines, it was operated by a hand crank. (See picture.) Very soon Singer invented a treadle to operate it. I. M. Singer and Company, founded the same year, adopted an aggressive sales policy that did much to popularize the sewing machine.

Three major lockstitch improvements were patented by Allen B. Wilson—the rotary hook (1851), the stationary bobbin (1852), and the four-motion cloth feed (1854). In 1853 Wilson and his partner Nathaniel Wheeler founded the Wheeler and Wilson Manufacturing Company, which became one of the leading 19th-century manufacturers of household sewing machines.

The first double-locked-stitch machine was patented in 1851 by two Boston tailors, William O. Grover and William E. Baker. Their company, the Grover and Baker Sewing Machine Company, produced the first portable sewing machine in 1856.

During the second half of the 19th century, most of the basic sewing machine attachments were developed, as well as the first overlock-stitch machine, the first zigzag machine, and the first flat-seam stitch machine.

The electric motor—used to power some machines as early as the 1870's—largely replaced the treadle in the early 1900's. Through the 1960's, there were gradual improvements in the sewing machine and its attachments. The first electronic sewing machine, featuring push-button selection of stitching patterns, was introduced by the Singer Company in 1975. Overlock sewing machines for use in the home were introduced in the 1970's but did not become popular until the 1980's.

See also HOWE, ELIAS; SINGER, ISAAC MERRIT; WILSON, ALLEN BENJAMIN.

A Book about the Sewing Machine

Saunders, Jan. *A Step-by-Step Guide to Your Sewing Machine* (Chilton, 1990).

Sex. See REPRODUCTION OF LIVING ORGANISMS, subtitle *Sexual Reproduction;* SEX EDUCATION.

Sex Education. Traditionally sex education has consisted of parents explaining the facts of human reproduction to children reaching the age of adolescence and of setting down the "do's" and "don't's" of sexual behavior. Increasingly, however, authorities in health education have come to consider such instruction inadequate. They believe that sex education should begin early in childhood. It should, they feel, include not only biological facts but also the basic principles of wholesome human relationships. In addition, these authorities believe, parental guidance should be supplemented by sex education programs in the schools and by counsel from the churches and other concerned institutions.

These authorities are of the opinion that early and comprehensive sex education is essential for many reasons. They believe it is important that children early be made aware of what it means to be a male or a female. These experts assert that sexuality—the quality or state of being male or female—is much more than a physiological process. It is a major aspect of personality and, as such, is closely tied to emotional and social adjustment and to physical development. Sexuality, they say, has a profound influence on the pattern of an individual's life within the family and in society.

Sex Education Programs

The primary goal of any well-rounded sex education program is to equip young people to use their sexuality responsibly, as individuals and as family members, in their present and future lives. Allied to this general goal are such specific aims as reducing venereal disease, illegitimate pregnancies, and broken marriages.

In the Home. Children will receive various information and impressions about sex from their everyday experiences whether parents wish it or not. Authorities are in general agreement that the loving atmosphere of the home is the best place for children to develop sound ideas and attitudes about the role of men and women in family and out-of-family situations. Parents should provide guidance not only to develop wholesome attitudes in their children but also to correct misinformation and to allay fears.

Most sex educators agree that to guide

children, parents themselves need to be adequately prepared. They feel it essential for parents to regard sex as a creative force, a natural and dignified part of life. In addition, parents need accurate information on the biological aspects of human sexuality and sound attitudes on marriage and family life. Above all, parents should be understanding about and responsive to the natural curiosity of a child and should be honest and factual in answering a child's questions. The information given should correspond to the child's level of maturity.

In the Schools. By the time children reach school age, they have accumulated various kinds of information on sex from their parents, from friends, and from television and movies. The schools are thus presented with the opportunity—and, many educators and others believe, the responsibility—to supplement the efforts of parents and correct any misconceptions children may have acquired.

In some communities, there has been resistance to any form of sex education in the schools. However, many parents, educational and health associations, and other groups have come to feel that the schools are ideally suited to provide basic factual information and to emphasize social standards and mores as part of the normal educational process.

Some authorities, while not against sex education, feel that teachers and curriculum directors on the whole are inadequately trained in this area and that some programs are educationally unsound. Many other people who object to sex education in the schools do so on moral or religious grounds; some feel that it encourages premarital sex.

In general, educators favoring sex education think the program should extend from kindergarten through 12th grade and even into college. It should deal scientifically and objectively at the appropriate levels of maturity with the biological, psychological, and social aspects of sexuality. This material can be integrated into normal classwork in the lower grades and can be given in special courses in upper grades.

Sex education often includes information on sexually transmitted diseases, with special emphasis often given to AIDS prevention. Some high schools, primarily those in the inner cities, provide their students with condoms and birth-control counseling.

In Religious and Other Institutions. Most supporters of sex-education programs agree

that, to be effective on a large scale, sex education requires the involvement of many institutions, including churches, community organizations, health and educational associations, and the news media. Working individually or collectively, these institutions can be important forces not only in furnishing facts but also in instilling responsible attitudes about sex and the part it should play in the life of an individual.

Information on Sex Education

Information on sex education can be obtained from such sources as the following:

American Medical Association, 535 North Dearborn Street, Chicago, Illinois 60610

Council for Sex Information and Education, Box 72, Capitola, California 95010

National Education Association, 1201 16th Street, N.W., Washington, D.C. 20036

Sex Information and Education Council of the United States, 80 Fifth Avenue, New York, New York 10011

See also ADOLESCENCE; BABY; BIRTH CONTROL; CHILD DEVELOPMENT; REPRODUCTION OF LIVING ORGANISMS.

Selected Books

For Parents

Engel, Beverly. *Beyond the Birds and the Bees: Fostering Your Child's Healthy Sexual Development* (Pocket Books, 1997).

Moglia, R. F., and Jon Knowles, editors. *All About Sex: a Family Resource* (Crown, 1997).

Vaughan, Peggy, and James Vaughan. *For Parents Only: Your Personal Handbook for Talking to Your Kids about Sex* (Dialog, 1996).

For Teenagers

Basso, M. J. *The Underground Guide to Teenage Sexuality: an Essential Handbook for Today's Teens and Parents* (Fairview, 1997).

Bourgeois, Paulette, Martin Wolfish, and Kim Martyn. *Changes in You and Me: a Book About Puberty, Mostly for Boys* (Andrews & McMeel, 1994).

Bourgeois, Paulette, Martin Wolfish, and Kim Martyn. *Changes in You and Me: a Book About Puberty, Mostly for Girls* (Andrews & McMeel, 1994).

Fenwick, Elizabeth, and Richard Walker. *How Sex Works: a Clear, Comprehensive Guide for Teenagers to Emotional, Physical, and Sexual Maturity* (D K, 1996).

Harris, Robie. *It's Perfectly Normal: Changing Bodies, Growing Up, Sex, and Sexual Health* (Candlewick, 1996).

Stoppard, Miriam. *Sex Ed* (D K, 1997).

For Younger Readers

Brown, L. K. *What's the Big Secret, Dinosaurs?: Talking about Sex with Girls and Boys* (Little, Brown, 1997).

Greene, Carol. *Why Boys and Girls Are Different*, revised edition (Concordia, 1995).

Hummel, R. S. *Where Do Babies Come From?*, 2nd edition (Concordia, 1995).

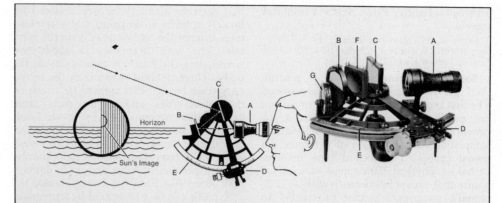

How a Sextant Works. Sighting through an eyepiece (A) the observer sees both the sun and the horizon in the horizon mirror (B). The left half is clear; the right half is silvered, reflecting the sun's image from the index mirror (C). This mirror is adjusted by moving the index arm (D) until the sun appears level with the horizon. The arm indicates the angle of the sun on the graduated arc (E). The circle *(above left)* shows what the observer sees when his sextant is adjusted. The photograph *(above right)* shows a marine sextant. Smoked lenses (F) and (G) mounted on both sides of the horizon mirror reduce the sun's glare.

Sextant, a navigation instrument used to measure angles, particularly the altitudes of the sun and stars above the horizon. A sextant is used by a navigator to find his position on the earth. There are two classes of sextants—marine and air.

A typical marine sextant consists of a triangular frame, with a curved scale, marked in degrees of arc, at the bottom. Mounted on the frame are an eyepiece and a piece of glass, called the *horizon mirror,* half of which is silvered and half clear. The sextant is held so that the horizon can be seen through the clear part of the glass when looking through the eyepiece. Attached to the frame is a movable arm that crosses the scale; on the arm is a second mirror. The arm is positioned so that the image of the reference body (the sun for example) appears in the horizon mirror to be just touching the horizon. The position of the arm along the scale gives the altitude of the body in degrees.

The time of the measurement is noted on an extremely accurate clock, called a *chronometer.* With the altitude of the body, the correct time, and a nautical almanac, the observer determines that the ship is somewhere on a *line of position.* By taking a second sextant reading an hour or two later, a second line of position is established. The intersection of the two lines, considered together with the ship's course and speed, indicates the latitude and longitude.

An air sextant serves the same purpose as a marine sextant. The horizon cannot be used while in flight, so an artificial horizon is provided. A spirit-level, a pendulum, or a gyroscope provides the artificial horizon from which the altitudes of the celestial bodies can be measured.

Sexton, Anne (1928-1974), a United States poet, one of the leading members of the confessional school of poetry. Sexton's poetry is known for its vivid images, intimate subject matter, and emotional intensity. Beginning with her first collection of poetry, *To Bedlam and Part Way Back* (1966), Sexton used her own life as subject matter. She revealed and examined in writing her personal relationships, struggle with mental illness, and feelings of despair and anger. Sexton was often hospitalized during periods of mental instability. She wrote candidly about this taboo subject, as well as about the physical aspects of womanhood and her desire for religious belief.

Sexton was born Anne Harvey in Newton, Massachusetts. She married Alfred Sexton in 1948. She taught creative writing at several colleges, including Boston University. Her collection *Live or Die* (1966) was awarded a Pulitzer Prize. Sexton committed suicide.

Other poetry collections include: *All My Pretty Ones* (1962); *The Death Notebooks* (1974); *The Awful Rowing Toward God* (1975).

Sexual Harassment, in law. In general, there are two types of sexual harassment. The first type, sometimes referred to as *quid pro quo* harassment, occurs when a job benefit is directly tied to an individual's submission to or rejection of a request for sexual favors. The second type involves verbal or physical harassment of a sexual nature that causes interference with an individual's work performance or creates an intimidating or offensive atmosphere in the workplace. Most victims of sexual harassment are women; the perpetrators generally are male coworkers or men who hold positions of authority over them.

A number of countries have laws prohibiting sexual harassment. In the United States, sexual harassment violates federal and state antidiscrimination laws. Sexual harassment was ruled to be a violation of federal law in 1980 when the Equal Employment Opportunity Commission declared that it violates the Civil Rights Act of 1964. This ruling was upheld by the U.S. Supreme Court in *Meritor Savings Bank* v. *Vinson* (1986). The problem of sexual harassment became a topic of national attention in 1991 during the Senate hearing on the Supreme Court nomination of Clarence Thomas, who was charged with sexually harassing behavior by a former employee, Anita Hill.

Sexual Reproduction. See REPRODUCTION OF LIVING ORGANISMS, subtitle *Sexual Reproduction.*

Sexually Transmitted Disease (STD), or **Venereal Disease,** any one of several highly contagious diseases contracted by sexual contact with infected persons. Syphilis, gonorrhea, chlamydia, herpes simplex type 2, and genital warts are the most common sexually transmitted diseases. AIDS and type B hepatitis can also be sexually transmitted. (See AIDS; HEPATITIS.)

Syphilis is caused by tiny, corkscrew-shaped bacteria called *spirochetes*. The disease is characterized by three progressive stages: primary, secondary, and tertiary. Within a few hours after exposure, the bacteria penetrate the skin or mucous membranes and enter the bloodstream and tissues. The first sign of infection is a sore called a *chancre*

that appears about three weeks after contact. It appears at the point where the bacteria entered the body—usually on the genitals. The sore disappears in about two weeks, but the bacteria remain inside the body. Three to eight weeks later the secondary stage begins. It is marked by a rash on the palms, soles, and mucous membranes and is often accompanied by fever, headache, and sore throat. Syphilis is infectious only during the primary and secondary stages. In the tertiary stage, intense pain, paralysis, and permanent heart and brain damage may occur. (See PARESIS; TABES DORSALIS.)

Syphilis can be transmitted by a pregnant woman to her unborn child. The baby may be born deaf or blind, or with other disabilities. A blood test for syphilis is required in most states prior to obtaining a marriage license; persons whose test results are positive are denied the license. Syphilis can be cured if treated in either of its first two stages with penicillin.

Gonorrhea is a bacterial infection that affects the genitals and urinary tract and can also infect the ovaries and testes. A discharge from the infected areas appears two to eight days after contact with an infected person. Gonorrhea is treated with penicillin or other antibiotics. A chlamydial infection usually occurs with gonorrhea, and it is treated at the same time. Untreated gonorrhea can result in sterility. Arthritis, meningitis, and blindness can develop if the infection spreads throughout the body. Gonorrhea can be transmitted during childbirth.

Chlamydia is caused by single-celled microorganisms called chlamydiae. The first symptom, a watery discharge from the genital organs, occurs 7 to 28 days after exposure. It is followed by painful urination and pain in the pelvis. In men, chlamydia is the leading cause of nongonococcal urethritis (NGU), an inflammation of the urethra. If untreated, NGU can lead to sterility. In women, chlamydia can cause an infection in the uterus. If untreated, the infection can spread to the fallopian tubes and cause sterility. The disease can be transmitted during childbirth, causing conjunctivitis (an eye infection) and pneumonia in the infant or, in some cases, death. Chlamydia is treated with tetracycline or erythromycin. If untreated, chlamydia can also cause *trachoma,* a chronic eye inflammation that can lead to blindness. (See TRACHOMA.)

Herpes Simplex Type 2, or **Genital Herpes,** is caused by a virus. Two to eight days after exposure to the virus, small red bumps appear on the genital organs, thighs, and buttocks. These bumps develop into painful blisters that rupture and form crusty sores. After 10 days the sores heal, but the disease is not cured. The virus goes into a dormant stage in the nerve cells of the spinal cord, remaining there for the life of the victim. Stress, exposure to the sun, or menstruation can trigger a recurrence of the symptoms months or years later. The disease can be transmitted during childbirth, causing permanent neurological damage to the child or its death.

The symptoms of genital herpes can be relieved by acyclovir, an antibiotic. Acyclovir decreases the severity of the initial outbreak and prevents or reduces the frequency of recurrent outbreaks.

Genital, or **Venereal, Warts** are caused by a virus. One to six months after exposure to the virus, pink or reddish warts appear on the genital organs. The warts begin as small bumps but may spread, becoming clusters that resemble a cauliflower. The virus that causes genital warts has been linked to cancers of the cervix, vulva, and penis. The disease can be transmitted during childbirth. Genital warts are treated with drugs such as podofilox, phodophyllum resin, 5-fluorouracil, and alpha interferon, applied to or injected into the affected area. They can also be removed by a laser beam.

Syphilis is caused by the spirochete bacterium *Treponema pallidum;* gonorrhea by the bacterium *Neisseria gonorrhoeae,* commonly called gonococcus; chlamydia by the bacterium *Chlamydia trachomatis;* herpes simplex type 2 by the virus *Herpesvirus hominis;* and genital warts by the human papilloma virus, *Condyloma acuminata.*

Seychelles (in full: **Republic of Seychelles**), sā-shĕlz′, an island country in the Indian Ocean near the Equator, some 1,100 miles (1,800 km) east of Africa. It consists of about 90 volcanic and coral islands, totaling 171 square miles (444 km²). Most of the people are of mixed black and European descent and live on the largest island, Mahé. The capital and only sizable city is Victoria, on Mahé. Agriculture and fishing sustain most of the people. Tourism is an important source of income. Seychelles is a member of the Commonwealth of Nations.

The Seychelles Islands were known to the Portuguese by about 1500. They were first settled, by the French and by black slaves, in 1770. Britain seized the islands during the Napoleonic Wars and acquired them by treaty in 1814. They were made a colony in 1903 and granted independence in 1976.

Population: 61,898.

See also FLAG (color page).

Seymour, a noble English family. Three members of this family became prominent during the reigns of Henry VIII (1509-47) and Edward VI (1547-53). All three were the children of Sir John Seymour.

Edward Seymour, Duke of Somerset (1506-1552). See SOMERSET, DUKE OF.

Thomas Seymour (1508-1549) was a soldier and statesman. He was knighted in 1537 and served as an ambassador during 1538-43. In 1547 he was made Baron Seymour of Sudeley and lord high admiral. After the death of Henry VIII, Seymour plotted to unseat his brother Edward, who was the head of government as lord protector. Seymour was convicted of treason and executed.

Jane Seymour (1509-1537) was queen of England as the third wife of Henry VIII. She married the king in 1536. Jane Seymour died shortly after giving birth to a son, who later became Edward VI.

Seymour, Horatio (1810-1886), a United States political leader. An important figure in New York politics for many years, he was the Democratic candidate for President in 1868. He was defeated by Civil War hero Ulysses S. Grant. Although the electoral vote was 80 for Seymour and 214 for Grant, Grant had an edge of only 306,592 popular votes. An analysis of the vote showed that Seymour was the choice of the majority of white voters, Grant's victory margin being provided by newly enfranchised blacks.

Seymour was born in Pompey Hill, Onondaga County, New York. He began his political career as a secretary to the governor of New York, 1833-39. He was a member of the state assembly in 1842, 1844, and 1845, and was assembly speaker in 1845. He was twice New York's governor, 1853-55 and 1863-65. During his second term, he helped end the New York City draft riots of 1863. In the 1870's he was active in the reform faction of the New York Democratic party.

Sforza, the ruling family of Milan, 1450-1535. The Sforzas were cunning politicians and able administrators. During their rule, Milan prospered. Two members of the family were especially notable:

Francesco (I) Sforza (1401-1466) was a prominent mercenary soldier. He married the daughter of the duke of Milan and became duke in 1450.

Ludovico (or Lodovico) Sforza (1451-1508), son of Francesco, was one of the wealthiest and most powerful figures of his time. He was duke of Milan from 1481 to 1499, when he was deposed by Louis XII of France. Ludovico is especially remembered as a patron of Leonardo da Vinci.

Sgraffito. See POTTERY AND PORCELAIN, subtitle *History:* United States.

Shabuoth, shä-voo′ŏth; shȧ-voo′ŏs, a Jewish religious holiday; other spellings are Shavuoth, Shabuot, Shebuoth, and Shavuot. The name is derived from the Hebrew for "weeks." The festival comes on the sixth day of Sivan (in May or June), upon the completion of seven weeks after the second day of Passover. Shabuoth celebrates both the giving of the Ten Commandments to Moses on Mount Sinai and the first fruits of the harvest. It is also called the Feast of Weeks, Pentecost (for the 50th day after the beginning of Passover), Festival of the First Fruits, and Season of the Giving of Our Torah. Shabuoth is observed for two days by Orthodox and Conservative Jews, one by Reform.

Shackleton, Sir **Ernest Henry** (1874-1922), a British Antarctic explorer. During 1907-09, he led an expedition attempting to reach the South Pole. Bad weather and lack of food forced his party to turn back. They had come, however, within 97 miles (156 km) of the pole—the farthest point south reached to that time. He was knighted upon his return to Great Britain.

Shackleton's next expedition, begun in 1914, was intended to be a transantarctic crossing, but before reaching the continent his ship, the *Endurance*, became trapped and was crushed by pack ice. The expedition made a perilous 200-mile (320-km) trip by sledge and boat to the South Shetland Islands. From there Shackleton and five crew members in small boats went 800 miles (1,300 km) by sea to South Georgia Island to send help to the rest of his party. He died while on his fourth Antarctic expedition.

Shackleton was born in Kilkee, Ireland. His first Antarctic exploration was with the Robert Scott expedition of 1901-04.

Shad, the name applied to several species of fish of the herring family. Shad are bony fish with deeply forked tails. They spend most of their lives in the ocean and feed mostly on plankton. In spring or early summer, shad leave the ocean and enter freshwater coastal rivers to spawn. The female sheds an average of about 30,000 pale pink or amber eggs. The eggs hatch in about 6 to 10 days. After spawning, the parent shad leave the river and go back to the ocean; the young stay until autumn, then migrate out to the ocean. Only mature shad that are four years of age or over are able to spawn.

Some shad are important food fish in North America and Europe. They are caught in nets as they enter coastal rivers to spawn. Most of the catch is sold fresh. The eggs of the shad, called *roe,* are considered a delicacy in North America.

The *American shad* is the largest and best-known shad of North America. It is native to the Atlantic coast from the Gulf of St. Lawrence to the St. Johns River in Florida. In 1871, it was introduced to the Pacific coast and is now found there from southern California to Alaska. The American shad is deep blue to blue-green on its back with silver sides. Behind the gills are a large dark spot and several smaller and lighter spots. The average American shad is about 24 inches (60 cm) long and weighs about 4 pounds (1.8 kg). (For record catch, see FISHING, table *Freshwater Fishing Records.*)

The American shad is *Alosa sapidissima.* Shad are of the herring family, Clupeidae.

See also FISHING, color page titled *North American Game Fishes.*

Shadow, a dark area within or next to an illuminated one. Shadows are caused by the blocking of light by an object. Large areas of shadow, as from trees, buildings, and other large bodies, are usually called *shade.* Because the heat-producing infrared rays from the sun are blocked as well as the visible light, it is usually cooler in the shade than in areas where the rays of the sun are not blocked. A full moon is bright enough to produce noticeable shadows, as are most types of illumination.

Most shadows consist of two parts, the *umbra* and the *penumbra.* In the umbra, all light from the source is blocked and an area of maximum darkness for the prevailing conditions results. In the penumbra, the opaque body blocks part of the light from the source, but not all of it. The penumbra,

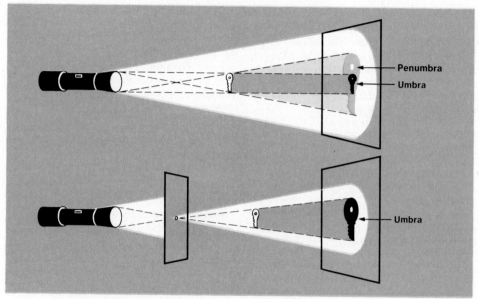

Shadows. Light from a wide source (top) produces two shadows—the penumbra and the umbra. Light from a point source (bottom) produces a single dark shadow—the umbra.

then, is an area of medium darkness. If the light comes from a point source, such as by shining a light through a pinhole in a piece of paper, the entire shadow is umbra; there is no penumbra.

Shadows play an important role in photography and art, where they may set a mood or strengthen a composition. By using trigonometry, it is possible to determine the height of the objects that cast shadows, a technique used to measure the heights of mountains on the moon. Shadows in aerial photographs help to bring out the three-dimensional character of the terrain. During a solar eclipse, the shadow of the moon falls on the earth. Special studies of the sun are possible during such eclipses.

See also ECLIPSE.

Shaduf, or **Shadoof.** See IRRIGATION, subtitle *History*.

Shaftesbury, shăfts′bẽr-i, **Earl of,** a title held by various members of the Cooper family of England. Among the prominent were the following:

Anthony Ashley Cooper (1621-1683), the First Earl of Shaftesbury, was a statesman important in the Commonwealth and Restoration periods. He entered the House of Commons in 1640. At first he supported Charles I, but later he joined Oliver Cromwell and the Puritans in the Civil War. After Cromwell's death, he helped Charles II restore the monarchy and was rewarded by being made Baron Ashley in 1661 and Earl of Shaftesbury in 1672. He served as chancellor of the Exchequer, 1661-72, and lord chancellor, 1672-73, being a part of the so-called Cabal ministry, 1667-73. (See CABAL.)

Dismissed as chancellor in a dispute with Charles II, Shaftesbury became a leader of the opposition in Parliament. He was mainly responsible for securing passage of the Habeas Corpus Act (1679) to reduce instances of unjust imprisonment. Shaftesbury became involved in the conspiracy to replace James, Duke of York (later James II), a Roman Catholic, with the Protestant Duke of Monmouth as heir to Charles II, and was arrested for treason in 1681. He was released, but the insecurity of his position led him to flee to Holland, where he died.

Anthony Ashley Cooper (1671-1713), the Third Earl of Shaftesbury, was an author and moralist, sometimes called "Lord Ashley." He was the grandson of the first earl. Shaftesbury was the proponent of an optimistic philosophy that held that humans have an innate moral sense and that all in nature is in harmony. His writings were collected in *Characteristics of Men, Manners, Opinions, Times* (1711).

Anthony Ashley Cooper (1801-1885), the Seventh Earl of Shaftesbury, was a philanthropist and statesman. He served in the House of Commons for 25 years, 1826-51, where he sponsored bills to help the working classes, the poor, and the insane. After succeeding to the earldom in 1851, he continued his philanthropic activities.

Shagbark. See HICKORY.

Shaggymane. See MUSHROOM, subtitle *Nonpoisonous Mushrooms* (and color page).

Shah Jahan or **Jehan,** shä jȧ-hän′ (1592-1666), an Indian emperor of the Mogul dynasty, reigned 1628-58. Considered one of the great Mogul emperors, he was most noted for the construction of many magnificent buildings, including the Taj Mahal. During his 30-year reign, Shah Jahan extended Mogul rule southward into the Deccan. He was overthrown by his son Aurangzeb in 1658 and spent his remaining years in prison.

See also TAJ MAHAL.

Shah Namah, shâh nâ-mȧ′, the Persian national epic, by Abul Kasim Mansur (who died about 1020). *Shah Namah* means Book of Kings. The poet was called Firdausi ("Heavenly") because of the beauty of his verse. The *Shah Namah* is based on earlier prose chronicles. It tells the legends and history of Persian kings and heroes from the earliest Persian dynasty to the beginning of the Turkish dynasties in Persia in the middle of the seventh century. The epic is the longest (60,000 couplets), most popular, and best of Persian literary works.

One of the stories told in the *Shah Namah* concerns the legendary hero Rustum and his son Sohrab. It is the basis of the poem *Sohrab and Rustum* by the English poet Matthew Arnold.

See also RUSTUM.

Shahn, Ben (1898-1969), a United States painter and graphic artist. He was known for his paintings and posters dealing with social and political themes. His concern with social issues can also be seen in the thousands of photographs he took for the Farm Security Administration. Many of his paintings, such as *The Red Stairway* and *Handball*—with their sharp lines, flat colors, and broad patterns—combine elements of realism, abstraction, and expressionism. Shahn believed that commercial art could be as beautiful as fine art and was one of the few artists to be successful in both fields.

Shahn was born in Lithuania, then part of czarist Russia. His family settled in Brooklyn in 1906, and he became an American citizen in 1918. Shahn was at first a

The Red Stairway, by Ben Shahn in 1944; tempera on hardboard, 16 × 23 5/16 inches (40.6 × 59.2 cm)

City Art Museum of St. Louis

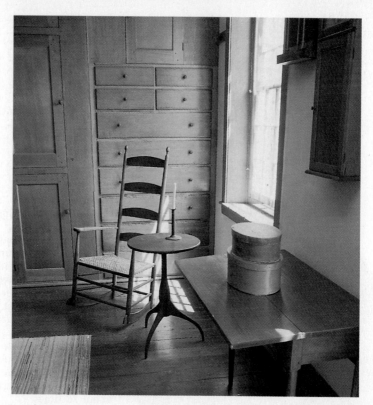

Shaker Furnishings. The elegant simplicity of the rocking chair, tables, and hat boxes are typical of Shaker designs. Also typical are the built-in drawers and cupboards.
Photo taken at Hancock Shaker Village. © Mark E. Gibson.

commercial lithographer. The series of paintings on the controversial Sacco-Vanzetti trial brought him fame. (For picture, see SACCO-VANZETTI CASE.)

Shaka, a 19th-century African chieftain. See ZULUS.

Shaker Heights, Ohio, a city in Cuyahoga County, adjoining Cleveland on the east. It is a fashionable residential community and has virtually no industry. Shaker Heights was laid out in 1905 as a residential suburb and took its name from a Shaker community located here early in the 19th century.

Population: 30,831.

Shakers, the common name for members of the United Society of Believers in Christ's Second Appearing. The Shakers were the most successful and longest-lasting communistic religious group in the United States. They believed in pacifism, celibacy, equality of the sexes, communal ownership of goods, and separation from the rest of the world. They considered work a form of prayer and stressed efficiency and excellence in achievement. The Shakers invented the flat broom and probably the clothespin, circular saw, and metal pen point. Shaker herbs and packaged seeds had wide sales. Their furniture and other handicrafts are highly prized by antique collectors. Also popular are Shaker reproductions.

The Shakers, known first as Shaking Quakers, originated in England in the mid-1700's as an offshoot of the Society of Friends. Their name resulted from their trembling and jerking (later modified to dancing and marching) during worship. Ann Lee, a convert, became recognized by them as the second incarnation of Christ and as the leader of the movement. "Mother" Ann arrived in New York with a few followers in 1774. They established themselves first near Albany, but later made their headquarters at New Lebanon. Many converts were made and several other villages were founded.

The Shakers lived in "families" of up to 100 persons. At the height of the movement, in the mid-1800's, there were 18 Shaker communities with a membership of about 6,000. By the 1990's only a handful of believers remained, at the last active Shaker community—Sabbathday Lake in Maine.

Three restored Shaker villages—Hancock (Massachusetts), Shakertown at Pleasant Hill (Kentucky), and Canterbury (New Hampshire)—are open to the public.

See also ANTIQUE, picture titled *Antique Furniture;* KENTUCKY, section "Interesting Places"; LEE, ANN.

Shakespeare

He was not of an age, but for all time!

Shakespeare, shāk'spēr, **William** (1564-1616), an English poet and playwright. He has long been recognized as the world's finest dramatist and a poet of high rank, and most modern critics consider him the world's greatest literary figure. His plays have been translated into all major languages and numerous minor ones; performed repeatedly in almost every country; and in Europe and America staged oftener than those of any other playwright. His plays have been made into motion picture, radio, and television productions and have formed the basis for operas and musicals. *Hamlet* and *Romeo and Juliet* have each been filmed about 25 times.

More has been written about Shakespeare than about any other author. The thousands of essays and books about him and his works include biographies; critical appraisals; Shakespeare encyclopedias; psychological and philosophical interpretations; and bibliographies. Poems in his praise—and some in his disparagement—have been written by leading poets of his own and later generations. Plays and stories have been based on his life and works. Several libraries have extensive collections of writings by and about Shakespeare, including copies of early editions of Shakespeare's plays. The largest such collections are in the British Library in London and the Folger Shakespeare Library in Washington, D.C.

Shakespeare's works have inspired more music than have those of any other author. Among musical scores for operas based on his plays are those of Rossini, Berlioz, Verdi, and Gounod. Composers of incidental music for his plays or of music for ballets based on his plays include Purcell, Mendelssohn, Liszt, Brahms, Tchaikovsky, Debussy, Humperdinck, Sibelius, Prokofieff, and Walton.

Shakespeare's Genius

Shakespeare shared the cultural advantages and limitations of the society in which he lived. During his lifetime the Renaissance in England was manifested by a period of literary excellence. Shakespeare's contemporaries included such brilliant men of letters as Edmund Spenser, John Donne, Christopher Marlowe, Ben Johnson, Sir Philip Sidney, and Sir Francis Bacon. But as a literary genius Shakespeare surpassed all of them.

While Shakespeare was still a young man England's supremacy on the seas was assured by the defeat of the Spanish war fleet, the "invincible Armada." England's great age of exploration and colonialism began, and the nation became a leading commercial power. There was also a flowering of intellectual interests, especially in the field of science. Along with this interest in science, however, went increased interest in astrology, alchemy, and other occult subjects; and the demonology of the Middle Ages was still an acceptable subject of investigation.

The people for whom Shakespeare wrote his plays—and he himself—were thus still bound to the superstitious past in some ways, while at the same time they were eager for new learning. He wrote of kings and heroes, peasants and artisans, witches and ghosts. It is understandable that his plays, dealing with matters familiar to his audiences, would have been popular in his times.

Shakespeare's reputation as a literary figure has increased since his death, time adding perspective to the value of his work. Once known merely as a popular playwright, Shakespeare is now recognized as one of the greatest writers of all time. His genius is evidenced in the appeal and meaning his dramas continue to have for contemporary audiences. He saw through outward differences to the inner nature and problems common to all mankind and expressed what he saw with power and clarity. The words of Ben Jonson have proved to be prophetic:

"He was not of an age, but for all time!"

Characterization. Among the qualities for which Shakespeare is valued are his understanding of human nature and his expression of it in characterizations so real they seem to take on a life of their own. Shakespeare's Richard III, physically deformed and the murderer of his two young nephews, overshadows the historical Richard, who was not deformed and probably did not kill the little princes. Shakespeare's genius, however, keeps Richard from being a melodramat-

ic villain; his speeches sparkle with satiric wit and his actions, although evil, are logical outgrowths of the character Shakespeare has created.

Shylock, in *The Merchant of Venice*, is almost monstrous in his greed and vindictiveness, but suggests a believably human basis for his cruelty when he accuses his Christian enemies of having taught him villainy and later asks: "Hath not a Jew hands, organs, dimensions, senses, affections, passions?" Whether predominantly good or evil, most of Shakespeare's characters are realistically complex. The personality of Hamlet, for example, continues to be argued about by actors, directors, critics, philosophers, and psychologists.

Language. Critics generally agree that Shakespeare's use of the English language is incomparable, and that he has had more influence upon the language than has any other writer. Shakespeare uses words poetically—with precision of meaning and freshness of imagery—but also makes them serve his dramatic purpose by fitting them to characterization and action.

That Shakespeare's use of English sometimes differs from correct modern usage does not show lack of knowledge on his part. In his day strict rules for English grammar and spelling had not been established. Even personal names were given various spellings. Shakespeare spelled his own name several ways, including "Shaksper," "Shakspere," and "Shakspeare." He was not breaking grammatical rules when he wrote, in *Julius Caesar,* "the most unkindest cut of all," and, in *Antony and Cleopatra,* "Is she as tall as me?"

The English vocabulary expanded rapidly during the Elizabethan period. Shakespeare exceeded all others before and since his time in adding new words and phrases to the language. Among the many words he is believed to have coined are *countless, dwindle, eventful, fitful, fretful, heartsick, hotblooded, lackluster, laughable, monumental* and *multitudinous*. Well-known phrases that Shakespeare was either the first to use or the first to write down include "heart of gold," "elbow room," "flaming youth," "beaten black and blue," "to be, or not to be," and "it's Greek to me."

Who Wrote Shakespeare's Plays?

In the late 18th century, when little was known of Shakespeare's life and times, a

Stratford-upon-Avon. The spire of Holy Trinity Church, where Shakespeare and his wife are buried, is seen in the background.

theory was advanced that Francis Bacon wrote the plays attributed to Shakespeare. The theory was based in part on the supposition that such great works could not have been written by a man from a small village, who was not a nobleman and who had not attended a university.

Doubt of Shakespeare's authorship was furthered and expanded in the 19th century. Claims were made for more than 50 individuals, including the most prominent Elizabethan writers and noblemen as well as Queen Elizabeth herself. Even in the 20th century, with Shakespeare's authorship established by sound scholarship, there are still some adherents to the "anti-Stratfordian theory." No prominent scholar has ever taken that theory seriously.

Shakespeare's Life

Early Years at Stratford

Birth and Parentage. William Shakespeare was born at Stratford-upon-Avon, Warwickshire, in 1564. He was baptized there in Holy Trinity Church on April 26. His birth date is not known, but is traditionally celebrated on April 23 because children were usually baptized a few days after their birth.

William's father, John Shakespeare, dressed leather and made and sold such leather goods as gloves and purses. He also dealt in grain and other agricultural products, owned several buildings in Stratford, and held some of the town's most important offices. His wife, Mary, was of the Arden family, prosperous farmers and landowners in the vicinity.

Schooling. Stratford was not a large town, but it was a thriving market place about 85

miles (137 km) from London. Its school, the Stratford Grammar School, had an excellent reputation, and education was provided free for boys between the ages of 6 and 16. As in other English schools of the time, Latin grammar and Latin literature were emphasized, with Greek sometimes taught in the upper forms (grades). There was instruction in logic, rhetoric, elocution, and history, but little or none in the sciences.

One of the many erroneous ideas about Shakespeare that developed in the 18th century was that he was almost totally lacking in formal education. It is true that there is no record of his attending grammar school. Leading researchers agree, however, that William, as the son of a citizen of Stratford, was entitled to go to the Stratford Grammar School and—considering his father's position in the community—undoubtedly did.

This assumption is strongly supported by evidence found in Shakespeare's writings. Various passages show his acquaintance with grammar school subjects as they were then taught, and his plays, especially the earliest, reflect a strong foundation in rhetoric. There is a story that he quit school at about the age of 13 to help his father support the family, but it cannot be proven. John Shakespeare had some financial difficulties at that time, but there is no indication that the family became poor.

Early Married Life. In November, 1582, William married Anne Hathaway, the daughter of a farmer near Stratford. A daughter, Susanna, was born to the couple in 1583. Hamnet and Judith, twins, were born two years later. Little else is known of Shakespeare's early married life.

The story told by John Aubrey, a 17th-century biographer of Shakespeare, that William taught school in the country is based on hearsay. It is given credence by certain passages in his plays that show familiarity with school teaching and include humorous comments on the profession that might be made by someone who had been a teacher.

Sometime in the late 1580's, Shakespeare went to London. According to one well-known story, he left Stratford to escape punishment for poaching (stealing live game) in the deer park at Charlecote, the estate of Sir Thomas Lucy. There was no deer park at Charlecote until 1618, and although Sir Thomas could have prosecuted Shakespeare for poaching in the forest near the estate, the legend was not recorded until nearly a century after his death and few scholars take it seriously. Modern researchers believe it more probable that Shakespeare simply left Stratford to seek his fortune. He did not break ties with his home town, and there is no indication that he lost contact with his family.

It is also probable that he left Stratford with the intention of seeking a theatrical career. He had had many opportunities to see plays staged by touring companies in Stratford and nearby towns.

Life in London

A Youthful Success. There is little direct knowledge of Shakespeare's life in London before 1594. However, reasonable assump-

tions have been made from records of later events. For example, researchers agree that Shakespeare is undoubtedly the unnamed actor and playwright satirized in a pamphlet, *A Groatsworth of Wit* (1592), by the playwright and novelist Robert Greene. The satirical passage includes the term "Shake-scene" in referring to the anonymous actor-dramatist and a parody of a line from Shakespeare's *Henry VI, Part 3*. Greene's bitterness reflects envy of someone more successful than himself.

In or shortly before 1594 Shakespeare joined a newly formed acting company, the Chamberlain's Men, composed partly of former members of another company, Strange's Men. The fact that Shakespeare joined the company as a part owner, dramatist, and one of three leading actors shows that he had already acquired experience and a professional reputation of some importance.

The theaters in London were closed most of the time from 1592 to 1594 because of outbreaks of the bubonic plague, and the acting companies toured the country during this period. It is believed that Shakespeare spent the time writing his two long narrative poems, *Venus and Adonis* (1593) and *The Rape of Lucrece* (1594).

As an actor Shakespeare was not as popular as the other leading actors in his company, Richard Burbage and William Kempe, and did not win critical acclaim equal to theirs. However, he was apparently competent and continued to act in his own and other dramatists' works until late in his career.

Most Productive Years. During the first 15 years after he joined the Chamberlain's Men Shakespeare wrote more than 20 plays,

The Droeshout Engraving of Shakespeare appears on the title page of the First Folio, 1623. It is one of only two likenesses of the poet considered authentic by historians. The other is the memorial bust in Holy Trinity Church. For a detail of the bust, see the opening page of this article.
The Folger Shakespeare Library

The Folger Shakespeare Library

The Globe Theatre, where most of Shakespeare's later plays were first staged. Shakespeare was a part owner of the Globe, which was built in 1599. This picture is a detail from Visscher's *View of London,* an early-17th-century engraving.

including his greatest tragedies and most of his comedies. His standing is indicated by the fact that after 1597, publishers put his name on nearly all editions of his plays, and even on plays he had not written.

In *Palladis Tamia: Wit's Treasury* (1598), the critic Francis Meres calls the poet "honey-tongued" and places him first among the English dramatists and lyric poets. In this book Meres mentions 12 of Shakespeare's plays, his two long poems, and his sonnets.

Shakespeare became prosperous during these years. In 1597 he bought New Place, the second largest house in Stratford, and moved his wife and daughters into it. His only son, Hamnet, had died the year before. Shakespeare himself continued to live in London.

Among Shakespeare's friends were England's theatrical and literary leaders, including the playwrights Ben Jonson, Francis Beaumont, and John Fletcher.

In 1599 a new theater, the Globe, was built in Southwark, at that time a suburb of London. Shakespeare became a part owner

of the theater, and some of his greatest plays were first performed on its stage. By the time of Queen Elizabeth's death in 1603 the Chamberlain's Men was known as the best of the acting companies. James I took the company—thereafter called the King's Men—under his patronage. In 1608 the company leased the Blackfriars Theatre for winter performances; this theater was one of the first in the vicinity of London to be entirely roofed over.

Last Years

Shakespeare no longer kept London lodgings after 1611, and spent most of his time in Stratford. Through the years he had made a number of investments in and near his hometown and now owned—in addition to New Place—a cottage, extensive farmland, and the right to rentals from other properties. He probably visited London in connection with theatrical business and other matters. In 1613 he bought a house near the Blackfriars Theatre, but there is no record of his living there.

He continued to write plays, but at a slower pace. His last play, written in collaboration with John Fletcher, was *Henry VIII*, which opened at the Globe Theatre on June 29, 1613. During the first performance the theater caught fire and burned to the ground. The Globe was rebuilt the following year, but it is likely that Shakespeare's active connection with the King's Men ended with the fire.

Shakespeare died on April 23, 1616, at the age of 52. There is no record of the cause of his death. He was buried near the altar in Holy Trinity Church, Stratford. His gravestone in the church floor is inscribed with four lines of doggerel verse, a warning intended to prevent violation of the grave to make room for new burials. It was once thought that Shakespeare wrote it himself or chose it to be put on his gravestone, but modern scholars believe the poet had nothing to do with it. His real epitaph, in Latin and English, is inscribed on the memorial bust of Shakespeare, which was erected in the church a few years after his death.

Shakespeare's granddaughter, Elizabeth, who died in 1670, was the last of his descendants.

Shakespeare's Works

Shakespeare's Plays

Shakespeare fitted style and language to his dramatic needs. He wrote mainly in *blank verse* (unrhymed iambic pentameter), but also used rhymed couplets and quatrains, and introduced short songs in various meters into his plays. Some of the speeches in his plays are in prose. The colloquial, often coarse, language of the common people contrasts with the stately speeches of kings and noblemen. Young lovers' speeches vary from simple and natural expressions to passages filled with rich and fanciful imagery.

The themes used by Shakespeare are also

Contemporary engraving of Elizabethan stage

Shakespeare's Plays with Probable Date of Writing
(according to the Shakespearean scholar Alfred Harbage)

Comedies
The Comedy of Errors (1587-92)
Love's Labour's Lost (1588-94)
The Taming of the Shrew (1590-94)
The Two Gentlemen of Verona (1590-94)
A Midsummer Night's Dream (1595)
The Merchant of Venice (1594-97)
The Merry Wives of Windsor (1597-1602)
Much Ado About Nothing (1598-99)
As You Like It (1598-1600)
Twelfth Night (1600-02)
All's Well That Ends Well (1602-04)
Measure for Measure (1604)
Pericles (1606-08)*
Cymbeline (1609-11)
The Winter's Tale (1610-11)
The Tempest (1610-11)
The Two Noble Kinsmen (1613)*
Tragedies
Titus Andronicus (1589-94)
Romeo and Juliet (1595)
Julius Caesar (1599)
Hamlet (1600-01)
Troilus and Cressida (1601-02)
Othello (1604)
King Lear (1605-06)
Timon of Athens (1605-08)
Macbeth (1606)
Antony and Cleopatra (1606-07)
Coriolanus (1608)
History Plays
Henry VI, Parts 1, 2, and 3 (1589-92)
Richard III (1593)
King John (1590-95)
Richard II (1595-96)
Henry IV, Parts 1 (1597) and 2 (1598)
Henry V (1599)
Henry VIII (1613)*
*Written in collaboration with others.

varied. There are, however, two general themes that recur in nearly all his plays. One is the necessity for human beings to recognize and accept a divine order in all things—religion, politics, social castes, and personal human relations. It is thought that Shakespeare derived many of his ideas about order from sermons called *homilies,* official texts for pastors, that were published from the mid-16th to the 17th century.

The second general theme of Shakespeare's plays is the difference, and sometimes the confusion, between pretense and truth, appearance and reality. Shakespeare not only creates a number of villains who are hypocrites—such as Richard III, Iago, and Edmund—but characters, such as Valentine in *The Two Gentlemen of Verona,* who deceive themselves. Valentine speaks scornfully of romantic love but falls victim to it.

In other ways the confusion between appearance and reality is portrayed. The lovers in *A Midsummer Night's Dream* are not sure whether they have dreamed their experiences or not. Throughout his plays, Shakespeare's characters repeat in various ways the idea that the world is a stage or that life is a dream. Hamlet says to his mother: "Seems, Madame? Nay, it is. I know not 'seems'," but later to Rosencrantz and Guildenstern: "there is nothing either good or bad but thinking makes it so."

Rich and varied characterizations helped make Shakespeare's works immortal.
Top, the tragic figure of King Lear as portrayed by
John Gielgud; *bottom right,* Richard III, presented as
treacherous but courageous; *bottom left,* the comic but pathetic Falstaff.
Photo: Angus McBeam; paintings: The Folger Shakespeare Library

History Plays. *History,* or *chronicle, plays* became popular in England in the 16th century when the people were filled with national pride. These plays were concerned only with English history from the Middle Ages onward, not with ancient times or with legends. Unlike tragedies based on history, the history plays stressed events rather than plots and characterizations. Some scholars believe that Shakespeare's *Henry VI* was the first history play.

Shakespeare's main sources for his history plays were Edward Halle's *The Union of the Two Noble and Illustrious Families of Lancaster and York* (1548) and the second edition (1587) of Rafael Holinshed's *Chronicles of England, Scotland, and Ireland.* For dramatic effect Shakespeare often simplified the events recounted in his sources and rearranged their sequence. He accepted the pro-Lancaster, pro-Tudor prejudices of his sources, but tempered them with his own ironic wit and deep understanding of human nature.

The dominant theme of Shakespeare's history plays is the evil that results from rebellion. Shakespeare modified the political lessons taught by the homilies, however. He never places his rulers above natural law and moral responsibility, but shows that even a rightful king can bring disaster upon his country through weakness or tyranny.

Comedies. Shakespeare's comedies vary greatly in mood and treatment: some are farcical, others are romantic. Still others are so somber that they are called "bitter comedies," or "dark comedies." *Pericles, Cymbeline,* and *The Winter's Tale,* although not "bitter," are sometimes called tragicomedies because of their plot reversal from impending tragedy to happy ending.

Two of the romantic comedies—*As You Like It* and *Twelfth Night*—are considered by critics the best of all Shakespeare's comedies. They are well constructed dramatically, and in language and ideas show a skillful balance between verse and prose, sentiment and wit, fancy and realism. In them are found some of Shakespeare's most human and appealing characters. These plays are grouped with *Much Ado About Nothing* and *A Midsummer Night's Dream* as "joyous comedies" because of their predominantly lighthearted mood.

Shakespeare adapted most of the plots, situations, and characters in his comedies from various sources: classical Greek and Roman and medieval and contemporary European. In the sources the plots are contrived, most of the situations artificial, and the characters stereotyped. Shakespeare, however, was able to overcome most of the weaknesses inherent in these borrowed elements and to give his adaptations freshness and vitality.

Tragedies. Shakespeare's first published play was a tragedy, *Titus Andronicus,* an imitation of the revenge and horror tragedies of the first-century Roman dramatist Seneca. Senecan elements are found in many of his other tragedies but are subordinated to masterful characterization and to ethical and philosophical themes.

Critics designate as the "great tragedies" *Hamlet, Othello, King Lear,* and *Macbeth.* In these dramas are found some of the world's greatest poetry, some of the subtlest yet most powerful characterizations, and some of the most absorbing and best-constructed plots. *Hamlet* is not only the most famous and popular play in the world, but is acclaimed by critics as one of the finest dramas of all time.

Romeo and Juliet has been as popular on the stage as the four great tragedies, and *Antony and Cleopatra* almost as fully admired by modern critics. The late tragedies, *Coriolanus* and *Timon of Athens,* are thought by some critics to be experiments in writing tragic satire rather than tragedy. Both these plays lack the warmth and power of Shakespeare's other tragedies.

The source of the tragedies on Roman themes was an English translation of *Parallel Lives,* biographies of Greek and Roman statesmen, by the first-century Greek biographer Plutarch. Most of the other tragedies derived from Holinshed's *Chronicles* and from continental works of fiction.

In most of his tragedies, as in his other plays, Shakespeare manipulates the sequence of events and selects or rejects details while staying close to his sources' basic plots. In his "great tragedies," however, he radically alters plots, not only for dramatic impact and characterization, but to emphasize his own moral and religious convictions.

For example, in Shakespeare's main source for *Macbeth*—Holinshed's *Chronicles* —Macbeth is the rightful heir to the throne. Partly to save his own life and partly to save the kingdom, he murders the incompetent king, Duncan, in open rebellion with the help of Banquo and others. Macbeth then reigns wisely for ten years before trying to kill Banquo. Shakespeare makes Duncan a just and able ruler and intensifies the horror of Macbeth's crime by making it secret, treacherous, and personal. Macbeth has potential for greatness and goodness but chooses sin; his downfall thus represents the destruction of evil and restores order to the kingdom.

Shakespeare's Poems

Narrative Poems. Shakespeare dedicated *Venus and Adonis* (1593) and *The Rape of Lucrece* (1594) to the Earl of Southampton, whose patronage he sought. Both poems are written in the conventional style of the times, with exaggerated and fanciful figures of speech and long, didactic passages. This style, popular in Elizabethan times, appeals to few modern readers. There are, however, lines of lyric simplicity in the poems, passages of sensuous description, and—especially in *The Rape of Lucrece*—evidence of the

The Rape of Lucrece. This illustration of the tragic poem is from a 17th-century engraving. The inset is a portrait of Shakespeare.
The Folger Shakespeare Library

author's developing dramatic skill. The stories told in the poems are from the Roman poet Ovid (43 B.C.-17 A.D.) and the Roman historian Livy (59 B.C.-17 A.D.).

Sonnets. Shakespeare's sonnets have aroused conjecture and controversy, some of it concerning the dates they were written. Two of them were published in 1599 in a collection of verses by various authors, but the sonnets were not published as a collection in themselves until 1609. There is no way of determining the dates of their composition, but most scholars believe that all but a few of the sonnets were written between 1593 and 1599.

Further discussion concerns the extent to which the sonnets portray events and persons in Shakespeare's life. Of the 154 sonnets, the majority are concerned with an idealized love for a young man; about 25 deal with an unhappy relationship with a mistress "color'd ill." This black-haired, dark-eyed woman is the antithesis of the Elizabethan blond ideal; her elusive love and unknown identity add to her mysteriousness. Scholars commonly refer to her as the "Dark Lady." There are also references in the sonnets to a rival poet.

Hundreds of essays and books have been written in an attempt to prove that one or another historical person was the original of the beloved friend, the unfaithful mistress, or the rival poet. None of the evidence is conclusive, and some of the arguments are extremely farfetched. Most critics agree, however, that the power and sincerity of the sonnets show them to be expressions of emotions actually felt by Shakespeare, whether they are strictly autobiographical or not. The best of them rank among the finest lyric poetry of all times.

Editions of Shakespeare's Plays

None of the original manuscripts of Shakespeare's plays has been discovered. In order to find out as nearly as possible what he wrote, scholars study the early editions of the plays. New editions are then published in the hope of correcting mistakes.

The task of reconstructing the exact texts of Shakespeare's plays is difficult. The plays were owned by the acting company, and Shakespeare himself was not concerned with their publication. Type was set by hand, letter by letter, making it difficult for the typesetter to follow the sense of what he was setting and thus catch and correct his own errors. Also, spelling and rules of grammar were not uniform. When errors were discovered during the printing process, corrections were made but the previously printed pages were not discarded.

Shakespeare himself apparently made numerous errors, perhaps through haste and failure to revise. Scholars find him guilty of frequent discrepancies in regard to places, dates, and the names and physical descriptions of characters. In some plays he introduces characters and then "forgets" them. For example, early texts of *Much Ado About Nothing* introduce the heroine's mother, Innogen, in the first scene. She is given no lines or action and does not appear again. Such obvious errors as these are corrected when possible in carefully edited texts of the plays.

Quartos. About half of Shakespeare's plays were published during his lifetime. They were printed separately in pamphlets called *quartos*. Some quartos were based on the author's original manuscripts or on promptbooks, corrected copies of the manuscripts with stage directions added. Scholars call these editions "good quartos." Some quartos were published without permission of the acting company and were probably reconstructed from the memory of actors or from notes taken by other persons. These "bad quartos" are marred by garbled passages, omissions, and the addition of spurious material.

Folios. The 17th-century editions of Shakespeare's collected plays were printed in books called *folios*. The *First Folio* was published in 1623 under the editorship of John Heming and Henry Condell, members of the King's Men. The 36 plays in the *First Folio* include those first printed in quartos. Copy used included good quartos as well as original manuscripts and promptbooks. About 1,000 copies of the *First Folio* were printed; more than 200 still exist.

The *Second Folio* was published in 1632 with more than 1,500 changes in the text. The *Third Folio*, published in 1663, was reprinted in 1664 with seven additional plays, of which only one—*Pericles*—is accepted as Shakespeare's by modern scholars. The *Fourth Folio* (1685) was based on the reprint of the *Third,* but contained 750 changes.

18th-century Editions. In 1709, Nicholas Rowe, an English dramatist, published Shakespeare's plays together with the first biography of Shakespeare. Rowe's edition was based on the *Fourth Folio,* but he made several valuable corrections, divided the plays into acts and scenes, and added stage directions. A second edition by Rowe (1714) included the narrative poems. Several other editions, including those of the poet Alexander Pope and the critic Samuel Johnson, were based on Rowe's text.

A more scholarly approach was made by editors who based their editions on a comparison of quartos and the *First Folio*. Among such editions are those of Lewis Theobald (1733), Edward Capell (1768), George Steevens (1773, 1778, 1785, 1793), and Edmund Malone (1790). Malone continued to collect material for a revision, but died before finishing the project.

19th-century Editions. Among outstanding Shakespeare publications are the *variorum editions,* which contain the text with the variations found in preceding editions and the comment of earlier editors. The *First* and *Second Variorums* (1803, 1813), edited by Isaac Reed, were based on Steevens' editions. The *Third Variorum* (1821), edited by James Boswell the younger, was based on Malone's edition and his collected material.

The first volume (*Romeo and Juliet*) of the *New Variorum* was published in 1871. It was edited by an American scholar, H. H. Furness, who published 18 volumes. After his death, his son carried on his work. In 1936 the Modern Language Association of America assumed sponsorship of the *New Variorum,* and has published several additional volumes.

Perhaps the most important critical edition of Shakespeare in the 19th century was *The Cambridge Shakespeare* (9 volumes, 1863-66), edited by British scholars W. G. Clark, John Glover, and W. A. Wright. It was based on Capell's large collection of quartos and became the standard text of Shakespeare. The text was reprinted in one volume as *The Globe Shakespeare* (1864).

Facsimiles (exact reproductions) of the quartos and folios were made possible in the 19th century by developments in photoengraving. The most important 19th-century facsimiles are those of the *First Folio* by Howard Staunton (1866) and J. O. Halliwell-Phillipps (1876), and of the quartos by Halliwell-Phillipps (1862-76) and F. J. Furnivall (1880-89).

A popular but unscholarly book was *The Family Shakespeare* (1807, 1818), edited by Thomas Bowdler, an English physician. Bowdler omitted words that he thought were not proper for all members of a family to read. "Bowdlerize," meaning to expurgate a literary work according to the editor's idea of propriety, was derived from his name.

20th-century Editions. A large number of critical editions of Shakespeare have appeared in the 20th century. Outstanding are the continuing *New Variorum* volumes; *The New Cambridge Shakespeare* (1921-66); *The Arden Shakespeare* (1951-82, revised from a series begun in 1899); *The Yale Shakespeare* (1959); *The Pelican Shakespeare* (1956-67, revised in one volume 1969); and *The Oxford Shakespeare* (1984).

Among notable facsimile editions is *The Norton Facsimile of the First Folio* (1968), edited by Charlton K. Hinman, an American scholar. It is based on 30 of the surviving *First Folio* copies. By analyzing different type-fonts, spelling preferences, and printing-house procedures Hinman discerned the work of five typesetters. Using the results of his studies, he determined how and in what order the plays were printed and which copies represented the final, corrected state of the *First Folio*.

Performances of the Plays

As early as the 18th century, Shakespeare's plays were being staged in Germany in translation. By the end of the 19th century they had been translated and acted in all the leading countries of Europe and in Japan and India. By the middle of the 20th century there were few countries in the world in which Shakespearean productions had not been staged in English or in local languages.

The following discussion is limited to English-speaking performances in the British Isles and North America.

In Shakespeare's Day. From what is known of the construction of playhouses in Elizabethan and Jacobean times, and from the texts of the plays themselves, it is conjectured that stage sets were generally simple. There were, however, such stage properties as movable furniture, utensils, weapons, carts, chariots, and even trees. Costumes were colorful, elaborate, and in the current fash-

ion rather than in that of the plays' time of action. Stages projected into the yard or auditorium. The stage had no front curtain or footlights.

It was considered improper for women to act. Women's roles were played by boys; those of old women were sometimes played by mature men.

For a description of Elizabethan theaters, see THEATER, subtitle *History:* Medieval and Renaissance Theater; illustration, *The Globe Theatre.*

Restoration Period and 18th Century. England's theaters were closed from the outbreak of the Great Rebellion in 1642 until the restoration of the monarchy in 1660. For many years after the Restoration, such playwrights as William Davenant, John Dryden, Nahum Tate, and Colley Cibber rewrote and often retitled Shakespeare's plays to suit their own dramatic theories and the taste of the Restoration audiences. Until early in the 19th century, Shakespeare's plays were usually presented in these adapted forms. Cibber's version of *Richard III* continued in popularity into the 20th century.

The efforts of scholars in the early 18th century to recover Shakespeare's original texts influenced some stage presentations, including those at the Covent Garden Theatre in London, where original versions of several of the plays were staged. David Garrick, England's most famous 18th-century actor and producer, and another outstanding actor-producer, John Philip Kemble, rejected many of the standard adaptations for versions closer to Shakespeare's texts, but also presented some of their own adaptations. One of Kemble's important theatrical contributions was his staging of Shakespeare's plays with historically accurate settings and costumes.

The outstanding actor of the Restoration period was Thomas Betterton. His wife, Mary Saunderson, was one of the first English actresses. She was noted for her playing of Lady Macbeth. Sarah Siddons, Kemble's sister, considered the greatest actress of the 18th century, was acclaimed for her Shakespearean roles.

19th Century. Sumptuousness and attempts at extreme realism marked the stag-

Shakespeare's plays may be effectively produced in various ways. *Facing page:* rehearsal of a stage production of *Macbeth* in stylized costumes; *upper left,* a modern-dress staging of *All's Well That Ends Well; lower left,* a battle scene from the motion picture *Henry V; below,* the method of staging at Shakespeare's time at the Globe Theatre with the stage thrust out into the audience.

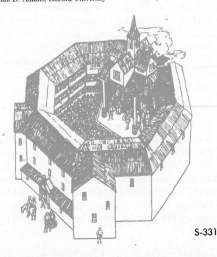

Royal Shakespeare Theatre, Stratford-upon-Avon, is the site of an annual Shakespeare festival. Similar festivals are held in Stratford, Ontario, and Stratford, Connecticut.

ing of Shakespeare's plays in the early part of the 19th century. Among noted actor-producers who presented lavish and spectacular performances were Sir Henry Irving and Sir Herbert Beerbohm Tree. Irving was generally considered the finest Shakespearean actor of his day.

A trend toward simpler staging began about the middle of the 19th century. Leaders in the movement were the actors Samuel Phelps, manager of Sadler's Wells Theatre, and Sir Francis Robert Benson, who was associated with the Shakespeare Memorial Theatre (later called the Royal Shakespeare Theatre). In 1894, William Poel founded the Elizabethan Stage Society for the purpose of staging Shakespeare's plays in the Elizabethan manner.

Among other leading British actors of the 19th century were Edmund Kean and his son Charles; Sir Johnston Forbes-Robertson; Fanny Kemble; and Dame Ellen Terry. Sarah Bernhardt, a French actress, was noted for playing the title role in *Hamlet.* The outstanding American Shakespearean actors of the day were Junius Brutus Booth and his son Edwin, E. H. Sothern, and Julia Marlowe.

20th Century. Modern Shakespearean productions use a variety of theatrical styles; staging and scenery range from the simple and symbolic to the ornate and naturalistic. One innovation that has become popular is to stage the plays in modern dress to add a sense of relevancy. A 1928 New York production of *The Taming of the Shrew* was one of the first of this kind. In 1937 Orson

Welles did a modern-dress version of *Julius Caesar* in which the costumes were Nazi uniforms.

Fresh interpretations of Shakespeare's plays and new emphases in their production have been influenced by modern literary criticism, an evolving understanding of the human psyche, and a global society in which diverse cultures are interconnected. For example, Sir Laurence Olivier, in a 1937 London performance of *Hamlet,* portrayed Hamlet as the victim of a paralyzing neurosis. Other contemporary productions have examined the role of women from a feminist perspective; incorporated flamboyant Kabuki makeup; and added the music of Dixieland bands and electric guitars.

Many of Shakespeare's plays have been made into motion pictures, some more than once. For example, *Hamlet* was filmed in 1948 (with Olivier in the title role) and again in 1990 (with Mel Gibson playing Hamlet). Other plays that have been filmed several times include *Richard III, Henry V, Julius Caesar, Romeo and Juliet, A Midsummer Night's Dream,* and *Othello.* Shakespeare's work has also been adapted for radio and television, making it accessible to a broad audience.

Twentieth-century actors of the English-speaking stage who won acclaim for Shakespearean roles include Walter Hampden, Dame Sybil Thorndike, John Barrymore, Dame Edith Evans, Morris Carnovsky, Dame Judith Anderson, Maurice Evans, Sir Ralph Richardson, Sir Donald Wolfit, Sir John Gielgud, Sir Laurence Olivier, Sir Michael Redgrave, Paul Scofield, Richard Burton, Derek Jacobi, Kenneth Branagh, and James Earl Jones.

The Royal Shakespeare Theatre in Stratford, England, is dedicated to Shakespeare's works and holds annual Shakespeare festivals. Another noted festival is held in Stratford, Ontario, each summer. The New York Shakespeare Festival Public Theater holds annual festivals and workshops in New York City.

For further information, see:

Plays

Articles on all the plays listed in the box *Shakespeare's Plays with Probable Date of Writing* (with the exception of *Pericles* and *Coriolanus*) are found in this encyclopedia.

Famous Shakespearean Players

BARRYMORE (family)	MANSFIELD, RICHARD
BERNHARDT, SARAH	MARLOWE, JULIA
BOOTH (family of actors)	OLIVIER, Sir LAURENCE
BURBAGE, RICHARD	SIDDONS, SARAH
EVANS, MAURICE	SOTHERN, EDWARD HUGH
FORREST, EDWIN	
GARRICK, DAVID	TERRY, Dame ELLEN
GIELGUD, Sir JOHN	TREE, Sir HERBERT BEERBOHM
GUINNESS, Sir ALEC	WELLES, ORSON
IRVING, Sir HENRY	
KEAN, EDMUND	
KEMBLE (family)	

Books about Shakespeare

Boyce, Charles. *Shakespeare A to Z: a Complete Guide to the Poems, the Plays, the Characters, the Life, and More* (Facts on File, 1990).

Burgess, Anthony. *Shakespeare* (Ivan R. Dee, 1994).

DeLoach, Charles, editor. *The Quotable Shakespeare: a Topical Dictionary* (McFarland, 1988).

Epstein, Norrie. *The Friendly Shakespeare: a Thoroughly Painless Guide to the Best of the Bard* (Viking Penguin, 1993).

Harrison, D. C. *Every Man's Shakespeare* (Winston-Derek, 1990).

Kay, Dennis. *William Shakespeare: Life and Times* (Macmillan, 1994).

Levi, Peter. *The Life and Times of William Shakespeare* (Holt, 1995).

McMurtry, Jo. *Understanding Shakespeare's England: a Companion for the American Reader* (Shoe String Press, 1989).

Rowse, A. L. *Shakespeare the Man,* revised edition (St. Martin's Press, 1989).

Van Doren, Mark. *Shakespeare* (1939; Greenwood reprint, 1982).

For Younger Readers

Lamb, Charles and Mary. *Tales from Shakespeare* (Folger Books, 1979).

McCaughrean, Geraldine, editor. *Stories from Shakespeare* (Simon & Schuster, 1995).

Perrone, Vito. *William Shakespeare* (Chelsea House, 1995).

Miscellaneous

BLACKFRIARS THEATRE	HOLINSHED, R.
BOWDLER, THOMAS	OBERON
FALSTAFF, Sir JOHN	PLUTARCH
FOLGER SHAKESPEARE LIBRARY	STRATFORD-UPON-AVON
GLOBE THEATRE	THEOBALD, LEWIS

Shaking Palsy. See PARKINSON'S DISEASE.

Shale, the most common type of sedimentary rock. Geologists estimate that between 70 and 83 per cent of the earth's sedimentary rock is shale. Shale is made up of particles too small to be seen individually. It tends to split into thin layers parallel or almost parallel to the plane in which the particles were deposited. Although most shale is gray or black, shale of other colors, such as red or yellow, is also found.

Shale is composed primarily of clay minerals and quartz. Various other minerals, such as carbonates and feldspars, as well as organic materials, may also be present. *Ferruginous shales* contain iron oxides. *Calcareous shales* contain calcite. Shale is formed from waterborne deposits of silt and mud that are compacted into rock by the pressure of overlying layers of sediments. Many shales contain abundant fossils. When shale is subjected to sufficient heat and pressure, it becomes slate. (See SLATE.)

Shale is used primarily as a source of clay minerals such as kaolin. *Oil shale* contains hydrocarbons that can be distilled to form substitutes for petroleum. (See OIL SHALE.)

Shallot, a perennial herbaceous plant native to western Asia. In the United States, the shallot is grown mainly in southern Louisiana. This plant has slender, green, tubular leaves and an underground bulb made up of separable, oblong sections called cloves. The cloves are used for flavoring in cooking and in pickling. The shallot is closely related to the onion but is milder in taste.

The shallot is *Allium ascalonicum* of the lily family, Liliaceae.

Shalom Aleichem. See ALEICHEM, SHALOM.

Shaman, shä'măn, a part-time religious leader considered to be a medium for spirits. The shaman's usual function is to cure illness. Shamanism is best known as a religious practice of peoples of the Arctic region, especially in Siberia, but it is also practiced by Africans and American Indians. "Medicine men" is commonly used to refer to the Siberian and American Indian shamans, even though among the American Indians women may also become shamans.

Shamans call upon spirits to enter their bodies or send them supernatural power, and then fall into trances, presumably possessed by spirits. Most use hypnotic singing and drum beating to help induce their trances and achieve possession, but some, especially among American Indian tribes, take hallucinogens to induce trances. Shamans believe that when they are possessed, they can exercise mastery over the spirits and thus achieve power to cure illness and bring bad or good luck.

Shamans conduct rites whenever their help is requested, usually for one person or a small group. Shamans generally receive no training; they usually achieve the status of shaman after experiencing a dream or trance that, they believe, gives them the required special ability.

Shamrock, a popular name for several clover plants having leaves divided into three small leaflets. The shamrock is a national emblem of Ireland, worn especially on St. Patrick's Day. According to legend, Saint Patrick used the three-sectioned leaf to illustrate the doctrine of the Trinity.

The suckling clover (*Trifolium dubium*) is widely regarded as the "true shamrock"; however, white-clover (*T. repens*) and the hop clover (*Medicago lupulina*) are also used as shamrocks. All are of the pea family, Leguminosae.

Shams ud-din Mohammed. See HAFIZ.

Shang Dynasty. See CHINA, section "History," subtitle *Early History*.

Shanghai, shăng'hī, China, the nation's largest city and principal seaport, and one of the most populous cities in the world. It is on the Huangpu Jiang (Huangpu River), which empties into the Yangtze River (Chang Jiang) estuary north of the city. Officially, Shanghai is a special municipality called a *shih* and is one of the 30 main administrative units into which China is divided. The municipality's boundaries lie far beyond the city proper and enclose suburbs, small rural communities, and farmland.

Shanghai proper lies on the west side of the Huangpu and, like the entire municipality, is situated on the flat, low floodplain of the Yangtze delta. Flowing through the city are several small streams, including the Wusong, which is crossed by many bridges and is much used by small boats. Shanghai's central business district lies near the junction of the Wusong and the Huangpu.

Extending along the west bank of the Huangpu is Zhong Shan Road, which before the Communists took over China in 1949 was known as the Bund. It was the principal center of the International Settlement, from where Western (mainly British, French, and American) interests controlled much of China's foreign commerce for about a century. Parts of the Settlement area, especially along Zhong Shan Road, have a somewhat European appearance. Nanjing Road, the principal commercial street, has a number of department stores, restaurants, and theaters. Port facilities and industrial areas line the banks of the Huangpu downstream from the business district.

Economy

Its location at the seaward end of the densely settled and highly productive Yangtze River valley has helped make Shanghai China's leading port and commercial city. Most of central China's goods destined for foreign or domestic ports pass through Shanghai, as do manufactured products headed for China's interior.

As a manufacturing city, Shanghai ranks first in China and among the most important in Asia. It has long been a center of light industry, especially the making of textiles. In the early 1960's the Chinese government

SHANGHAI

| 0 | Miles | 1 |
| 0 | Kilometers | 1 |

Park

Major Street

Jiangsu

Zhejiang

SHANGHAI MUNICIPALITY

Area of Main Map

East China Sea

Lu Xun Tomb

0 Miles 50
0 Km 50

Central Railway Station

Shanghai Mansion

Wusong Jiang

Peace Hotel

Beijing Road

People's Nanjing Road

Acrobatic Theater

People's Park

Shanghai Museum

Yan'an St.

Library

People's Square

Xizang St.

Huangpu Jiang

Zhong

Oriental Pearl Television Tower

Museum of Nat. History

Pudong

Shan Rd. (Bund)

Yu Yuan Garden

Old Town

To Hongqiao International Airport

Fuxing Park

Central Shanghai is divided by the Huangpu River. The city's skyline is dominated by the Oriental Pearl Television Tower and other structures in Pudong, a new financial and business district (left). The People's Heroes Memorial Tower appears in the foreground.

© Keren Su/China Span

began intensive efforts to develop heavy industry in Shanghai. Many factories were enlarged and modernized and new ones were built. Shanghai is a major producer of iron and steel, ships, motor vehicles, chemicals, electrical equipment, petroleum products, and such consumer goods as electric appliances, bicycles, and paper goods. Shanghai is also a major printing and publishing center.

Three major transportation routes—two railways and the Yangtze River—link Shanghai with the interior. The Yangtze is navigable by large ships for 630 miles (1,010 km) to Wuhan. Hongqiao International Airport, southwest of the city, is one of China's largest air terminals.

Places of Interest

Two of Shanghai's prominent landmarks are hotels on or near Zhong Shan Road—the Shanghai Mansion, a vast structure on the Wusong's north bank, and the Peace Hotel. On the east bank of the Huangpu is another major landmark, the Oriental Pearl Television Tower, which rises more than 1,500 feet (460 m). Near the center of the city is the old town district, a roughly circular area about one mile (1.6 km) in diameter that was once enclosed by walls. It is a maze of narrow streets and contains a number of traditional Chinese gardens and temples. The splendid Yu Yuan Garden dates from the 16th century.

Two public areas, People's Square and People's Park, occupy the former site of the British-built racecourse on Nanjing Road. Facing the square and park are the Municipal Library and the Workers' Cultural Palace. The Shanghai Art and History Museum, occupying a former bank building, has extensive displays on the evolution of Chinese art. Also in Shanghai are the tomb of the poet Lu Xun, an acrobatic theater, a museum of natural history, and a zoo.

Shanghai is one of China's leading educa-

Facts about Shanghai

Name—From the Chinese words meaning "up from the sea."

Location— Shanghai is about 670 miles (1,080 km) southeast of Beijing, China's capital. Downtown Shanghai is located at 31° 15′ N., 121° 30′ E., about the same latitude as Savannah, Georgia.

Area—Shanghai municipality has an area of 2,388 square miles (6,185 km²); Shanghai proper (the densely settled section corresponding to the city itself) occupies about 300 square miles (780 km²).

Climate—Average temperatures vary from about 39° F. (4° C.) in January to 82° F. (28° C.) in July and August. Average annual precipitation is about 43 inches (1,090 mm), most of which falls as rain during spring and summer.

tional centers. Among institutions of higher learning are Fudan, Shanghai, and Tongji universities and colleges of engineering, education, foreign languages, medicine, and textile science. There are also a number of research institutes of the Chinese Academy of Sciences.

History

Shanghai was an unimportant trading center from Ming times (1368-1644) until the mid-19th century. By the Treaty of Nanking (1842), which ended the Opium War between China and Great Britain, Shanghai was made a treaty port, opening the city to foreign trade. (See TREATY PORT.) In 1843 a section of Shanghai was leased in perpetuity to the British for commercial and residential purposes. Later, similar "concessions," as the special leases were called, were granted to France and the United States.

In 1863 the British and American concessions were joined to form the International Settlement. Under the foreign concessions, which were enlarged several times, Shanghai developed rapidly, becoming the financial and commercial center of the Far East.

In 1932 the old town district was attacked and partially destroyed by Japanese troops. Intimidated, the Chinese ended the trade boycott against Japan that they had begun after the Japanese invasion of Manchuria in 1931. Japan invaded China in 1937, and Shanghai was under Japanese occupation until 1945. Britain and the United States relinquished their concessions in 1943 and France in 1946.

Shanghai was taken by the Chinese Communists in 1949 and they seized the extensive foreign holdings in the city, forcing most foreigners to leave. Following the Chinese government's introduction of economic reforms in the late 1980's and early 1990's, Shanghai became an important international trade and finance center.

Population: Shanghai proper, 7,780,000; the municipality, 9,750,000.

Shannon River, shăn′ŭn, the longest and the most important river in Ireland. It begins in the Iron Mountains near the boundary of Northern Ireland and flows southward and westward for about 230 miles (370 km) to the Atlantic Ocean. The Shannon passes through several lakes, the largest of which are Lough Ree and Lough Derg. West of Limerick, the main city on the Shannon, the river broadens into an estuary, which is navigable by oceangoing ships. There is a hydroelectric station between Lough Derg and Limerick.

Shaper. See MACHINE TOOL, subtitle *Kinds of Machine Tools.*

Shapiro, shȧ-pĭr′ō, **Karl** (Jay) (1913-   ), a United States poet and critic. In 1945 he won the Pulitzer Prize for his *V-Letter and Other Poems,* written while he was serving in the U.S. Army. He provoked controversy with *In Defense of Ignorance* (1960), an attack on overintellectualism in poetry. In *To Abolish Children* (1968), he censures the revolt of university students against academic authority.

Shapiro was born in Baltimore, Maryland, and attended Johns Hopkins University. He edited *Poetry: A Magazine of Verse,* 1950-56. He taught at various universities, including Johns Hopkins, Nebraska, Illinois, and California.

Among his other works are: Poetry—*Person, Place, and Thing* (1942); *Poems* (1935); *Poems 1940-1953* (1953); *The Bourgeois Poet* (1964); *Selected Poems* (1968); *Love & War/Art & God* (1985). Criticism—*Beyond Criticism* (1953); *Prose Keys to Modern Poetry* (1962); *The Poetry Wreck* (1975). Novel—*Edsel* (1971).

Shapley, shăp′lē, **Harlow** (1885-1972), a United States astronomer. His studies of stars in globular clusters and of Cepheid variable stars led to a new understanding of the structure of the universe. From these studies he determined the size and shape of the Milky Way and placed the solar system far from the galaxy's center. He introduced the theory that the Cepheid variable stars undergo changes in brightness because they pulsate, alternately growing and shrinking in size. He also developed a method of determining the physical properties of eclipsing binaries.

Shapley was born in Nashville, Missouri. After attending the University of Missouri, he received a Ph.D. from Princeton in 1913. He was a staff astronomer at Mount Wilson Observatory in California and then directed the Harvard College Observatory, 1921-52. Shapley wrote numerous technical and popular books. *Through Rugged Ways to the Stars* (1969) is his autobiography.

Share. See STOCK.

Sharecropping. See TENANT FARMING.

Shark, a fish found in almost all oceans of the world but chiefly in warm water. Sharks inhabit both deep and shallow water. Open-water species must move constantly to

Whale Shark

American Museum of Natural History

breathe and stay afloat. Some migratory species swim up river to spawn. Sharks range in size from less than 2 feet (60 cm) to 60 feet (18 m) or more. Large sharks may weigh more than 13 tons (11,800 kg).

Contrary to popular belief, most sharks are not aggressive toward humans. Unprovoked attacks are rare; sharks tend to retreat when confronted unless they are threatened. Of the more than 350 species, only about 20 are known to attack humans. These species are usually attracted by blood or by any unusual movement in the water. Many types of shark protection have been developed. Examples include the shark billy, a stick used to push sharks away; the shark dart, which is fired from a gun and explodes upon contact with the shark; the shark screen, a polyvinyl bag, supported by an inflatable collar, that surrounds a person in the water, making him undetectable to sharks; and protective suits made of steel mesh.

Shark meat is used as food in many parts of the world, and commercial fishing of sharks is common in the Far East. The fins serve as the main ingredient in shark-fin soup. Shark skeletons are dried and processed for use in fertilizer and animal feed. *Squalene,* an oil extracted from the liver, is used to treat burns and as a base for cosmetics.

Description and Habits

The typical shark body is torpedo-shaped with the upper half of the tail fin longer than the lower half. In male sharks, the pectoral fins have been modified into *claspers,* a pair of sexual organs containing sperm. Most sharks are black, brown, or gray, usually with lighter undersides. Some species, however, such as the leopard shark, whale shark, and swell shark, have blotches and markings on their bodies.

Sharks have many anatomical features that set them apart from most other fish. For example, the skeleton lacks bone; it is made up of cartilage. The skin is embedded with *placoid scales,* horny structures that, unlike the scales of most fish, do not overlap. Each bears a tiny toothlike projection called a *denticle.* Like most other fish, sharks

Great White Shark

Mako

Leopard Shark

Hammerhead
(top view)

Hammerhead
(bottom view)

Top two courtesy of the American Museum of Natural History; bottom three courtesy of the Field Museum of Natural History

breathe through gills, but unlike most other fish, which have four pairs, sharks have five to seven pairs of gills, with a corresponding number of gill slits opening at the sides of the head. Most sharks are cold-blooded. Sharks have numerous rows of teeth and produce new teeth throughout their lifetime. Teeth of the outer row periodically break off or wear away and those of the next row advance in position to take their place.

Most sharks are powerful swimmers and chase their prey. Most eat fish, mollusks, crustaceans, and occasionally, seals. Sharks have sensitive pores, called *ampullae of Lorenzini,* on the chin and nose. These sensory organs are used to detect weak electric currents in the water, helping the shark locate prey.

Sharks reproduce by sperm and eggs. A few species are *viviparous*—the females give birth to live young. Some are *oviparous* —the females expel the fertilized eggs. The eggs are contained in leathery cases, popularly called mermaid's purses, that are sometimes found on the seashore. Most species are *ovoviviparous*—the female retains the fertilized eggs within her body until birth.

Kinds of Sharks

The largest of all sharks—and of all fish— is the *whale shark,* which reaches an average of 40 feet (12 m) in length. It is found throughout tropical waters of the world. It is one of the few sharks with its mouth at the tip of the snout rather than on the underside. Second in size is the *basking shark,* which averages a length of about 25 feet (7.6 m). It is found in temperate waters. Both feed on plankton and are relatively harmless.

The shark that is most dangerous to humans is the *great white shark* (also called the *man-eater* and *tommy*). It is a warm-blooded species. This shark averages about 18 feet (5.5 m) in length. It is most abundant in tropical waters. Other extremely dangerous sharks are the bull, tiger, and oceanic white-tip sharks.

The *mako,* another warm-blooded species, is a popular game fish. It occurs in tropical and temperate waters of the Atlantic Ocean, and is primarily a deep-sea fish. The mako averages about 12 feet (3.7 m) in length. The *leopard shark* is a generally timid shark often found along the coast of California. Several species of small sharks commonly found close to shore are called *dogfish.* (See DOGFISH.)

Among the most unusual sharks in shape are the *hammerheads*. The head is extended laterally to form flattened lobes. At the end of each lobe are an eye and a nostril. The largest species of hammerhead is the *great hammerhead,* averaging about 15 feet (4.6 m) in length. It is found in tropical and subtropical waters in both the Atlantic and the Pacific.

Sharks make up several families of the class Chondrichthyes. The whale shark is *Rhincodon typus;* the basking shark, *Cetorhinus maximus;* the great white shark, *Carcharodon carcharias;* the great hammerhead, *Sphyrna mokarran;* the mako, *Isurus oxyrinchus;* the leopard shark, *Triakis semifasciata.*

See also FISHING, table *Saltwater Fishing Records.*

Shark Sucker. See REMORA.

Sharkskin, a fabric. See TEXTILE (table).

Sharp-shinned Hawk. See HAWK, subtitle *Hawks of the United States:* Short-winged Hawks.

Sharpsburg, Battle of. See ANTIETAM, BATTLE OF.

Shasta, Mount, shăs'tȧ, a snowcapped dormant volcano in the Cascade Range in northern California. It was named for the Shasta Indians, who once inhabited the area. Mount Shasta is one of California's most impressive mountains, rising some 10,000 feet (3,000 m) above the surrounding land and 14,162 feet (4,317 m) above sea level. On its upper slopes are five glaciers, one about two miles (3 km) long. On Shasta's western flank is Shastina, a younger volcanic peak 12,433 feet (3,790 m) high. Mount Shasta Recreation Area, centering on Mount Shasta, offers mountain climbing, skiing, and camping.

The first white man to view Mount Shasta was Peter S. Ogden, a Canadian fur trader who explored the area in 1827. The peak was first climbed in 1854 by E. D. Pearce.

Shasta Daisy. See BURBANK, LUTHER, subtitle *Burbank's Contributions;* DAISY.

Shatt al Arab, a river in southeastern Iraq. It is formed by the junction of the Tigris and Euphrates rivers and flows about 115 miles (185 km) to the head of the Persian Gulf. The river's lower course, which is navigable by oceangoing ships, marks a section of the boundary between Iraq and Iran. Major cities on the Shatt al Arab are Basra, the chief port of Iraq; and Abadan, Iran, one of the world's largest petroleum-refining centers.

Shaughnessy, shô'nĕ-sĭ, Thomas George, First **Baron** (1853-1923), a Canadian railway official. As president (1899-1918) and chairman (1910-23) of the Canadian Pacific Railway and director of associated companies, he played an important part in the development of Canada. He presided over the railroad during the period of its greatest consolidation and expansion.

Shaughnessy was born in Milwaukee, Wisconsin. He worked for the Chicago, Milwaukee, and St. Paul Railroad, 1869-82, before moving to Montreal to join the Canadian Pacific Railway. He was knighted in 1901 and was made a baron in 1916.

Shaw, Anna Howard (1847-1919), a United States reformer, physician, and preacher. Active in the movement for woman suffrage—she was president of the National American Woman Suffrage Association, 1904-15—she did much toward obtaining the vote for women.

Anna Shaw was born in England and was brought to Michigan by her parents at the age of four. She graduated from the theological school of Boston University and in 1880 became the first woman to be ordained in the Methodist Church. After receiving a medical degree from Boston University in 1886, Anna Shaw gave up preaching and spent most of her time lecturing on women's rights. During World War I, she was chairman of the women's division of the Council of National Defense and in 1919 was awarded the Distinguished Service Medal for her contributions to the war effort.

Shaw, George Bernard (1856-1950), a British playwright, critic, essayist, and social reformer. He has been called the greatest dramatist writing in English since Shakespeare and the greatest British satirist since Jonathan Swift. His drama criticism influenced the trend of 20th-century playwriting. In 1925 Shaw was awarded the Nobel Prize for literature.

Shaw was a master of clear, direct prose. His writings sparkle with wit and playfulness, but he was also capable of brutal irony. He attacked capitalism, militarism, hypocrisy, and the artificiality of moral and social conventions. He ridiculed marriage and romantic love, and found fault with the church, the legal and medical professions, and many of the theories and findings of science. He supported vegetarianism and was an ardent antivivisectionist.

Shaw adopted other men's ideas, but he interpreted and presented these ideas with originality. The British novelist Samuel Butler's opinion that poverty is a crime had great effect on Shaw. Such philosophers as the Germans Arthur Schopenhauer and Friedrich Nietzsche and the Frenchman Henri Bergson gave Shaw the belief that human will and a natural life force can transform mankind through a process its exponents called "creative evolution." From the Norwegian playwright Henrik Ibsen he adopted a belief in the right of the individual to self-realization. Ibsen's plays also convinced Shaw that ideas of social reform can be effectively presented in drama.

Shaw also called for reforming the English language, believing communication in English could be made more exact and efficient with a new alphabet. Shavian, an alphabet of 48 symbols, was invented by Kingsley Read after Shaw's death. Shaw's advocacy

George Bernard Shaw
caricature by Sir Bernard Partridge
© *Punch*, London 1925

of unusual and unpopular ideas and causes, as well as his deliberately eccentric behavior, made him one of the best-known and most controversial figures of his time.

Shaw's Major Plays

Shaw prefaced many of his plays with a long essay expanding the ideas presented in the play. Even in the plays themselves he was more concerned with ideas than with telling a story. However, his dramatic skill was such that his best dramas have seldom lacked enthusiastic audiences. In some plays, his characters are little more than mouthpieces for the expression of ideas. But he also created such real and memorable characters as Candida in *Candida,* Caesar in *Caesar and Cleopatra,* Barbara Undershaft in *Major Barbara,* Eliza Doolittle and Henry Higgins in *Pygmalion,* and Joan of Arc in *Saint Joan.*

Arms and the Man (1894) is a mild satire on romantic love and military heroics. It introduces one of Shaw's favorite character types—the man-trapping woman—in the person of Louka, the heroine's maid. Oskar Straus's operetta *The Chocolate Soldier* (1908) is based on this play.

Candida (1897) is one of Shaw's best plays from a dramatic standpoint. In it he creates several notable characters. Candida, the wife of a successful clergyman, is loved by a temperamental young poet who begs her to elope with him. She decides to stay with her husband, not for conventional reasons, but because she realizes he is the weaker of the two men and needs her more.

Caesar and Cleopatra (1899) is also important for its characterizations. Caesar is portrayed as an intelligent, practical man who tries to bring a primitive and childlike Cleopatra to a recognition of her responsibilities as a ruler.

Man and Superman (1905), considered Shaw's masterpiece by many critics, develops the theme of woman—as an agent of the life force—in pursuit of reluctant man. The third act, made up largely of the hero's dream, contains some of Shaw's most powerful satire. It is sometimes presented alone as *Don Juan in Hell.* Like many of Shaw's plays, *Man and Superman* was published some years before it was performed. The date given here is of first performance.

Major Barbara (1907) is one of Shaw's more perplexing and paradoxical plays. Barbara, the daughter of a munitions manufacturer, rejects her father's ruthless way of life and joins the Salvation Army. At the play's end, however, she renounces the Army as hypocritical and ineffectual. Barbara's father is portrayed as diabolical, and yet there are indications that he has deeper and stronger religious ideals than those of his daughter. The play expresses Shaw's belief that poverty cannot be wiped out by charity but only by a practical economic and political system.

Pygmalion (1913) satirizes the social caste structure. Henry Higgins, a professor of phonetics, transforms an ignorant flower girl into an elegant lady by teaching her to speak English correctly. The musical comedy *My Fair Lady* (1956) is based on this play.

Back to Methuselah (1923) is a cycle of five plays. Shaw felt it was his most important work but critics and the public find it wordy and didactic. It is a fantasy on one of Shaw's favorite themes—mankind's ability to become perfect. The theme is developed more effectively in the play's preface than in the play itself.

Saint Joan (1923) is one of Shaw's most popular plays and dramatically one of the best constructed. Joan is depicted realistically as a simple peasant girl who yet reflects spirituality and wisdom. She dies because she poses a threat to feudalism with her nationalistic ideals and to the Church with her claim of direct contact with spiritual forces without churchly mediation.

Shaw's Life

Shaw was born in Dublin of a Protestant family. He quit school at the age of 15 and for five years worked in a land agent's office. In 1872 his mother left his alcoholic father and went to London, where she taught music. Shaw joined her in 1876. His mother supported him for several years while he wrote five unsuccessful novels.

He became interested in Socialism, joined the newly formed Fabian Society in 1884, and wrote and lectured on Socialism. In 1889 he began a career as a critic of music, art, and drama for various London publications. His drama criticism for one of these, *The Saturday Review,* sparked controversy and made famous the initials G.B.S. with which he signed his reviews.

Shaw's first play was *Widowers' Houses* (1892), an attack on slum landlords. It was not a success—nor were any of his plays that

were produced in the 1890's successful at the time they were first staged. Not until 1904, when they began to be produced under Harley Granville-Barker's management at the Court Theatre, did Shaw's plays receive critical and popular acclaim.

Shaw married Charlotte Payne-Townshend in 1898. Before and during his marriage, however, he carried on long and ardent friendships, mainly through letters, with several women—including the actresses Ellen Terry and Mrs. Patrick Campbell.

Shaw's other works include: Plays—*The Devil's Disciple* (1897); *Mrs. Warren's Profession* (1902); *Androcles and the Lion* (1912); *Heartbreak House* (1921); *The Apple Cart* (1929). Novels—*Cashel Byron's Profession* (1886); *An Unsocial Socialist* (1887). Political writings—*Fabian Essays in Socialism* (1889); *The Intelligent Woman's Guide to Socialism and Capitalism* (1928). *Shaw's Music* (3 volumes, 1981) is a compilation of his reviews and articles on music. His *Collected Letters* (1965-88) were published in four volumes.

Books about George Bernard Shaw

Grene, Nicholas. *Bernard Shaw: a Critical View* (St. Martin's Press, 1984).
Hill, E. C. *George Bernard Shaw* (Twayne, 1978).
Holroyd, Michael. *Bernard Shaw* (3 volumes; Random House, 1988-91).
Weintraub, Stanley. *Bernard Shaw: a Guide to Research* (Pennsylvania State University, 1992).

Shaw, Henry Wheeler. See BILLINGS, JOSH.

Shaw University. See UNIVERSITIES AND COLLEGES (table).

Shawinigan, shȧ-wĭn'ĭ-găn, Quebec, Canada, a city in St. Maurice County. It is on the St. Maurice River about 85 miles (137 km) northeast of Montreal. Shawinigan is an important industrial center producing aluminum, chemicals, paper, wood pulp, textiles, and clothing. The city was founded in the late 1890's after a hydroelectric plant was built on the river. Industries were attracted by the abundant power supply.

Population: 21,470.

Shawn, shôn, **Ted** (Edwin Meyers Shawn) (1891-1972), a United States dancer and choreographer who helped promote the dance as an art for men. He was one of the first to create dances on American themes, such as *Cowboy Tommy* and *Feather of the Dawn.* Shawn was born in Kansas City, Missouri, and began his professional career in 1912. With his wife, Ruth St. Denis, he founded the Denishawn schools and dance troupe in 1915. Shawn founded a dance school at Jacob's Pillow, near Lee, Massachusetts, in 1933. The Jacob's Pillow Dance Festival (founded 1941) became an annual summer event.

See also DANCE, subtitle *Development of Western Dance:* Early 20th-century Dance; ST. DENIS, RUTH (photograph).

Shawnee, shô'nē, Oklahoma, the seat of Pottawatomie County. It lies on the North Canadian River about 35 miles (56 km) southeast of Oklahoma City. Shawnee is the trading and processing center for a farming and ranching area and has a variety of light manufacturing industries. Oklahoma Baptist University is here. Shawnee was founded in 1895. It has the council-manager form of government.

Population: 26,017.

Shawnee Indians, a North American tribe of the Algonquian language family. "Shawnee" is from an Indian word meaning "southerners." When the Shawnees were first seen by Europeans in the 17th century, they lived along the Cumberland River in what is now Tennessee and numbered about 3,000. An outlying band lived along the Savannah River in what is now South Carolina. Conflicts with the Cherokee and Catawba Indians caused the Shawnees to move northward and to settle eventually as one group along the upper Ohio River in present-day Ohio and Pennsylvania.

The Shawnees sided with the British in the American Revolution. Afterward about half the tribe moved west to what is now Missouri, while another large group settled in what is now Indiana. Two Indiana Shawnees, Tecumseh and his brother Tenskwatawa (called the Prophet), set out to form a confederacy of Indian tribes to resist white encroachment. However, the Indians were badly beaten at the battle of Tippecanoe in 1811, and after the death of Tecumseh in the War of 1812 most of the Shawnees accepted peace terms with the United States. They eventually settled in Indian Territory (what is now Oklahoma), where many joined the Cherokee Nation. The Shawnee in Oklahoma presently number about 3,700.

See also TECUMSEH.

Shaw's Garden. See MISSOURI BOTANICAL GARDEN.

Shays' Rebellion, 1786-87, an uprising of debt-ridden farmers in western Massachusetts. It reflected the widespread discontent during the depression that followed the Revolutionary War, particularly the antagonism between debtors and creditors. Although the rebellion was put down, many grievances eventually were redressed. The rebellion also helped to pave the way for the U.S. Constitution by demonstrating the need for a strong central government, which could suppress such uprisings and could also remedy the economic causes.

Massachusetts was the state most seriously affected by the postwar economic crisis. Many farmers and small property owners were losing their land and being threatened with jail for nonpayment of debts and taxes. They demanded reduction of taxes, court reforms, and revision of the state constitution. Some called for a large quantity of paper money to be issued to make debt payment easier. When their pleas were ignored by the legislature, mobs of farmers attempted to prevent courts from hearing debt cases.

In September, 1786, about 500 insurgents, led by Daniel Shays (1747-1825), a destitute farmer and former army captain, gathered at Springfield and forced the Massachusetts supreme court to adjourn. They were declared outlaws by Governor James Bowdoin. In January, 1787, Shays and some 1,200 men marched on Springfield to seize the federal arsenal. The poorly armed rebels were driven off by the militia and were pursued by a large force under General Benjamin Lincoln. The rebellion was soon crushed. Shays fled to Vermont.

Ultimately all involved were granted amnesty. A newly elected legislature enacted laws to reform taxation, lower court fees, and exempt household goods and workmen's tools from the debt process.

Shearing, George (Albert) (1919-), an English-born pianist and composer, known especially for his melodic jazz arrangements of popular standards. His jazz quintet, organized in 1949, became internationally known for its unique harmonic blending of piano, vibraphone, guitar, bass, and drum. He arranged many songs and composed "Lullaby of Birdland" (1952). Shearing, who was born blind, studied music in his native London. While a teenager he heard recordings by Fats Waller and Teddy Wilson and turned to jazz. Shearing became Britain's most popular pianist. He settled in the United States in 1947 and became a citizen in 1956.

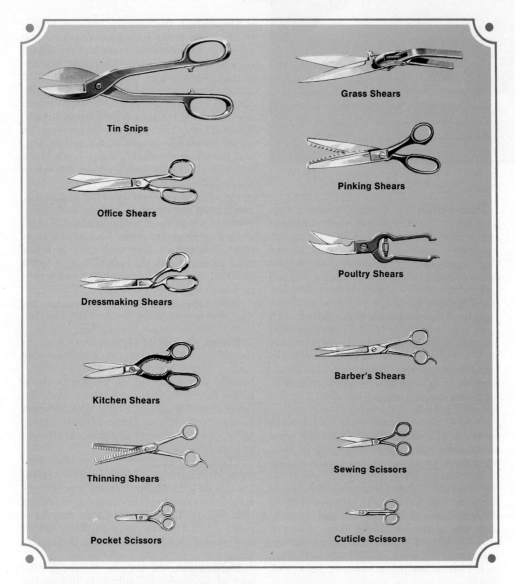

Tin Snips

Office Shears

Dressmaking Shears

Kitchen Shears

Thinning Shears

Pocket Scissors

Grass Shears

Pinking Shears

Poultry Shears

Barber's Shears

Sewing Scissors

Cuticle Scissors

Shears, a cutting instrument. The most familiar type is hand shears, or scissors, which have opposed metal cutting edges that slide past each other, severing material caught between them. The two blades, beveled to form sharp inner edges, are crossed and held together by a pivot pin or screw. The other ends of the blade strips are shaped into handles. Pressing the handles together causes the blades to close.

Shears are usually made of steel. There are many kinds and sizes, most designed for a specific purpose. For example, pinking shears have serrated cutting edges that make a saw-toothed cut; cuticle scissors have short, curved blades that cut and shape the cuticle.

The blades of early shears were not crossed, but connected at one end, and had to be squeezed together to cut. Cross-blade shears were developed early in the Christian Era, but did not become common until much later. Modern developments include machine shears for industrial purposes and electric shears for home use.

See also PRUNING, illustration.

© Brian Rogers/Visuals Unlimited
White Sheathbills

Shearwater, the common name of a family of birds; also the common name of a genus of the family. Members of this genus are sometimes referred to collectively as the "true shearwaters." The family, with a total of more than 50 species, includes the fulmars and certain species of petrels as well as the true shearwaters.

Birds of this family are drab colored, with sooty gray, brown, or black upper parts and generally white underparts. They have short legs, webbed feet, and large hooked beaks with tubular nostrils. Shearwaters are usually about 15 to 25 inches (38-64 cm) in length, with long pointed wings that span 2 to 2½ feet (60-75 cm) from tip to tip.

Shearwaters are found on all the unfrozen oceans of the world. When a steady wind blows, they will glide with it for more than one mile (1.6 km), just skimming the surface of the water. They feed chiefly on small marine animals. Some feed while floating on the water's surface; others perform shallow dives in search of food. Shearwaters come to land only to nest, returning to the shores or offshore islands where they were reared. One chalky white egg is laid in the nest, built in a burrow in the ground or in a rock crevice.

In some countries, such as Australia and New Zealand, several species of the true shearwaters are called *muttonbirds* because they are used for food. The *sooty shearwater* of the Atlantic and Pacific oceans is a muttonbird. It annually breeds on land in the Southern Hemisphere and each spring and summer migrates to the subarctic waters of the Northern Hemisphere.

The shearwater family is Procellariidae; the shearwater genus is *Puffinus*. The sooty shearwater is *P. griseus*.

See also FULMAR; PETREL.

Sheathbill, the common name of a family of shore birds found on the antarctic shores and subantarctic islands of the Atlantic and Indian oceans. The sheathbills are plump, snow-white birds about 14 to 17 inches (36-43 cm) in length. They have pink-rimmed eyes and short, stubby bills, which are covered at the base with a horny sheath. There are only two species in the family—the *white sheathbill,* which has a yellow bill, and the *lesser sheathbill,* which has a black bill and is slightly smaller than the white sheathbill.

Sheathbills feed on seaweeds, mussels, small crustaceans, and the eggs and sickly young of penguins. They build a nest of grass in rock crevices and under boulders. Two or three pale brown eggs with gray or black speckles are laid in the nest. The eggs hatch in about 28 days. The young chicks are covered with a gray down.

Sheathbills make up the family Chionididae. The white sheathbill is *Chionia alba;* the lesser sheathbill, *C. minor.*

Sheba, Queen of (10th century B.C.), in the Bible (I Kings 10:1-13), a woman who visited King Solomon of Israel. She was supposedly very beautiful. In the Koran she is called Bilkis, in Ethiopian legend Makeda. According to tradition, Sheba bore Solomon a son, from whom Haile Selassie (1892-1975), the last emperor of Ethiopia, claimed to have been descended.

The ancient kingdom of Saba (called Sheba in Hebrew) was in southwestern Arabia, the site of present-day Yemen. Inscriptions from Saba do not mention any queens ruling that region. The Biblical queen may have ruled a Sabaean colony in northern Arabia and visited Solomon to discuss trade relations.

Sheboygan, shě-boi′găn, Wisconsin, the seat of Sheboygan County. It lies at the mouth of the Sheboygan River on Lake Michigan's shore, about 50 miles (80 km) north of Milwaukee. Sheboygan is a Great Lakes port and a commercial center for a major dairy region. Factories in or near the city produce furniture, plumbing fixtures, food products, plastics, clothing, and leather goods. Lakeland College is here. The city has the mayor-council form of government. Sheboygan was settled in the 1830's, primarily by German immigrants, and was incorporated as a city in 1853.

Population: 49,676.

Sheeler, Charles (1883-1965), a United States painter and photographer. Sheeler painted factories, dams, trains, and other machine-age subjects with sharp, precise lines and austere, simplified forms that became associated with the Precisionist School. Some of his works, such as *River Rouge Plant* and *Rolling Power,* are photographically realistic. Others, such as *Golden Gate,* are more abstract with their emphasis on geometric form. His photographs, mostly of industrial subjects, are as precise and sharp as his paintings.

Sheeler studied applied design and painting in his native Philadelphia. He made several trips to Europe and was influenced by the Cubists. Success as a painter came slowly, and Sheeler turned to photography to earn a living.

Sheen, Fulton J. (John) (1895-1979), a United States Roman Catholic bishop, educator, and author. He became one of the best-known figures of the Catholic Church in the United States as a result of his sermons on radio; his television program, *Life Is Worth Living;* and his more than 70 books and pamphlets on Christian living. He won many converts to Catholicism, waged a vigorous fight against Communism, and worked for social justice.

Sheen was born in El Paso, Illinois. After becoming a priest in 1919, he taught philosophy at the Catholic University of America, 1926-50. He entered broadcasting in 1930 on *The Catholic Hour,* a network radio program. Sheen was national director of the Society for the Propagation of the Faith, 1950-66. He served as bishop of Rochester, New York, 1966-69, and then returned to lecturing and writing. He was given the title archbishop in 1969.

His works include: *Peace of Soul* (1949); *Life Is Worth Living* (5 volumes, 1953-57); *The Power of Love* (1964); and *Parents and Children* (1970).

Sheep, a mammal that is closely related to the goat. Sheep, like cattle, are *ruminants;* that is, they chew a cud. Their stomachs have four chambers for digesting the grass and other plant material they eat. Their hooves are split into two parts, making them cloven-hoofed.

There are both domestic sheep and wild sheep, and there is a great difference in their appearance. Domestic sheep have long tails (which are usually removed at an early age) and, usually, a woolly coat; wild sheep have shorter tails and a coat made up of stiff hairs. Male sheep are called *rams;* females, *ewes.* Domestic sheep under one year old are usually called *lambs.*

Domestic Sheep

Sheep have a natural inclination to assemble in flocks and to follow a leader—characteristics that enable a lone shepherd to handle hundreds of them. Sheep have been domesticated since very early in human history.

Importance. Sheep are raised in almost all parts of the world, especially in temperate regions. They provide humans with food,

Rolling Power, by Charles Sheeler in 1939; oil on canvas, 15 by 30 inches (38 × 76 cm)

Smith College Museum of Art

Merino Ram

Hampshire Ewe and Lamb

Dorset Ewe and Lamb

Young Corriedale Ram

clothing, and many other products. The flesh of young sheep is called lamb; the flesh of older sheep, mutton. (See LAMB; MUTTON.) Sheep's wool is sheared from their bodies and can be woven into various types of fabrics and carpets. (See WOOL.) The skins of sheep are used to make numerous leather goods, such as shoes, coats, gloves, and hats. (See LEATHER.) Furs obtained from sheep may be unsheared or sheared. (See FUR, table titled *Some Important Furs*.)

Description. Mature ewes generally weigh from 120 to 250 pounds (55 to 115 kg). Mature rams range from 175 pounds (80 kg) to 350 pounds (160 kg) or more. Weight depends on the breed and the individual. The fleece is usually white but sometimes gray, tan, or black. Some sheep have fleece covering the head and legs, others do not. In some breeds the hind legs are covered with fleece while the forelegs are bare of wool and covered with hair. In those that have bare faces or legs, or both, legs and faces may be white, black, gray or brown. Some breeds have horns (usually a single pair); others do not. In some breeds only the males are horned; in others, both sexes are.

Breeds. There are more than 200 breeds of domestic sheep, but only about a dozen are of significant economic importance. The various breeds can be classified in many different ways. A common way of classifying breeds is by the products for which they are primarily raised, as follows:

Wool-producing. These breeds are raised primarily for their fine wool. To this category belongs the most famous of all breeds—the Merino, which produces the finest wool. This breed was developed in Spain and has been the basic stock for the development of other types of Merinos, including the American Merino and the Delaine Merino.

Fur-producing. The only breed that is raised primarily for its fur is the Karakul. (See KARAKUL.)

Meat-producing. Most of these breeds are of English origin. They are raised primarily for their meat, although their wool is used also. Included in this group is the Hampshire breed. Hampshires have black or brown faces. The lambs grow exceptionally fast and produce meat of fine quality. Other breeds in this group are the Suffolk, Oxford, Southdown, and Dorset.

Dual-purpose. These breeds are raised both for their wool, which is of a good quality, and for their meat. The Rambouillet is a dual-purpose breed developed from the Spanish Merino. The Rambouillet has also been extensively used for crossbreeding. The rams usually have large spiral horns; some ewes have stubby horns, but most are hornless. The Corriedale, developed in New Zealand, is considered a good dual-purpose breed. This white-faced breed has fairly long wool covering the body. Horns are lacking in both

LEADING SHEEP-RAISING COUNTRIES

Millions of Sheep*

	0	20	40	60	80	100	120	140

China
Australia
India
Iran
New Zealand
Great Britain
Sudan
Pakistan
Turkey
South Africa

*Average for 1997-99.
Source: FAO.

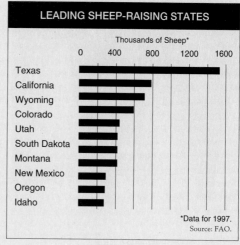

LEADING SHEEP-RAISING STATES

Thousands of Sheep*

	0	400	800	1200	1600

Texas
California
Wyoming
Colorado
Utah
South Dakota
Montana
New Mexico
Oregon
Idaho

*Data for 1997.
Source: FAO.

Mouflon Ram

sexes. Other dual-purpose breeds are the Columbia and Romney.

Triple-purpose. These breeds are raised primarily in Europe and the Near East. They are raised for their milk as well as for their meat and wool.

Some highly specialized breeds are raised primarily for their milk. Examples are the Awassi and the East Friesian. Some breeds in northern Africa and in Asia produce a coarse wool especially suited to carpet making. Many of these breeds store fat in their tails and are called "fat-tailed" breeds.

Sheep Raising. In the United States, sheep are raised in practically every state, primarily for meat. Some sheep raisers specialize in purebred stock for breeding purposes.

Sheep are usually bred during the late summer or early fall. Some, however, are bred twice a year. Only one ram is needed for a flock of about 35 to 50 ewes. The lambs are born after a gestation period of about five months. Single births are usual, but twins or triplets are not uncommon. For cleanliness, lambs' tails, which would otherwise grow quite long, are usually docked (cut off) within the first two weeks. For better meat production and easier management, male lambs raised for meat are castrated; they are then called *wethers*.

Lambs raised for meat are marketed when they are four to seven months old. Those weighing about 100 to 120 pounds (45 to 54 kg) are sold to packinghouses. Smaller ones are sold to "feeders" who take them to feedlots where they are fed grain for rapid weight increase. While meat is the primary product, the wool, skin, bones, intestines,

and other parts of the slaughtered lambs are used for various products. (See MEAT PACKING and table titled *Some By-products of Meat Packing.*)

Lambs allowed to reach maturity are raised for breeding and for their wool. Some are also raised for mutton. Sheep are usually shorn of their wool in the spring but sometimes in both spring and fall. (See WOOL, subtitle *Shearing and Processing.*)

The size of flocks varies greatly. Farm flocks are usually small, ranging from 10 to several hundred animals. Range flocks, consisting of some 2,000 to 10,000 or more sheep, are raised on the open range where they feed on pasture. In these flocks the ewes usually give birth on the open range but in some cases may be provided with sheds. Farm flocks, on the other hand, are allowed to graze on pastures at certain times of the year, but at other times are provided with sheep barns and with feed such as alfalfa, clover, or silage. The ewes generally give birth in the sheep barns.

Although sheep require little care except at lambing time, they are susceptible to various diseases. These include foot rot, foot-and-mouth disease, internal parasites, bloat, and infestation with ticks, lice, mites, grubs, and maggots. (See FOOT-AND-MOUTH DISEASE; FOOT ROT; MANGE.)

History. There were domesticated sheep in southwestern Asia about 11,000 years ago. The origin of domestic sheep is not definitely known, but most zoologists believe that they are descendants of relatives of the wild sheep known as urial, argali, and mouflon. Domestic sheep spread from Asia to Europe between 3000 and 1000 B.C.; they were brought to Europe by the ancient Greeks. Sheep were important animals in Biblical times and figure in Jewish and Christian symbolism.

The first sheep were brought to the New World by Columbus on his second voyage in 1493. In what became the United States, the first sheep were introduced, into the Southwest, in the early 16th century by Spanish troops. The American colonies had sheep early in their history.

Wild Sheep

Wild sheep are found in North America, Asia, northern Africa, and certain parts of Europe. They are of no commercial importance although in Africa and Asia they are sometimes killed for their meat and hides.

There are eight species. Wild sheep range in body length from about 4 feet (1.2 m) to more than 6 feet (1.8 m), not including a 3- to 10-inch (7.5- to 25-cm) tail. Weight is from about 110 to 440 pounds (50-200 kg), depending on the species, individual, and sex. Wild sheep, like domestic sheep, live in flocks. Often it is difficult to tell wild sheep from wild goats; the two are closely related.

The aoudad, or Barbary sheep, lives in rough, barren, rocky areas of northern Africa. It has a reddish-tan color and a unique feature—a mane of long, soft hairs on the throat, chest, and upper parts of the forelegs. The horns, found on both male and female, are heavy and ridged and curve outward, backward, and then inward.

The bharal, also called burrhel, or blue sheep, is found in central Asia at elevations of about 12,000 to 16,000 feet (3,700-4,900 m). This species is distinguished by the shape of its horns, which are rounded and smooth, and curve backward and outward. They are borne by both sexes. The animal is blue-gray on the upper body and on the outside of the legs. The underparts and inside of the legs are white.

The other six species of wild sheep are all of the same genus and are sometimes referred to collectively as true sheep. This genus includes the bighorn sheep, Dall sheep, argali, urial (also called red sheep and Asiatic mouflon), Laristan sheep, and mouflon. In these species, color varies from whitish to gray or brown. Some have lighter markings. The males have massive spiral horns; the females have short horns that are only slightly curved. These sheep are found in fairly dry upland and mountainous areas.

(It is from members of this genus that most zoologists believe the domestic sheep developed.)

Two species are found in North America —the bighorn sheep and the Dall sheep. (See BIGHORN.) The Dall sheep is found in Alaska and northwestern Canada. It is usually white all over, although gray individuals are found occasionally.

The domestic sheep and true sheep belong to the genus *Ovis*. The domestic sheep is *O. aries;* the Dall sheep, *O. dallii*. The bharal is *Pseudois nayaur;* the aoudad, *Ammotragus lervia*. All are of the family Bovidae.

Books about Sheep

Clark, J. L. *The Great Arc of the Wild Sheep* (University of Oklahoma, 1994).

Ensminger, M. E. *Sheep and Goat Science*, 6th edition (Interstate, 1997).

Smith, Barbara, Mark Aseltine, and Gerald Kennedy. *Beginning Shepherd's Manual,* 2nd edition (Iowa State, 1997).

For Younger Readers

Hansen, A. L. *Sheep* (Abdo and Daughters, 1997).

Kalman, Bobbie. *Hooray for Sheep Farming!* (Crabtree, 1997).

Murray, Peter. *Sheep* (The Child's World, 1997).

Sheep Tick. See MITES AND TICKS.

Sheepdog. See DOG, subtitle *Breeds of Dogs:* Herding Dogs (Belgian Sheepdog, Old English Sheepdog, and Shetland Sheepdog).

Sheepshead, a food and game fish of the Atlantic and Gulf coasts of North America. Its black-banded body is a dark olive-green above and a dull silver below. The sheepshead attains a length of about 30 inches (76 cm) and a weight of about 20 pounds (9 kg). The chief foods of the sheepshead are shellfish such as crabs, mussels, and barnacles. Its prominent front teeth, which resemble those of a sheep, enable it to pick apart the

**Dall Sheep
(Rams)**
© Patrick J. Endres/
Visuals Unlimited

© Science
Visuals Unlimited

Sheepshead

shellfish and to scrape the barnacles off wharf pilings and rocks.

The sheepshead is *Archosargus probatocephalus* of the porgy family, Sparidae.

Sheet Metal Workers' International Association. See LABOR UNION (table).

Sheffield, England, a city in South Yorkshire. It lies on the Don River about 140 miles (225 km) northwest of London. Sheffield is a major industrial center, noted for the production of high-quality steels and cutlery. Heavy steel products, tools, and silverware are also manufactured.

Prominent buildings in Sheffield include Cutlers' Hall, completed in 1832, and the Cathedral of Saints Peter and Paul, which dates in part from the 1300's. Castle Hill is the site of the castle where Mary, Queen of Scots, was held prisoner, 1569-84. Housed in Graves Art Gallery is one of the foremost collections of paintings in northern England. The University of Sheffield, founded in 1905, specializes in metallurgy, engineering, and related sciences.

Sheffield was well known for cutlery as early as the 14th century. The invention here of Sheffield plate (silver fused on a copper base) and crucible steel in the 1740's brought rapid industrial growth to the city. It became a major steel center after Henry Bessemer put his steelmaking process into operation here in 1858. The first stainless steel was made on an experimental basis in Sheffield in 1913.

Population (district): 530,400.

Sheffield Plate. See SHEFFIELD.

Sheikh, or **Sheik,** both shēk, Arabic title of respect. It is used by Muslims throughout the Arab world. In the Arabian Peninsula, the title is applied to rulers of small Persian Gulf states, whose territories are called *sheikhdoms*. Tribal chiefs, village headmen

and elders, religious leaders, and others are also given the title.

Shelburne, William Petty, Second **Earl of** (1737-1805), a British statesman. As prime minister, 1782-83, Shelburne favored a policy of conciliation toward the United States. In 1783 he negotiated the Treaty of Paris, which recognized the independence of the former British colonies. Shelburne's political rivals used the unpopularity of the treaty in Parliament to build opposition to him, and he resigned his office.

Shelburne was born in Dublin. He attended Oxford and took his seat in the House of Lords in 1761. He was made Marquis of Lansdowne in 1784.

Shell. See AMMUNITION, subtitle *Artillery Ammunition*.

Shell (boat). See ROWING, subtitle *Competitive Rowing*.

Shell, the hard outer covering of various animals and of eggs. With the exception of turtles, most of the animals that have shells are either *crustaceans* (such as lobsters, shrimp, and crabs) or *mollusks* (such as clams, oysters, snails, and scallops). In its most common usage and in the remainder of this article, shell refers to the outer covering, called exoskeleton, of mollusks. For other shells, see CRUSTACEAN; EGG; TURTLE.

Some shells are so small they can hardly be seen without a microscope; the largest shell—that of the giant clam—may be four feet (120 cm) wide and weigh 500 pounds (230 kg). Most shells are either *bivalves* (made up of two parts hinged together, as in clams) or *univalves* (one part, as in snails). One group of mollusks, the chitons, have shells made up of eight plates.

Although not all mollusks have shells, there are thousands of species that do. The purpose of the shell is to provide protection. No two species have the same kind of shell, there being great variation in both shape and color. Often there are differences within the same species. Some shells have a tough glassy, porcelain-like surface; others have numerous spiny projections; still others have rough, granular, or ridged surfaces. Some species, such as the nautilus, have shells made up of many chambers.

Shell-bearing mollusks are found in seawater and freshwater, on land, and on plants. Univalves can be found in almost any type of habitat. Bivalves are mostly marine, although some species such as cer-

Scallop (*Chlamys senatorius*). Actual size.

tain clams and mussels are found only in fresh water. There are no land- or plant-dwelling bivalves. The warmer sea waters contain the largest number of species of shelled mollusks and the most colorful shells.

For description and classification of mollusks, see MOLLUSK.

Structure and Formation

A shell is typically made up of three distinct layers. The outer layer, called *periostracum,* is made up of a protein-like material called *conchiolin*. The two layers under the periostracum are composed of a framework of conchiolin in which is deposited calcium carbonate (the chief component of limestone) with traces of calcium phosphate and magnesium carbonate. In some mollusks, the molecules of the innermost layer are arranged in such a way that it is hard and iridescent; such a layer is commonly called mother-of-pearl.

Mollusks begin secreting their shells very early in life—while still in the larval forms. The shell is formed by various specialized cells in the mantle—a thin layer of tissue that covers all or part of the soft portion of the mollusk's body. The materials secreted by the mantle quickly solidify into the appropriate layer of shell. The shell increases in size when new material is added to the edge of the existing shell. In general, the older the animal, the larger the shell.

Uses of Shells

Shells are widely collected, traded, or bought for their beauty and rarity. Shells are often collected on beaches where they are cast ashore by waves. They are also collected by diving or dredging, digging at low tide, or, in the case of land mollusks, by searching for them in their natural habitat. Shells obtained with the animal still inside should be cleaned. In most instances, the animal is removed after the shell is boiled in

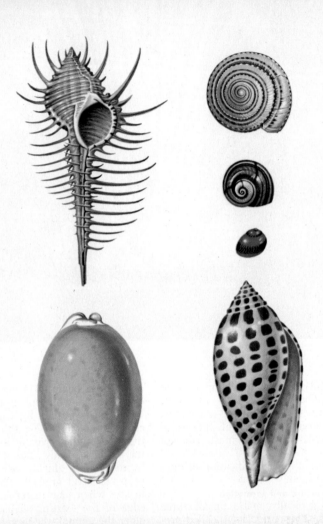

Clockwise from top left: **Venus Comb** *(Murex tenuispina)*, **Sundial** *(Archi-tectonica maximum)*, **Cuban Land Snail** *(Polymita picta)*, **Neritina** *(Neritina communis)*, **Junonia** *(Scaphella junonia)*, **Golden Cowrie** *(Cypraea aurantium)*

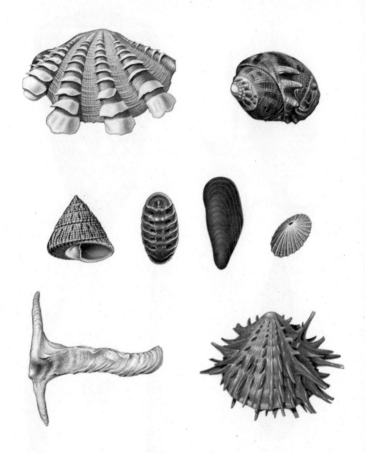

water for a few minutes. The shell's exterior can be cleaned with a stiff brush.

Shells have many uses in the arts. Their designs appear in many paintings and other works of art. Jewelry and decorative inlays on musical instruments and other objects are made from mother-of-pearl. Shells can be used as ornaments in themselves or to decorate various objects.

Cultures that have little advanced technology often use shells as domestic utensils, and certain peoples of Africa and the South Seas have used shells as money. Some of the American Indians used shells to make wampum. (See WAMPUM.)

Shells are used to make roadbeds in some parts of the world. They are burned and slaked to make lime for fertilizer, and they are crushed for use in animal feed. Shells can be useful in archeological studies. For example, shells known to be from a certain area but found in distant burial sites or ruins can help determine such things as trade routes. The fossil remains of shells play an important role in geology and paleontology.

See also ABALONE; ARGONAUT; CHITON; CLAM; COCKLE; CONCH; CONE; COWRIE; GEODUCK; LIMPET; MUSSEL; NAUTILUS; OYSTER; SCALLOP; SNAIL; WHELK.

Books about Shells

Buyer, R. L., and M. M. Towers. *Seashells* (Stackpole, 1996).
Harasewych, M. G. *Shells: Jewels from the Sea* (Courage, 1996).
Meinhardt, Hans. *The Algorithmic Beauty of Sea Shells* (Springer Verlag, 1995).
For Younger Readers
Lember, B. H. *The Shell Book* (Houghton Mifflin, 1997).
Tibbitts, C. K. *Seashells, Crabs, and Sea Stars* (Gareth Stevens, 1998).

Shell Oil Company, one of the largest companies in the United States oil industry. It is a leading producer of crude oil, natural gas, and natural-gas liquids. Shell Chemical Company, a division, manufactures petrochemicals, plastics, resins, and synthetic rubber.

Shell Oil Company had its origin in two companies formed in 1912. In 1939 these and another company combined to form Shell Oil Company. The new company was owned in part by the Royal Dutch Petroleum Company; in 1985 Royal Dutch became the sole owner. Shell headquarters are in Houston, Texas.

See also ROYAL DUTCH PETROLEUM COMPANY.

Shellac. See LAC.
Shellbark. See HICKORY.
Shelley, Mary Wollstonecraft Godwin. See SHELLEY, PERCY BYSSHE.
Shelley, Percy Bysshe (1792-1822), an English poet and social reformer. One of the greatest of England's Romantic poets, he is known best for such superb lyrics as "Ode to the West Wind," "The Cloud," and "To a Skylark." *Adonais* (1821), written on the death of the poet John Keats, is considered one of the greatest elegies in English literature. Shelley's poetry is rich in symbolism, and his images—drawn mostly from nature—are precise and striking. His poetry is predominantly serious and often melancholy, but some of it is witty and satirical.

Shelley hated tyranny and felt that all social institutions—including governments—tend to prevent human beings from cooperating with each other. He thought that a better society could be established only through mutual understanding and sympathy, not through coercion. He expressed these beliefs in prose as well as in such poetic works as *Prometheus Unbound* (1820), an allegorical drama based on the myth of the Titan who defied the gods to bring fire to mankind. Shelley did not advocate the violent overthrow of existing institutions but rather the gradual attainment of social improvement through democratic processes.

Shelley's theories were drawn from several sources. He was influenced by such philosophers as Plato, Baruch Spinoza, and George Berkeley. William Godwin, an English philosopher and author who became his father-in-law, perhaps exerted the strongest influence on Shelley's thought. Many of Shelley's ideas were impractical, but some of the reforms he advocated became part of English law.

Shelley's Life
Shelley was born at Field Place near Horsham, Sussex, the son of a country gentleman. He attended Eton, and in 1810 entered Oxford University. He and a friend, Thomas Hogg, were expelled in 1811 for writing and circulating a pamphlet titled *The Necessity of Atheism.*

In the same year, Shelley married Harriet Westbrook, a 16-year-old friend of his sisters. For more than two years the couple traveled in the British Isles, with Shelley spending much of his time writing pamphlets advocating political and social reform. During this

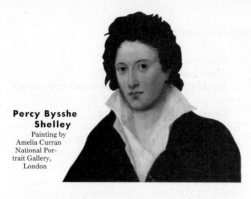

Percy Bysshe Shelley
Painting by
Amelia Curran
National Portrait Gallery,
London

time Shelley met Godwin, with whom he had corresponded for some time. In 1813 Shelley published *Queen Mab,* an imitative but powerful poem attacking what he felt was the tyranny of church and government.

Shelley and Harriet became estranged, and in 1814 he went to Switzerland with Godwin's daughter, Mary. For the next two years they divided their time between England and Switzerland, and Shelley wrote his first important poem, *Alastor* (1816). While in Switzerland Shelley met and began a friendship with the poet Lord Byron.

In 1816 Harriet drowned herself and shortly afterward Shelley and Mary were married. The following year Shelley was declared unfit to have custody of his two children by Harriet. They were placed in the care of Harriet's mother. Shelley had been in bad health for some time and he now became depressed. He and Mary left England permanently in 1818.

They settled in Italy, and during the remaining four years of his life the poet did his best work, which includes most of his short lyrics. Longer works of this period include—in addition to *Prometheus Unbound* and *Adonais—The Cenci* (1819), a tragedy in five acts, and *Epipsychidion* (1821), a poem inspired by his brief love for a young Italian noblewoman. Shelley's best prose work, *A Defence of Poetry,* was written in 1821 but not published until 18 years after his death, in 1840.

In the summer of 1822 the Shelleys were living in a villa on the Gulf of Spezia. On July 8 Shelley and a friend were caught in a sudden squall while sailing and their boat was overturned. The bodies were washed ashore and were burned on a pyre by Lord Byron and other friends. Shelley's ashes were buried near the grave of Keats in the Protestant cemetery in Rome.

Mary Wollstonecraft Shelley (1797-1851), Shelley's second wife, was a novelist. Her

best-known work is a Gothic novel, *Frankenstein* (1818). She was the daughter of William Godwin and Mary Wollstonecraft, an author and proponent of women's rights.

The Letters of Mary Wollstonecraft Shelley (three volumes) was published during 1980-88.

See also FRANKENSTEIN, OR THE MODERN PROMETHEUS.

Books about Percy Bysshe Shelley

Blank, G. K. *The New Shelley: Later Twentieth-Century Views* (St. Martin's, 1991).
Morley, Margaret. *Wild Spirit: the Story of Percy Bysshe Shelley* (Trafalgar Square, 1992).

Shellfish, a name given to various edible water animals that have a hard outer covering called a shell. Most of the animals called shellfish are either crustaceans (such as lobsters, shrimp, and crabs) or mollusks (such as oysters, clams, and mussels).

For further information, see CRUSTACEAN (and references); MOLLUSK (and references).

Shelter. See HOUSING.

Shem, in the Bible (Genesis 5-11), the oldest son of Noah. According to Hebrew tradition, Shem was the ancestor of the peoples now called *Semites,* a term derived from his name.

Shenandoah National Park. See NATIONAL PARKS, section "United States."

Shenandoah River, shěn′ăn-dō′a, a river of Virginia and West Virginia, known especially for its scenic and historic valley. It begins near Front Royal, Virginia, at the junction of the North Fork Shenandoah and the South Fork Shenandoah rivers. From here the river flows northeastward for 55 miles (89 km) to the Potomac River at Harpers Ferry, West Virginia.

The valley, which is a highly productive agricultural area noted for apples, is part of the Great Valley of the Appalachians. On the east it is bounded by the Blue Ridge Mountains; on the west, by the Shenandoah Mountains. Skyline Drive, winding through Shenandoah National Park in the Blue Ridge Mountains, affords spectacular views of the upper part of the valley.

During the Civil War the valley was the scene of two significant campaigns. Confederate General Stonewall Jackson defeated three small Union armies there in 1862. In late 1864 and early 1865 Union General Philip H. Sheridan routed Confederate forces and devastated the valley.

Shenandoah University. See UNIVERSITIES AND COLLEGES (table).

Shenyang, shŭn'yäng' (*Manchu:* **Mukden,** mōōk'dĕn'), China, the capital of Liaoning province. It is in southern Manchuria on the Hun River, 400 miles (640 km) east-northeast of Beijing, the national capital. Shenyang is a major railway and road junction. Located near sources of steel, iron, coal, and other industrial materials, it is one of China's chief industrial centers. Shenyang's many factories produce heavy machinery, machine tools, and other products. Its public library and museum are among the largest in China. Liaoning University is in Shenyang.

Shenyang was a Chinese settlement for centuries before the Manchus made it their capital (1625-44). Industrialization began in about 1900, while Manchuria was under Russian dominance. In 1905, during the Russo-Japanese War, Japan won a major battle at Shenyang. In 1931 Japan claimed that Manchurian troops had blown up a section of a Japanese-owned railway near the city and used the "Mukden Incident" as a pretext to seize the city and the rest of Manchuria. The Chinese Nationalists gained control of Shenyang after World War II but lost the city to Communist forces in 1948.

Population: 4,669,737.

Shoel. See HELL.

Shepard, Alan B. (Bartlett), **Jr.** (1923-1998), a United States astronaut. On May 5, 1961, he became the first American in space, riding in the *Freedom 7* capsule to an altitude of 115 miles (185 km). In 1971 he commanded the *Apollo 14* moon flight and became the fifth man to walk on the moon.

Shepard was born in East Derry, New Hampshire. After graduation from the U.S. Naval Academy in 1944, he served aboard a destroyer during World War II. He took flight training in 1947 and became a naval test pilot in 1950. Shepard was chosen as one of the seven astronauts in the Project Mercury program in 1959. During 1963-69, he was chief of the Astronaut Office at the Manned Spacecraft Center at Houston. Shepard was promoted to rear admiral in 1971. He retired from the navy in 1974 and became a business executive.

Shepard, Helen Miller Gould. See GOULD (family).

Shepard, Sam (Samuel Shepard Rogers) (1943-   ), a United States playwright and actor. Shepard's plays—surreal, violent, poetic, and experimental—embrace American history, the family, and popular culture. *Buried Child* (1978), for which he won a Pulitzer Prize, deals with a decaying rural family that harbors guilty secrets of incest and infanticide. Shepard was born at Fort Sheridan, Illinois, and was raised in California. He appeared in such films as *The Right Stuff* (1983), *Country* (1984), and *Fool for Love* (1985), the film version of his play of the same name.

Other plays include: *Cowboys* (1964); *Chicago* (1966); *Icarus's Mother* (1966); *Red Cross* (1966); *La Turista* (1967); *Operation Sidewinder* (1970); *The Tooth of Crime* (1972); *Action* (1974); *Curse of the Starving Class* (1977); *True West* (1979); *A Lie of the Mind* (1985); *Simpatico* (1994). Other writings include the short-story collections *Motel Chronicles* (1982) and *Cruising Paradise* (1996).

Shepherd College. See UNIVERSITIES AND COLLEGES (table).

Sheraton, shĕr'ȧ-t'n, **Thomas** (1751-1806), an English furniture designer. His books on design, including *The Cabinet-Maker and Upholsterer's Drawing Book* (1791-94) and *Cabinet Dictionary* (1802), influenced cabinetmakers in the rest of Europe and in America as well as in England. His strong, graceful, well-balanced furniture often featured straight lines, slender tapering legs, and ornamental porcelain plaques. Sheraton emphasized usefulness and designed folding tables, writing desks, and other furniture.

Sheraton was born in Stockton-on-Tees. Little is known of his life. It is thought he was trained as a cabinetmaker. There is no evidence that Sheraton ever owned a workshop.

See also FURNITURE, subtitle *Period Styles of Furniture:* England.

Sheraton Sideboard (about 1790)
Needham's Antiques, Inc.

Sherbet. See ICE CREAM.

Sherbrooke, shûr'brŏŏk, Quebec, Canada, the seat of Sherbrooke County. It is in southern Quebec at the junction of the Magog and St. Francis rivers, about 85 miles (137 km) east of Montreal. Sherbrooke is a commercial center and an industrial city, producing textiles, machinery, processed foods, clothing, and rubber products. The University of Sherbrooke, founded in 1954, is here. Near the city are extensive facilities for skiing and other winter sports.

Sherbrooke was founded in 1794 by Gilbert Hyatt, a Loyalist from Vermont, and was first called Hyatt's Mills. The name was later changed in honor of Sir John Sherbrooke, who was governor general of Canada, 1816-18. Sherbrooke was incorporated as a city in 1875.
Population: 76,429.

Sheridan, Philip Henry (1831-1888), United States army officer. A daring and aggressive cavalry officer, "Little Phil," as he was called by his men, was one of the most successful Union commanders in the Civil War.

Sheridan's Shenandoah Valley campaign of August, 1864 to March, 1865, resulted in the destruction of a Confederate army under

NEW STANDARD Collection
Philip Henry Sheridan

General Jubal A. Early and the devastation of the valley, which had been a major Confederate supply source. It was during this campaign that Sheridan made a ride of 14 miles (22.3 km) from Winchester, Virginia, to Cedar Creek in the midst of battle to rally his faltering troops and personally lead them to victory. His drive southward to block Lee's withdrawal from Petersburg helped force the Confederate surrender at Appomattox Court House, April 9, 1865.

Sheridan was born in Albany, New York, the son of Irish immigrants. He spent his boyhood in Ohio and won appointment to the United States Military Academy. After his graduation in 1853, he served as a lieutenant of infantry in Texas and in campaigns against the Indians in the Northwest.

Sheridan was an infantry captain in Missouri at the outbreak of the Civil War. He held various administrative posts before being appointed a colonel of cavalry. After a victory at Booneville, Mississippi, in 1862, Sheridan was transferred to the Army of the Cumberland, where he won promotions to brigadier general and to major general. Sheridan's success at Chickamauga and Chattanooga in 1863 led General Grant to name him commander of cavalry for the Army of the Potomac. He held this post until given direction of the Army of the Shenandoah in August, 1864.

Following the war, Sheridan was named commander of the military district of the Gulf and military governor of Texas and Louisiana. He pursued such stern Reconstruction policies, however, that President Johnson transferred him to Missouri. There Sheridan launched military operations against hostile Indians and forced them to settle on reservations. In 1884 he succeeded General Sherman as commanding general of the U.S. Army. Sheridan was made a full general in 1888. Also in that year his *Personal Memoirs* was published.

Sheridan, Richard Brinsley (1751-1816), an English playwright and politician. He was the most notable English dramatist of the 18th century. His witty, well-constructed plays are in the tradition of the 17th-century Restoration comedy of manners, ridiculing the foibles of fashionable society. Sheridan's reputation is based largely on *The Rivals* (1775) and *The School for Scandal* (1777), which are distinguished for their ingenious plots, brilliant dialogue, and colorful characterizations.

Sheridan was born in Dublin, the son of Thomas Sheridan, an actor, and Frances Sheridan, an author. His family later moved to England, where he attended Harrow School. *The Rivals, St. Patrick's Day,* and *The Duenna* (a comic opera) were all produced at Covent Garden in 1775. The following year Sheridan became part owner of the Drury Lane Theatre in London; he later became manager. His other plays, including *The Critic* (1779), were produced there. The theater burned in 1809, leaving him heavily in debt.

Sheridan was a member of Parliament from 1780 to 1812. He opposed the continuation of the war against the American colonies. He was known for his oratory and made two eloquent speeches urging the impeachment of Warren Hastings, governor general of India.

Sheriff, in the United States, a public official, usually elected, who is in charge of law enforcement in a county (or parish). A sheriff's principal duties are to enforce the law and to carry out decisions of the county court. A sheriff serves legal papers, summons jurors for the county court, and maintains the county jail. One or more deputy sheriffs may be appointed, and other persons may be deputized when needed. The office originated in England in about the ninth century. A sheriff was the king's overseer in a *shire,* the old term for county.

Sherlock Holmes. See DOYLE, Sir ARTHUR CONAN.

Sherman, Cindy (1954-   ), a United States photographer. She became known for unusual photos of herself that comment on female stereotypes in Western society. In *Untitled Film Stills,* a series of black-and-white photos created between 1977 and 1980, she used costumes, wigs, makeup, and lighting to portray herself as schoolgirl, housewife, librarian, film star, and other characters. Other photographic series, most in large color format, include *Rear Screen Projections, Centerfolds,* and *History Portraits.* In the 1990's she began using masks, mannequins, and other devices to create surreal, often grotesque, images.

Cynthia Morris Sherman was born in Glen Ridge, New Jersey, and attended the State University of New York at Buffalo, 1972-76. She settled in New York City in 1977.

Sherman, James Schoolcraft (1855-1912), the 27th Vice President of the United States. Sherman was born in Utica, New York. After he graduated from Hamilton College, he studied and later practiced law. A Republican, he was a U.S. Representative from New York, 1887-91 and 1893-1909. Sherman was elected Vice President as William Howard Taft's running mate in 1908. He was renominated in 1912 to run again with Taft but died before the election.

Sherman, John (1823-1900), a United States statesman and financial expert. He is best known for the two laws bearing his name, the Sherman Anti-Trust Act and the Sherman Silver Purchase Act. Sherman was especially influential in financial legislation, and he was known for his ability to reconcile differences by compromise. A prominent Re-

publican from Ohio for nearly 50 years, Sherman served in the U.S. House of Representatives (1855-61) and in the U.S. Senate (1861-77, 1881-97). He also served as secretary of the treasury (1877-81) and secretary of state (1897-98).

John Sherman, the younger brother of William Tecumseh Sherman, was born in Lancaster, Ohio. He was admitted to the bar in 1844.

Sherman, Roger (1721-1793), a United States patriot and statesman. He was the only person to sign all four of the documents that were most significant in the formation of the United States: the Association (a compact to boycott British goods, adopted 1774), the Declaration of Independence (1776), the Articles of Confederation (1781), and the Constitution of the United States (1787).

Sherman was born in Newton, Massachusetts, and became a shoemaker in early life. In 1743 he moved to Connecticut, where he practiced law and became prominent in business and politics. He was one of the first to deny that the British Parliament had a right to make laws for the colonies. Sherman

New Standard Collection
Roger Sherman

was an influential member of the Continental Congress (1774-81), serving on the committee that drafted the Declaration of Independence and helping to draw up the Articles of Confederation.

At the Constitutional Convention (1787) Sherman helped sponsor the Connecticut Compromise, settling the dispute between the large and small states over how much representation each state should have in Congress. (See UNITED STATES CONSTITUTION, subtitle *History:* The Constitutional Convention.) Sherman served in the first U.S. House of Representatives (1789-91) and in the U.S. Senate (1791-93).

Sherman, William Tecumseh (1820-1891), a United States army officer who was one of the great Union generals of the Civil War. A tough, tenacious soldier, Sherman sought to cripple the Confederacy's will to fight through a policy of total war. He was the first to use this tactic, now a part of modern warfare, when he deliberately laid waste

Library of Congress
William Tecumseh Sherman

the territory through which his army marched. Sherman's march to the sea— from Atlanta to Savannah—in 1864 hastened the collapse of the Confederacy, and left lasting bitterness in the South because of the devastation it caused. Sherman said at the time of the burning of Atlanta, "War is cruelty, and you cannot refine it." (He made his famous statement "War is hell" in 1880.)

A Soldier of Three Wars

Sherman was born in Lancaster, Ohio; his younger brother was John Sherman (later to be a United States senator). After graduation from the U.S. Military Academy in 1840, Sherman served in the Second Seminole War in Florida. He was an aide to Philip Kearny during the Mexican War but saw little action.

Sherman resigned his commission in 1853 to become a partner in a San Francisco bank; it failed in 1857. He practiced law briefly and unsuccessfully, then became superintendent of a Louisiana military academy (now the state university) in 1859. The state's secession from the Union in January, 1861, compelled him to resign his post. Although he hoped war could be averted, he felt that preservation of the Union was of the utmost importance.

During the months that preceded the outbreak of the Civil War, Sherman held the presidency of a St. Louis street railway company. In May, 1861, he reentered the army as a colonel of infantry. He fought at Bull Run in July, 1861. A month later, Sherman was made a brigadier general of U.S. Volunteers and commanded troops in Kentucky and Missouri. His courage at the battle of Shiloh (1862) won him promotion to major general of volunteers. Sherman was advanced to brigadier general in the regular U.S. Army for his leadership in the battle of Vicksburg in 1863. As commander of the Army of the Tennessee, he participated in the victorious Chattanooga campaign.

When General Grant became commander in chief in 1864, he put Sherman in charge of operations in the West. Sherman drove the Confederate forces back toward Atlanta

and, after winning a series of bitter battles, captured and burned the city. On November 12, 1864 he began the march through Georgia. Sherman and his troops cut a swath of devastation 20 to 25 miles (32 to 40 km) wide for more than 300 miles (480 km). (See CIVIL WAR, AMERICAN, map titled *The War in the West and Deep South*.) He reached Savannah and the sea on December 21, 1864, having broken the Confederate supply system. Sherman received the surrender of General Joseph E. Johnston's army, the only large Confederate force left in the field, in North Carolina on April 26, 1865.

Sherman was promoted to lieutenant general in 1866 and in 1869 succeeded Grant as commanding general with the rank of full general. He held that post until his retirement in 1884.

Sherman's *Memoirs* appeared in 1875.

Sherman, Texas, the seat of Grayson County. It is near the Oklahoma boundary in the Red River Valley. Sherman is the trade center for an agricultural region producing grains, cotton, and livestock. The city's manufactured goods include processed foods, electronic equipment, surgical supplies, and textiles. Austin College is here. Sherman was founded in 1846.

Population: 31,601.

Sherman Antitrust Act. See ANTITRUST LAWS.

Sherpas, a Tibetan people who live on the southern slopes of the Himalaya Mountains, in northeast Nepal and Sikkim. Sherpas have aided explorers as guides and porters for mountain-climbing expeditions since the 1920's. (For the best-known Sherpa, see TENZING NORGAY.) According to tradition, the Sherpas migrated from Tibet to Nepal about 600 years ago. Their religion is Lamaism, a form of Buddhism.

Sherrington, Sir **Charles Scott** (1857-1952), a British physiologist. For his research on the neuron, he shared the 1932 Nobel Prize for physiology with Edgar D. Adrian. Sherrington graduated from Cambridge and taught at several universities. He was knighted in 1922. His work *The Integrative Action of the Nervous System* (1906) became a classic in physiology.

Sherry. See WINE, subtitle *Types and Classes of Wine:* Appetizer Wines; Dessert Wines.

Sherwood, Robert Emmet (1896-1955), a United States playwright. He won four

Pulitzer Prizes—three for drama (*Idiot's Delight* in 1936; *Abe Lincoln in Illinois* in 1938; *There Shall Be No Night* in 1941) and one for biography (*Roosevelt and Hopkins* in 1948). Many of Sherwood's plays comment on the consequences of war. His interest in world peace led him to government service during World War II. He became associated with President Franklin D. Roosevelt and helped write many of his speeches.

Sherwood was born in New Rochelle, New York. He left Harvard University in 1917 to serve with the Canadian Expeditionary Force in World War I. Sherwood was on the editorial staffs of several magazines before the success of *The Road to Rome* (1927), his first Broadway play, induced him to spend all his time writing. A number of plays followed, including the comedy *Reunion in Vienna* (1931) and the melodrama *The Petrified Forest* (1935).

During World War II Sherwood served as director of the overseas division of the Office of War Information. After the war he wrote scripts for several motion pictures, including the Academy Award–winning *The Best Years of Our Lives* (1946). He collaborated with Irving Berlin on the musical comedy *Miss Liberty* (1949). In the 1950's he wrote a number of television plays.

His other plays include: *The Queen's Husband* (1928); *Waterloo Bridge* (1930); *The Rugged Path* (1945).

Sherwood Forest. See ROBIN HOOD.

Shetland Islands, a group of more than 100 islands in the Atlantic Ocean, forming the northernmost part of Scotland. The bleak, virtually treeless islands lie about 110 miles (180 km) northeast of the Scottish mainland. The total area is 550 square miles (1,425 km²). Only 16 of the islands are inhabited. Mainland, the largest, is the site of Lerwick, the principal town. Other islands include Yell, Unst, Fetlar, Whalsey, and Bressay.

The islanders live primarily by fishing and the raising of sheep and cattle. Only a few hardy crops, such as barley, oats, and potatoes, are grown. The Shetlanders are noted for their handmade knit goods and as the original breeders of Shetland ponies. North Sea oil has brought previously unknown prosperity to the islands. A large oil terminal is at Sullom Voe.

The Shetlands were originally settled by the Picts in about 200 B.C. In 875 A.D. the islands were annexed by the king of Norway. They remained a Norwegian possession until 1468, when they were mortgaged to Scotland as collateral against the payment of the dowry of Princess Margaret of Norway. The dowry was never paid, and Scotland annexed the islands in 1472.

Population: 22,017.

Shetland Pony. See HORSE, section "Breeds of Horses," subtitle *Important Breeds: Ponies* (and picture).

Shetland Sheepdog. See DOG, subtitle *Breeds of Dogs:* Herding Dogs.

Shevardnadze, she-värd-näd′ze, **Eduard** (1928-   ), a Soviet and Georgian statesman. In 1985 he came to international prominence as the Soviet Union's foreign minister. Shevardnadze was known for his diplomatic skill and his work toward improving foreign relations, particularly with Western nations. Amid growing political instability he resigned as foreign minister in 1990 but resumed the post for a short period in 1991 before the collapse of the Soviet Union that year. In 1992 Shevardnadze returned to his native Georgia, which had become an independent republic. He was elected head of the ruling council after the military ouster of President Zviad Gamsakhurdia and in 1995 was elected president.

Shevardnadze was born in Mamati, Georgia, then part of the Transcaucasian Soviet Federated Socialist Republic, and attended the Kutaisi Pedagogical Institute. He was first secretary of the Georgian Communist Party from 1972 to 1985.

Shevchenko, shĕf-chän′kô, **Taras** (1814-1861), a Ukrainian poet and artist. His poems calling for Ukraine's freedom from Russian domination made him a hero among his people and established his reputation as a nationalist author. His paintings and engravings reflect his hatred of serfdom.

Shevchenko was born a serf in the province of Kiev. His master, aware of Shevchenko's talent, apprenticed him to a portrait painter in St. Petersburg in 1832. Artist friends bought Shevchenko's freedom in 1838. He then entered a St. Petersburg art academy. *Kobzar* (1841) was his first collection of poems and *The Dream* (1844), his first important revolutionary poem. In 1847 his affiliation with a secret nationalist society was discovered; he was forced to enter the army and was sent to Central Asia. He returned to St. Petersburg in 1858.

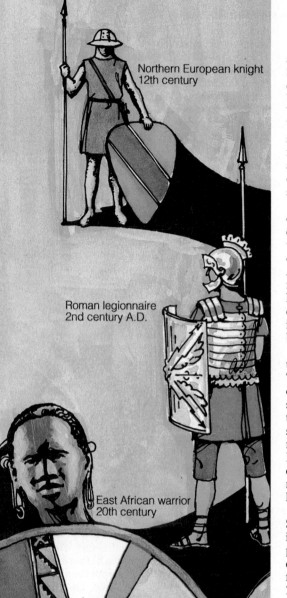

Northern European knight
12th century

Roman legionnaire
2nd century A.D.

East African warrior
20th century

Shield, a piece of armor carried on the free arm or in the hand not holding a weapon. Shields were used from early times to ward off missiles, such as arrows and spears, and blows from swords, clubs, or other weapons. With the development of effective firearms, beginning in the 14th century in Europe, shields ceased to be of value and gradually fell into disuse in the Western world, but they are still used in some places. In the mid-20th century the use of shields was revived in some areas for the protection of riot police.

The earliest shields were made of wood or of animal hides stretched tightly on a wooden frame. In the Far East shields made of woven wicker were common. Metal shields came into use in the latter part of the Bronze Age, about 1400 B.C. These usually were made of bronze hammered into a thin circular sheet. A *boss* (knob or spike) was placed on the outside center; opposite it on the inside was either a handle or straps. This became a common form of shield.

The Greek *hoplite* (heavily armed infantryman) carried a large round or oval shield. The Roman legionnaire first carried a flat, oval shield and later an oblong one with the sides curved in, which gave better protection. In Europe during the Middle Ages, shapes and sizes of shields varied greatly; the most common shape was roughly triangular. Knights marked their shields with symbolic designs, or *bearings,* by which they could be recognized. This practice was the origin of heraldry.

Shields, Carol (1935-   ), a United States–born Canadian author. In her writings Shields often focuses on the common people society overlooks, the details of domestic life, and the search for emotional fulfillment and personal identity. Her novel *The Stone Diaries* (1993) is the life story of a woman who has lived in Canada and the United States, experienced personal tragedies, and finds meaning in small triumphs. This book won a Pulitzer Prize in 1995 and brought Shields international recognition.

Shields was born Carol Warner in Oak Park, Illinois. In 1957 she graduated from Hanover College in Indiana and married Donald Shields, a Canadian citizen. She obtained Canadian citizenship in 1971.

Other works include: Novels—*The Box Garden* (1977); *Happenstance* (1980); *Swann* (1987); *The Republic of Love* (1992); *Larry's Party* (1997). Short-story collections—*Various Miracles* (1985); *The Orange Fish* (1989).

Shih Tzu. See DOG, subtitle *Breeds of Dogs: Toy Dogs.*

Shiitake. See MUSHROOM, subtitle *Non-poisonous Mushrooms.*

Shiites. See ISLAM, subtitle *Divisions.*

Shijiazhuang, also **Shihchiachuang** and **Shih-chia-chuang,** shĭr'jĭ-ä'jwäng', China, the capital of Hebei province, about 160 miles (260 km) southwest of Beijing. Shijiazhuang is a railway junction and manufacturing center. The city was a small agricultural village until early in the 20th century, when it became the junction point of two newly constructed railways.

Population: 1,300,000.

Shilling, a former coin of Great Britain and most other nations of the British Commonwealth. In the historical British coinage system, 12 pence equaled one shilling, and 20 shillings equaled one pound.

Originally, the shilling was an accounting unit; it came into use at about the time of the Norman Conquest (1066). British silver shillings were first minted during the reign of Henry VII (1485-1509). In 1946 an alloy of copper and nickel was substituted for silver. In 1968, as Britain began changing to a decimal coinage system, the shilling was replaced by a piece worth five new pence.

Several coins called shillings were minted in colonial North America; among them were pine tree and Maryland shillings.

See also COIN; NUMISMATICS (pictures); PINE TREE MONEY.

Shiloh, Battle of, shī'lō, or **Battle of Pittsburg Landing,** April 6-7, 1862, a decisive battle of the American Civil War. Confederate General Albert Sidney Johnston, driven out of Kentucky and most of Tennessee, gathered an army at Corinth, Mississippi, for a counteroffensive. Twenty miles (32 km) away, in Tennessee, camped around Shiloh Church, a Union army led by General U. S. Grant was awaiting the arrival of reinforcements under General Don Carlos Buell. Johnston's strategy was to defeat Grant before Buell could arrive.

The Confederate troops caught Grant's army off guard and almost won the battle on the first day, although Johnston was killed. The next day the Union troops, supported by Buell's army, which had arrived during the night, defeated the Confederates, then commanded by General P. G. T. Beauregard.

The battle, one of the bloodiest of the war, cost the Union about 13,000 casualties out of

about 55,000; the Confederacy, about 10,000 out of about 40,000. The defeat of the Confederates prevented the South from regaining Kentucky and Tennessee and assured further Union advances in the west.

The site of the battlefield is a national military park.

Shiloh National Military Park. See NATIONAL PARKS, section "United States."

Shimmy, See DANCE (table).

Shimonoseki, shĭm'ō-nō-sĕk'ĭ, Japan, a city in Yamaguchi prefecture. It lies on the southwestern tip of the island of Honshu on Shimonoseki Strait. Railway and highway tunnels under the strait link the city with Kitakyushu on Kyushu. Shimonoseki is a major port and an industrial center with foundries, shipyards, seafood-processing plants, and chemical works.

In 1185 the Minamoto clan annihilated the ruling Taira clan here and went on to establish a shogunate (military government), the form of government that ruled Japan for nearly 680 years. In 1864 the city was bombarded by American, British, French, and Dutch ships in retaliation for attacks by the daimyo (baron) of Choshu on foreign vessels passing through the strait. The treaty ending the Sino-Japanese War was negotiated and signed in Shimonoseki in 1895.

Population: 262,635.

Shimonoseki, Treaty of. See SINO-JAPANESE WAR, 1894-95.

Shiner. See MINNOW.

Shingle, a small, thin, flat or tapering piece of material used in surfacing roofs or exterior walls. Most shingles are of composite material. Asphalt shingles, for example, consist of roofing felt saturated with asphalt and covered with small pebbles on the exterior. Shingles are usually are nailed in place in an overlapping pattern. The amount of overlapping depends on the angle of the surface—the steeper the surface, the less overlapping is required.

Wood shingles are sometimes used, chiefly for decorative effects. *Shakes* are shingles that have been split from a piece of wood and show a rough, raised grain pattern; ordinary wood shingles are relatively smooth. Cedar is a common wood for shingles and shakes.

Shingles, or **Herpes Zoster,** in medicine, a viral infection of nerve tissue. Shingles is caused by the same virus that causes chicken pox. After a chicken pox infection, the virus remains dormant in nerve cells.

Revue
by Everett Shinn in 1908
oil on canvas
detail, about 17 by 10½ inches
(43.2 by 26.7 cm)
Whitney Museum of American Art, New York

Shinn, Everett (1876-1953), a United States painter and illustrator. He belonged to the group of painters derisively called the Ashcan School and was known especially for his paintings of the entertainment world, such as *London Hippodrome* and *Revue*. Shinn was born in Woodstown, New Jersey. He studied art in Philadelphia, and began his career as a newspaper illustrator there. Shinn also designed stage sets, painted murals, and wrote several plays.

Shinto, shĭn'tō, or **Shintoism,** a major Japanese religion. It is based on tradition and social institutions, and has no formal doctrine. Worship takes the form of a purification rite at a shrine.

Shinto, which means "Way of the Gods," began as a simple form of nature worship. Foremost among its thousands of deities was Amaterasu, the sun goddess. Added later were the spirits of a few emperors and national heroes. After Japan came under strong Chinese influence in the sixth century A.D., ancestor worship, Confucian ethics, and magical elements of Taoism were incorporated into Shinto. The religion was also influenced by Buddhism. By the ninth century Buddhist ideas permeated Shinto.

In the 1600's, a movement developed to make Shinto, with all Buddhist elements removed, a national faith. This movement made little headway until 1868, when the emperor abolished the shogunate (military government), and an official cult called State Shinto was organized. It was based on the heroic traditions of the Japanese people, and its purpose was to promote loyalty to the state. The emperor was worshiped as a descendant of the sun goddess. With Japan's defeat in World War II, Allied authorities forced the emperor to renounce his professed divinity and abolished the official status of Shinto.

Following the war, most of the shrines organized themselves into the Association of Shinto Shrines. Shinto also experienced a great increase in the number of sects.

Years later, the virus may again become active, causing shingles. Reactivation typically occurs in persons more than 50 years old who are ill from other diseases or who are experiencing stress. Blisters containing the virus form on the skin over infected nerves. Blisters that open release the virus, which can then cause chicken pox in persons who come in contact with the virus.

Fever, headache, and upset stomach usually appear three to four days before the blisters form. The blisters are typically limited to a band on one side of the face or on one side of the body from the middle of the chest or abdomen to the middle of the back. In three to five weeks the blisters dry up and disappear, and the pain ceases. However, in some cases, particularly in elderly persons, the pain can persist for months or years. This chronic nerve pain, called postherpetic neuralgia, usually indicates nerve damage. Complications of shingles include corneal damage and temporary facial paralysis.

Shingles is commonly treated with aspirin, to relieve pain, and calamine lotion, to relieve itching. Antiviral drugs, such as acyclovir, can usually lessen the severity and shorten the duration of a shingles attack.

Shingles is caused by the varicella-zoster virus, a herpesvirus.

Ship

Ship, a large oceangoing vessel. The term is also used for large vessels plying coastal waters or inland lakes and rivers. A boat is generally smaller than a ship, but there is no clear distinction between the two terms. An oceangoing tugboat, for example, may be much larger than a naval patrol ship. This article discusses large vessels used on oceans and inland waters such as the Great Lakes. Smaller vessels are discussed in the article BOATS AND BOATING.

Throughout history, men have used ships to trade, explore, and wage war. Until the development of the telegraph in the 19th century, ships provided the only means of communicating across oceans. Until air

Glossary

Aft, at, near, or toward the stern.

Amidships, at or near the middle of a ship.

Ballast, weight put in a ship to improve its stability; usually water carried in tanks serves as ballast.

Beam, the greatest width of a ship.

Bilge, the curved part of a ship's hull where the sides meet the bottom.

Bow, the forward part of a ship.

Bowsprit, a short pole extending forward from the bow.

Bridge, a superstructure amidships; also, the place from which a ship is navigated.

Bulkhead, any vertical partition, or wall, on a ship.

Capstan, a vertical, cylindrical winch used to move or raise anchors or other heavy objects.

Davit, a shipboard crane that projects over the side of the ship; used to raise and lower boats, cargo, and other items.

Deck, any horizontal partition, or floor, on a ship.

Deckhouse, any structure above the weather deck, surrounded by open deck.

Draft, the vertical distance from the waterline to the lowest part of a ship's bottom.

Fathom, a measure of length equal to six feet, used mainly to measure water depth.

Forecastle, a superstructure at the bow.

Freeboard, the distance from the waterline to the freeboard deck.

Freeboard Deck, the uppermost continuous deck, with permanent means of closing all openings exposed to the weather.

Galley, a ship's kitchen; also an ancient and medieval ship. See separate article, GALLEY, in this encyclopedia.

Hatch, an opening through a deck.

Helm, the wheel used to steer a ship; also, the entire steering gear and the rudder.

Hold, a compartment below decks for storing cargo or ballast.

Hull, the lower body of a ship.

Keel, the main structural part of a ship, consisting of a metal or wooden beam extending along the bottom centerline of the vessel.

Knot, a speed of one nautical mile per hour. See in this encyclopedia KNOT.

Pilot House, the place from which a ship is navigated.

Poop, a superstructure at the stern.

Port, the left side of a vessel, looking forward.

Porthole, a circular opening with a hinged cover in the side of a ship.

Starboard, the right side of a vessel, looking forward.

Stem, the forward edge of the bow.

Stern, the back part of a vessel.

Superstructure, any structure stretching the full width of the ship above the freeboard deck.

Ton, a measure of a ship's weight or volume. See illustration titled *Tonnage*.

Watch, a working period, usually four hours long; a dog watch is a two-hour working period. At sea, the day is usually divided into six watches, but sometimes into five watches and two dog watches. Bells sound every half hour during a watch. For the bell system, see in this encyclopedia CLOCK, subtitle *Special Kinds of Clocks:* Striking Clocks.

Waterline, a line painted on a ship's side indicating the level to which it sinks in the water.

Weather Deck, the uppermost continuous deck exposed to the weather.

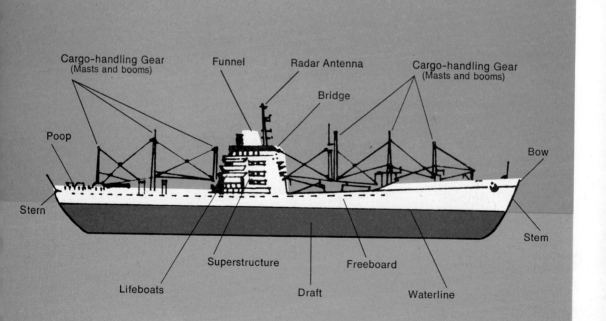

transportation became a reality in the 20th century, ships were the sole means of carrying travelers and cargo across oceans. Most of the world's great empires have been sea powers—masters of the seas in both commerce and war.

Parts of a Ship

Structure

Hull. The hull, or body, of a modern ship is usually made of steel. It houses cargo, fuel, machinery, and—on passenger and naval vessels—some of the living spaces. The hull's interior is subdivided by crosswise and lengthwise *bulkheads* (walls) and by one or more *decks* (floors). The uppermost continuous deck that has permanent means for closing all openings exposed to the weather is called the *freeboard deck*. On cargo ships the freeboard deck is usually also the *weather deck*—the uppermost continuous deck—but on passenger liners the freeboard deck may be one or more decks below the weather deck. Large ships have a *double bottom,* a series of compartments between the outer plating and the inner bottom that are used to carry fuel oil, fresh water, and water ballast.

Superstructures and Deckhouses. The part of a ship above the freeboard deck is commonly called the *superstructure*. Technically, however, the term superstructure is used only for a part of the ship's upper structure that extends the full width of the ship. A structure that does not extend the full width—that is, a structure surrounded by open deck—is called a *deckhouse*. The upper part of a ship may be composed of one or more superstructures or deckhouses, usually made of steel, but sometimes of aluminum.

There is much variation in the layout of the superstructures and deckhouses on different types of ships. Common superstructures include the following:

Forecastle (pronounced fōk′s′l), a partly or completely enclosed space at the bow.

Poop, a partly or completely enclosed space at the stern.

Bridge, a partly or completely enclosed space amidships.

The forecastle and poop contain living quarters, machinery, or supplies. The navigating and communications equipment is usually located at the top of the bridge, or in one or more deckhouses set on the bridge. In bridgeless vessels, the navigating and com-

Tonnage

Methods of Measuring Ships and Ship Capacity

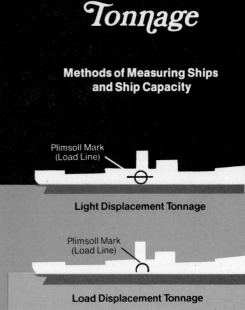

Plimsoll Mark
(Load Line)

Light Displacement Tonnage

Plimsoll Mark
(Load Line)

Load Displacement Tonnage

Displacement Tonnage is the weight of water displaced by a ship, which is equal to the weight of the ship itself. Displacement tonnage is expressed in *long tons* (a long ton equals 2,240 pounds), or *metric tons* (or *tonnes;* a metric ton equals 2,205 pounds). A ship's *light displacement* is its weight when empty. Its *load displacement* is its weight when fully loaded; it includes cargo, fuel, crew, and provisions. The size of warships is generally given in load displacement tons.

Deadweight Tonnage is the weight of cargo, fuel, stores, passengers, and crew a ship may legally carry. The deadweight tonnage is expressed in long tons or metric tons. It is equal to the difference between the ship's load displacement and light displacement. The size of freighters and tankers is generally given in deadweight tons.

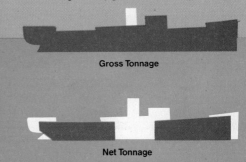

Gross Tonnage

Net Tonnage

Gross Tonnage is most of the internal volume of a ship's enclosed spaces. Gross tonnage is expressed in *register tons* (a register ton equals 100 cubic feet of space). The size of passenger ships is normally given in gross tons.

Net Tonnage is the gross tonnage minus the volume of most noncargo and nonpassenger spaces. The net tonnage, also given in register tons, is roughly equal to the volume of the ship's money-earning spaces. Harbor and canal fees are based on net tonnage.

munications gear is located in a midship deckhouse or in one or more deckhouses set on the forecastle or poop. Regardless of where the major pieces of navigating equipment are located, that place is usually called the *navigating bridge* or the *pilothouse*. Supplementary navigating gear is in a nearby compartment, called a *chart room* or *chart house*. Communications equipment is located in the *radio room*.

Propulsion and Steering Machinery

Propeller. Projecting from the hull are one or more propellers. There are two types in use today—the *screw propeller* and the less common *cycloidal propeller*.

A screw propeller consists of two to six blades mounted on a hub attached to the end of a drive shaft projecting from the stern. As the drive shaft turns, the blades rotate to push the ship forward. When the rotational direction of the drive shaft is reversed, the blades rotate in the opposite direction, moving the vessel backward. A screw propeller with movable blades, called a *controllable-pitch propeller,* can be adjusted to move a vessel backward without reversing the motion of the drive shaft. Most ships have one propeller, but some use multiple propellers (generally two or four).

A cycloidal propeller consists of a number of vertical blades mounted around a ring on the bottom of a vessel. The blades' pitch can be adjusted so the propeller will move the vessel forward or backward, turn it to the left or right, or hold it stationary in a strong current or tide. Cycloidal propellers are used mainly on tugboats and oceanographic research ships.

Propulsion Engines. Each propeller shaft is turned by one or more propulsion engines, located below decks in the *engine room*. Steam turbines are used as engines on most of the world's large ships and, in the United States, on medium-sized vessels also. Diesel engines are favored for medium-sized ships outside the United States.

A simple steam turbine power plant consists of an oil-fueled boiler for heating water to steam, a steam turbine, and a condenser for turning the steam back into water. A steam turbine, when used at greatest efficiency, turns too fast to operate the propeller directly and is therefore linked to the propeller shaft through a speed-reducing device—either a set of reduction gears (in the geared turbine) or an electric generator connected to a low-speed electric motor (in the turbo-electric drive).

A diesel engine burns diesel fuel. The engine may operate the propeller shaft directly or turn it through a set of reduction gears (in the geared diesel engine) or an electric generator-and-motor combination (in the diesel-electric drive).

Other engines used on ships include the steam engine, the gas turbine, and the nuclear reactor power plant (the reactor heats water for a steam turbine).

Engine Room Control Console aboard a naval vessel. The engineering officer (in white hat) is starting the main engine.
Deborah J. Huston
Bath Iron Works Corp.

© Cameramann International, Ltd.

Navigation Bridge of a cruise ship. The officer is monitoring a radar screen to detect any nearby vessels.

See also DIESEL ENGINE; STEAM ENGINE (and illustration); TURBINE, subtitles *Steam Turbine Power Plant* and *Gas Turbine.*

Rudder. Attached to the stern of a screw-propeller ship, behind the propeller or propellers, is the *rudder.* This is a flat plate or a streamlined structure formed by two slightly curved plates. It is pivoted to the right or left to steer the ship. The rudder is controlled by a steering wheel on the navigating bridge (or in the pilothouse) or by a device called an *automatic pilot.* The rudder is turned by a steering engine at the stern.

A cycloidal-propeller ship does not have a rudder.

Navigating and Communicating Equipment

Navigating-bridge Equipment. Instruments and equipment commonly found on the navigating bridge (or in the pilothouse) include the following:

Magnetic Compass, which indicates the direction the ship is traveling with reference to magnetic north. (See COMPASS, subtitle *The Magnetic Compass.*)

Gyrocompass Repeater, which indicates the ship's direction with reference to true north. The repeater is operated by the ship's master gyrocompass, installed below decks. (See COMPASS, subtitle *Nonmagnetic Compasses:* The Gyrocompass.)

Wheel, for steering the ship. Out at sea, some ships use a gyrocompass-controlled automatic pilot that keeps the vessel on a predetermined course, sending

orders to the steering engine whenever necessary. (See AUTOMATIC PILOT; COMPASS, subtitle *Nonmagnetic Compasses:* The Gyrocompass.) However, a ship still has a wheel for use in emergencies and when maneuvering is necessary.

Ship-control Console, for controlling the speed of the ship. In most modern ships, the engines are controlled directly from the bridge. In other ships, engine speed orders are transmitted by a signaling device to a person on watch in the engine room who operates the engine controls.

Depth Sounder, which shows the depth of the sea in feet, fathoms, or meters.

Radio Navigational Instruments, which use radio waves to determine the ship's location. (See DIRECTION FINDER; GLOBAL POSITIONING SYSTEM; LORAN; RADIO BEACON.)

Radar Scope, which shows the direction and distance of objects in the ship's vicinity. (See RADAR.)

Log Speed Indicator, which shows the speed of the ship in knots. (See LOG, subtitle *Mechanical Logs.*)

Log Distance Recorder, which shows the distance the ship has traveled. (See LOG, subtitle *Mechanical Logs.*)

Tachometer, which shows the rotational speed of the engine drive shafts. (See TACHOMETER.)

Telephones or Voice Tubes, for communicating with other parts of the ship.

Chart-room Equipment. The chart room (or chart house) usually contains the chronometer, sextant, and marine charts. The chronometer is a highly accurate clock used to keep Greenwich mean time. (See CHRONOMETER.) The sextant is an instrument for making celestial observations to determine the ship's location. (See SEXTANT.) The marine charts depict well-traveled waterways, showing such details as depth of water, rocks, shoals, and islands; currents, storm paths, and prevailing winds; and beacons and lighthouses.

Radio-room Equipment. The radio room usually contains three types of equipment— a radiotelephone, for sending and receiving voice messages; a radiotelegraph, for sending and receiving coded messages using the dots and dashes of the International Morse Code; and a radio teletypewriter, for sending and receiving typewritten messages.

Other Equipment

Stabilizers. To reduce rolling (rocking from side to side) in rough seas, a ship is equipped with stabilizers. Common stabilizers include the following:

Bilge Keels, a pair of fixed fins, one running along each side of the ship.

Gyro-controlled Fins, a pair of small, movable fins activated by a gyroscope within the ship. As the ship begins to roll, the gyroscope senses the movement and tilts the fins up or down to counteract the roll. The fins are retracted into the hull when they are not needed.

Antiroll Tanks, a pair of large tanks, one built into each side of the ship, connected by a duct or a center tank. Each tank is partially filled with water or other liquid. As the ship rolls from side to side, the liquid slowly flows from one side of the ship to the other. The liquid shifts at a rate that is slightly slower than the ship's rate of roll, thus retarding the roll.

Gyro-controlled Antiroll Tanks, similar to antiroll tanks, except that gyroscope-controlled pumps begin transferring the liquid from one tank to another as a roll begins. The rapid shifting of the liquid thus partially counteracts the ship's tendency to roll.

Deck Machines. Winches, capstans, and windlasses are hand- or power-driven machines with one or more revolving drums. Winches are used primarily for hoisting cargo; capstans, for handling heavy ropes; and windlasses, for raising and lowering anchor chains.

Cargo-handling Gear. Most ships transfer cargo by means of booms supported by masts or kingposts. Some ships use cranes or conveyor belts to transfer dry cargo. Liquid cargo is loaded and unloaded by pumps.

Anchor. A ship normally carries three anchors, two at the bow and one at the stern. (See ANCHOR.)

Other Apparatus. In addition to the propulsion and deck equipment, a ship has apparatus to provide heating, lighting, ventilation, air conditioning, refrigeration, fresh water, and water drainage.

Types of Ships

Ships vary in length from about 100 feet (30 m) to more than 1,000 feet (300 m). Their maximum speed ranges from about 10 knots (12 mph, or 19 km/h) to more than 30 knots (35 mph, or 56 km/h). Nearly all ships are displacement-type vessels; that is, they are buoyed up by a force equal to the weight of the water they displace. Some, however, travel above the surface of the water, supported by a cushion of air or by wings, called *hydrofoils,* projecting down from the hull. (See AIR CUSHION VEHICLE; HYDROFOIL CRAFT.)

All ships have certain characteristics in common, but the size and design of ships may differ radically. There are many ways of classifying and identifying the various types of ships. The most common ways are by use, type of propulsion, number of propellers, and type of construction.

Classification by Use

Ships are grouped into two main categories by use—*naval ships* and *merchant ships*. The navies of the world have a large variety of vessels for combat, for keeping the com-

batant ships ready to fight, and for performing special tasks, such as breaking channels through ice or doing oceanographic research. For a description of United States naval vessels, see NAVY, UNITED STATES, subtitle *Ships and Aircraft*.

Merchant vessels are divided into the following categories:

Passenger Ships, which are defined by international safety regulations as oceangoing vessels carrying 13 or more passengers. The U.S. Maritime Administration classes a vessel as a passenger ship if it carries 100 or more passengers. Passenger ships range from combination passenger-cargo vessels with a small passenger capacity to *ocean liners,* ships carrying hundreds of passengers and very little cargo. Some passenger ships operate on a fixed schedule, providing transportation over a specific route. Others, called *cruise ships,* make leisurely round-trip cruises with stops for sightseeing ashore. Some ships make regular transatlantic runs in the summer and cruises in the winter.

A large ocean liner, called a *superliner,*

Some Types of Ships

The ships pictured here are examples of their types. Within a type there may be wide variance in size and speed.

Supertanker; 990 feet (302 m); typical speed, 16 knots

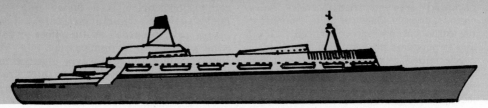

Passenger Superliner; 900 feet (274 m); typical speed, 27 knots

Containership; 810 feet (247 m); typical speed, 26 knots

Great Lakes Ore Carrier; 730 feet (223 m); typical speed, 16 mph*

Tanker; 520 feet (158 m); typical speed, 16 knots

Freighter; 480 feet (146 m); typical speed, 16 knots

Oceangoing Tug; 120 feet (37 m); typical speed, 11 knots

*The speed of vessels on the Great Lakes and inland waters is measured in statute miles per hour; 16 mph equals about 14 knots.

carries some 1,000 to 2,000 passengers. Such ships require a large crew, usually 500 to 1,000 persons. In addition to the dining and recreational facilities found on smaller passenger ships, a superliner may have a bank, hospital, chapel, large movie theater, art gallery, gymnasium, shooting gallery, sauna bath, beauty shop, barber shop, dog kennel, and shops.

Freighters, which carry packaged dry cargo and bulky goods such as lumber and machinery. On a conventional freighter, the packaged cargo is carried in crates, bales, cartons, barrels, bags, or rolls. Sometimes the cargo packages are palletized (stacked and strapped on platforms called pallets).

Specialized freighters are of various types. The *reefer* has refrigerated holds for carrying perishable goods. The *car carrier* carries loaded railway freight cars. The *container- ship* transports goods in standardized containers. The *roll-on-roll-off ship* has ramps for rolling motor vehicles or wheeled cargo containers on and off the ship. There are also giant freighters that carry loaded barges; the barges and their cargo can travel on inland waterways before and after the sea voyage.

A multipurpose freighter carries cargo in two or more ways—as, for example, in containers and in palletized shipments. Most freighters operate on a fixed schedule. However, some freighters, called *tramps,* travel to wherever cargo is available and wherever it is to be shipped.

Bulk Carriers, which transport unpackaged dry cargo. Common types of cargo include sugar, ore, coal, grain, and cement.

Tankers, which are fitted with tanks for carrying liquids or semiliquids in bulk. Their most common cargo is oil, but tankers also carry such products as molasses, wine, liquid sulfur, liquefied natural gas, and wood pulp. Some tankers have refrigerated, heated, or pressurized tanks. Large tankers, called *supertankers,* are the biggest ships afloat. An increasing number exceed 1,000 feet (300 m) in length and 100,000 tons in deadweight. (See TANKER.)

Other Classifications and Types

Type of Propulsion. A ship with a steam engine or steam turbine is called a *steamship.* A vessel with a diesel or other internal-combustion engine is a *motor ship.* A nuclear-powered ship is a *nuclear ship.* The *sailing ship,* propelled by the effect of the wind on sails, is a disappearing type. A commercially unsuccessful type invented in the 20th century was the *rotor ship,* propelled by the effect of the wind on revolving metal cylinders, called rotors.

The name of each ship is usually preceded by a set of initials designating its type of propulsion—"SS" for steamship, "MS" for motor ship, or "NS" for nuclear ship. Not all sets of initials, however, indicate the type of propulsion. Those with other meanings include "USS," for United States ship; "HMS," for His (or Her) Majesty's ship; "FV," for fishing vessel; and "TSS," for twin-screw ship.

Number of Propellers. Screw propeller ships are classed as single-screw, twin-screw, or multiple-screw vessels.

Type of Construction. The layout of a ship's superstructures and deckhouses gives rise to such classifications as *three-island ship* (with forecastle, bridge, and poop); *quarter-deck ship* (with combined bridge and poop); and *trunk-decked ship* (with small forecastle, no bridge, and large poop), a design common to tankers and bulk carriers.

Operation of a Ship

Crew Organization

A ship is commanded by an officer called a *master,* who is by courtesy addressed as "Captain." He supervises the work of the crew, which ranges in size from some 30 men on a cargo vessel with the maximum amount of automated equipment to more than 1,000 persons on a superliner. A typical cargo ship carries a crew of 36 to 55 men.

The crew is divided into four main departments. The *deck department* navigates the ship and does hull and deck maintenance work. The *engine department* operates and maintains all the ship's machinery. The *steward's department* does cooking and housekeeping, and the *radio department* transmits and receives radio messages. In addition, large passenger ships have a *purser's department,* which does bookkeeping and takes care of the comfort of the passengers, and a *medical department.*

Running a ship is a 24-hour job, so the day is divided into *watches* (working periods), each of which is usually four hours

Cargo Handling. *Above,* deck machinery hoisting containerized cargo, which will be stowed in the hold or on deck. *Right,* deckhand directs the loading of wheat.

© Cameramann International, Ltd.

long. A crew member of a typical cargo ship works two watches a day; he is usually on duty for one watch and then off duty for two watches.

The crew of a typical cargo steamship includes the following persons:

Deck Crew. The *first mate* assigns work to the crew, supervises the handling of cargo, and helps the captain bring the ship in and out of port. The *second mate* is in charge of the navigating equipment. The *third mate* takes care of the navigating bridge (or pilothouse), the chart room, and the lifesaving equipment. The mates take turns navigating the ship and keeping a record of the ship's operation in the deck logbook. (For the methods of navigating, see Navigation.)

The *boatswain* (pronounced bō's'n) supervises the deck work crew, which is usually composed of one or more *carpenters,* six *able-bodied seamen,* and three *ordinary seamen.* Carpenters on modern steel vessels are concerned primarily with repairing and maintaining the bracing that keeps the cargo from shifting. Able-bodied seamen act as lookouts, take turns at steering, and do maintenance work. Ordinary seamen do maintenance and odd jobs.

Engine Crew. The *chief engineer* is responsible for all of the ship's machinery. He usually has three assistants, who take turns controlling the main engines and supervising the work of the engine-room gang. This gang consists of *oilers,* who oil the machinery; *water tenders,* who regulate the water in the boilers; *firemen,* who regulate the oil burners under the boilers; and *wipers,* who do odd jobs. On some modern ships, one crew member controls the main engines, boilers, and oil burners from a central control panel in the engine room.

Steward's Crew. The *chief steward* purchases food and supervises the work. The *cooks* prepare meals. *Utility men* and *messmen* do the other cooking chores and the housekeeping.

Other Crew Members. A typical cargo ship has one radio officer. (International law requires that the radio be monitored only during certain hours.) Some cargo ships have a *purser,* an officer who does bookkeeping, or a *purser-pharmacist,* a purser qualified to give first aid and treat minor physical ailments.

Dangers at Sea

The gravest dangers at sea are collision and grounding, fire, and storms and rough seas. Any of these may make it necessary to abandon ship. Each ship must carry at least one life preserver for each person on board and enough lifeboats to hold the passengers and crew.

Collision and Grounding. To reduce the possibility of colliding with an obstacle or running aground, a ship's officers use marine charts, navigation instruments, and man-made landmarks—such as lighthouses, buoys, and radio beacons—to keep on a safe course. When visibility is poor, a ship posts lookouts in addition to using its radar to detect approaching ships, icebergs, and other obstacles. Ships in the North Atlantic obtain reports on the movement of icebergs from the U.S. Coast Guard.

To prevent ship collisions, ships follow traffic rules established by the world's maritime nations for ocean travel and by individual nations for coastal and inland-water travel. These *rules of the road* give directions for passing another vessel; for crossing the course of another vessel; for indicating the presence and course of one's own ship; and for sending distress signals.

At night, for example, a moving power-driven ship carries *running lights*—a red light on its port side, a green light on its starboard side, two white range lights on its masts, and one white light at its stern. An anchored vessel carries a white anchor light at its bow and, if longer than 150 feet (45.7 m), at its stern. During fog and other conditions of poor visibility, a moving ship sounds blasts on a whistle, siren, or fog horn; an anchored ship rings a bell and, sometimes, a gong. In coastal and inland waters, approaching ships indicate their planned courses by sound signals. On the high seas, approaching ships use sound signals to indicate changes of course.

In case of minor damage from collision or grounding, a ship is protected from sinking by its hull construction. The hull is divided into a series of buoyant compartments by watertight bulkheads and decks. If one compartment—or, sometimes, more than

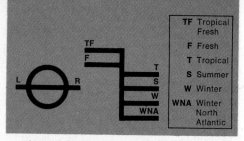

TF	Tropical Fresh
F	Fresh
T	Tropical
S	Summer
W	Winter
WNA	Winter North Atlantic

Plimsoll Mark. The line bisecting the circle is the load line for summer salt water. It is marked with the initials of the authorizing body, in this case, Lloyd's Register of Shipping. Beside it are lines for other types of water.

one—is flooded, most ships can still stay afloat. The passageways through the watertight bulkheads are covered by sliding watertight doors, which can be simultaneously closed from the navigating bridge.

Fire. Fire is one of the greatest dangers to a ship alone at sea. Ships have smoke- and fire-detecting equipment, fire mains and hoses, hand fire extinguishers, and, sometimes, automatic extinguishing systems. Fire-resistant and fireproof materials are used wherever possible.

Overloading. To prevent dangerous overloading, merchant ships must abide by certain load limits. A ship may carry more cargo when it navigates calm seas than when it navigates rough seas. In summer, for example, a heavier load is permitted than in winter because the ocean is usually calmer in summer than in winter.

Each cargo ship has a set of markings on its side, called a *Plimsoll mark,* indicating how deep in the water the ship may ride for various voyages. The markings show the maximum depth in the water (and thus the maximum load) for voyages in tropical fresh water, summer fresh water, tropical salt water, summer salt water, winter salt water, and winter-North Atlantic salt water. An oceangoing passenger ship usually has only two markings, one for salt water and one for fresh water.

Shipbuilding

Japan dominates the shipbuilding industry, usually accounting for almost half of the tonnage launched annually. Other major shipbuilders are South Korea, Germany, Italy, and Denmark.

Designing

The general design of a new ship depends upon the purpose for which the ship will be used, the depth of the harbors and canals it will visit, and the owner's specifications regarding such factors as speed and carrying capacity. Following those guidelines, a naval architect draws up detailed plans for the vessel. In the course of this work, the architect may make and test scale model ships in a small indoor tank to determine the best shape for the hull and the size of engines required.

Manufacturing

A ship's parts may be manufactured in several ways:

Shipbuilding. Steel parts, cut to shape by following patterns, are laid out in a large workroom before assembly *(above)*. In the conventional method of assembly, sections called subassemblies are constructed and then joined on the shipway *(below)*.

E. Mirsch/Newport News Shipbuilding

Conventional Method. The lines shown on the architect's plans are drawn full-scale on the floor of a large room called a *mold loft*. From the full-size drawing, workers then make a wooden or paper template (pattern) of each part of the ship's hull and superstructure. In a separate lay-off area, each template is laid on a plate of steel and outlined in chalk or paint. Then the template is removed and the steel is cut and shaped to make the part.

Other Methods. In the photo lay-off process, each of the architect's drawings is photographed and the resulting negative is made into a glass slide. Each slide is then used to project a full-size outline of the drawing on a steel plate. Workers trace the outline on the steel and cut out the part. In the photoelectronic lay-off process, each of the architect's drawings is fed to a machine that simultaneously "reads" the drawing and by remote control guides torches that cut the part out of a steel plate.

Assembling

In the conventional method of assembly, the parts are welded and riveted into large units, called *subassemblies,* some as big as houses. Then cranes move the subassemblies outdoors to a platformlike structure, called a *shipway* or the *ways*. There the subassemblies are riveted and welded together, from

S-375

Launching takes place when the steel shell of the ship is completed. The ship shown here is being launched sideways. The ship is then towed to an outfitting pier, where workers finish its construction.

the keel subassemblies up, to form the hull. As the hull takes shape, workers usually start to install some of the ship's internal equipment. In a few modern shipyards, assembly time is greatly reduced by using a moving assembly line to carry parts from one operation to the next.

When the hull and superstructures are finished, the ship is christened and launched. It may be launched by sliding it from the shipway end first or sideways, or by flooding the shipway to float it out. (The choice of launching method is made before construction begins.) At launching, a ship is generally only two-thirds completed. It is towed to an outfitting pier, where workers install the rest of its internal equipment. (A time-saving technique used in some yards is to install most or all of the internal equipment as the hull is being constructed, rather than after launching at its outfitting pier.) The completed ship is then given sea trials to check its performance before delivery to its owner.

History

Ancient Ships

When people first ventured on water, they probably rode astride logs or other floating objects, such as bundles of reeds or inflated animal skins. Later, they lashed several floating objects together to form rafts. They also learned to hollow out logs to make dugouts and to stretch animal skins over wooden frames to make hide boats. When people first used such craft, they probably poled or paddled them along, then they learned to row them. The sail was invented in Egypt about 4000 B.C., for traveling against the current on the Nile River.

The first people known to have built large vessels were the Egyptians. By 2500 B.C., they were constructing ships some 100 feet (30 m) in length. Lacking tall trees, they pegged together short lengths of timber to make a long hull, which they strengthened with a rope pulled taut from bow to stern. Egyptian ships had several pairs of oars for rowing and one or more pairs of oars lashed to the sides of the stern for steering. A single square sail was hoisted for sailing before the wind.

The Phoenicians and Greeks built sturdy vessels equipped with oars, a single square sail, and a pair of side rudders. Their warships were long, narrow vessels called *galleys,* while their merchant ships were shorter, wider craft. In combat, the galley's sail was lowered and the craft was propelled by oarsmen sitting on each side of the ship, sometimes in several tiers. The merchantman relied mainly on its sail for propulsion, but was rowed when becalmed. Both types of ships were *carvel-built,* that is, made with planks joined smoothly edge to edge, not overlapping.

Through ancient and medieval times, the narrow galley and beamy merchantman were the two main types of ship on the Mediterranean. The Romans improved both types by adding a second square sail, called an *artemon;* it was hoisted on a pole that slanted forward over the bow. The artemon provided little extra pulling power, but it helped in steering. The Romans also added a raised lookout platform to the bow or stern of some of their ships. Some Roman galleys reached a length of 200 feet (60 m).

Medieval Ships

After the fall of the Roman Empire, the Byzantine navy dominated the Mediterranean. Little is known about Byzantine ships in early medieval times. The best-known ship from that period is the Viking *longship,* a long narrow vessel with oars and a single square sail. Some longships have been preserved in the burial mounds of Norse chieftains. The Vikings also had shorter, sturdier vessels for cargo carrying. Unlike the carvel-built Mediterranean vessels, the Viking ships were *clinker-built,* that is, made of overlapping planks. Viking ships were steered by a single rudder that was usually set on the right side, giving that side the name *steerboard* ("steering side"), later *starboard.* The rudderless side was turned to the quay in port, giving the left side the name *port.*

As northern European ocean commerce grew, the Viking types gave way to a sturdier craft with a larger cargo capacity. A raised fighting platform, called a *castle,* was built at each end of the ship for defense. Sometime during the 12th or 13th century, the stern rudder was introduced, perhaps from the Far East. It made the ship easier to maneuver. By the early 14th century, the typical merchant and war vessel in northern and western Europe was the *cog,* a sturdy clinker-built ship with a single square sail, a stern rudder, forecastle, and aftercastle (or poop).

Meanwhile, an important change occurred in Mediterranean galleys and merchantmen. Between the 9th and 13th centuries, the square sail gave way to the *lateen sail,* a fore-and-aft triangular sail hung from a long pole supported by a short mast. The lateen sail made it possible for a ship to sail closer to the wind (that is, more nearly into the wind) than with a square sail. The exact origin of the lateen sail is unknown, but it may have come to the Mediterranean from China, the East Indies, or Arabia.

About the same time, Mediterranean shipbuilders added a forecastle and poop to some of their ships, as well as one or two extra masts. By the 13th century, the typical Mediterranean merchantman was a carvel-built vessel with two lateen sails, a pair of side rudders, forecastle, and poop. A slimmer Portuguese version of the lateen merchantman, called a *caravel,* was the type of ship Prince Henry the Navigator sent to explore the African coast in the 15th century.

Golden Age of Sail

During the 14th century, the cog was introduced to the Mediterranean. By the late 15th century, features of the cog had been combined with those of southern merchantmen to produce the *carrack,* a sturdy carvel-built vessel with three or four masts, stern rudder, overhanging forecastle, high poop, and, usually, *bowsprit,* a short pole extending forward from the forecastle. A four-masted carrack carried at least six sails—a square sail on both the bowsprit and the foremast; two square sails on the mainmast; and a lateen sail on each of the aftermasts.

The carrack opened the seas of the world to navigation. The divided-sail plan enabled the crew to regulate more accurately the amount of sail exposed to the wind, making the ship safer and easier to handle. The hull was large enough to hold the crew and supplies for a long voyage.

The carrack set the pattern for sailing vessels through the early 19th century. From the 16th century on, sailing ships were mainly refined versions of the carrack, with more complicated sail plans and reduced superstructures. The *galleon,* for example, was slimmer than the carrack and had a lower forecastle and poop. It had a beaklike struc-

Egyptian Sailboat. The Egyptians first hoisted sail over a papyrus craft such as this about 4000 B.C.
The British Museum

Historical Merchant Ships

Egyptian Wooden Ship
about 2500 B.C.

Roman Grain Ship
1st-2nd century A.D.

Mediterranean Merchantman
with lateen sails
13th century

Northern Cog
with stern-post rudder
14th century

Carrack
combining Mediterranean
and Northern features
15th century

First Oceangoing Steamship
Savannah (1819)

Mauretania (1907), the first modern luxury passenger liner

Scale: 1 inch = 180 feet; 1 cm = 21.6 m

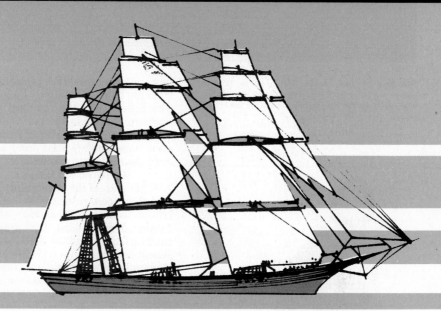

Clipper Ship, mid-19th century

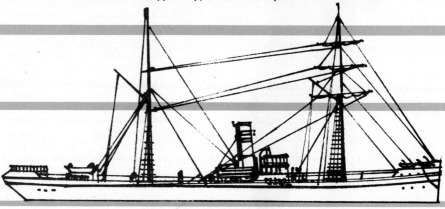

Cargo Ship, early 20th century

Scale: 1 inch = 73 feet; 1 cm = 8.76 m

The Age of Sail. Boston Harbor in the 1850's, *above,* was filled with sailing vessels of all sizes. Many ships of the era had figureheads, such as the one shown below.

Painting by Fitz Hugh Lane, M. & M. Karolik Collection of American Painting, 1815-1865, Courtesy Museum of Fine Arts, Boston
Figurehead: The Mariners' Museum, Newport News, VA.

ture, called a *beak-head,* projecting forward from the bow in imitation of a galley's ram. The galleon was the standard warship of northern Europe in the late 16th and early 17th centuries. On the Mediterranean, however, oared galleys were used as warships until the early 18th century.

From Sail to Steam

At the start of the 19th century, the seas of the world were ruled by the beamy, blunt-bowed wooden sailing ship. After Robert Fulton demonstrated the practicality of steam transportation in 1807, paddle-wheel steamboats came into wide use on lakes and rivers. (See STEAMBOAT.) Oceangoing steamships, however, developed slowly.

The first steamship to cross an ocean was the *Savannah,* a three-masted American sailing ship with auxiliary steam engines and paddle wheels. The *Savannah* crossed the Atlantic Ocean from west to east in 1819, using sails for most of the trip. In 1827 the Dutch paddle-steamer *Curaçao* made the first transoceanic trip entirely under steam.

The early steamship boilers used seawater to produce steam for the engine and it was necessary to stop the engine periodically and clean out the accumulated salt in the boilers. The invention of the surface condenser (1834), which collected for reuse the water condensed from the steam, enabled a steamship to operate continuously on a supply of distilled water. The English paddle-steamer *Sirius,* one of the first steamships fitted with surface condensers, made the first transatlantic crossing under continuous steam power in 1838.

The first steamship to make regular transatlantic trips was the English paddle-steamer *Great Western* (1838), built for the Great Western Railway Company by the engineer Isambard Kingdom Brunel. Another important Great Western liner was Brunel's *Great Britain* (1843), the first oceangoing ship with an iron hull and the first deep-sea vessel with a screw propeller. (The screw propeller was developed in England in the late 1830's by Francis Smith and John Ericsson, working independently.) The success of the Great Western company led to the formation of many transatlantic steamship companies.

In the mid-19th century, the growth of trade with the Far East and the discovery of gold in California and Australia created a demand for a ship faster than the steamship or the blunt-bowed sailing vessel. The need was met by the development in America of the *clipper ship,* a slim, sharp-bowed vessel regarded as the most glamorous sailing ship ever built. Soon American and British clippers ruled the long-distance sea routes, coursing along at speeds as high as 20 knots —faster than many 20th-century ships.

The clipper ship was expensive to operate, however, requiring a large, highly skilled crew and more maintenance work than slower, sturdier ships. The building of the fastest type of clipper ships, the *extreme clippers,* was over by the middle 1850's, when falling freight rates turned owners to slightly wider ships—called *medium* or *half clippers*—in which capacity was as important as speed. From 1865 to 1890 large numbers of medium-sharp-bowed sailing vessels, known as *down easters,* were built in Maine. With nearly the speed of the extreme clipper and a good cargo capacity, the down easter represented what many regard as the highest development of the sailing merchant ship.

During the second half of the 19th century, steamships generally replaced sailing vessels on the world's trade routes, although most steamships continued to carry auxiliary sails. All-purpose merchant vessels, carrying both passengers and cargo, were joined on the deep seas by such specialized ships as tankers and bulk carriers. The screw propeller took the place of the paddle wheel, and metal hulls—first iron and then steel—

replaced wooden hulls. The largest ship of the 19th century was Brunel's *Great Eastern* (launched in 1858), a 692-foot (211-m) steamship with both paddle wheels and a screw propeller, six masts, and space for 4,000 passengers. (See GREAT EASTERN.)

For the development of steam-driven naval vessels, see NAVY, subtitle *History of Navies:* Steam and Armor.

Modern Ships

During the first half of the 20th century, the steam turbine and diesel engine were widely adopted for ship propulsion. The era of the large luxury liner began in 1907 with the *Mauretania,* a 790-foot (241-m) turbine-powered, quadruple-screw steel ship with space for some 2,000 passengers. Cargo ships grew larger and more specialized. For the development of modern naval vessels, see NAVY, subtitle *History of Navies:* World War II; After World War II.

By the mid-20th century, oil fuel had replaced coal on most steamships. In the 1960's nations began building experimental nuclear-powered ships and vessels powered with gas turbines. By the early 1980's, regular passenger service on the oceans had virtually disappeared, and the only passenger liners still being built were cruise ships.

During the 1960's and 1970's, the development of new kinds of cargo ships revolutionized ocean and inland shipping. Most significant was the containership, which carries goods in large metal boxes that can be easily handled. Other new ships were the roll-on-roll-off ship, which carries large containers on wheels, and giant vessels for transporting barges across the ocean.

For further information, see:

Equipment

ANCHOR	RADIO, section "Uses
AUTOMATIC PILOT	and Regulation of
CHRONOMETER	Radio," subtitles
COMPASS, subtitles	*Communication*
The Magnetic	*and Navigation*
Compass and	SEXTANT
Nonmagnetic	STEAM ENGINE
Compasses:	TACHOMETER
The Gyro-	TELEGRAPHY, subtitle
compass	*Sending and Receiv-*
DERRICK	*ing Equipment:*
DIESEL ENGINE	The Morse Tele-
DIRECTION FINDER	graph
LIFE PRESERVER	TURBINE, subtitles
LIFEBOAT	*Steam Turbine*
LOG	*Power Plant*
LOGBOOK	*and Gas Turbine*
LORAN	WINDLASS
RADAR	

NEW STANDARD photo by Donald R. Downey

Model Ship. The model was placed inside the bottle with the masts lying against the deck. Wires were then used to pull the masts erect. The shape of the bottle causes the model to appear somewhat distorted.

Books about Ships

Hoehling, A. A. *Ships That Changed History* (Madison Books, 1992).
Innes, P. B. and W. D., editors. *Bridge Across the Seas* (Devon, 1995).
Kemp, Peter, editor. *The Oxford Companion to Ships and the Sea* (Oxford University, 1994).
Mellott, Jack. *Historic Ships of America* (Howell Press, 1996).
Pedraja Toman, Rene De La. *A Historical Dictionary of the U. S. Merchant Marine and Shipping Industry Since the Introduction of Steam* (Greenwood, 1994).
For Younger Readers
Baxter, Leon. *Famous Ships* (Hambleton-Hill, 1993).
Grady, S. M. *Ships: Crossing the World's Oceans* (Lucent Books, 1992).
Richards, Roy. *Ships Through Time* (Raintree, 1996).

Ship, Model, a three-dimensional replica of a ship or boat. Most model ships are built by hobbyists for display or sailing. Some are built professionally as decorator items for offices and homes. Model ships are divided into two main classes—static, or display, models and operating models. Of the two, static models are the more common.

Static models are built of many types of ships and boats, the most common being sailing ships of historical interest (such as USS *Constitution*) or great beauty (clipper ships). Some model kits consist of preformed plastic parts requiring only assembly. Others are produced in wood with metal fittings; the wood may be preshaped or may require carving. Some modelers work directly from blueprints, doing all of the forming by hand. There are no standard sizes for ship models; the size chosen depends on the amount of detail the builder wishes to include.

Operating models are produced of many pleasure boats, yachts, and working vessels. Such operating models frequently have gasoline engines or electric motors. Operating models may be radio-controlled or may be controlled by a clock mechanism that moves the rudder after a preset length of time.

Shipbuilding. See SHIP, section "Shipbuilding."

Shippensburg State University of Pennsylvania. See UNIVERSITIES AND COLLEGES (table).

Shipping. See FREIGHT.

Shipworm, or **Teredo,** tĕ-rē'dō, name for a family of shelled marine animals. Although they resemble worms, shipworms are mollusks. A shipworm has a long slender body and a small two-part shell attached to the anterior (front) end of the body. The body is very long in relation to the shell; for example, one species commonly found in North American waters can grow up to two feet (60 cm) long, but its shell is only one-half inch (13 mm) long. There are more than 65 shipworm species, ranging in length from 10 inches (25 cm) to more than three feet (90 cm). Shipworms are found in all but polar seas.

The small shells function as boring tools that shipworms use to burrow into submerged wood, such as in wharf piles and boats. Once they attach themselves to a wooden structure, they burrow deeper and deeper. They can eventually so weaken the wood that it breaks apart. The wood is the main food source for shipworms.

Shipworms make up the family Teredinidae.

Shiraz, shē-räz', Iran, the capital of Fars province. It lies in a basin in the Zagros Mountains in southwestern Iran, about 420 miles (680 km) south of Tehran. Shiraz is a commercial, governmental, and manufacturing center. Rugs, textiles, and metalwork have long been made here. Shiraz is also a tourist city noted for fine mosques and the tombs and gardens of the poets Sadi and Hafiz. About 40 miles (64 km) to the northeast are the majestic ruins of Persepolis, a capital of ancient Persia.

Shiraz probably dates from the sixth century B.C., but rose to prominence only after the Arab conquest of Persia in the seventh century A.D. It prospered under the Safawid dynasty and reached its greatest splendor as the capital of Persia during the Zand dynasty (1750-94).

Population: 965,117.

Shire, a breed of horse. See HORSE, section "Breeds of Horses," subtitle *Important Breeds:* Draft Horses.

Shirley, William (1694-1771), a British official in the American colonies. He was governor of Massachusetts, 1741-49 and 1753-56. During King George's War, Shirley planned the capture in 1745 of the French fort of Louisbourg (on Cape Breton Island off Nova Scotia), Britain's first and most decisive victory. With the money Massachusetts received from Parliament for its war expenses, Shirley was able to give the colony a sound currency for the first time in decades. In the French and Indian War, he led an unsuccessful expedition to Niagara against the French (1755) and was briefly commander of all British forces in America. He was governor of the Bahama Islands, 1761-67.

Shiva. See BRAHMAN.

Shizuoka, shē-zōo-ō̄-kä, Japan, the capital of Shizuoka prefecture, about 90 miles (145 km) southwest of Tokyo. Shizuoka is the trading and processing center for an agricultural area that produces tangerines and green tea. The city is noted for its lacquerware and bamboo goods. Shizuoka University is here.

Population: 472,196.

Shoat. See HOG.

Shock, a condition in which the vital functions of the body are greatly depressed. Shock is a reaction of the body to serious injury, surgery, disease, or emotional upset (such as fright). Many of the symptoms of shock are caused by a reduction in the flow of blood to the vital organs. Symptoms include cold, clammy, pale skin; a chilly feel-ing or shaking chills; perspiration on the forehead and the palms of the hands; shallow breathing; weak, rapid pulse; and, frequently, nausea or vomiting. If the state of shock continues over a period of only a few hours, it may cause serious damage to vital body organs and it may even be fatal.

While awaiting professional medical treatment, the victim should be given first aid to lessen shock. If possible, the cause of shock should be corrected. For example, it is advisable to attend to a severe wound and try to control bleeding. A victim of shock should be moved as little as possible. If the cause of shock is unknown or if a head or neck injury is suspected, the victim should be kept lying flat. In most other situations, the victim's legs should be raised about 12 inches (30 cm) to maximize the flow of blood to the head. The victim should be covered to protect against loss of body heat. Sips of water should be given if the victim is conscious and able to swallow and has no abdominal injury. Alcoholic beverages should never be given to a person showing signs of shock.

Professional medical treatment for shock may include the administration of drugs, oxygen, blood, plasma, or fluids.

Shock, Electric. See ELECTRIC SHOCK.

Shock Absorber. See AUTOMOBILE, section "How an Automobile Runs," subtitle *Running Gear:* Suspension System.

Shock Therapy, or **Convulsive Therapy,** the use of drugs or electricity to treat certain forms of mental illness by causing convulsive seizures. Injections of insulin and metrazol have been used in treating anxiety and schizophrenia. *Electroshock therapy,* or *electroconvulsive therapy* (ECT), is used mainly to treat severe depression. In ECT, the patient is first given a muscle relaxant and an anesthetic to minimize discomfort. Electrodes are then placed on the patient's temples; the electrodes send a 70- to 130-volt current through the brain, causing the convulsive seizure. ECT is usually administered three times a week for two to four weeks. Partial memory loss sometimes occurs with treatment.

Shock therapy was introduced in 1938. It was formerly used to treat many illnesses that are now treated with psychotherapy and relatively mild drugs.

Shock Wave, a compression wave that moves through a material at a speed greater

Shoebill
© Phil Degginger

than the speed at which the material transmits ordinary sound waves. The material may be a gas, liquid, or solid. Shock waves are caused by sudden, strong disturbances generated by such phenomena as explosions, earthquakes, and lightning. Shock waves are also created by aircraft flying faster than the speed of sound. These shock waves are often heard as *sonic booms*.

The passage of a shock wave is marked by a sharp increase in pressure, density, and temperature. Strong shock waves transfer a considerable amount of energy to anything in their path. Much of the damage done by explosions and earthquakes is caused by the shock waves they produce.

See also AIRPLANE, section "Why an Airplane Flies," subtitle *Supersonic Flight*.

Shockley, William. See NOBEL PRIZES (Physics, 1956).

Shoe. See FOOTWEAR.

Shock Wave. The lines show the shock waves set up by a missile of this shape traveling at 2,500 miles per hour (4,000 km/h).
Adapted from a NASA photo

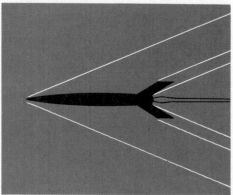

Shoebill, or **Whalehead,** a large bird of eastern Africa. The shoebill stands about 50 inches (1.3 m) high on long, thin legs. It has a large head with a huge, flattened bill that somewhat resembles a man's shoe. The shoebill has blue-gray plumage and a small crest of feathers at the nape of its neck.

The shoebill, which lives mostly on land, flies only short distances. It lives in swampy areas where it wades in water in search of such food as fish and frogs. The shoebill makes its nest on the ground out of water plants it gathers together into a mound about three feet (90 cm) high.

The shoebill is *Balaeniceps rex* of the family Balaenicipitidae.

Shoemaker, Willie (William) (1931-), a United States jockey. He won 8,833 races during his career, more than any other jockey in racing history. He also won more than $123,000,000 for his mounts. Shoemaker was born in Fabens, Texas. He began racing in 1949 and became successful immediately. In 1953 he won a record 485 races. In 1959 he became the youngest jockey to be elected to horse racing's Hall of Fame. Shoemaker retired in 1990.

Shogun, shō'gōōn', the military governor of Japan for most of the period from 1192 to 1868. Japan since the fifth century B.C. had been ruled by an emperor, but under the shogunate the emperor reigned but held no power. In theory, the shogun was appointed by the emperor, but in practice the title was hereditary. Shoguns were of the samurai class.

There were three dynasties of shoguns—Kamakura, Ashikaga, and Tokugawa. The Kamakura dynasty was founded by Minamoto Yoritomo, who after winning a civil war became supreme ruler in Japan in 1185. He took the title shogun in 1192. The Kamakura shogunate was overthrown by the emperor in 1333, but in 1336 Ashikaga Takauji seized power from the emperor, and two years later he made himself shogun. The Ashikaga shogunate survived until 1573. In 1603, following years of civil war, a powerful lord, Tokugawa Ieyasu, reunited the country and became shogun. His dynasty lasted to 1868, when supporters of Emperor Mutsuhito overthrew Shogun Tokugawa Yoshinobu and reestablished imperial power.

Sholapur, shō'lä-pōōr, India, a city in Maharashtra state, about 220 miles (354 km) southeast of Bombay. Sholapur is an important center of cotton-textile manufacturing and also produces metalwares, leather goods, and chemicals. A 14th-century Muslim fortress is the city's most notable structure. From the 15th century until India became independent in 1947, Sholapur was ruled in turn by Persians, Moguls, Hyderabad princes, Marathas, and the British. Population: 604,215.

Sholes, Christopher Latham (1819-1890), a United States inventor and journalist. Sholes developed the first commercially practical typewriter. He and two associates, Carlos Glidden and Samuel W. Soulé, developed a working model in 1867. After making improvements, he tried to manufacture and market the machine, but was unsuccessful and sold his patent rights to E. Remington and Sons in 1873. Sholes was born in Pennsylvania and later moved to Wisconsin, where he became a newspaper editor and legislator.

For picture of 1872 model, see TYPE-WRITER, subtitle *History*.

Sholokhov, shôl'ŏ-kôf', **Mikhail** (1905-1984), a Russian novelist and short-story writer. He was awarded the 1965 Nobel Prize for literature. He is best known for *The Quiet Don* (four volumes, 1928-40), a powerful novel about the life of the Don Cossacks during and after the Russian revolution. Some critics, however, question his authorship of that work, believing that he plagiarized parts or even all of the book.

In the novels *Seeds of Tomorrow* (1932; also titled *Virgin Soil Upturned*) and *Harvest on the Don* (1960), Sholokhov deals with the Don Cossacks' problems in regard to the Soviet collective farm program. His writings are believed to have influenced the Soviet government to restore to the Cossacks certain privileges that they had had under the czars.

Sholokhov was born in a village in the Don River region of southern Russia.

The Quiet Don was published in English translation as And Quiet Flows the Don (1934) and The Don Flows Home to the Sea (1940).

Sholom Aleichem. See ALEICHEM, SHALOM.

Shooting Star. See COWSLIP.

Shooting Star. See METEOR (introduction).

Shop Steward. See LABOR UNION, subtitle *Organization and Work of a Union*.

Shore Crab. See CRAB, subtitle *Life of the Crab* (Green, or Shore, Crabs).

Shore Patrol, a unit of the U.S. Navy that performs police functions. It maintains order in shore areas where there are naval installations or forces. The Shore Patrol also aids civilian police in handling naval personnel on liberty or leave. Its members have the rank of petty officer and wear an armband bearing the letters "SP" in yellow.

Short Circuit. See ELECTRICITY, subtitle *Electric Circuits*.

Short Story, a brief fictional narrative in prose. Short stories vary in length from about 1,000 to 10,000 words. Narratives longer than 10,000 words but too short to be novels are usually called *novelettes* or *novellas;* they have more in common with novels than with short stories. Short stories of less than 2,500 words are sometimes called *short-short stories*.

Short stories vary also in style, theme, and emphasis. Some of them—such as the detective story and the adventure story—are concerned almost entirely with action and plot. Others are predominantly character studies. Still others stress atmosphere and mood. In spite of their differences, however, most short stories have in common certain characteristics imposed by their brevity. A short story usually has only one plot (no subplots) and one theme. It has few incidents and the number of characters is extremely limited.

Some critics make a distinction between various kinds of short fiction, calling only the compact, well-plotted narrative a short story. According to them, a loosely constructed narrative, especially if unrealistic, is a *tale*. A narrative without a well-defined plot and stressing atmosphere or character is a *sketch*. Most modern critics, however, accept the broader definition of the short story.

Development of the Short Story

Early Period. Stories were collected and written down early in history. Perhaps the oldest collection is the Egyptian *Tales of the Magicians,* written between 4,000 and 6,000 years ago. A Greek collection, *Milesian Fables,* was compiled in the second century B.C. The Hindu *Panchatantra,* written between 300 and 500 A.D., contains fables and other short prose tales.

Stories were popular during the Middle Ages. Some of them, such as the *exemplum* and the beast fable, are moralizing tales

The *fabliaux,* which originated in France, are comic, often ribald, stories in verse; they inspired much prose fiction. The Italian *novella* of the Middle Ages is similar to the fabliau but is in prose.

Gesta Romanorum (Deeds of the Romans) is a collection of stories—only a few of them about Romans—compiled in 13th-century England. Many authors, including Geoffrey Chaucer and William Shakespeare and the Italian Giovanni Boccaccio, derived plots from this collection. Boccaccio's *The Decameron* (1348-53), a collection of stories retold from fabliaux, fables, and folk tales, and Sir Thomas Malory's *Le Morte d'Arthur (The Death of Arthur;* 1485), a collection of romantic legends about King Arthur, also provided material for many writers.

During the Renaissance and the 18th century a few collections of medieval stories were still being compiled. One of the most outstanding was *Tales of Mother Goose,* published in 17th-century France by Charles Perrault.

The 19th Century marked the rapid development of the short story as a distinct, recognized literary form. Increasing numbers of periodicals supplied an outlet for short fiction. America, France, and Russia led in mastery of the short story.

Washington Irving gave his stories realistic settings, a strong sense of atmosphere, and rich characterization. Nathaniel Hawthorne made use of symbols and showed psychological insight in his stories. The first attempt to define the short story and set up rules for it was made by Edgar Allan Poe, who stressed brevity and unity. Poe's "The Murders in the Rue Morgue" (1841) was the first detective story. Among others who greatly influenced the development of the short story were the Frenchman Guy de Maupassant with his carefully constructed Realistic narratives, and the Russian Anton Chekhov with his Impressionistic stories.

The regional short story was developed in the United States by such authors as Bret Harte, who wrote of California gold-rush days; Joel Chandler Harris, with his legends set in the South of slavery times; and Sarah Orne Jewett and Mary E. Wilkins Freeman, who portrayed the lives of New England villagers. The British authors Robert Louis Stevenson and Rudyard Kipling aroused interest in foreign settings with their adventure stories.

The 20th Century. O. Henry's journalistic style and his mannerism of ending each story with an ironic twist were much imitated. Chekhov's objectivity and restraint are reflected in the delicate stories of Katherine Mansfield as well as in the Naturalistic stories of Sherwood Anderson and James Joyce. Ernest Hemingway's simplified, dramatic, and powerful style was highly influential and was especially suited to the short story. In contrast to Hemingway's understatement are the discursive regional stories, set in the South, of William Faulkner, Eudora Welty, and Carson McCullers.

The Realism that prevailed in short stories in the early part of the century gave way to Impressionism and Symbolism as the belated influence of the Austrian Franz Kafka began to be felt. Kafka's nightmarish view of life is in some respects similar to that of the French authors Jean-Paul Sartre and Albert Camus, whose stories reflect their belief that life is absurd.

After the middle of the century the popularity of the short story declined with the rise of interest in nonfiction. In the United States, short stories with literary merit found an audience mainly in quarterly journals with only a small readership.

Books about the Short Story

Hills, Rust. *Writing in General and the Short Story in Particular* (Houghton Mifflin, 1987).
For Younger Readers
Bauer, M. D. *What's Your Story? a Young Person's Guide to Writing Fiction* (Houghton Mifflin, 1992).

Short Ton. See TON.

Short-eared Owl. See OWL, subtitle *Kinds of Owls:* Typical Owls.

Shorter College. See UNIVERSITIES AND COLLEGES (table).

Shorthand, any system of writing rapidly by substituting characters, symbols, or abbreviations for letters, words, or phrases. There are several shorthand systems, some written by hand, some employing a machine. Their purpose is to enable the writer to keep pace with a speaker in order to take down an accurate record of what is spoken. The taking of shorthand notes and the transcribing of them (making a written, printed, or typed copy) is called *stenography.*

Shorthand is widely used in business and government to record correspondence, meetings, conferences, and official proceedings of all kinds. A writer of shorthand is called a

Speedwriting Secretarial School

	Pitman	Gregg	Speedwriting
Pay the bill.			
I know you will cover each package.			
Get a bill and pay for the file.			
The file is rather cheap.			
Lock the silver case and cover it.			
I know you will check the cover.			
The check for the package is due.			

Shorthand Systems and how they differ

stenographer. "Shorthand reporter" is the term applied to individuals who take down records of official proceedings.

Handwritten Systems

The two most widely used symbol systems are Pitman and Gregg. A stenographer using these systems averages about 100 words per minute. Pitman shorthand is based on strictly phonetic principles, with a character for each sound or combination of sounds. Shading and position of the characters with relation to the ruled lines on the paper are important. The consonants are grouped according to light and heavy sounds and are assigned light and heavy strokes. For example, | is "t," | is "d."

Vowel sounds are divided into phonetic groups and assigned positions above the line, on the line, and through the line to indicate the general groupings. For example, ⌐ is "by," ⌐ is "be."

Pitman shorthand has been adapted to many languages other than English.

The Gregg system is based purely on linguistic principles, with characters representing letters of the alphabet rather than sounds. The characters are designed to be joined easily in the combinations in which they normally occur in the language. For example,

the symbols for "j" / , "u" ⌐ , and "n" — can be combined to form ⌐ , June.

Brief (shortened) forms are used for many commonly occurring words. For example, the symbols for "e" ∘ and "v") are joined in) to form "every."

Gregg characters are not shaded and may be written on unlined paper, as position in relation to line of writing is not significant. Gregg shorthand is the most widely used system in the United States and Canada.

Various simplified and abbreviated systems have been developed. Speedwriting, for example, uses letters of the alphabet and only a small number of arbitrary symbols. In general, only what is heard is written; silent and unessential letters are omitted. In addition, single letters are often used to represent combinations of sounds.

Machine Systems

Machine systems, such as Stenotype and Stenograph, can record speeches or dictation at a rate of more than 200 words per minute. The shorthand machine has 22 keys, which can be pressed singly or in groups to record syllables, words, or phrases. The machine prints onto a paper tape, and may also be connected to a computer-aided transcription system, which automatically translates the shorthand into readable English and displays it on a video screen. The sentence "Walt was a Scout" would appear as follows on the machine's paper tape:

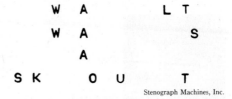

Stenograph Machines, Inc.

Machines are most widely used in the field of shorthand reporting, where high speeds are necessary to record court trials, hearings, conferences, and legislative proceedings.

History

Shorthand was used as early as 2,000 years ago in modern Greece and Egypt. In the fourth century B.C., Marcus Tullius Tiro, a Roman, devised a system with which he took down the speeches of Cicero. This method, known as Tironian, was employed by other writers to record the proceedings of the Roman Senate. It continued to be used as late as the 11th century A.D. in France.

Although shorthand systems are used in several modern languages, modern shorthand is of English origin. In the 16th century, Timothy Bright devised the first system that approached fully phonetic writing. Samuel Pepys, the noted 17th-century diarist, wrote in a form of shorthand to ensure secrecy. Well over 1,000 shorthand systems have been introduced in English-speaking countries, the largest number of them in England.

The best-known English system, that of Isaac Pitman, was introduced in 1837 as *Stenographic Sound Hand.* It was soon renamed "phonography" (from the Greek words for sound and writing). Benjamin Pitman, Isaac's brother, introduced the system, with slight modifications, in the United States in 1853. The Pitman system was the basis for later phonetic systems, such as Graham and Munson. In 1888, in Great Britain also, John Robert Gregg published his first book, setting forth a linguistically based shorthand. He brought his system to the United States, where he published *Gregg Shorthand* in 1893. This work, revised and updated, is still in use today.

About 1913 shorthand written by machine was introduced. It was known as machine shorthand or stenotypy (later, touch shorthand). With the demand for greater speed, there was a trend toward simplified and abbreviated systems. A simplified version of Gregg was introduced in 1949 (revised in 1963). The use of shorthand machines became widespread in the latter part of the 20th century. Although dictating machines and ordinary tape recorders have replaced the use of shorthand for many purposes, shorthand still remains the best system when absolute accuracy is required.

See also PITMAN, Sir ISAAC.

Books about Shorthand

Knapp, M. H. *The Complete Court Reporter's Handbook,* 2nd edition (Prentice Hall, 1991).

Pitman New Era Shorthand, anniversary edition (Trans-Atlantic, 1988).

Pullis, J. M., and Linda Bippen. *Principles of Speedwriting Shorthand* (Macmillan, 1994).

Zoubek, C. E., and Gregg Condon. *Gregg Shorthand,* centennial edition (3 volumes; McGraw-Hill, 1989).

Shorthorn. See CATTLE, subtitle *Breeds of Beef Cattle.*

Short-horned Grasshopper. See GRASSHOPPER, subtitle *Economic Importance.*

Shortleaf Pine. See PINE, subtitle *American Hard Pines:* Two-needled Hard Pines.

Shortnose Gar. See GAR.

Shoshonean Languages. See INDIANS, AMERICAN, section "Language Groups and Tribes."

Shoshoni Indians, shŏ-shō'nē, a North American tribe of the Shoshonean division of the Uto-Aztecan language family. They lived originally in the Great Basin between the Sierra Nevada and Rocky Mountains, where they subsisted on the meager resources of their largely barren land. After 1700 some Shoshoni acquired horses and moved eastward onto the Great Plains, where they became buffalo hunters. In the early 19th century, they numbered about 8,000. Friendly to the white settlers, the Shoshoni were given reservation land of their own choosing. Today they live on reservations and tribal lands in Idaho, Nevada, and Wyoming and number more than 7,000. Some members of other tribes have intermingled with them.

See also SACAJAWEA.

Shostakovich, shŏ-stŭ-kô'vĭch, **Dimitri** (1906-1975), a Russian composer. He became internationally known for his symphonies and other orchestral works. A prolific composer, Shostakovich wrote cantatas, chamber music, and ballet and film music. Because of the political pressures of Soviet life, his music has an uneven quality. Many of his works, such as *Symphony No. 4*

Dimitri Shostakovich
Novosti
Press Agency

SHOT PUT

(composed 1936, first performed 1962) and *The Execution of Stepan Razan* (1964), are marked by lyrical melodies, dissonance, and great dramatic power. Other works, which many critics consider inferior, conform to official Communist party standards of art and were designed to appeal to the masses and inspire patriotism.

Shostakovich was born in St. Petersburg and attended the conservatory there, 1919-25. His *Symphony No. 1*, composed as a graduation piece, brought him worldwide fame when it was first performed in 1926. Throughout his career, Shostakovich was both highly praised and severely criticized in his native land. His operas *The Nose* (1930) and *Lady Macbeth of the District of Mtsensk* (1934; revised and renamed *Katerina Ismailova*, 1963) were denounced by Soviet critics as "decadent" and "bourgeois." *Symphony No. 4*, condemned as "too modern," was withheld from performance for 26 years. With his *Symphony No. 5* (1937), however, he regained favor. *Symphony No. 7* (1942), composed during the siege of Leningrad (St. Petersburg), was widely played during World War II.

His music was attacked as too "formalistic" in 1948. After confessing artistic error, Shostakovich was again given critical approval. *Symphony No. 13* (1962), based on "Babi Yar" and other poems by Yevgeny Yevtushenko, was not permitted a second performance until changes that pleased the party were made. *Symphony No. 14* (1969) is for chamber orchestra and voices. *Symphony No. 15* (1972) contains passages from works of other composers. In the last years of his life, Shostakovich dictated his memoirs to the music critic Solomon Volkov. *Testimony: the Memoirs of Dimitri Shostakovich* was published in 1979.

Shot Put, in track and field sports, a weight-throwing contest in which athletes *put* (throw with an outward pushing motion) a metal ball called a *shot* for distance. The standard shot for men weighs 7.257 kilograms (16 lb); for women, 4 kilograms (8 lb, 13 oz). High school boys use a 12-pound (5.4-kg) shot; high school girls, an 8-pound (3.629-kg) shot.

Success in putting the shot depends upon the strength and body control of the putter. Standing at the back of a circle 2.135 meters (7 ft) in diameter, the shotputter balances the shot upon the central fingers and palm of one

Shot Put Technique. (1) Begins facing back of circle. (2) Crouches and swings left leg out. (3) Hops back on right foot. (4) Begins pivot and comes down on left foot. (5) Pivots to the front of circle. (6) Releases shot.

hand, hops backward into the center of the circle on one foot, pivots, and coming down on his other foot at the front of the circle releases the shot at approximately a 45-degree angle. The distance recorded is the space between the nearest point on the circle and the point where the shot lands.

For record, see TRACK AND FIELD SPORTS (table).

Shotgun, a shoulder weapon used primarily for hunting birds and small game. Shotguns are also used in hunting deer, in the sports of skeet shooting and trapshooting and, to some extent, in police work. A shotgun has a smooth-bore barrel from which small metal pellets, called *shot,* are usually fired. (For deer hunting, a lead slug is used in place of shot.) A cartridge, or shell, holds the shot (or slug) prior to shooting.

Shotguns are made in both single-barrel (in single-shot and repeating types) and double-barrel models. The size of the bore of a shotgun barrel is stated as its *gauge.* Gauge has a historical origin. It was defined as the number of round balls with the same diameter as the bore that could be molded from one pound of lead. Common shotgun sizes include (in order of descending size) 12 gauge (.725 inch), 16 gauge (.665 inch), and 20 gauge (.615 inch). Shotgun sizes in countries using the metric system generally are referred to by caliber. The calibers corresponding to 12, 16, and 20 gauge are 18.2 mm, 16.8 mm, and 15.7 mm.

Most shotguns have some *choke,* or narrowing of the bore near the muzzle. The choke affects the rate at which the shot spread after they leave the barrel. Many double-barrel shotguns have a different choke in each barrel, giving a choice for short or long range. Some single-barrel models have adjustable choke.

The shotgun developed from the blunderbuss, a large-bore gun with a bell-shaped muzzle, popular in the 18th century.

See also AMMUNITION, subtitle *Small-arms Ammunition* and illustration *A Shotgun Shell;* TRAPSHOOTING AND SKEET SHOOTING.

Shoulder Blade. See ANATOMY (illustration, #60).

Shovel, a hand tool used for digging and lifting. Shovels are used for such purposes as gardening and snow removal. A shovel consists of a metal dish, or blade, attached to a wooden or metal handle. Shovel blades are made in a variety of shapes for different uses. (See illustration.)

The term *spade* is often used interchangeably with *shovel,* but specifically refers to a heavy-weight shovel designed to be pushed into the ground with the foot. On many spades, there is a lip at the top of the blade to make pushing the spade into the ground easier.

Shovel, Power. See POWER EXCAVATORS.

Shoveler. See DUCK, subtitle *Wild Ducks* (Shoveler).

Showboat. See STEAMBOAT.

Shrapnel. See AMMUNITION, subtitle *History:* Early Artillery Ammunition.

Shreveport, shrēv'pōrt, Louisiana, the state's third largest city and the seat of Caddo Parish. Shreveport is on the Red River in northwestern Louisiana, near the Texas and Arkansas borders. It lies on the west side of the river, opposite Bossier City. Cross Lake, a man-made reservoir, adjoins Shreveport on the west.

Shreveport is the principal refining and distributing center for the extensive petroleum and natural-gas fields of northern Louisiana. In addition to refineries, there are chemical plants, and firms that make oil-field machinery and pipeline equipment. Other major activities are the processing of cotton and grains, lumber milling, the making of wood products, and the manufacture of electrical equipment.

Two annual events bring many visitors to Shreveport—the Louisiana State Fair, held in the fall, and the Holiday in Dixie festival, held in the spring to commemorate the Louisiana Purchase. On the state fairgrounds are an art gallery, a planetarium, and the State Exhibit Museum, which contains displays illustrating the state's economy and natural resources.

The privately sponsored R. W. Norton Art Gallery has a collection of American

Shotgun
This trapshooter is using a single-barrel, 12-gauge shotgun.

Remington Arms Co., Inc.

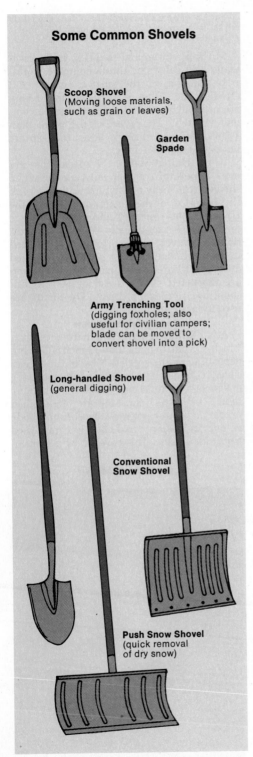

Some Common Shovels

Scoop Shovel
(Moving loose materials, such as grain or leaves)

Garden Spade

Army Trenching Tool
(digging foxholes; also useful for civilian campers; blade can be moved to convert shovel into a pick)

Long-handled Shovel
(general digging)

Conventional Snow Shovel

Push Snow Shovel
(quick removal of dry snow)

and European painting and sculpture. Centenary College of Louisiana is one of the oldest colleges west of the Mississippi River.

History

Shreveport was founded in 1837. It was named for Henry Shreve, a riverboat captain who arrived in the vicinity in 1833 to clear obstructions from the Red River. Opening of the river to steamboats stimulated growth of the new town, and it was incorporated in 1839. During the Civil War, Shreveport served as the state capital. Discoveries of nearby oil and gas in the early 1900's marked the beginning of industrial development.

Population: 198,525.

Shrew, a small predatory mammal of the family Soricidae. There are about 250 species. Some animals that are not members of the family Soricidae are also called shrews, but are not discussed here. For an example, see TREE SHREW.

Shrews have long, narrow bodies; thin tails; and heads with long, pointed snouts. The smallest shrew—as well as the smallest mammal in the world—is Savi's pygmy shrew, which is about 2½ inches (6.4 cm) long, including a 1-inch (2.5-cm) tail, and weighs 1/14 ounce (2 g). One of the largest shrews is the African giant shrew, which is about 9½ inches (24 cm) long, including a 4-inch (10-cm) tail. It weighs about 2 ounces (57 g). Shrews have tiny eyes and ears, which are often concealed by fur. They have poor vision. The fur is short, thick, and very soft, and is usually gray or brown.

Shrews are found in the temperate and tropical areas of all major continents of the world except Australia. There are more than 40 species in North America; one of the most common is the short-tailed shrew. Most shrews are land animals, but several species are aquatic. Aquatic shrews have stiff hairs on the feet that trap air bubbles, allowing the animal to run on the surface of the water. The Tibetan water shrew is the only shrew with webbed feet. Shrews live mostly in moist areas such as swamps and bogs, and on the moist, leaf-covered floors of deciduous forests. They hide under vegetative covering, logs, or large rocks, or in underground burrows.

The shrew is a fast-moving, excitable animal that uses up so much energy that it must eat day and night in order to keep alive. It eats two or three times its own

© Bill Ivy/Tony Stone Images
Short-tailed Shrew

weight in food each day—mostly insects, mice, and other small animals. Some shrews have poisonous saliva that paralyzes their prey. Shrews have a pair of scent glands on their hind legs; the glands secrete an acrid, musky odor that repels predators.

Shrews have a maximum life span of about two years. They reach maturity when they are about a year old. In the tropics, shrews breed throughout the year; in temperate climates the breeding season is usually from March to November. As many as four litters are born a year, with from two to 10 young in a litter.

The shrew family, Soricidae, is in the order Insectivora. Most species belong to the genus *Sorex* or the genus *Crocidura*, which includes the African giant shrew, *C. flavescens*. Savi's pygmy shrew is *Suncus etruscus;* the short-tailed shrew, *Blarina brevicauda;* the Tibetan water shrew, *Nectogale elegans.*

Shrike, the common name of a family of birds found in North America, Europe, Asia, and Africa. There are about 70 species. Shrikes are small birds of prey with large heads and strong, hooked bills. Their plumage is usually a combination of gray and black. Shrikes have a melodious warbling song, which they often interrupt with sharp cries or shrieks. They feed chiefly on insects, mice, and smaller birds. Shrikes are often called *butcherbirds* because they impale their prey on sharp twigs, thorns, or barbed wire much as a butcher hangs meat on a hook. The shrike builds a cup-shaped nest of twigs, grasses, and moss in a bush or a tree. The female lays two to eight eggs.

The two North American species are the *northern shrike* and the *loggerhead shrike.* The average length of the northern shrike is 10 inches (25 cm); of the loggerhead shrike, 9 inches (23 cm). Birds of both species are gray with black-and-white wing and tail feathers and broad black bands on either side of the head.

Shrikes make up the family Laniidae. The northern shrike is *Lanius excubitor;* the loggerhead shrike, *L. ludovicianus.*

Shrimp, an animal found in both freshwater and saltwater throughout the world. Like its relatives the lobsters, crabs, and crayfish, the shrimp is a crustacean. Shrimp are a popular seafood and a valuable commercial item. However, of the more than 1,900 species of shrimp, fewer than 20 are important commercially.

In the United States, the species that are most important commercially are the white shrimp, the brown shrimp, and the pink shrimp. Most of the shrimp marketed in the United States are bred and raised in large tanks under scientifically controlled conditions. However, some shrimp are still fished in the traditional manner; special nets, called otter trawls, are used to catch them. Shrimp are marketed chiefly fresh or frozen, but some are canned or dried. The shells are used to make animal feed.

Description and Habits

Adult shrimp range in length from less than 1 inch (2.5 cm) to more than 12 inches (30 cm), depending on the species. Most of the species caught commercially have an adult length of 3 to 9 inches (7.5 to 23 cm). Those that are more than 5 inches (13 cm) long are often called *jumbo shrimp,* or *prawns.* The shrimp's body is long and narrow and slightly compressed from side to side. It is covered by a translu-

Loggerhead Shrike

© Joe McDonald/Visuals Unlimited

cent shell called an exoskeleton. Shrimp periodically molt (shed their outer covering). Shrimp may be gray, white, pink, brown, or green, often with various markings. Many species can change color to blend with their surroundings.

The body of the shrimp is divided into two distinct regions—the *cephalothorax* (a fused head and thorax) and the *abdomen*. (It is the abdomen that is usually eaten, often after the vein found on the back is removed.) The cephalothorax bears a pair of compound eyes and usually 13 pairs of appendages. Listed from front to back, these appendages are: two pairs of antennae (one pair much longer than the other); a pair of jaws (called mandibles); two pairs of accessory jaws, called maxillae; three additional pairs of accessory jaws, called maxillipeds; and five pairs of legs. (The accessory jaws serve many functions, including grasping, biting, and swimming.)

The abdomen also bears appendages—five pairs of swimmerets (called pleopods and used for swimming); a pair of uropods (also used for swimming); and a telson, or tailpiece. The uropods and telson together make up the tail fan.

Shrimp are usually found on muddy or sandy bottoms. Some species burrow in the sand or mud; others burrow into rock and coral crevices. Many of the smaller species live inside sponges. Shrimp eat both plant and animal material. Reproduction is by eggs and sperm. Females usually carry the fertilized eggs on their swimmerets until they hatch.

Shrimp make up the suborder Natantia of the order Decapoda, class Crustacea. The white shrimp is *Penaeus setiferus;* the brown, *P. aztecus;* the pink, *P. duorarum. Crangon vulgaris* is a common European species.

Shriners, members of the Ancient Arabic Order, Nobles of the Mystic Shrine, a fraternal organization for Masonic Knights Templar and 32nd-degree Scottish Rite Masons. The Shriners founded and operate more than 20 charitable hospitals for badly burned and disabled children; funds come from the Shriners themselves, fund-raising events, and private contributions. The fraternity was founded in 1872. There are about 635,000 members. National headquarters are in Tampa, Florida.

Shroud of Turin, a cloth showing what is thought to be the image of the front and back of a bearded man with arms folded. The

shroud is a yellowed linen cloth 14 feet, 3 inches (434 cm) long and 3 feet, 7 inches (109 cm) wide. Since the first documented appearance of the cloth, at a church in Lirey, France, in the 1350's, it was believed by many to be the cloth used to wrap the body of Jesus Christ after his crucifixion. Through the centuries, there was controversy over its authenticity. Believers held that the image of Jesus was miraculously imprinted on the cloth at the time of his resurrection; others called it a 14th-century artistic fake. The shroud has been kept at the cathedral in Turin, Italy, since 1578.

Scientific investigations into the origin of the shroud began in the 1970's. In 1988 a small strip of the cloth was subjected to radiocarbon dating by three scientific teams. Tests by all three groups indicated that the cloth dated from some time between 1260 and 1390. In 1998, the shroud was put on display for the first time in 20 years.

Shrove Tuesday, in the Christian Church, the last day before Lent. It was formerly a day of confession; *shrove* is from an old English word for *confession*. In many countries Shrove Tuesday is the last day of the *carnival,* a time of feasting and merrymaking before Lent begins. In French, Shrove Tuesday is called *mardi gras.* (See MARDI GRAS.)

Shrub, a perennial plant, often referred to as a bush. Unlike an herb, a shrub has woody tissue in its stems, which last from season to season. Unlike a tree, a shrub is low growing and has many woody stems, which branch from a point at or near the ground.

Some shrubs, such as the blackberry, blueberry, currant, raspberry, and gooseberry, are grown for their fruit. Others are used in landscaping. Some flowering shrubs are the honeysuckle, rose, forsythia, mock orange, hydrangea, and lilac. The yew and

Jumbo Shrimp
© Alex Kerstitch/Visuals Unlimited

the juniper are evergreen shrubs often used as ground cover and for decoration around buildings. The privet and the barberry make good hedges.

See also FLOWERING PLANT, subtitle *Flowering Shrubs and Trees;* GARDENING AND LANDSCAPING, subtitle *Shrubs and Trees;* HEDGE.

Shubert Brothers, United States theater owners and Broadway producers. Lee (1875?-1953), Sam (1876-1905), and Jacob (1880?-1963) built the Shubert Theatrical Corporation, one of the largest theatrical production companies in history. Their Broadway theaters included the Shubert, the Winter Garden, and the Princess.

The brothers were born in eastern Europe and as young children moved to the United States, following their father, who had emigrated a year before. With very little education, they began working in the theaters of Syracuse, New York. In 1900, Sam moved to New York City, where he was hired to manage the Herald Square Theater. His brothers soon followed. After their first hit, the Shuberts started buying theaters both in New York and around the country. By 1914 they controlled 75 per cent of all the theaters in the United States.

Shuffleboard, a game in which two players or two teams of two players each use cues to shove disks into scoring zones marked on a smooth, rectangular court. A shuffleboard court may be indoors or outdoors. The game is often played in retirement communities and at resorts. Many parks, playgrounds, churches, and schools have courts.

A shuffleboard court usually has a surface of concrete or wood. The court is 6 feet (1.8 m) wide and 52 feet (15.8 m) long. At each end is a 20-foot (6.1-m) playing zone; in the middle, a 12-foot (3.7-m) neutral zone. Each playing zone has a triangular scoring area

with numbered sections worth 7, 8, or 10 points. Eight small wooden or composition disks are used. The players' cues have curved pushing devices at the end.

Each player—or, in doubles, one member of each team—in turn slides a disk from one end of the court toward the opposite end until all eight disks have been played. Points are then scored for each disk that rests in the scoring area. (During play, one disk may knock another out of the scoring area.) Across the base of the scoring triangle is the minus, or "10-off," section. Ten points are deducted for each disk ending up in that section. Disks stopping in the neutral zone are removed from play. The eight disks are played from alternate ends of the court until one player or team reaches a predetermined score, usually 50, 75, or 100 points.

Shuffleboard was played by the aristocracy in England in the 15th century and was first called shovegroat and shovelboard. It became a popular game on ocean liners and at resorts early in the 20th century. Official rules of the game were established in St. Petersburg, Florida, by the National Shuffleboard Association in 1931.

Shula, Don (1930-   ), a United States football coach. His career total of 347 victories was a National Football League (NFL) record. Shula became the first coach to lead a professional football team through an undefeated season (the Miami Dolphins in 1972). He also set the NFL coaching record of six appearances at the Super Bowl—once with the Baltimore Colts and five times with the Miami Dolphins.

Shula was born in Grand River, Ohio. He graduated from John Carroll University in Cleveland in 1951. That same year he began his football career playing for the Cleveland Browns. He began coaching in professional football in 1960 as the defensive coordinator for the Detroit Lions. He was the head coach

Shuffleboard. In doubles play, one member of each team stands at one end of the court, and his or her partner stands at the opposite end. Opponents' disks are of different colors.

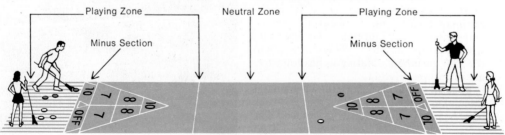

of the Baltimore Colts (1963-70) and the Miami Dolphins (1970-96). Shula was inducted into the Pro Football Hall of Fame in 1997.

Shull, Clifford G. See NOBEL PRIZES (Physics, 1994).

Shultz, George P. (Pratt) (1920-   ), a United States statesman. He was appointed secretary of state by President Ronald Reagan in 1982. He had previously served in the Nixon administration, as secretary of labor, 1969-70; director of the Office of Management and Budget, 1970-72; and secretary of the treasury, 1972-74. Shultz was born in New York City. He graduated from Princeton in 1942 and received a Ph.D. from the Massachusetts Institute of Technology (MIT) in 1949. He taught at MIT, 1946-57, and at the University of Chicago, 1957-68. He was a business executive, 1974-82.

Shushan. See SUSA.

Shute, Nevil, the pen name of Nevil Shute Norway (1899-1960), a British author and aeronautical engineer. His most important novel is *On the Beach* (1957), a story of the possible effects of a nuclear war. Shute was born in Ealing, a borough of London. In 1931 he founded an airplane construction firm and served as its managing director until 1938. His most successful early novel was *Pied Piper* (1942), about an elderly Englishman who safely escorts children out of France during World War II. Among Shute's other novels are *A Town Like Alice* (1948), *No Highway* (1949), and *Trustee from the Toolroom* (1960).

Shuttle. See WEAVING, subtitle *How Cloth Is Woven* and illustration.

Shuttlecock. See BADMINTON.

Shylock. See MERCHANT OF VENICE.

Shyness, a common personality trait characterized by a tendency to be self-conscious and uncomfortable in social situations. The shy person often feels anxious, embarrassed, confused, or tongue-tied when meeting people or when asked to speak before a group. Shy individuals are afraid they will be viewed as foolish, unattractive, unintelligent, or unworthy.

Most people experience some degree of shyness at some time in their lives. Individuals who suffer from *situational shyness* have problems some of the time and only under certain circumstances. Persons who suffer from *chronic shyness* are distressed in almost all social circumstances. Researchers believe that shyness is a serious problem for at least two million people in the United States. For these people, shyness inhibits social and professional growth.

Researchers have identified three potential sources of shyness: (1) heredity, (2) lack of social skills, and (3) social development that fosters low self-esteem instead of self-confidence. The circumstances of an individual's upbringing often determine the extent of that person's shyness. For example, parents who constantly criticize a child can undermine the child's self-esteem.

With professional counseling or individual effort, shy persons can develop the self-confidence necessary to face social situations. They can build self-esteem by such activities as focusing on their strong points, identifying and then sharpening specific social skills, and learning methods of relaxation.

SI. See METRIC SYSTEM.

Si River. See XI RIVER.

Sialkot, sī-äl′kōt, Pakistan, a city near the Kashmir border, about 65 miles (105 km) north of Lahore. Sialkot is a trading center and has light manufacturing industries, producing primarily sporting and surgical goods. An ancient city, it was reputedly the capital of the Bactrian Greek ruler Menander in the second century B.C. In the early sixth century A.D. it was the capital of Mihiragula the Hun, who ruled a large part of northwestern India.

Population: 296,000.

Siam. See THAILAND.

Siamang. See GIBBON.

Siamese Cat. See CAT, subtitle *The Domestic Cat:* Breeds (Short-haired Cats).

Siamese Fighting Fish, a tropical freshwater fish of Thailand (formerly Siam). It is one of a group of tropical fish called *bettas*. The Siamese fighting fish is yellowish brown and patterned with bright greens, blues, and reds. It has a rounded tail and short fins. The adult is about 2½ inches (6.4 cm) long.

The male of the species is the fighter. When two males meet they attack each other, nip each other's fins and gills, and often lock jaws. In Thailand large sums of money are bet at fish fights. A contest ends when one of the two fish flees.

Although it obtains oxygen from the water, the Siamese fighting fish also occasionally surfaces to gulp air. Before mating, the male builds a "bubble nest" by blowing saliva-coated bubbles to the surface of the water, where the bubbles form a frothy mass. The male places the fertilized eggs in the nest and guards the nest for about two days until the eggs hatch. The nest usually contains from 100 to 500 eggs.

The Siamese fighting fish is *Betta splendens* of the family Belontiidae.

Siamese Twins, a common name for *conjoined twins,* twins born joined together. The name was derived from twin boys, Chang and Eng, born in Siam (Thailand) in 1811; they were joined at the chest. In 1829 the boys were brought to the United States, where they were exhibited at circuses and sideshows. They took the last name Bunker and became American citizens. In 1843 they married sisters; each had several children. Chang and Eng died within a few hours of each other in 1874.

Siamese twins develop when a single fertilized egg fails to separate completely into two sections. (If the separation of the egg were complete, identical twins would result.) The degree of union varies; for example, the twins may share a single set of internal organs or there may be a set for each twin. Most conjoined twins are joined at the chest, lower back, or head. In many cases, conjoined twins can be separated so that each twin can live independently. When certain organs are shared, separation may result in the death of one or both of the twins.

Sian. See XI'AN.

Sibelius, sĭ-bā′lĭ-ŭs, **Jean** (1865-1957), a Finnish composer. He was known for his symphonies and symphonic poems that captured the spirit and flavor of his native land. *En Saga* (1893), *The Swan of Tuonela* (1893), and *Lemminkäinnen's Return* (1895) are among the early symphonic poems that established his reputation as a nationalist, Romantic composer. Although Sibelius never used folk tunes, many of his works con-

Jean Sibelius
Embassy of Finland

tain haunting, folk-like melodies. The stirringly nationalistic *Finlandia* (1900) became identified with Finland's struggle for independence. (Finland was controlled by Russia until 1917.) Many of his later works, such as *Symphony No. 4 in A minor* (1911), are less dramatic and are marked by a more restrained orchestration.

Sibelius was born in Hämeenlinna, Finland, and began to study music at the age of nine. In 1885 he entered the University of Helsinki to study law but left within a year to attend the Helsinki Conservatory. He later studied music in Berlin and Vienna. In 1892 he began composing *Kullervo,* the first of many symphonic poems based on the Finnish epic poem *Kalevala.* For a time Sibelius taught theory at the Helsinki Conservatory. After receiving a government grant in 1897, he devoted all his time to composing.

Sibelius composed seven symphonies. Other works include *Violin Concerto in D minor* (1904) and the symphonic poems *Pohjola's Daughter* (1906) and *Tapiola* (1926). He also wrote incidental music for plays; "Valse Triste," written for the play *Kuolema* (1903), became one of his best-known pieces. He composed much choral music, more than 80 songs, and many short piano pieces.

Siberia, sī-bēr′ĭ-á, the mainland part of Russia in Asia. Siberia is a geographic region rather than a political unit; it lies entirely within Russia. Because of their close association, geographic and economic ties, Sakhalin and the northern part of Kazakhstan are sometimes considered part of Siberia.

With an area of some 5,000,000 square miles (13,000,000 km²), Siberia makes up about 75 per cent of the territory of Russia and is more than a third larger than the United States. It extends from the Ural Mountains to the Pacific Ocean (a distance of as much as 3,800 miles [6,100 km]) and from China and Mongolia northward to the Arctic Ocean (some 2,000 miles [3,200 km]).

Physical Geography

Land. Siberia can be divided into three sections: Western, Central, and Eastern Siberia.

Western Siberia lies between the Urals and the Yenisey River valley and consists primarily of the low-lying, flat plains of the West Siberian Lowland. Except for parts of the far north, Western Siberia is drained by the sluggish Ob-Irtysh river system. Much of the land is swampy. In the extreme southeast, the terrain becomes increasingly rugged, particularly in the Altai Mountains,

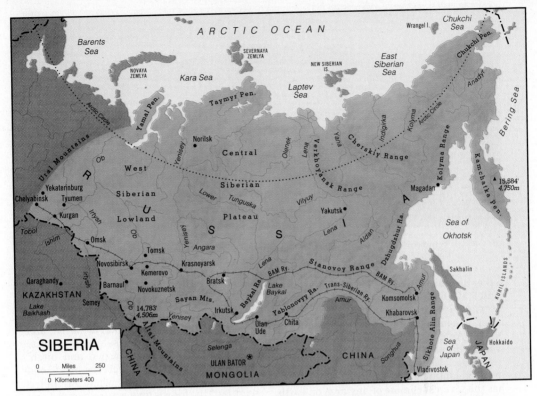

SIBERIA

0   Miles   250

0   Kilometers 400

which rise to almost 14,800 feet (4,500 m) above sea level.

Central Siberia is roughly the area drained by the Yenisey and Lena rivers and consists chiefly of the eroded Central Siberian Plateau. Here elevations are generally well below 3,000 feet (900 m). Numerous mountains, including the Sayan Mountains and the Baykal and Yablonovyy ranges, make up the extreme south. Peaks in the Sayans reach heights of up to about 11,400 feet (3,470 m).

Eastern Siberia occupies the area between the Lena River and the Pacific Ocean. Except for several broad river valleys, most of Eastern Siberia is made up of low mountains; elevations rarely exceed 7,000 feet (2,100 m). Among the more prominent ranges are the Sikhote Alin, Dzhugdzhur, Stanovoy, Verkhoyansk, Cherskiy, and Kolyma ranges. On the Kamchatka Peninsula are numerous volcanoes, both active and dormant, including snowcapped Klyuchevskaya Sopka (almost 15,590 feet [4,750 m] high), the loftiest peak in Siberia.

Water. Most of the great rivers of Russia are in Siberia. The Lena, Ob, Irtysh, and Yenisey all exceed 2,000 miles (3,200 km) in length. More than a dozen others, including the Amur, Kolyma, Lower Tunguska, Vil-

yuy, Aldan, and Angara, have courses of 1,000 to 2,000 miles (1,600 to 3,200 km). Except for the eastward-flowing Amur, all the major Siberian rivers drain northward to the Arctic Ocean. In the extreme north, the Arctic rivers remain frozen as long as nine months each year, blocking the flow of water from warmer areas to the south. As a result, flooding is widespread each spring.

Small lakes dot many areas, especially the western lowlands. The only large lake is

Siberian Landscape. Ice fishing on the Amur River, in eastern Siberia.

© B. & C. Alexander/Black Star

Reindeer are among the many large wild animals found in Siberia. This herd is on the Chukchi Peninsula near the Bering Strait.

Lake Baykal (Baikal), in the south. More than 5,300 feet (1,600 m) deep, up to 50 miles (80 km) wide, and almost 400 miles (640 km) long, it contains about as much water as North America's Great Lakes. It is the world's deepest lake.

Climate. Because of its northerly location in the gigantic landmass of Eurasia, Siberia has the severest climate of any area on earth, excluding Antarctica. Winters are long and bitterly cold; average January temperatures range from about 0° F. (−18° C.) in some parts of the south to well below −50° F. (−46° C.) in the northeast. At Oymyakon, on the Indigirka River, temperatures as low as −96° F. (−71° C.) have been reported.

Summers are short and vary from warm to cool, depending on location. During July, the warmest month, temperatures are occasionally high, but generally average from about 70° F. (21° C.) in some southerly localities to about 38° F. (3° C.) in the north. Where summers are briefest and coolest, notably in the far north, permafrost (permanently frozen ground) lies near the surface.

Precipitation comes mainly during summer as rain and is scanty over most of Siberia—some 4 to 20 inches (100 to 500 mm) a year. Only in a few mountain areas, mainly along the Pacific coast, does it amount to as much as 40 inches (1,000 mm). Snow covers the land for about six to nine months each year.

Plants and Animals

Vegetation in the tundra—a treeless zone along the Arctic coast—consists chiefly of mosses, lichens, short grasses, and small shrubs. Similar vegetation occurs above the tree line in many of Siberia's mountains.

South of the Arctic tundra lies the taiga, a vast coniferous forest which in some places is more than 1,000 miles (1,600 km) wide. The predominant species are pine, fir, larch, and spruce. In some parts of southern Siberia, deciduous trees, such as aspen and birch, occur mixed with the evergreens or in solid stands. In the southwest, where rainfall is scantiest, the forests give way to wooded and grassy steppes. There are also sizable steppe areas in some of the valleys and intermountain basins of the south and southeast.

Being largely wilderness, Siberia is the home of a great variety of animals. Moose, elk, reindeer, deer, bears, and wolves are among the principal large animals of the taiga. Though comparatively rare, tigers and leopards are found in some of the remote mountainous areas. Animals valued for their fur—for which Siberia has long been famous—include fox, kolinskies (minks), martens, otters, sables, squirrels, and rabbits and hares. The Arctic coast is the breeding ground for a multitude of birds, especially ducks, geese, and coots.

Economic Development

Despite its many adverse conditions, such as harsh climate, rough terrain, and great distances, Siberia is undergoing rapid development. The region has an enormous wealth of resources, especially fuel and metallic minerals, timber, and water power. Virtually all of the economic development has come since 1928, when the Soviet Union began a planned economy with its first Five Year Plan. Many groups, including ardent pioneers as well as convicts in forced-labor camps, have contributed to Siberia's partial conquest.

Trans-Siberian Railway greatly aided the development of Siberia. Shown is a passenger train near Ulan Ude, south of Lake Baykal.

During World War II, while the European part of the Soviet Union was heavily damaged, Siberia's development was speeded up. Many industrial activities were moved from European Russia to Siberia to prevent their destruction by the Germans. After the war, large amounts of equipment, even entire factories, were brought in from the countries of eastern Europe. Government investment in Siberia has been particularly heavy since the 1950's.

Most of the industrialization has occurred along or near the Trans-Siberian Railway in the south. Of major importance is the southern part of Western Siberia. It contains the bulk of Siberia's population, most of its large industrial cities, and several connecting railway lines. The heart of the region is the Kuznetsk Basin. Its enormous supply of coal and its reserves of iron ore and other minerals provide the foundation for heavy industries. In or near the basin are such centers as Novosibirsk, Siberia's largest city (1,436,000 inhabitants in 1989), Novokuznetsk, Barnaul, Kemerovo, and Tomsk. Other major cities include Omsk, with a population of 1,148,000, and Krasnoyarsk, with 912,000.

Elsewhere in Western Siberia are Russia's most productive oil and gas fields. In the late 1980's almost two-thirds of the Soviet Union's petroleum output came from the Ob fields northeast of Tyumen.

A number of industrial and urban areas are located along the Trans-Siberian Railway to the east. Irkutsk, at the southern end of Lake Baykal, is the hub of a rapidly growing industrial complex based largely on hydroelectric power. Farther east are Ulan Ude, Chita, Khabarovsk, and the Pacific port of Vladivostok. Some centers, because of abundant minerals or other resources, are developing at some distance from the Trans-Siberian. They are, however, usually linked to it by branch lines. Bratsk, on the Angara River at the site of one of the world's largest hydroelectric dams, is an example.

A second railway, the Baykal-Amur Mainline (BAM), runs 2,000 miles (3,200 km) across southeastern Siberia, north of the Trans-Siberian. Construction began in 1974 and was completed 10 years later, opening up rich mineral and timber resources.

Farming, like manufacturing, is concentrated in the southwest, where conditions are favorable to dry farming. Wheat is the chief

Pipeline Under Construction. Western Siberia supplies Russia with much of its petroleum and gas.

Traditional Towns and Modern Cities. Wooden buildings and unpaved streets are typical of virtually all towns and villages. Only the major cities have a modern appearance. Shown are Novosibirsk and a village near Lake Baykal.

crop. In 1954 a program was begun in southwestern Siberia and the adjacent part of Kazakhstan that eventually brought 100 million acres (40 million hectares) of virgin land into wheat production. Other grains, sunflower seeds for oil, and sugar beets are also significant crops.

Mining, lumbering, fur farming, and trapping are carried on in some far-north localities. The only sizable northern city is Norilsk (181,000), a nickel-producing center near the mouth of the Yenisey River. Throughout the far north transportation is primarily by water during summer. There is also air service to several Arctic ports and remote towns. Commercial fishing is becoming increasingly important in the cold waters along the Pacific coast.

People

There are more than 40 million people in Siberia, most of whom are Russians, Ukrainians, and other Slavs. The Slavic population lives predominantly in cities. Throughout Siberia, but mainly in rural areas, are various indigenous peoples, most of them belonging to Turkic, Mongol, or other Altaic-speaking groups.

The Turkic-speaking peoples include the Tatars in the west, the Tuvinians in Central Siberia, and the Yakuts in the northeast. The largest of the Mongol groups are the Buryats. They are found, along with the Tungus-Manchurians, in the southeast. The Tuvinians, Yakuts, and Buryats each have their own state.

Siberia has numerous nomadic tribes in the northern regions. They live chiefly by

S-400

hunting, fishing, and reindeer herding. The majority are of Finno-Ugrian stock. In the northeast are peoples of Paleo-Asiatic stock, including the Chúkchi and the Koryak.

History

Southern Siberia was a part of the vast Mongol Empire conquered by Genghis Khan in the 13th century. To the Europeans, who referred to the conquerors as Tatars, Siberia became known as Tatary. Russian fur traders first penetrated the wilds of western Siberia in the 1500's. During 1581-84, Cossacks conquered western Siberia for Russia, defeating the forces of an independent khan at his capital, Sibir. This town gave Siberia its name.

Market Vendor. This Buryat woman belongs to one of the many Mongoloid ethnic groups in Siberia.

This conquest ended the last organized resistance to the Russian advance eastward. Following exploration by the fur traders, the Cossacks established garrisons throughout the wilderness and exacted tributes in furs from surrounding tribes. By the mid-1600's, Russia's frontiers had been extended to the Pacific Ocean.

After reaching the Pacific, the Russians moved south and encountered serious opposition from the Manchurians in the Amur River basin, where the Chinese aided local tribes to resist Cossack forces. By a treaty with China in 1689, Russia agreed to stay out of this region. In 1860 Russia was finally able to force a much weaker China to give up the Amur basin and a coastal region on the Sea of Japan. Vladivostok was founded the same year.

Siberia's vastness and severe climate hampered Russian settlement for centuries. Much colonization resulted from the czarist policy of exiling criminals and political offenders to the area. Mass settlement of voluntary colonists did not begin until the construction of the Trans-Siberian Railway, 1891-1915. In the civil war that followed the Russian Revolution of 1917, Siberia was used as a base by Russian White armies opposing the Bolshevik regime. By the end of 1921, the Bolsheviks had won firm control of the region.

The Bolsheviks continued the practice of exiling prisoners to Siberia. Under Stalin, the penal system was vastly enlarged and millions of people were exiled to Siberia to work at slave labor. After Stalin died in 1953, most of the slave labor camps were dismantled and the Soviet government promoted colonization and development of the region. When the Soviet Union collapsed in 1991, some Siberian groups urged independence. In response, the Russian government granted Siberia greater independence.

Siberian Husky. See DOG, subtitle *Breeds of Dogs:* Working Dogs.

Sibley, Henry Hastings (1811-1891), a United States public official. Sibley helped to establish Minnesota Territory and in 1849 became its first territorial delegate to the U.S. Congress. When Minnesota became a state, he served as its first governor (1858-60). In 1862 Sibley led a force of state militia that put down a Sioux uprising, and he eventually helped to negotiate a peace treaty with the Sioux. For his service he was given the rank of brigadier general by President Lincoln.

Sibley was born in Detroit. In 1834 he moved to Minnesota (then part of Michigan Territory) and opened a branch of the American Fur Company at Mendota. After his military service ended in 1866, he served a term in the state legislature and was later involved in several business ventures.

Sibyl, sĭb'ĭl, in Roman mythology, a female prophet. Sibyls were usually priestesses of the god Apollo, who was said to inspire their prophecies. The most famous of them was the sibyl of Cumae, in Italy, who was said to have lived for a thousand years. According to legend, she wrote the Sibylline Books, important prophecies concerning the destiny of Rome.

Sibylline Books. See SIBYL.

Sicilies, Kingdom of the Two, a former kingdom consisting of the island of Sicily and southern Italy. In the 11th century, Norman adventurers conquered territory in southern Italy, holding their lands as vassals of the pope. The Norman knights, led by Roger de Hauteville (also called Roger Guiscard), then invaded Sicily, and Roger became its ruler. His son Roger II combined Sicily with the Norman conquests in Italy, and in 1130, with papal approval,

---

For further information, see:

Land

ALTAI MOUNTAINS	SIKHOTE ALIN RANGE
KAMCHATKA	URAL MOUNTAINS
PENINSULA	YABLONOVYY RANGE

Water

ALDAN RIVER	KARA SEA
AMUR RIVER	LENA RIVER
BAYKAL, LAKE	OB RIVER
BERING SEA	OKHOTSK, SEA OF
BERING STRAIT	TUNGUSKA
JAPAN, SEA OF	YENISEY RIVER

Regions

ARCTIC REGIONS	TAIGA	TUNDRA

Cities

ANGARSK	NOVOKUZ-	OMSK
IRKUTSK	NETSK	TOMSK
KRASNOYARSK	NOVOSIBIRSK	VLADIVOSTOK

Miscellaneous

BERING, VITUS	TRANS-SIBERIAN RAILWAY

Books about Siberia

Bobrick, Benson. *East of the Sun: the Epic Conquest and Tragic History of Siberia* (Simon & Schuster, 1992).

Forsyth, James. *A History of the Peoples of Siberia: Russia's North Asian Colony* (Cambridge University, 1992).

Matthiessen, Peter. *Baikal: Sacred Sea of Siberia* (Sierra Club, 1992).

a kingdom was created and named the Two Sicilies. Norman expansion on the mainland continued until the kingdom consisted of everything south of the Papal States. Islamic culture, prevalent in Sicily, continued to flourish under the Normans and penetrated into Europe.

In 1194 the kingdom passed to the German Henry VI, Holy Roman Emperor, through marriage. Frederick II, his son, made Sicily his home and ruled the empire from his capital at Palermo.

In 1266-68 the Two Sicilies were conquered by Charles, count of Anjou, brother of King Louis IX of France. An uprising against the French (an event known as the Sicilian Vespers) broke out in 1282. The revolt, aided by the Spanish house of Aragon, was successful in Sicily, but the Angevins continued to hold southern Italy, renamed the Kingdom of Naples. Naples was reunited with Sicily under Spanish rule in the 1440's.

In the Peace of Utrecht (1713) ending the War of the Spanish Succession, Austria received Naples; it later acquired Sicily. Spanish control over the Two Sicilies was restored in the 1730's by the Bourbons. In the mid-19th century, insurrections against Bourbon rule broke out in Sicily. In 1860 Garibaldi helped drive the Spanish rulers out of the kingdom, which became part of a united Italy.

See also ALFONSO, subtitle *Aragon:* Alfonso V; FERDINAND, subtitle *Two Sicilies:* Ferdinand I and II; FREDERICK, subtitle *Holy Roman Empire:* Frederick II; HENRY, subtitle *Germany:* Henry VI.

Sicily, sĭs'ĭ-lĭ, (*Italian:* Sicilia), the largest island in the Mediterranean Sea. Politically, it is part of Italy. It lies off the southern tip of the Italian mainland, separated from it by the narrow Strait of Messina. Sicily is roughly triangular in shape and has an area of 9,926 square miles (25,708 km²).

The island is a rugged land of mountains and hills, with little flat land except along the coast. The principal ranges cross northern Sicily, reaching elevations of nearly 6,500 feet (1,980 m). Southward, the ranges give way to the lower mountains and hills that make up most of the island's terrain. Sicily's highest peak is the massive Mount Etna, a 10,902-foot (3,323-m) active volcano near the east coast. With few exceptions, Sicily's rivers are short; many of them are dry during summer. The climate is of the Mediterranean type—the winters are cool and rainy and the summers are hot and dry.

With its limited resources, relatively high population, and isolated location, Sicily is one of Italy's poorer regions. Sicilians have long been dependent primarily on farming—an occupation that provides only bare subsistence to many. Although industrial development is beginning to raise the low income level in some parts of the island, many people continue to live by farming. Wheat is the chief field crop, followed by barley and oats. The coastal lowlands of the north and east produce a large part of Italy's citrus fruit crop. There are also extensive olive groves and vineyards.

The discovery of petroleum in the 1950's marked the beginning of gradual economic change in Sicily. Oil fields near Ragusa and Gela, which account for most of Italy's domestic production of crude oil, brought about the building of refineries and petrochemical plants on the coast. In the area between Catania and Syracuse were built manufacturing plants producing such items as drugs, paper, and electronic equipment. Other factories have been established at Palermo and Messina, which also have sizable shipbuilding and food-processing industries. Trapani and Syracuse are commercial fishing ports.

Sicily's population in 1991 was 4,966,386. The largest cities were Palermo, the capital, 697,162; Catania, 330,037; and Messina, 272,461.

SICILY

⊕ Capital

| 0 | Miles | 40 |
| 0 | Km | 40 |

EUROPE
Sicily

Tyrrhenian Sea

Stromboli

Lipari Islands

Egadi Islands

PALERMO

Trapani

6,492' 1,979 m

Nebrodi Mts.

Messina

Reggio di Calabria

Marsala

Mt. Etna 10,902' ▲ 3,323 m

Strait of Messina

Caltanissetta

Salso

Catania

Gela

Ragusa

Siracusa (Syracuse)

MEDITERRANEAN   SEA

© Gary Yeowell/Stone

Taormina, Sicily, a resort on the east coast. The town is on the cliffs above the beach.

History

Sicily's strategic location brought successive waves of colonists and invaders. Trading posts were established by the Phoenicians, about 900 B.C. In the eighth century B.C., Greek colonists began to arrive, and the Phoenicians were forced to withdraw to the western part of the island. Rivalries gradually developed among the flourishing Greek cities. Syracuse, in the east, came to dominate most of Sicily and rivaled Athens in culture and military power.

In 409 B.C., Carthaginian invaders overran most of Sicily. Following the First Punic War (264-241), fought between Rome and Carthage, Sicily became a Roman province. Beginning in the fifth century A.D., it was invaded by Vandals and Goths. Byzantine forces eventually freed Sicily from the barbarians. During the ninth century, Muslim invaders from North Africa gained control.

Islamic culture flourished, and Sicily became a trade center. In the 11th century, the Normans, who had conquered southern Italy, added Sicily to their domain, which became the Kingdom of the Two Sicilies in 1130. (For the history of Sicily as part of the Kingdom of the Two Sicilies, see SICILIES, KINGDOM OF THE TWO.)

Following the overthrow of the kingdom's Spanish monarchy in 1860, Sicily became part of a unified Italy.

See also CATANIA; ETNA, MOUNT; MAFIA; MESSINA; MESSINA, STRAIT OF; PALERMO; SYRACUSE.

Sickle. See REAPING AND THRESHING, subtitle *Hand Reaping.*

Sickle-cell Anemia. See ANEMIA, subtitle *Causes and Kinds.*

Siddhartha Gautama. See BUDDHA.

Siddons, Sarah (Kemble) (1755-1831), an English tragic actress—the greatest of the

18th century. Her most outstanding role was that of Lady Macbeth. She was born in Wales, the daughter of actor-manager Roger Kemble. At 18 she married William Siddons, a fellow actor in her father's troupe. Mrs. Siddons' first London success was in 1782 at the Drury Lane Theatre. In 1806 she joined her brother John Philip Kemble at Covent Garden Theatre, where he was co-manager.

For Sir Joshua Reynolds' painting *Sarah Siddons as the Tragic Muse* see REYNOLDS, Sir JOSHUA. Gainsborough also painted her portrait.

See also KEMBLE (family).

Sidereal Time. See TIME, subtitle *Units and Systems of Time Measurement.*

Sidesaddle Flower. See PITCHER PLANT.

Sidestroke. See SWIMMING, subtitle *Styles of Swimming.*

Sidewinder. See RATTLESNAKE, subtitle *Kinds of Rattlesnakes.*

Sidney, Sir **Philip** (1554-1586), an English author, statesman, and soldier. His important writings were published after his

Library of Congress
Sir Philip Sidney

death. *Arcadia* (1590), a pastoral romance in prose and verse, furnished plots and characters for works by Spenser, Shakespeare, and others. *Astrophel and Stella* (1591) includes some of the most structurally perfect and emotionally powerful sonnets in English. They greatly influenced the sonnets of Shakespeare. *An Apology for Poetry* (1595) is the first significant example of English literary criticism.

Sidney was born in Penshurst, Kent. He attended Oxford from 1568 to 1571. Sidney was knighted by Queen Elizabeth in 1583 and was sent by her on several diplomatic missions. In 1585 he was appointed governor of Flushing, a commune in the Netherlands. The following year he was fatally wounded in the Battle of Zutphen while aiding the Dutch against the Spanish. Sidney was greatly admired as a person. The story is told that as he lay wounded he refused a drink of water and asked that it be given to a soldier whose need he thought was greater than his own.

Sidon. See PHOENICIA.

Siegbahn, Kai. See NOBEL PRIZES (Physics, 1981).

Siegbahn, Karl Manne Georg. See NOBEL PRIZES (Physics, 1924).

Siege, a military action in which a hostile force *invests,* or surrounds, a fort or town. The purpose is to cut off help or communications from the outside so that the besieged forces may be defeated by direct and repeated assault or compelled to surrender by lack of food, water, or ammunition. A siege is *lifted* when the attacking force abandons the attempt. Sometimes the besieged forces are *relieved* by an outside force, which drives off the attackers.

Besiegers in ancient times sometimes built a wall around the besieged place and another around their own position to shield themselves from attack by relief forces. Catapults were used to hurl large rocks, wooden beams, and other objects at the defenders. To assault the walls, soldiers used ladders or rode on high, movable towers. Attackers would normally try to make a *breach* (gap) in the wall. This was attempted by either pounding with a battering ram or undermining by *sapping*—digging under a wall to cause its collapse.

Long sieges were common in the Middle Ages, when strong castles were won more often by starving the defenders than by direct attack. With the introduction of gunpowder in the late Middle Ages, sapping, by making use of explosives, became more effective. With the development of artillery, however, sapping fell into disuse because concentrated bombardment proved sufficient to make a breach. Because artillery fire from

Some Famous Sieges

Location	Date	Length	Conflict	Defenders	Attackers	Result
Troy (Asia Minor)	1194 B.C.?-1184 B.C.?	10 years	Trojan War	Trojans	Greeks	Fell
Tyre (Phoenicia)	332 B.C.	7 months	Alexander the Great's Conquests	Phoenicians	Macedonians	Fell
Syracuse (Sicily)	213 B.C.-211 B.C.	2 years	Second Punic War	Greek allies of Carthage	Romans	Fell
Orléans, France	1428-29	7 months	Hundred Years' War	French	English	Relieved
Gibraltar	1779-83	43½ months	American Revolution	British	French and Spanish in support of United States	Siege Lifted
Sevastopol, Russia	1854-55	11 months	Crimean War	Russians	Anglo-French Sardinian Turkish	Fell
Vicksburg, United States	1862-63	186 days	American Civil War	Confederates	Union troops	Fell
Paris, France	1870-71	130 days	Franco-Prussian War	French	Germans	Fell
Port Arthur, Manchuria	1904-05	241 days	Russo-Japanese War	Russians	Japanese	Fell
Verdun, France	1916	298 days	World War I	French	Germans	Siege Lifted
Leningrad, Russia	1941-44	28 months	World War II	Russians	Germans	Relieved
Stalingrad, Russia	1942-43	166 days	World War II	Russians	Germans	Relieved
Dienbienphu, Vietnam	1954	55 days	Indochina War	French	Viet Minh	Fell
Khe Sanh, Vietnam	1968	76 days	Vietnamese War	U.S. Marines	North Vietnamese	Relieved

the besieged forces made assault at ground level hazardous and the use of movable towers impracticable, attacking troops were moved up to the walls through zigzag approach trenches.

The development of coordinated attacks by air and ground forces, by which cities normally could be taken in a matter of days, virtually ended siege warfare in its original form. Nevertheless, it was shown in World War II at Leningrad and Stalingrad that determined defenders sometimes could still hold a city against besiegers.

See also BATTERING RAM; CATAPULT; FORT AND FORTIFICATION.

Siege Perilous. See ROUND TABLE.

Siegfried, sēg'frēd, a legendary German hero. His deeds are almost identical with those of Sigurd, a hero of Scandinavian mythology. Siegfried is the central figure of the first part of the *Nibelungenlied,* a 13th-century German epic, while Sigurd is the hero of the 13th-century Icelandic *Volsunga Saga.* Siegfried's story is also told in Richard Wagner's *Siegfried* and *Götterdämmerung,*

the third and fourth operas in the *Ring of the Nibelung* series.

See also LITERATURE, GERMAN, picture titled *Siegfried Slaying the Dragon;* NIBELUNGENLIED; RING OF THE NIBELUNG.

Siegfried Line. See WORLD WAR II, section "The War with Germany and Italy, 1942-45," subtitle *Breakthrough in France: Southern France Invaded.*

Siemens, sē'mĕnz, the family name of four German brothers who were inventors and industrialists.

Werner von Siemens (1816-1892) invented a method of electroplating; devised a unit of measurement of electrical conductance; and developed a method of using electromagnets to generate an electrical current. He also constructed the first telegraph line in Germany and that country's first electric railway.

Sir William Siemens (1823-1883) invented the bathometer (for measuring water depths) and an electric thermometer, and helped develop the open-hearth process of steel production. He designed the ship that laid the Atlantic cable of 1874. Originally named

Karl Wilhelm, he became a British subject and in 1883 was knighted as Sir William.

Friedrich Siemens (1826-1904) received a patent in 1856 for a method of heat-regeneration that led to the development of the open-hearth process of steel and glass production.

Karl von Siemens (1829-1906) directed the Russian branch of Werner's firm.

Siemens AG, one of the world's largest electronics companies. The company provides products and services in many areas, including transportation, communications, and power generation and transmission. Its consumer products include computers and household appliances. Siemens's numerous products and services for businesses include various telephone lines and systems, lighting design, and software development.

The company was founded in Berlin in 1847 by Werner von Siemens and Johann Georg Halske to construct telegraph equipment. Werner's brother Sir William Siemens directed the company's London subsidiary and another brother, Karl von Siemens, established subsidiary factories and directed the Russian division of the company. Siemens was implicated in World War II German atrocities and, after the war, most of its plants were taken or destroyed by other nations. In the 1950's the company began to recover financially. Siemens has production sites worldwide. Headquarters are in Munich.

Siena, sĭ-ĕn'à (*Italian:* syâ'nä), Italy, a city in Tuscany, about 115 miles (185 km) northwest of Rome. Siena is primarily a tourist and art center, little changed since the 15th century. Medieval walls enclose the city with its narrow, winding streets lined by Gothic- and Renaissance-style buildings. Outstanding among Siena's landmarks are the central square, the cathedral, and the 14th-century town hall. The Palio delle Contrade, a colorful horse race and festival held since 1656, attracts numerous visitors each summer.

Siena was founded as a Roman colony in the first century B.C. After the fall of Rome in the fifth century A.D., it was ruled in turn by Lombards, Franks, and its own counts. Between about 1125 and 1500 Siena rivaled Florence as a trading and banking center. During this period Siena was the seat of a school of painting that included such artists as Duccio di Buoninsegna and Simone Martini.

In the mid-1500's Siena was conquered by the Medicis of Florence. They ruled Tuscany until their line died out in 1737, and their holdings passed to the family of Hapsburg-Lorraine. In 1860 Siena, with the rest of Tuscany, was annexed by the Kingdom of Sardinia, the nucleus of united Italy.

Population: 61,349.

Sienkiewicz, shĕn-kyĕ'vĕch, **Henryk** (1846-1916), a Polish novelist. In 1905 he was awarded the Nobel Prize for literature. He is perhaps best known in English for *Quo Vadis?* (1896), a novel about persecution of the Christians under Nero in Rome. It has been dramatized and filmed a number of times. Poland's 17th-century struggle for national existence was pictured in his trilogy: *With Fire and Sword* (1884), *The Deluge* (1886), and *Pan Michael* (1887-88).

Sienkiewicz was born in Russian Poland. He graduated from the University of Warsaw in 1870 and then began a career in journalism. From 1876 to 1878 he lived in the United States, studying the problems of Polish immigrants. He was a leader in Poland's struggle for independence.

Sierra Club, a United States organization concerned with the preservation of the world's natural environment. The club's main concern is the protection of forests, wilderness areas, bodies of water, and other natural sites, and of wildlife. The club promotes conservation programs, publishes books and produces films about ecology, initiates legal proceedings to prevent the destruction of scenic and natural resources, and lobbies for conservation legislation. It offers numerous outdoor activities for members.

The Sierra Club was founded by the naturalist John Muir in 1892. It was influential in the establishment of the National Park Service, the U.S. Forest Service, and the National Wilderness Preservation System. It has approximately 650,000 members. Publications include a biweekly news report and a bimonthly magazine, *Sierra*. Headquarters are in San Francisco, California.

Sierra Leone, sĭ-ĕr'à lē-ōn', officially **Republic of Sierra Leone,** a country in western Africa. It is bordered by the Atlantic Ocean, Guinea, and Liberia. Its area is 27,699 square miles (71,740 km²). The name is from the Portuguese for "Lion Mountain."

Sierra Leone's coast, which is 210 miles (340 km) long, has numerous bays, estuaries, and mangrove swamps. Inland are wide, rolling grasslands and scattered areas of scrub forest. In the extreme east are hills and low mountains marking the edge of western

SIERRA LEONE

Africa's broad plateau. This region of Sierra Leone averages 1,500 to 2,000 feet (460 to 600 m) above sea level; a few peaks, such as those in the Loma Mountains, reach 6,000 feet (1,800 m) or more. Nearly all of the major rivers, including the Rokel, Jong, and Sewa, flow to the Atlantic from the eastern mountains.

The climate is tropical, with heavy, although seasonal, rainfall. Nearly all the rain occurs between April and November, and the greatest accumulations are along the coast. Freetown receives about 150 inches (3,800 mm) annually, but parts of the interior may get only half that amount. Grass and secondary scrub growth have replaced most of the tropical rain forest that once covered nearly all the land.

The Economy

Sierra Leone is an underdeveloped nation with a largely rural population. Most of the people live and work on small farms, producing barely enough food to provide for their own needs. Rice is the main food crop. It is supplemented by cassava, sweet potatoes, and other vegetables. Commercial crops, including palm kernels and fiber, cacao, and coffee, are raised chiefly for export.

Mining is the chief nonagricultural activity, with minerals accounting for a large share of exports. Rutile, a titanium ore, leads all other minerals in value of export. It is produced near Moyamba and Bonthe. Sierra Leone is a major producer of diamonds of both gem and industrial quality. Bauxite and gold are also produced in significant amounts.

Manufacturing, the least developed part of the economy, centers on Freetown and is devoted chiefly to processing agricultural and mineral products.

Inadequate transportation is a serious problem in Sierra Leone. Only a small part of the road system has been paved; the rest is subject to frequent damage from heavy rains. Most foreign trade moves through Freetown, the chief seaport. Bonthe is also an important seaport. An international airport is at Lungi, 10 miles (16 km) north of Freetown.

Sierra Leone's basic currency unit is the leone.

People

Sierra Leone's population in 1985 was 3,517,530; that of Freetown, the capital and

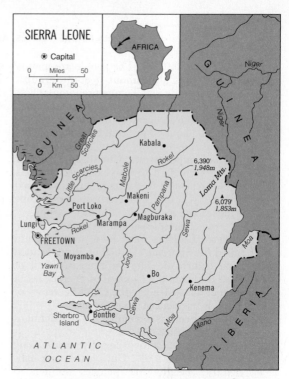

King Jimmy Market, Freetown
© Pedro Coll/The Stock Market

largest city, 469,776. The people are mainly blacks, representing about 18 ethnic groups, with the Mende and Temne predominant.

English is Sierra Leone's official language, but numerous indigenous dialects are spoken. Although about 40 per cent of the people are Muslims, the majority follow animist beliefs. A small minority are Christians. Primary schools provide a seven-year program, secondary schools a five-year program followed by a two-year one. University of Sierra Leone is the leading institution of higher learning.

Government and History

Sierra Leone is ruled by a military junta called the Supreme Council of State, headed by a chairman. The Supreme Council of State appoints the Council of Secretaries, a cabinet whose leader, the Chief Secretary of State, is the head of government.

Sierra Leone is a member of the Commonwealth of Nations.

The Portuguese first began to trade along the coast about 1500. During the next half-century, neighboring peoples subjugated many of the local peoples and established kingdoms. The British arrived in 1562 in search of slaves, and soon many Europeans were trading in the region. In 1787, British philanthropists bought land at the site of Freetown to establish a settlement for freed slaves. The colony prospered and became an important center for trade and missionary activity. In 1896 the British proclaimed a protectorate over the area that is modern Sierra Leone.

Sierra Leone became independent in 1961, and throughout the 1960's was beset with political instability. Sieka Stevens came to power in 1968 and gradually imposed authoritarian rule. In 1978 he created a one-party state. He retired in 1985.

In 1991, the Revolutionary United Front engaged in fighting to overthrow the government. The ensuing civil war continued through the 1990's. In 1999, a peace agreement was reached, and the United Nations established a peacekeeping operation to assist in the implementation of the agreement.

See also FLAG (color page); FREETOWN.

Books about Sierra Leone

Fyfe, C. M. *The History of Sierra Leone* (Trafalgar Square, 1993).
For Younger Readers
Milsome, John. *Sierra Leone* (Chelsea House, 1988).

Sierra Madre, sĭ-ĕr'*à* mä'drä, the name of three mountain ranges in Mexico that bor-

der the Central Plateau. The Sierra Madre Occidental is in the west, the Sierra Madre Oriental is in the east, and the Sierra Madre del Sur in the south.

See also MEXICO, subtitle *Physical Geography:* Land.

Sierra Nevada, syĕr'rä nȧ-vä'tħä, a mountain range in southern Spain, part of the Cordillera Penibética. It lies some 15 to 25 miles (24 to 40 km) north of the Mediterranean coast, extending eastward from the vicinity of Granada for about 50 miles (80 km). One of Spain's most rugged ranges, the Sierra Nevada has several peaks exceeding altitudes of 10,000 feet (3,000 m) above sea level. Snowcapped Mount Mulhacén, at 11,411 feet (3,478 m), is the highest peak in continental Spain.

Sierra Nevada, sĭ-ĕr'*à* nĕ-văd'*à*, a mountain range in the United States. It lies almost entirely in California; a small section near Lake Tahoe juts into Nevada. The range is some 400 miles (640 km) long and 40 to 80 miles (65 to 130 km) wide. For most of its length it rises abruptly from the Great Basin on the east and slopes gently toward the Central Valley of California on the west. In the southern section, called the High Sierras, are 11 peaks more than 14,000 feet (4,270 m) high. One of these is 14,494-foot (4,418-m) Mount Whitney, the highest point in the United States outside Alaska.

Numerous rivers originate in the Sierra Nevada. Most of them flow westward to the Central Valley. Lumbering and grazing in the range are of major economic importance. The Sierra Nevada contains some of the finest scenery in the United States, including that of Yosemite, Sequoia, and Kings Canyon national parks and Lake Tahoe.

See also TAHOE, LAKE; WHITNEY, MOUNT; YOSEMITE NATIONAL PARK.

Sieyès, syä-yâs', **Abbé Emmanuel Joseph** (1748-1836), a French clergyman and statesman. Sieyès was a conspirator in the coup d'etat of 1799 that overthrew the Directory and brought Napoleon to power. He was a consul in Napoleon's first government and was later made a senator and count of the empire. Following Napoleon's overthrow, he lived in exile until 1830. Sieyès wrote *What Is the Third Estate?* (1789), a revolutionary pamphlet, and helped write the Declaration of the Rights of Man of the French Revolution.

Sight. See EYE (and cross references).

Sight, in weaponry. See RIFLE, subtitle *How a Rifle Works*.

Sigismund, sĭj'ĭs-mŭnd (1368-1437), king of Hungary (1387-1437), Holy Roman emperor (1411-37), and king of Bohemia (1419-37). He was the son of Emperor Charles IV of the House of Luxemburg. After gaining the Hungarian throne through marriage to Mary, queen of Hungary, he tried unsuccessfully to stop a Turkish invasion of the Balkans.

The ecumenical Council of Constance was called in 1414, under Sigismund's auspices. It ended the Great Western Schism in the papacy and dealt with the heresy of John Huss. The emperor was bitterly condemned by the Hussites for permitting Huss—after promising him safe conduct and protection —to be burned at the stake. After Sigismund succeeded his brother Wenceslaus to the throne of Bohemia in 1419, the Hussites' refusal to accept him led to 15 years of warfare. He was finally accepted as king in 1436.

Sigma Xi, The Scientific Research Society, sĭg'má zī, an honorary organization dedicated to research in the pure and applied sciences. Individuals are elected to membership on the basis of their achievement or potential achievement in scientific research. The society publishes *American Scientist,* a bi-monthly. The organization was founded as Sigma Xi in 1886. In 1974 it absorbed the Scientific Research Society of America. Membership is approximately 110,000. Headquarters are in Research Triangle Park, North Carolina.

Sigmoid Colon. See INTESTINE, and illustration.

Sign Language, a method of communicating by gestures, especially of the hands. A sign language was used by the Indians of North America who lived on the plains between the Rocky Mountains and the Mississippi River. Since each tribe had its own spoken language, the tribes used a common sign language when they came in contact with each other. The Kiowas were considered the most eloquent and fluent in the sign language.

Deaf persons are sometimes taught a sign language. See DEAFNESS, subtitle *Education of the Deaf* (and illustrations titled *Signing* and *American Manual Alphabet*).

Signac, sē'nyȧk', **Paul** (1863-1935), a French painter. He was the leading spokesman for pointillism, or neo-impressionism.

Quay at Clichy, by Paul Signac in 1887; oil on canvas, 18¼ by 25¾ inches (46.4 × 65.4 cm)

Baltimore Museum of Art

His book *From Eugène Delacroix to Neo-Impressionism* (1899) explains the pointillist theory of applying color in dots of relatively uniform size.

Signac was born in Paris. At first he painted in the Impressionist style. In 1884 he met Seurat and adopted his pointillist technique, painting such works as *Quay at Clichy* and *The Harbor*. In 1900 Signac began a series of pencil and watercolor sketches that are marked by simplicity and spontaneity. Many art historians feel these are among his best works.

Signal Corps, the branch of the U.S. Army responsible for communications. Common means of electronic communication used by the corps are telephone, facsimile, radio, and computer systems. The corps also uses messengers and hand signaling. Signal Corps troops may be assigned to any type of unit, but most are attached to signal units, which operate and maintain communications for brigades or larger units.

Functions of the Signal Corps other than communications include preparing psychological-warfare materials, data processing, taking photographs, and producing training films and videotapes. Where United States troops are stationed in foreign countries, the corps operates radio and television networks for their entertainment.

The Signal Corps was established as a separate branch of the army during the Civil War. The corps pioneered in the use of balloons and airplanes for observation purposes. The army's aviation section was a part of the Signal Corps until 1920, when a separate air service was formed.

Signaling, a form of communication not requiring the ordinary use of written or spoken language. A signal, also frequently referred to as a sign, consists of something sighted or heard (or, occasionally, felt) that instantly conveys meaning or that transmits a message to a point beyond the range of human voice or in circumstances requiring silence. In distance transmission a code is used. (See CODE, in communications.)

Lights, flags, hand gestures, and sound devices such as horns, bells, and whistles are common means of signaling. When used to transmit code, radio and telegraphy are also signaling methods. Some signals are completely natural and universally understood—an arm motion meaning "come here," for example, or a whistle to attract attention.

Some signals in the form of symbols are equally well understood, such as an arrow sign signaling direction. (See SYMBOL.)

Some simple signals are meaningless without prior knowledge—a busy signal on the telephone, for example. Visual signals may depend on shape, color, and an established word or phrase to convey a message, such as a triangular yellow road sign bearing the world "Yield," which tells a motorist that other traffic has the right-of-way. Information may also be transmitted by patterns of sound or movement, as when a certain sequence of blasts is sounded on a ship's whistle to signal "passing to starboard." Most codes are based on pattern.

Signaling systems that depend on code require study and training to understand and use. Besides learning the signals for the letters of the alphabet, numerals, and punctuation, practice is necessary to execute them so they will always be recognized. In addition to such signals with permanent, fixed meanings, a code signal may be improvised for one-time use—for example, the "one if by land, two if by sea" lanterns in Longfellow's poem about Paul Revere.

Signals are an important part of everyday life—such signals as the ring of the telephone or doorbell, the pilot light indicating that an electric appliance is turned on, and the hand gestures of a traffic officer.

Hand signals are used to conduct certain kinds of business, such as trading on the floor of a stock exchange or commodity exchange. (For picture, see STOCK EXCHANGE.) In auctions of art and antiques, bidding is mainly by hand or head signals, which sometimes are known only to the bidder and the auctioneer. (When hand gestures are part of a system by which conversation can be carried on, they are considered to be sign language rather than signals.) Hand signals are often used in military operations when silence is essential or when the noise of combat makes voice communication impossible.

Signals are widely used in transportation. Self-propelled vehicles of all kinds are equipped with lights or sound devices to signal the vehicle's movements to other traffic or to signal a malfunction to the operator. A train crew uses whistles, hand signals, and lanterns or flashlights for exchanging operating orders and information. (Walkie-talkies have reduced the need for such sig-

Flags and Pennants of the International Flag Code*

Each letter and numeral has a code name by which it is known for signaling purposes. The names of the numerals combine a foreign word with the English word.

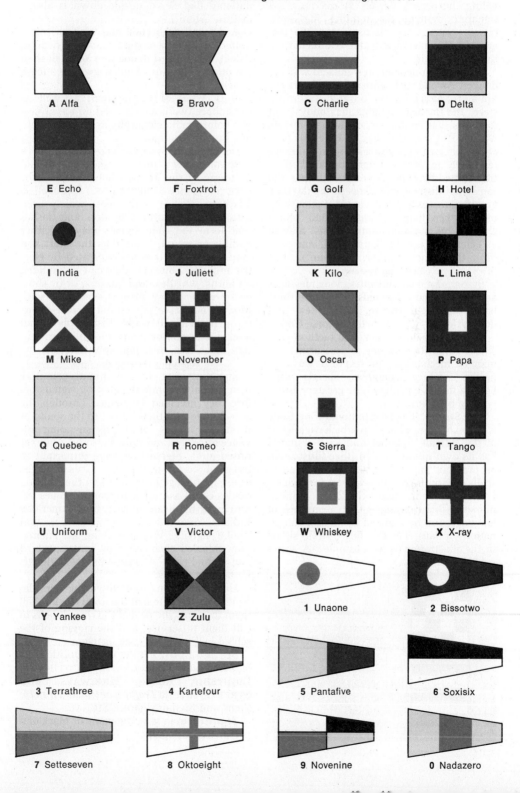

A Alfa   **B** Bravo   **C** Charlie   **D** Delta

E Echo   **F** Foxtrot   **G** Golf   **H** Hotel

I India   **J** Juliett   **K** Kilo   **L** Lima

M Mike   **N** November   **O** Oscar   **P** Papa

Q Quebec   **R** Romeo   **S** Sierra   **T** Tango

U Uniform   **V** Victor   **W** Whiskey   **X** X-ray

Y Yankee   **Z** Zulu   **1** Unaone   **2** Bissotwo

3 Terrathree   **4** Kartefour   **5** Pantafive   **6** Soxisix

7 Setteseven   **8** Oktoeight   **9** Novenine   **0** Nadazero

naling, however.) Vessels at sea may use signaling systems for sending messages. (These systems are discussed later in this article.) Motor-vehicle traffic is directed entirely by signals.

People often depend on signals to warn of danger. Among such warning signals are the fire alarm at school, the burglar alarm in a store, and the beacon lights, bell buoys, and foghorns that enable vessels to stay in safe waters. If a ship founders, it relies for help on an international distress signal—the letters SOS in Morse International Code—transmitted by radio. A vessel without radio can signal distress with flags in the daytime or with flares at night. An aircraft pilot, who uses spoken language rather than Morse Code in his radio communications, may in an emergency use the signal word "mayday" (from the French *m'aider,* "help me").

Signaling Systems

Systems for communicating long messages are based on coded signals. There are three basic types—semaphore, flag codes, and dot-and-dash systems such as Morse Code.

Semaphore System is a visual method consisting of positioning one or two arms, human or mechanical, in specified ways. A person sending semaphore signals often holds a flag in each hand for greater visibility. (See SEMAPHORE.)

Flag Systems. The International Flag Code is based on a set of flags in which each letter of the Roman alphabet and each numeral has its own unique design. (See illustration on previous page.) Flags can be hoisted to spell out messages in various languages. Even more important, the code contains numerous brief messages that, regardless of language, can be signaled by certain combinations of flags. The two-flag distress signal in the illustration is an example. (A ship's national flag flown upside down is also a distress signal.)

A dot-and-dash code may also be transmitted by use of a single flag, which denotes a dot when dipped to one side and a dash to the other. The Boy Scout wigwag is such a system.

Both types of flag system, as well as semaphore, were widely used on naval vessels before radiotelegraphy and radiotelephony became common.

Dot-and-dash Systems. The concept of a code consisting of long and short signals had its origin in the Morse Code, designed for telegraphy. (See MORSE CODE.) It proved so adaptable that it is the most widely used system in the world. The dots and dashes that form the code signals may be either audible or visual. If audible, the short and long sounds are commonly created by electric impulse; however, they can be sounded on horns, whistles, and buzzers, or by shots or by raps. Many prisoners familiar with Morse Code have tapped out conversations through their cell walls. Visible short and long signals can be made with blinker, lantern, flashlight, or heliograph (reflector).

Signaling Through the Ages

Signaling is as old as mankind; primitive men probably communicated by signals before they invented language. Through the ages men fought their battles to the sound of trumpets, bugles, or drums signaling advance or retreat and rallied around a banner raised aloft. Signal fires were important in times of crisis; during the Crusades, for example, besieged Crusaders in their hilltop castles could ask for help from 50 miles (80 km) away by means of their fires. American Indians communicated by signal fires and smoke signals. When stalking an enemy, they signaled each other by imitating bird and animal calls. African tribes sent signals by beating drums.

Until the recent past, town dwellers depended on the chime of the town clock to tell them the time, the peal of the church bells to call them to service, and the ringing of the school bell to signal time for class.

See also BUOY; FIREWORKS, subtitle *Uses of Fireworks;* HELIOGRAPH; LIGHTHOUSE; LIGHTSHIP; ROADS, HIGHWAYS, AND STREETS, subtitle *Traffic Control and Safety:* Signs and Signals; SMOKE SIGNAL.

Signature, in law, the name or mark of a person on a document, indicating that the

The hoist NC (November Charlie) signals "I am in distress and require immediate assistance."

The Damned (detail), by Luca Signorelli in 1503-04; one of a series of frescoes in Orvieto Cathedral in Italy

signer agrees to its contents. Laws covering many types of documents require a handwritten signature, or autograph. An illiterate person is permitted to make his mark, usually a cross, in the presence of witnesses. The most common use of legal signatures is on checks and charge slips.

See also FORGERY.

Signature, in music. See MUSIC, subtitle *Elements of Music:* Melody (Key).

Signature, in publishing. See BOOK, subtitle *How Books Are Made.*

Signorelli, sē′nyô-rĕl′lĕ, **Luca** (1445?-1523), an Italian Renaissance painter. His simple, yet powerful, drawings and paintings of the human figure influenced Raphael, Michelangelo, and other painters of the High Renaissance. Signorelli's frescoes in Orvieto Cathedral, depicting the end of the world and the last judgment, are considered his masterpiece. Signorelli was born in Cortona. He may have studied with Piero della Francesca. About 1475 he went to Florence, where he was influenced by Antonio Pollaiuolo's figure studies.

Other paintings include *Madonna and Child,* *Crucifixion with the Magdalen,* and *Eunostos of Tanagra.*

Sigsbee, sĭgz′bĕ, **Charles D.** (Dwight) (1845-1923), a United States naval officer. In the 1870's Sigsbee developed a number of devices for sounding and dredging that advanced the science of oceanography. After teaching at the U.S. Naval Academy, he was chief hydrographer for the Navy Department (1893-97). He was commander of the battleship *Maine* when it was destroyed in Havana Harbor in 1898. In 1903 he was made a rear admiral. Sigsbee was born in Albany, New York. He graduated from the U.S. Naval Academy in 1863 and served in the Civil War.

Sigurd. See SIEGFRIED.

Sika. See DEER, subtitle *Kinds of Deer.*

Sikhism, sēk′ĭz′m, an Asian religion, centering in the Punjab region of India and Pakistan. Sikhs believe in one God. Their sacred scripture is the *Granth Sahib* (Lord Book). Sikh men wear long hair, untrimmed beards, and turbans.

Sikhism originated in the Punjab. Nanak (1469-1538), founder of the sect, was originally a Hindu. His intention was to unite Hindus and Muslims. Amritsar, founded in 1577, soon became a holy city. Under Govind Singh (1666-1708), the Sikhs became a militant body in order to fight persecution. By 1800 they controlled most of the Punjab and had established an independent state. In 1849 they were conquered by the British, and many Sikhs joined the British military and police forces in Asia.

During the 1980's, violent conflict between Sikhs and Hindus repeatedly occurred in the Indian state of Punjab. The worst outbreak of violence took place in 1984. In an attempt to suppress a terrorist Sikh group, the Indian army stormed the Sikhs' sacred temple at Amritsar, where a large group of terrorists was holding out. Some 600 defenders were killed in the battle. In retaliation, Sikh extremists assassinated Prime Minister Indira Gandhi; outraged Hindus, in turn, slaughtered large numbers of Sikhs.

See also AMRITSAR.

Sikhote Alin Range, sē'kǒ-tā ä-lēn, a mountain range in southeastern Siberia. It extends along the Sea of Japan for about 650 miles (1,050 km), roughly from the mouth of the Amur River to Vladivostok, and is up to 160 miles (260 km) wide. The range attains a maximum elevation of slightly less than 6,600 feet (2,000 m). Heavily forested, the Sikhote Alin is an important lumbering area. The range also contains valuable mineral deposits, especially lead and zinc.

Sikkim, sĭk'ĭm, an Indian state in the Himalayas. It is bounded by Bhutan, the Indian state of Bihar, Nepal, and the Chinese province of Tibet. Sikkim has an area of 2,744 square miles (7,107 km²). It consists primarily of high, snowcapped mountains separated by deep valleys. The loftiest peak, 28,208-foot (8,598-m) Kanchenjunga, lies on the Nepalese border. The only large river is the Tista, a tributary of the Brahmaputra. On the Tibetan border is Natu Pass, a key route between eastern India and Tibet. Sikkim's climate varies from subtropically warm and humid in the valleys to extremely cold in the high mountains.

The Sikkimese live mainly by raising livestock, including yak, and grains and fruits. The only industry is of the handicraft type. There are a few good roads, but in general transportation is poorly developed.

In 1991 Sikkim had a population of 406,-457; Gangtok, the capital and largest town, had a population of 24,971. About three-fourths of the people are of Nepalese origin. The rest are mainly Lepchas (the indigenous

Lamaistic Monastery, Sikkim. Lamaism, a form of Buddhism, is practiced by nearly a quarter of the people of Sikkim.

© John Paul Kay/Peter Arnold, Inc.

Igor Ivan Sikorsky
Sikorsky Aircraft

inhabitants) and Bhotias from Tibet. Nepali and several Tibeto-Burman languages are spoken. Lamaism is the faith of the Lepchas and the Bhotias, Hinduism the faith of the Nepalis.

Sikkim's governor is appointed by the president of India. There is an elective legislative assembly.

Little is known of Sikkim's history before the 17th century, when Bhotias from Tibet and Lepchas established a government headed by a maharaja. Sikkim was dominated by Tibet until Great Britain extended its control into the country from India during the 1800's. After about 1870, Nepalis migrated into Sikkim and eventually became the country's largest ethnic group. However, the Bhotias and the Lepchas continued to dominate the government. A treaty in 1950 made Sikkim a protectorate of India. In 1965 the maharaja declared himself *chogyal* (king). In 1975 India annexed Sikkim and abolished the monarchy.

Sikorsky, sĭ-kôr′skĭ, **Igor Ivan** (1889-1972), a Russian-American aeronautical engineer and aircraft manufacturer. Sikorsky made a number of important contributions to aviation. In 1913 he built and flew the world's first multiengined airplane. During the 1930's he designed and manufactured long-range amphibious planes, called "flying boats," that were used for transoceanic passenger service. He designed and in 1939 flew the first practical helicopter. (See HELICOPTER, picture titled *VS-300*.) He later produced several types of helicopters used in World War II, the Korean War, and the Vietnamese War.

Sikorsky was born in Kiev. He studied engineering and during World War I built airplanes for the Russian army. He left Russia during the Revolution and came to the United States in 1919, becoming a citizen in 1928. In 1923 he formed an aircraft manufacturing company, which later merged with United Aircraft Corporation.

Siksika Indians. See BLACKFEET INDIANS.

Silage, or **Ensilage,** food for livestock that consists of plant material preserved by fermentation. Silage is used to feed livestock primarily in winter months when green forage crops are not available. It is made by chopping corn, sorghum, legumes, or other crops into fine pieces with a *silage cutter*.

The chopped plant material is tightly packed into a silo, which is made as airtight as possible. A certain amount of moisture is needed to assist in packing and to hasten fermentation. If the crop is too dry, water is added; if too moist, the crop is wilted on the field before cutting and storing. Silage preservatives, such as molasses or phosphoric acid, are usually added to control the rate of fermentation.

Silesia, sĭ-lē′zhȧ, a historic region of east-central Europe. It occupies the upper valley of the Oder River and is bounded on the south and west by the Sudeten Mountains. All of lower Silesia (the northern two-thirds of the region) and most of upper Silesia (the southern part) are now part of southwestern Poland; a small section of upper Silesia lies in the Czech Republic. Upper Silesia is primarily industrial and contains some of Europe's richest coalfields; lower Silesia is primarily agricultural. Wrocław and Katowice are the area's chief cities.

Slavic tribes had settled in Silesia by the sixth century A.D. In the 11th century the region was conquered by Poland, but Polish rule weakened and in the 14th century Silesia passed to Bohemia. Silesia came under control of Austria in 1526.

In 1740 Prussia invaded Silesia, initiating the first of three Silesian Wars with Austria. The first two wars were part of the War of the Austrian Succession. The first war ended in 1742 when Silesia was ceded to Prussia. Austria failed to recover the territory in the second war (1744-45) and the third (1756-63), which was part of a more general conflict, the Seven Years' War.

When the German Empire was formed in 1871, Silesia, as part of Prussia, was incorporated into it. After World War I small sections of upper Silesia went to Poland and Czechoslovakia. After World War II, changes in boundaries placed the German portions of Silesia in Poland.

See also SEVEN YEARS' WAR; SUCCESSION WARS, subtitle *War of the Austrian Succession*.

Silesian Wars. See SILESIA.

Silhouette, sĭl′ōō-ĕt′, an outline picture filled in with black or some other solid color.

Museum of the City of New York
Silhouette of Lyman Beecher by Auguste Edouart

It may be painted or cut out from black paper and pasted on white board. The technique was named for Étienne de Silhouette (1709-1767), the finance minister of France under Louis XV. He was noted for his frugal economic policies and his name was linked derisively with the inexpensive pictures.

An ancient art, silhouettes are found in the cave paintings of prehistoric humans. Egyptian artists used the technique in decorating tomb and temple walls, and the Greeks used it in decorating vases and other pottery. The silhouette became a popular art form in Europe during the Industrial Revolution when paper and scissors became readily available. Silhouettes by such artists as Auguste Edouart and John Miers are highly valued. The development of photography in the 19th century led to the decline of the silhouette as a fine art form. Silhouettes have been used by commercial artists in the 20th century to convey instant recognition of a product or service.

Silica. See SILICON.

Silica Gel. See SILICON.

Silicon, sĭl´ĭ-kŏn, a lustrous, grayish-black chemical element that has both metallic and nonmetallic properties. Silicon is hard and brittle. It is a semiconductor; that is, its electrical conductivity is intermediate between that of a conductor and that of an insulator. Chemically, silicon is relatively inert at ordinary temperatures. It resists attack by all acids except hydrofluoric acid, and is not easily oxidized by air. At high temperatures, silicon can combine with many other elements.

Silicon is the second most abundant element on earth (after oxygen). It makes up about 28 per cent of the earth's crust. In

nature, silicon is always found combined with other elements. It usually occurs as *silica* (silicon dioxide) or as *silicates,* compounds containing silicon, oxygen, and one or more metals. Most common rocks, soils, and clays consist mainly of silicates. Silica occurs chiefly as quartz, a common igneous rock-forming mineral and the chief constituent of sand and sandstone.

Silica is found in many plants, and is necessary to build strong cell walls. The shells of diatoms and the skeletons of certain sponges consist mainly of silica. Trace amounts of silica occur in such animal parts as feathers and hair.

Silicon (from the Latin *silex,* "flint") was first isolated in 1823 by the Swedish chemist Jöns J. Berzelius. Most commercial silicon is produced by heating sand with coke in an electric arc furnace. The silicon thus obtained, about 98 per cent pure, is used primarily for alloying purposes. Silicon of higher purity is usually prepared by heating silicon tetrachloride or trichlorosilane with hydrogen gas.

Uses

Silicon is widely used in alloys. Copper, when alloyed with silicon, becomes stronger and easier to weld; aluminum, easier to cast; and alloy steels, harder and stronger. Ferrosilicon alloys are used as deoxidizers in steelmaking and as reducing agents in preparing such metals as magnesium and chromium. Highly pure silicon crystals are used as semiconductors in such devices as transistors, power rectifiers, and solar batteries.

Silicon minerals and compounds have many commercial uses. Quartz is used as a flux in metallurgy, and in the manufacture of glass, enamels, mortar, and many other substances. Many silicates are important ore minerals. Some are used to make cement, brick, pottery, porcelain, electrical insulation, and heat-resistant fabrics. Certain silicates (such as emerald and topaz) and some forms of silica (such as opal and amethyst) are highly prized gems. *Diatomite,* a soft rock composed of fossilized diatom shells, is used as a filter for liquids, as a mild abrasive, and as heat insulation.

Silica gel, a porous form of silicon dioxide, is used as a drying agent. A typical use is for keeping packaged instruments dry by taking up any moisture in the package. *Silicon carbide,* an extremely hard substance, is used as an abrasive for grinding, cutting, and polishing metal. *Sodium silicate,* also called *water glass,* is used as a coating to preserve eggs and as an industrial adhesive. The *silicones* are organic silicon compounds that are important oils, resins, and rubber-forming substances.

Symbol: Si. Atomic number: 14. Atomic weight: 28.0855. Specific gravity: 2.33. Melting point: 2,570° F. (1,410° C.). Boiling point: 4,271° F. (2,355° C.). Silicon has three stable isotopes: Si-28 to Si-30. It belongs to Group IV-A of the Periodic Table and may have a valence of +2, +4, or −4.

See also DIATOMITE; QUARTZ; SILICONE; SILICOSIS; WATER GLASS.

Silicon Bronze. See BRONZE.

Silicone, sĭl'ĭ-kōn, the name for a number of man-made oils, resins, and rubber-forming substances; also, products, including certain greases, plastics, and rubbers, based on these substances. The silicones are organosiloxanes; that is, chemical substances consisting of silicon, oxygen, carbon, and hydrogen. The chemical bonds in silicones are much stronger than those in ordinary organic compounds. Silicones are little affected by extreme temperatures, are nonpoisonous, and do not conduct electricity. They resist moisture, weathering, aging, and oxidation. Excellent release properties prevent them from sticking to most organic substances. Commercial silicones were introduced in 1943 by Dow Corning Corporation.

Silicone oils and *silicone greases* are resistant to many solvents and are good electrical insulators. They do not corrode metals. The oils are used as lubricants and as hydraulic fluids, and to waterproof fabrics. Because of their low surface tension, they are used to control foam in making food concentrates and synthetic rubbers. Silicone oils are also used in cosmetics, lotions, adhesives, paints, electrical insulation, and automobile and furniture polishes. Silicone greases serve as lubricants, stable at both high and low temperatures.

Silicone resins resist extreme heat and are excellent electrical insulators. They can be made into films, coatings, rigid foams, and molded objects. Silicone molded plastics resist heat better than organic plastics. Silicone resins are widely used in heat-resistant paints, varnishes, and enamels; in coatings for electrical and electronic components; and in coatings for non-stick baking pans and waffle irons. Textiles and leather treated with the resins are water- and stain-

repellent. Silicone resins have many other uses—in electrical insulation; adhesives and sealants; heat insulation for aircraft; heat shields for space vehicles; and parts for electrical switches, plugs, and sockets.

Silicone rubbers are tough and durable, and resist ozone. They remain flexible at low temperatures and are more resistant to chemicals and heat than natural rubber. Silicone rubbers are used as adhesives and sealants, in protective coatings for electronic equipment, and to make gaskets, rollers, conveyor belts, and electrical insulation. Because they resist body fluids and are not toxic to body tissues, they have important uses in medicine—for example, as prostheses (artificial replacements for damaged body parts, such as ear cartilage and arteries); as protective coatings for heart pacemakers; and as tubing for heart-lung machines.

The silicones are *polymers*—substances composed of extremely large molecules. The molecules contain *siloxane* groups joined together to form chains, rings, or network structures. (A siloxane group consists of a silicon atom linked to an oxygen atom and to two organic groups.) Silicones are made by *polymerization*—the process of changing compounds of low molecular weight and simple structure (such as methyltrichlorosilane) into polymers.

Silicosis, sĭl-ĭ-kō'sĭs, a disease of the lungs caused by the inhaling of silica dust. It is an occupational disease, affecting workers in such occupations as stonecutting, sandblasting, mining, and glassmaking. The particles of silica become embedded in the lungs and abnormal nodules are formed. As the disease progresses more and more of the lung tissue becomes affected and the lungs cannot function properly. Silicosis develops slowly; it takes from 5 to 10 years of inhalation before significant changes in the lung tissues occur.

In the early stages of the disease symptoms may include shortness of breath and coughing, but usually there are no symptoms. In later stages, labored breathing, chest pain, weakness, and loss of appetite occur. Persons with silicosis are often susceptible to tuberculosis and other diseases of the respiratory tract. Silicosis, if allowed to progress, can be fatal. There is no cure for the disease, but it can be arrested or prevented by eliminating the silica dust through proper ventilation in work areas or by filtering out the dust with a mask.

Silique. See FRUIT, subtitle *Kinds of Fruits:* Simple Fruits (Dry Fruits).

Silk

Silk, a fine, lustrous fabric. It is composed of filaments, or fibers, also called silk, produced by the caterpillar of the silkworm moth when it spins its cocoon. Since World War II synthetic fibers have replaced silk in many products, but silk fabrics are still desired for many kinds of specialty apparel.

The production of silk fabric is intricate, requiring much hand labor. Silk is therefore expensive in comparison with synthetics. Because of the great decline in the use of silk, it is no longer classed as a major textile fiber in the United States.

Raising the Silkworm

The silkworm is the caterpillar of the silkworm moth (*Bombyx mori*). It is a domesticated species that is raised by silk farmers and does not exist in the wild. The raising and cultivating of silkworms for commercial purposes is called *sericulture*. Silkworms are susceptible to several diseases and must be raised in a sterile, temperature-controlled environment.

The female silkworm moth is cream-colored and has a two-inch (5-cm) wingspan.

Several days after mating, she lays 300 to 500 eggs. Three days later, she dies. A human worker places the eggs in a cool place where they develop into larvae. Under normal conditions, the larvae hatch in 20 to 32 days. Larvae are dark gray to black and about an eighth of an inch (3 mm) long. They are voracious eaters, consuming large quantities of mulberry leaves, their main source of food. It takes approximately 30 days for the larvae to develop into caterpillars. During this time, they molt (shed their skin) four times. A full-grown caterpillar is about 3½ inches (9 cm) long.

When the silkworms are ready to begin spinning their cocoons, they stop eating and they raise their heads and weave them slowly in a figure-eight pattern. The caterpillars are placed on trays and provided with twigs or bits of straw to which they attach them-

The Japan Silk Association, Inc.
Top of page, silkworm cocoon, about three-fourths actual size. *Opposite*, elaborate handweaving.

Silkworm Life Cycle

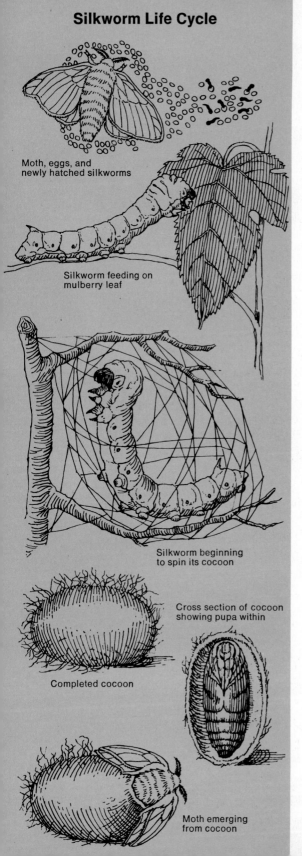

Moth, eggs, and newly hatched silkworms

Silkworm feeding on mulberry leaf

Silkworm beginning to spin its cocoon

Completed cocoon

Cross section of cocoon showing pupa within

Moth emerging from cocoon

selves. The fiber that makes up the cocoon is secreted through the *spinneret,* an opening under the jaws of the silkworm.

The material that makes up the silk fiber comes from a pair of glands that run lengthwise in the caterpillar's body, one on each side. This proteinlike material, called *fibroin,* is mixed with a gummy substance, called *sericin,* from another pair of glands. The liquid material from all four glands is secreted at the same time and comes out as one fiber from the spinneret. The fiber hardens upon contact with air. The sericin cements the fiber together to form the cocoon.

When the caterpillar begins its cocoon, the filament it produces is coarse and rough. Gradually the strand becomes soft and fine. The cocoon fiber may be 300 to 1,600 yards (270 to 1,460 m) long. In about three days the caterpillar has completed the cocoon, which is about the size of a hen's egg. Cocoons vary in color and texture, depending on the breed of silkworm.

During the next two weeks, the pupa inside the cocoon develops into a moth. Cocoons that are going to be used to produce another generation of breeding adults are allowed to develop fully and the adult moths break out of them. Cocoons that are to be used for their silk, however, are treated before the moths fully develop.

Treating the Cocoons

The cocoons that are to be used for silk are *stoved* (exposed to dry heat) or *stifled* (steamed) to kill the pupae inside. (If allowed to live, they would develop into moths and break out of the cocoons, thus damaging the silk fibers.) The cocoons are then aired to dry the dead pupae inside. The dried cocoons are taken to a *filature,* a factory where the silk is reeled.

At the factory, the cocoons are sorted according to color, size, shape, and texture. Next, they are soaked in hot water to soften the gum (sericin) in the filaments. After the cocoons have been soaked, the free end of the filament is attached to a reeling machine. Usually five to eight cocoons are unwound at the same time. The filaments from these cocoons are combined into one thread and wound onto a frame. About one-third of the total filament in a cocoon is usable.

The thread is next removed from the frame and twisted into a bundle called a skein. The skeins are packed into small bundles called books. The books are then

Above, the Chicago Pub. Lib.; right, The Japan Silk Assn., Inc.

Above: In the past the filaments from the cocoons (soaking in basin) were unwound, combined to form a thread, and reeled onto a silk frame by hand. *Right:* In modern silk manufacture, filaments from the cocoons (shown soaking at bottom) are automatically unwound, combined, and reeled onto frames (shown at top).

combined to form bales, each weighing about 140 pounds (64 kg). The raw silk is now ready for manufacture into yarn and fabric.

Manufacture of Silk

The skeins are sorted for size and color. They are soaked in warm water with soap or oil to soften the threads. Then the skeins are dried and the threads are wound onto bobbins. During winding the fibers are given a twist, a process called *silk throwing.* By throwing, several different kinds of yarn can be made, depending on the type of twist and number of threads combined.

The bobbins are taken to the fabric manufacturer for the silk yarn to be woven into fabric. Thrown silk threads still contain a substantial amount of sericin, most of which must be removed in a soap bath. The process, called *degumming,* may be done after the yarn is thrown or after the fabric is woven. As much as 25 per cent of the weight of the reeled silk is lost in degumming.

Mineral salts may be added to the yarn to increase the silk's finished weight, making it firmer. This process, called *weighting,* is done during dyeing. Weighted silk is generally considered inferior to *pure-dyed* silk,

silk that is dyed without the addition of salts. Weighting is no longer practiced in the United States, but some European yarns, particularly those used in neckties, are still prepared this way.

Spun Silk. Only about one-third of the cocoon is used for ordinary silk fabrics, but good use is made of the remaining fiber. In addition, the pierced cocoons of the moths used for breeding, and other scraps left from the reeling and throwing, are used. This waste silk is carded, combed, and spun together much like cotton or wool to make yarn called spun silk. Spun silk is not as lustrous, strong, or elastic as reeled silk, but it is less expensive.

Wild, or **Tussah, Silk** is produced by the caterpillar of the wild silkworm moth, also called the tussah silkworm moth (*Antheraea paphia*). The larvae feed on oak leaves. The silk produced by the caterpillars is tougher and more durable than that of the silkworm caterpillar but is difficult to dye or bleach. It is usually left in its natural tan color, but is occasionally dyed. This silk is less lustrous and is cheaper than ordinary silk. Wild silk fabrics, such as shantung and pongee, are durable and have an irregular surface.

S-421

Uses and Production

Silk fiber is used in many woven fabrics, including crepe, taffeta, chiffon, peau de soie, and satin. Beautiful silk brocades are often considered works of art. Silk fabric can be made into almost any type of wearing apparel, including suits, dresses, scarves, shirts, and ties. Silk is also used to make ribbon, laces, trimmings, and thread. Silk yarn is also used to weave fabrics in combination with other yarns, such as cotton or wool. Silk is also used to make sheets, sutures, fishing line, parachutes, and tires for racing bicycles. For information on the various types of silk fabrics, see TEXTILE (table).

Major producers of silk are China, Japan, India, North Korea, and Brazil. For some time Japan was by far the largest export-er of silk, but domestic demand for silk is so high that it has greatly reduced the amount available for export, and Japan has been importing some silk, primarily from China.

The United States imports silk mainly from China, Japan, and Brazil. Silk fabrics, however, account for a very small percentage of the output of the textile industry in the United States.

History

The art of silk culture and weaving was first developed in China. According to legend it was discovered about 2600 B.C. by a young empress. She accidentally dropped a silkworm cocoon into a basin of hot water and found that it unraveled into a long, slender filament of remarkable strength and beauty. The empress then invented a means

Above, The Japan Silk Assn., Inc.; right, Bettmann Archive
Above: Silk yarn of various colors. Unlike most other fibers, most silk can be dyed well in any color with either natural or synthetic dyes. *Right:* A print of Hsi-ling Shih, the Chinese empress who according to legend discovered the art of silk culture.

Secrets of sericulture were smuggled out of the Far East to Byzantium by two Greek monks who hid silkworm eggs and mulberry seeds in their bamboo staffs.

Bettmann Archive

of joining the delicate filaments into a yarn thick enough for weaving into cloth.

For nearly 3,000 years the Chinese guarded the secret of making silk. Other countries were eager to buy the luxurious fabric. Camel caravans carried it along a trade route—called the Silk Road—across Asia to Persia. From there it was traded to countries bordering the Mediterranean Sea. In Rome silk was literally worth its weight in gold.

The secret of silk production finally became known outside China when it spread to Japan in the fourth century A.D. and later to India. It was about 550 A.D. before silk culture was introduced in the West. The Byzantine emperor Justinian sent two monks to China; they stole mulberry seeds and silkworm eggs and smuggled them out in hollow staffs. A flourishing silk industry soon developed in the Byzantine Empire.

The Muslims were introduced to silk culture when they overran Persia in the seventh century; they carried it to North Africa, Spain, and Sicily. The demand for silk grew rapidly, and the industry expanded throughout Europe. The manufacture of silk in Italy was fostered by prominent families. In the 14th century, it became the most profitable industry in cities such as Florence, Milan, and Venice. The French silk industry received royal patronage and was soon rivaling that of Italy. The city of Lyon became one of the greatest silk manufacturing centers of the world. England also started to produce silk during the Middle Ages. In the 17th century, the English silk industry gained the expertise of Huguenot (Protestant) textile workers who fled religious persecution in France and settled in the London district of Spitalfields.

In the 17th century, King James I of England sent silkworms to Virginia to start a silk industry there, but the venture failed. However, manufacture of cloth from imported raw silk was successful. The first silk mill in the United States was built in 1810. In the mid-1800's, protective tariffs placed on imported fabric caused rapid growth in the American silk industry. Meanwhile, Asia continued to be the leading producer of raw silk. By the mid-20th century, silk had been largely replaced by man-made fibers.

Silk-cotton Tree. See KAPOK TREE.

Silk-screen Printing, a method of printing in which paints or inks are forced through the uncovered parts of a fabric screen onto the surface to be printed. It is called silk-screen printing because originally silk was the fabric used for the screen. Today, the screen is usually made of such materials as wire mesh, nylon, or polyester.

Silk-screen printing is a stencil process; the stencil covers a part of the screen, forming printing and nonprinting areas. To print, a rubber tool called a squeegee is drawn across the screen, forcing ink through the open parts of the stencil. Only one color can be printed at a time. For a multicolor print, a separate stencil must be made for each color.

Commercial silk-screen printing, often simply called screen printing, is used in printing limited quantities of large designs, such as posters, and in printing on such materials as textiles, leather, metals, and glass. When artists create their own designs and stencils and make their own prints the process is called *serigraphy*. The print is called a *serigraph* to distinguish it from commercial silk-screen reproductions.

There are several techniques an artist may use to make a screen stencil. The artist may

Silk-screen Printing

Tusche and Washout Technique

1. Areas to be printed are painted directly on the screen with *tusche*, a greasy black liquid.

2. A layer of glue is spread over the entire screen to block out non-printing areas. (The glue does not adhere to the tusche.)

3. The screen is washed with a paint thinner, dissolving the tusche and thus uncovering the areas of the screen that will print. Printing paper is then positioned.

4. Color (ink or oil paint) is forced through the exposed areas of the screen with a squeegee and the design appears on the paper.

5. The screen is removed and the print is ready to be hung to dry.

cut out the design from paper or from a special lacquer stencil film. Or the stencil may be prepared photographically from a light-sensitized gelatin. A popular technique, the tusche and washout, is shown in the illustration. It allows the artist to create fine details.

Silk-screen printing is a 20th-century development of the basic stencil technique known to artists for centuries. At first a commercial technique, silk-screen printing developed as a fine-art medium in the late 1930's.

Silkworm. See SILK, subtitle *Raising the Silkworm*.

Silky Terrier. See DOG, subtitle *Breeds of Dogs:* Toy Dogs.

Sillanpää, Frans Eemil. See NOBEL PRIZES (Literature, 1939).

Sills, Beverly (1929-), a United States operatic soprano known for the wide range and flexibility of her coloratura voice and her emotionally vivid acting. She was born Belle Silvermann in Brooklyn, New York, and was a child radio star. Sills performed with many musical touring companies before joining the New York City Opera in 1955. After gaining national fame in 1966 as Cleopatra in Handel's *Julius Caesar,* she made guest appearances throughout the world. In 1975 she joined the Metropolitan Opera. Sills was director of the New York City Opera, 1979-89. She became chairwoman of the Lincoln Center for the Performing Arts in 1994. *Bubbles: A Self-Portrait* (1976) is her autobiography.

Silo, in agriculture, a waterproof structure designed for storing crops and converting them into silage. (Silage is a fermented feed for livestock. See SILAGE.) Corn, legumes, sorghum, and other crops are placed in silos. Silos provide economical crop storage and the silage produced is excellent feed, particularly for dairy herds and beef cattle. The common types are the upright silo and the horizontal silo.

Upright silos are built above ground. They are cylindrical structures about 30 to 90 feet (9 to 27 m) high and 10 to 25 feet (3 to 7.6 m) in diameter. Upright silos are constructed of such materials as tile, concrete slabs or blocks, or glass-lined steel. They are completely sealed to exclude air and water. Fresh crops from the fields are placed in the silo from the top and are covered with an air-tight material such as a plastic sheet.

Silage can be removed from the bottom or the top of the silo, depending on the design of the particular silo.

There are two kinds of horizontal silos—trench silos and bunker silos. Trench silos are constructed partially or completely below ground level. Bunker silos are constructed above ground. Both types have slanting walls, the silos being wider at the top than at the bottom. Horizontal silos are usually from 6 to 8 feet (1.8 to 2.4 m) in depth. Bottom widths vary from about 10 to 28 feet (3 to 8.5 m), top widths from 14 to 30 feet (4.3 to 9 m). The length of a horizontal silo is determined by the quantity of silage to be made. Walls are constructed of concrete, stone, earth, or wood; floors, of wood, asphalt, concrete, or sometimes earth.

After the crops are placed in a horizontal silo, they are covered with plastic on which wet hay, soil, or crushed rock is placed to hold spoilage to a minimum. However, more spoilage occurs in horizontal silos than in upright ones. Horizontal silos are generally cheaper to construct than upright silos.

Silos were first used in the United States about 1875, in Michigan and Maryland.

Silone, sḗ′lō′nȧ, **Ignazio** (1900-1978), the pen name of Secondo Tranquilli, an Italian novelist and social reformer. *Bread and Wine* (1937), his best-known novel, and its sequel, *The Seed Beneath the Snow* (1940), tell of the underground movement against Fascism. *Fontamara* (1930) deals with Fascist exploitation of Italian peasants. *A Handful of Blackberries* (1952) and *The Secret of Luca* (1956) attack Communism. *Emergency Exit* (1965) is a collection of essays about Silone's political experiences. Other works include plays, a history of Fascism, and a satirical study of dictatorship. Silone was one of the founders of the Italian Communist Party, but broke with Communism in 1930. He lived in Switzerland, 1931-44.

Silt, See SOIL, subtitle *Physical Properties: Texture.*

Silurian Period, sĭ-lū′rĭ-ăn, a division of geologic time that began about 430,000,000 years ago and lasted about 35,000,000 years. It is the third period of the Paleozoic Era, coming just after the Ordovician Period and just before the Devonian Period. The Silurian Period is named after the Silures, an ancient people who lived in Wales, where rocks of this period were first studied.

Climate during the early Silurian Period was mild over much of the earth. Large shallow seas covered large portions of the continental land areas. Shales, limestones, sandstones, and conglomerates and quartzites were widely deposited. Toward the end of Silurian times the seas began to dry up, leaving many salt deposits where their shores had been.

Great Silurian rock formations are found in Pennsylvania and New York State and surrounding areas. Other extensive Silurian deposits are found in Great Britain and in the Czech Republic. Salt, iron, and some gas and oil are recovered from Silurian rock formations.

Animal life in Silurian times included primitive mollusks, sponges and corals, brachiopods, and early crustaceans such as trilobites.

See also GEOLOGY, chart *Earth's History Outlined.*

Upright Silos

Bunker Silo

Boltin Picture Library
Silver Candlesticks from Colonial Mexico

Silver, a metallic chemical element. Like gold and platinum, silver is a precious metal because of its beauty and scarcity. Silver is harder than gold but not as hard as copper. Of all the metals, pure silver is the best conductor of heat and electricity. It is ductile (can be drawn into wire), malleable (can be hammered or rolled into a thin sheet), and an excellent reflector of light.

Silver is one of the most corrosion-resistant metals. It resists attacks by alkalies and all acids except nitric acid and hot concentrated sulfuric acid. Silver is not easily oxidized by air, and is insoluble in water. Because of its softness, silver must be alloyed with other metals for uses that subject it to wear.

Silver for centuries has been used in the arts and for coinage. *Silversmithing,* the art of producing decorative silver objects, was highly developed in Egypt by the 16th century B.C. Jewelry, tableware, vases, religious articles, and many other items are made of pure silver or alloys containing a high percentage of silver. The most important use of silver compounds is for the light-sensitive materials used in photographic films and papers.

The use of silver for coinage has virtually disappeared because of its high price. In the United States, silver was eliminated from

dimes and quarters in 1965 and from half dollars in 1971. Silver certificates, last issued in 1963, were paper bills redeemable in silver until 1968. In 1986, a silver dollar weighing one troy ounce (31.1 g) was issued for collectors and investors. The coin's metal value is much higher than its face value, so it does not circulate.

Silver tarnishes on contact with sulfur or most sulfides. Unprotected silver will tarnish in air because of hydrogen sulfide gas, which comes mainly from the combustion of coal or oil in furnaces. To help prevent tarnish, silver objects may be stored in specially treated paper or felt, or in airtight containers. Display pieces are often coated with clear lacquer or silicone. Tarnish may be removed either by a fine abrasive polish or by various chemical processes.

Pure silver is called *fine* silver. The proportion of silver in jewelry, coins, and bullion is usually expressed in terms of *fineness* (the number of parts of silver in 1,000 parts of alloy). Example: an alloy that is 95 per cent silver is said to be 950 fine.

Uses of Silver and Its Alloys

Silver is widely used in alloys. *Sterling silver,* an alloy of 92.5 per cent silver and 7.5 per cent copper, is used for tableware, jewelry, and decorative items. Silver coins usually consist of silver-copper alloys and silver-copper-nickel alloys. Silver solders, which consist primarily of silver, copper, and zinc, are strong alloys that resist heat and corrosion. They are used for joining metals in car radiators, air conditioners, rocket nozzles, and other products. Silver-cadmium alloys are used for bearings. Silver amalgams are silver-mercury alloys used for dental fillings. Silver is alloyed with palladium, cadmium oxide, gold, or nickel to make electrical contacts. Some silver-gold alloys are used for jewelry and dental fillings.

Silver metal is used as a catalyst in the manufacture of chemicals, and to make electrical contacts, electrical wire, and silver compounds. Mirrors are often coated with silver. Because of its ability to resist corrosion, silver is used to line pipes, vats, and nozzles for chemical and food processing equipment. Silver powder is used in coatings for watch and clock dials and to decorate glass. Silver paints are used to make printed circuits for portable radios and television sets. Storage batteries made with silver-zinc or silver-cadmium cells are used in guided missiles, telemetry equipment, jet aircraft, and portable television cameras.

Silver plate is a base metal coated with pure silver or a silver alloy. The coating is used to improve the appearance or electrical conductivity of metal objects or to protect them from corrosion. Most silver plate is made by an electrolytic process known as electroplating. (See ELECTROPLATING.) Jewelry, tableware, trays, musical instruments, and novelties are plated with silver to make them more attractive. Silver is used as a protective coating for bearings, surgical instruments, and many electrical and electronic devices.

Silver Compounds

Silver compounds have many commercial uses. *Silver nitrate* is used for silvering mirrors, for coloring porcelain, and in the manufacture of photographic chemicals, hair dyes, indelible inks, glass, and other silver compounds. A solution of silver nitrate is used as an astringent and as an antiseptic. It is put on the eyes of children at birth to prevent eye infection.

Silver bromide, silver chloride, and *silver iodide* are used as light-sensitive substances in photographic emulsions. In artificial rainmaking, silver iodide crystals are dispersed into clouds to produce rainfall. *Silver cyanide* is used in silver plating. *Silver fulminate,* a high explosive, is sometimes used as a detonator for dynamite and other explosives. Several silver compounds, including *silver sulfate* and *silver chromate,* are used as reagents in chemical analysis. *Silver oxide* is used in storage batteries, in water purification, as a catalyst in the manufacture of chemicals, and to color and polish glass.

Occurrence and Production

Silver sometimes occurs free (chemically uncombined) in nature, but is usually found combined with other elements. The principal ores of silver are *argentite,* consisting of silver and sulfur; *polybasite, stephanite,* and *pyrargyrite,* consisting of silver, antimony, and sulfur; *proustite,* consisting of silver, arsenic, and sulfur; and *cerargyrite,* consisting of silver and chlorine. Small amounts of silver occur in most gold ores and in various base metal ores, chiefly those of copper, lead, and zinc.

Silver deposits that lie far underground are mined by using deep shafts. Sometimes uncombined silver or silver ores occur as small nuggets or flakes that lie on or near the surface of the earth. Such deposits are worked by placer mining methods. (See MINING, subtitle *Types of Mining:* Surface Mining [Placer Mining].)

Most of the world's silver is produced as a by-product in the refining of base metals, chiefly copper, lead, and zinc. Substantial amounts of silver are obtained from silver ores and in refining gold. The leading silver-mining countries are Mexico, the United States, and Peru. Silver is mined in about 20 states; Nevada, Idaho, Montana, and Arizona usually account for two-thirds to three-fourths of the United States output.

The largest percentage of silver is obtained from the electrolytic refining of copper. The silver collects in the anode slimes and is recovered by smelting. Silver in lead ores is recovered by the *Parkes process.* In this process molten lead that has been partially purified is treated with zinc. The zinc combines with the silver and any gold that may be present, forming an alloy that rises to the surface. The alloy is skimmed off, and then distilled to remove the zinc. Silver and gold are separated either by chemical processes or by electrolysis. Silver in zinc or gold ores may be recovered by various metallurgical processes.

Silver is usually extracted from its ores by the flotation process, and then refined by smelting. (See FLOTATION.) Silver is sometimes obtained from its ores by the cyanidation process and the amalgamation process.

Cyanidation Process. Crushed ore is treated with a dilute cyanide solution to dissolve the silver. Lime is usually added to the mixture to control acidity and to reduce chemical reactions between the cyanide and the impurities. After the silver dissolves, the mixture is filtered to remove the solid impurities. Zinc powder is added to precipitate the silver. The silver is then refined by electrolysis.

Amalgamation Process. Crushed ore is passed over copper plates coated with mercury. The mercury combines with the silver to form silver amalgam. The amalgam is washed, and then distilled to drive off the mercury. The silver is refined by electrolysis.

The recovery of silver from scrap is increasingly important to the world silver supply. Much silver is recovered from the wastes of manufacturing processes and the arts. Silver is also recovered from various used products, including batteries, mirrors, silverware, and jewelry. Also, considerable amounts of silver have been recovered from silver coins that have been withdrawn from circulation.

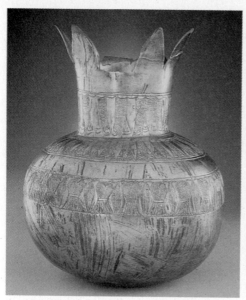

Silver Objects. *Left,* a vase from the tomb of the ancient Egyptian pharaoh Tutankhamen. *Right,* 18th-century American teapot by Paul Revere.

History

Silver was one of the first metals known to humans. It was used for jewelry and ornaments in the Near East as early as 3500 B.C. The metal was first used in coins about 600 B.C. The silver mines at Laurium, Greece, were worked for several centuries after 1000 B.C., and their output provided much of the wealth of Athens. Silver was mined extensively by the Romans. Production was relatively small during the Middle Ages.

World silver production increased greatly after the discovery of the New World. During the 16th century rich deposits were mined in Bolivia, Peru, and Mexico. Bolivia was the largest producer until the beginning of the 18th century. Silver production in the United States was small until the discovery of the Comstock Lode in Nevada in 1859.

Symbol: Ag (from *argentum*, Latin for silver). Atomic number: 47. Atomic weight: 107.8682. Specific gravity: 10.5. Melting point: $1,763.4°$ F. $(961.9°$ C.). Boiling point: $4,013.6°$ F. $(2,212°$ C.). Silver has two stable isotopes: Ag-107 and Ag-109. It belongs to Group I-B of the Periodic Table and may have a valence of $+1, +2, +3$.

See also ASSAYING; BIMETALLISM; BUL-

Books about Silver

Blair, Claude. *The History of Silver* (Ballantine Books, 1987).
Schwartz, Jeri. *The Official Identification and Price Guide to Silver and Silverplate,* 6th edition (Ballantine Books, 1989).

For Younger Readers

Rickard, George. *Silver* (Rourke, 1985).

LION; COIN; MONEY, subtitles *Monetary Standards* and *History.*

Silver Certificate. See MONEY, subtitle *Types of Money:* Credit Money.

Silver Fox. See FOX, subtitle *Kinds of Foxes:* The Red Fox.

Silver Maple. See MAPLE, subtitle *North American Maples.*

Silver Plate. See SILVER, subtitle *Uses of Silver and Its Alloys.*

Silver Spring, Maryland, an unincorporated community in Montgomery County, just north of Washington, D.C. It is a residential suburb with some manufacturing.

Population: 76,046.

Silver Springs, Florida. See FLORIDA, section titled *Interesting Places in Florida.*

Silver Star. See DECORATIONS AND MEDALS, subtitle *United States Awards:* Decorations.

Silver State, a nickname for Nevada.

Silverfish, a small, wingless insect that is covered with tiny silvery scales. The body is slender and tapers toward the back part. The silverfish moves rapidly on three pairs of thin, jointed legs. Extending from its head is a pair of antennae and trailing from the rear of its body are three long, bristly appendages. The silverfish is about one-half inch (13 mm) long exclusive of the tail appendages.

Silverfish are common household pests. They live in dark, cool places, such as in basements, behind baseboards, and in closets. They are also often found around plumbing fixtures. Silverfish are usually unnoticed because they move about only in the dark. They feed on starchy materials and often damage clothes, books, and wallpaper. They can be controlled with insecticides.

The silverfish is *Lepisma saccharina* of the family Lepismatidae, order Thysanura.

See also INSECT (picture page).

Silver-leafed (or White) **Poplar.** See POPLAR, subtitle *Poplars of North America.*

Silverpoint. See DRAWING, subtitle *Drawing Materials* (Silverpoint).

Silverside, the common name of a family of chiefly marine fish found along the shores of temperate and tropical seas. There are more than 150 species, some of them also commonly called silversides. A well-known member of the family is the grunion. (See GRUNION.) The silversides have slender, usually greenish bodies with wide silver bands on the sides extending from head to tail. The *Atlantic silverside* is a common species found along the north Atlantic coast of the United States. It is about three to six inches (7.5 to 15 cm) in length.

The Atlantic silverside is *Menidia menidia* of the silverside family, Atherinidae.

Silver-spotted Skipper. See BUTTERFLIES AND MOTHS, subtitle *Kinds of Butterflies:* The Skippers.

Silviculture. See FOREST, subtitle *Forestry.*

Silvius, Aeneas. See PIUS (Pius II).

Simbirsk. See ULYANOVSK.

Simeon Stylites, Saint. See HERMIT.

Simeon (I) **the Great** (?-927), a ruler of Bulgaria (893-927). During his reign, Bulgarian territory was expanded from the Black Sea to the Adriatic. His first campaign, 894-97, was a successful war against the Byzantine Empire, which was forced to pay a yearly tribute to Bulgaria. Simeon's armies then overran Macedonia, Albania, and Thrace, and finally Serbia.

Simeon was educated in Constantinople and admired Greek culture. He encouraged the translation of Greek literature into Slavic and made his capital, Preslav, a cultural center. He made the Bulgarian church independent of the patriarch in Constantinople. Simeon was the first Bulgarian ruler to take the title czar.

Simi Valley, California, a city in Ventura County. It is in the San Fernando Valley, about 35 miles (56 km) northwest of downtown Los Angeles, and is primarily a residential community. Settlement of the area dates from the early 19th century. Simi Valley was established in 1969 by the incorporation of the communities of Simi, Santa Susana, and Susana Knolls.

Population: 100,217.

Simile. See FIGURE OF SPEECH, subtitle *Kinds of Figures:* Metaphor and Simile.

Simmel, zĭm'ĕl, **Georg** (1858-1918), a German philosopher and sociologist. Through his lectures at the University of Berlin and his writings he was influential in the development of sociology as a field of study. Many of his works were translated into English by Albion W. Small, who established the first department of sociology in the United States. Simmel emphasized the importance of scientific study of small groups and of the interactions between individuals. This line of study contributed to the development of social psychology.

Simmons College. See UNIVERSITIES AND COLLEGES (table).

Simms, William Gilmore (1806-1870), a United States author. One of the South's most important 19th-century literary figures, Simms wrote novels, poems, plays, histories, biographies, and literary criticism. He is best known for his novels—historical romances that give a colorful but realistic picture of pioneer and Revolutionary War times in the South. The most popular was *The Yemassee* (1835), which shows sympathy for the Indians in the face of white encroachment. *Views and Reviews of American Literature, History, and Fiction* (1846) is representative of his critical works.

Simms was born in Charleston, South Carolina. He studied law there and in 1827 was admitted to the bar, He was a member of the Charleston School, a group of writers who supported slavery.

Simon, Saint, one of the 12 disciples of Jesus. Little is known about him, except that he belonged to the anti-Roman faction known as the Cananeans, or Zealots. (In the Gospels of Matthew and Mark, he is called Simon the Cananean; in Luke and Acts, Simon the Zealot.) According to tradition, he preached in Egypt and later went to Persia, where he suffered martyrdom. His feast day in the Roman Catholic Church is October 28, in the Eastern Orthodox Church May 10.

Simon, Herbert. See NOBEL PRIZES (Economic Science, 1978).

Simon, Neil (1927-   ), a United States playwright known for his humorous dialogue and depiction of middle-class life. Many of his plays have been adapted as motion pictures, including *Barefoot in the Park* (1967); *The Odd Couple* (1968); *The Sunshine Boys* (1975); *California Suite* (1978); and *Chapter Two* (1979). His semiautobiographical trilogy—*Brighton Beach Memoirs* (1983), *Biloxi Blues* (1985), and *Broadway Bound* (1986)—is noted for incorporating humor with themes of loss and personal responsibility. In 1991 his play *Lost in Yonkers* was awarded a Pulitzer Prize. Simon was born in New York City and attended New York University. He worked as a comedy writer for television, a job he portrayed in *Laughter on the 23rd Floor* (1994), before becoming a full-time playwright. *Rewrites* (1996) is his memoir.

Simon de Montfort. See MONTFORT, SIMON DE.

Simon Peter. See PETER, Saint.

Simons, Menno. See MENNONITES.

Simplon Pass, sĭm′plŏn, a pass in the Alps of southwestern Switzerland. It reaches a maximum elevation of almost 6,578 feet (2,005 m) and forms part of a principal route linking the Rhone Valley in Switzerland and the Po Valley in Italy. The pass was seldom used until the Middle Ages, when it became a trade route for merchants from Milan. The first carriage road over the Simplon was built early in the 1800's. Snow usually closes the pass from December until May.

The 12.3-mile (19.8-km) Simplon Tunnel, which runs beneath Monte Leone from Brig (Switzerland) to Iselle (Italy), is one of the world's longest railway tunnels. It consists of two adjacent tubes, the first completed in 1905, the second in 1922.

Simpson, O. J. (Orenthal James Simpson) (1947-   ), a United States football player and actor. He was one of the greatest running backs in National Football League history, noted for his speed and power. Simpson played for the Buffalo Bills, 1969-79, and broke several rushing records. He was named to the Pro Football Hall of Fame in 1985. After retirement, he was a television sports commentator and an actor.

In June, 1994, Simpson was arrested for the murder of his former wife, Nicole Brown, and her friend Ronald Goldman; he was linked to the murders by physical evidence and a history of spousal abuse. The trial—televised from January to October, 1995—was frequently complicated by accusations of racial bias on both sides of the case. In a controversial verdict, a predominantly black jury found Simpson, also black, not guilty of the killing of the two white victims. The families of the victims filed a civil suit against Simpson, and in 1997 he was found liable for the deaths of his former wife and Goldman.

Simpson was born in San Francisco. He played football at the University of Southern California and won the Heisman Trophy as the top college player in 1968.

Simpson, Wallis Warfield. See EDWARD (Edward VIII).

Simpson College. See UNIVERSITIES AND COLLEGES (table).

Sims, William S. (Sowden) (1858-1936), a United States naval officer and naval reformer. Through his efforts the U.S. Navy revolutionized its gunnery techniques and introduced other improvements prior to World War I. During the war, Sims was commander of U.S. Navy forces in Europe. He helped persuade the British to adopt the convoy system, which largely overcame the German submarine menace to Allied shipping.

Sims was born in Port Hope, Ontario, to parents who were from the United States. He graduated from the U.S. Naval Academy in 1880. As a rear admiral he served as president of the Naval War College (1917, 1919-22). He was temporarily a full admiral in 1918. Sims retired in 1922. *The Victory at Sea* (1920), which he wrote with Burton J. Hendrick, won the Pulitzer Prize in history.

Sin, an offense against the will of God. The concept of sin appears in all religions that believe in the existence of a god or gods. At the core of Christianity is the belief that Jesus Christ died for human salvation—to save people from their sins. The notion of breaking a taboo, as found among primitive peoples, is closely related to that of sin.

Sin produces a separation from God, and a person must seek reconciliation through atonement or repentance. In Judaism and in most Protestant denominations, atonement is made directly to God. In the Roman Catholic church, forgiveness of sins is gained through the sacrament of penance (confession and absolution). In Catholicism a distinction is also drawn between *mortal sin* and *venial sin.* (See ROMAN CATHOLIC CHURCH, subtitle *Beliefs and Practices*.)

Original sin, in Christian theology, is the original offense against God committed by

Adam and Eve in the Garden of Eden. By this sin, which is transmitted from generation to generation, human nature has been corrupted and is capable of further sin.

See also ATONEMENT; BAPTISM; CONFESSION; TABOO.

Sinai, Church of. See EASTERN ORTHODOX CHURCH, subtitle *Branches of the Church.*

Sinai Peninsula, sī′nī, a historic area of Asia that forms a land bridge to Africa. It is part of Egypt. Since 1948 the Sinai has been a strategic battlefield in the Arab-Israeli conflicts. In 1956 Israeli forces routed the Egyptians from the Sinai, but then withdrew under a peace agreement. In 1967, following the Six Day War and the defeat of the Egyptian army, Israel occupied the region. After the Yom Kippur War of 1973, Egyptian sovereignty was reestablished over parts of the Sinai adjacent to the Suez Canal. Under a 1979 peace treaty between Egypt and Israel, Israel began a step-by-step withdrawal from the Sinai. In 1982 the last troops were removed and Egypt regained sovereignty over the entire peninsula.

Since earliest times the largely arid Sinai has been only sparsely inhabited, mostly by nomads. Around 2800 B.C., Egypt began mining copper and turquoise in the southern Sinai's mountain region. The mines were worked periodically for centuries before Egypt finally abandoned them in the 12th century B.C. From the miners, many of whom were captives of war from Semitic lands, came one of the world's earliest alphabets. Their inscriptions, which were probably written around 1500 B.C., were found by archeologists in 1905.

According to Biblical accounts, Moses led the Israelites from Egyptian bondage into the Sinai, where they lived for 40 years before entering Canaan (Palestine). The Biblical Mount Sinai, where Moses received the Ten Commandments, has traditionally been identified as Gebel Musa (Mount of Moses), but other peaks have been suggested also.

Over the centuries, the Sinai was ruled by many peoples, including Romans, Byzantines, Arabs, and Turks. The Arabs were the only masters of the region to have more than a negligible influence, converting the Bedouins (nomads) to Islam sometime after the seventh century A.D. Following World War I, the Sinai was taken from the Ottoman Empire and put under Egyptian rule.

Wide World; Viking Press

Frank Sinatra and **Upton Sinclair.** Sinatra is shown as Maggio in *From Here to Eternity* (1953).

Sinatra, Frank (Francis Albert Sinatra) (1915-1998), a United States popular singer and actor. His easygoing stage manner and his sincerity in expressing the lyrics of a song helped establish a male singing style popular in American music for more than 20 years. Sinatra was born in Hoboken, New Jersey. He became a teen idol in the early 1940's singing with Tommy Dorsey's band.

Sinatra's popularity declined in the late 1940's but revived after he won an Academy Award as Best Supporting Actor for his role in the film *From Here to Eternity* (1953). He then made one of the most notable comebacks in show business history, singing in nightclubs and on television and starring in many motion pictures. His hit songs include "Night and Day" (1943), "Nancy" (1945), "All the Way" (1957), "My Way" (1969), and "New York, New York" (1980).

"Sinbad the Sailor." See ARABIAN NIGHTS.

Sinclair, Upton (Beall) (1878-1968), a United States author and social reformer. He was one of the best-known of the muckrakers—writers who exposed social evils in the early 20th century. *The Jungle* (1906), his most famous book, is a Naturalistic novel about the meat-packing industry in Chicago. The novel was written primarily as an attack on deplorable working conditions, but it had no immediate effect on labor legislation. It did, however, lead to the passing of meat-inspection and pure-food laws in 1906 as a result of its portrayal of unsanitary packing practices.

In *The Profits of Religion* (1918) Sinclair accused organized religion of being a tool of capitalism. He attacked corruption in journalism in *The Brass Check* (1919) and in the oil industry in *Oil!* (1927).

Beginning with *World's End* (1940), Sinclair wrote a long series of historical novels centering on a hero, Lanny Budd, who expresses the author's political and social convictions. One novel of the series, *Dragon's Teeth,* dealing with the rise of Nazism in

Germany, was awarded the 1943 Pulitzer Prize for fiction.

Sinclair was born in Baltimore. He graduated from the College of the City of New York in 1897 and attended Columbia University. In 1906 he helped found a cooperative society in New Jersey, but it lasted only a year. Sinclair moved to California in 1915. He ran for various public offices as a Socialist during the 1920's. In 1923 he founded the Southern California branch of the American Civil Liberties Union. As the Democratic candidate for governor of California in 1934 he ran on his own EPIC (End Poverty in California) platform and almost won the election.

His numerous books include *The Metropolis* (1908); *King Coal* (1917); *Boston* (1928); *What God Means to Me* (1936); *The Flivver King* (1937); *Expect No Peace* (1939); *What Didymus Did* (1955); *Theirs Be the Guilt* (1959); *The Autobiography of Upton Sinclair* (1962); *The Cry for Justice* (1963).

Singapore, or **Republic of Singapore,** sĭng'gȧ-pōr, an island country of southeast Asia. Most of the country's people live in the capital and largest city, which is also called Singapore.

Physical Description

The Country. Singapore Island and a number of smaller adjacent islands make up the country. They lie just north of the Equator at the tip of the Malay Peninsula. With an area of only 224 square miles (580 km²)—about the size of Chicago—Singapore is one of the smallest independent countries in Asia.

Outdoor Food Market in Singapore. Because cropland in this small nation is limited, much of the food supply comes from neighboring countries.

Ostman Agency: Jack Cannon

Singapore Island is separated from the southern tip of the Malay Peninsula by the narrow Johor Strait. To the south beyond Singapore Strait, the major link between the South China Sea and the Strait of Malacca, are islands of Indonesia. Singapore Island is generally low-lying and flat; its few hills reach less than 600 feet (180 m) above sea level. Because of the equatorial location, Singapore's climate is tropical. High temperatures and humidity prevail, and there is almost daily rainfall.

The City. On the southern coast of the island is the densely settled city of Singapore, its inhabitants crowded into an area of less than 40 square miles (100 km²). The city is a busy seaport and commercial center with docks, warehouses, and other harbor facilities lining much of the waterfront. Winding through the city is the narrow Singapore River, its banks often cluttered with barges that serve ships anchored offshore.

The downtown area is near the mouth of the river. Many of the buildings here are modern high-rises. Wide avenues enclose shopping areas, parks, and attractive squares. Hotels and clubs along Beach Road face the harbor, and tall apartment buildings are visible in many areas. Of interest are the Botanical Gardens, noted for tropical plants; the National Museum, with exhibits on Malayan and Indonesian culture; and several large amusement districts with theaters and other types of entertainment facilities.

Economy

Singapore has a thriving economy that is stronger than that of many larger, more populous countries of Asia. The people have one of the highest standards of living in Asia, and there is relatively little poverty.

At the core of the economy is the city of Singapore's *entrepôt* port (a port that specializes in the storing, processing, and reshipping of goods moving between other countries). A strategic location on one of the world's chief shipping routes has long made the port one of the world's busiest. Largely because of international shipping, Singapore has become a key financial center for southeastern Asia. Insurance and finance companies, as well as dozens of banks, including foreign banks, operate in Singapore. In addition, thousands of business travelers and tourists visit the country each year, making tourism a major source of income.

SINGAPORE

Until the early 1960's, when Singapore's government launched an economic development program, manufacturing was largely limited to food processing and the simple processing of raw materials. Under the program, industries of many kinds began to establish plants in Singapore. They range from such basic activities as oil refining and the making of iron and steel to the production of complex electronic equipment. Other industries include shipbuilding and ship repair, and the making of pharmaceuticals.

Agriculture is limited by the country's small size. Vegetables, tropical fruits, and various other food crops are intensively cultivated. Orchids, grown primarily for export, are the chief specialty crop. Pig and poultry farming provide much of the local meat supply, but most other foods must be imported.

Transportation within Singapore is chiefly by bus and auto over a network of paved roads. Singapore also has a mass-transit rail line, which links the city of Singapore with outlying areas. An important link with Malaysia is the causeway over Johor Strait, which carries a road and rail line. Singapore's international airport is at Changi. The national air carrier is Singapore Airlines.

The basic currency unit of Singapore is the Singapore dollar.

People and Government

About three-fourths of the population is Chinese. The largest minorities are Malay and Indian. In 1990 the population of Singapore was 2,705,115, the vast majority of whom lived in the city of Singapore.

Under the constitution of 1958 as amended, Singapore is a republic, with a parliament elected by universal adult suffrage. The prime minister is the leader of the political party controlling parliament. The head of state is a president, elected by the people to a six-year term. The Supreme Court is the highest judicial body.

History

Singapore was a Malay trading center as early as the 12th century, when it was a part of an empire based on Sumatra. The city was leveled by Javanese invaders in 1376. The site remained uninhabited until 1819, when Thomas Stamford Raffles, an agent of the British East India Company, leased it from a Malay sultan and founded a trading post. In 1824 the island was ceded to the company, which in 1829 made it part of the

Straits Settlements (the company's possessions in Malaya). In 1867 the Straits Settlements became a British crown colony.

Throughout the 19th century Singapore flourished because of its strategic location as a transshipment center for goods. Steady immigration, mainly from China, swelled the population, and Singapore became one of the largest Chinese cities outside China. After World War I, the British made the colony an important naval base. In World War II the strongly fortified city easily fell to the Japanese, who attacked from the land side. (The large guns intended to defend the city could only be fired seaward.) In 1946 the British made Singapore a separate crown colony upon the dissolution of the Straits Settlements.

In 1959 Singapore was given internal self-government. Lee Kuan Yew, leader of the ruling People's Action Party (PAP), became prime minister. Upon gaining independence in 1963, Singapore merged with Malaya, Sarawak, and Sabah to form the Federation of Malaysia. The federation, however, was torn by dissension between its Malay and Chinese populations. In 1965 Singapore seceded and became an independent member in the Commonwealth of Nations. In 1971 the British-Malaysian defense treaty, which provided British troops for Singapore's defense, expired.

Under Lee, Singapore, which had long been dependent on the *entrepôt* trade and income from British military bases, was extensively industrialized. By the 1980's, he had made Singapore one of the most prosperous nations in Asia. In 1990 Lee stepped down as prime minister and in 1992 he resigned as head of PAP. The financial crisis that began in Thailand in 1997 and that debilitated many economies in Southeast Asia had only a limited impact on Singapore, which had a more fundamentally sound financial sector than its neighbors.

See FLAG (color page); RAFFLES, Sir THOMAS STAMFORD.

Singer, Isaac Bashevis (1904-1991), a Polish-born United States novelist and short story writer. He was awarded the Nobel Prize for literature in 1978. His works portray Jewish life in Poland and are rich in Jewish folklore. Most of his writings were originally in Yiddish and were first published in periodicals; first publication dates of English translations are given here.

Singer's first and perhaps best-known novel is *The Family Moskat* (1950), a story of a family in Warsaw from the beginning of the 20th century until World War II. *Satan in Goray* (1953) is about religious persecution in 17th-century Poland. Singer received National Book Awards in 1970 and 1974— for *A Day of Pleasure,* an autobiographical story collection, and *A Crown of Feathers and Other Stories.* Several of his works were adapted for the stage or screen.

Singer was born near Warsaw. The son of a rabbi, he attended a rabbinical seminary but early in life turned to journalism. He came to the United States in 1935 and joined the staff of *The Jewish Daily Forward* in New York City. He became a United States citizen in 1943.

His other books include:

Novels—*The Magician of Lublin* (1960); *The Manor* (1967); *The Estate* (1969); *Enemies* (1972); *Shosha* (1978); *The King of the Fields* (1988); *Scum* (1991); *The Certificate* (1992); *Meshugah* (1994); *Shadows on the Hudson* (1998).

Short-story Collections—*Gimpel the Fool and Other Stories* (1957); *The Seance and Other Stories* (1968); *Passions* (1975); *The Power of Light* (1980); *The Collected Short Stories of Isaac Bashevis Singer* (1982); *The Image* (1985); *The Death of Methuselah* (1988).

Children's Books—*Mazel and Schlimazel* (1967); *When Schlemiel Went to Warsaw and Other Stories* (1968); *Alone in the Wild Forest* (1971); *Stories for Children* (1984).

Memoirs—*In My Father's Court* (1966); *A Young Man in Search of Love* (1978); *Love and Exile* (1984).

Singer, Isaac Merrit (1811-1875), a United States inventor. He was responsible for manufacturing the first sewing machines that were truly practical. His improvements on devices of other inventors, his development of a satisfactory home-style machine, and his imaginative selling techniques gave his machines worldwide preeminence.

Singer was born in Pittstown, New York, and became a machinist. He had patented machines for drilling rock and for carving when in 1850, in Boston, he was asked to repair a sewing machine. Instead, he redesigned it, devising a lockstitch machine with a device that fed cloth continuously beneath the needle. Financed by two partners, he set up a manufacturing company and began to sell the machine to garment factories.

Singer's original partners were replaced in 1851 by Edward Clark. Although the company lost a patent-infringement suit to Elias Howe in 1854, it suffered no setback. A home-style machine was put on the market in 1858, and to encourage its sale Clark offered customers installment terms and trade-in allowances. (Although he did not originate these practices, he was the first to use them with great success.) Singer continued to make improvements on his machines until his retirement in 1863. The company was headed by Clark until his death in 1882. By that time the Singer dominated the American market and was being sold throughout the world.

See also SEWING MACHINE, picture titled *Early Sewing Machines.*

Singing. See CHORUS; GLEE; VOICE.

Single Tax. See GEORGE, HENRY; TAXATION, subtitle *Single Tax.*

Sink, or **Sinkhole,** a funnel-shaped hollow in the earth's surface. Sinks are formed by the seepage of water in soluble rocks, such as limestone, dolomite, and gypsum. Usually they drain surface water into underground cavities. Some sinkholes, however, become blocked and form ponds or small lakes. Occasionally, a sinkhole is created by the collapse of a cavern ceiling.

Sinn Fein, shĭn fān (Gaelic for "Ourselves Alone"), an Irish political party. It played a leading role in the revolt against British rule in Ireland that resulted in the establishment of the Irish Free State. Sinn Fein was founded in 1905 by Arthur Griffith. In 1917 Eamon de Valera, a leader in the independence movement, became president of Sinn Fein, which in 1919 declared Ireland independent and began fighting the British.

After Britain recognized the Irish Free State in 1922, Sinn Fein split into factions. Extremists committed to immediate revolution eventually gained control of the party. By the late 1960's Sinn Fein had become the political arm of the Irish Republican Army

(IRA), joining its attempt to end British rule in Northern Ireland. (See IRISH REPUBLICAN ARMY.) In 1994, after the Provisional IRA announced an end to hostilities, representatives from Sinn Fein and Britain began negotiations. In 1997 Sinn Fein won two seats in the British Parliament. On April 10, 1998, Sinn Fein, along with seven other Northern Ireland political parties, signed an agreement creating the Northern Ireland Assembly, designed to replace direct rule from London. In the first elections to the Assembly, Sinn Fein won 18 of its 108 seats.

Sino-Japanese War, 1894-95, a conflict between China and Japan over domination of Korea. It marked the beginning of Japanese expansionism on the Asian mainland. The war had its origin in Japan's ambition to gain an empire. The Japanese had found a pretext several times for sending troops into Korea, for centuries a semi-independent vassal of the Chinese Empire, which moved to defend it. In 1894, following a series of armed clashes in Korea, each side declared war. Japan's superior equipment brought about China's defeat within eight months. By the Treaty of Shimonoseki (1895), Japan was given Taiwan and the Pescadores Islands. Also, the treaty required that China recognize the independence of Korea, thus making it possible for Japan to bring the nation into its sphere of influence.

Sino-Japanese War, 1937-45, a war between China and Japan, fought in China, that became merged with World War II. For the Chinese aspects, see CHINA, section "History," subtitle *Japan Invades China.*

For its relationship to World War II, see WORLD WAR II, section "The War with Japan, 1941-45," subtitles *Introduction* and *Offensive Against Japan, 1943-44:* China and Burma.

Sino-Tibetan. See LANGUAGE, subtitle *Language Families.*

Sinus, sī'nŭs, a cavity in a bone. The term is usually used to refer to the *paranasal sinuses,* cavities in bones of the skull; they drain into the nasal cavity and pharynx. There are four types of paranasal sinuses, named for the bones in which they occur. The *frontal sinuses* are located in the forehead over each eye. The *maxillary sinuses* are on each side of the nose in the cheek regions. The *sphenoid sinuses* are located behind the nasal cavity. The *ethmoid sinuses* are clusters of air pockets located in the roof of the nasal cavity.

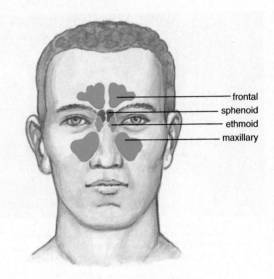

frontal
sphenoid
ethmoid
maxillary

Location of the Paranasal Sinuses

The sinuses are lined with mucous membrane—the same type of tissue that lines the nasal cavity. Often, the membranes of the sinuses—especially the frontal and maxillary—become inflamed, resulting in a disorder known as *sinusitis.* The inflammation interferes with the drainage and ventilation of the sinuses. Sinusitis can be caused by influenza, the common cold, pneumonia and other infectious diseases; allergies; and nasal obstructions, such as polyps and cysts.

In many cases, the symptoms of sinusitis are so mild as to cause little discomfort and the inflammation clears without any treatment. In severe attacks, symptoms include headache; pain and tenderness in the affected area; a thick discharge of mucus and, occasionally, pus into the nose or pharynx; and fever. Treatment includes use of medications to combat infection and relieve pain and moderate use of nasal sprays or nose drops that open up the congested passages. In some instances badly congested sinuses may have to be drained by a physician. When sinusitis is caused by a nasal obstruction, the obstruction may be removed surgically.

Sinyavsky, sĕ-nyăv'skī, **Andrei** (1925-1997), a Russian writer. His early works, notably *The Trial Begins* (1956) and *The Makepeace Experiment* (1964), were critical of Soviet ideology. These works were written under a pseudonym, Abram Tertz, and smuggled out of the country for publication.

Bureau of Indian Affairs: Martha Roberts
Powwow at Flandreau Santee Sioux Reservation, near Sioux Falls, South Dakota. The powwow, held each July, features traditional dancing and chants.

In 1965 Soviet authorities discovered that Tertz was Sinyavsky's pseudonym, and Sinyavsky was convicted of publishing anti-Soviet material. After serving six years in a prison camp, he was released in 1971. In 1973 he emigrated to France, where he lived until his death.

Other works include: *A Voice from the Chorus* (1973), *Strolls with Pushkin* (1975), and *Goodnight!* (1984).

Siouan Languages. See INDIANS, AMERICAN, section "Language Groups and Tribes."

Sioux City, Iowa, the seat of Woodbury County. It lies at the junction of the Big Sioux and Missouri Rivers, where Iowa, Nebraska, and South Dakota meet. Sioux City is the trading center for a large tri-state area and an important market for grain and livestock. Food processing, especially meatpacking, is the principal industry. The city lies at the head of barge navigation on the Missouri River. Historic sites in Sioux City include the grave of the Sioux Indian chief War Eagle and a monument, 175 feet (53 m) high, to Sgt. Charles Floyd, a member of the Lewis and Clark Expedition who died there in 1804. Morningside and Briar Cliff colleges are here. Settlement of the Sioux City area began around 1850.

Population: 80,505.

Sioux Falls, South Dakota, the state's largest city and the seat of Minnehaha County. It is located at a falls on the Big Sioux River in southeastern South Dakota, near the Iowa and Minnesota boundaries. Sioux

Falls is the commercial and industrial center of the state, serving a large livestock- and grain-producing region. Meatpacking and other food processing are the primary industries. The city is served by rail, air, and Interstate highways. The University of Sioux Falls and Augustana College are here.

Sioux Falls was founded in 1856 but was abandoned during an Indian uprising in 1862. In 1865 Fort Dakota was established there, and the town was resettled around it.

Population: 100,814.

Sioux Falls College. See UNIVERSITIES AND COLLEGES (table).

Sioux Indians, sōō, a North American Indian tribe of the Siouan language family. The name "Sioux" comes from a Chippewa word for "adder" or "enemy." The tribe calls itself by a Siouan word meaning "allies" —the word is spelled (depending on which Siouan dialect is being used) Lakota, Dakota, or Nakota. The Sioux are one of the best-known Indian tribes in American history. They were one of the largest and most warlike groups on the Northern Plains and under such leaders as Red Cloud, Crazy Horse, and Sitting Bull won notable victories against the U.S. Army.

The earliest known homeland of the Sioux was the upper Mississippi Valley in what is now Minnesota. Beginning in the 1600's, many Sioux were forced westward by the Chippewa (or Ojibway). By the late 1700's the main body of Sioux, called the Teton (or Western) Sioux, were centered in the Black Hills of South Dakota. To the east were the Wiciyela (or Middle) and the Santee (or Eastern) Sioux. At that time the total group numbered about 25,000.

The Teton Sioux were nomadic horsemen who depended upon the buffalo for food, clothing, tepee coverings, and a wide variety of tools, ornaments, and ceremonial objects. There were seven Teton bands: the Oglala (the band of Red Cloud and Crazy Horse); Hunkpapa (the band of Sitting Bull); Brulé; Sans Arcs; Oohenonpa, or Two Kettle; Miniconjou; and Sihasapa, or Blackfoot (not to be confused with the Blackfeet tribe of the Algonquian family).

The Wiciyela, consisting of two bands— the Yankton and Yanktonai—and the Santee, with four groups, were village dwellers who farmed and hunted small game.

Relations between the Sioux and the United States were largely peaceful until large numbers of whites began settling in Sioux territory, and the Indians were forced onto reservations by the government. In 1862 Santees led by Little Crow rose against the whites in Minnesota, killing more than 400 settlers. In retaliation, the United States government confiscated the Sioux lands in Minnesota and sentenced some 300 Santees to death. (All but 38 were eventually pardoned by President Lincoln for lack of evidence.)

In 1866 there was an uprising of Teton Sioux when forts were built along the Bozeman Trail, which crossed their hunting grounds and led to the gold fields of Montana. The Indians, under Red Cloud, eventually forced the government to abandon the trail. (See also RED CLOUD.)

Armed clashes continued at intervals, reaching a climax in 1876. At the Battle of the Little Bighorn, a force under Lieutenant Colonel George A. Custer was wiped out by Sioux and Cheyenne bands led by Crazy Horse, Sitting Bull, and Gall. Within a few months, however, the U.S. Army had forced the Indians onto reservations, except for those few who fled to Canada.

In the late 1880's, many Teton Sioux joined an Indian religious movement, known as the Ghost Dance, that promised the return of the buffalo and the disappearance of all white men. The government, fearing an uprising, sent large bodies of troops into Sioux territory. In December, 1890, the troops massacred nearly 300 Sioux who had gathered at Wounded Knee Creek in South Dakota. The massacre ended both the Ghost Dance movement and armed Indian resistance to the United States.

In 1973 militant Indians occupied the village of Wounded Knee until assured that provisions of the 1868 treaty creating the Sioux reservations would be honored.

Most Sioux live on reservations in South Dakota; the rest, in North Dakota, Montana, Minnesota, and Nebraska. Their economic status is low, and government and tribal leaders are working to develop agriculture, industry, and natural resources on the tribal lands. The tribe is the second largest (next to the Navajos) in the United States, numbering some 48,000.

See also CRAZY HORSE; CUSTER, GEORGE A.; GALL (Pizi); RED CLOUD; SITTING BULL; WOUNDED KNEE, BATTLE OF.

Sioux State, a nickname for North Dakota.

Siphon, sī'fŭn, a bent tube used to move a liquid over an obstruction to a lower level without pumping. A siphon is most commonly used to remove a liquid from its container. The siphon tube is bent over the edge of the container, one end in the liquid and the other outside end at a lower level than the surface of the liquid in the container. If the tube is once filled, a flow of liquid from the container through the tube will be set up. Several methods can be used to fill the tube. A small pump may be used. (The pump is no longer necessary once the flow has begun.) Water or any other harmless liquid may easily be siphoned through a small, short tube by sucking it through the tube with the mouth, as through a drinking straw, until the flow is started. The tube may also be filled by submerging it completely and then covering both ends while it is placed in position.

Siphons are sometimes used in irrigation to lift water from the irrigation canal, over a dike, and into a field. Wine may be siphoned from the top of large winemaking vats without disturbing the sediments on the bottom. Aqueducts sometimes act as siphons in carrying water over elevations.

How a Siphon Works

Siphons operate by atmospheric pressure. The container from which the liquid is siphoned must therefore be open to the air. When the tube is filled, the liquid will run

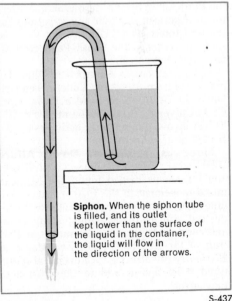

Siphon. When the siphon tube is filled, and its outlet kept lower than the surface of the liquid in the container, the liquid will flow in the direction of the arrows.

out of the lower end. (The greater weight of the liquid in the arm outside the container determines the direction of flow of the liquid.) As the liquid starts to flow, the fluid pressure at the top of the tube is lowered. A liquid always flows from an area under higher pressure to an area of lower pressure. The liquid in the container (under atmospheric pressure) flows up into the tube (an area of lowered pressure). This liquid in turn will flow out the outside end of the tube, again lowering the pressure at the top of the tube.

Once the flow has begun, it will continue if undisturbed as long as the inside end of the tube remains below the surface of the liquid. The flow can be cut off by raising the outside end of the tube above the level of the surface of the liquid in the container.

One limit to the use of siphons is imposed by the height to which atmospheric pressure can lift a given liquid. At sea level, atmospheric pressure can raise water to a height of about 30 feet (9 m). At higher altitudes the pressure is less, as is the height to which the water can be raised. Liquids heavier than water cannot be raised as high as water. Thus at sea level, mercury can only be raised about 30 inches (760 mm).

Siple, Paul A. (Allman) (1908-1968), a United States explorer, geographer, and biologist. He distinguished himself as an authority on climatology and the problems of subfreezing environments. As a member of the Byrd Antarctic expeditions and as director of American scientific investigations for the 1957 International Geophysical Year, he spent six years in the South Polar regions, more than anyone else.

Siple was born in Montpelier, Ohio. He graduated from Allegheny College, Pennsylvania, in 1932 and received a Ph.D. from Clark University. From 1946 until his death, he was involved in scientific activities for the United States government.

Siqueiros, sě-kě′ě-rōs, **David Alfaro** (1896-1974), a Mexican painter. With Rivera and Orozco he helped found the Mexican mural movement in the 1920's. A technical innovator, Siqueiros experimented with industrial and synthetic paints, spray guns, and curved surfaces in such murals as *Portrait of the Bourgeoisie.* In *The March of Humanity in Latin America* his metal sculptured relief figures add to the illusion of movement.

Siqueiros was born in Chihuahua, and studied art in Mexico City and in Paris. Siqueiros served as a revolutionary soldier in his teens and remained a political activist throughout his life; he was imprisoned several times by the Mexican government.

His other murals in Mexico City include *Burial of a Worker,* National Preparatory School; *New Democracy,* National Palace of Fine Arts; *The Revolution against the Porfirian Dictatorship,* National Museum of History. His major easel paintings include *Proletarian Mother* and *Our Present Image.*

Siren, a noisemaking device capable of producing a loud and continuous sound. A simple form of siren consists of two cylinders—one inside the other—with matching holes. The outer cylinder is rotated as a stream of air is forced through the siren. When the holes in the two cylinders line up, the air flows through; when they do not match up, the flow is interrupted. The regular interruption of the flow produces the sound. The faster the cylinder rotates, the higher the pitch of the sound.

Sirens are effective outdoor warning devices and are used as fog signals and for civil defense warnings. Emergency vehicles, such as fire trucks, ambulances, and police cars, use sirens to get through traffic safely. On many emergency vehicles, however, sirens have been replaced by electronic noisemaking equipment.

Sirens, in Greek mythology, sea nymphs who by their bewitching songs lured mariners to destruction. There were thought to be three sirens, each having the legs and wings of a bird and the head and body of a maiden. According to legend, they inhabited an island in the narrow strait between Sicily and Italy. In the *Odyssey,* Ulysses resisted them by sealing the ears of his crew with wax and having himself lashed to the mast of his ship so he could not change course. The sirens, upon being defied for the first time, threw themselves into the sea and became dangerous rocks.

Sirius, sĭr′ĭ-ŭs, the brightest star in the night sky. It is called the Dog Star, being the chief star of the constellation Canis Major ("great dog"). Sirius can be seen in the Northern Hemisphere during the evening in winter and early spring. After early spring it cannot be seen until around midsummer, when it becomes visible at dawn. In ancient Egypt, the reappearance of Sirius heralded the annual flooding of the Nile and marked the beginning of the new year.

Sirius is about 8.6 light-years from earth. It is actually a double star, but only the brighter of the pair of stars is visible to the unaided eye. The brighter star has an apparent magnitude of −1.5; the fainter star an apparent magnitude of 8.7. (The larger the magnitude number, the fainter the star.) The faint companion of Sirius, a *white dwarf* star, is from one-half to twice the size of the earth and has a mass approximately equal to that of the sun. The two stars revolve around each other with a period of 50.1 years.

That Sirius is a double star was detected first by irregularities in its motion. The existence of the faint companion was proposed in 1844; the companion was first seen by Alvan Clark in 1862.

See also ASTRONOMY, *Index to Star Maps;* CANIS MAJOR.

Sirocco, sĭ-rŏk′ō, a southerly wind in the region of the Mediterranean Sea, blowing from the Sahara. In North Africa the wind is exceptionally hot and dry and is frequently laden with dust. If sufficiently strong, the wind continues across the sea, picking up moisture but remaining hot and dusty. Siroccos may occur at any time of the year but are most frequent and severe during spring. They usually last a day or two. By their withering effect, siroccos can inflict great damage to vegetation. Local names for the wind include khamsin, in Egypt; gibleh, in Libya; and chili, in Tunisia.

Sisal, sī′săl, the name of a plant and also the name of the fiber obtained from its leaves. The fiber is used to make cord, rope, binder twine, and some floor coverings. The plant is native to Mexico and is named after the Mexican seaport of Sisal. Sisal is also cultivated in Central America, the West Indies, Brazil, eastern Africa, India, and Indonesia. A closely related plant, similar in appearance to sisal, is *henequen,* which is cultivated in Cuba and its native Mexico. It yields a fiber similar to sisal and is often called Mexican, or Cuban, sisal.

The leaves of the sisal plant are stiff, fleshy, and sword-shaped, and end in thorny tips. They grow in a rosette from a central bud at the base of the plant. Each leaf is about five feet (1.5 m) long and four inches (10 cm) wide and about two inches (5 cm) thick at the base. Green, funnel-shaped flowers are borne in spiked clusters on a long, single stalk that rises 15 to 20 feet (4.5

Robert & Linda Mitchell

Sisal

to 6 m) in the air. Bulbils (aerial buds) are borne among the flower clusters on the stalk. The bulbils and suckers (small shoots that form at the base of the plant) are used to propagate new plants.

Sisal is grown on large plantations. The plants are about three years old when their leaves are first harvested; they continue to produce new leaves for 6 to 15 years, depending on the local soil and climatic conditions. The outer, mature leaves of each plant are cut off twice a year, and the pulp is removed by machines. Then the fibers, about three feet (90 cm) long, are hung out in the sun to dry. They bleach from a greenish color to a creamy-white. The dried fiber is baled and sent to market. The yield of fiber is only about 3 or 4 per cent of the weight of the leaf.

The sisal plant is *Agave sisalana;* the henequen plant, *A. fourcroydes.* Both plants are of the agave family, Agavaceae.

Siskin. See PINE SISKIN.

Sisley, Alfred (1839-1899), an Impressionist painter. His landscapes of the French countryside, such as *Early Snow at Louveciennes,* have pure, luminous color and smooth brush strokes. Sisley's skill as a draftsman can be seen in his drawings and etchings and in many oil paintings, such as *Flood at Port-Marly.*

Zoe Dominic

Sitar. Ravi Shankar, a virtuoso Indian sitarist, helped popularize the instrument and Indian music, especially ragas, in Western countries. The sitar is used both as a solo instrument and in ensemble, or group, performances.

Sisley was born in Paris of English parents. He was sent to London in 1857 to prepare for a business career, but returned to Paris in 1862 to study painting. He met Monet, Renoir, and other Impressionists. Sisley spent most of his life in France but remained a British subject. Never winning popular success, he lived in poverty.

Sister Kenny. See KENNY, ELIZABETH.

Sisters and Nuns, members of religious orders of women. Traditionally, they live together in convents, wear a distinctive garb, or habit, and engage in various kinds of religious and charitable work. A small number of such groups exist in certain Protestant churches, particularly in Europe. In some Protestant denominations, women called deaconesses perform similar duties. Most such religious orders, however, are in the Roman Catholic Church.

In common speech, the terms "sister" and "nun" are often used interchangeably. Roman Catholic canon law, however, distinguishes between a sister and a nun. Sisters profess "simple" vows of poverty, chastity, and obedience that are less restrictive than the "solemn" vows taken by nuns. Usually, sisters also have more contact with the world, working in such places as schools, hospitals, and missions; nuns generally devote more time to quiet prayer and contemplation. Modernization of religious communities, however, has led to greater freedom for both in choice of activities, dress, and residence.

The first religious communities of women

were founded in Egypt early in the Christian era. The oldest existing religious order was established by Saint Basil in Capadocia (now part of Turkey) in the fourth century A.D. In the Middle Ages, the European monastic movement was expanded to include women. They mainly pursued a secluded life, devoted to prayer and contemplation. Later, orders were established to reach out and serve humanity. The first such group was the Sisters of Charity, founded by Saint Vincent de Paul in France in 1633. They aided the sick and the needy. Most orders established since 1800 have engaged in teaching or in charitable or missionary work.

Following the Second Council of the Vatican (1962-65), efforts were made to adapt the life of women in religious orders to the conditions of the modern world.

See also RELIGIOUS ORDERS..

Sistine Chapel. See VATICAN CITY, subtitle *Center of Culture*.

Sistine Madonna. See MADONNA (color picture).

Sitar, sĭ'tär, an Indian stringed musical instrument that is similar to the European lute. It has a long teakwood neck with a large gourd sound chamber at one end and a smaller gourd at the upper end. There are 18 to 20 movable frets. The sitar has 19 or 20 steel and brass strings. There are 6 or 7 playing, or main, strings under which are 12 or 13 sympathetic, or resonating, strings. The strings are plucked with the fingers or a wire plectrum. The sitar has a subtle, gentle tone. It was probably introduced into India from western Asia or Persia. The present form developed about the 13th century.

Sitdown Strike. See STRIKE, subtitle *Types of Strikes*.

Sitka, sĭt'kȧ, Alaska, a town on Baranof Island in the Panhandle, in the southeastern part of the state. Commercial shipping reaches Sitka by way of an arm of the Inside Passage, Alaska's coastal shipping route. Tourism and fishing are the mainstays of the economy. Nearby is Sitka National Historical Park, site of the Tlingit Indians' last stand against Russian settlers in 1804.

Sitka, the oldest town in Alaska after Kodiak, was founded in 1799 by Aleksandr Baranov as an outpost of the Russian-American Fur Company. In 1804 it was made Alaska's capital. The formal transfer of Alaska from Russia to the United States took place here in 1867, and the town remained the capital until 1900. Few buildings of the Russian era still stand.

Population: 8,588.

Sitka National Historical Park. See NATIONAL PARKS, section "United States."

Sitka Spruce. See SPRUCE.

Sitter, Willem de (1872-1934), a Dutch astronomer. He was a pioneer in applying Albert Einstein's theory of relativity to astronomy and developed a model of an expanding, curved universe. De Sitter's theoretical model led to further development of the theory of the expanding universe. De Sitter studied at the University of Groningen and became a professor at the University of Leiden in 1908. Later, he served as director of its observatory.

Sitting Bull (1834?-1890), a Sioux chief, warrior, and medicine man. He was the best-known Indian leader of his era because of his efforts to protect tribal lands, his leadership at the Battle of the Little Bighorn, and his appearances in the Wild West shows of Buffalo Bill (William Cody).

Sitting Bull was a member of the Hunkpapa band of Teton Sioux. He was fiercely opposed to white encroachment on Indian lands. In 1868 Sitting Bull accepted a treaty that restricted the Sioux to reservations but guaranteed them hunting rights off the reservation. When whites poured onto Sioux lands in the Black Hills following the discovery of gold in 1874, he became head of a war council of Sioux and Cheyennes formed to resist the whites. It was said that before the Battle of the Little Bighorn in June, 1876, Sitting Bull had a vision of the fight and of the Indian victory. The Sioux believed that he helped them win by "making medicine"—invoking supernatural assistance—during the battle. Within a few months, however, they were forced onto reservations, and Sitting Bull and his followers fled to Canada.

Gradually, however, they returned, and in 1881 Sitting Bull himself went onto a Dakota reservation. In the mid-1880's he made many personal appearances in eastern states, including those with Buffalo Bill's show. Then, when he was converted to the Ghost Dance, a mystical religion that promised restoration of Indian lands, government agents ordered his arrest. He was shot and killed in December, 1890, during a gun battle between his followers and Indian police sent to arrest him.

Dame Edith Sitwell
Rollie McKenna

Sitwell, sĭt'wĕl, the family name of three English authors, a sister and two brothers. Edith and Sacheverell were born in Scarborough, Osbert in London. Edith was privately educated; Osbert and Sacheverell attended Eton College. Sacheverell also attended Oxford. During World War I Edith edited and she and her brothers contributed to *Wheels,* a poetry magazine. The Sitwells were known for their eccentric behavior as well as for their writings. Edith wore dramatic hats, dresses that resembled medieval robes, and Baroque jewelry.

Dame Edith Sitwell (1887-1964) was best known for her poetry, but she also wrote criticism, biography, and history. Influenced by the French Symbolists, she used striking and original images in her poems and experimented with rhythm, meter, and tempo. Her early verse is light and witty, but her later poems—beginning with *Gold Coast Customs* (1929), a bitter social satire—are deeper in meaning, some of them markedly religious. In 1954 she was named a Dame Commander of the British Empire.

Her other books include: Poetry—*Bucolic Comedies* (1917); *Sleeping Beauty* (1918); *Street Songs*

Sitting Bull with Buffalo Bill in 1885
Denver Public Library: William McFarlane Notman

Winter Skate, photographed in waters off the coast of Maine

(1942); *The Canticle of the Rose* (1949); *Facade, and Other Poems, 1920-1935* (1950); *Gardeners and Astronomers* (1953); *Collected Poems* (1930, 1954, 1957, 1968). Prose—*Alexander Pope* (1930); *Aspects of Modern Poetry* (1934); *Fanfare for Elizabeth* (1946); *The Queens and the Hive* (1962). *Taken Care Of* (1962) is a book of memoirs. *Selected Letters 1919-1964* was published in 1970.

Sir Osbert Sitwell (1892-1969) wrote poems, essays, novels, and short stories. His best work is his five-volume autobiography published under the general title *Left Hand, Right Hand!* (also the title of the first volume), 1945-50. Osbert served in the Grenadier Guards during World War I. He inherited his title (he was a baronet) from his father, who died in 1943.

Sir Sacheverell Sitwell (1897-1988), a poet and essayist, was acclaimed for his travel books and criticism of art, architecture, and music. Such books as *Spanish Baroque Art* (1931), *Portugal and Madeira* (1954), and *Golden Wall and Mirador* (1961) combine travel sketches with art discussion. He succeeded to the baronetcy at Osbert's death.

Siva. See BRAHMAN.

Six Nations. See FIVE NATIONS.

Six-man Football. See FOOTBALL, subtitle *Other Types of Football.*

Six-shooter. See PISTOL.

Sixtus, the name of five popes. The most important were:

Sixtus IV (Francesco della Rovere; 1414-1484), pope 1471-84. He was a patron of the arts and learning and built the Sistine Chapel. However, he also was responsible for lowering the moral prestige of the papacy by his displays of favoritism and by his maneuvering for political power.

Sixtus V (Felice Peretti; 1521-1590), pope 1585-90. His reign was marked by reform of the government of the church and of the Papal States. He also built and restored many important structures, including the Lateran Palace and the Vatican Library.

Skagerrak, skăg'ēr-ăk, a strait in northern Europe forming part of the link between the North Sea and the Baltic Sea. It lies chiefly between Denmark and Norway and measures about 75 miles (120 km) in width at most points; its eastern waters touch the coast of Sweden. On the southeast another strait, the Kattegat, continues the connection to the Baltic Sea. The Skagerrak is relatively shallow near the Danish coast but reaches depths of 2,000 feet (600 m) or more near Norway. The strait is extensively used for shipping and fishing. The main ports are Oslo and Kristiansand in Norway.

Skagway, skăg'wā, Alaska, a coastal town in the southeast. It lies about 80 miles (130 km) northwest of Juneau, the capital, at the northern end of the Inside Passage, a coastal shipping route. Majestic peaks of the Coast Mountains rise directly behind the town. Skagway was founded in 1897 as the gateway to the Klondike goldfields of the Yukon, Canada, and soon became a boomtown of some 10,000 inhabitants. Though its prosperity was brief, Skagway retained much of the gold rush flavor and now is primarily a summer tourist center. Nearby is treacherous Chilkoot Pass, part of the main route to the goldfields until the opening of a railway between Skagway and Whitehorse (in the Yukon) in 1900.

Population: 692.

Skald, or **Scald,** skôld, as used in English, a name applied to poets of the courts of Scandinavian kings and chieftains from about the 9th century to the 14th century. (In Old Norse and in Icelandic, *skald* refers to any poet, not necessarily a court poet.) The skalds were skilled in the construction of complicated verse forms. Their poems, recited and sung, dealt with the heroic deeds of kings and noblemen, with romantic love, and with religious themes. Few complete skaldic poems have been preserved, but many fragments still exist. Material derived from skaldic poems is included in the Younger Edda and in certain sagas.

See also EDDA; SAGA.

Skateboarding. See SKATING, subtitle *Skateboarding.*

Skates and Rays, fish closely related to sharks. Like sharks, skates and rays have skeletons of cartilage rather than bone. Most skates and rays have bodies that are flattened from top to bottom. Their large pectoral fins, often called wings, are attached to the head. Skates live in cold seas; rays in warm seas and in some tropical rivers. There are about 100 species of skates and about 240 species of rays.

Skates range in length from a few inches to about 8 feet (2.4 m). Most, however, are less than 2 feet (60 cm) long. Rays range in length from less than 6 inches (15 cm) to more than 35 feet (11 m). Skates and rays are usually brown or gray above, often with various markings. They are whitish below, blending in well with their environment.

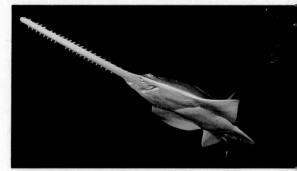

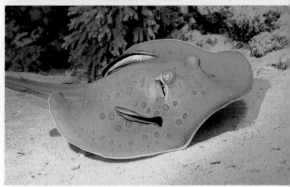

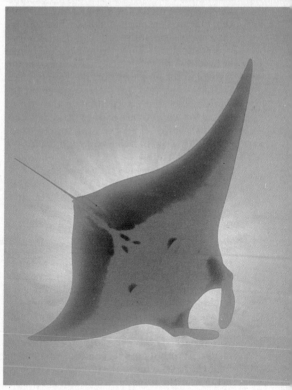

Rays. *From top:* sawfish; ribbontail ray, or bluespotted stingray; manta, or devil ray.

Skates and most rays live on the bottom of the waters they inhabit. Skates are sluggish animals that either lie on the bottom or slowly cruise, looking for the clams, snails, shrimp, and other small animals that they eat. Rays are far more active, constantly moving about and often rolling and jumping along the ocean floor. Their food is similar to that of skates and they sometimes take a heavy toll of clam and oyster beds.

The mouth in almost all skates and rays is on the underside of the body. Skates and bottom-dwelling rays take in water through openings, called spiracles, at the top of the head. The water is transferred to the gills, on the underside of the head. Those rays that do not live on the bottom take in water through the mouth, like other fish. Skates and rays have five pairs of gill slits.

The skin of skates is generally covered with numerous scales, but some skates and most rays have smooth skin. The tail is often slender and whiplike. Most rays have one or more sharp barbs on the ends of their tails; the barbs can inflict painful on humans. Sometimes these barbs contain poison. Skates do not have barbed tails, but some have organs along the sides of the tail that can produce an electric shock. The voltage they emit is generally low.

Young skates hatch from eggs contained in leathery, protective capsules. Rays do not lay eggs, but give birth to live young.

Skates and rays are eaten throughout the world. They are not popular in the United States for food but are used to make fertilizer and fish meal. The pectoral fins of some species are used to make imitation scallops in the United States.

Some Interesting Skates and Rays

The *little skate* is found in the Atlantic from North Carolina to Nova Scotia. It is one of the smaller skates, reaching a length of about 20 inches (50 cm) and a weight of little more than one pound (450 g). The *winter skate* has a similar range. It grows up to 3½ feet (1.1 m) in length and can weigh 12 pounds (5.4 kg). The *big skate*, found off the Pacific coast of North America, can reach a length of about 8 feet (2.4 m). The upper side of each wing is marked with a dark spot surrounded by a white ring.

The *electric rays*, or *torpedoes*, have an electricity-producing organ on each wing near the head. One of the largest electric rays is the *Atlantic torpedo*, which can grow up to

S-444

6 feet (1.8 m) long. This ray can discharge an electrical shock of about 200 volts. Electric rays use their electric organs to stun their prey and to defend themselves against predators.

The *sawfish*, found in tropical waters, is a ray with an elongated snout that bears teeth on either side and resembles a double-edged saw. The sawfish uses its "saw" to dig up the sea floor in search of food and to club its prey. It can inflict painful wounds and is of concern to fishermen because it damages fishnets. (Despite many cartoons on this subject, sawfish do not saw holes in wooden boats.) Some sawfish can grow to more than 35 feet (11 m) long and weigh more than 5,000 pounds (2,270 kg).

Among the rays with venomous barbs at the ends of their tails are the *stingrays*. Stingray venom affects the circulatory system of the victim, especially the heart. The venom can be fatal to humans. Most stingrays are shallow-water species. The bluntnose stingray is an Atlantic species; the ribbontail ray (or blue-spotted stingray) is found in the Pacific and Indian oceans.

The *mantas*, or *devil rays*, are quite active, often jumping out of the water. Many devil rays are extremely large and powerful with large wings. (One of the largest devil rays known measured 22 feet [6.7 m] between wing tips.) These fish are capable of overturning small boats. Mantas are found in warm-temperate to tropical seas.

Skates and rays make up the order Rajiformes, or Batoidei. Skates make up the family Rajidae. The little skate is *Raja erinacea;* the winter skate, *R. ocellata;* the big skate, *R. binoculata.* Electric rays make up the family Torpedinidae. The Atlantic torpedo is *Torpedo nobiliana.* Sawfish make up the family Pristidae. Stingrays make up the family Dasyatidae. The bluntnose stingray is *Dasyatis sayi;* the ribbontail ray, *Taeniura lymma.* Mantas make up the family Mobulidae.

Skating. There are three kinds of skating —*ice skating,* on blades attached to shoes; *roller skating,* on wheels attached to shoes, and *skateboarding,* on wheels attached to a board. Skateboarding is an outdoor sport; ice skating and roller skating may be done either indoors or outdoors.

Ice skating is a popular form of recreation in many countries, where persons of all ages can skate either on indoor rinks or on frozen streams, ponds, and small lakes. Competitive skating includes ice hockey (see HOCKEY), figure skating, and speed skating

Figure Skating demands grace and technique. Competitive skaters normally spend several hours each day practicing jumps, spins, and other dance-like maneuvers to develop an individual style.

Phil Cole/Allsport

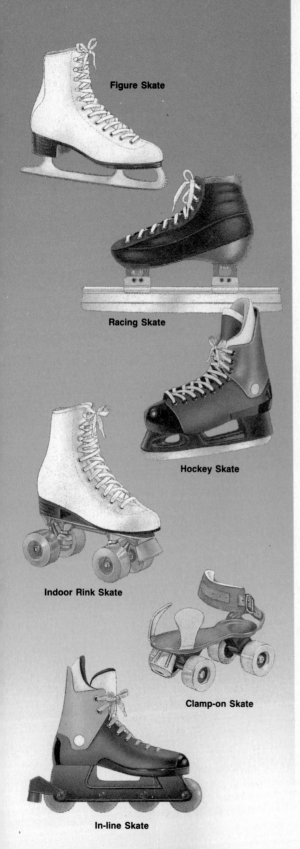

Figure Skate

Racing Skate

Hockey Skate

Indoor Rink Skate

Clamp-on Skate

In-line Skate

(racing). Figure skating is also done noncompetitively as a theatrical entertainment. Figure skating, speed skating, and ice hockey are Olympic events.

Roller skating is popular around the world. Some people roller skate regularly as a form of exercise. Skateboarding is popular mainly in the United States. Although there are competitive events in both roller skating and skateboarding, neither is an Olympic sport.

Ice Skating

An ice skate consists of a steel blade fastened to a leather or hard plastic boot. *Figure skates* have sharp, rocker-shaped blades. Each blade has a saw-toothed area, called a *toe pick*, at the front. Toe picks are used in certain jumps and spins. *Racing skates* have blades that are long, thin, and straight. *Hockey skates* have slightly curved blades. The boot of the hockey skate is reinforced with steel or hard plastic in the toe and heel. Figure skates and hockey skates are commonly used for recreational skating. There are also double-bladed skates, made for beginners.

Figure Skating is a graceful, artistic form of ice skating in which skaters perform intricate maneuvers. Figure skating competitions consist of singles, pairs, and ice dancing events. All events are skated to music.

In singles competition, skaters perform two programs: a *free skating* and an *original* program. The free skating program, also called the long program, consists of various jumps, spins, and other maneuvers. The skater is free to combine basic patterns with original movements, as in ballet. This program lasts from 4 to 4½ minutes. The original program consists of certain required maneuvers. This program, also called the short program, lasts from 2 minutes to 2 minutes, 40 seconds.

In pairs skating, two persons skate together and perform free skating and original programs as a couple.

In ice dancing, skaters perform three programs: compulsory, original, and free dancing. The compulsory and original programs are performed by two persons skating together to popular ballroom rhythms in the style of ballroom dancing. All competitors skate the same predetermined dance in the compulsory program. In the free program, couples are allowed to design their own dance.

In the original program of singles and pairs, and in the compulsory program of ice dancing, competitors are judged on how well

Speed Skating. Because of the wide area needed for turns in long-track, Olympic-style speed skating, the competitors do not race as a group, but in pairs, with the overall winner being the skater with the best time.

they execute the required maneuvers and on their general presentation. In the other programs, skaters are judged mainly on gracefulness, originality, and style.

Speed Skating is racing on skates. In competition, skaters race around an oval course—sometimes reaching speeds of up to 30 miles per hour (48 km/h). There are two types of speed skating, long track and short-track. Long-track speed skating includes both Olympic-style racing and pack, or mass-start, racing. The oval track is 400 meters (437 yards) in circumference. In an Olympic-style race the track is separated into two lanes. Two skaters compete for time in distances ranging from 500 meters (547 yards) to 10,000 meters (10,936 yards). In a pack race there is only one lane; six to eight skaters compete at the same time. In short-track speed skating four to six skaters race against each other rather than the clock. The track is 111 meters (121 yards) around. Races are skated in heats and range from 500 to 3,000 meters (3,280 yards). There are also relay events. For Olympic speed skating records, see OLYMPIC GAMES, table *Olympic Records.*

History of Ice Skating. The first ice skates may have been animal bones tied to the feet with thongs and used by humans as a means of transportation. In the Middle Ages ice skates with wooden blades were used. Skates with iron blades were introduced in about the 16th century, probably by the Dutch or the Scots. The first ice skating club was founded in Edinburgh, Scotland, in

1742. The sport probably was introduced into North America in the 18th century.

The introduction of skates with steel blades in about 1850 helped popularize the sport. Figure skating developed in Europe in the 1860's. Both figure skating and speed skating were events in the first Winter Olympics, held in 1924. Professional ice shows were made popular in the 1930's by Sonja Henie, a world champion figure skater. (See HENIE, SONJA.) Women's speed skating events were not included in the Winter Olympics until 1960. In 1992 short-track racing became an Olympic event. The clap skate, a speed skate with a hinged blade, was introduced in 1996.

Roller Skating

A person can roller skate on any hard, smooth surface except ice. Roller skating is popular with young and old alike. There are two types of roller skates—traditional, which have two wheels at each end of the skate; and in-line, which have three or four wheels mounted, one in front of the other, in a bladelike structure under the boot. Most roller skate wheels are made of hard rubberlike plastic. On some children's skates, the wheels are made of metal, and on some racing skates, of wood.

There are two types of traditional skates used by children outdoors—*clamp-on skates,* which are attached with straps and clamps to street shoes; and *shoe skates,* which come with attached shoes or boots. Children also use in-line skates outdoors. Most adults use

Skateboarder performing a maneuver at a skate-board park. He is wearing appropriate protective equipment—helmet and elbow and knee pads.

in-line skates outdoors but some use shoe skates with either boots or low-cut shoes resembling running shoes.

Indoor rink skates have narrower wheels than outdoor skates. A toe-stop—a round bumper used for starting, stopping, and turning—is attached to most indoor skates. (A few outdoor skates also have this feature.) All indoor skates are of the shoe or boot type. In-line skates can be used in some indoor rinks.

There are three types of competitive roller skating—speed skating, roller hockey, and artistic skating. Traditional four-wheel (quad) skates are used for most events, but in-line skates are sometimes used, especially in roller hockey and speed skating. Events in speed skating are similar to events in competitive speed skating on ice. Roller hockey is played much like ice hockey. Artistic skating has programs and events that are similar to those in competitive figure skating.

The *roller derby* is a form of racing in which touring professional teams of men and women compete on banked indoor tracks.

History of Roller Skating. Roller skating probably began in Holland as a warm-weather version of ice skating, a favorite sport in that country. The first skates had crude wooden rollers. In 1863 J. L. Plimpton of New York developed a skate with four small wooden wheels. Ball-bearing wheels were introduced in the 1880's. In the 20th century roller skating became a popular pas-

time. Thousands of indoor rinks were built in the United States, Canada, and other countries. Figure skating and racing competition came into prominence in the 1930's.

After World War II, the roller derby became immensely popular for a time. Roller derby's appeal faded in the mid-1970's. In-line skating, originally done as training by figure skaters and hockey players, became very popular in the late 1980's and 1990's.

Skateboarding

A skateboard is a narrow board about two feet (61 cm) long with one pair of skate-type wheels at each end. It is usually made of wood, fiberglass, or plastic. Wheels made of hard, resilient plastic and a special suspension make the board highly responsive to shifts in the rider's weight, making possible the performance of elaborate stunts. On level surfaces, a rider keeps one foot on the board and propels with the other; when used on inclined surfaces, skateboards require only occasional foot propulsion. Skateboarding is done on driveways, sidewalks, and streets and in *skateboard parks*—curved, sloping roadways designed to permit skateboarders to perform a great variety of maneuvers.

The first skateboards, developed in the 1960's, used roller skate wheels and were suitable only for straight-line riding. Improved designs in the 1970's made skateboards more versatile and greatly increased the popularity of the sport.

The United States Figure Skating Association, founded in 1921, is the governing body for the sport in the United States. Headquarters are in Colorado Springs, Colorado. The Amateur Speedskating Union of the United States, founded in 1927, sanctions national and regional competitions. Headquarters are in Glen Ellyn, Illinois. U.S. Speedskating, the governing body affiliated with the U.S. Olympic Committee, was founded in 1966 and has headquarters in Rocky River, Ohio. USA Roller Skating (USAC/RS) sponsors and regulates roller skating competition. It was founded in 1971 and has headquarters in Lincoln, Nebraska.

Books about Skating

Ryan, Pat. *Extreme Skateboarding* (Capstone, 1998).

Berman, Alice. *Skater's Edge Sourcebook: Ice Skating Resource Guide,* 2nd edition (Skater's Edge, 1998).

Dugard, Martin. *In-Line Skating Made Easy* (Globe Pequot, 1996).

For Younger Readers

Gutman, Bill. *Skateboarding to the Extreme!* (St. Martin's, 1997).

Gutman, Dan. *Ice Skating: from Axels to Zambonis* (Viking Penguin, 1997).

Skiing, skē'ĭng, a winter sport in which a person glides over snow on a pair of long, narrow, flat runners called skis. There are two main types of skiing: Alpine, or downhill, skiing; and Nordic skiing, which includes cross-country skiing and ski jumping. A third form of skiing, freestyle skiing, generally involves various combinations of acrobatics, stunts, and dance.

Millions of persons throughout the world ski for recreation or competition. Ski vacations are popular with individuals and families. Some countries have national teams of ski racers who compete in the Winter Olympics and International Ski Federation tournaments. Some racers compete for prize money in ski circuits.

Downhill Skiing

Equipment. Essential equipment consists of a pair of skis with bindings and brake, ski boots, and two ski poles.

Skis are usually made with a wood, metal, or foamed plastic core, and are strengthened with layers of such materials as fiberglass, metal, plastic, or Kevlar. Layers of hard plastic are laminated to the top surface of the skis to protect them from scratches. The bottom surface is coated with a polyethylene plastic, to which wax is applied to help improve glide.

The curved front part of a ski is called the *tip* or *shovel;* the rear part is the *tail.* Narrow steel strips, called *edges,* run along the bottom edges of the ski to grip the snow and aid in turning. *Bottom camber* is the arch of a ski that supports the skier's weight and distributes it along the entire length of the ski. *Side camber* is a narrowing of the ski toward the middle.

Typical downhill skis are three to four inches (7.5 to 10 cm) wide and about one inch (2.5 cm) thick in the middle, tapering to about one-fourth inch (6 mm) at the tip and tail. The proper length of a ski depends on the size and skill of the skier: the heavier, taller, and more skilled the skier, the longer the ski. In general, a ski should be six to eight inches (15 to 20 cm) longer than the skier's height, except for beginners, who sometimes start on skis as short as three feet (90 cm).

Ski boots are heavy and rigid and are designed to quickly transmit the movement of the lower body to the skis. Most boots have a hard plastic outer shell and a composite rubber and cloth inner liner. Some have

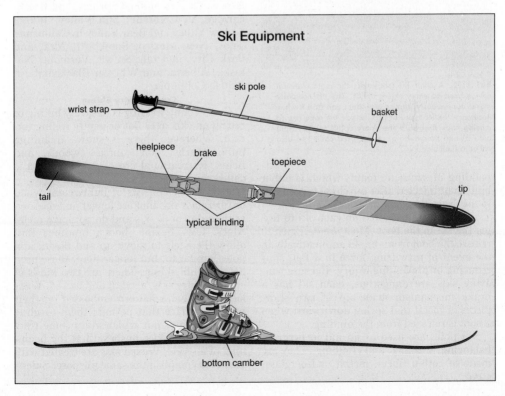

Ski Equipment

ski pole

wrist strap

basket

heelpiece

brake

toepiece

tail

tip

typical binding

bottom camber

with plastic or rubber molded grips and leather wrist straps. Each pole has a blunt metal tip and, slightly above it, a basket (a round webbing or disk that keeps the pole from sinking too deeply into the snow).

Ski Areas. Persons may ski for recreation wherever there are snow-covered hills, but most skiers travel to developed ski areas or ski resorts. Skiing areas vary from small hills with only a few slopes and minimum facilities to vast complexes having numerous slopes and trails and designed to handle thousands of skiers per hour. *Ski lifts* are mechanical devices that pull or carry skiers uphill. The most common type is the *chair lift,* a chair suspended from a moving cable. Ski schools are available at many areas to offer professional instruction.

Most ski areas have slopes and trails for beginner, intermediate, and expert skiers. Ski runs are usually marked with signs designating their degree of difficulty. Most areas have first-aid facilities, and the local Ski Patrol—composed of specially trained expert skiers, mostly volunteers—will take injured skiers off the slopes to the nearest facility. The Ski Patrol also enforces safety rules.

Major ski areas in North America include Aspen, Vail, Steamboat Springs, and Breckenridge, in Colorado; Sun Valley, Idaho; Squaw Valley and Bear Valley in California; Taos, New Mexico; Snowbird, Alta, and Park City, in Utah; Stowe, Vermont; Nakiska, Alberta, and Whistler/Blackcomb, in British Columbia.

Cross-country Skiing

Cross-country skiing is basically hiking or racing on skis over flat or gently rolling terrain, wherever there is snow—including public parks, golf courses, woods, and fields. Recreational cross-country skiing is called *ski touring.*

Equipment consists of lightweight wood or fiberglass skis that are longer and narrower than downhill skis and do not have metal edges; low, flexible boots; bindings that allow the heels to move up and down; and poles similar to, but longer than, those used for downhill skiing. There are two kinds of cross-country skis, *waxless* and *waxed.* Waxless skis have a pattern embossed on their bottom surface that permits them to glide forward easily, but which gives some traction when the skier pushes off at the beginning of a stride. Waxed skis are treated with wax to accomplish the same purpose. Skiers

© Mark Gibson

Ski Lift. A chair lift (shown) is the most common device used to carry skiers uphill. The lift normally moves continuously, but an attendant can stop it when necessary. Other types of lifts include the rope tow (a moving rope that pulls the skiers uphill as they hold onto it) and the gondola, an enclosed cable car also called a funicular.

padding of synthetic foam, which is either built in or injected after purchase to conform to the exact shape of the skier's foot.

Bindings are mounted on each ski to fasten the ski to the boot. Most are designed to release the boot from the ski automatically in the event of a twisting force in a fall, thus reducing or preventing injury. Because runaway skis are dangerous, each ski has a brake mechanism made up of two short pieces of metal that spring downward when a boot is released from the binding.

Ski poles are used as an aid in turning, balancing, walking, and climbing. They are made of cotton fibers, metal, or fiberglass,

Common Ski Terms

Base, the packed (hard) snow underneath new snow.

Check, a braking maneuver done before turning.

Christie, an advanced turn in which the skis slide together during the last part of the turn.

Diagonal Stride, a cross-country technique in which the skier pushes off on one ski while gliding on the other. The skis move in a parallel fashion.

Edging, putting a ski on its long side so that one edge digs into the snow to prevent slipping.

Fall Line, an imaginary line that a freely sliding object would follow from the top of a hill to the bottom; it is used as a reference in describing various kinds of maneuvers and courses.

Geländesprung, a jumping maneuver in which the poles are used to help the skier leap.

Hardpack, snow that has been compacted solidly, usually by the weight of many skiers.

Herringbone, a method of climbing a hill; the skis are moved alternately uphill while kept in a V-position and edged to prevent slipping backwards.

Moguls, mounds formed by snow displaced as skiers turn in the same tracks down the slope.

Parallel, a style of skiing in which the skis are kept parallel and close together through an entire turn.

Powder, light, fluffy snow.

Schuss, to ski downhill without turning.

Skate Skiing, a cross-country technique in which the skier's motion is similar to that used in ice skating.

Side Step, a method of climbing a hill; the skis are kept at right angles to the fall line and are stepped alternately uphill with the poles used for support.

Snowplow, a maneuver used by beginners to slow down, turn, and stop. The ski tips are close together and the tails wide apart, forming a V-position with edges applied to the snow.

Stem, a maneuver in which the tail of the uphill ski is opened from the parallel position to a V-position in preparation for and during a turn.

Traverse, skiing across the slope instead of down the fall line.

Wedeln, or Wedel, a series of short, quick turns down the slope in a zigzag pattern; done to develop a steady skiing rhythm.

---

who use waxed skis usually carry several different types of wax for use in varying snow conditions.

Ski Jumping

In ski jumping the skis are longer and heavier than downhill skis. Each ski has two or three grooves on the bottom for stability, but no steel edges. Jumpers wear lightweight, flexible boots. Bindings allow the heels to be raised so the jumper can lean forward over the skis to reduce wind resistance. Poles are not used. In competition, jumpers slide down a steep chute, or *inrun*, and from the end of it soar through the air

Cross-country Skiing is increasingly popular as a form of recreation, but as a racing event it requires great stamina.

Ski Jumping. In competitive jumping correct form is extremely important because it increases distance and earns scoring points.

Focus on Sports

for up to 300 feet (90 m). A jumper is in the air for three to five seconds.

Ski Competitions

In the United States a number of ski clubs conduct local tournaments. NASTAR (National Standard Race) is a racing program for recreational skiers. The National Collegiate Athletic Association holds annual downhill, cross-country, and ski jumping championships. The International Ski Federation (Fédération Internationale de Ski, or FIS) supervises international competition.

Competitive Alpine ski events consist of the *slalom, giant slalom, super giant slalom, downhill, Alpine combined,* and *speed skiing.* In the slalom, skiers are timed as they race down a zigzagging course marked off by sets of poles called *gates.* The slalom course is about 630 yards (575 m) long. The course used for the giant slalom is longer than that used for the slalom and has fewer gates. The super giant slalom course is similar to that of the giant slalom except that it is steeper and longer. The course for the downhill race is 1,800 to 5,000 yards (1,600 to 4,600 m) and is relatively straight, with only a few gates to mark its route. The Alpine combined is made up of a downhill and a slalom race. The speed skiing course is about one mile (1.6 km) long. It is extremely steep and has no gates. Skiers often reach speeds of 130 mph (209 km/h).

Competitive Nordic events include cross-country races, biathlon and ski jump events, and the Nordic combined. Cross-country races are of various distances over natural courses. There are individual and relay competitions. In the biathlon, teams and individual contestants ski courses of from 7.5 to 30 kilometers (4.7 to 18.6 miles), stopping at intervals to shoot at targets from a distance of 50 meters (164 feet). Scoring for ski jumping is based on the total distance of several jumps and on style. The Nordic combined consists of a cross-country race and a ski-jump event.

Competition in freestyle skiing includes the mogul event (skiing down a steep, bumpy course), the ballet event (dancing to music while skiing down a gentle slope), and the aerial event (performing acrobatic stunts while skiing off a jump).

USSA (U.S. Ski and Snowboard Association) sanctions Olympic skiing and snowboarding. Headquarters are in Park City, Utah.

History

The first skis may have been tree branches that were strapped to the feet and used by prehistoric humans as a means of staying on top of the snow. Northern Europeans were probably the first to wear skis. The oldest known skis date to about 5,000 years ago. During the Middle Ages, Scandinavian armies sometimes wore skis in winter warfare. Troops on skis were used in World War II.

Skiing as a sport probably began in the 18th century. The first United States ski club was formed in 1872 in Berlin, New Hampshire. The National Ski Association of America, now the U.S. Ski and Snowboard Association, was founded in 1904. In 1924 a

Soldier on Skis. Scandinavian soldiers used skis as early as the Middle Ages. Skis of different lengths reportedly increased maneuverability, but improved equipment and techniques eventually made this feature obsolete.

Editor's Digest

munities, such as Vail and Aspen, Colorado, grew around ski areas. In the late 1970's cross-country skiing also gained widespread popularity.

See also SNOWBOARDING; WATER SKIING.

Books about Skiing

Gamma, Karl. *The Handbook of Skiing,* revised edition (Knopf, 1992).

McCallum, Paul and C. L. *The Downhill Skiing Handbook* (Betterway Books, 1992).

Tejada-Flores, Lito. *Breakthrough on Skis: How to Get Out of the Intermediate Rut* (Random House, 1993).

Wicks, David. *Making Tracks: an Introduction to Cross-Country Skiing* (Pruett, 1994).

For Younger Readers

Evans, Jeremy. *Skiing* (Macmillan, 1992).

Godlington, Douglas. *Skiing* (Sterling, 1991).

Skimmer, or **Scissorbill,** a long-winged shorebird with brownish-black plumage above and white plumage below. It has small, orange feet. The lower part of the long, slender bill is slightly longer than the upper part. The base of the bill is orange, and, depending on the species, the tip may be yellow or black. The *black skimmer* of temperate and tropical America is 16 to 20 inches (40 to 50 cm) long and has a black-tipped bill. Its call is similar to a dog's bark. There are two other species of skimmers,

number of countries formed the International Ski Federation. That same year Nordic and ski jumping events were included in the first Winter Olympics. Alpine ski events were not included in the Winter Olympics until 1948.

Interest in Alpine skiing grew rapidly following the development of ski lifts in the 1930's. After World War II hundreds of recreational ski areas were opened. In the United States particularly, entire resort com-

Alpine Competition. Snow flies as this skier speeds through a gate during a giant slalom race.

Brooks Dodge/Sports File

found in Africa and in India and Southeast Asia.

All skimmers live along seacoasts and large rivers and lakes. As the name "skimmer" implies, they skim across the water, scooping up such food as fish and shrimp with their bills. Skimmers breed in colonies. Their nests—slight depressions in the sand—may hold from two to five pale and darkly blotched eggs.

The black skimmer is *Rynchops nigra* of the skimmer family, Rynchopidae.

Skin, the outer covering of the body of a vertebrate (an animal with a backbone). The skin is the largest organ of the body. In an average-sized adult person, it has an area of about 2 square yards (1.7 m²) and weighs from 6 to 7½ pounds (2.7 to 3.4 kg); its thickness varies from $\frac{1}{32}$ of an inch (0.8 mm) on the eyelids to $\frac{1}{8}$ of an inch (3.2 mm) on the soles.

Hair, nails, sweat glands, and sebaceous (or oil) glands are structures derived from the human skin. In other groups of animals additional derivatives of the skin include horns, scales, feathers, beaks, claws, and hooves. (See FEATHER; HAIR; HOOF; HORN; NAIL.) The skins of various animals provide many useful products. (See FUR; LEATHER.)

The skin is composed of two distinct layers—the outer layer is called the *epidermis* and the inner layer the *dermis*. Most vertebrates shed the outer part of the epidermis throughout their lifetime. It may be shed in fragments of different sizes, as in humans, or it may be shed all at once, as in snakes. In most vertebrates the epidermis consists of several layers of cells. Cells in the outer layers produce an insoluble protein called *keratin*. This substance, which accumulates in the cells, makes the skin waterproof, preventing entrance of water into the body and excessive loss of water from the body.

The dermis, also composed of several layers of cells, contains the blood vessels, nerves, and sensory receptors. In addition, the dermis gives the skin its strength and elasticity.

The Human Skin

The skin covers the body and protects the deeper tissues from injury and drying. It offers protection from invasion by infectious organisms and is important in temperature regulation. It contains many sensory nerve endings that provide a person with information about the environment. The skin, through its numerous sweat glands, also has excretory functions, eliminating water and salts through perspiration. (See PERSPIRATION.)

The human skin, like that of other vertebrates, is made up of epidermis and dermis. Underlying the skin is a layer of tissue called the *subcutaneous tissue,* which is in most parts of the body composed largely of fat.

Epidermis. The epidermis, also called *cuticle,* is made up of living and dead epithelial cells. (These specialized cells also form the mucous membranes that line the mouth and interior passages of the body.) The dead cells form the outer surface of the skin. These flake off constantly and are replaced by new cells made in the living (lower) layer of epidermis. There is no blood supply in the

Human Skin. *Left,* photo of a cross section, greatly enlarged. *Right,* block diagram of structures of the skin.

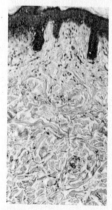

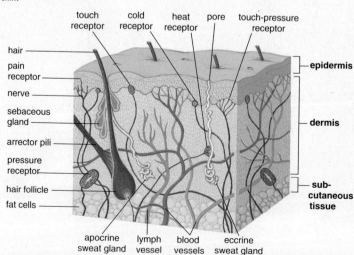

epidermis—that is why an injury to this layer causes no bleeding. There are, however, numerous nerve endings, such as those that register pain, among the inner layers of the epidermis. The cells of the epidermis obtain nourishment from lymph fluid that filters in from the dermis.

A brownish-black pigment, *melanin,* is produced in *melanocytes,* living cells of the epidermis. Skin and hair color depend on the amount of melanin produced here. Freckles and suntan are due to increased melanin production. (See FRECKLES; SUNTAN.) Fingernails and toenails are composed of clear, horny cells and are derivatives of the epidermis.

The surface of the epidermis is marked by a network of ridges. In the tips of the fingers the pattern of the ridges is unique for each person. Therefore these patterns are used as a means of identification. (See FINGERPRINT IDENTIFICATION.) Similar ridges appear on the soles of the feet, and footprints are used in hospitals to identify babies.

Dermis. The dermis, also called *corium,* contains numerous blood vessels, lymph vessels, nerves, glands, and hair follicles. The surface area of the dermis is increased by numerous elevated protrusions called *papillae.* The entire layer of dermis is richly supplied with blood and lymph vessels that expand and contract with body temperature changes. The dermis contains sensory receptors that, depending on their type, respond to such stimuli as heat, cold, touch, pressure, and pain.

Located in the dermis are the follicles from which hairs grow and the arrectors pili, muscles that control the movements of the hairs, as when goosebumps are formed. Also in the dermis are the sebaceous glands— glands that secrete an oil that keeps the skin and hair soft and lubricated. The ducts of some of these glands open onto the skin surface, but the ducts of most of the glands open into the hair follicles.

Sweat glands extend from deep within the dermis, where they produce sweat, to the tiny pores on the surface of the skin, where sweat is secreted. They are found throughout the skin, but are most numerous in the palms and soles. There are two types of sweat glands, the *eccrine* and the *apocrine.* Eccrine glands secrete sweat primarily in response to elevated body temperature. They function from the time of birth and are common on the forehead, upper lip, neck, and back. The apocrine glands, which do not become active until puberty, respond to emotional stress. They open into hair follicles and are most numerous in the armpits and groin. Modified sweat glands in the external canal of the ear secrete the wax found in ears. The hair follicles and glands, although located in the dermis, develop from the same type of epithelial cells that make up the epidermis and are considered to be derivatives of the epidermis.

Disorders and Care of the Skin

Doctors often judge a person's general health by the color and condition of the skin, for the skin often reflects internal disturbances and diseases. For example, chronic liver disease often gives the skin a yellowish cast, and many allergies show up as hives or rashes on the skin. Diseases such as measles and scarlet fever produce visible changes in the skin.

The skin itself can become the site of various diseases and disorders, such as psoriasis and eczema. The study of the skin and its diseases is called *dermatology;* physicians who specialize in skin disorders are *dermatologists.*

Any inflammation of the skin is called *dermatitis.* The inflammation may take on the appearance of reddening, crusting, oozing of fluids, scaliness, blisters, or cracking. Such inflammations may be caused by physical and mechanical conditions such as heat, cold, chafing, and scratching. Dermatitis may also be caused by viruses, bacteria, and fungi. Some inflammations result from infection by small animals such as mites, ticks, lice, fleas, bedbugs, and hookworms. Dermatitis may be caused by contact with various chemicals, such as soaps and petroleum products, and with dust. It may result from malnutrition, such as that caused by the lack of certain vitamins.

Various kinds of cancer affect the skin; the three main kinds are *basal cell carcinoma, squamous cell carcinoma,* and *malignant melanoma.* Basal cell carcinoma, the most common skin cancer, produces small, round bumps or scarlike growths. It is rarely fatal. Squamous cell carcinoma produces red, scaly bumps. Malignant melanoma, the most deadly type of skin cancer, usually produces irregularly shaped moles; the cancer quickly spreads to the lymph nodes. Most cases of skin cancer are caused by excessive exposure to the ultraviolet rays of sunlight.

Certain accessory organs of the skin, such as sebaceous glands and hair follicles, may become diseased, and such conditions as acne or baldness may develop. The nails are sometimes the site of infections. *Albinism* results when melanin is not produced in the epidermis. (See ALBINO.) *Vitiligo,* a condition in which patches of skin appear lighter than the surrounding areas, is caused by the destruction of melanocytes.

Vital to a healthy, attractive skin is cleanliness. Bathing washes away dirt, sweat, oil, and dead skin. Equally important are good nutrition and adequate sleep. Even when the general rules for good health are observed, however, skin problems may still occur. Many adolescents, for example, will have some form of acne.

Many harmless blemishes, such as birthmarks, can be covered with cosmetics or be removed through surgery or laser treatment. Excess hair can be removed or bleached so that it is not easily visible. Cosmetic preparations can help reduce excessive oil or lubricate especially dry skin. (See COSMETICS.)

Wrinkling of the skin is a natural process; as a person grows older the skin becomes thicker, drier, and less elastic. Because there is less fatty tissue under the skin, the skin sags, and wrinkles form. Many wrinkles can be removed by plastic surgery but eventually they recur.

For information on disorders involving the skin, see:

ABSCESS	ELEPHAN-	PSORIASIS
ACNE	TIASIS	RINGWORM
ALLERGY	ERYSIPELAS	ROCKY
ATHLETE'S	FROSTBITE	MOUNTAIN
FOOT	GANGRENE	SPOTTED
BIRTHMARK	HIVES	FEVER
BLISTER	IMPETIGO	SCARLET FEVER
BURN	LUPUS	SHINGLES
CALLUS	MANGE	SMALLPOX
CANCER	MEASLES	TYPHOID FEVER
CHICKEN POX	PELLAGRA	TYPHUS
COLD SORE	PRICKLY	ULCER
DANDRUFF	HEAT	WART
ECZEMA		

See also POISON IVY; SUNTAN.

Skin Diving. See DIVING, subtitle *Diving with Breathing Apparatus.*

Skink, a family of small, ground-dwelling lizards. Skinks are usually less than one foot (30 cm) in length, and have conical or blunt-shaped heads, cylindrical bodies, and tapering tails. There are about 1,280 species,

S-460

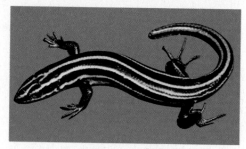

Carolina Biological Supply Co.
Five-lined Skink

found on all continents except Antarctica. Skinks are most numerous in Africa, Asia, Australia, and the islands of the western Pacific.

Many skinks have two pairs of well-developed limbs; some have only small hind limbs; and others are limbless. Skinks are usually some shade of olive or brown and are often marked with stripes, crossbars, or spots. The smooth, flat, overlapping scales covering their bodies give skinks a glossy or shiny appearance.

The skink's tail often serves as a protective device. When seized it easily breaks off and the skink escapes. A new tail grows shortly afterwards. Most skinks feed on small invertebrates, mainly insects. Some are vegetarians. Some skinks lay eggs; others bear live young.

There are 15 species in the United States. Among them are the *sand skink,* which is tan or white with dark stripes; the *five-lined skink,* black with light stripes; and the *ground skink,* brown with black stripes.

Skinks make up the family Scincidae. The sand skink is *Neoseps reynoldsi;* the five-lined skink, *Eumeces obsoletus;* the ground skink, *Scincella lateralis.*

Skinner, B. F. (Burrhus Frederic) (1904-1990), a United States psychologist. Skinner was one of the leaders of the behaviorist school and his research greatly influenced experimental psychology and education. (See BEHAVIORISM.) Skinner developed what came to be known as the Skinner box. An animal placed in this device would automatically be rewarded (with food, for example) when it performed a desired task. Applying the principle involved—that rewarded behavior is repeated—to human learning, he created teaching machines that reward students by immediately informing them when they give a correct answer. (See TEACHING MACHINE.)

Skinner was born in Susquehanna, Pennsylvania. He received his Ph.D. degree in

1931 from Harvard University, where he became a professor of psychology in 1948. He retired from teaching in 1974.

Among his other works are: *Walden Two* (1948; revised editions, 1960 and 1976); *Science and Human Behavior* (1953); *The Technology of Teaching* (1968); *About Behaviorism* (1974); *Enjoy Old Age* (1983). *Particulars of My Life* (1976), *The Shaping of a Behaviorist* (1979), and *A Matter of Consequences* (1983) are autobiographies.

Skinner, Cornelia Otis (1901-1979), a United States actress and author. She was the daughter of Otis Skinner (1858-1942), a United States actor known for his versatility in playing roles ranging from the comic to the tragic. Cornelia Otis Skinner gained fame for her solo performances—dramatic monologues about famous people from history—that she wrote, produced, and acted. These works included *The Wives of Henry VIII* (1931) and *The Loves of Charles II* (1933). She also starred in such plays as *Candida* and *Major Barbara*. Skinner wrote several humorous books, beginning with *Tiny Garments* (1932).

Skinner was born in Chicago. She attended Bryn Mawr College and also studied at the Sorbonne, Paris.

Her other books include: *Excuse It, Please* (1936); *Soap Behind the Ears* (1941); *The Ape in Me* (1959); *Our Hearts Were Young and Gay* (1942), with Emily Kimbrough, about a trip they took to Europe; *Family Circle* (1948), an autobiography; *Madame Sarah* (1967), a biography of Sarah Bernhardt.

Skipper. See BUTTERFLIES AND MOTHS, subtitle *Kinds of Butterflies:* The Skippers (and illustration).

Sklodowska, Marie. See CURIE, PIERRE AND MARIE SKLODOWSKA.

Skokie, Illinois, a municipality in Cook County, 13 miles (21 km) northwest of downtown Chicago. Skokie is a residential and industrial suburb with such industries as printing and publishing and the manufacturing of drugs, chemicals, and electronic equipment. A settlement was founded here around 1831 and was incorporated as the village of Niles Center in 1888. It remained a small community until after World War II. The name Skokie, an Indian word, was adopted in 1940.

Population: 59,432.

Skopje, skōp′yĕ, the capital of the Republic of Macedonia. It lies on the Vardar River, in the northern part of the republic near its border with Yugoslavia. Skopje is an important trade and transportation center with varied industries, including food processing, metallurgy, and chemical manufacturing. The city has a university, several museums, and numerous mosques.

Skopje dates from at least the third century A.D., when it was a Roman colony. After being destroyed by an earthquake in 518, it was rebuilt and flourished as part of the Byzantine Empire. Skopje was captured by the Slavs by 695, but in the next 700 years it changed hands many times. Late in the 14th century the Ottoman Turks conquered the city. They held it until 1913, when it was granted to Serbia by the Treaty of Bucharest. After World War I, Skopje became part of the Kingdom of the Serbs, Croats, and Slovenes (Yugoslavia). It became capital of an independent country when Macedonia seceded from Yugoslavia in 1991.

Population: 563,301.

Skua, skū′å, a seabird of Arctic and Antarctic regions. The skua (also called *great skua*) is nearly two feet (60 cm) long. It has dark-brown plumage, a hooked bill, and strong, sharply taloned feet.

The skua preys upon the eggs and the young of other seabirds. It also eats fish and will either catch the fish itself or steal it from another bird. The skua comes on land only to breed. A hollow in the ground serves as a nest. Usually two spotted, grayish-brown eggs are laid.

The skua is *Catharacta skua* of the family Stercorariidae.

Skull, the rigid framework of the head of vertebrates (animals with backbones). The structure of the skull varies greatly in the different groups of vertebrates. In most mammals there are about 35 separate bones that make up the skull. In the human skull there are 22 named bones plus some tiny, irregularly shaped bones collectively called *sutural,* or *Wormian, bones*.

The human skull has 8 bones in the cranium, or brain case, and 14 in the anterior region, or face. Some of the facial bones have air-filled cavities called sinuses. (See SINUS.) Except for the mandible, or lower jaw, the bones of the skull are joined together by immovable joints called *sutures*. The only skull bones not shown in the accompanying illustration are the two *palatine bones* (which make up the posterior part of the hard palate, part of the floor and wall of the nasal cavity, and part of the floor of the eye sockets).

The skull of an adult female usually

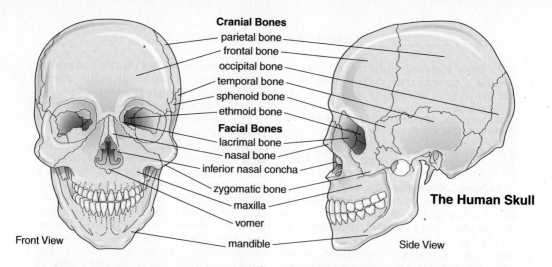

Cranial Bones
parietal bone
frontal bone
occipital bone
temporal bone
sphenoid bone
ethmoid bone

Facial Bones
lacrimal bone
nasal bone
inferior nasal concha
zygomatic bone
maxilla
vomer
mandible

The Human Skull

Front View

Side View

weighs less and is smaller than that of an adult male. The skull of a newborn infant is large in proportion to the other parts of the skeleton, and its cranium is large in proportion to the facial portion. In an infant's head there are six regions, called fontanels, that are covered by membranes rather than bone. The largest of these regions, the anterior fontanel (often called the "soft spot"), is at the front top of the skull. The five other fontanels become covered with bone within a month or two after birth, but the anterior one is not completely closed until about the middle of the second year.

See also TREPHINATION.

Skullcap. See HAT (picture).

Skunk, a mammal found only in the Americas and noted for its offensive odor. Skunks are black or blackish with various types of white markings and have long, bushy tails. Adult skunks range in length from 4½ to 19 inches (11 to 48 cm), not including a tail that is 2½ to 19 inches (6 to 48 cm) long. Weight ranges from a half pound to 10 pounds (225 g to 4.5 kg). There are 10 species: two species of spotted skunks, a striped skunk, a hooded skunk, and six species of hog-nosed skunks. Skunks are sometimes called polecats.

Skunks produce an unpleasant-smelling oil in a pair of glands located under the skin below the tail. The oil may be squirted at will, in extreme cases for a distance of 12 feet (3.7 m) or more. Skunks use this liquid for defense; they usually squirt it only when frightened. The liquid can cause intense smarting and burning sensations in the eyes, nose, and mouth.

Skunks usually live in burrows they line with vegetation. Several skunks may share

S-462

the same burrow. Skunks eat both plants and animals and are active mainly at night. Some skunks found in cold areas sleep through much of the winter. The young are usually born in the spring. Litter size is usually four or five.

The most common skunk in the United States is the *striped skunk,* found in Mexico, throughout the United States, and into southern Canada. It is about 12 to 18 inches (30 to 46 cm) long with a tail 5 to 19 inches (13 to 48 cm) long.

Skunks are inquisitive, somewhat playful animals, and people keep them as pets even when the scent glands are not removed. (Skunks, however, can be carriers of rabies.) Skunk fur is used to make various garments and trimmings.

Skunks belong to the family Mustelidae. There are three genera—*Spilogale* (spotted skunks), *Conepatus* (hog-nosed skunks), and *Mephitis* (striped and hooded skunks). The striped skunk is *M. mephitis.*

Skunk Cabbage, a perennial herb that grows in swamps and other wet areas in North America and Asia. Tiny flowers occur on a structure called a spadix. The spadix is partially surrounded by a hood called a spathe. Large leaves develop after the spadix and spathe have formed. The plant gives off a foul odor, which draws insects that pollinate the flowers. As the plant grows, the buds generate their own heat, reaching a temperature as much as 27° F. (15° C.) warmer than the surrounding air.

The *common skunk cabbage,* which grows in eastern and central North America, has a knoblike spadix and a mottled, purplish-green spathe. Its leaves are one to three feet (30 to 90 cm) long. The *yellow skunk cabbage,* which grows in western North America, has a spikelike spadix and a yellow or cream-colored spathe. Its leaves are one to five feet (30 to 150 cm) long. (For picture, see FLOWERING PLANT.)

The common skunk cabbage is *Symplocarpus foetidus;* the yellow skunk cabbage, *Lysichitum americanum.* Both are of the arum family, Araceae.

Škvorecký, shkvôr'ĕk-skē, **Josef** (1924-), a Czech author. In *The Cowards* (1958), his first novel, Škvorecký uses ironic humor and frank language to portray characters caught in an absurd world in which they turn to jazz music for meaning. The book both established his reputation and aroused the disapproval of the Communist government. In later works Škvorecký frequently used satiric humor, detective-story elements, and personal experiences to depict ordinary people who are struggling to have lives with meaning in an oppressed society. Škvorecký was born in Náchod, Czechoslovakia (now in the Czech Republic). He emigrated to Canada in 1968.

Other works include: novels—*The End of the Nylon Age* (1967); *Miss Silver's Past* (1969); *The Tank Battalion* (1971); *The Miracle Game* (1972); *The Engineer of Human Souls* (1977); *The Return of Lieutenant Boruvka* (1980); *The Bride of Texas* (1992); short-story collections—*The Mournful Demeanor of Lieutenant Boruvka* (1966); *The End of Lieutenant Boruvka* (1975). *Headed for the Blues* (1996) is a memoir.

Sky, the atmosphere and space as seen from the earth. The clear sky is blue during daylight hours because sunlight, which contains all colors, is scattered by the molecules of air as it strikes the upper atmosphere. Blue light is scattered the most and illuminates the whole sky. At night the sky is black since no sunlight is striking the visible portion of the atmosphere.

The sun and stars appear to move across the sky and are commonly described as doing so; actually, this apparent motion is caused by the movements of the earth.

See also ATMOSPHERE.

Sky Waves. See RADIO, section "How Radio Works," subtitle *Transmitting Radio Signals:* Amplifying and Transmitting; and picture titled *Ground and Sky Waves.*

Skydiving. See PARACHUTE, subtitle *Skydiving* (and picture).

Skye. See HEBRIDES.

Skye Terrier. See DOG, subtitle *Breeds of Dogs:* Terriers.

Skyjacking. See HIJACKING.

Skylark. See LARK, subtitle *The Skylark.*

Skyrocket. See FIREWORKS.

Skyscraper. See BUILDING CONSTRUCTION, subtitle *Large Buildings.*

Slag. See SMELTING.

Slag Wool. See MINERAL WOOL.

Slaked Lime. See LIME.

Slalom. See SKIING, subtitle *Ski Competitions.*

Slander. See LIBEL AND SLANDER.

Slang, words and phrases in general informal use that are not fully accepted as standard or that have nonstandard meanings. *Blooper,* meaning an embarrassing error, is of the first type—a nonstandard word; it is a coined word used only as slang. *Beef* is of the second type—a standard word with a nonstandard meaning; it is slang when used to mean a complaint but standard when it means the flesh of cattle.

Slang is used for many reasons. The speaker may feel that it is more forceful or colorful, or less formal or sentimental than its standard equivalent. Using slang may give the speaker a sense of belonging to a certain group. A new discovery or invention may have no short or easily pronounced name, and a slang word is applied to it. Often a speaker simply uses a familiar word or phrase without realizing it is slang.

Most slang is short-lived. *Skidoo,* for example, was extremely popular in the United

Striped Skunk
© Richard & Susan Day/Anmimals Animals

States in the early years of the 20th century but was out of fashion by 1920. It first meant "go away" but later came to be a nonsense word. Some slang however, persists, either as slang or as accepted standard speech. The expression *O.K.* or *okay* was used as slang during the 19th century and in the 20th became a standard but informal expression. Among other standard English words that once were slang are: *strenuous, clumsy, wangle, blimp,* and *skyscraper.*

Slang is found in all languages. English, French, and Spanish have unusually large slang vocabularies. United States slang is the most widely known and used around the world. The origin of the word *slang* is unknown. Some researchers say it is derived from the Norwegian phrase *slengja kjeften,* meaning "to sling the jaw; to abuse with words."

Sources of Slang

Much slang comes from *argot* (or *cant*), the informal speech peculiar to a certain group. For example there is baseball argot, teenagers' argot, jazz musicians' argot, soldiers' argot. Some argots—such as that of the underworld—originate as secret languages. When words or phrases of an argot become widely understood and used outside the group in which they originate, they become slang. For example, *stool pigeon* or *stoolie,* once confined to the underworld and meaning one who informs to the police, is now a slang expression for one who informs against others to any authority.

Ethnic and regional groups contribute many slang expressions, some of them from foreign languages. From Yiddish come such words as *chutzpah* (impudence; brashness) and *schlemiel* (an awkward, foolish person). Examples of black Americans' additions are *chick* (a young woman) and *gig* (a job). London's Cockneys are noted for their rhyming slang—*trouble and strife,* for example, means "wife," and *Rosy Lee,* "tea."

Some slang expressions originate as *euphemisms* (mild or indirect words used in place of unpleasant or taboo words) such as *heck* (hell). Others are *dysphemisms* (disagreeable or disparaging expressions substituted for agreeable or neutral ones) such as *heap* (car). Other sources of slang are abbreviations and clipped words. For example, *deejay* is from the abbreviation "d.j.," for *disc jockey*—itself a slang expression for one who conducts a radio show of recorded music. *Vet* for veteran and for veterinarian, *fridge* for refrigerator, and *mike* for microphone are clipped words. Among clipped words that have become standard are *van* (caravan), *cab* (cabriolet), and *bus* (omnibus).

Books about Slang

Chapman, R. L., editor. *Thesaurus of American Slang* (HarperCollins, 1989).
Simpson, John, and John Ayto, editors. *The Oxford Dictionary of Modern Slang* (Oxford University, 1993).

Slapstick. See COMEDY, subtitle *Types of Comedy.*

Slash Pine. See PINE, subtitle *American Hard Pines.*

Slate, a common metamorphic rock that splits into thin, even sheets. Slate consists primarily of such minerals as muscovite (mica), chlorite, and quartz. Other minerals that may also be present in lesser amounts include hematite, rutile, and tourmaline. Slate is usually gray or black but also occurs in such colors as red, green, brown, and yellow. It is fine-grained rock; the individual grains cannot be seen with the unaided eye.

Slate forms when shale, volcanic tuff, or other fine-grained rocks are subjected to great heat and pressure in the earth's crust. The grains of the original rock are squeezed into flakes by the pressure and new minerals form parallel to the flakes. The slate will split along the flakes, which lie at right angles to the direction of the pressure that formed the slate.

Slate is quarried in blocks and then separated into thin sheets. There are large slate quarries in Pennsylvania, Virginia, and the New York–Vermont area. Sheets of slate are used for roofs, blackboards, flagstones, and billiard-table beds. Crushed slate is used in abrasives, shingles, and pigments.

Slate-colored Junco. See BIRD, picture page B-247; JUNCO.

Slater, Samuel (1768-1835), an English-American manufacturer called the father of American manufacturing. He founded the cotton-textile industry in the United States.

Slater was born in Derbyshire, England. While apprenticed to a partner of Richard Arkwright, he learned the Arkwright cotton-spinning method. In 1789 he left to make his home in the United States. Because England forbade the exportation of textile information and the emigration of textile workers, Slater committed the design of the machin-

Captives of War in ancient times often faced a lifetime of slavery. In this detail from a Roman sculpture, two women and a child are led away by victorious soldiers.

Column of Marcus Aurelius, in Rome; photo from German Archaeological Institute

ery to memory and traveled disguised as a farmer. After joining a firm in Pawtucket, Rhode Island, he successfully reproduced the machinery in 1790 and began operations in an old fuller's mill. In 1793 he and his partners built a large water-powered cotton mill. In 1798 he formed S. Slater and Company, which constructed textile factories throughout New England.

Slater Fund. See SOUTHERN EDUCATION FOUNDATION.

Slatkin, Leonard (Edward) (1944-   ), a United States conductor and pianist. He is known for his interpretations of 20th-century music—especially American, British, and Russian music—and for promoting arts education. Slatkin was born in Los Angeles and attended Indiana University and the Juilliard School. He made his conducting debut at Carnegie Hall in 1966 with the Youth Orchestra of New York. Slatkin joined the St. Louis Symphony Orchestra as an assistant conductor in 1968 and was music director there, 1979-96. He became music director of the National Symphony Orchestra in Washington, D.C., in 1996.

Slaughterhouse. See MEAT PACKING.

Slav. See SLAVS.

Slave Lake. See GREAT SLAVE LAKE.

Slave River. See MACKENZIE RIVER.

Slave-holding Ant. See ANT, subtitle *Kinds of Ants.*

Slavery, a system under which an individual is held as the property of another to be used or disposed of at the will of the owner, or master. Slavery has existed throughout most of human history and is still practiced in some parts of the world. It originated in prehistoric times, when it was found to be more profitable to enslave than to slaughter captives of war. The term "slave" dates from the Middle Ages, when it came into common

usage in Europe because of the large numbers of Slavs who had been forced into servitude.

Warfare was the original source of slave labor. When slavery proved economically advantageous, it was extended to include debtors and criminals. To insure a continuous and plentiful supply of slaves, a slave trade was established, with people being seized and sold into slavery. Children born of slaves were also enslaved.

The status of slaves and their treatment varied greatly in different times and places. In some societies, slaves were considered merely *chattels,* pieces of property. They had no rights; their lives and labors belonged to their owners. In other social systems, slaves were recognized as human beings. Thus they received certain protections under the law, and manumission (release from slavery) was sometimes possible.

Slaves were utilized in agriculture, industry, commerce, domestic service, and the armed forces. The conditions of their labor ranged from the highly privileged position held by the well-educated teacher slaves of Rome to the miserable existence of those who worked in the mines.

Throughout history various legal, social, economic, and philosophical arguments—typically involving prejudices of race, color, nationality, or religion—were made to justify slavery. The view that enslavement was an inherent moral evil was not forcefully propounded until an antislavery movement began to develop late in the 18th century.

Slavery in the Ancient World

Ancient peoples of many different civilizations practiced some form of slavery, and in many areas—such as Egypt, Babylonia, Assyria, Greece, Rome, India, and China—it was an established institution. The Greek philosophers Aristotle and Plato regarded

Historical Pictures Service

Slaves, chained to their oars and often mercilessly flogged, provided manpower for galley warships used in the Mediterranean from the 15th to the 18th century. The Spanish novelist Miguel de Cervantes (*center*) toiled briefly as a galley slave after his capture by corsairs in 1575.

mastery over the weak by the strong as natural and inevitable. Slaves made up a significant part of the population of Athens in the fourth century B.C. and were an integral element of social and economic life. The military society of Sparta could not have existed without its slave laborers, the helots.

Ancient Rome during the period of the Republic began the practice of using large slave gangs to work huge plantations. Such work, however, was not the lot of most Roman slaves. Some toiled alongside their farmer masters. Others worked as minor city officials, private tutors, servants, factory laborers, and gladiators. Slaves performed nearly all the duties at the courts of the Roman emperors. By the reign of the emperor Trajan (98-117 A.D.), one out of three persons in Rome was a slave. Roman law precisely defined the status of a slave and was the basis for later slave codes.

Slavery in the Middle Ages

Toward the end of the Roman Empire, slavery began to decline as slave labor became increasingly scarce and expensive. Although disrupted by the barbarian invasions of the early Middle Ages, slavery continued to exist in western Europe and in the Byzantine Empire. The Christian Church did not oppose the institution of slavery, considering it a part of the divine order of the world. However, the Church asserted the equality of both master and slave before God and sought to mitigate some of the evils of servitude.

As early as the sixth century A.D., slav-

ery in Europe began to be replaced by serfdom, a system that proved better suited to the emerging feudal agricultural economy. Serfs were in a state between slave and free, bound to the soil (that is, they could not leave the land of their own free will) and more or less subject to the will of their lord. (See also FEUDALISM.) However, the religious wars between Christians and Muslims helped to keep slavery alive, as each side enslaved prisoners of the opposing religion. In the late Middle Ages, warfare against the Turks and a demand for domestic servants revitalized slavery for a time in some parts of Europe. The Mediterranean slave trade reached its peak in the 14th and 15th centuries.

American Slavery

Slavery in the Americas began shortly after the first European settlers arrived in the New World. In some areas Native American slave labor was used at first, but soon the Europeans began to import slaves from Africa. Several European nations became engaged in a profitable slave trade in Africans. An especially barbarous aspect of the slave trade was the passage from Africa to America on overcrowded, poorly supplied vessels and the consequent disease and death. From the early 16th century to the mid-19th century, about 15 million Africans were transported to the New World. (See also AFRICAN SLAVE TRADE.)

In North America. The first Africans were brought to what is now the United States in 1619. They were not slaves but indentured servants. However, it was not long before Africans were being brought in as slaves. Slavery existed in both the North and the South during the colonial period. However, it was the introduction of large-scale cotton farming in the South after the Revolutionary War that made slavery profitable.

Only a minority of Southern whites, less than one-fourth, held slaves, and most of them owned only one or two. Large-plantation owners were the exception, although as a class they dominated social, economic, and political life in the pre–Civil War South. Not all slaveholders were white; some Indians had black slaves, and even some free blacks held slaves. At the time of the Civil War, there were about four million slaves— approximately one-third of the population of the slaveholding states.

Slavery varied from place to place. Not

all slaves labored on plantations; some worked as domestic servants, skilled artisans, and factory hands. For the vast majority, however, bondage meant submission and degradation. It was a physically and psychologically brutalizing experience. In general, blacks' existence as human beings was given no recognition. They had little or no protection under the law and little hope of emancipation. There were few slave revolts, but many thousands of slaves fled the South.

A complicated set of laws grew up to safeguard the property interests of slaveholders. Slavery gradually became a highly emotional political issue in the North-South struggle for power that was taking place in the national government. The importation of slaves after 1808 was forbidden by the U.S. Congress. Abolitionist agitation began early in the 19th century. However, it was the defeat of the South in the Civil War that resulted in the abolition of slavery by the 13th Amendment in 1865. Although the blacks were freed, the racism accompanying slavery persisted.

In South America and the West Indies. Indigenous people were enslaved in South America in the early period of European colonization. Gradually, Africans replaced them. Millions of blacks were transported as slaves to the Spanish, Portuguese, French, and English colonies, especially to the West Indies and Brazil. The first were brought in 1502, to the island of Hispaniola.

Most blacks labored on plantations in tropical areas. Slave codes provided that the slave was not the absolute property of the owner, but the slave's treatment was not markedly better than that of the slave in the Southern United States. However, manumission generally was easier and was encouraged by some governments. Hispaniola was the first to abolish slavery in the Western Hemisphere, in 1793; Brazil was the last, in 1888.

Modern Slavery

By the end of the 19th century slavery had been abolished in the British Empire, Europe, and the Americas. It has continued to exist legally in parts of Asia and Africa and illegally in other areas of the world. Various organizations, such as the Anti-Slavery Society for the Protection of Human Rights, headquartered in London, and the United Nations Commission on Human Rights,

have sought its elimination. It is estimated that several million humans still exist under varying conditions of slavery, including chattel slavery, serfdom, and debt bondage.

For further information, see:

ABOLITIONIST	JANISSARIES
AFRICAN SLAVE TRADE	MAMELUKES
BLACK AMERICANS,	PEONAGE
subtitle *History to 1900*	SOUTH, THE
CIVIL WAR, AMERICAN	SPARTACUS
COMPROMISE OF 1850	TURNER, NAT
DRED SCOTT DECISION	UNDERGROUND
EMANCIPATION	RAILROAD
PROCLAMATION	UNITED STATES,
FEUDALISM	section "History," picture ti-
FUGITIVE SLAVE	ry," picture ti-
LAWS	tled *Slavery*
HELOTS	VESEY, DENMARK

Books about Slavery

Botkin, B. A., editor. *Lay My Burden Down: a Folk History of Slavery* (1945; Dell reprint, 1994).

Dudley, William, editor. *Slavery: Opposing Viewpoints* (Greenhaven, 1992).

Goodheart, L. B., and others, editors. *Slavery in American Society,* 3rd edition (Heath, 1993).

Huggins, N. I. *Black Odyssey: the Afro-American Ordeal in Slavery* (Vintage, 1990).

For Younger Readers

Hamilton, Virginia. *Many Thousand Gone: African-Americans from Slavery to Freedom* (Knopf, 1993).

Meltzer, Milton. *Slavery: a World History* (Da Capo, 1993).

Slavs, slävz, a group of peoples speaking the languages of the Slavic branch of the Indo-European language family. Slavs are divided into three main branches: the East

Shackled Slaves are driven through the streets of Washington, D.C. Washington was a slave market until 1850.

Library of Congress

Slavs, of European Russia; the West Slavs, of the Czech Republic, Slovakia, and Poland; and the South, or Balkan, Slavs, of Bulgaria and Yugoslavia.

The origin of the Slavic peoples is obscure. However, it is known that they inhabited the region between the Vistula and Dnieper rivers in the first century A.D. The Slavs were loosely organized into clans and tribes. Through migrations, they became divided into three distinct groups. Those who came to be known as East Slavs gradually spread throughout European Russia. They established trading settlements that, by the mid-ninth century, spread from the Black Sea to the Baltic.

Other tribes migrated westward, as far as the Elbe River. The West Slavs settled in central Europe, while in the sixth century numerous groups crossed the Danube River and moved southward into the Balkan Peninsula. Gradually, the other peoples of that area were dispersed or assimilated—except for the Greeks, who gradually absorbed the immigrants into their own culture. The rest of the South Slavs soon emerged as Serbs, Croats, Slovenes, and Bulgarians. The Serbs and Bulgarians formed kingdoms in the 9th century, but by the end of the 10th century their domains were provinces of the powerful Byzantine Empire. From the 14th to the 20th century, the South Slavs were subject to the Ottoman Turks.

Meanwhile, the West Slavs founded a number of kingdoms in central Europe. The Czechs established themselves in Bohemia. In the ninth century, Moravia formed the center of a kingdom that included Bohemia and Slovakia. About 900 it was destroyed by Magyars, Asian invaders who settled in Hungary. The Slovaks were among the Slavic peoples who were included in the Hungarian kingdom. Farther to the north, several Slavic tribes were united under the Polani tribe in the second half of the 10th century to form the Polish kingdom.

During the Middle Ages, many German principalities in central Europe expanded to the east. By the 12th century, the Germans had conquered and annexed Bohemia and penetrated into northwestern Poland. During the 14th century, the Hapsburgs of Austria conquered Slovenia, Bohemia, Hungary, and Croatia. In the 18th century, a series of partitions divided Polish territory among Austria, Russia, and Prussia.

In the 19th century, the Pan-Slavic movement arose to free Slavic territories from foreign domination and create a confederation of states based on Slavic cultural unity. Russia viewed this idea as an opportunity to expand its influence in the Slavic community at the expense of Austria. By the early 20th century, competition between Russia and Austria for Slavic territories created some of the tensions that caused World War I.

As part of the peace settlement following World War I, Poland was reestablished and Slavic peoples formed two new nations. Czechoslovakia included the historic regions of Bohemia, Moravia, and Slovakia. The Serbs, Croats, and Slovenes formed a kingdom that later became Yugoslavia. Shortly after World War I the Soviet Union was formed out of most of the territory that had made up Russia.

During the early 1990's many of the changes that had occurred after World War I were undone. The Soviet Union, Yugoslavia, and Czechoslovakia all broke up. The Soviet Union split into 15 independent nations. Three of these new nations were Slavic (Russia, Ukraine, and Belarus). Civil war erupted in Yugoslavia between various Slavic groups, and, four of its constituent states—Bosnia and Herzegovina, Croatia, Macedonia, and Slovenia—became independent. Czechoslovakia peacefully split into two Slavic nations, the Czech Republic and Slovakia.

For further information, see:
> ALPHABET, subtitles *Modern Alphabets:* Roman and Cyrillic Alphabets, and *History of the Alphabet:* The Alphabet in Europe
> BELARUS, subtitle *Government and History*
> BOHEMIA
> BULGARIA, subtitle *History*
> CZECH REPUBLIC, subtitle *History*
> LANGUAGE, section "Major Languages of the World" (Slavic Languages)
> MORAVIA
> POLAND, subtitle *History*
> RUSSIA, section "History," subtitle *Early History (to 1505):* Kievan Russia
> SERBIA
> SLOVAKIA, REPUBLIC OF
> SLOVENIA
> UKRAINE, subtitle *History*
> WENDS
> YUGOSLAVIA, subtitle *History*

Sled, a vehicle, usually mounted on metal runners, designed to glide across ice and snow. Sleds are not self-propelled; they are used for sliding or racing downhill, as a recreation or competitive sport, or are pulled by animals to provide transportation. A light, horse-drawn sled is called a *sleigh*. A large, heavy sled, usually with wood runners and commonly used for hauling, is called a *sledge*. A *snowmobile* is similar to a sled but is self-propelled. (See SNOWMOBILE.)

The *coaster sled*, used by children for coasting down hills, has metal runners and is built to carry one person. Another sled for coasting is the *saucer sled*, a concave disk with no runners. The *toboggan* is a runnerless sled usually built to hold several persons. (See TOBOGGAN.) The *bobsled* and *luge* are used in competition. (See BOBSLED; LUGE.) Distinctive types of transportation sleds include the Russian *troika*, pulled by three horses, and the Eskimo dogsled.

The first sleds were runnerless sledges made of logs, used on smooth terrain (not necessarily snow or ice) before there were wheeled vehicles. Sledges continued to be used for heavy loads; in ancient Egypt, stone blocks for the pyramids were transported on them. Meanwhile, the sled with runners became the common winter vehicle in colder regions; it was widely used until the advent of self-propelled vehicles. Long after sleighs had been given metal runners, children's sleds continued to have wooden ones. The introduction of metal runners for coasting sleds in the latter half of the 19th century led to the development of bobsleds and sledding as a competitive sport.

Sleep, an interruption of wakefulness. People normally sleep for a long interval—between five and eight hours or more at a stretch—once in every 24 hours. Not everyone needs the same amount of sleep, but in order to maintain physical and mental health, all persons must sleep. Sleep is a basic biological function of humans and of most other animals. (It is believed that some animals, such as shrews, do not sleep.)

Infants and children sleep a great deal, which helps to conserve the large amount of energy needed for their growth and development. It is not unusual, for example, for newborn infants to sleep as much as 20 hours a day. The need for sleep decreases as the child grows older, but even a child four years old usually sleeps as much as 12 hours a day. Children, like adults, vary in the amount

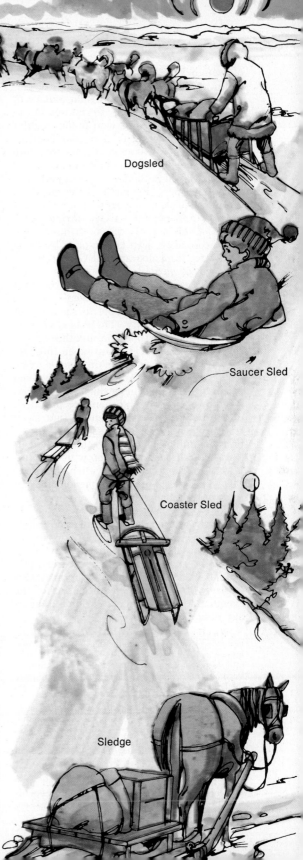

Dogsled

Saucer Sled

Coaster Sled

Sledge

of sleep they need, and naps may or may not be the norm, depending on the child.

The establishment of a regular pattern of sleep is beneficial not only to children but to adults as well. Persons who follow regular sleeping habits—that is, a regular bedtime and a regular awakening time—are more likely to avoid problems of insomnia.

Sleep was long thought to be a period of unconsciousness. Research in the mid-20th century, however, showed that there is great physical and mental activity during sleep. Much of this activity has been discovered and recorded in sleep laboratories by using an electroencephalograph (EEG). Electrodes attached to various portions of the scalp record the several types of brain waves characteristic of various stages of sleep.

Just what causes people to sleep is not known with certainty. There is a definite relationship between fatigue and the onset of sleep, but persons can sleep when they are not fatigued and can remain awake when they are fatigued. Many scientists involved in sleep research believe that sleep is triggered by one or more biochemicals produced in the body. They also believe that sleep results when a "wakefulness center" in the brain is inhibited, perhaps by these biochemicals. The alternation of sleep with wakefulness is an example of a circadian rhythm—that is, a series of biological phenomena that recur on a daily basis.

Stages of Sleep

A night's sleep is made up of various phases that scientists can identify in terms of different types of activity in the sleeper's brain and body. While asleep, a person constantly drifts back and forth through various stages of sleep. Following is a description of the events that typify a night's sleep of an average adult.

Sleep is preceded by a period of relaxed wakefulness in which the brain produces a pattern of waves known as the *alpha rhythm*. As the individual sinks into sleep, relaxed wakefulness gives way to Stage 1 sleep. In this stage, which lasts only a few minutes, the body muscles relax, respiration grows even, and the heart rate becomes slower.

Stage 2 lasts about 10 minutes. During this stage the heart rate, respiration, blood pressure, and temperature fall slowly. In Stages 1 and 2, which are light transitional levels of sleep, the sleeper is quite easy to awaken; if awakened he may insist that he was not really sleeping.

In Stage 3 the muscles are relaxed, breathing is even, and blood pressure, temperature, and heart rate continue to decline. At this stage the sleeper is still not deeply asleep but is more difficult to awaken.

Next comes the deep, oblivious sleep of Stage 4. This stage is also called *delta sleep* for the large waves (called delta waves) recorded at this time by the EEG. This is the deepest sleep, and it is difficult to arouse a person from it. The muscles are very relaxed, while other physiological functions are still becoming slower. Although it is the deepest stage of sleep, EEG recordings indicate the brain shows a high response to outside stimulations such as noise. But the portions of the brain that register the stimuli as conscious sensations do not appear to be working. Researchers have found that terrifying nightmares may occur during delta sleep.

About 60 to 90 minutes after falling asleep the person begins to enter the lighter phases of sleep again—Stage 3, then Stage 2. The person spends 20 to 30 minutes in the light stages of sleep and then the EEG begins to register wild oscillations. The sleeper at this time turns over and moves about. The eyes begin to make rapid darting movements. The sleeper has entered into a special variety of Stage 1 called REM (Rapid Eye Movement) sleep. These rapid eye movements are a signal that the sleeper is experiencing a period of intense dreaming. Although he or she may be hard to awaken, the sleeper's brain waves paradoxically resemble those of wakefulness.

During this dreaming period, heart rate, respiration, and blood pressure become exceedingly variable, often fluctuating wildly. Body muscles, however, are exceedingly limp.

An average adult dreams about every 90 minutes, and each REM period lasts about 10 to 40 minutes. (Dreaming, dreamlike experiences, and images occur in all phases of sleep, but they are not intense.) After the dreaming period, the sleeper enters Stages 2, 3, and 4 and the foregoing cycle is repeated four or five times during a night's sleep. As morning approaches, each dreaming period is longer and more vivid.

There is no consistent time schedule for the different stages of sleep, and individuals vary even from night to night in how much time they spend in each sleep stage. Evidence from a number of studies, however, indicates that each individual may have a distinctive EEG sleep pattern.

Sleep Disorders

The most common sleep disorder is *insomnia,* the inability of a person to fall asleep or to remain asleep throughout the night. Insomnia may be caused by a variety of physical and mental conditions that prevent complete relaxation. Persistent insomnia is one of the more common symptoms experienced by the emotionally disturbed. (See INSOMNIA.)

Another sleep disorder sometimes associated with emotional problems is *hypersomnia,* excessive frequency or duration of sleep. Hypersomnia is much rarer than insomnia. It can be caused by such diseases as encephalitis (a type of sleeping sickness). Persons with encephalitis often exhibit another type of sleep disorder—their sleep cycle is reversed; that is, the patient sleeps by day and is awake at night. (See ENCEPHALI-TIS.)

In *sleep apnea,* a sleeping person repeatedly stops breathing for brief periods. Sleep apnea typically occurs in persons whose airway muscles have poor tone; the muscles become excessively relaxed during sleep and block the flow of air. Severe cases can lead to a heart attack or stroke.

Narcolepsy is a condition in which a person falls suddenly and uncontrollably asleep at inappropriate moments. (See NARCOLEP-SY.)

In the past it was thought that in *somnambulism,* or *sleepwalking,* the sleepwalker was acting out a dream. Research in sleep laboratories, however, has shown that sleepwalking begins when the person is in Stage 3 or Stage 4 sleep, two stages that are not associated with intense dreaming.

The brain waves of a sleepwalking person are not like those typical of any of the normal stages of sleep. The waves resemble those of the alpha rhythm. These findings have led researchers to propose that there is another stage of sleep in which there is reduced awareness of the environment but in which complex acts requiring interaction with the environment may be performed. It is best not to awaken sleepwalkers unless they are in danger. Upon awakening, sleepwalkers usually have no memory of their activities.

Effects of Sleep Loss

Studies of total deprivation of sleep show that as sleeplessness is prolonged, a person progressively suffers mental deterioration and psychological change. Lapses of attention and microsleep intervals (periods of sleep lasting a few seconds) become frequent. There is a tendency to withdraw from activity and to become disoriented in time and place. Visual illusions and changes in depth perception are also symptoms. Eventually, prolonged sleeplessness results in vivid hallucinations.

The extent of the effects of sleeplessness is influenced by environmental factors and by

Sleep Laboratory. Electrodes attached to the sleeping subject are wired to an electroencephalograph (EEG) (*right foreground*) where traces of the activities of the brain and eyes are recorded. The EEG tracings (*right*) show the activity of eyes and brain during REM sleep, a period of intense dreaming. Although the brain waves (bottom two tracings) are low, the eye movements (top three tracings) show intense activity.

National Institute of Mental Health

the mental stability of the individual. Age also seems to be a significant factor; there is some evidence that it is easier for young persons to withstand and recover from long vigils.

After prolonged sleeplessness, stress hormones in the blood show an elevation, and other biochemical changes occur in the body. The metabolism of the body is altered, showing a severe decline after about 120 hours of sleeplessness, coinciding with the onset of such psychotic symptoms as hallucinations.

Although a single night of sleep appears to erase most of the symptoms of sleeplessness, it has not been determined what subtle mental and physical aftereffects may persist.

A person, such as a student studying for exams, who for several days limits sleeping to four hours or less does not experience the sudden and dramatic results that occur after prolonged total deprivation of sleep. However, a variety of rather mild symptoms may appear after several days. Such symptoms include irritability, the feeling of pressure around the head, and momentary illusions. In addition, such a person will not exhibit the usual sleep pattern of Stages 1 through 4 and REM. The person will spend more time in deep sleep and less in REM sleep and in the transitional light levels.

Many experiments have also been done in which individuals were deprived only of their dreaming sleep. On subsequent nights these individuals dreamed considerably more than they had on normal sleeping nights. They appeared to be making up for lost dreams. (For further information on dreams and dreaming, see DREAM.)

The term "jet lag" refers to the discomfort felt when normal sleep patterns are disrupted by rapid travel across time zones. This condition is discussed in the article BIOLOGICAL CLOCK.

See also HYPNOTIC; SNORING.

Books about Sleep

Dotto, Lydia. *Losing Sleep: How Your Sleeping Habits Affect Your Life* (Morrow, 1990).
Edelson, Edward. *Sleep* (Chelsea House, 1992).
Thorpy, Michael, and Jan Yager. *The Encyclopedia of Sleep and Sleep Disorders* (Facts on File, 1990).
For Younger Readers
Showers, Paul. *Sleep Is for Everyone* (Crowell, 1974).
Silverstein, Alvin and Virginia. *The Mystery of Sleep* (Little, Brown, 1987).

Sleeping Bear Dunes National Lakeshore. See NATIONAL PARKS, section "United States."

"Sleeping Beauty, The," a fairy tale. The most familiar version is the one in Charles Perrault's 17th-century collection of Mother Goose tales. Another version, "Briar Rose," is in the 19th-century collection of fairy tales by Jacob and Wilhelm Grimm. The story tells of a young princess who falls into an enchanted sleep because of a fairy's magic spell. After 100 years, a prince finds the princess and breaks the spell by awakening her with a kiss. They marry and live happily ever after. Tchaikovsky's *Sleeping Beauty* (1890), a ballet, is based on the story.

Sleeping Car. See RAILWAY, section "Railway Equipment," subtitle *Passenger-train Equipment:* Passenger Cars.

Sleeping Pill. See HYPNOTIC.

Sleeping Sickness, the common name of two different diseases that can cause a sleeplike state in the victim. One of these diseases, encephalitis, is an inflammation of the brain. (See ENCEPHALITIS.) The other disease, African sleeping sickness, is dealt with in this article.

African sleeping sickness, also called *African trypanosomiasis,* is caused by a parasite called a *trypanosome.* Two types of the disease (Gambian and Rhodesian) occur in tropical Africa in wild game, domestic animals, and humans. The parasites are transmitted chiefly by the bite of the tsetse fly. Early symptoms of the disease include headache, fever, swollen lymph glands, and skin rash. As the disease progresses, the parasite invades the central nervous system and brain, causing lethargy and sleepiness. If untreated, the disease can cause convulsions, coma, and, eventually, death.

The disease is treated with such antimicrobial drugs as suramin and pentamidine. An injection of pentamidine every three to six months can prevent the Gambian type of the disease.

The Gambian type of African sleeping sickness is caused by the protozoan *Trypanosoma brucei;* the Rhodesian type, by *T. b. rhodesiense.* The protozoans are of the order Kinetoplastida.

See also TSETSE FLY.

Sleepwalking. See SLEEP, subtitle *Sleep Disorders.*

Sleepy Daisy. See XANTHISMA.

Sleet, frozen or partly frozen rain. Sleet occurs in cold weather when raindrops

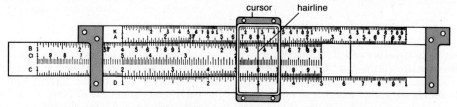

cursor　　hairline

Using a Slide Rule for Multiplication. As explained in the text, multiplication on the slide rule is done by adding lengths representing logarithms. The illustration shows how to find 2 × 3 = 6. Set the 2 on the C scale over the 1 on the D scale. The number on the C scale directly above the 3 on the D scale is the answer, 6.

freeze as they fall through cold air. The ice pellets that form are generally ⅕ inch (5 mm) or less in diameter. Sleet differs from *freezing rain,* which occurs when raindrops freeze upon landing on a cold surface. It also differs from *hail,* which consists of small lumps of ice that form during thunderstorms in warm weather.

See also HAIL.

Sleigh. See SLED.

Sleight of Hand. See MAGIC (in entertainment).

Slide Fastener. See ZIPPER.

Slide Rule, a device formerly in wide use by scientists, engineers, and others for making rapid calculations. It has largely been replaced by the portable electronic calculator, which is faster and more versatile and provides a greater degree of accuracy. Slide rule settings are accurate only to three significant digits.

The slide rule is based on the principle that numbers can be multiplied or divided by adding or subtracting their logarithms. (See LOGARITHM.)

The common slide rule consists of a body, a movable slide, and a cursor with a hairline indicator. (See illustration.) There are also circular slide rules. The simplest slide rule would have only the C and D scales, which are sufficient for multiplication and division. The CI scale is graduated like the C scale but from right to left. The A and K scales are useful in computations involving square roots and cube roots.

Slidefilm Projector. See PROJECTOR, subtitle *Transparency Projectors.*

Slidell, John. See TRENT AFFAIR.

Slime Mold, an organism with some characteristics similar to those of fungi, and other characteristics similar to those of protists. There are more than 500 species of slime molds. They creep on decaying wood and in moist soil, ingesting bacteria and decaying vegetation. There are two major groups of slime molds: plasmodial, or true, slime molds and cellular slime molds.

Plasmodial Slime Molds

The body of a plasmodial slime mold is the *plasmodium,* a thin, flat mass of protoplasm as long as 12 inches (30 cm). It does not have any cells, but its protoplasm contains structures similar to cell nuclei. The plasmodium is slimy to the touch and may be yellow, red, purple, or colorless. In response to adverse conditions (such as a lack of moisture), the plasmodium produces *sporangia,* typically round structures borne on stalks. Through an asexual process, sporangia produce structures called spores. The spores are scattered by the wind. When there is a sufficient amount of moisture, the spores develop into reproductive cells called gametes. Through a sexual process, the fusion of two gametes produces a new plasmodium.

Several species of microscopic, parasitic slime molds known as plasmodiophorans are classified with plasmodial slime molds by some biologists. Plasmodiophorans cause club-root disease in cabbage roots and powdery scab in potato plants.

Cellular Slime Molds

The body of a cellular slime mold consists of many cells. They form a sluglike mass called a *pseudoplasmodium.* The pseudoplasmodium eventually transforms itself into

Plasmodial Slime Mold (sporangia)
Carolina Biological Supply Co.

a stalklike structure called a *sorocarp,* which releases spores. Amoeboid cells emerge from the spores. After feeding for some time, the amoeboid cells gather together to form a new pseudoplasmodium. A cellular slime mold does not usually have a sexual stage in its life cycle.

Classification

Most biologists place slime molds in the kingdom Protista. Some biologists, however, place slime molds in the kingdom Fungi. Plasmodial slime molds are usually placed in the phylum Myxomycota; cellular slime molds in the phylum Acrasiomycota. Plasmodiophorans are placed in the phylum Myxomycota or the phylum Plasmodiophoromycota. The species of plasmodiophoran that causes club-root disease is *Plasmodiophora brassicae;* the species that causes powdery scab, *Spongospora subterranea.*

Slipher, slī'fĕr, **Vesto Melvin** (1875-1969), a United States astronomer. He made perhaps more basic contributions in various fields of astronomy than any of his contemporaries. Slipher is best known for his fundamental spectroscopic discoveries, especially of the rotations and atmospheres of planets. He also pioneered in the measurement of the rotations of galaxies and their movement through space, providing observational evidence for the expanding-universe theory. Slipher was born in Clinton County, Indiana, and graduated from Indiana University. He served as director of the Lowell Observatory at Flagstaff, Arizona, 1917-52.

Slipped Disk. See BACKACHE.

Slippery Rock University of Pennsylvania. See UNIVERSITIES AND COLLEGES (table).

Sloan, slōn, **Alfred P.** (Pritchard), **Jr.** (1875-1966), a United States industrialist and philanthropist. He was president of General Motors Corporation, 1923-37, and chairman of the board, 1937-56. Sloan was born in New Haven, Connecticut, and graduated from the Massachusetts Institute of Technology in 1895. *My Years with General Motors* (1964) is his autobiography.

The Alfred P. Sloan Foundation was established by Sloan and his wife in 1934. (See FOUNDATIONS, table.) In 1945 he and Charles F. Kettering founded the Sloan-Kettering Institute for Cancer Research.

Sloan, John (1871-1951), a United States painter. He was one of the most promi-

nent members of the Ashcan School—the group of painters known for their realistic scenes of everyday city life. Sloan captured the color and movement of New York City in such paintings as *Pigeons; Backyards, Greenwich Village;* and *Sunday, Women Drying Their Hair.*

Sloan was born in Lock Haven, Pennsylvania. He studied art and was a newspaper illustrator in Philadelphia before settling in New York in 1904. Sloan taught at the Art Students League for many years and helped found the Society of Independent Artists. He wrote *The Gist of Art* (1939).

For a reproduction of *Sunday, Women Drying Their Hair,* see ASHCAN SCHOOL.

Sloan Foundation. See FOUNDATIONS, table titled *Some Major Foundations.*

Slobodkin, slŏ-bŏd'kĭn, **Louis** (1903-1975), a United States illustrator, author of children's books, and sculptor. He was awarded the Caldecott Medal in 1944 for his pictures in James Thurber's *Many Moons.* Slobodkin was born in Albany, New York, and studied sculpture in New York City and Paris. He did sculpture for public buildings, including *Young Abe Lincoln* for the Department of the Interior in Washington. He began his illustrating career in 1941 with pictures for Eleanor Estes' *The Moffats.*

Among the books Slobodkin wrote and illustrated are *The Adventures of Arab* (1946); *The Space Ship Under the Apple Tree* (1952); *The Late Cuckoo* (1962); *Round Trip Space Ship* (1968). Slobodkin wrote several books with his wife Florence, including *The Cowboy Twins* (1960) and *Sarah Somebody* (1969). He also wrote *Sculpture: Principles and Practice* (1949).

Sloe, or **Blackthorn,** a shrub or small tree native to Europe and western Asia. The sloe grows to about 15 feet (4.6 m) in height and has short, thorny branches. Its small white flowers bloom in April, usually before the leaves begin to appear. The round, blue-black fruit is about one-half inch (13 mm) in diameter. A liqueur known as *sloe gin* is made from the pulp of this rather bitter fruit. The dark brown wood of the sloe is sometimes used to make walking sticks and other items.

The sloe is *Prunus spinosa* of the rose family, Rosaceae.

Sloop. See SAILING, subtitle *Sailing a Fore-and-aft-rigged Boat,* and illustration titled *Main Types of Fore-and-aft Rigs.*

Slot Machine, a device with a mechanism set in motion by the insertion of a coin in a slot. The term is usually applied to coin-operated gambling devices. The most common kind of slot machine is sometimes called a "one-armed bandit." The player deposits a coin and pulls down on an "arm," or lever, at the side of the machine. This motion sets three wheels spinning. Each wheel has a number of symbols around its outside. The wheels stop and a series of three symbols appears in a small window in the front of the machine. One combination of symbols pays a "jackpot" of a large number of coins; a few combinations pay off a small number of coins; most pay nothing. Such gambling devices are illegal in most parts of the United States.

Sloth, an extremely slow-moving mammal native to the forests of Central and South America. The sloth has a small, round head. The toes of its limbs end in strong, curved claws. Its most notable characteristic is that it spends much of its life upside down, hanging by the claws of all four of its limbs from the branches of a tree. Tiny green organisms called algae grow on the sloth's hair, giving it a greenish color and causing the animal to blend in well with its leafy surroundings.

Sloths usually sleep during the day, either curled up in the fork of a tree or hanging from branches. At night, they move about in the tree, slowly feeding on leaves, flowers, or fruits. Because its feet curve inward, a sloth is unable to walk with ease upon the ground and will descend a tree only to get to another tree in search of food. In such a case, it either shuffles clumsily about on all fours or drags itself by its forelimbs across the ground. The chief enemies of sloths are eagles and jaguars. Some sloths breed in the spring while others breed throughout the year. The female generally gives birth to one young.

There are two genera of sloths—the *three-toed sloth,* or *ai;* and the *two-toed sloth,* or *unau.* Both have three toes on their hind limbs, but differ in the number of toes on the forelimbs. The three-toed sloths, of which there are three species, have small, stumpy tails and a body length of up to about 20 inches (50 cm). The two-toed sloths, of which there are two species, are tailless and grow up to about 25 inches (64 cm) long. Almost all other mammals have seven vertebrae in their necks, but three-toed sloths have nine and two-toed sloths have six.

© Buddy Mays/Travel Stock
A Three-toed Sloth

Sloths make up the family Bradypodidae. The three-toed sloths make up the genus *Bradypus;* the two-toed sloths make up the genus *Choloepus.*

Sloth Bear. See BEAR, subtitle *Kinds of Bears:* Other Bears.

Slovakia, slō-vä′kĭ-à, **Republic of,** a country in east-central Europe. From 1918 until 1993 it was a part of Czechoslovakia. Slovakia is bordered by Poland, Ukraine, Hungary, Austria, and the Czech Republic. The area is 18,934 square miles (49,035 km²), about the size of New Hampshire and Vermont combined.

Physical Geography

Slovakia's terrain is generally mountainous. Most of the country is covered by the

Tatra Mountains form a backdrop for the city of Poprad in northern Slovakia.

© Eastcott/Momatiuk—Woodfin Camp & Assoc., Inc.

Carpathian Mountains and branches of this range, including the Tatra and Nizke Tatry mountains. Gerlachovský Peak, in the Tatra Mountains, is Slovakia's highest point; it reaches 8,711 feet (2,655 m). Lowlands occur in the Danube Basin in the southwest, and near where the Slovakian, Ukrainian, and Hungarian borders meet.

Major rivers in Slovakia include the Dan-

Glassworker. Slovakia has long been noted for its fine glassware.
© Eastcott/Momatiuk—Woodfin Camp & Assoc., Inc.

ube (which forms part of Slovakia's border with Hungary and with Austria), Váh, Hron, Hornád, and Laborec. Most of these rivers are important sources of hydroelectric power.

Slovakia has a continental climate. Average temperatures in Bratislava, the capital, range from 70° F. (20° C.) in July to 31° F. (−1° C.) in January. Average annual precipitation is generally between 25 and 30 inches (645 and 760 mm).

Economy

Until the Communists came to power in Czechoslovakia in 1948, Slovakia's economy was dominated by agriculture. By the mid-1970's, the Slovakian economy had been transformed into one based on manufacturing; especially important were such heavy industries as metalworking and chemical production. After Czechoslovakia broke apart Slovakia suffered from numerous economic problems, largely because its factories were inefficient and the production of consumer goods was negligible.

Manufacturing is concentrated in and around Bratislava, Kosice, Komarno, and Nitra. Products made here include machinery, electrical equipment, cement, refined petroleum, chemicals, and beer. Fine glassware is an important specialty product.

About a third of the land is cultivated. The main crops are wheat, barley, corn, sugarbeets, rye, oats, and potatoes. Cattle, pigs, and sheep are the most numerous livestock. The production of timber is important.

Metals are Slovakia's most important mineral resources. They include antimony, copper, iron ore, lead, manganese, and zinc. Petroleum, natural gas, and lignite are produced in small amounts.

Slovakia is well served by roads, and railroads link most of the major cities. Slovakia's main airport is in Bratislava. Bratislava and Komarno are the chief river ports.

The People

In 1991 the population of Slovakia was 5,310,154; that of Bratislava, the capital, 444,482.

About 85 per cent of the people are Slovaks. Hungarians, who account for about 10 per cent of the population, are the largest minority. Other groups include Czechs, Ruthenians, and Ukrainians. Slovak, a Western Slavic language, is the official language. German and Hungarian are also spoken. Roman Catholicism is the predominant religion. Comenius University of Bratislava is Slovakia's largest institution of higher learning.

Government and History

Under the constitution of 1992, Slovakia is a parliamentary democracy. The parliament is made up of 150 members. The president is the head of state and is elected by the parliament. The prime minister is the head of government and is appointed by the president.

The area that is now Slovakia was first settled by Illyrian, Germanic, and Celtic tribes. Western Slavic tribes first settled in the region during the sixth and seventh centuries. In the ninth century Slovakia was included in a Slavic kingdom created by Moravia. The Moravian kingdom was conquered by Magyars in the 10th century and Slovakia became a part of their Hungarian kingdom, which in 1526 came under Hapsburg rule. With the dissolution of the Austro-Hungarian Empire after World War I, Slovakia became a part of the new nation of Czechoslovakia.

During 1939-45 Slovakia was a nominally independent state dominated by Nazi Germany. In 1948 Slovakia, along with the rest of Czechoslovakia, came under Communist rule. In 1989 the Communist government of Czechoslovakia fell from power and was replaced by a democratic regime. During 1990-92 nationalist sentiment among Slo-

vaks intensified, and in 1993 Slovakia became an independent nation.

See also CARPATHIAN MOUNTAINS; CZECHOSLOVAKIA; DANUBE RIVER; KOSICE; MORAVA RIVER.

Slovenia, slȯ-vē′nĭ-ȧ, a country on the Balkan Peninsula, in southeastern Europe. Slovenia is bordered by Austria, Hungary, Croatia, and Italy. From 1946 to 1992 Slovenia was a constituent republic of Yugoslavia. In 1992 Slovenia became independent. The total area is 7,819 square miles (20,251 km²). Slovenia is a mountainous country. The Karawanken and the Julian Alps in the north and west gradually give way to wooded hills in the south and plains in the east. Agriculture, manufacturing, and tourism are the mainstays of the economy. Most of the people speak Slovenian, a Slavic language. Roman Catholicism is the predominant religion. In 1991 Slovenia's population was 1,962,606. Ljubljana, with 286,681 inhabitants, is the capital and largest city. Slovenia has a parliamentary form of government with an elected president.

The Slovenes, a Slavic people, settled in Carinthia, at the head of the Adriatic Sea, in the sixth century. They soon came under attack from the Avars, Asian nomads who had settled in Hungary. After Charlemagne, king of the Franks, defeated the Avars in the late eighth century, he made Slovenia a part of Germany. Eventually, the Hapsburgs of Austria gained control of it. After World War I Slovenia joined other South Slavs in forming the Kingdom of the Serbs, Croats, and Slovenes, later renamed Yugoslavia.

Shortly after World War II, the Slovenian

Common Garden Slug

government, like the federal Yugoslav government, came under Communist control. In 1990 Slovenia held its first multiparty elections in more than 50 years, which resulted in the fall of the republic's Communist government. The new government sought to negotiate greater independence from the federal government, which was still controlled by Communists. Negotiations broke down, and in 1991 Slovenia declared independence. The federal army invaded Slovenia but was unable to defeat Slovenian forces and a cease-fire was signed. Slovenia's independence was recognized in 1992.

See also LJUBLJANA; YUGOSLAVIA, subtitle *History*.

Slow-down Strike. See STRIKE, subtitle *Types of Strikes*.

Slowworm, a limbless lizard that inhabits forests and grasslands of Europe, western Asia, and Algeria. It has the sinuous, gliding movements of a worm or a snake. The slowworm reaches a length of about 20 inches (50 cm). It is covered with smooth, shiny scales and is bronze or greenish-bronze above and black below. It has long, sharp teeth and feeds on slugs, earthworms, and insects. Mating occurs in the spring; the young, usually numbering from 6 to 20, are born live in the late summer. The slowworm burrows into the ground and hibernates there over the winter.

The slowworm is *Anguis fragilis* of the family Anguidae.

Slug, the common name of various mollusks that are related to snails, but lack a shell or have only a fragmentary shell embedded under the skin. There are both land- and sea-dwelling slugs.

Land slugs are slow-moving animals with soft bodies. They are one to eight inches (2.5 to 20 cm) long, depending on the species. Projecting from the head are two pairs of tentacles; the front pair is sensitive to touch, the other pair bears eyes. Land slugs hide in moist, dark places during the day and come out at night to feed. Some eat insects and earthworms but most feed on leafy plants and often become serious garden pests. In winter, slugs burrow into the ground to hibernate.

Sea slugs (a term that refers to both *nudibranchs* and related animals called *sea hares*) are found in all oceans, where they either crawl on the bottom or swim with sinuous movements. There are about 2,500 species. They range in length from ⅜ of an inch to 39 inches (1 cm to 1 m) and are often brightly colored. Most sea slugs have two pairs of tentacles: (1) cephalic tentacles (sense organs) located just behind the mouth and (2) rhinophores (respiratory organs) located farther back on the head. Sea slugs are hermaphroditic (each individual has both male and female reproductive organs).

Most nudibranchs have brilliantly colored, fingerlike projections (called cerata) on their backs; these projections are respiratory organs. Immature nudibranchs have delicate external shells, which they lose as adults. Nudibranchs are carnivores, feeding on such things as sponges, sea anemones, barnacles, and fish eggs.

Sea hares have thin internal shells, and rhinophores that are more prominent than those of nudibranchs. Sea hares eat only algae.

Slugs belong to the class Gastropoda. Land slugs are of the order Stylommatophora. Nudibranchs make up the order Nudibranchia; sea hares, the order Anaspidea.

Sluice. See DAM.

Slum Clearance. See CITY, subtitle *City Planning:* Redevelopment.

Slur, or **Legato.** See MUSIC, subtitle *Notation of Music:* Other Signs and Symbols.

Sluter, slü'tĕr, **Claus** (1340?-1406?), a Dutch sculptor who worked for the Duke of Burgundy. He introduced realism into late Gothic sculpture and greatly influenced the 15th-century school of Burgundian sculpture. Sluter's most important works were done for the Carthusian Monastery of Champmol in Dijon. His figures ornamenting the chapel doorway and those making up the *Well of Moses* have vigorous facial expression and dramatic force. Little is known about Sluter's life. He was born in Haarlem and worked in Brussels before settling in Dijon in 1385.